£8

German
**Liberalism
in the
Nineteenth
Century**

James J.
Sheehan

German
Liberalism
in the
Nineteenth
Century

METHUEN

First published in 1978 by The University of Chicago Press

First published as a University Paperback in 1982 by
Methuen & Co. Ltd
11 New Fetter Lane, London EC4P 4EE

© 1978 The University of Chicago

Printed in Great Britain at
the University Press, Cambridge

British Library Cataloguing in Publication Data
Sheehan, James J.
  German liberalism in the nineteenth century.
  —(University paperbacks 765).
  1. Liberalism—Germany—History
  I. Title
  320.5′1′0943   JN3925

ISBN 0-416-32910-1

This book is for Elena

Contents

V

Division and Decline
1877–90

VI

The Wilhelmine Age
1890–1914

Acknowledgments

It is a great pleasure to express my gratitude to those who have helped me while I was writing this book.

The Council for Intersocietal Studies at Northwestern, the National Endowment for the Humanities (under Grant H5426 and with a summer fellowship), the Institute for Advanced Study at Princeton, and the Faculty Research Committee at Northwestern provided funds for leave, travel, and research assistance.

James Bailey, Anita Lotz, Ruth Oldberg, Marilyn Shevin, and Myrtle Yedor all helped in preparation of the manuscript. Marjorie Carpenter of the Northwestern University Library deserves special mention, not only because of her tireless efforts on my behalf but also because she best personifies the virtues I found among librarians from California to Cologne.

George Dalton fought a long, twilight struggle against the vagaries of my prose style. T. W. Heyck and Robert Wiebe read the manuscript with great care and posed hard questions about its organization and analysis. Hans-Ulrich Wehler helped from start to finish. He encouraged me when the project was first taking shape and read the final draft almost a decade later.

Finally, I wish to acknowledge my debt to Felix Gilbert and Hans Rosenberg. For many years they have given me moral support and material assistance. Much more important, they have nourished my commitment to the historian's craft by giving me models of scholarly excellence and personal integrity.

Evanston, Illinois
April 1977

Introduction
Liberalism in an
Illiberal Society

The origins of liberalism were part of that cluster of developments often subsumed under the term "modernization": the expansion of administrative institutions and participant politics, population growth and social mobility, economic development and urbanization, scientific progress and cultural secularization. As an ideology, liberalism was one of the first and most influential attempts to understand and evaluate these changes. And, like every important ideology, liberalism was also a call to action which quickly developed an organizational base. Liberalism, then, was an attempt both to understand and to change the world, an ideology and a movement, a set of ideas and a set of institutions.

Liberal ideas and institutions can be found in almost every country where the erosion of traditional forms and values weakened what Edmund Burke called "the ancient opinions and rules of life."[1] But it was in western Europe and North America that the roots of liberal thought struck deepest, here that the social soil was the most nutritious and the political climate the most beneficial. It was only natural, therefore, that liberals in Germany and elsewhere should turn to the west for inspiration and guidance. Robert von Mohl's description of his political views as those of "an English Whig, a member of the French left-center, an American Federalist" is just one of many examples which could be cited to show how Germans tried to understand their own past, present, and future in terms borrowed from the Atlantic states.[2] But while German liberals looked to the west for models of progress and hints of the future, they also had to look inward, toward the particular values, traditions, and problems in their own society. This dual vision is common to modernizers of every persuasion since they all must "translate" western ideas and experiences into their own terms. And, as so often happens in the process of translation, the original has to be adapted, perhaps even distorted, before it can become comprehensible to the translator and his audience. The farther liberalism moved away from its western European source, the more problematic this process of translation became.

In Germany, the difficulties involved in adapting liberalism to local conditions were often underestimated, at least until the middle of the nineteenth century. After all, it did not seem difficult to find German equivalents for French and English concepts. *Staat*, *Volk*, *Mittelstand*, *Partei*, *Bewegung* all seemed to be part of a common European vocabulary of politics. But in fact the meaning of these German terms was affected by a complex web of traditions, assumptions, and national preoccupations. Similarly, it seemed as though a number of developments in Germany were part of a common European experience: the expansion of constitutional government, the quickened pace of economic development, the spread of popular political participation. But the meaning of these developments, like the meaning of the terms with which they were described, was profoundly affected by historical traditions and existing structures. We can hope to understand the distinctive character of German liberal thought and action, therefore, only if we understand the distinctive character of Germany's emergence as a modern state and society.

The purpose of this book is to examine the relationship between liberalism and German society. Chronologically, the emphasis is on the nineteenth century, although there are brief discussions of the years before 1815 and after 1914. Geographically, the analysis covers those parts of German-speaking central Europe that were eventually united in the Kaiserreich of 1871. The focus includes liberal leaders and, whenever possible, the sources of the movement's popular support.

When I began work on the liberals many years ago, I did not plan to define my project so broadly. But every time I tried to study a piece of the movement, a single party or a specific period, I became convinced that it could not be understood without reference to another. Finally, I decided that the best way to contribute to the historiography of German liberalism would be to attempt a synthesis which would describe how German liberalism looked when all of its components were seen together. In the end, the price of synthesis has often been uncertainty. Much of what I have to say is tentative, designed to pose questions rather than to provide answers. I hope that what I have written accurately reflects what is known about the subject, but I also hope that my work will encourage others to extend this knowledge and indicate where I have been wrong.[3]

Unlike a great deal of recent scholarship on German liberalism—especially work done by American historians since 1945—my book does not attempt to explain the liberals' failure in terms of their moral deficiencies. Nor do I dwell on the specific mistakes liberals made during the revolution of 1848, the Prussian constitutional conflict, and the critical period after 1867. Obviously, a number of liberals were shortsighted and selfish; many more showed bad judgment and political ineptitude. I do not wish to apologize for these failures of intellect and will. But I am not convinced that these failures sealed liberalism's fate. I wish I did think so, if only because it would make a better story. Moreover, it is somehow comforting to feel that if a small group of men had acted differently, their fortunes might have been reversed. This does not seem to me to have been the case. I am much more impressed by the way in which the historical situation narrowed liberals' choices and often precluded alternatives that might have enabled them to save themselves and their ideals. Certainly one reason for this point of view is that I have been concerned with the apparently necessary evolution of long-range trends rather than the potential for change which seems to exist at specific historical moments. I suspect another reason is the fact that I worked on this book during the late 1960s and early 1970s, a time when there was little in my own political experience to suggest that reality was malleable and that individual action could change the direction of events. Those historians who studied German liberals during a more promising stage in the evolution of American political life may have found it easier to blame them for not doing more and doing it better.

I The Origins of German Liberalism 1770–1847

Because *liberalism* always meant different things to different people, it is impossible to define simply. It is one of those words which, to borrow a line from T. S. Eliot, "slip, slide, perish, decay with imprecision . . . will not stay still." Given the difficulties involved in defining *liberalism*, it is not surprising that many historians have evaded the issue by assuming that the word refers to a thing, a discrete object waiting patiently to be studied. Others have taken refuge behind some vague generalizations about the core of liberal ideology ("individualism," "beginnings of a new personal ego") or the social basis of the movement ("the bourgeoisie," "the new economic class"). Most of these definitions fail, either because they do not accurately describe liberalism or because they describe liberalism as well as a number of other political movements.[1]

The problem of definition is especially burdensome when one deals with liberalism in the first half of the nineteenth century. During this period, political terminology was extremely imprecise and inconsistent. Thus even after *liberal* began to take on a political meaning in the late 1820s, a number of unlikely converts, including Goethe and the young Bismarck, used the word to refer to themselves.[2] Similarly, the political direction of organizations was often uncertain, and popular political preferences remained amorphous. In short, we have a great deal of trouble defining liberalism during the movement's formative period because the liberals were having a great deal of trouble defining themselves.

One can try to resolve these problems by formulating a set of least common denominators for the liberals. This can be done by operating at a high level of abstraction—using terms like "constitutionalism," "individualism," and "progress"—but as soon as one tries to be more concrete, anomalies and exceptions begin to multiply. It seems more useful to think of liberalism as a "family" of ideas and behavior patterns. This is a metaphor suggested by Ludwig Wittgenstein to illuminate words which refer to "a complicated network of similarities, overlapping and crisscrossing: sometimes overall similarities, sometimes similarities of detail."[3] Seen together, these similarities enable us to recognize liberals, just as, during the movement's formative era, they enabled liberals to recognize one another. Of course, as in most families, there were those who shared more common features than others; and there were also those who at first seemed to belong but on closer inspection were identified as outsiders.

The next three chapters are about liberals' initial efforts to define their ideology and to form the basis for a collective existence. Our first task will be to examine the emergence of liberal institutions and to see how these institutions fostered certain attitudes about the nature and purpose of political action; then we will turn to the social composition of the movement and try to understand how this helped to shape liberals' ideas about social and economic change; finally, we will consider liberal politics, with particular emphasis on how liberals tried to put together those two key elements in the political equation, the *Staat* and the *Volk*.

1   *Partei* and *Bewegung*

> Everyone has had enough of the liberals'
> pretty speeches and critical clichés.
> Everyone longs for the liberal party to do
> something.... But is there a liberal
> party in Germany? Can there ever
> be one?
>
> Arnold Ruge (1843)[1]

The intellectual ancestry of German liberalism can be traced into the seven-teenth century, but for our purposes the best place to begin is the last third of the eighteenth. At this time, we can find signs of a "political public," a small but significant group of men who tried to establish ties outside of the existing administrative, ecclesiastical, and corporate establishments. This was the *Öf-fentlichkeit* to which men such as Immanuel Kant looked with such hope; if only this public could be free to debate and disseminate ideas, Kant believed, it could enlighten itself and eventually all of society.[2]

The clearest evidence for the emergence of this public was a new vitality in German cultural life. Not only was there an extraordinary cluster of genius in poetry, philosophy, drama, and music, there was also a dramatic quantitative growth in cultural consumption. Between 1764 and 1800, the number of new books published annually tripled, the number of magazines founded grew from 411 in the 1750s to 1,225 in the 1780s; the number and circulation of newspapers showed a comparably significant increase.[3] The audience for these publications also patronized the new organizations which proliferated in this period: lodges and clubs, scientific societies and professional organiza-tions, and, most characteristic of all, reading societies, of which there were several hundred by the turn of the century.[4]

The political content of these publications and institutions was often hidden and always subdued. This was a necessary prerequisite for survival in the repressive political climate which prevailed in most of central Europe. Never-theless, many writers introduced unmistakably critical motifs into their work, and many organizations devoted themselves to the spread of new ideas about public affairs. Taken together, these ideas and institutions mark the beginning of a new political awareness among men who sought, as the program of one new society put it in 1777, "to make Germans acquainted with themselves and to turn their attention toward their own national affairs."[5]

When the effects of the French Revolution began to be felt east of the Rhine, the search for new forms of political expression took on greater rele-vance and urgency.[6] The events of the years 1789–1815 had global historical scale and an immediate effect on the character of daily life. In Frankfurt and Cologne, for example, the traditional leadership faced challenges to its authority from within the city at the same time that there was a radical shift in the relationship between the city and the outside world.[7] In the south and southwest, Napoleonic hegemony produced a massive transfer of territory, the secularization of church lands, and the end of aristocratic sovereignties. The newly enlarged state of Bavaria, for example, absorbed six ecclesiastical principalities and as many free cities, two duchies, and after 1815 one additional principality, a former duchy, and the Palatinate. Baden, a rather insignificant splinter state in 1803, became a full-fledged *Mittelstaat* with the addition to it of four times its former territory.[8] The severing of old loyalties produced by these changes often had a profound impact on those involved. Thus the young Karl von Rotteck responded to the experience of seeing his hometown of Freiburg passed around to various states with a lifelong commitment to political opposition and liberal ideals.[9] In fact, throughout the nineteenth century we find that many of the most important centers of liberalism—Baden, the Bavarian Palatinate, parts of Württemberg and Hanover, and the western provinces of Prussia—were territories in which the disruption of traditional loyalties during the revolutionary era had heightened people's political awareness and increased their inclination to political opposition.[10]

We should not overestimate the number of those actively engaged in politics in the early 1800s; most Germans remained the unfortunate but passive pawns of processes they only dimly understood. But in the course of the revolutionary era, a significant minority began to acquire some profoundly important insights into political life. As several German states crumbled upon impact with the French armies, these men gained a sense of the fragility of political structures. As new laws were promulgated, new boundaries drawn, and new institutions established, they recognized the malleability of human affairs and thus acquired one of the basic assumptions of political life. In his New Year's Day sermon for 1800, one progressive pastor expressed this feeling when he said that "The unmistakable character of our century is the vital, free struggle for something new and better."[11]

The French conquest of central Europe affected German public life by weakening old certainties, shattering old loyalties, and also by evoking a surge of patriotic enthusiasm. Of course, much of the mass participation in the so-called "wars of liberation" was produced by government compulsion or old-fashioned dynastic and regional loyalties. But for some young men the campaign against the French invader produced a taste for political action and a new commitment to the ideals of freedom and national unity.[12] After 1815, German university students tried to institutionalize these ideals in the

Burschenschaften, which they hoped would provide models for a free and national political life.[13] Even after the Burschenschaften were repressed, the historical memory of the war lived on in ceremonies which celebrated its victories and in stories of how the nation, mobilized by reform and infused with national enthusiasm, could shape its own destiny.[14] The power of this memory, reaffirmed by ritual and myth, continued to be important for many liberals and helped to sustain their belief that national power and domestic reform were inexorably linked, a belief which lasted until Bismarck disproved it in 1866.

In the wake of the French triumphs, many leading German statesmen tried to stimulate political consciousness and popular involvement in public affairs. They needed the power which they believed "slumbered in the heart of the *Volk*" as an ally, not only against the French conqueror but also against domestic rivals such as the landed nobility, the churches, and traditional local authorities. This was especially true in the *Mittelstaaten*, where officials hoped that representative institutions would help to integrate newly acquired territories into the state. The constitutions drafted for these states, therefore, established parliaments which provided carefully limited but potentially very significant new avenues to political participation.[15] In Prussia the situation was more complicated. During his brief tenure in office, Freiherr vom Stein succeeded in promulgating a law setting up representative bodies in the cities, but neither he nor his successors were able to extend these to the national level. Despite the promises made by the king, Prussia remained without a constitution or a parliament, although provincial Landtage were established as surrogates for the state-wide institutions that had been the reformers' final goal.[16]

The Prussian reformers' defeat on the issue of a state parliament was part of a broad reactionary wave which engulfed central Europe after 1815. Once Napoleon's defeat had removed the main impetus for change, conservative forces in almost every state returned to power and tried to set tighter limits on political activity. The participatory energies which had once been seen as a necessary source of state power were now condemned as the source of unrest and revolution. In individual states and in the newly created Germanic Confederation, strict laws were passed against dangerous ideas and organizations. The Burschenschaften and similar groups were crippled or disbanded. Publications were censored and sometimes banned. Public organizations were supervised and their leaders sometimes arrested.[17]

Despite these repressive measures, there was a good deal more room for political action in Vormärz than there had been in the eighteenth century. Censorship, for example, was applied unevenly, to newspapers more than to books, to shorter more than to longer publications, and in some states more

than in others. At times it was relaxed—as in Prussia in 1842, for example—
and then later reimposed. Furthermore, a great many organizations did find
ways to establish themselves, and a large number had at least latent political
significance. Generally speaking, therefore, liberalism took shape in a climate
which had enough restrictions to be frustrating but not enough to cut off
political life entirely.

This interplay of opportunity and restriction can also be seen in Vormärz
representative institutions. The very existence of these bodies was a
significant advance from the arid political landscape of the eighteenth century.
The government of every state, however, sought to inhibit the parliament's
effectiveness as a source of political mobilization and expression. In the
Mittelstaaten, the government controlled parliamentary procedures and retained the legislative initiative in the presentation of bills and the arrangement
of debates. The situation varied somewhat from one state to another, but
everywhere efforts were made to keep clear-cut political groupings from
coalescing: like-minded men were usually prevented from sitting together, the
order of speaking was designed to hinder sustained debate, and limitations
were imposed on the publication of parliamentary proceedings.[18] Restraints
on parliamentary life were even more pronounced in Prussia. The city councils, for example, were prohibited by law from dealing with matters outside of
their communities. Similarly, everything possible was done to separate the
deliberations of the provincial Landtage from the political public: these bodies
met infrequently and in closed sessions, the publication of their decisions was
delayed until well after the session had closed, and any discussion of general
political issues was discouraged.[19] In short, conservative rulers and officials
tried to contain the pressures for participant institutions within the traditional
confines of the old regime's corporate bodies. This is what King Frederick
William IV of Prussia had in mind when he told the meeting of the United
Provincial Landtage in 1847 that "you have been called together to represent
rights—the rights of your estates and those of the throne. It is not your task to
represent opinions."[20]

Suffrage arrangements were also designed to limit the ability of the new
parliaments to mobilize political opinion. Except in Baden, all of the *Mittelstaaten* retained some corporate elements in their electoral laws, thus assur-
ing that the aristocracy and clergy were overrepresented. Even in Baden,
property restrictions and an indirect system of voting kept a large part of
society from political participation.[21] In some of the smaller states, suffrage
restrictions were even more stringent. Nassau, for example, had such high
property requirements that in one election no eligible candidates could be
found in twelve of the twenty electoral districts, while in the entire state there
were only seventy men qualified to be candidates. The Prussian provincial

Landtage were also elected by a narrowly defined group. Voters in Westphalia were divided into four groups: in the first, *Standesherren* had the right to a seat without election; representatives of the other three (the *Ritterschaft,* the cities, and the rural areas) were elected, but in each there were special limits as well as age, property, and residence requirements. In 1826, about one-fifth of the adult males in the province could vote; among those excluded were most officials and other members of the educated elite who did not own property or some kind of business enterprise.[22]

As so often is the case, external restrictions were reinforced by deeply-rooted popular attitudes. Centuries of domination had produced a political culture in which the role of subject, of *Untertan,* seemed proper and inescapable, while the role of citizen seemed alien and uncomfortable.[23] Even where a tradition of participation existed, as in the self-governing cities of the south and southwest, there was little interest in abstract programs and distant political struggles. Liberal spokesmen, therefore, had to contend with repressive laws and also with distrust and passivity in the population at large.

These were formidable obstacles, and it is not surprising that liberalism's growth was slow, difficult, and discontinuous. During the 1820s, when the word *liberal* first began to be used to designate a political position, the movement consisted of small and scattered groups trying desperately to protect the hopes born during the era of revolution and reform. Characteristically, the fate of these efforts was sealed by government oppression and profound public apathy. In the *Mittelstaaten,* most people showed little concern for the constitutional struggles which attended the transition from "reform" to "restoration."[24] Participation in elections was almost aways very low: in a Württemberg district, for example, it was once impossible to have an election because a quorum of electors did not show up.[25] A similar atmosphere of public apathy permeated the Prussian city councils during the first two decades of their existence. In the councils, as in most other representative institutions, the prevailing mood reflected the heritage of absolutism much more than the opportunities and ideals created during the era of reform.[26]

The high point of political activity between 1815 and 1840 was the flurry of excitement evoked by the French revolution of 1830. The news that the Bourbon monarchy had fallen produced popular disorder in some cities and encouraged advocates of liberal reform in a number of state parliaments.[27] But if the events of 1830 showed that there were important reservoirs of discontent in Germany, they did not signal the emergence of sustained political movements. Popular unrest was quickly suppressed, and much of the energy displayed in the parliaments soon dissipated.[28] Throughout the thirties there were other brief episodes of political action: the Hambach demonstrations in favor of free expression in 1832, parliamentary agitation produced

by issues like the Zollverein, and a few scattered outbreaks of popular unrest
such as those which occurred in Frankfurt in 1834.[29] By and large, however,
David Hansemann's assessment of the situation in the Rhineland was also true
for almost every German region: "Nowhere," he wrote in 1840, "is there
real political freedom or a strong party prepared to fight for it."[30]

During the 1840s, sustained political agitation finally began. This was in
part due to the cumulative efforts of liberals in cities and towns throughout
Germany; their slow and painstaking labors at last began to be felt in a number
of state parliaments and local organizations. More important was the growing
sense of crisis which spread throughout much of Europe in the years preceding
the revolution of 1848; economic dislocation, social unrest, and intense religious controversy began to engage the attention of a larger and larger public.
In the course of the decade almost every indicator of public interest in political
life showed a sharp increase: newspaper circulation, book publishing, the formation of political organizations, parliamentary debates, and popular demonstrations.[31] In Königsberg, for example, a young physician named Johann
Jacoby published a pamphlet in 1841 which demanded "the legal participation of independent citizens in the affairs of the state." His work caused a
considerable stir throughout eastern Prussia and provided a program for those
who were beginning to make political demands in city councils and other local
organizations. During the next few years, Jacoby appeared as the defendant in
a series of political trials which helped to dramatize the need for reform and to
enlist popular support.[32] At least among certain groups and in some places,
the impulse to political involvement was great. In the words of one participant, by 1842 it was no longer possible "not to become identified with a
religious and political party."[33]

Obviously a great deal of the political interest generated in the forties was
not associated with liberalism; the riots and demonstrations which made such
an impact on contemporaries often reflected social and economic discontents
rather than support for any political program. Moreover, habits of passivity
remained widespread. Those citizens of Halle who, when handed a copy of
Jacoby's pamphlet, threw it in the street rather than risk being involved,
probably still represented the majority of Germans.[34] Nevertheless, by the eve
of the revolution, German liberals could look back with some satisfaction on
the growth and vitality of their movement.

Behind this national trend of liberal growth was a complex pattern of regional
diversity. The level of social and economic development, the prevailing social
climate, and the legal limitations on public life all varied among and often
within states. This meant that the intensity of liberal political action different
from one locality to another. In some places—a few large cities, parts of

Baden, and the Rhineland—liberalism was vigorous and rather broadly based. Elsewhere, it was a frail movement, limited to a small and isolated minority. Moreover, the character of liberalism was shaped by different forces in different places. Inevitably, centuries of political and social fragmentation left their mark on the emerging movement, which reflected differences between north and south, east and west, Protestant and Catholic, urban and rural, prosperous and impoverished.

The long-term effects of regional diversity were increased by the fact that liberals' practical experience remained locally oriented. Liberals may have felt part of a national movement, but almost all of them acted within the confines of their own communities. One reason for this was governmental repression. Police surveillance, censorship, and legal restrictions all hampered the evolution of a national nexus within which ideas could be freely exchanged and a common course of action determined and pursued. The communications network remained relatively undeveloped in the first half of the century, travel was difficult, mail service slow and undependable. Finally, Germany lacked a cultural or political center like London or Paris, a place toward which talented and ambitious men were drawn and where they could get to know one another.[35]

Throughout the twenties and thirties, contact between various liberal groups was infrequent and intermittent. A few men acquired regional or even national prominence because of their parliamentary activity or because of their professional reputation; a few journals and some publications, like the *Staatslexikon,* gained a fairly wide circulation.[36] After 1840, the growing intensity of political action, improvements in the communications network, and a cumulative increase in the number of personal ties among various liberal notables produced some signs of a national liberal elite.[37] However, when the revolution suddenly created a national political forum in 1848, the bonds uniting liberals were still very slender and the predominant source of institutionalized activity closely followed the contours of local life.

In most communities, the center of liberal activity was an organization apparently devoted to some nonpolitical purpose. In order to avoid legal sanctions, liberals had to operate in social clubs, professional societies, and recreational associations.[38] Johann Jacoby, for example, entered public life through the Thursday Club, which was supposedly a social organization. The Leipzig *Schillerfest* of 1841 was billed as a cultural and literary event, but under the influence of men like Robert Blum it quickly took on political overtones. Much the same thing happened in singing clubs and gymnastic societies, banquet groups and reading circles, educational associations and lecture series.[39] Quasi-official economic groups like the Chambers of Commerce sometimes became "debating grounds for the parties, forums for the

discussion of public issues, the real center of public interest.''[40] Professional
associations of teachers and lawyers, the annual meetings of literary critics or
legal scholars became ways of gathering like-minded men in the political
opposition. The Lichtfreunde, whose manifest purpose was religious reform,
became a vehicle for political agitation. As Rudolf Haym put it:

> The agitation for a free organization of church life served at the same time
> to prepare the ground for participation in public affairs as a whole.
> Liberalism in the church was the training school for political liberalism.[41]

In fact, all of these various organizations were "training schools" for liberals
during the first half of the century. Within this diffuse and heterogeneous
institutional network the first generations of liberal leaders learned to think
and to act politically. It was here that their ideas about the proper form and
purpose of political participation first took shape.

A distinctive feature of these ideas was the inclination of liberals to see
political participation in spiritual terms. The purpose of participation, many
of them believed, was the spread of enlightenment and moral improvement;
its form should be educational, the transmission of enlightened opinions to a
public of independent and reasonable men. In the minds of many liberals,
therefore, politics was closely associated with *Bildung,* a concept which combined the meaning carried by the English word *education* with notions of
character formation and moral cultivation.[42]

This tendency to link political progress and spiritual enlightenment had
been part of liberalism since its beginnings in the last third of the eighteenth
century. Kant had seen political change as a process of opinion formation and
moral betterment, a goal which was pursued by his contemporaries in lodges,
reading societies, and a variety of other educational associations.[43] The Prussian reformer Stein supported representative institutions because he believed
that political participation "is for adults what schools are for the young." It
will create "love for the constitution, a reliable public opinion concerning
affairs of state, and administrative abilities in many citizens."[44] During this
early stage in the evolution of *Bildung* as a political category, the emphasis
was clearly on reform, not opposition. The goal of political education was
most often seen as a reconciliation of the citizen with the state, not the
mobilization of opinion against the existing order.

By the 1820s, liberals had begun to give political education a more critical,
oppositional impetus. But the link between participation and *Bildung* remained intact. The liberal professors and officials—the *Gebildete*—who
served as the movement's first national leaders emphasized the close relationship between spiritual and political reform. Note, for instance, how Georg
Gervinus explained the revolution of 1830:

The world opens before our eyes . . . every day brings new experiences.
The gradual but inevitable ripening of *Bildung* in Europe is coming to
fruition. Spiritual endeavors forcefully penetrate the existing order of
things and envelop them and by slowly learning the lessons of history and
experience despotism and obscurantism bow their heads.[45]

Liberals continued to see reading societies and other educational enterprises as
the surest way to bring the fruits of liberty to their own society. As one
contemporary put it: *"Volksbildung* is *Volksbefreiung."* And in the *Staatslexikon* we read that "The spread of correct and basic knowledge in all branches
of learning must work to the advantage of liberalism; indeed it cannot advance
without this."[46] An educational orientation also existed in many of those
organizations designed to uplift the lower orders of society, as well as in a
number of bodies without an overt cultural purpose. The Chambers of Commerce, for example, saw one of their primary functions as the dissemination
of information and a proper point of view on economic affairs.[47] Liberal
student groups wanted to encourage the growth of freedom and justice in the
nation "by means of moral, scientific, and physical education in the universities."[48] Many of their teachers agreed that academic activities and political
education should be joined. Thus in 1847, Heinrich von Sybel called for a
"true academic politics" which would "infuse every discipline with an interest in public affairs and keep in view its value for national concerns." To
historians like Sybel, Gervinus, and Dahlmann, to scientists like Justus von
Liebig, to publicists like Karl Biedermann, there was no disharmony between
scholarship and politics, learning and life.[49]

The liberals' image of themselves as a *party* derived from this association
of political action and spiritual enlightenment. For most liberals, party membership implied certain shared ideas and values, not a common institutional
commitment. Among Königsberg liberals, Ferdinand Falkson tells us, "the
source of community was what was then called sensibility [*Gesinnung*] . . . the weapons were the printed and spoken word."[50] When Karl
Rosenkranz gave a lecture to the German Society in 1843 on "The Concept of
the Political Party," he stressed the origins of parties in religious and intellectual controversies and their importance for the expression of opinion, but he
had little to say about their organizational dimension.[51] Ten years earlier,
Heinrich von Gagern had written along the same lines to his father: "I don't
deny being a party man; what else does that mean besides having an opinion
and seeking to work for its success?"[52]

Liberals, of course, recognized that there were different points of view
within their movement. But they believed that these differences were much
less important than the ideals they all shared. To quote Falkson once again:
"Certainly there were different shades of opinion in our ranks, but not dif-

ferent parties. The liberal party in Königsberg was a unified one—which was
natural enough given the generality of its program."[53] This assertion of unity
is confirmed by the impression one gets from reading contemporary de-
scriptions of political groups, which usually emphasize abstract ideals while
paying almost no attention to substantial tactical or theoretical differences
among liberals.[54] Similarly, an enterprise like the *Rheinische Zeitung,* which
in the 1840s brought together liberals and radicals from a bewildering variety
of groups, would have been unthinkable after mid-century.[55]

Because liberals saw themselves as the spokesmen for enlightened views,
their image of political conflict was essentially a dualistic one:

> Overall we see two opposing parties confronting one another: on the one
> side, the rulers and the aristocracy with their inclinations toward caprice
> and their commitment to old, irrational institutions; and on the other side,
> the people with their newly awakened feeling of power and their vital
> striving toward free development.[56]

In this confrontation between the forces of light and darkness, liberalism
represented not just one possible viewpoint but rather reason, progress, and
enlightenment—in sum, the good of the nation as a whole. Liberals were
convinced that their opponents had special interests and selfish motives, while
they themselves spoke for the real *Volk.* Their party was, therefore, the only
legitimate party. In Paul Pfizer's words: "liberalism directs the state back to
what the whole nation in its rational interest wants or must want [*will oder
wollen muss*]."[57]

Liberals believed that they represented not simply the common good but
also the forces of history which would insure the gradual triumph of
enlightenment and freedom. Their goals coincided with the direction of
change. "Liberalism," wrote Theodor Mundt in 1834, "wants nothing but
history's future." Paul Pfizer expressed a similar confidence when he wrote:
"Freedom has now become a necessity and no earthly power can hope to
deflect those world-moving ideas, which will force their way through all
limits and inhibitions until they follow the course set by a higher power."[58]
When liberals thought of themselves as a movement, they tended to fuse two
common meanings of the word. They were a group of men united by a
common goal and the current of time flowing in a set direction. They were,
therefore, the "party of movement" whose eventual victory was guaranteed
by the same logic of development which would consign their opponents to
historical oblivion.[59] Characteristically, liberals spoke of the progressive
trends they represented in spiritual terms: "Everything," wrote Benzenberg
in 1815, "is in flux—a vital spirit is at work throughout the nation, and what
moves the world will conquer the world." Karl Rotteck said much the same

thing a few years later: "There is in the movements of our time a predominately spiritual quality, a battle of ideas."[60]

Liberals' emphasis on the spiritual character of their movement was often accompanied by a certain distrust for practical implications of political organization and action. The term *party*, for example, took on a negative connotation when it was used to refer to something other than an ideological community. As the Brockhaus encyclopedia put it in 1846: "There is nothing to be said against collaborations which arise and are sustained naturally by a similarity of attitudes or endeavors. But a great deal can be said against organized, consciously calculated parties."[61] This fear of membership in a "party" is an important leitmotif in many liberals' writings about public affairs. Georg von Vincke, for example, celebrated the fact that he was "acting in agreement with public opinion" but made clear that "I recognize no party and regard it as an honor that I do not belong to one." Similarly, an anonymous contributor to the *Grenzboten* in 1846 celebrated the backwardness of German political life and pointed out the advantages which flowed from not having organized political groups such as existed in western Europe.[62] Liberals frequently complained that parties would interfere with their freedom of decision by enforcing conformity and imposing external discipline. Other were afraid that organized parties would encourage selfishness and personal ambition at the expense of public service. This is what was on Friedrich Murhard's mind when he rejected a proposal for closer cooperation in the Baden Landtag because he feared that "instead of a noble striving for objectives and for the realization of ideas" there would be "an unedifying race for ministerial posts," "the interest of the Volk" would be "subordinated to the interest of the party or of individual ambitions."[63]

The association of politics and *Bildung,* the concept of the party as an ideological community, the identification of liberalism with the inevitable spread of enlightenment—all these aspects of the liberals' political vision helped to sustain them during the long and difficult years before 1848. These beliefs gave them the strength to stand against the powerful forces of privilege and repression and the confidence that somehow their clubs and reading societies would help to create a better world. Considering the limitations on political action during Vormärz, it is understandable that spiritual enlightenment should have become what Hans Rosenberg once called a "surrogate for the parliamentary life they missed and so urgently desired."[64]

But these attitudes, as necessary as they may have been in Vormärz, had some unfortunate consequences for liberalism's future as a political movement. The liberals' view of themselves as the only legitimate political party made it difficult for them to formulate a pluralistic conception of the political process and to recognize the inevitability and potential creativity of party conflict. Their tendency to see political life as a dualistic struggle between good and evil inhibited the development of that willingness to compromise and bargain which is such a necessary part of parliamentary politics.[65] Finally, and most important, the liberals' spiritual view of political participation encouraged widespread disdain for the everyday world of organization and agitation. Too often, their confidence in *Bildung* became a refuge, not simply from the restrictions of a reactionary state, but also from the dangers of a restless *Volk*. To understand why that happened, we must turn to a discussion of liberalism's social dimensions.

2 Social Change and the *Mittelstand*

> The misery of the German status quo
> comes from the fact that until now no
> one class has been strong enough . . .
> to represent the interests of the nation
> as whole. All the estates and classes
> which have made a historical appearance
> since the tenth century . . . exist next to
> one another.
>
> Friedrich Engels (1847)[1]

For over a hundred years, from its origins in the political public of the late eighteenth century until the formation of the Bismarckian Reich, German liberalism's most prominent spokesmen came from university-educated elites and especially from those employed in the administrative or judicial bureaucracy. Members of these groups predominate among the authors of periodical articles on social and political affairs in the 1770s and 1780s; they were present in large numbers in the lodges, reading societies, and other early opinion-making bodies.[2] Their influence continued after the turn of the century and can be seen in the first self-consciously liberal groups within Vormärz parliaments. In Baden, for example, state officials often held a majority of seats in the parliament and provided the leadership for the liberal opposition as well as for the progovernmental faction. The same situation seems to have existed in states such as Württemberg and Kurhessen, although in neither was liberalism as powerful as it was in Baden.[3] It is difficult to be very precise about the role of officials in Prussian liberalism because Prussia did not have a national representative institution before 1848 and officials did not play much of a role in the provincial Landtage. Nonetheless, most contemporaries agreed that liberalism was widespread in the judicial and administrative bureaucracies, assessments which were born out by the success of liberal officials in 1848 during the first state-wide elections.[4]

Other members of the educated elite were also well represented among those who first helped to popularize liberal ideas and form liberal organizations. Every history of German liberalism discusses Vormärz's politically active professors, who used their university positions and sometimes ancillary roles as editors or publicists to spread liberal ideas. Their significance, of course, was far greater than their rather small number. We know much less about those in the lower ranks of the teaching profession, although some of them also seemed to be active supporters of liberalism, especially in local institutions.[5] The same was true of physicians and pastors, whose names appear among those of local liberal leaders but who did not, at least before 1848, often come into national prominence.[6] The influence of lawyers varied

widely from one region to another. In Hanover, the legal profession became a
refuge for men refused admittance to the bureaucracy, often on political
grounds; as one might imagine, this heightened the profession's oppositional
inclinations. Frankfurt's jurists also seem to have taken the initiative in
spreading liberal ideas in the 1830s and 1840s.[7] Finally, in the period after
1830 a number of *Gebildeten* found their way into journalism, which emerged
as a profession for the first time. These men contributed to the marked intensification of liberal agitation in newspapers and periodicals that can be seen in
the years immediately preceding the revolution of 1848.[8]

What drew these members of the *Bildungselite* into political opposition?
Obviously no single answer could apply to all of them. Johann Jacoby's
commitment to political reform was inseparable from his desire to complete
the emancipation of the Jews.[9] For others reform was part of a campaign for
greater religious freedom or a response to the regional antagonisms generated
by the territorial shifts that took place during the Napoleonic era. For some
officials, liberalism became an ideological weapon in the century-old struggle
against local autonomy and the lingering powers of traditional institutions.[10]
But combined with these various motives was usually that particular blend of
privilege and frustration which characterized the educated man's position in
German society. Educational reforms in the late eighteenth and early
nineteenth century had institutionalized the privileges of the *Gebildeten*: university education was made a prerequisite for a number of key occupations
and for receiving special privileges such as one-year military service. The
state's investment in instructional institutions leading to the university was
increased until it became dramatically disproportionate to the resources used
for other kinds of schools.[11] But state support and state control went together.
The self-esteem of educated men was affirmed by their acknowledged importance to the state and society, but their independence was frequently cir-
cumscribed by frustrating regulations and restrictions. This was true for
teachers, pastors, and journalists, whose effectiveness as purveyors of
enlightenment was often hindered by censorship and other forms of harassment. It was also true of officials, who conceived of themselves as representatives of the common good, but who found that their superiors were often
reluctant to allow them to pursue this common good as they saw it.

In the 1830s and 1840s, dissatisfaction among the *Gebildeten* was sharpened by an increase in the number of educated men looking for suitable
employment. Thus in 1839, the Prussian minister of justice warned all pro-
spective candidates for the judicial service that, because of an oversupply of
applicants, only the most outstanding aspirants had any hope of a post.[12]
Vigorous competition for jobs and a significant slowdown in promotions
within the bureaucracy led many young men into other fields. In some cities

the number of lawyers almost doubled from 1820 to the mid-1830s; in Frankfurt, there was one lawyer for every 468 inhabitants. Moreover, a number of disappointed jurists turned to journalism, where they often became associated with a periodical committed to political opposition.[13] The strains caused within the lives of Germany's educated elites could not help but have profound political implications. For men whose occupations were closely tied to the state in one way or another, career frustrations almost inevitably became political frustrations.

In order to understand the prominence of the *Gebildeten* in the liberal movement, it is also necessary to ask why large sectors of the political public were willing to acknowledge them as leaders. The most obvious reason, of course, is the prestige conferred by state employment. Professors shared the prestige of state service, and all university-educated men could exploit the well-established link between *Bildung* and social status. But education and state employment gave men more then just status. In a society without an extensive communications system, without national markets, a national press, or unified political institutions, it was university education, professional relationships, and above all, the nexus of the state's bureaucratic institutions that were of great practical significance for the development of supralocal personal and political ties.[14]

Another aspect of the educated elites' advantage over potential competitors was what Max Weber called *Abkömmlichkeit*, that is, the availability of an individual for a political role.[15] State employees could apply for leave to participate in parliamentary life, lawyers could seek to combine a practice with political activity, and journalists could try to make a living writing about events in which they took part. Men responsible for an economic enterprise, on the other hand, had great difficulty leaving their communities for any length of time. Throughout the late eighteenth and early nineteenth centuries, there was a severe shortage of qualified labor at all levels, and this made it imperative for most owner-managers to stay close to their work. One need only recall the trials and tribulations of a politically active entrepreneur like Friedrich Harkort in order to get a sense of the risks a businessman took if he left his enterprise in the hands of others. For men with small businesses, political activity away from home involved even greater dangers and hardships.[16]

These practical advantages help explain why the educated elites provided so many of liberalism's most prominent spokesmen. However, we must always be careful not to confuse prominence and typicality. When we look at liberals who were active in institutions closer to the concerns of local life, we find that the *Gebildete* were important but not so decisively as has often been assumed. This was even true for some of the representative institutions in the

smaller states: Siegfried Büttner has been able to identify eighteen liberals in
the Landtag of Hessen-Darmstadt elected in 1826. They included nine local
officeholders (most of whom also listed another occupation, usually farming),
three farmers, two manufacturers, and a retail merchant, a notary, a hospital
administrator, and a civil servant. Our evidence for the other parliaments does
not allow such clear correlations of social position and political alignment, but
in the Baden Landtag of 1831 almost two-fifths of the members were engaged
in some kind of economic activity; this Landtag was generally regarded as
overwhelmingly liberal. Wolfram Fischer has recently listed the Badenese
entrepreneurs who played an important role in parliamentary life in Vormärz,
although they remained a minority among the total membership.[17]

For most businessmen, local government provided the most congenial
forum for political action. Data on the social composition of the city councils
during Vormärz show a more diverse and economically active leadership than
was respresented in most state parliaments. Because of the variety of political
traditions and socioeconomic conditions in German cities, generalizations
about municipal institutions are hazardous. However, two patterns seem to
have prevailed in much of Germany. In cities where old and established local
elites existed, these tended to persist despite the institutional reforms which
occurred in the first decades of the nineteenth century: Hamburg, Münster,
and Krefeld would fall into this category.[18] In cities where the local leadership
was less well established, there was often very little initial response to reforms
in local government; usually an apathetic electorate chose as its representatives a few willing craftsmen, shopkeepers, and other small businessmen.
This was the situation in most Prussian cities after Stein's Städteordnung,
whose suffrage arrangements favored the Kleinbürgertum.[19] In the years after
1830, the growing strength of liberal ideas in the cities introduced a new
vitality and sense of political purpose into a large number of city councils. In
Hamburg this was expressed in a generational shift, as younger businessmen
and jurists, most of them with close personal ties to the existing leadership,
began to press for liberal reform. In Berlin, on the other hand, there was both
a generational and a social shift. Representatives of the existing leadership
(the master baker Kochhann, for instance) allied themselves with groups that
had hitherto shown little interest in local affairs—entrepreneurs, journalists,
and some men from the ranks of the Gebildeten.[20] Whatever the precise social
ingredients of the councils, the evidence points to an inclination toward
liberalism among a rather broadly based and diversified group of men.

Scattered data on liberal supporters below the level of the elected leadership
also suggest the movement's social diversity. For example, in 1832 the
authorities made a list of those residents of the Palatinate who participated in
the Hambach Festival: 29 were from assorted academic professions, 57 were

university students, 101 were in some kind of economic activity, of whom 36 were shopkeepers and merchants and 34 were listed as *Handwerker*.[21] A rather similar picture emerges from the occupational makeup of those who signed a petition circulated in Breslau in 1845 protesting the persecution of the Lichtfreunde.[22] About a thousand master craftsmen, businessmen, and *Gebildete* belonged to the liberal Bürgergesellschaft in Königsberg in the 1840s which was dissolved by the government because of its political character. At about the same time the Städtische Ressource was formed in Breslau, where men from a variety of social groups met to discuss current problems under the leadership of liberal members of the municipal government.[23]

It cannot be assumed that everyone who demonstrated at Hambach, signed the Lichtfreunde petition, or joined the clubs in Königsberg and Breslau would have been willing to identify himself as a liberal. But it is probable that most of them would have considered themselves part of a diffuse and diverse movement of political opposition which drew its main ideas and leadership from the liberals' ranks. The impression of social diversity suggested by these data is confirmed by contemporary accounts emphasizing the extent to which liberalism had come to attract widespread support in the years just before the revolution. Hans Viktor von Unruh, for example, believed that by the 1840s liberalism had not only become fashionable among the educated but had spread into the lower ranks of the *Bürgertum*. Stephan Born agreed that the *"kleinbürgerliche Mittelstand* had become thoroughly liberal and shared the views of the *Honoratioren*, merchants, and officials." Recalling the emergence of the liberal movement in Königsberg on the eve of the revolution, F. Falkson stressed the involvement of both commercial and artisan groups. Even Friedrich Engels, while emphasizing the role of the "bourgeoisie" in liberalism, recognized that "in Germany, the composition of the different classes of the people which form the ground work of every political organization is more complicated than in any other country."[24]

This social complexity of which Engels spoke can be illustrated by comparing the biographies of a few liberals. Heinrich Karl Jaup and Ludwig von Liebenstein were prestigious and well-placed officials, while Hermann Schulze was a young *Patrimonialrichter* whose career was tied to local affairs and whose life-style was as modest as that of the farmers and artisans among whom he lived. Rotteck and Welcker were famous professors and publicists, while Carl d'Ester was a poorly paid physician. Rhenish liberals like Hansemann, Camphausen, and Mevissen were energetic entrepreneurs, as was the Bremen railroad pioneer Duckwitz, but the movement also included patricians like Johann Hüffer and Friedrich Bassermann, small businessmen like the Berlin baker Kochhann and small-town innkeepers like Philip Thiebauth. Nor should we forget men like Theodor Fontane, then a pharmacist's apprentice in

Berlin, who recalls how, dressed in his Sunday best, he used to spend his free afternoons in a café reading newspapers and feeling especially fortunate ''to be able to participate in the awakening of political life'' in Germany.[25]

German liberals, therefore, tended to belong to what might be called the ''middle strata,'' the middle ranks of Germany's economic and status hierarchies: members of a university-trained elite, small and large businessmen, manufacturers, shopkeepers, craftsmen, independent farmers, and the like. There were a few liberal aristocrats, but they were exceptions. Similarly, some skilled workers belonged to a liberal organization, but in general the masses of the population—the urban poor, landless laborers, most wage earners, servants, and apprentices—were either uninterested in or excluded from liberal activities.[26]

Because of the range of groups to be found among liberalism's leaders and constituency, it does not seem very useful to identify the movement with the ''middle class'' or ''bourgeoisie.''[27] In the first place, these terms suggest a common set of economic interests arising from a similar relationship to the means of production. This communality did not exist among German liberals. Second, the use of these terms assumes that the groups to which they refer are roughly similar in different countries, that the German ''bourgeoisie'' is a somewhat weaker version of its western European counterpart. But the groups which made up the middle strata in Germany were not dim, Teutonic reflections of analogous classes in more ''mature'' societies. Instead, they quite vividly reflected the distinctive features of their own social world.[28]

Like the German social structure as a whole, the middle strata differed significantly in character from one region to another.[29] In most communities in the south, southwest, and in eastern Prussia, the middle strata would be composed of a handful of *Gebildeten* and few shopkeepers and craftsmen. In larger cities, they would include a more complicated array of social groups and usually an established commercial elite. In a few areas, parts of the Rhineland, for example, one can find the beginnings of an entrepreneurial elite. This regional diversity was intensified by the process of social and economic growth which occurred in the first half of the century. As often happens in the early stages of development, the most advanced regions—or, more accurately, some enterprises within these regions—were drawn into foreign economic systems while their neighbors remained locally oriented. Commercial agriculture in eastern Prussia or the metal industry in Westphalia, for example, turned outward, toward England and western Europe, for customers and competition. The farmers and artisans of the southwest, on the other hand, operated within a smaller, much more narrowly defined regional economy.[30] The growth of a better network of internal communications after 1830 had some effect on this situation, but until well after mid-century words

like "German society" or "the German economy" represent notational con-
veniences rather than historical realities.

Although the character of the middle strata was regionally diverse, it is
clear that most of them lived in a preindustrial world of state service, artisanal
production, and small enterprise. Despite some impressive signs of economic
development, aggregate data on production and consumption portray a predominately rural, relatively backward economy.[31] Demographic data show
that more Germans lived in small and medium-sized towns during Vormärz
than at any other time before or since; the main effect of population growth
was to overcrowd these places rather than to increase the size of large urban
centers. Investment patterns suggest that, while railroads may have captured
the popular imagination, most Germans preferred to put their money in
government bonds or to support familiar forms of economic activity like
brewing and agriculture. This same persistence of traditional forms can be
also found in the social vocabulary, which reflected the difficulties many had
in seeing the distinction between craft and industry, workshop and factory,
master and entrepreneur, journeyman and worker.[32]

Most of the middle strata in Vormärz seemed to have preserved a rather
simple and relatively homogeneous style of life.[33] Again and again, writers in
the late nineteenth century recall how social forms were plainer before 1850
and division of wealth less apparent. Carl Peterson, for instance, wrote in
1885: "It is striking how much narrower was the difference between living
conditions in 1783–85 and 1825–27 on the one side and 1825–27 and today on
the other. In 1825 Hamburg was still a patriarchal city, today it is a modern
one."[34] Of course such memories are often misleading since they reflect
present attitudes as well as past realities. But even if one corrects for nostalgic
distortion, the evidence points to a social world in which the middle strata
could see the differences within their ranks as being of degree rather than
kind.[35]

This feeling was reaffirmed by the fairly high degree of mobility which
seems to have existed within the middle strata. A rather large number of
liberal leaders, for example, moved from the lower reaches of these groups
into positions of power and prominence: Karl Biedermann, Sylvester Jordan,
P. Siebenpfeiffer, Heinrich Christian Meyer, Ludolf Camphausen, and David
Hansemann are just a few of the names that could be mentioned.[36] Data on the
social backgrounds of university students and the members of learned professions confirm the impression one gets from these biographical illustrations,
while the evidence on the family origins of leading Vormärz entrepreneurs
shows that a great many leaders of early industrial development came from
modest beginnings.[37]

Liberal members of the middle strata were also drawn together by the hostility most of them felt toward those above and below them in the social order. In the eighteenth century, criticism of aristocratic morals and privileges had been one of the most prominent features of the literary and journalistic statements produced by the first wave of political opposition.[38] This theme remained important after 1815, even though liberals differed as to whether the nobility should be dissolved or merely reformed and integrated into an enlightened society.[39] Even more important was their collective hostility to the uneducated and unpropertied masses, to those who remained outside of the diverse but still relatively thin middle ranks. Dependent men—servants, day laborers, the worthy and unworthy poor—formed a constant shadow on the liberals' image of society and a constant reminder that beyond their own social world lay another, separated from them by a far larger gap than any which existed within their own ranks. The nobility and the masses, therefore, set the boundaries for the *Mittelstand* or *Mittelklasse*, the terms liberals most often used to define their own social identity and to describe their movement's social location.

The *Mittelstand*, most liberals believed, was the source of enlightenment and progress; on it the power of the state, the growth of the economy, the expansion of freedom would ultimately depend. It was, wrote Friedrich Dahlmann, the "core of the nation," which combined the wisdom of the old clerical estate with the wealth and power of the traditional nobility.[40] Just as the liberal party was the only legitimate party, the political expression of enlightened opinion, so the *Mittelstand* was more than one social group among others. It was the center of society, the seat of social virtue, the vehicle of harmony and compromise. As one liberal teacher put it in 1839:

> The citizen of the middle class is found in the administration of the affairs of the community. . . . In the meetings of the Estates he takes part in legislation. There is no matter and no task that is so high and so difficult that his advice cannot be sought . . . . If this is so, what we are here discussing is not the interests of the middle class but of the whole public weal.[41]

The liberal concept of the *Mittelstand* was both a social and a moral category. It depended less on objective criteria than on the existence of shared moral virtues. These virtues meant that the *Mittelstand* coincided with what liberals often called "the real *Volk*," those enlightened and progressive men whose political and social virtues would eventually triumph, producing that liberal world to which the movement was committed.

But while liberals believed that the *Mittelstand* stood for the interests of society as a whole, they knew that it included only certain segments of society. They acknowledged that there were certain material preconditions for membership, even though they disagreed as to what these actually were. Almost all of them would have regarded some measure of "independence" as necessary for membership—this was the prerequisite for having what Kant called a "civil personality." But who was *independent*? Some liberals would have excluded only the most obviously dependent groups in society: women, children, servants. Others would have extended the list to include apprentices and day laborers; a few would have drawn the boundaries of independence even more narrowly and limited it to those with wealth or education.[42] But for all liberals there was a certain tension between the moral and the material dimensions of *Mittelstand*, between its function as the embodiment of the common good and its reality as a minority within the social order.

This same tension existed in the political manifestation of the *Mittelstand*, its existence as the "real nation," *das eigentliche Volk*. Frolinde Balser has enumerated five meanings assigned to the term *Volk* during the first two-thirds of the century: a particular linguistic or ethnic group; the romantics' *Volkstum*, with its poetic and mystical overtones; the common people; the lower classes, as opposed to the government: and the politically active sectors of the nation.[43] Within this multiplicity of meanings, one ambiguity was particularly important to the liberals: the ambiguity between the *Volk*, whose well-being legitimized the liberals' opposition and whose support would provide their strength, and the *Volk* as *eine unbestimmte Menge*, the *Volk* of the masses, the *Pöbel*.[44] Liberals used the same word to refer to both of these groups because they liked to think that their interests coincided, that the liberal *Volk* was the "real *Volk*." But most of them knew that distinctions had to be made between the active political nation and the masses. They had great difficulty making this distinction, however, both in the language of social analysis and in the world of political action.

The clearest example of these difficulties is to be found in liberal ideas about suffrage, an issue which forced them to define that sector of the nation they wanted to have an active role in the life of the state.[45] On the far left of the movement there were a few liberals who would have been willing to give all male adults the right to vote; a few on the other extreme wanted nothing more than a reform of the traditional corporate bodies which still existed in some states. Characteristically, the majority of liberals were somewhere in between these two positions. For them, the problem was to find a way of protecting the state from the dangers of the mob without excessively narrowing the opportunities for political participation. One way of doing this, many believed, was to have an indirect system of voting. This would impose an extra step between the electorate and their representatives, a step through which the influence of moderate men might be reaffirmed. In addition, most liberals recognized that some kind of property restrictions might be necessary.

Karl von Rotteck, for example, asserted that the ownership of property would have to be made a prerequisite for voting in large cities to avoid conferring political power on the urban masses.[46] Some liberals, however, were worried about property restrictions because they did not want to see political affairs dominated by businessmen who would be overly concerned with their own self-interest.[47] A few tried to avoid favoring those with wealth by suggesting that the vote should be given only to those who controlled their own source of income. But such a literal definition of "independence" clashed with the social realities of the movement since it seemed to imply that officials should not vote, a position few liberals would have been willing to accept.

Liberal attitudes about the suffrage show how categories like *Mittelstand* and "the real *Volk*" fractured when they were moved from the moral realm of political discourse into the world of political reality. Liberals were deeply divided among themselves about who did and did not fit within the social and political boundaries of their movement. Furthermore, they were afraid that unless some boundaries were drawn, the *Mittelstand* would be overwhelmed by the masses of dependent, unenlightened men. These themes of internal division and underlying anxiety appear again and again in liberal social thought during the first half of the century.

On the surface of their thought, almost all liberals seemed to believe in social progress and in the blessings of economic growth and development. The Westphalian entrepreneur Friedrich Harkort, for instance, regarded, industrialists as a new aristocracy whose skill and good fortune would change the world by eliminating the lingering residues of "feudal" privilege and absolutism.[48] Other liberals pointed to the value of commerce as a source of social and political change and as a bond that would tie Germans close together. Hermann von Beckerath stressed this point when he proclaimed in 1846 that "The spirit of the *Volk* in material form strives for the unity of the nation." Trade, Friedrich Murhard wrote, will create "bonds of nationality" which "would include all the German people and through which Germans would recognize each other."[49] The chief symbol of the bonds among Germans to be generated by technological progress was the railroad. Thus the liberal journalist Heinrich Brüggemann expressed satisfaction over the opening of a new rail line in essentially political terms: "Our joy," he wrote, "is a liberal joy, a pleasure over new triumphs which will increase the power of liberal and humane principles." Karl Biedermann recalled in his memoirs how stirred he had been by the coming of the railroad to Leipzig. It brought economic and political vitality to the city and benefited those who held shares as well as many others who simply felt part of a larger network of relationships symbolized by the shining rails.[50]

But despite their eloquent statements in praise and expectation of progress, only a few liberals were unambiguous exponents of economic growth and industrial development. Even an outspoken advocate of economic progress such as Friedrich List could recognize that a great many good things were being lost as the world of crafts gave way to the world of factories. Other intellectuals, such as Karl Mathy and Robert von Mohl, were much more cautious in their endorsement of the new industrial order. They acknowledged that industry was the way of the future but were disheartened by the cultural defects and social dangers they saw in factory life.[51] This uneasiness about industrialism extended into the ranks of those actively engaged in economic enterprises. Ludolf Camphausen, for one, decried the *Menschenanhäufung* in factories and feared the concentration of wealth this process would bring about. The successful Badenese textile magnate Karl Mez ran his giant enterprise with great energy but, in theory, opposed an excessive concentration of factories and wanted a decentralized economic system.[52] Along these lines it is worth recalling that one of the most popular novels of the thirties and forties was Karl Immermann's *Epigonen* (1836), which carefully records the triumph of an entrepreneur but ends with the destruction of his factories and the return of his workers to crafts and agriculture.[53]

Liberal uncertainty about the implications of industrialization was connected to the diverse views on agriculture which existed in the movement. There were those like Friedrich List who were convinced that rural life bred intellectual stagnation and national impotence.[54] Others believed that improvements in agriculture were the most secure basis of material progress.[55] Rotteck, for example, viewed agriculture as "the most natural, congenial, beneficial occupation for individuals and the richest, most independent, and secure basis for national prosperity." Mohl had no illusions about stopping the expansion of industry but maintained that farmers lived in a more natural, less corrupted world than factory workers.[56] Liberal images of the city were equally diverse. To Heinrich von Gagern "cities are the seat of intelligence, the cradle of civilization, the center of freedom." Welcker agreed: "Life in cities engenders higher achievements in commerce, industry, and civilization . . . . Men become strong and cultivated only through close contact with their fellow humans."[57] But there were those who saw another, more dangerous side of urban life. To them the close contact of men with one another did less to strengthen civilization than to heighten the chances for epidemics, not simply of disease but also of discontent, criminality, and barbarism.[58]

Anxiety about the consequences which would follow from the unrestrained growth of factories and cities led a great many liberals to qualify their support for a totally free economy. Most liberals recognized the anachronistic and detrimental effects of guild privileges, but some were reluctant to see a total dismantling of these institutional limits on the growth of enterprises. Rotteck, for example, wanted a reform of the guilds but feared the results of their total abolition:

> With the dissolution of the guilds, total war within society will break out. The satisfying, honorable, and calm joy with which so many thousands are blessed will disappear. The poor will be reduced to wage servitude in the factories and the unwholesome aristocracy of wealth will be favored.[59]

Many liberals, especially those living in the south and west where traditional limitations on enterprise continued throughout Vormärz, tended to endorse *Gewerbefreiheit* in theory but were willing to see it significantly restricted in practice. In Baden, both the government and the opposition agreed that the local economy was simply not mature enough to do without some direction from the state.[60] Theoretical endorsement combined with practical hesitation can also be seen in liberal attitudes towards free trade. Some liberals questioned commercial freedom because they feared it would encourage large firms at the expense of smaller ones. This perception caused Johann Adam von Itzstein to oppose the Zollverein, which he, like many south Germans, regarded as an invitation to deleterious economic growth.[61]

The sense that classical economics was valuable in principle but dangerous in practice informs most of liberal economic thought during the first half of the nineteenth century. As Marie Vopelius has recently demonstrated, the first generations of liberal economists in Germany praised the effects of economic freedom but remained aware of the potential problems involved in its consistent application to the German scene.[62] Most of them were unwilling to abandon totally the reliance on the state which had pervaded German economic thought and action during the cameralist era. Karl Heinrich Rau, for example, accepted *Gewerbefreiheit* as an ideal but carefully pointed out the educational and protective role of the state. Moreover, Rau had no doubt that the state should interfere if economic freedom seemed to threaten the interests and well-being of society as a whole.[63] By the 1840s, there were economists in Germany who were willing to embrace classical economic doctrines more or less in toto. John Prince Smith, a transplanted Englishman, is the best-known advocate of a free market economy.[64] But Prince Smith was not typical and even many of those liberals who supported certain aspects of his program—free trade, for example—held back from embracing the full implications of laissez-faire.

During the 1840s liberals' uneasiness about the consequences of unrestricted economic growth was increased by what a number of them began to call the "social question." The social disturbances of the forties were the result of both long- and short-term dislocations in German social and economic development: the gradually building pressures of population growth, structural decline in certain trades, shortages caused by crop failures, and a commercial recession. Food riots in some cities, violent strikes in certain regions, and a disturbing rise in crime and pauperism produced a growing fear of what one contemporary called those "titanic forces, hostile to all man holds dear, which threaten a vast upheaval."[65]

Liberals reacted to those "titanic forces" in a variety of ways. Some managed to ignore them completely and saved their energies for political or religious controversies. Others acknowledged that there were new sorts of trouble in society but saw these problems as a spiritual crisis to be addressed with cultural improvement, or as a political threat to be met with an alliance between the *Mittelstand* and the state.[66] A number of liberals regarded social dislocation as an inevitable part of progress. Prince Smith suggested that the main causes of poverty were the poor's "aversion to labor" and their "rudeness." Poor relief would only encourage these vices, so the only answer to social problems was a more consistent application of the market mechanism.[67] Even some of those who were a good deal more compassionate than Prince Smith were inclined to argue that the problems of the 1840s could best be solved by quickening the pace of economic development and thereby raising the general level of prosperity. The suffering attendant upon this course was sure to be less than that produced by hindering industrial progress. Friedrich List expressed this viewpoint when he argued that "there are many worse things than having a proletariat: empty treasuries, national impotence, servitude, death." The sharpest suffering, List maintained, existed not where there was the greatest progress but where there was the least. The choice facing Germany was to grow economically or face the ghastly sufferings inflicted upon the Irish by their backwardness.[68]

However, a great many liberals—and they were more characteristic of the movement as a whole during Vormärz—did not accept the notion that social problems could best be met by increasing the pace of economic development. These men tended to view social dislocation as the product of development itself, not as a symptom of its insufficiency.[69] For them, the crises of the 1840s strengthened the misgivings about industrialization that had been latent in the movement for some time. The focus of their concern was usually that sector of society most vulnerable to uncontrolled growth: small tradesmen, master craftsmen, and farmers—in other words, those who had been regarded as important parts of the traditional *Mittelstand*. Johann Hoffmann, for example, an early advocate of *Gewerbefreiheit* in Prussia, argued in 1844 that the maintenance of a "numerous, independent, and prosperous lower *Mittelstand*" of craftsmen and farmers was the best defense against social upheaval.[70] A great many liberals agreed. Only a few saw industrial workers as the central element in the social question because the distinction between industrial and artisanal categories was only gradually emerging.[71] Moreover, even when a man like Mohl recognized the social importance of factory workers, he continued to argue that the best way to ease their discontents was to increase their opportunity to become self-employed. The ideal of many liberals, therefore, was not a dynamic industrial society but rather a society of prosperous small enterprises, which would avoid the cultural disorganization of factories and which would enable the social order to rest firmly on a broad stratum of independent men, each in control of his own firm.[72]

Liberals believed that if nothing was done to preserve and expand the *Mittelstand*, there would be a steady growth in its social antithesis, the group that some contemporaries began to call the "proletariat." Predictably, liberals did not agree about what this term meant. Some used it to mean all the discontented elements in society, others limited it to workers, apprentices, and masters without apprentices. As one liberal pointed out in 1847, the concepts which relate to "the slogans of our time, *pauperism, proletariat, communism, socialism,* organization of work" are "dark and confused."[73] But almost all liberals used *proletariat*, like *Mittelstand*, as both a moral and a social category. The essential characteristic of the "proletariat" was material poverty and spiritual degradation. Karl Biedermann defined the proletariat as those "without a firm position in life, without an independent business, without their own property." And he saw that with this lack of material independence went a moral inability to reach rational decisions.[74] The proletariat, therefore, was the opposite of the *Mittelstand*: dependent, irrational, rootless. And this is what made its members so dangerous to the social order. Since they had no stake in the status quo and no way of reaching an enlightened opinion, they were always susceptible to temptations to act against society as criminals, revolutionaries, or as political tools of unscrupulous demagogues.

Because the proletariat was an economic and a moral problem, most liberal reform proposals had both material and educational dimensions. Friedrich Harkort, for example, wanted to improve German schools in order to remedy the cultural deprivation of the poor and to spread those skills necessary for economic improvement.[75] But for Harkort and many other liberals, better education for the poor meant not only improved formal schooling but also involved the creation of associations, which became the liberals' most characteristic institutional response to the social question of the forties. Associations designed for adult education, cooperative saving, the learning of special skills, and the improvement of moral life were thought to be the best way to replace those corporate institutions which were being destroyed by the forces of socioeconomic development. These bodies would help men pool their resources, teach them to cooperate, give them new skills, and, most important of all, help them to overcome that sense of alienation which cut them off from the existing social order. At the very least, associations would keep the poor from utter destitution and reconcile them to their inferior position in society.[76] But the ultimate goal was to give as large a number of men as possible the skills and spiritual qualities necessary for admission to the *Mittelstand*. In the words of one educational society in Hamburg:

> So unite together, German workers, journeymen, helpers, or whatever else you call yourselves. Put your pennies together in order to attain education and training and thereby to become the pride and honour of the state in a golden *Mittelstand*.[77]

Although liberals had great hopes for the educational power of associations, many of them realized that these institutions might not be sufficient to stem the tide of social discontent. Only the state would be strong enough to assist associations and other forms of cooperative self-help in defending the social order. The state, Karl Biedermann believed, was the ''natural guardian of the workers'' with clear responsibility for social reform.[78] In the crisis atmosphere of the forties, many liberals were willing to concede that these reforms would involve restricting some of the social freedoms which they endorsed in theory. Freedom of movement, for example, was a well-established liberal goal, long asserted in opposition to those traditional institutions which wanted to retain a community's right to decide who could reside within it. But after 1840 some liberals began to fear that the growth and mobility of the population was a grave threat to the social order; they were willing, therefore, to advocate new restrictions on population movement. They had, of course, only one place to turn for the power to impose these restraints. Mevissen advocated a decentralization of industry which was to be encouraged by the state's planned dispersal of enterprises. And Mohl, that famous advocate of the *Rechtsstaat*, was ready to go even farther. As a last defense against overpopulation, he was prepared to see the state force people to emigrate and even to impose restrictions on their right to marry. The Berlin city council, which was regarded as politically liberal in the forties, considered asking the state to prohibit movement into the city so that it would not become a ''magnet for poverty.''[79]

The crises of the 1840s increased liberals' fears of social unrest, their doubts about social progress, and their inclination to look to the state for protection. But these attitudes had always been leitmotifs in liberal thought. Probably the sharpest and most influential formulation of this inclination is in Hegel's *Philosophy of Right* (1821), where he acknowledges the importance of economic activity and freedom but insists that the state must be prepared to check the disruptive forces latent in "civil society." For this reason political authority should remain in the hands of officials who were members of a "universal estate" and thus committed to defending the common good against egotism.[80] A similar orientation appears in various forms throughout liberal social thought: a contributor to the *Staatslexikon*, for example, called for state initiative in social reform because the state "represents society in its unity." Gustav Mevissen saw the difference between *staatlich* and *sozial* as the contrast between the universal and the individual, between unity and conflict.[81] Even when liberals' sympathies clearly rested with social freedom and a market economy, they retained the lingering fear that without the strong hand of the state these forces might lead society to chaos.

3 The *Staat* and the *Volk*

> Many men seem to believe that . . . the state can give without taking anything in return . . . . Those who expect and demand from the state everything they wish or require are like guests who believe that they have been invited to a free meal but are surprised when a bill is presented after they have eaten.
>
> K. S. Zachariä (1839)[1]

By the 1770s, when liberalism first emerged as ideology and movement, the bureaucratic state was already firmly established as the most significant political force in central Europe. From the beginning, liberalism's relationship to state power was intense and problematic. On the one hand, liberals saw the state as their enemy, the defender of the status quo and the instrument of repression. On the other hand, they recognized that the state could be a valuable ally, a source of progressive change and of protection against dangerous opponents. Liberals' ambivalence about the state reflected the historical role bureaucrats had come to play in eighteenth-century German states. As the tools of princely absolutism, officials had often acted against those who opposed the royal will. But as the "servants of the state," officials strove for goals shared by many progressive Germans: administrative efficiency, legal equality, and material prosperity. Commitment to these goals led many administrators and judges to take part in the organizations which signalled the arrival of a progressive public in the late eighteenth century. Like other elements of the educated elite, these officials wanted to build enlightened opinion to support their struggle for reform.[2]

Until the turn of the century, the influence of these reform-minded officials was severely limited by divisions within their own ranks, the strength of traditional institutions, and the timidity or hostility of their princely superiors. The era which opened with the French conquest of central Europe brought them new and unparalleled opportunities. Amid the political debris produced by military defeat, liberal bureaucrats emerged in many German states as the most effective instruments of change and cohesion. Opponents of reform within the administration were in disarray, traditional institutions were disrupted, and the rulers' hostility to reform was weakened by the desperate situation in which they found themselves. In Prussia, for example, an extension of bureaucratic power seemed to be the only way to survive the punishing defeats of 1806. In the *Mittelstaaten* of the Rhenish Confederation, vestiges of aristocratic and urban independence were absorbed into a cluster of administratively integrated states under Napoleon's patronage. The bureaucracy's

power was increased by a tightening of the officials' control over their own
institutions, by a further undermining of aristocratic power in the countryside
and of local authority in the towns, and by a substantial centralization of
power over social, economic, and cultural life.[3] The so-called era of reforms,
therefore, usually meant reform by, and frequently for, the administration.

In the words of Count Maximilian Montgelas, a leading Bavarian reformer,
the purpose of these changes was to "bring all subjects into a beneficient
union with the common [Bavarian] fatherland, and provide for them the
advantages of nearer association with administrative authority." As another
contemporary put it in 1809:

> The state is the highest rule of unity . . . and therefore will tolerate no
> competing states within itself. Even as a concept, the state excludes every
> independent association of members, every alien purpose, every kind of
> autonomous power.[4]

During this critical period of German history, therefore, the state's role as the
primary agent of political change was significantly enhanced.

After the defeat of Napoleon at Waterloo, many of the enemies of bureaucratic reform hoped for a rollback of administrative power and a "restoration" of traditional institutions. These men—Prussian Junkers, south German
Standesherren, religious leaders, and the defenders of local autonomy—had
some success, especially in the years immediately after 1815. But they were
never able to convert tactical victories into strategic ones: from 1815 to 1848
traditional power was not restored and the Beamtenstaat flourished. During
this period the bureaucracy occupied the center of a complex field of social
and political forces. Officials were used as the chief enforcers of the reactionary policies personified by Metternich but carried out, to some extent, in all of
central Europe. This frequently made them allies of the revolution's aristocratic enemies, with whom they continued to skirmish over questions of local
autonomy and the power of corporate institutions. A similar pattern of conflict
and collaboration obtained in the relationships of the bureaucracies to the
emerging liberal movement: the officials' role as guardian of the reactionary
status quo generated deep enmity between them and the liberals, but the
persistence of the reforming impulse in certain bureaucratic policies, as well
as in the political thinking of many individual officials, provided the basis for
cooperation.

· Closest to the surface of the liberals' relationship to the state in the years
after 1815 was the hostility almost all of them felt for the excesses of bureaucratic rule and especially for bureaucratically enforced restrictions on the
development of an enlightened public. No liberal program was complete
without a denunciation of censorship and no liberal spokesman's career was

without frustrating, humiliating, and often dangerous run-ins with state censors.[5] Censorship prevented the free flow of information and thereby the true expression of public interests and needs. The censor not only inhibited the liberal movement (which liberals saw as the political expression of these interests) but also deprived the state of the information it needed to function effectively. Even a cautious man like Friedrich Dahlmann regarded any limitations on the freedom of the press as mistaken, because, as he put it, "a fleck of dust can easily disturb the eye of the spirit."[6] To appreciate the depth of the liberals' hatred for the censor it is necessary to realize that to many liberals the question of publicity and publication had an almost sacred quality: "*Newspapers*," wrote August Ludwig Schlözer at the end of the eighteenth century, "I write this word with a feeling of awe. Newspapers are one of the great cultural instruments through which we can become European." To a later generation, newspapers, periodicals, and pamphlets were the cultural nourishment through which "Germans could become Germans" and public opinion could make itself felt within the state.[7]

The persistent antagonisms generated by censorship were part of a wider pattern of liberal frustration with the trivial and sometimes serious abuses of bureaucratic power they saw around them. At times this was simply annoyance over examples of official pendantry; imagine the dismay of enlightened men when they heard that Badenese bureaucrats were busy putting numbers on trees and posting signs that said "It is permitted to travel on this road."[8] Frequently the cause for complaint was more serious. A respectable businessman like David Hansemann, for example, was harassed by the police when there was some minor trouble with his travel documents; Robert von Mohl and a rather significant number of his colleagues were removed from teaching posts because of political unreliability; Sylvester Jordan, Friedrich Murhard, and scores of others faced arrest and imprisonment for their political convictions. More than one-sixth of the liberal elite that was elected to the Frankfurt parliament in 1848 had been persecuted by the state at one time or another in their careers.[9] Of course, persecution in Vormärz was not up to the higher standards set in our own century. Sometimes those arrested were acquitted by progressive judicial officials. Nevertheless, the wages of political commitment were not infrequently a broken career, personal anguish, and sometimes imprisonment or exile. The fact that to be a liberal required civic courage, a rare enough quality in any time or place, is too often overlooked by those who dismiss German liberalism as empty phrases or the mask of material self-interest.

Because the power of the bureaucracy was so broad and deep in the first half of the nineteenth century, the potential for conflict with the liberal movement was not confined to purely political affairs. Religion, for example, was a

matter of great significance both for the state and for many of its opponents.
Religious reform had been an important ingredient in the German enlightenment and continued to motivate many of those who began to identify themselves with the liberal opposition after 1815. At the same time, the religious
authority of the state, a traditional feature of German Protestantism, increased
along with the rest of bureaucratic power. When the state attempted to use its
power to defend doctrinal and institutional orthodoxy, religious conflicts were
transformed into political ones.[10] Inevitably, those who wanted more
tolerance for theological diversity and more flexible patterns of governance in
the church were forced into opposition to the state. Similarly, even those who
were indifferent to theological issues could be drawn into theological controversies which they saw as contests between bureaucratic authority and the
rights of the individual. Demands for religious freedom, therefore, became
part of the liberal effort to create a free public in which men would be able to
follow the dictates of their own enlightened opinion. The Lichtfreunde
controversy during the 1840s is a good example of the way in which political opposition and religious dissent could join and become mutually
reinforcing.[11]

For some of those in the liberal movement, the state's involvement in
economic affairs was a more important source of political opposition than its
religious policies. This was especially true in economically dynamic regions
of Germany such as the Rhineland, where businessmen continually complained about the state's insensitivity to and harmful interference in economic
affairs. These men often felt threatened by what they saw as a basic hostility
to their activities shown by some officials. This was certainly the feeling some
Barmen industrialists brought home with them from Berlin when they were
told by a minister that industry was a "cancer" eating at society's vitals.[12]
Businessmen were also exasperated by the inconsistencies of state economic
growth. Some officials were sympathetic to economic growth, but suspicious
of certain kinds of commercial activity such as joint stock companies and
banks. Others were more vigorous defenders of economic freedom than the
entrepreneurs themselves and denied them the protection they felt was necessary. Others protected what entrepreneurs regarded as the wrong sectors of
the economy at the expense of what they saw as the most dynamic and significant ones. Liberal businessmen's views of the state were by no means
consistent and homogeneous, but the majority of them did feel they were
being discriminated against by the *Beamtenstaat* and constantly explored the
limits of its willingness to tolerate or promote their activities.[13]

Opposition to the restrictions imposed on Germans' lives by the political,
cultural, and economic policies of the bureaucratic state provided what many
contemporaries regarded as the most important single impetus for the liberal

movement. In the Prussian provincial *Landtage*, in the parliaments of the
south German *Mittelstaaten*, in the correspondence of liberal leaders, and in
an increasing number of books and pamphlets, we find a litany of complaints
about the *Beamtenkaste* and its unwarranted limitations on the free development of enlightenment and progress.[14] This opposition to bureaucratic excesses helped to blur the differences within the liberals' own ranks by
encouraging them to put aside internecine conflicts in the face of this powerful
common enemy. Moreover, the liberals profited from the fact that their opposition to the bureaucracy was shared by a number of other groups in Germany.
Young aristocrats like Heinrich von Gagern and Rudolf von Bennigsen were
drawn into the movement by their distaste for official arrogance and sterility.
Sometimes Catholics were attracted to the political opposition because they
felt its insistence on limiting state power would protect their church from
official interference. And in a number of areas, the Rhineland for example,
liberalism's appeal came in part from the antipathy men felt to a central
bureaucracy whose activities were made especially obnoxious by regional
antagonisms.[15]

Despite the manifest importance of liberal protests against the excesses of
the Vormärz *Beamtenstaat*, it is incorrect to define the movement in terms of
its desire "to push back the power and influence of the state for the sake of the
liberty of the individual."[16] Certainly there were always a few consistent
enemies of the state among German liberals, but most of their positions were a
good deal more complicated. Most liberals, while hostile to the abuses of state
power, acknowledged the state's importance in shaping fundamental social,
economic and political institutions. For a clear majority in the movement, the
problem was how to reconcile their hatred for official despotism with their
recognition that state power had been, and could still be a way of fulfilling
some of their most cherished ideals. Friedrich Dahlmann once described
Prussia as a state with "the magic spear which heals as well as wounds," a
striking image which many of his contemporaries might have applied to the
bureaucratic phenomenon in general.[17]

The deep ambivalence which characterized most liberals' attitudes toward
the state was frequently expressed in the political literature published during
the first half of the nineteenth century. In Paul Pfizer's famous *Briefwechsel
zweier Deutschen*, this ambivalence appears in the conflicting assessment of
the state given by the two "correspondents"; taken together their views
represented the contrasting impulses which Pfizer, like many of his contemporaries, tried to combine in his own thought.[18] Similarly, the influential
Staatslexikon contains frequent attacks on the bureaucracy, but very few of its
contributors were willing to see the state reduced to a guardian of law and
order. Theodor Welcker, for instance, combined opposition to the officials'

Kastengeist with the conviction that the state had a "positive moral function" without which it would be like a legal marriage without love. Karl Mathy agreed that the state should play an important role in the social and economic life of the nation.[19] One of the best statements of these themes was an article, "Über Bureaukratie," which Robert von Mohl published in 1846. Mohl traced the increasing use of the term "bureaucracy" whose negative connotations reflected the growing antipathy many Germans felt toward the public administration. He acknowledged the validity of these complaints and pointed to the need for greater popular participation in the political process. But Mohl also recognized the positive accomplishments of the state and argued that the best way of dispelling criticism of the administration was not to dismantle it but rather to employ better-qualified officials.[20]

The ambivalence which individual liberals displayed toward the state was reproduced within the movement as a whole. On one extreme was a minority which wholeheartedly opposed the state and was willing to see its functions severely limited. At the other extreme, some liberals maintained that the state was the most important source of progress, despite its occasional abuses in practice. To a liberal official like Otto Camphausen, for example, the rigorous selection process and relative independence of the Prussian administration produced "a sort of aristocracy of achievement," which served as the "true representative of the common good." Johann Gustav Droysen agreed, calling the Prussian bureaucracy "the most noble spiritual force in the fatherland," although, it should be noted, Droysen also recognized the need for greater popular participation in political life.[21]

The complexity of liberal attitudes can be illustrated by examining liberal views of the state's role in a few key areas of life during the first half of the nineteenth century. A good place to begin is with education, which liberals regarded as of the greatest importance for the future. "Where schools flourish," predicted one liberal spokesman, "slow, gradual, but inevitable progress is assured."[22] A great many bureaucrats agreed; as Lorenz von Stein once put it, the state came to realize that it needed "education, just as it needed money, the army, and roads."[23] In the late eighteenth and early nineteenth centuries, therefore, bureaucrats in a number of German states devoted themselves to expanding the school system and, at the same time, to increasing their own power over its operation. As we might expect, liberals complained bitterly about the use of the educational system for reactionary purposes; they denounced the harassment of teachers whose political views appeared insufficiently orthodox. However, liberals recognized that the power and resources of the state were essential if Germany was to have the kind of schools they wanted. In a widely read pamphlet on educational reform, Friedrich Harkort argued that schools were obviously a *Staatsangelegenheit*; the

teacher must stop being the "pastor's assistant" and must become a "servant
of the state." Much the same message emerges from the long sections on
education in the *Staatslexikon* which combine criticism of the state's abuse of
its powers with the demand that the state support, encourage, and even inspect
and control the schools.[24] Perhaps the best single example of these attitudes is
provided by the career of Wilhelm von Humboldt, the author of a famous
treatise on the limitations of state power, who was responsible for the
bureaucratically-inspired educational measures passed in Prussia during the
era of reforms.[25]

The principal reason why many liberals were willing to acknowledge the
state's power in educational affairs was their belief that it was a necessary ally
against other, even more dangerous influences at work in German life, such as
the Catholic church, whose hold over its members had to be broken before an
enlightened public could emerge. "The state," argued Harkort, "has to replace the church in matters of education in order for its independence to be
assured." Droysen believed that "only the state could be tolerant in matters of
religion." At times, this "tolerance" might have to have a repressive dimension. Many liberals, for example, were willing to have the state use its power
to expel the Jesuits, even though they condemned this kind of repression when
it was turned against their own institutions. On the radical left of the movement were many who viewed an extension of the state's power over both
Protestant and Catholic churches as a necessary step toward the secularization
of society.[26] And even among more moderate and religiously inclined liberals
there was a tendency to acknowledge that if the state and the church should
find themselves in conflict, the state should always have the final say. Thus a
progressive theologian like Schleiermacher could argue that it is "the state
[which] joins the individual to the universal good and the divine order."[27]

There were also many in the liberal movement who looked to the state for
the emancipation of Germany's Jews. This was the position taken in C. W.
Dohm's *Über die bürgerliche Verbesserung der Juden* (1781), and it was
repeated in much of the literature on emancipation written after the turn of the
century. In fact, the bureaucratic state confronted Jews with precisely the
same combination of progressive action and repression which characterized its
role in so many other aspects of German life. Official decrees granting Jews
legal equality had been an important part of the reform era, while reactionary
bureaucrats often enforced limitations on this equality after 1815. It is not
surprising, therefore, that the initial political stance of many Jews mixed an
inclination toward radical protest with a sense that the state was the primary
instrument for future reform and their emancipation.[28]

Just as the liberals' cultural and religious attitudes combined protests
against censorship and enforced orthodoxy with a desire for progressive initia-

tives on the part of the state, so liberals' economic views were a composite of complaints about the bureaucracy and calls for collaboration with the state. Both theorists and businessmen sought to make the state a partner in their quest for social progress and personal enrichment. Perhaps the most famous theoretical statement of the need for state action came from Friedrich List. Although List was aware that in some circumstances administrative interference with economic life could have unfortunate results, he maintained that the prevailing backwardness of the economy made state protection necessary if the growth of German industries was not to be inhibited by the more developed nations.[29] Protection and active subvention were also demanded by many businessmen, especially those active in enterprises like the railroads which involved large-scale capital investment and complex jurisdictional disputes. On the basis of his experience as an entrepreneur in the Rhineland, Gustav Mevissen believed that "only a powerful state policy will be able to give economic life the basis for expansion." Both Mevissen and David Hansemann assigned the state a role in building up the infrastructure upon which future growth would be based.[30] Friedrich Harkort extended this to include the spiritual as well as the material basis for development: the state, he argued, had to introduce the educational measures necessary to create skilled workers and receptive consumers. To him, liberalism was not primarily free markets and economic mobility but the creation of a "protective *bürgerlich* state."[31]

Perhaps the most consequential instance of liberals' ambivalence toward the state was their view of its role in creating national unity. Most liberals realized that the bureaucratic establishments in the various German states provided formidable barriers to the attainment of the nation many of them ardently desired. Some believed that to dismantle these barriers it would be necessary to liberate the political energies of the German *Volk*: "Only freedom will be able to increase national feeling enough to dissolve provincial differences and especially to direct every competing national loyalty toward the new fatherland to which it belongs."[32] Other liberals, however, were not so sure. In practice, of course, it had not been "freedom" but the bureaucracies of Prussia and the *Mittelstaaten* which had so successfully destroyed regional institutions during the era of reform. And to a liberal like Paul Pfizer, state power still represented the best hope for carrying on this process at the national level. "It is doubtful," Pfizer wrote, "whether personal freedom in the constitutional state would lead us to unity." It would be better, he felt, to have "the most violent of despots" ruling a unified nation, since once unity had been achieved, "no power in the world" would be able to halt "the progressive dissemination of liberal ideas and institutions."[33] In practice, liberal uncertainty about the role of the state in the struggle for national unity was often expressed in their conflicting attitudes about Prussia, which was condemned by some as the "gendarme of absolutism," but praised by others as a potential ally in the service of freedom and unity.[34]

Liberal attitudes toward the state, therefore, were the product of two conflicting sets of pressures. On one side was the antistatist impulse of western European liberal thought and the frustrations caused by the repressive realities of bureaucratic absolutism. On the other side, however, was the record of progressive reforms sponsored by the state and, equally important, the conviction shared by many liberals that the state remained an indispensable ally in a society as culturally, religiously, and economically backward as their own. Most German liberals did not want to limit or destroy the power of the state but rather to purge it of abuses and turn its power toward liberal aims. "Who does not wish the state well?" asked one liberal in 1842:

> We all want it to be great, mighty, powerful, and rational. We all have no other wish than to be absorbed into the state, and to devote our strength to it. Our highest goal is to become citizens and to think and act as such.[35]

It is significant that the word for *citizen* here is *Staatsbürger*, which gathers to a terminological point the opposing strands of liberalism's relationship to the state.[36] From the beginning of modern political life in Germany, it had been the state which had created the foundations for citizenship by weakening the restraints imposed by traditional society, breaking down the power of regional loyalties and institutions, creating laws which linked the individual to the central polity. Liberalism's main problem was how to build upon these achievements of the *Staat* and at the same time to fulfill the promise implied by the word *Bürger*, the promise of a participant public willing and able to define its own destiny.

Almost every liberal in the first half of the nineteenth century would have regarded as the first step toward making the state "mighty, powerful, and rational" the creation of a rule of law, a *Rechtsstaat*, in which all the organs of government would be governed by principles of justice. In fact, the concept of the *Rechtsstaat* was first formulated by bureaucrats, who saw the rule of law as a weapon against the parochial customs of traditional society and the arbitrary whims of the ruler. By the end of the eighteenth century, however, the idea of the *Rechsstaat* was also applied to the relationship between the state and its citizens. Kant used this notion to synthesize his hopes for freedom in society with his respect for the authority of the state. A few liberals after 1800 saw the *Rechtsstaat* as the final goal of progressive politics; through it bureaucratic excess would be limited but the state's ultimate and autonomous power would also be reaffirmed.[37] For most liberals, however, the attainment of a just state required more than this. For them, justice inevitably involved the creation of political institutions through which enlightened public opinion could be expressed and absorbed into the policy-making process.[38]

Liberals by no means agreed on these issues. On one extreme were those who recognized the value of representative institutions but wanted to keep their influence over political affairs as limited as possible. For example, the author of an article on "Constitutional Questions," which appeared in the *Deutsche Vierteljahrsschrift* in 1846, argued that the public would value the parliament more if it was not involved in political decisions and thus did not have an opportunity "to make mistakes and earn the enmity of the crowd." This writer also believed that it would be a great mistake to sacrifice the bureaucracy's knowledge and experience in favor of parliamentary committees. The answer was not to increase the autonomous power of the parliament but to give its members a chance to participate in administrative affairs as *Beisitzer*.[39] Friedrich Dahlmann had an equally modest role in mind for representative institutions. He believed that they should "restrain the arbitrary power of the ruler but not weaken the power of the government."[40] Some liberals, however, were willing to go a great deal farther than this. John Prince Smith spoke of political progress in terms of the "participation of the *Volk* in determining the business of the state." And of course there were even those on the extreme left of the liberal movement who believed that the legitimate source of political power and sovereignty was to be found in the *Volk*.[41] But most liberals were probably somewhere in between these extremes. Characteristically, the moderate majority struggled to combine in their own thought and action the alternatives sharply posed on the movement's far right and left.[42]

A good place to observe this struggle is in Baden, the German state with the most progressive constitution and the most advanced parliamentary life during the first half of the century. In the course of a Landtag debate in 1821, liberal delegates maintained that the government could not rule in the long run without the support of public opinion, which one of them defined as "developed and active reason." The art of the statesman, they argued, was to ascertain and be guided by this opinion. But, responded a member of the government, isn't this a demand for rule by the parliament? The liberals denied that this was their intention, asserting instead that parliamentary debates would allow enlightened opinion to manifest itself and then the wise statesmen would follow its beacon.[43] In this exchange we can see some characteristic ingredients of liberals' views on representative government: faith in the enlightened character of public opinion, a defense of its importance in public life, and a deep reluctance to specify the mechanism through which its influence could be imposed. The same complex of views can be found in the political thought of Karl von Rotteck. He regarded the

Gesamtwille as one of the central pillars of political life, and he recognized that electoral politics were the clearest and "most unquestionable way" this will could be expressed. But when faced with the problem of how the *Gesamtwille* and the government related to one another, he sought refuge in the belief that no ruler could long resist the power of his citizens' enlightened will. Rotteck, moreover, continually emphasized that the government had to maintain its "independence." Even a republic would become "dangerous and uncontrollable" if "the executive did not have a certain independence from the community and the representative institutions."[44] Rotteck's coeditor of the *Staatslexikon*, Theodor Welcker, provided a concise summary of this position when he defined the state as the "sovereign, moral, personal, vital social association of a *Volk*, united in a freely constituted parliament, "under the leadership of an appropriate and constitutionally independent government."[45]

These attempts to affirm the power of the *Volk* and the independence of the *Staat* were characteristic of a great many liberals' political thought throughout the nineteenth century. Some, like Welcker and Rotteck, simply stated their faith in both and their belief that conflict between them was unlikely. Others took refuge in an organic conception of the state which joined in some unspecified fashion representative institutions and bureaucratic power. Still others looked to a unified German nation as the means through which these elements might be reconciled. Whatever the specific formulation, the same unwillingness to define the final location of sovereignty can be found, an unwillingness which came from the liberals' reluctance to confront the full practical and theoretical implications of their desire to represent the *Volk* against the state. Most of them, therefore, were unable to devise clear alternatives to the monarchical power which was unambiguously enshrined in the constitutions of the *Mittelstaaten* and in the political practice of those states, such as Prussia, which did not have a constitution before 1848.[46]

As with other aspects of their thought and action in Vormärz, the liberals' political vocabulary often masked their ambiguities. As one contemporary put it: "Public life is new to us, so new that even the language itself is strange. Particularly with regard to concepts which are associated with the words *sovereignty* and *constitution* there is great confusion."[47] A good example of this confusion is the liberals' demand for ministerial responsibility, which many of them took to be an important way of guaranteeing the responsiveness of the state to the needs of enlightened opinion.[48] Most of those who used this term, however, never made clear *to whom* the government was to be responsible and what should happen if it behaved in an "irresponsible" fashion. Their defense of governmental "independence" implied that the political responsibility of the government would be rather

limited. Most of them seemed to have thought in terms of a responsibility to
follow the law rather than to follow the political will of the nation's representatives; in this view, irresponsible action by the government would result in
legal action, not in political conflict between parliament and state.[49] Mohl was
one of the few liberals to recognize the fragility of this conception. After a
long and arduous process, which included a seven-hundred page book on the
purely legal aspects of ministerial responsibility, he was able to present a clear
picture of a parliamentary system and was willing to offer it as a way of
resolving the inconsistencies in German thought and action. But Mohl himself
was not free from the liberals' reluctance to engage in a direct struggle with
the state. As we saw in the last chapter, he was prepared to see the state take
extraordinary measures to prevent social unrest. Moreover, in the years after
1850 Mohl's faith in the parliamentary system waned, and he began to place
important qualifications on his demand that it be introduced in Germany.[50]

A revealing symptom of that persistent obscurity about the ultimate locus of
power which informs so much liberal political thought was their inability to
grasp the essential character of English institutions. An anglophile like Friedrich Dahlmann, for example, did not fully comprehend the parliament's role
in English public life and consequently overestimated the importance of the
monarch. Similarly, most German observers misunderstood the significance
of ministerial responsibility in England and tended to see it in terms of their
own legal categories. These misconceptions were partly due to the unsettled
character of British constitutional developments during the first half of the
nineteenth century. But they were also an example of a process which is of
great importance for understanding the transmission of liberal ideas east of the
Rhine. The way in which German liberals formed a distorted view of English
reality suggests how concepts and perceptions change as they are refracted
through men's experience. German liberals' misconceptions about England,
therefore, are part of a wider and more complex set of problems involved in
the attempt to use western European concepts in a very different historical
setting.[51]

An important clue to the reasons why so many liberals were reluctant to see
representative institutions as the source of power and sovereignty can be
found in the political writings of Karl Zachariä. Zachariä was not insensitive
to the dangers of dependence on the state, as his remarks used for this
chapter's epigraph make clear. Although he was a defender of the parliament's importance in the political system, he shared the characteristic liberal
hesitancy to define the precise modes through which parliament and government were to interact. He also acknowledged that, in case of a conflict between them, the government would almost certainly prevail. It is enlightening
to examine the way in which Zachariä expressed the distinction between these

two organs of government: "The hereditary rule [*erbliche Einherrschaft*] relates to the representative institutions as stability to change, rest to movement, nature to art, unity to diversity, public power to public freedom."[52] These dichotomies appear in the political thought of many liberals for whom the state was a necessary source of continuity, security, and order. With this often went the muted (and sometimes not so muted) fear that the *Volk* could be too fluctuating, chaotic, volatile, unstable. Thus Paul Pfizer, who sometimes seemed to favor popular government, insisted that the monarch had to be strong "in order that he can grasp or pull in the reins every time the *Volk* lacks the decisive will or, because of factionalism or flaccidity, approaches the dangers of dissolution."[53]

This sense of risk is a leitmotif in the thought of many liberals, coexisting uneasily with their eloquent words in praise of public opinion and enlightenment. It suggests an anxiety born of the liberals' sense that beyond the enlightened ranks of the nation were those shadowy and hostile groups which might force society into chaos, the mob which Welcker regarded as "a more savage enemy of the common good than any other." Even so progressive and committed a liberal as Friedrich Murhard could write, "I am myself born a commoner and I am true to the interests of the citizens until my dying day; still, nothing is more repellent to me than when I see those who would replace the decent pride of princes with the coarse pride of the mob."[54]

This fear of the mob made most liberals extremely reluctant to acknowledge the right of citizens to rebel against unjust authority. Some of them did defend this right: Murhard did so, but only after a long and difficult intellectual struggle and the bitter experience of imprisonment for his political views.[55] Most liberals, however, saw in rebellion the potential for terror and tyranny which had perverted the French Revolution, a historical example that was burned into their political imagination.[56] Just as liberals left unresolved the problem of a confrontation between state and *Volk*, so too they ignored the unhappy possibility that the forces of reaction might prove too strong to be conquered by the evolving power of enlightened opinion.

Liberals' uneasiness about rebellion, their reluctance to pose a clear parliamentary alternative to monarchical rule, and their inclination to view the bureaucratic state as a potential ally were shaped by their historical position. The fact that so many of the movement's most prominent spokesmen were employed by the state meant that liberal theory was defined by men who tried to combine an official position with political opposition, to criticize institutions on which they themselves depended. To do this often required courage, but it also set limits on liberals' ability and willingness to think beyond and act against state power. By the time liberalism began in Germany the state was already a potent force in political life—in contrast to the English setting of

classical liberal theory. In many parts of central Europe, the repressive power
of the state made resistance dangerous, while its positive role evoked hopes
for fruitful collaboration. Finally, liberals' attitudes about bureaucratic authority reflected their sense that Germany's moral and material backwardness
required the state's assistance not only against the lingering influences of
traditional forces but also against the dangers of mob rule. Liberals' assessment of the state, therefore, was inseparable from their assessment of German
society. Deference to authority and anxiety about disorder, the pull of the
Staat and the fear of the *Volk*, were interrelated and mutually reinforcing parts
of the same political vision.

Despite what they were up against, German liberals accomplished a great deal
during Vormärz. In newspapers, magazines, and publications such as the
Staatslexikon, they were able to formulate some basic questions about Germany's future. In state and local parliaments, they began to form factions,
define programs, and discuss strategies. In cities and towns across central
Europe, they started to build an institutional base in clubs, educational
societies, and similar organizations. But despite these impressive accomplishments, German liberalism continued to bear the marks of the hostile
environment in which it took shape. Behind liberals' brave hopes for a powerful *Partei*, a united *Bewegung* propelled to victory by the reliable winds of
historical progress, was the continued fragmentation of their political experience and the unyielding narrowness of their popular support. Behind their
identification with the common good and their proclamation of themselves as
the enlightened *Mittelstand* were complex social and economic divisions
and lingering anxieties about the direction of social change. Behind their
promise of a reconciled *Volk* and *Staat* were deeply rooted fears about the
implications of popular rule and a pervasive unwillingness to challenge the
ultimate authority of the state. As long as liberals remained in opposition,
forced to communicate in censored abstractions and to act within a diffuse set
of local institutions, these problems could remain latent; they are certainly
much clearer to us now than they were to most contemporaries then. After
1848, however, these problems would manifest themselves with increasing
clarity as liberals tried to use their ideas and organizations to transform German political and social life.

II Revolutionary Overture 1848–49

One of the most remarkable things about the revolutions of 1848 was the fact that they were anticipated by so many contemporaries. As an American diplomat reported from Europe in 1847: "All well-informed people express the belief that the existing crisis is so deeply interwoven in the events of the present that 'it' is but the commencement of that great revolution, which they consider sooner or later is to dissolve the constitution of things."[1] Specter, storm, volcano—these were the words men used to describe the inevitable cataclysm which would divide the present from the future. When, during those unseasonably warm days in March 1848, the storm seemed finally to have come, many German liberals were filled with the hope that a new age, their age, was about to begin. During the opening stages of the revolution this hope was a necessary source of strength and courage. But as time went on and the revolutionary spring gave way to summer and autumn, it became increasingly clear that liberals' hopes for a new age rested upon cruel and debilitating illusions.

Gradually it became apparent that the revolutionary storm had left most of the world of Vormärz in place. Despite a brief national election campaign, Germany remained a fragmented political system, in which local loyalties, regional diversity, fragile institutional ties, and rudimentary communications inhibited collective action. Despite widespread dissatisfaction with prevailing conditions, Germans were deeply divided by a tangled set of special economic interests and incompatible social values. Despite the governments' initial impotence, the instruments of their power remained, their armies held together, their administrative apparatus continued to function. Furthermore, the world of Vormärz also persisted in the liberals' own attitudes, habits, and values. Few of them had had the kind of experience which might have helped them to deal effectively with the problems they had to face. They were, after all, accustomed to talking to one another within the narrow institutional confines of a local club or state assembly; now they had to act on a national forum and reach out to the broad masses of the nation.[2] They were enmeshed with the state—in their careers, their ideals, and their emotions—and now they had to shed these habits of deference and to think of themselves as the legitimate source of political power.[3]

Perhaps if liberals had been better able to transcend their own past, if they had been less shortsighted and more courageous, they might have emerged victorious. Certainly they could have left a more heroic legacy to their heirs in the second half of the century. Nevertheless, as we follow the unhappy story of the liberal revolutionaries' ultimate collapse, it is well to keep in mind the formidable barriers which stood in their path.

The Coming of
the Revolution

Our time of political innocence, of
trusting deference is over—but the era
of political freedom has not yet begun.

Johann Jacoby (June 5, 1848)[1]

By the end of 1847, many liberals were convinced that a new stage in the evolution of German political life was about to begin. As an anonymous contributor to the popular periodical *Grenzboten* put it, freedom in Germany has ceased to be a poet's dream and has begun to acquire a base among the masses of society.[2] In many ways, 1847 had seen an awakening of political consciousness without parallel in German experience. Perhaps the most dramatic single event was the meeting of the so-called United Landtag in Berlin, a gathering of the representatives from the various provincial parliaments called by the Prussian king in an attempt to calm the rising waves of opposition in his realm. The United Landtag had precisely the opposite effect: not only did it give some liberal spokesmen a national forum from which to broadcast their demands, but its eventual dissolution significantly increased the level of discontent within Prussia.[3] By the autumn of 1847, pressures for reform had become manifest throughout the kingdom. In November, for example, a large number of city councils used their newly attained right to hold public meetings as the occasion for popular demonstrations in support of constitutional change.[4] These political activities occurred against the background of increasing concern for social and economic issues; throughout 1847, there were several spontaneous demonstrations expressing discontent with food shortages and other economic problems. That year, disagreements about tariff policy led to the formation of the first independent economic interest group in Prussia, John Prince Smith's Freihandelsverein.[5]

The excitement generated by events in Berlin, together with the growing momentum of local movements, sharply increased political activity throughout the smaller states of the south and southwest. In Württemberg there was an extraordinary session of the Landtag in which the political opposition played an unusually active role. In Saxony and Hesse-Darmstadt, liberals participated in a series of confrontations with the government on a variety of issues. In Bavaria, popular discontent, evoked in part by hostility to the king's mistress, Lola Montez, helped to force the resignation of the reactionary Abel ministry; that autumn a special session of the Bavarian parliament was convened.[6]

There was also a marked increase in the number of regional and even national organizations and relationships. In the summer, physicians, lawyers, philologists, philosophers, foresters, and gymnasts held national conclaves which all had political overtones. Moreover, the informal contacts among liberals from various parts of Germany increased as men began to consult with one another about the future course of events.[7]

An important expression of this new vitality occurred in September, when political leaders from a number of southwestern states met in Offenburg to formulate a program. In addition to the usual call for an end to censorship and repression, the Offenburg statement demanded the representation of the *Volk* at the Germanic Confederation and the introduction of popular [*volkstüm-liche*] administration. There was no effort to spell out what these words might mean, no mention of suffrage laws or constitutional models, but the emphasis on government by and for the *Volk* was clear. A month later, a different collection of notables gathered at Heppenheim. These men did not produce a formal program, but the *Deutsche Zeitung* did publish an extended report on their discussion, which was generally regarded as a moderate reply to the Of-fenburgers. Overall, the differences between the two documents are matters of tone and emphasis, barely visible behind vague generalities and abstract exhortations. But the differences were prominent enough to suggest that one product of renewed political consciousness was a sharper definition of the divisions within the opposition. The Heppenheimers, for example, viewed the Prussian-led Customs Union (Zollverein) rather than the Confederation as the proper foundation for a new nation, a preference which reflected their pro-Prussian orientation as well as their inclination to stress the economic advantages of nationhood. Like the Offenburg program, the Heppenheim discussion acknowledged the need for representative institutions but seemed somewhat less prepared to put unqualified faith in the creative power of the *Volk*.[8]

In a variety of ways, therefore, political activity on the eve of the revolution was beginning to shatter the restrictive confines of Vormärz institutions. In provincial and state parliaments, city councils, clubs and associations, and in the private correspondence of liberal notables, we can detect a new sense of crisis and opportunity. In this already volatile setting, the revolutionary violence which began in Italy and France during the first weeks of 1848 had an immediate catalytic effect. At the end of February, the news of the French monarchy's fall set off widespread political agitation and popular disorder east of the Rhine. For better or worse, people throughout central Europe were about to begin their first large-scale effort at effecting fundamental political change from below.

The energy and initial success of the revolution came from the fact that many different groups in German society were brought together by their dissatisfaction with the status quo. Like almost every modern revolution, 1848 was a "revolution of conflicting expectations," carried out by men who did not share a common vision of how discontents might be dissolved.[9]

From the beginning, there were important differences between those who saw the revolution as primarily a political phenomenon aimed at constitutional reform and those who saw it as a way to relieve economic and social problems. The relative importance of and relationship between these groups, which Bruno Bauer called the "national" and "social" elements of the revolution, varied from place to place.[10] In a few regions there was not a great deal of social unrest, and liberals remained the only visible spokesmen for change. But sometimes popular unrest swept aside or simply ignored the liberals: this happened in the south and west where peasants attacked manor houses to express their hatred of seignorial obligations and in cities where artisans destroyed machines which they felt threatened their livelihood; elsewhere men seized the opportunity created by the revolution to assault an unpopular official or protest against an unpopular policy. These outbreaks of popular violence were an intensification of the social unrest which had erupted sporadically throughout Vormärz.[11] In some areas, political and social discontents fused, if only briefly. This happened, for example, in Berlin, which is the best known but certainly not the most characteristic revolutionary episode. Here counterrevolutionary violence, widespread hatred for the army, and longstanding frustrations with the regime created a broadly based coalition directed against the government. In other Prussian cities, such as Cologne, moderate liberals opposed mass disorder almost from the start.[12]

To suggest, as some scholars have, that liberals "led" the masses during the opening phase of the revolution is to oversimplify the diverse and often inchoate relationships between the political and social movements.[13] It is true that some, especially those on the extreme left of the Vormärz opposition, would have liked to lead the masses in a revolutionary assault on the existing order. But this happened only for a short time and in a few areas. On the other hand, there were those on the opposition's right wing who were frightened from the start by what Ludolf Camphausen called the *Kommunistencliquen*. Camphausen and others like him swiftly became convinced that only a joint effort between reformers and the state could restore public order.[14] The majority of liberals were to be found somewhere between these extremes. Most of them were uneasy about popular violence but still hopeful that the "onwards rushing revolution" could be diverted to a "reformist path."[15]

In addition to these complex relationships between the political and social components of the revolution there were a series of conflicts and divisions within the political opposition itself. Here again it is important not to lose sight of regional diversity. In some places, the alignment of forces present in

Vormärz continued and the basic framework of participatory institutions remained virtually unchanged. Here liberals used clubs, municipal institutions,
and various informal organizations to generate support and petition the states
for reform. Elsewhere, however, these institutions quickly collapsed under
the weight of the agitation they suddenly had to carry. New associations were
founded, disagreements erupted between radical and moderate elements, and
new men emerged to challenge established liberal notables.[16] In Württemberg, for example, disagreements between moderates and radicals found expression as soon as the revolution began. The former tended to be increasingly
frightened of popular unrest and therefore willing to act with the state; the
latter distrusted existing institutions and came to view any cooperation with
them as playing into the hands of the reactionaries. Even in Württemberg,
however, these disagreements did not find institutional expression right away;
only gradually did there develop a set of *Vereine* clearly linked to a political
program.[17]

The most prominent and best articulated political divisions occurred among
those notables who met, first at Heidelberg and then in the so-called *Vorparlament* at Frankfurt, in order to decide how a national constitution should be
established. Initially, moderate leaders such as Heinrich von Gagern and
Friedrich Bassermann opposed the idea of a constituent assembly, which they
feared would lead to republicanism and chaos. They wanted a national constitution but were reluctant to bypass the established order. Even the experience of revolution was not enough to overcome the deference toward the *Staat*
that was so deeply rooted in the minds of some liberals. Eventually, however,
most moderates had to admit that a national parliament was inevitable. The
incompetence of the Confederation, the apparent weakness of the various
states, and the power of popular movements precluded any other alternative. It
became necessary, as one contemporary put it, "to become revolutionary in
order to avoid a revolution."[18]

Although they agreed to the creation of a national parliament, many liberals
continued to be uneasy about the extent of popular participation in political
life. This was clearly reflected in the Vorparlament's statement on the suffrage question. The majority rejected any limitation on the right to vote, but
the final declaration gave the suffrage to all "independent" Germans. It is not
known how the word "independent" got into the final draft. Possibly·there
was some kind of chicanery involved, but probably it was another example of
the conceptual obscurity and ideological uncertainty which had always characterized liberals' attitudes toward the *Volk*. The moderates at the Vorparlament may well have assumed that "all citizens" meant all "independent"
citizens, just as they assumed, without explicitly saying so, that all citizens
meant all male citizens.[19] If the liberals' ambivalence toward the *Volk* was

revealed by the wording of the election regulations, the enforcement of these regulations demonstrated their dependence on the states. Since the Vorparlament lacked the power to put its decisions into practice, it had no choice but to ask the various states to administer the elections.

Because the states were free to interpret "independent" any way they wished and because they could choose to make the voting either direct or indirect, the elections were administered rather differently in the various German states. Frequently, efforts were made to qualify the democratic implications of the Vorparlament's decisions. For instance, most states decided to use an indirect voting procedure because they believed that the interposition of an electoral college between the mass of voters and their elected representative would exert a moderating influence. And, in a number of areas, "independence" was defined so as to exclude important sectors of the population.[20]

More important than the election law and its application were those habits of mind and action which shaped Germans' relationship to their political system. It is hardly surprising that a political culture which had developed over decades was not suddenly transformed by an election campaign lasting a few weeks. In some areas (and these are the ones we tend to know the most about), the local leadership was able to generate considerable interest in the campaign. But elsewhere apathy and habits of deference persisted and popular involvement in the political process remained rather low.[21] Overall, it seems probable that less than half of the adult males in the population took advantage of their right to vote.[22]

The election campaign in various parts of Germany suggests that a great many liberal leaders, no less than the masses of the electorate, remained closely tied to the habits of the prerevolutionary era. It is true that in some regions—especially in parts of the southwest and in some of the larger cities—the campaign produced specific programs and revealed sharp divisions within the liberal camp. We can find, especially on the far right and left of the Vormärz opposition, clearly stated positions on the future role of the existing states, monarchical institutions, and popular participation.[23] But most moderate liberals continued to express their hopes for a reconciliation of popular participation and state power with characteristic vagueness. For instance, Rudolf Haym told his supporters that "the worth and security of the princes will grow, the more deeply the ringing spirit of freedom permeates into the lowest depths of the *Volk*."[24] At about the same time, the citizens of Hamm were given a vivid example of the liberals' ambivalence about the state and the *Volk* and of their desire to avoid choosing between the two:

In order to realize our ideas of freedom and equality, we want above all a strong and powerful government, which, based on the legislative principle of popular sovereignty and strengthened by the authority of a hereditary monarchy, will be able to repress with an iron hand any disorder [*Zügellosigkeit*] and any violation of the law.[25]

Political discourse during the spring of 1848 continued to display that imprecision and tendency toward abstraction which had obscured the divisions within liberalism during the preceding decades. In Hildesheim, for example, everyone who opposed absolutism called himself a "democrat." Similarly, Rudolf Virchow proudly proclaimed his republicanism, but added that he thought the republic should have a hereditary president.[26] For a great many liberals the purpose of the elections was not to clarify programs and debate tactical alternatives but rather to elect enlightened men of good will who could then reason together and formulate a new political order. Thus an election pamphlet distributed in Dortmund urged voters to select "determined, free men, who will not be deflected from the right course by fear or by interests, men who have the political maturity and judgment to understand the events of the present."[27] Even the sudden opening of political opportunity did not change the liberals' penchant for turning problems of political ideology into questions of moral attitude.

Besides these impediments to the clarification of political thought and action, political expression was also inhibited by a number of practical considerations. The relative backwardness of the communications network and the weakness of supralocal ties between political groups continued to prevent the development of a nationally recognized political elite. This meant that when there was no local political leader willing and able to become a candidate, voters tended to choose some national celebrity, about whom they knew very little, or perhaps a prominent man from a nearby city.[28] All these factors help to explain how such a homogeneous parliamentary elite could emerge from elections carried on in a fragmented political system and under a variety of electoral regulations.

As can be seen in table 4.1, men in government service were especially prominent at Frankfurt. This was because, more than any other group in Germany, they combined local prestige with supralocal ties and, equally important, because they were able to accept a mandate without abandoning their regular occupation.[29] The social composition of the Berlin Assembly was also dominated by educated elites (9.5 percent administrators, 24 percent judges, 25.4 percent other professionals), although more of the Berlin delegates tended to come from the lower ranks than those at Frankfurt. There was also a much larger number (22 percent) of artisans and farmers in Berlin. We have no way of knowing whether the differences between these two simultaneously elected bodies reflected the voters' sense of their different functions

Table 4.1   **The Social Composition of
the Frankfurt Parliament**

	No. of Members (%)
Officials	
Administrative*	157 (19.7)
Judicial	119 (14.9)
Professors, teachers	123 (15.4)
Lawyers	130 (16.3)
Clergy	45 (5.6)
Writers, journalists	36 (4.5)
Physicians, etc.	25 (3.1)
Businessmen	75 (9.4)
Landowners	68 (8.5)
Army officers	15 (1.9)
Miscellaneous, unknown	6 (.7)
Total	799 100

SOURCE: Eyck, *Frankfurt* (1968), p. 95.
* Includes a rather small number of
local officials.

or if it was simply easier for men with more modest means to serve in the Prussian parliament.[30]

As was the case in Vormärz, local groups were more socially heterogeneous than the national leadership. In the electoral colleges chosen to select parliamentary delegates and in the political *Vereine* which began to spread over central Europe, we find the same range of occupations which provided the basis for the political opposition before the revolution: officials and other *Gebildete*, businessmen, manufacturers, shopkeepers, and artisans.[31] Despite the obvious importance of educated men in national affairs, therefore, it should not be assumed that those who sat in the Frankfurt and Berlin parliaments were somehow typical of the movement as a whole.

The problem of *Abkömmlichkeit* is one reason why it is very difficult to know how well the political composition of the revolutionary parliaments reflected the opinion of the electorate. It may be, for example, that the liberals' relative strength in Berlin and Frankfurt came from the fact that they were disproportionately strong among those sectors of the population that were both interested in and able to hold national office, that is, among the *Gebildeten*. Moreover, voting involves a choice between alternatives and, given the vagueness of the electoral programs in many regions, we cannot be sure that alternative political positions were presented to and understood by the electorate. It is possible to cite instances where the same group of voters elected men with very different views, perhaps only because they were all locally prominent and willing to serve. The best example of this was the outcome of the voting in Cologne, where electors chose Archbishop Geissel, the right-wing liberal Camphausen, and a democratic *Justizrat* to represent them in Berlin and sent the radical Raveaux to Frankfurt with the local chief of police as his alternate.[32] Finally, the indirect method of voting gave the final decision to a fairly small group of local notables and thereby further separated the successful candidates from the mass of the voters.

But after all of these questions and qualifications have been noted, the fact remains that the spring elections of 1848 were a clear-cut victory for the Vormärz political opposition in general and for the liberal movement in particular. During the first stages of the proceedings at Frankfurt, only about 15 percent of the delegates could be identified as belonging to either the extreme right or left, another 27 percent had no clear political affiliation, and the rest gravitated toward some shade of the liberal spectrum.[33] In Berlin, the center of political gravity was somewhat further to the left, but even there liberals seemed to be a clear majority.

Many took these electoral victories as a sure sign that the "real" *Volk* had spoken and had entrusted to the liberals the task of creating a new nation. Equally important, the appointment of men from the political opposition to ministerial posts in almost every German state seemed to fulfill the liberals' hopes for a reconciliation of governmental power and enlightened opinion. Two months after the outbreak of revolution, therefore, the triumph of liberalism seemed at hand.

The Frankfurt Parliament and the Dilemmas of Liberty

Is there really a *Volk* which those men
in the Nationalversammlung and the
other parliaments represent?

Bruno Bauer (1849)[1]

On May 18, 1848 the Frankfurt parliament assembled for its first formal meeting. After electing temporary officers in the old town hall, the delegates moved in solemn procession to the Paulskirche, which would remain the site of their deliberations for most of the next eleven months. In many ways, the church was a poor choice: its size and acoustical deficiencies made debate on or from the floor very difficult; there were no rooms for informal meetings among delegates or for caucuses and committees; the galleries were so large that the presiding officer often had trouble maintaining order.[2] But on the day the parliament began its work, few realized these disadvantages. Indeed many delegates regarded Paulskirche as the perfect setting for a collection of enlightened men, unencumbered by factions, to address their colleagues about Germany's future, while a grateful *Volk* observed from the galleries and applauded the gradual emergence of a new political order.

It did not take long for some delegates to realize that things were not going to work out that way. Some measure of internal organization was obviously necessary in order to regulate the discussion and prevent complete oratorical chaos. At first, efforts to make the parliament more efficient reflected the distrust of organized ''parties'' that was so deeply engrained in the minds of many liberals. The procedures adopted in the first weeks of the session divided the delegates by lot into fifteen ''sections'' that could be used to elect committees, validate election results, and carry on other types of parliamentary business which the full assembly might find cumbersome and excessively time-consuming.[3] Eventually, however, parliamentary factions did emerge. In part this was because the hundreds of strangers who suddenly found themselves facing a series of common tasks needed to discover congenial companions and reliable allies.[4] Moreover, political alignments began to take shape as the parliament debated the major questions on its agenda about its own power and jurisdiction, the present and future role of the existing states, and the proper definition of political freedom and popular sovereignty.[5] Over the summer, like-minded men formed factions which took their names from the inns and restaurants where groups of delegates met each evening to plan for

Table 5.1   **Political Alignments in the Frankfurt
                                          Parliament (September 1848)**

	No. of Members (%)
Cafe Milani (right)	50 (12)
Kasino (right-center)	120 (30)
Landsberg (right-center)	40–50 (10)
Augsburger Hof (center)	45 (11)
Württemberger Hof (left-center)	36 (9)
Westendhalle (left-center)	40 (10)
Deutscher Hof (left)	50 (12)
Donnersberg (extreme-left)	25–30 (6)
Total	406–21

SOURCE: Kramer, *Fraktionsbindungen* (1968),
pp. 283–85. The numbers and the identifying
labels should be viewed as rough estimates.
It should also be noted that almost half of
the parliament is not included in this table,
undoubtedly because the commitment of those
members to a club was too uncertain
or unstable.

the following day's proceedings.[6] By the autumn, the delegates had grouped themselves in roughly the fashion shown in table 5.1.

As these groups coalesced, they formulated rules to govern their own deliberations, selected leaders, and tried to agree on common policies. In September, the importance of the *Fraktionen* was significantly enhanced by changes in the rules governing debate which virtually ended the eloquent anarchy of a purely individualistic speaking order. At the end of the year, one delegate's wife observed that "all questions are now decided outside of the sessions, in the clubs, and it is rare if a vote turns out differently than expected . . . . the debates are a formality since everyone has decided how he will vote."[7]

Despite the obvious importance of *Fraktionen*, the fluidity that had characterized Vormärz political groupings was never entirely absent from Frankfurt.[8] At least a hundred delegates refrained from joining a *Fraktion*. Those who did join were more likely to act with their colleagues on political matters than on regional, religious, social, or economic issues.[9] Generally speaking, the left was rather successful in formulating and enforcing rules to control its adherents.[10] But in the middle range of the political spectrum, uncertainties and divisions about key ideological problems continued to produce a constantly shifting set of alignments and the inclination to schism. Furthermore, while many moderate liberals were willing to accept the need for some kind of institutions outside of the plenum, they still retained their distrust of "parties" and overly organized political activity. This was the basis of Rudolf Haym's arguments against efforts in the "Kasino" to define a specific program and a body of rules to discipline its members: "If we seek to bind ourselves with a program, we will destroy the essence of our society, because what holds us together is not a particular view [*Ansicht*] but rather essentially the same sensibility [*Gesinnung*]."[11] To men like Haym, even the need to build a movement cohesive enough to define and attain Germany's political future did not dispel the old notion of liberalism as a *Gesinnungsgemeinschaft*, a moral community of shared ideals.

The need to build a political movement was not, of course, confined to the environs of Paulskirche. Delegates not only had to learn how to deal with one another but also how to relate to their supporters in the nation. Once again, the left seemed best able to respond to this task. In organizations like the Märzverein, and in a series of national congresses, the democratic factions in Frankfurt tried to construct a permanent basis for support in German society.[12] More moderate members moved in this direction with greater reluctance, but many of them sent messages to their constituents and wrote articles for local newspapers; eventually all the *Fraktionen* began to publish their own reports on the parliament's activity. In turn, voters sent petitions, declarations, and sometimes votes of no confidence to the parliament. Nevertheless, poor communications interfered with a delegate's relationship to his district, and the inchoate nature and often thin institutional basis of political activity continued to limit the ties between *Abgeordneter* and those at home. Equally important, the fact that Frankfurt was seen as a unique institution, not part of a regular rhythm of election and reelection, also diminished a constituency's ability to influence its representative, just as it diminished his need to stay in contact with his voters. In sum, the institutional bonds between Frankfurt and the nation are impressive if we compare them to the sort of relationships that existed in Vormärz, but they remained slender and uneven.[13]

The relationship between members of the Nationalversammlung and the nation was further complicated by the fact that while the debates continued in Paulskirche, political life in the various states went on. State parliaments continued to meet, elections were held, and political alignments developed in response to events over which the men at Frankfurt had little or no control. The parliament meeting in Berlin was undoubtedly the most significant of these parallel institutions. Its relationship to Frankfurt was obscure from the start and became even more uncertain in the autumn of 1848 when the Prussian king sent troops into the capital, effectively restored his own authority, changed the ministry, and called new elections for the Prussian parliament. This counterrevolutionary coup not only radically altered the balance of power

between the traditional forces of order and the revolutionaries, it also significantly broadened the distance between the Prussian parliament and the
Frankfurt Nationalversammlung.[14]

The restoration of royal power in Prussia was only one instance of
Frankfurt's inability to shape public life in the nation it was supposed to
represent. Something of the same process was at work in other state parliaments, where new elections reflected revised suffrage regulations, different
local political conditions, and the changing character of the revolution. In
Kurhessen, for example, elections held under a restricted suffrage in late
November, after the successful counterrevolution in Vienna and Berlin, reduced the left to a small minority, with a "constitutionalist" group, leaning to
the right, clearly in control. In Württemberg on the other hand, democratic
elections in 1849 gave the left a two-to-one edge over the constitutional
liberals. The Bavarian elections of December 1848 produced a Landtag without a clear political majority but with a social composition dramatically different from that of the educated elite which was debating Bavaria's future in
Frankfurt.[15]

Below the level of the state Landtage, the situation was even more complex
and discontinuous. By and large, the pattern of political alignment already
apparent in the spring seems to have persisted through the rest of 1848. The
right wing of the prerevolutionary political opposition became increasingly
obsessed with the dangers of disorder and mass action, with what one of them
called the "new enemy" which "has arisen in our midst." Many of these
men were prepared to accept an alliance with the forces of order on almost any
terms.[16] On the far left, a growing impatience with the parliamentary process
was expressed in meetings like the Berlin *Gegenparlament* of October 1848
which urged secession from all representative institutions.[17] These two currents grew in the course of revolution, reinforcing each other. In between
these two extremes, however, the composition and ideological commitment of
many local organizations continued to be fluid and uncertain. The Württemberg constitutionalists, for example, still spoke of reconciling the monarchy
with a "popular and free spirit," thus continuing that Vormärz tendency to
blur questions of sovereignty and power.[18] While some local groups became
more exclusive and programmatically precise, others continued to use prerevolutionary procedures and to caution their followers against excessive commitment to a party. In the words of one Prussian election statement of January
1849: "Vote for electors who stand above party passions ... [men] who
combine courage with insight and calm, who can express their opinion freely
and coolly."[19]

The evidence on local political life during 1848 and 1849 reveals a remarkable amount of activity among liberals. But the impact of this activity

on national affairs was blunted by the existence of important differences on
tactical and ideological issues within the movement and by the persistence of
that institutional fragmentation characteristic of Vormärz. As Veit Valentin
put it, "The new particularism of the various parliaments, the parties, the
thousands of clubs created a fragmentation in the new Germany that was
almost worse than that produced by the old particularism."[20] Of course,
"new" and "old" particularism both flowed from the same characteristics of
the German situation: the lack of a political center; weaknesses in the communications network and in the institutional basis of participant politics; the
tenacity of local loyalties and alignments nurtured by Germany's economic,
social, and cultural diversity. In the highly charged political climate of 1848
these factors helped to produce an overlapping and intersecting pattern of
political conflict which prevented liberals from giving effective institutional
expression to their ideas and aspirations.

The problems arising from the liberals' inability to create a national political
movement were compounded by their growing estrangement from important
groups in German society.

As we saw at the end of the last chapter, the spring elections of 1848 seemed
to show widespread popular support for liberalism. Throughout the summer,
the Berlin and Frankfurt parliaments were deluged with petitions which
suggested that many Germans continued to look to their elected representatives for leadership and assistance. Paul Noyes quotes from a typical document, sent to Frankfurt in June by 193 artisans from Krefeld:

> Convinced that the Exalted Assembly will regard it as one of its deserving
> tasks to act against the increasing impoverishment of the artisan class,
> which was once without doubt a stalwart mainstay of the state and can still
> be an adequate protection, the undersigned venture to present to the
> Exalted Assembly the following as points which appear most significant.[21]

As the wording of this petition suggests, the artisans of Krefeld regarded
the primary issues of the revolution to be social and economic, not constitutional. To them and to thousands of others who addressed the parliaments
during the spring and summer, the aim of the revolution was to alleviate the
painful realities of their everyday life, to restore a prosperous and secure
social world which they felt had been threatened by the endemic social crises
of Vormärz. In some regions, religious issues also played an important role,
producing petitions which asked the parliaments to protect the churches from
the unwholesome pressures of the *Beamtenstaat*.

A number of liberals recognized that a response to these popular discontents
would be a necessary part of their task. At the Vorparlament, several dele-

gates had urged that action be taken to assist the economically distressed and socially uprooted. But the Vorparlament could not agree on any concrete proposals. Its members contented themselves with high-sounding phrases in support of "The protection of labor with measures and regulations which would protect those unable to work from privation and provide the unemployed with an opportunity to earn wages, and which would enable the structure of enterprises and factories to conform to the demands of the times."[22] As would so often be the case, consensus among liberals was reached by a statement of general principles, the practical implications of which could be interpreted in a variety of ways.

When the Frankfurt parliament began its work, some of its members insisted that the promise of social reform declared at the Vorparlament be fulfilled. Their efforts resulted in a committee on *Arbeiter-, Gewerbs- und Handelsverhältnisse,* whose activities were supposed to parallel the work of the Constitutional Committee and thus ensure that the parliament would not lose sight of social and economic problems. On June 3, the first chairman of this committee on "Workers, Manufacturing, and Commerce," Friedrich von Rönne, stated the assumptions behind its activities:

> The *Volk* has sent us here to create a new political structure. But this must be constructed on the solid foundation of improved material and social conditions. A purely political settlement would be extremely fragile as long as the various German states did not become economically interdependent and as long as material interests did not bind them together initimately.[23]

Implicit in von Rönne's remarks are two lasting characteristics of the committee's activities. First, it tended to see the problem of workers and artisans as part of a general concern for "improving social and economic conditions." By the time von Rönne spoke, the committee had widened its focus to include the entire range of economic, social, and commercial issues and had changed its name to the "Economics Committee." Second, the committee, like the parliament as a whole, viewed social and economic issues as being enmeshed with political problems, and especially with the problem of political unity (note how easily von Rönne moves from one to the other). For the businessmen and professors who dominated the Economics Committee, the "social question" was no doubt important, but it was part of, and perhaps necessarily subordinated to, larger issues of political and economic development. This conception helps to explain why the Economics Committee, despite its extraordinary vigor and diligence, was rarely able to play a creative role at Frankfurt. As long as social reform was seen as an aspect of political change, constitutional issues (and therefore the Constitutional Committee)

would almost always take precedence. This was especially true during the
crucial debates on the constitution in early 1849, but it was already apparent
during the parliament's first confrontation with social issues in its discussions
of the *Grundrechte*, which began in July 1848.[24]

The notion that the constitution should begin with a declaration on "basic
rights" had compelling precedents in the great political documents of the
eighteenth century and in the constitutions promulgated by the *Mittelstaaten*
during the era of reform.[25] Moreover, some of the most influential men at
Frankfurt saw two additional reasons for starting their deliberations with a
discussion of basic rights. First, many felt that the parliament was not ready to
tackle fundamental constitutional problems and should, therefore, begin with
issues on which agreement could be more easily reached. Second, there was a
feeling that a declaration of basic rights would help to assuage the pressures
generated by the masses of the *Volk*. Georg Beseler, who presented the
Constitutional Committee's draft to the assembly, made this point in his
opening statement:

> We believe that it is necessary to say something with regard to the great
> social movement which has gripped all of Germany, to find the limits
> beyond which this movement should not be allowed to proceed.

Later in his remarks, Beseler pointed out what would be the fundamental
tension in the debate over the *Grundrechte*:

> We want the Basic Rights to remove abuses, but here there are voices
> which warn us to pay attention to well-established rights and to disturb
> these only when it is absolutely necessary . . . . The abuses of the state
> power should be stopped, as should despotism and domination. But what
> is necessary for the security of political life should not be removed, espe-
> cially during the transitional period in which we find ourselves, under the
> social conditions in which we must act.[26]

Beseler's formulation vividly reflected the persistent ambivalence many liberals felt about freedom. In 1848, as in Vormärz, the primary concern of men
like him was to find a way of putting together reform and security, liberty and
order.

The supposed advantages of beginning the parliament's proceedings with a
statement on basic rights turned out to be illusory. The problems involved
proved to be far more complex and divisive than most delegates had imag-
ined. The debate, which began on July 3 with lengthy majority and minority
reports by both the Constitutional Committee and the Economics Committee,
dragged on for the next eight months.[27] Nor could the ambivalent and often
obscure products of this debate create those limits for the social movement

which Beseler had promised. The prolonged discussion of basic rights was paralleled by a growing gap between the parliament and many of those who had initially looked upon it with hope and expectation.

It is not necessary for us to consider the full range of issues covered by the *Grundrechte*, which included pronouncements on civil and judicial rights, the reform of rural society, limitations on aristocratic privilege, and many other important matters. Instead, our focus will be on those three aspects of the debate which seem most important for understanding liberals' long-range problems in the nineteenth century as well as the immediate difficulties they faced in their relationship with popular movements during 1848 and 1849: the problem of community power and freedom of movement (*Freizügigkeit*), the protection of labor and freedom of enterprise (*Gewerbefreiheit*), and the relationship between the Catholic church and the state.

The first line of the Constitutional Committee's draft of the *Grundrechte* gave every German "common German citizenship." What could be a more natural point of departure? Could anyone doubt that the principle of German citizenship was the foundation on which the parliament's constitutional endeavors would have to rest? Of course not. But almost at once the delegates were faced with what would become a familiar problem in the months ahead: a principle which seemed universally acceptable in the abstract could become extremely divisive when its practical implications were examined. Thus to some men the social implications of citizenship were the right to move and settle anywhere in Germany; but to others—especially those in the Hansa cities and the "hometowns" of the south and southwest—citizenship meant membership in a community, with each community retaining the freedom to protect itself from overcrowding, to decide who was to participate in its affairs, and to restrict the allotment of its resources for poor relief. In asserting the freedom to move, therefore, the parliament would be forced to trespass upon liberals' belief in local government. These difficulties generated a long and complicated debate, which crossed ideological lines and underscored again the degree to which liberals were internally divided on questions of social freedom and order. In the end, the parliament decided to sacrifice community control in favor of freedom of movement. This was clearly the orientation that best represented the experience and interests of those supra-local elites gathered at Frankfurt. This solution also reflected the parliament's inability to agree about how limitations on *Freizügigkeit* should be defined and how they could be institutionalized. The principle of freedom was qualified, not by specific limitations, but by the promise of a future law (*Heimatsgesetz*) that would seek to find practical measures to protect local communities from the possible disadvantages of liberty.[28]

The question of communal control over local rights of citizenship was closely tied to that of trade regulations. To those who argued for greater mobility, it was obvious that the freedom to reside wherever one wished and the freedom to practice any trade were both ways of insuring the most efficient allocation of resources in society.[29] The opponents of this kind of freedom maintained that it violated the rights of particular groups to regulate their own affairs and to protect their collective interests. The opposition to *Gewerbe-freiheit*, however, had a much broader basis in German society than the opposition to *Freizügigkeit*. Communal autonomy was not important in a number of regions, including Prussia, because it had been destroyed long ago by the expansion of the bureaucratic state. But limitations on the practice of a trade existed in many parts of Germany, albeit with considerable variation in strength and effectiveness. Furthermore, even where the authority of trade organizations over their own affairs had dwindled to the point of inconsequence, the memories lingered on, as did the hopes of those who viewed a revitalization of guilds as the best way to relieve their present discontents.[30]

From the end of July until the following February the Economics Committee considered various opinions on the question of trade regulations. Representatives of the committee met with the spokesmen for various trades, attended congresses held by different social groups, and studied the petitions which continued to flow into Frankfurt from throughout Germany. Most of those who claimed to speak for various groups in German society were agreed that the present situation was intolerable and that new regulations were necessary to improve it. But there was no clear consensus on the nature, purpose, or extent of these regulations since the interests of each group differed so markedly from those of the others. The positive proposals for reform, therefore, reflected the extraordinary diversity within the German social structure, a diversity produced by the unevenness of legal, social, and economic development in the various regions, by the different conditions prevailing in various kinds of enterprise, and by the complex set of horizontal cleavages separating masters, journeymen, and wage-earners.[31]

In December, Moritz Veit, a committee member, prepared a summary of prevailing views on *Gewerbefreiheit* in order to guide the final stage of the committee's discussions. Veit underestimated the diversity within German society and also, as we might expect, tended to regard social and economic problems as political ones. His report did, however, touch the heart of the matter when he called for an industrial order "which avoided equally the exclusiveness of privilege and the unbridled anarchy of laissez faire."[32] But the Economics Committee was deeply divided as to how these undesirable extremes were to be avoided. At the center of their disagreements was that subtle interplay of hope and anxiety with which so many liberals had viewed the promise and danger of social liberty. In the end, the committee's report accepted the principle of economic freedom, although not without certain vague limitations. The report did not have majority support and it was submitted, on February 26, with minority statements attached.[33] By this time the parliament was fully occupied with the political aspects of the constitution. The report was never debated, and in the final constitutional draft the promulgation of a *Gewerbeordnung* was postponed until some future date. Earlier in February, resolutions favoring the right to work and greater protection for labor had been debated but not passed.[34]

The problems which liberals faced in their attempt to regulate the relationship between the Catholic church and the state resembled the difficulties which arose in the debates on socioeconomic issues. Like communal autonomy and freedom of trade, the role of the church directly touched the lives of many Germans, proved to be extremely divisive within the parliament itself, and in the end helped to alienate sectors of German society from the political opposition.

During the early stages of the revolution, Catholics—like defenders of communal rights and guild privileges—hoped that the freedom promised by the revolution's spokesmen might also mean enhanced freedom for their own institutions.[35] But as the debate over the religious sections of the *Grundrechte* illustrated, the liberals had a rather different notion of what this promised freedom should be. To most liberals, religious freedom meant the right of each individual to follow his own conscience on religious matters. In order to insure that this would be the case, the churches had to be separated from public institutions. Civil marriage, for example, should be compulsory because it freed individuals from the need to identify themselves with a particular denomination. Similarly, secular education was necessary because it made certain that the church would not be able to exercise undue influence over the formation of public opinion. Some liberals, especially those on the left, were willing to go even further. They believed that it was necessary for the state to expel religious organizations, like the Jesuits, which constituted a threat to liberty. Obviously, the defenders of the church's interests saw religious freedom very differently; to them the main point was the protection of the church from state domination. They regarded compulsory civil marriage and secular education, not to mention the prohibition of the Jesuits, as interference by the state in those areas of life which rightfully belonged to the church.[36] For neither the first nor the last time in their history, therefore, liberals' efforts to give concrete form to the promise of liberty in Germany revealed that one man's freedom seemed inseparable from another's compulsion.

By the time the parliament had completed its long and convoluted debates on the basic rights, many Germans had decided that they had little to gain from the promises of a new constitutional order. Catholics, advocates of communal autonomy, and many other social and economic pressure groups became increasingly concerned with their own specific interests.[37] Inevitably, this worked to the advantage of the existing states, which were in a position to grant or promise concessions to these groups. The scope of this popular estrangement from the constitutional process should not be exaggerated. As the struggles over the constitution in the spring of 1849 would show, the political opposition retained its popular support in some regions and among certain social groups. Nonetheless, a shift of opinion away from the liberal parliamentarians is unmistakable. This shift was significant not only because it helped to set the stage for the revolution's failure but also because it foreshadowed the liberals' ultimate inability to meet the social, economic, and religious needs of large numbers of their fellow countrymen.

The alienation of these groups from the political opposition was particularly unfortunate for the liberal spokesmen at Frankfurt, but they were not the only ones to suffer from it. The Berlin parliament was no more able than its Frankfurt counterpart to deal with social and religious discontents. Nor was the radical wing of the political opposition able to harness popular discontent to its own demands for political democracy.[38] Why was this so? Why did the men at Frankfurt and Berlin, liberals and radicals, moderates and democrats, have so little success in stopping that hemorrhaging of popular support which weakened their struggle against the robust forces of reaction? One answer is certainly to be found in the social backgrounds of these groups' national spokesmen. As we know, the men elected in the spring of 1848 were hardly representative of their constituencies, indeed their interests and experiences separated them in many important ways from the masses of the German people. Those with a background in business were usually part of that small entrepreneurial elite whose interests called for an end to local privileges and the creation of a national system. The administrators, judges, and professors who made up the core of parliamentary liberalism also had a great deal of trouble understanding and sympathizing with the values of communal autonomy, the hopes and discontents of guildsmen, the suffering of journeymen, and the religious loyalties of devout Catholics. Instead, they tended to think in political terms and to hope that a constitutional system might somehow provide the basis for accommodating these various needs at some future time. Moreover, they too readily sought refuge from the pressure of these discontents in the abstractions which had been so much a part of prerevolutionary social and political discourse.

But liberals' inability to respond to the needs of large parts of the population did not merely reflect the limitations inherent in their own interests and experience. Equally important were the intrinsic difficulties involved in defining freedom in the German setting. What would have happened, for example, if the Frankfurt parliament had acknowledged the importance of local control and imposed some limitations on *Freizügigkeit*? Would that not have alienated those who felt frustrated and constrained by the restrictions which these communities could have imposed? And what if liberals had accepted the call for greater limitations on *Gewerbefreiheit*? Would that not have alienated those journeymen and workers who felt oppressed by the power of the guild masters? And if the liberals had accepted the demands of the Catholic church, would not that have alienated those whose freedom was restricted by the power of religious institutions? To recognize these difficulties is not to deny that the liberals in 1848 might have done better. Surely they could have been more compassionate and clear-sighted. But we should be wary of those who place all the blame for the revolution's failure on the liberals' manifest deficiencies of intellect and will. Whatever course the liberals might have chosen, it is difficult to see how they could have transcended a historical situation in which it was impossible to define freedom for some without restricting the freedom of others.[39]

During the winter of 1848–49, while popular support for the parliament was beginning to ebb, the men at Frankfurt turned their attention from what Georg Beseler called "the deeper levels of public life" to "the peaks of the highest power," from the problem of basic rights to questions of constitutional authority.[40] But even when the focus of debate shifted, the problems the parliamentarians faced remained strikingly similar. In dealing with the constitution, as in their efforts to define basic rights, the delegates had to find ways of relating their experience in Vormärz to the new demands of a revolutionary situation. Moreover, in the political as in the social and economic realm, they eventually had to confront the distance separating their hopes and ideals from the intractable realities of German life.

It was apparent in the opening days of the parliament that many liberal delegates remained within the ideological framework erected during Vormärz. They wanted the new constitution to remove the abuses of the existing political system but they were content to leave monarchical authority and the states more or less intact. This cast of mind informed the constitutional draft prepared in April by Friedrich Dahlmann for the so-called "Committee of Seventeen." In the foreword to his proposals, Dahlmann left no doubt as to where he felt the center of political power should continue to reside: "To our princely houses belong not only the old habits of obedience ... in truth they are the only possibility to lead gradually this multifaceted and diverse Germany into a unified state." And how was this authority of the princes to be related to the power of the *Volk*? Dahlmann answered this problem with a characteristic evasion: "The fullness of the imperial power is joined in the ruler of the Reich and in the parliament.''[41] Throughout the proceedings in Frankfurt, Dahlmann and many like him would continue to display uncertainty about the creative function of representative institutions, a deep respect for monarchical authority, and an inclination to rhetorical obscurity.

But the left wing of the Frankfurt parliament was not prepared to let this point of view go unchallenged. An articulate minority rejected the moderates' dualistic view of sovereignty, a view which clouded the issue of parliamentary authority and thereby left the direction of the state in the hands of the ruler. These men wanted popular sovereignty, a democratic suffrage, and a ministry politically responsible to the parliament. Their views, which seemed to conform to the revolutionary origins of the Frankfurt assembly itself, generated tensions throughout the long debate over the future political order.[42]

The shape of the debate and a clue to its eventual resolution could be seen on the second day of the parliament's existence when the radical delegate Raveaux proposed that the Frankfurt assembly declare itself the only legitimate instrument for constitutional change. To many moderate liberals this seemed to preclude what they hoped would be the creative role of the states and the princes and to give too much potential power to the untested parliament of which they were themselves a part. After some delay, the issue was resolved with a compromise which seemed to accept the left's call for Frankfurt's constitutional preeminence. But the practical impact of this decision was far less certain. As we know, state parliaments went on meeting and the rulers continued to act more or less independently of the Nationalversammlung.[43] This same blend of theoretical radicalism and practical moderation emerged from the second major debate on constitutional issues, that over the provisional central power. As the left demanded, the parliament assumed the right to create a temporary executive for the Reich. But the post was given to an Austrian archduke and efforts to make his office politically responsible to the parliament failed.[44] In effect, the men at Frankfurt handed the new nation's fragile executive authority to an *Ersatz-Monarch*, whose position is reminiscent of the answer to a similar constitutional problem given by the Weimar assembly seven decades later.

The parliamentary alignments that began to take shape during the debate on the provisional central power were tested and somewhat revised in September by the crisis following the armistice between Prussia and Denmark that had been signed at Malmö. The Prussian action, which defied the parliament by abandoning the struggle for Schleswig-Holstein, drove a number of moderates, led by Dahlmann, into opposition. This shift to the left forced the resignation of Prince Karl Leiningen's ministry. But the internal divisions within the assembly prevented the creation of a new government based on a parliamentary majority. The September crisis also showed that in political, no

less than in social, economic, and religious affairs, the parliament had to
contend with internal divisions and the pressures of external events. In mid-
September riots swept through Frankfurt and seemed to threaten the very
existence of the assembly. These disorders demonstrated with considerable
psychological impact that the assembly could not control the *Volk*. Nor could
it control the states: Prussia ignored the parliament's protests and, even more
important, the delegates had to depend on the states for protection against
popular disorder.[45] The September events revealed for a moment the three
roots of the parliament's ultimate failure: its own divisions, its alienation from
the populace, and its dependence on its enemies—conditions which also bring
to mind the difficulties faced in 1918 by another generation of Germans who
sought to erect a liberal political order in central Europe.

All of these problems worsened in the months following the September
crisis. Frankfurt's popular support was narrowed by the growing apathy of
some and the growing animosity of others within the nation. At the same
time, the reassertion of monarchical authority in Vienna and Berlin marked
the recovery of antirevolutionary forces in those two key states. But to many
men at Frankfurt the meaning of these developments was not as obvious as it
now seems in retrospect. The confidence of the left was sustained by its apparent support in various organizations throughout Germany. The moderates
noted with satisfaction that the coup in Berlin had not been followed by excessive reaction but rather by the granting of a constitution which sought—in the
words of one observer—to synthesize "the new freedom of 1848 with the
authority of the crown."[46] As the parliamentarians were drawn further into
their own task, they seemed more and more inclined to ignore outside reality
and concentrate on the immediate demands of constitution making. Perhaps it
was only natural, as their debates grew more heated and complex, that those
involved would begin to confuse a solution to their own internal problems
with a solution to the problems of the political world outside Paulskirche.
Moreover, an inclination to withdraw from the world of power and action into
a realm of abstract disputation came naturally to men whose political consciousness had been shaped by the educationally oriented institutions of Vormärz liberalism.

Before the question of how the constitutional debate at Frankfurt reflected
long-standing liberal attitudes about the relationship between the *Volk* and the
Staat can be considered, it is necessary to recall that in 1848 this issue was
inseparable from the problem of the nation's relationship to the existing states.
The creation of a united Germany had, of course, long been an important item
on the liberals' agenda. Most of them had assumed that national unity would
be part of a reform of the political order in which the energies and desires of
the *Volk* would find expression. They also assumed that the profound advan-

tages of nationhood would dissolve the parochial loyalties men felt toward their own states. As in the case of social, economic, and religious freedom, liberals failed to see that what they regarded as the marvelous freedom to be a German might appear to others as the compulsion to stop being Austrian, Bavarian, and so on. Here again, liberals greatly overestimated the universality of their own image of emancipation and underestimated the strength of rival loyalties and institutions. The debates at Frankfurt over the nation quickly revealed these problems. From October 1848 until January 1849 the delegates searched for a formula which would resolve the tension between Prussia and Austria, between the exponents of a "small" Protestant nation centered in Berlin and a larger Catholic nation including Austria. The issue was further complicated by the multinational character of the Austrian empire and the riddle posed by the future of Austria's non-German subjects.[47] These problems were not resolved until the last stages of the constitutional debate, when they could be postponed no longer. The decision became unavoidable at that point where the issues of state and *Volk* and of state and nation intersected: the question of who was to be the ruler of the new Germany.

As the debate moved into its decisive stage, a number of influential moderates, many of them from Prussia and the smaller states of the southwest, began to cooperate in what came to be called the *Erbkaiserpartei*. The core of their position was support for the king of Prussia as hereditary emperor of the nation. Although they knew that this would give Prussia a preeminent position in the Reich, some of them hoped that a federal relationship with German-speaking Austria might still be possible. By and large, the Erbkaiserpartei also accepted the main elements of Vormärz liberalism's moderate program: suffrage limited to "independent" male adults and a strong executive coexisting with an important but ultimately subordinate parliament.[48] The great advantage of this group was derived from the fact that although their opponents were numerous, they were also deeply divided. On the right of the assembly, there were those who objected to Prussia but not to a hereditary monarchy; on the left, there were those who wanted a more centralized state but also a more democratic one.

At the end of January, a motion favoring a hereditary emperor was defeated by a vote of 263–211. Following this defeat, the pro-Prussian faction attempted to mobilize as much support in the parliament as possible; there was some reordering of party alignments, but the Prussian solution still lacked a majority. For a time it seemed that the assembly was hopelessly deadlocked, but a way out emerged when some of the Erbkaiserpartei's opponents on the left offered their support for a hereditary emperor in return for concessions on other aspects of the constitution.[49]

The first, and in some ways the most painful, compromise between these

groups was reached in February, when the assembly debated the law that
would regulate elections to the national parliament. In the deliberations of the
Constitutional Committee and later in the parliament itself, a number of
liberals had rehearsed their old arguments against universal suffrage which
recent events seemed to make even more persuasive. As the spokesman for
the Constitutional Committee put it:

> No state, no matter if it be a republic or a monarchy, can exist or can
> attain any kind of stability if the decision over all political questions is put
> in the hands of the masses, who all too often allow themselves to be led
> without a will of their own and temperamentally shift their allegiance
> from one leader to another from one day to the next.[50]

In the end, however, the assembly rejected the committee's proposal for a
limited ballot and voted for universal, direct, and secret suffrage. In addition
to their desire for a compromise with the left, liberals abandoned this key
element in their program for two reasons. First, popular support for a democratic suffrage was considerable, as shown by the fact that even the Prussian
constitution that had been decreed in December did not tamper with it. Second, the debate made clear that the liberals could not agree on where the line
should be drawn between the politically active and the politically passive
Volk. A number of speakers demonstrated that the Constitutional Committee's
attempt to exclude those who were not "independent" had little practical
meaning.[51] For the history of nineteenth-century liberalism, this failure to
define "independent" is probably the most interesting aspect of the suffrage
debate. Like so many of their concepts and ideals, the liberals' notion of a
politically active class of "independent" men evaporated when they tried to
apply it to the complexities of German life. In this regard, the debate on the
suffrage reconfirmed what the discussions of communal power and trade
regulations had already suggested: liberals could not draw convincing boundaries around their constituency, the Mittelstand, that "core of the nation" on
whom they depended for support and for whom they claimed to speak.

Compared to the suffrage issue, the constitution's definition of the relationship between monarch and parliament was much more in keeping with the
main lines of Vormärz liberal political thought. In the course of the discussions of this issue, which continued on and off from the summer of 1848
until March 1849, there were repeated examples of the uncertainty about the
final location of authority that characterized liberal thinking about the relationship of Staat and Volk before and after the revolution. In the final stages of
the debate, the left was able to prevent a provision granting the monarch an
absolute veto over legislation, which some liberals had argued was necessary
to preserve the stability of the state in times of turmoil (in December

Dahlmann had called it "ein Recht der rettenden That"). But if the monarch
was deprived of his ability to block legislation (he did have a suspensive
veto), the other limitations on his power were much less certain. The
monarch, moreover, retained ample emergency powers which could be used
to counter internal instability and disorder.

As in Vormärz, the key to the question of parliamentary power was the
meaning of "responsibility": the Frankfurt constitution required minister and
monarch to cosign laws; the ministers were declared "responsible" to the
parliament, but they were appointed by the crown. Was it necessary for the
ministry to have the support of a majority of the parliament? The constitution
did not say. Could a minister be forced from office by a vote of no-
confidence? Once again the constitution was silent; when this kind of responsibility was proposed in the course of the discussions, it met no support. In
short, the constitution granted the parliament significant power, but stopped
short of establishing a parliamentary system.[52] In this fundamentally important way, the left-liberal compromise was clearly a product of the same
political tradition that had produced the Prussian constitution of December
1848 and that would inform the Bismarckian constitution of 1867.

In most of non-Austrian Germany, liberals greeted the constitution with
enthusiasm. Many probably had their doubts about some of the accommodations with the left, but they accepted these as the price necessary to create a
German nation and hoped that future revisions and amplifications would be
possible. In short, the moderates accepted the compromises with the left for
the same reasons that would lead them to embrace a compromise with Bismarck less than two decades later. But in 1849, unlike in 1866, the liberals'
willingness to compromise did not bring them the power necessary to put the
results of the compromise into practice. The left could deliver the votes
necessary to pass the Erbkaiserliche constitution at Frankfurt but it did not
have the force necessary to make this constitution a reality. As they did so
often, both before and after 1848, liberals were forced to turn for the fulfillment of their program to the Prussian state. There would rest the final decision
about the revolution's fate, not with the crowds who cheered the parliament's
deputies on their journey to Berlin, nor with the proud city councilmen who
joined them in their procession through the Prussian capital. At the end of this
hope-filled expedition the liberal representatives of the Volk found once again
that the state was a powerful but fickle ally. The king of Prussia categorically
refused the crown they offered.[53]

When the king denied the Frankfurt parliament the power necessary to
impose its will, the liberals' impotence was suddenly revealed. In the wake of
this revelation, the revolution ended as it had begun, with a disconnected
series of protests, meetings, demonstrations, and armed uprisings.[54] As in the

preceding spring, different groups engaged in a variety of activities which
ranged from the outraged proclamations of law-abiding Rhenish notables to
the desperate violence of the revolutionary armies in the southwest. As in the
spring of 1848, men were moved to action by a number of different discontents. In some regions, the constitution served as a rallying point for a rather
broadly based popular movement; elsewhere social and economic issues provided the basis of the revolts. But in 1849 these various groups did not act
with the energizing illusion of unity; moreover, in 1849 they confronted not
frightened and uncertain governments but a renewed and confident coalition
prepared to defend the established order. Unable to build a national political
movement, unable to tame and direct the forces of popular discontent, and
finally abandoned by the power of the state, liberals faced the unhappy alternatives of doomed resistance or acquiescence. Let us not forget those who had
the courage to choose the former and paid dearly for their choice. But most
liberals were like C. H. Alexander Pagenstecher, former Burschenschaftler,
member of the Vormärz opposition, and delegate to the Frankfurt parliament.
The "unhappy experiences of 1848–1850" convinced him that

> now was the time to establish a worthy life, to cultivate intellectual con-
> cerns, to educate one's family and make them happy, to acquire like-
> minded friends, to live in peace with those around one and offer patriar-
> chal hospitality, in short, now was the time to lead a purely human
> existence.[55]

After the violent hopes and disappointments of the revolutionary era, liberals
returned to the familiar patterns of their lives, some with relief, some with
reluctance, some with despair.

III

Old Problems
and New Realities
1850–66

The final collapse of the revolution led some contemporaries to proclaim the end of the liberal movement. Friedrich Engels, for example, declared that "Political liberalism . . . is forever impossible in Germany."[1] Engels' bitter assessment corresponded to the fervent wish of those on the other end of the political spectrum who tried to demonstrate that the liberal interlude was only an episodic break in the continuity of their own power. At Frankfurt, representatives to the reconstituted Germanic Confederation met and solemnly abrogated the revolutionary parliament's "basic rights." Throughout most of Germany, censorship was restored, political organizations dissolved, and electoral participation discouraged. Elections were held, but turnouts were small and apathy prevailed.[2]

Even during the darkest days of reaction, many liberals continued to hope that the future might still be theirs. Of course they knew that they had lost a battle, but they were not convinced that the struggle was over. As early as December 1848, a writer sympathetic to the liberal cause expressed the mixture of immediate despair but ultimate confidence that sustained many in the following decade: "I shudder at the prospect of a long journey through the wilderness, but I believe in the promised land of freedom and a happier future." And, to take three other examples from different sectors of the movement, Schulze-Delitzsch in July 1849, Alexander von Soiron in December 1850, and L. K. Aegidi in January 1851 all wrote to friends with much the same message: we represent the great historical ideas, let us have faith because in the end they will triumph.[3]

By the end of the 1850s reactionary pressures had begun to ease and Germans were talking about a "new era" filled with promise and opportunity. Public interest in political affairs revived and liberal organizations flourished. Even old Dr. Pagenstecher temporarily left the delights of domesticity to participate in a new liberal government in Baden.[4] Those who returned to public life after 1858 found the political and social world at once deceptively familiar and significantly altered. Many of the problems liberals had faced in Vormärz remained. But both the shape and the setting of these problems had been transformed by the revolution and its aftermath. Economic development, for example, had entered a new phase after mid-century and had begun to have an unmistakable impact on values and behavior. The Prussian Landtag, created during the revolution and retained in modified form after 1849, provided a new and significant focus for political activity north of the Main River.[5] Finally, the Crimean War of 1854–56 shattered the international system which had regulated European affairs after 1815 and ushered in a period of diplomatic turmoil and violence.[6]

In the period from 1850 to 1866, from the revolution to the *Reichsgründung*, liberals had to come to terms with a complex mixture of continuity and innovation, in the world around them and within their own ranks. Our problem in tracing liberalism's evolution during this period is to keep in mind the lines of historical continuity without losing sight of the forces which were reshaping German political life and society. We will begin by examining the impact of economic growth on liberalism, then consider the evolution of liberal institutions, and finally analyze those critical constitutional conflicts which revealed, once again, the liberals' problematic relationship to the *Volk* and the *Staat*.

The Search for a Liberal Society

> ... the *Mittelstand* is and remains the most indispensable and most valuable material for the construction of a German state; nothing is more unpolitical than making political plans based on an idealized view of the material at hand and assuming the existence of this material in any unexplored sectors of society.
>
> L. A. von Rochau (1853)[1]

"At the present time," wrote the Prussian statistician Dieterici in 1855, "industry is penetrating human affairs with such power and significance that a comparison with earlier conditions is scarcely possible."[2] In fact, as a number of contemporaries realized, the German economy had entered a new stage in its development by the early 1850s. Within a very brief period, the basis for future growth was established and, for the first time, we catch a glimpse of that extraordinary economic vitality which will remain a distinctive feature of German economic life for the next century. Between 1850 and 1869, the production of coal grew from 5.1 to 26.7 million metric tons, pig iron from .2 to 1.4; steam power capacities increased from 260,000 to 2,480,000 horse power and railroad lines from 3,639 to 10,834 statute miles. At the same time, there was an impressive growth in banking and commerce, changes in the structure of enterprise, and important advances in technology.[3]

As significant as all of these changes were, lines of continuity linking the fifties and sixties with the world of Vormärz remained. In the first place, despite its impressive growth, the German economy was still relatively backward when compared to Great Britain's: as late as 1870, per capita consumption of coal in Germany was only 17 percent of that in the United Kingdom, per capita production of pig iron 16 percent, cotton yarn 13 percent, and woolen yarn 39 percent.[4] Furthermore, Germany remained a predominantly rural and agrarian society throughout this period: the percentage of Germans living in small towns and villages, for example, did not begin to decline until after 1871 and, despite the growth of some cities, only about 5 percent of the population lived in communities with more than a hundred thousand inhabitants. Social and economic development also continued to be very uneven. As with Vormärz, this is easiest to see in regional terms: between 1849 and 1861, the population of an economically dynamic region like Saxony grew by over 13 percent, while the populations of Baden and Württemberg either remained stable or declined slightly.[5] A similar if more complex pattern of uneven growth existed in various branches of manufacturing. In some, factory production posed a very serious threat to craftsmen, while in others traditional forms could hold their own or even expand. Overall, the number of master craftsmen in Prussia remained stable between 1849 and 1861, while the number of apprentices increased by 37 percent.[6]

Changes taking place in the economy had an immediate and obvious effect on the structure of society. Contemporaries were quick to note, for example, that a new business elite emerged after 1850, entrepreneurs who seemed more aggressive and profit-oriented than their predecessors, more willing to disregard community obligations and religious values, more given to luxury and ostentation in their private lives. Their wealth, social position, life-style, and economic function set them apart from the social and economic world of the small manufacturer and merchant.[7] At the same time that this new business elite was beginning to move away from the more modest ranks of the *Mittelstand*, an analogous process was at work in the lower ranks of society. Here men engaged in manual labor began to think of themselves as *workers* with an economic position and social identity that were clearly separate from those of the master craftsman and his apprentices.[8]

Obviously neither of these processes began suddenly in 1850 and neither was completed within the period we are now considering. Residues of traditional values and institutions remained well into the 1860s. The self-image of the entrepreneur, for example, took shape only gradually and it was not until after 1871 that *Unternehmer* in Berlin began to use this term in a way that captures its modern connotation of technical and organizational innovation. Gustav Freytag's famous novel of commercial life, *Soll und Haben,* did not celebrate the international banker or great industrialist but rather had as its hero a thrifty and reliable merchant who would have been much more at home with the Fuggers than with Siemens or Krupp.[9] Similarly, August Bebel noted that well into the 1860s journeymen continued to think of themselves as future masters rather than as belonging to a subordinate class of manual workers.[10] Changes in the conceptual framework with which men tried to understand society after 1850, therefore, remained as uneven and incomplete as the changes in the social and economic landscape itself.

This complex interplay of innovation and continuity can be seen in the social composition of the liberal movement in the fifties and sixties. Some of those entrepreneurs whose activities were changing the commercial and industrial scene also played an important role in political life. A few, such as Friedrich Hammacher and Franz Peter Buhl, became nationally recognized liberal spokesmen.[11] Although it is difficult to determine how widespread liberalism was among businessmen, the evidence suggests that a majority of politically active business leaders probably identified with the liberal movement before 1866. A study of the *Wahlmänner* in Berlin, for example, indicates that in 1862 almost 90 percent of the business leaders in that city voted for a liberal candidate.[12] Obviously Berlin was not a "typical" German city, any more than 1862 was a "typical" election year, but the data on other Prussian elections between 1858 and 1866 show that in most cities there was a high degree of liberal support among urban groups who voted in the first of the three suffrage classes, that is, among those who paid the most taxes. Moreover, businessmen figure prominently in the scattered data available on the social basis of liberalism's local leaders in other states.[13] Finally, throughout these years liberalism drew a great deal of its strongest support from city councils which often represented the economic elite of various cities throughout Germany.[14]

Despite the increasing importance of businessmen in many areas, the national spokesmen for the liberal movement continued to be drawn from the *Gebildeten*, just as they had in the years before 1848. This was even true of the Kongress deutscher Volkswirte, an organization formed to further economic interests and enlightenment, which was initially dominated by officials, judges, and journalists. By 1861, the number of industrialists and merchants at the Kongress had increased significantly, but they still made up only about one-third of the participants.[15] Data on the social composition of the Nationalverein show much the same blend of educated and economic elites.[16]

The most dramatic instance of the educated elites' continuing importance is to be found in the Prussian Landtag, as can be seen in table 6.1, which gives the occupations of delegates elected during the highpoint of liberal activity in the early 1860s. No wonder that to Karl Marx's unsympathetic eye the Prussian parliament looked like a combination schoolroom-bureaucratic office.[17] In none of the other states was this predominance of the *Gebildeten* so apparent, but they did play a considerable role in most representative institutions. In the Saxon Landtag of 1864, for example, the left was composed of six jurists, five farmers, eight businessmen, and one physician; the seventeen-man Progressive *Fraktion* in the Bavarian parliament had seven *Gebildete*, five businessmen, two farmers, one *Posthalter*, one innkeeper, and a retired mayor. We do not have any reliable statistics for Baden, but it appears that the traditional importance of Badenese officials in the liberal movement decreased but by no means disappeared during the late fifties and early sixties.[18]

Why did educated men continue to be so important, even after the economy had begun to create the basis for a new business elite? The persistent problem of *Abkömmlichkeit* is surely one reason: after 1850, as before, the primary concern of businessmen was business, and this remained difficult to combine with a parliamentary career. Moreover, the prestige of a university education and a government post continued to be important in most regions, especially where participatory institutions were weak and traditional political styles continued.[19] Finally, even in places where there were important changes in the

Table 6.1   **The Social Composition of the Liberal
                                                 Factions in the Prussian Chamber
                                                 of Deputies (1862)**

	No. of Members (%)
Officials	
Administrative	14 (5)
Judicial	82 (29)
Local	15 (5)
Retired	17 (6)
Professors, teachers	10 (3.5)
Lawyers	16 (5)
Physicians and other academics	13 (4)
Writers, editors, bookdealers	4 (1.4)
Businessmen and *Rentier*	37 (13)
Agricultural occupations	
Rittergutsbesitzer	39 (13.6)
Others	32 (11)
Miscellaneous, unknown	6 (2)
Total	285*

SOURCE: Hess, *Parlament* (1964), pp. 65ff.
* These 285 delegates (out of a total member-
ship of 352) include members of the Deutsche
Fortschrittspartei (135), "Left-Center" (103),
Free Parliamentary Association (21), and
Constitutionalists (26).

conduct of electoral politics, where organizations grew and agitation intensified, it was often a member of the educated elite who could best respond to
the new demands of political life. Thus we find in this period the development
of a new subgroup within the *Gebildeten* composed of men who came close to
devoting themselves full-time to political affairs even while drawing their
income from a profession or local office. This group included publicists and
interest-group employees like Viktor Böhmert and Schulze-Delitzsch,
lawyers like the young Eduard Lasker, and city government officials like
Forckenbeck and Becker. The number of these men remained relatively small
but their importance for the movement was often considerable.[20]

While the liberals' national leadership continued to come from educated
elites many of whom still held government jobs, the movement's social base
continued to span Germany's middle strata.[21] As usual, the evidence does not
yield precise or comprehensive conclusions, but there are enough data to show
that liberals drew their support from a relatively large and rather heterogeneous sector of the *politically active* population. The final modifier deserves its
italics because, as will be argued later on, the most important single fact about
electoral politics before 1866 was that the majority of those eligible to partici-

pate did not do so. Nevertheless, in a great many areas those who did vote voted for a liberal candidate. The material from the Prussian three-class electoral system demonstrates that the extent of liberal support did not vary greatly from one economic group to another. The most important factor was not the amount of a voter's taxable income but whether he lived in a rural or an urban community. Table 6.2 shows that within urban and rural districts, liberals did almost equally well in all three voting classes. The composition of these three classes varied from one region to another, but it is clear that in most places the second and third classes would have included large numbers of craftsmen, small manufacturers, farmers, shopkeepers, minor officials, and so on.[22] The material available on liberal *Wahlmänner* in Prussia and on liberal supporters in other German states tends to confirm that the middle strata provided the movement's rank and file.[23]

Table 6.2	Voting Patterns in the Prussian Landtag Elections of 1863 (percentage of votes cast)			
	Voting Class			
	I	II	III	Total
Urban districts				
Liberals	65.17	67	67.67	67.39
Conservatives	21.77	20.87	19.39	19.8
Rural districts				
Liberals	43.89	41.13	35.6	37.36
Conservatives	34.56	33.36	38.5	37.19
All districts				
Liberals	50.5	50	48.2	48.8
Conservatives	30.5	29	30.9	30.5

SOURCE: Gagel, *Wahlrechtsfrage* (1958), pp. 177–78.

Until we have more detailed and congruent local studies, we will be unable to answer the important questions which remain about the liberal constituency: What were the alternatives open to voters and what was the political meaning of their decision to vote for a liberal candidate? How did liberal support vary from one region to another? What occupations seem disproportionately represented among liberalism's supporters and why?

The same mixture of continuity and innovation which characterized liberalism's social composition also defined the contours of liberal social thought between the revolution and the *Reichsgründung*. Just as we see the beginnings of an aggressive group of entrepreneurs and of a self-conscious

working class in this period, so too do we find new attitudes about social and
economic life which were to be of great importance in the movement after
1866.

During the 1850s the public and private statements of many liberals contain
a new emphasis on the importance of economic and social change. One reason
for this was the obvious contrast between the dynamism of the economy and
the stagnation of German political life. Gustav Mevissen pointed out this
contrast in 1851 when he spoke of the parliament's "total impotence" and
concluded that economic activity offered "the only way a better future can be
achieved."[24] As they surveyed the world amid the ruins of their hopes, many
liberals were inclined to agree. Ludwig Bamberger, for example, was deeply
impressed by Bastiat's classical economic tract, *Sophisme économique,* when
he studied it shortly after having fled Germany to avoid persecution for his
part in the 1849 uprisings. After the failure of Bamberger's political
endeavors, Bastiat's confident promise of economic progress must have made
reassuring reading.[25] As the economic boom of the fifties progressed, the
reasons to celebrate its potential became ever more apparent. "What idealistic
efforts strove in vain to do," proclaimed a contributor to the liberal *Nationalzeitung* in 1856, "materialism has accomplished in a few months."[26]

Even when political activity began again in the late fifties, this new concern
for economic developments remained in the minds of many liberals. Indeed,
the renewal of political energies found one of its first institutional expressions
in the Kongress deutscher Volkswirte, whose leaders contrasted their practical
concern for the material basis of progress with the Frankfurt parliament's
pursuit of "wishes and ideas."[27] Most of the programmatic statements formulated by liberal parliamentary groups in the early sixties contained some
reference to economic issues. In 1860 the Badenese liberals called for the
creation of a ministry to deal with economic affairs because, they believed,
"material interests have become so important they can no longer be dealt with
as an administrative and financial side issue."[28] Similar sentiments can be
found in a number of liberal periodicals and in publications such as
Bluntschli's *Staatswörterbuch,* which paid a good deal more attention to the
economy than they had before 1848. Even the postrevolutionary edition of the
Staatslexikon, that paradigmatic expression of Vormärz liberalism, treated
commercial and industrial affairs in greater depth and detail. In the third
edition, for instance, the editors deleted the entry on "Secret Societies"
(*Gesellschaften, geheime*) and replaced it with one on "Joint Stock Companies" (*Gesellschaften*).[29]

For an important group of liberals, this new awareness of economic developments was attended by a growing faith in the progressive impulses of a
free economy. After 1850, John Prince Smith found increasing support for his

view that "the solution of political conflicts as well as the alleviation of material want can only be done with a healthy economic policy."[30] Even those who refused to accept this reduction of political and social problems to economic ones, acknowledged the basic validity of the classical economists' free market economy. Many liberals believed it was only necessary to liberate the resources of society in order to insure progress and prosperity; limitations on the free play of the market's laws, which governed the allocations of these resources, were unproductive and ultimately disastrous. Obviously, the strongest support for this view came from representatives of commercial and industrial interests, who expected to profit if the state's interference with their economic activity ceased. But a faith in economic freedom was shared by many others as well—intellectuals, bureaucrats, even some craftsmen and small manufacturers—who believed that they could prosper in a free economic environment.[31] Those who saw economic freedom as the proper direction of change could draw a great deal of encouragement from the events of the fifties and sixties: one state after another lowered tariffs, signed commercial agreements, and removed or weakened remaining restrictions on economic activity. An age of *Gewerbefreiheit* and *Handelsfreiheit*, freedom of enterprise and of trade, seemed to have arrived. By the mid-sixties, a contributor to the *Staatslexikon* could summarize the prevailing climate of opinion by saying that if a belief in economic freedom was not yet universal, it was "essentially dominant."[32]

Despite the power exercised on the minds of many liberals by the concept of a free economy, it would be incorrect to equate liberalism after 1850 with laissez-faire economics or the special interests of a capitalist bourgeoisie. Certainly these ideas and interests had greater influence over the movement than they had before mid-century, but the breadth and depth of their influence was limited by the persistence of older habits and behavior patterns. Consider, for example, the Kongress deutscher Volkswirte, which has often been viewed as the forum for Manchester economic doctrines in Germany.[33] As we know, the Kongress reflected a growing awareness of economic problems and a widespread desire among liberals to give their search for freedom in Germany a more practical orientation. Some of the leading members of the Kongress certainly resembled the stereotype best personified by John Prince Smith. But in several important ways the Kongress resembled an educationally oriented *Verein* from the first half of the century much more than an economic interest group from the imperial era. Its procedures were designed to facilitate the discussion and dissemination of information about the economy. Meetings were open to all who wished to attend, membership was unrestricted, and a wide variety of views were represented. The publications sponsored by the Kongress were scholarly rather than popular. To Wilhelm

Lette, a Prussian official and moderal liberal who was the first chairman of
the Kongress, the purpose of the organization was to improve society by
spreading enlightenment, not unlike the aim of the Zentralverein für das
Wohl der arbeitenden Klassen, which Lette had helped to establish during the
1840s. Moreover, a number of those who attended the meetings of the Kongress were men like Julius Wiggers, a theologian and linguist without much
interest in economic matters, who enjoyed the company of the other members
of the Kongress, was pleased to meet well-known liberals from various parts
of Germany, and felt that his participation demonstrated support for the liberal
ideals rather than for a specific program.[34]

As the procedures of the Kongress suggest, many liberals continued to
believe that their activities were educational and that it was wrong to overem-
phasize material interests and issues. The *Grenzboten,* for example, carried a
number of articles on economic, social, and scientific subjects during the
fifties, but also went out of its way to warn against emphasizing what one
contributor called a one-sided "acquisitive and speculative spirit" at the
expense of a "genuinely human and organically legal and moral occupational
spirit [*Berufsgeist*]." In a similar vein, Schulze-Delitzsch stressed the importance of the "whole moral power of society" even when he rejected the
theoretical preoccupations of Vormärz. Gustav Mevissen, who was busy making a great deal of money in the fifties, continued to use the ethical and
spiritual categories of an earlier age: he recommended the formation of joint
stock companies not simply because they provided a source of greater economic power but also because of what he called their "ethical-social
spirit."[35] Even Ludwig August von Rochau, generally regarded as the apostle
of materialism and Realpolitik, did not deny the role of spiritual forces in
political and social life. When Rochau spoke of the importance of power in
human affairs, he included spiritual power as one element and praised the
Bürgertum both for its material and its educational attainments. Ideas, Rouchau
realized, drew their strength from real social forces, but that did not keep him
from believing that "under all circumstances the spirit of the age [*Zeitgeist*]
has the decisive influence on the general direction of politics."[36]

As in Vormärz, after 1850 there were many in the movement who questioned the desirability of total economic freedom. As the debate over the
Franco-Prussian commercial treaty of 1862 demonstrated, free trade was by
no means unanimously endorsed in liberal circles.[37] Moreover, there were
still some social groups which were drawn to liberal political and cultural
goals, but which regarded a totally unrestrained market economy as a threat to
their own livelihood and social position.[38]

Resistance to the spread of complete laissez-faire liberalism also continued
on the theoretical level. Robert von Mohl, for one, did not deny the impor-

tance of a free economy, but he did try to find a middle ground between the chaotic individualism of laissez-faire and the outmoded restrictions of traditional society. This was the focus of Mohl's influential essay on "The Political and the Social Sciences," which was first published in 1851 and reprinted in somewhat revised form four years later. Here Mohl tried to show that there was a sphere in between that of "the individual personality and the organic unity of the nation." This was the social sphere, a set of institutional relationships that were both independent of the state and above the interests of individuals.[39] In many respects, these institutions resembled what Hegel had called "corporations." For Mohl, as for Hegel, their purpose was to establish sources of cohesion which built upon but ultimately transcended the individualistic impulses at work in the market economy.[40]

Some liberals rejected the delicate balance between individualism and cohesion which Mohl tried to find in the social sphere and argued that the only defense against the potential dangers of social and economic liberty was the state. This was the basis of Heinrich von Treitschke's attack on Mohl's essay. Treitschke denied the theoretical distinction between the political and social sciences because he believed that the state, properly understood, had to contain and dominate the full range of institutional relationships within it.[41] Rudolf Gneist was prepared to accept the distinction between the state and society, but he agreed that the former must take priority. Germany, Gneist wrote in 1860, is "the last refuge in Europe where the state can make itself heard over the economy, where the character of the nation still has a place against the one-sided views of a transforming society."[42] This deference to the state, which was a central element in liberal social thought during the first half of the century, continued to shape the attitudes reflected in Bluntschli's widely cited *Staatswörterbuch*. Bluntschli's own article on "Corporations," for example, presents these institutions as valuable expressions of social interests and worthwhile defenses against both despotism and revolution. But there is never any doubt that the state should protect its essential unity from being disrupted by these bodies: "In no way should the functions of the state become dependent upon the special interests of the corporation." Johannes Huber's article on "Socialism and Communism" makes the same point: "The state, as the element which consciously struggles toward humanity's highest goals and which can see beyond the blind commands of society's elementary powers, has to rule these forces and make them serve its own purposes."[43]

This resistance to the model of a free social and economic system drew its strength from the liberals' continued unwillingness to overlook the potential dangers of unrestrained social and economic forces. Anxiety about the direction of social change, about the turbulent masses, about the growth of cities and spread of factories, remained an important leitmotif in German thought after 1850, where it found expression in such popular novels as Wilhelm Raabe's *Der Hungerpastor* (1864) which contains an eloquent indictment of big-city life. To a man like J. G. Droysen, whose sensibilities had been shaped in the first half of the century, the economic boom of the fifties represented a grave threat rather than a bright promise. In his essay on "The European Crisis," written in 1854, Droysen warned that "economic and moral ruin approaches with increasing speed and horror." He pointed to economic swindles, the excessive power and irresponsible use of money, and the impoverishment of the lower classes as forces which would destroy the old order of things.[44] Probably only a minority of liberals in the fifties and sixties shared Droysen's bleak assessment of the present. But even many of those who welcomed the emergence of a new social and economic world still retained some of that fear of social and economic freedom which was so apparent in liberalism before 1848. This blend of confidence tempered with a sense of impending danger infuses Wilhelm Kiesselbach's striking portrait of life among three generations of merchants in Bremen. Writing in 1860, Kiesselbach realized that the world his grandfather lived in was narrower and more limited than his own, but he could not suppress a certain nostalgia for those simpler and less demanding times. In the end, Kiesselbach faced the future with fond hope that its promise might be fulfilled, even though he warned that the present was a trying time full of threatening forces.[45]

An increased sense of material interests and a continuing concern for spiritual values, a greater faith in the free market and a traditional reliance on the ordering power of the state, a broader confidence in social progress and a lingering anxiety about the implications of social change—these, then, are the discordant elements which made up liberal social thought in the fifties and sixties.

The liberals' conception of themselves as a social movement was also shaped by a discordant mixture of new trends and familiar habits. After 1850, a number of liberals stressed the importance of economic interests and elites for the movement's present and future. Kiesselbach, for instance, criticized old-fashioned liberalism for failing to see that "a politically independent *Bürgertum* must be based on economic independence." Julius Fröbel went farther when he argued that liberalism was essentially a "system in the special interest of quite specific elements of society which are assembled in the commercial and industrial middle class." Returning to Germany after a decade of exile abroad, Friedrich Kapp affirmed the significance of these groups. The past few years had transferred the responsibility for Germany's future from the hands of the *Gebildeten* "to the young technicians, industrialists, and skilled craftsmen."[46] In these views we can find the beginnings of that self-conscious class of economically oriented men who would form the industrial and commercial *Bürgertum* of the imperial era. However, other attempts to describe the social basis of liberalism contain echoes of the pre-revolutionary *Mittelstand*. Theodor Welcker, for instance, believed that the *Mittelstand* was still the "core and power of the nation." A contributor to the *Grenzboten* in 1861 tried to distinguish between what he called the *Honoratioren* and the *Kleinbürgertum*, but concluded by arguing that their essential interests were the same.[47] And the author of the *Staatslexikon*'s article on political parties firmly rooted liberalism's social base in a *Mittelstand* that he saw as the source of social harmony and collective interest:

> The political influence for which the [*Mittelstand*] contends is not based upon a political division of the estates but on a natural law. The *Mittelstand* has nothing exclusive about it, it is not divided from the masses of the nation by a rigid frontier.... Nothing is more a part of the properly-understood interests of the *Mittelstand* than the dissemination of enlightenment and prosperity among all sectors of the population and the ability of all to employ fully their political rights.[48]

Even many of those who saw a need to revise the concept of liberalism's social basis did not fully abandon liberal attitudes popular before 1848. Thus Karl Mittermaier emphasized the importance of economic functions in his article on the *Bürgertum* in the new edition of the *Staatslexikon*, but he still emphasized the importance of *Bildung* and the inclination towards freedom as hallmarks of this social group. Johann Bluntschli took a similar tack in his *Staatswörterbuch*. For him, as for Mittermaier, membership in the *Bürgertum* was derived from both occupation and *Gesinnung*. He thereby retained that blend of social and moral qualities which characterized liberalism's social vocabulary in the first half of the century.[49] Finally, note the analysis of the *Mittelstand* in Rochau's work on Realpolitik: Rochau was far more aware than most earlier writers that the groups included in the German *Mittelstand* had some profound weaknesses and divisions. The experience of the revolution had shown him "the shadowy side of their character." Nonetheless, he was convinced that without the *Mittelstand* "no political idea is ready to be realized, no political change has a chance to be realized and sustained without its support. The most important task of every political party is to win the *Mittelstand* for itself."[50] Rochau recognized, therefore, that the *Mittelstand* was not necessarily enlightened or even liberal. But he remained true to the liberals' fundamental contention that this social group "is and remains the indispensable and most valuable material for the construction of the German state."

There is no doubt that liberals became more aware of material interests and their own social divisions after 1850, but a number of factors prevented these perceptions from totally destroying the image of a *Mittelstand* in which the

liberal movement and the common good might be based. First of all, as we
have seen, changes produced by economic development in the fifties and early
sixties had not been sufficient to displace the heritage of Vormärz. The social
structure, the terminological framework, and the social composition of
liberalism itself retained many of the characteristics of the movement's formative era. Second, the social dissensus among liberals was obscured by the
continued priority given to political goals. As long as national unity remained
unrealized and constitutional conflicts persisted in a number of states, liberals
from different social and economic groups could join in a politically directed
alliance which transcended their differences on specific social and economic
issues. Finally, the liberals' sense of themselves as a *Mittelstand* continued to
be sustained by their common hostility to groups above and below them in the
social hierarchy. In the fifties and sixties, hostility to the aristocracy remained
an important part of liberals' thought and was frequently fused with their
political struggle against reaction. At the same time, liberals' distrust of the
masses continued; indeed it was deepened by the unhappy memories of the
revolution. Liberal attitudes toward the nobility and the masses were characteristically diverse, but the presence of these two groups continued to provide a basis of communality for "independent" men of property and culture.

The final aspect of liberal social thought to be considered is their attitudes
toward what contemporaries called the "social question." These attitudes are
important not only because they contributed to the growing split between
liberalism and labor after 1871, but also because they provide a vantage point
from which we can derive another look at the diversity and ambiguities of
liberal social thought as a whole in the years between 1850 and 1866.[51]
   The increased popularity of economic liberalism after 1850 strengthened
the hand of those who were willing to accept social and economic privation as
the regrettable but inevitable by-product of progress. As usual, John Prince
Smith was a representative spokesman for this group of businessmen and
publicists. In 1864, he published an essay entitled "The So-called Worker
Question" in which he argued that social ills, like bodily ones, are subject to
certain unyielding laws. To disregard these laws in search of some solution to
social discontent is to risk doing a great deal more harm than good. Prince
Smith believed that the only way to diminish the level of suffering in society
was to improve the kind of education provided workers and to raise the
general level of prosperity through the free operation of the market.[52]
   Even liberals who were not fully committed to laissez-faire principles
doubted that the social question should be first on their agenda. Benedikt
Waldeck, for example, one of the leaders of Prussian liberalism's left wing,
called the social question a "swindle" and implored liberals not to be dis-

tracted from more fundamental political and national issues.[53] This belief in the priority of political change was also prevalent in the Democratic parties of Saxony and Württemberg. The leaders of these organizations were eager to have workers as allies in the struggle for political emancipation but showed little understanding for the economic and social discontents of laboring men.[54] As in 1848, therefore, both the moderate and the democratic wings of the political opposition found it extremely difficult to formulate a social program which would strengthen their campaigns for constitutional change by addressing problems of great concern to industrial workers and the urban poor.

This failure to respond to the social question was in part the product of the liberals' own narrow experiences and interests. As in the first half of the century, the educated elites who spoke for the movement were separated from the masses of the German people by a social distance great enough to impede an understanding of workingmen and effective interaction with them. And as liberal businessmen began to feel the effects of workers' discontent in the form of strikes and unions, their social and economic antagonisms hardened. Liberals' unwillingness to see the significance of social unrest was also a product of the historical setting, which was marked by the uneven and incomplete character of German industrialization and the inchoate nature of class consciousness and social relations. In this regard, it is important to remember that the institutional expressions of social discontent were still extremely weak before 1866. Ferdinand Lassalle, for example, created quite a stir with his call for an independent labor movement in 1863, but his practical success was very modest indeed.[55] Similarly, although tensions between liberals and workers existed in a number of areas and organizations, liberals could draw some encouragement from the fact that the majority of workers who took an interest in politics seemed to do so within the confines of liberal clubs, educational societies, and the like. As August Bebel recalled in his memoirs, most workers in the sixties remained more interested in economic freedom than in the state-sponsored producers' cooperatives which Lassalle recommended.[56] The weakness of an autonomous labor movement may have provided the liberals with an unparalleled opportunity to mobilize working-class support for their cause, but this same weakness also concealed the dangers involved in not taking advantage of this opportunity.[57]

There were, however, some liberals who saw the opportunities as well as the dangers posed by the social question. In 1865, one contributor to a collection of essays entitled *Unsere Tage* argued that the labor issue was and would remain the central problem of the age, far more significant than the constitutional issues which absorbed the attention of most contemporaries.[58] Eight years earlier, Franz Vorländer had called the social question the modern riddle of the Sphinx and doubted that a single Oedipus would be able to resolve an issue which was "so tightly bound up with all the developments of social progress."[59] We have no way of knowing how many liberals shared this sense of the social question's importance. But it is clear that a significant number of them did become involved in educational societies, cooperatives, and other organizations which sought answers to the problems of modern society.

For many contemporaries, the man who personified liberals' continuing concern for social reform was Hermann Schulze, from Delitzsch. Like many others, Schulze returned from the political struggles of the revolution with the conviction that the way to reform was to be found in social and economic rather than political life.[60] During the fifties, he was harassed by the police, prevented from practicing law, and thus suffered considerable personal hardship. These experiences deepened the sympathy he felt for the displaced and poverty-stricken handicraftsmen living around him. But Schulze also became convinced by the arguments of the liberal economists and accepted the notion of a market economy ruled by inflexible laws. He hoped that the cooperative movement would provide a way of achieving social reform within a free economy. Schulze argued that cooperatives would enable the poor and underprivileged to pool their resources and thus to overcome their individual economic weaknesses. Early in the fifties, therefore, he began to sponsor cooperatives in Delitzsch and elsewhere and to advocate their creation in periodicals like the *Grenzboten*, organizations like the Kongress deutscher Volkswirte, and eventually in the Prussian Landtag.

As a practical solution to the social question, cooperatives had a rather mixed record in the fifties and sixties. Only the credit associations really prospered, increasing from 4 (with 1,019 members) in 1854 to 532 (with 193,712 members) in 1866.[61] Cooperatives created to obtain raw materials for small producers, to manufacture goods, or to market products did not flourish as their advocates had hoped. Nevertheless, cooperatives continued to play a central role in the social thought of an extraordinarily diverse group of men, including conservatives such as V. A. Huber, radicals such as Lassalle, Catholics such as Bishop Ketteler, and a variety of liberals such as Leopold Sonnemann, Karl Biedermann, Friedrich Harkort, Johannes Miquel, Gustav Schmoller, and Viktor Böhmert.[62] The cooperative idea seems to have conformed to the way these men formulated the essential problem facing German society; by giving members of the lower classes a place within some kind of organization, by giving them a way of pooling their resources and of learning how to act together, cooperatives would alleviate both the material and spiritual malaise caused by the decline of traditional society. Friedrich Harkort captured the essence of the cooperatives' appeal to many of their sponsors when he wrote in the 1850s: "If the proletarian is given property of some kind, he will join the existing order, the *Bürgertum*."[63]

Cooperatives also had other virtues in the eyes of some socially concerned members of the liberal movement. In the first place, they were not incompatible with a belief in a free market economy. Unlike the old guilds, cooperatives did not require compulsory membership, nor did they impose restrictions on production or marketing. They could be seen, therefore, as freely organized extensions of the market, subject to the law of supply and demand and ultimately resting upon the self-interest of their members. At the same time, however, cooperatives appealed to those who still valued the older liberal notions of enlightenment and moral reform. To these men, cooperatives were a particularly effective kind of association, essentially an educational institution through which men could learn to overcome their spiritual isolation and ignorance.[64] An important source of Schulze-Delitzsch's popularity was his ability to express both of these themes: sometimes he stressed the conformity of cooperatives to the model of economic freedom; on other occasions he spoke of their spiritual function as a defense against the evils of unrestrained selfishness and materialism.[65]

Another reason for the widespread faith in cooperatives was that they seemed to fit the needs of both impoverished artisans, hard hit by competition from industrialism, and industrial workers, alienated by the inhumanity of the factory system. Cooperatives had the advantage of dissolving the distinction between the two groups by offering a way for both craftsmen and workers to acquire material and moral access to the stable ranks of the *Mittelstand*. Although many liberals in the fifties and sixties continued to be uncertain about which of these groups should be the proper focus for their efforts, there was a growing awareness that industrial labor was the most dangerous source of social discontent. By the mid-sixties, Lassalle's agitation and an outbreak of strikes in several key regions strengthened the conviction that the "social question" was now the "worker question."[66]

This evolution can be traced in Schulze's career as he moved from a concern for the craftsmen he knew in semirural Delitzsch to an emphasis on the working class. But for Schulze, as for many other liberal social reformers, concern for industrial labor did not mean abandoning the idea that social stability ultimately rested upon a large and powerful *Mittelstand*. This conviction, so central to liberal social thought in Vormärz, continued to shape liberals' response to the postrevolutionary social and economic world. Schulze's own views are nicely summarized in a speech he gave to a Berlin "workers' meeting" in November 1862. After expressing his commitment to bettering the condition of laboring men, Schulze concluded by stressing the common interests of workers and the *Mittelstand*:

> Because we must have a *Mittelstand* in Germany through which our character, consciousness, and education can develop according to the deepest

roots of Germany's nature as a *Volk*—for that reason we need a working
class [*Arbeiterstand*] whose existence is no longer in danger.[67]

The echoes of Vormärz can be distinctly heard in this statement: the view of
the *Mittelstand* as the true embodiment of the common good, the inclination to
mix moral and material categories, and the implication that in some ways the
workers' well-being was a subordinate goal, at best a prerequisite for the
solution of society's real ills. These lingering habits of mind come out even
more clearly in Schulze's famous response to the problem of workers' membership in the liberals' Nationalverein:

> The *Mittelstand* is the main source of the national essence and idea, and
> the most central part of the *Mittelstand* is made up, more or less, of
> workers. . . . If a worker asks me if he should join a workers' association
> or the Nationalverein, I answer: Dear friend, you will serve the cause of
> the nation much better if you first think about your own material im-
> provement, because our national cause will benefit from nothing more
> than an improvement of the working class. If you have some money left
> over, we will welcome you with open arms. . . . And real workers who
> use your savings for this, I welcome you in the name of the Executive
> Committee as spiritual members, as honorary members of the
> Nationalverein.[68]

Schulze was a decent man, and his remarks reflected a sincere desire to
improve the lot of the working class. And yet it is not hard to see why Schulze
and those like him proved to be unable to forge an alliance between liberalism
and labor. One cannot overlook the patronizing tone in his remarks, nor can
one overlook his inability to formulate an image of industrial workers as a
distinct group with its own interests. Schulze's conceptual failures had an
institutional dimension: the liberals' advocacy of cooperatives and educational
societies proved insufficient to meet the needs of laboring men to define their
identity and express their interests as an autonomous social group. Until 1866
these failures of the liberal reformers were hidden by the still inchoate nature
of social and economic relations in Germany, but as the process of social and
economic change penetrated ever deeper into German society the estrangement between liberalism and industrial workers would become increasingly
apparent.

7 The Search for a Liberal *Volk*

> The question of the *true*, the *real Volk*
> is a very familiar one for all the parties,
> and every party finds the *true*, the
> *real Volk* where it finds its own point
> of view or at least willing tools for its
> own purposes.
>
> L. A. von Rochau (1853)[1]

When reactionary policies began to ease in the late 1850s, the liberal movement reemerged with extraordinary speed and vitality. As early as the fall of 1858, one observer celebrated the "happy sense of relief" which was sweeping the land.[2] In the next few years Heinrich Schulthess' *Europäischer Geschichtskalender*, which was itself a product of the "new era," could report with unconcealed satisfaction an almost unbroken string of liberal election victories. In Prussia, liberals' electoral potential began to be apparent in 1858; by the mid-sixties they had reduced their opponents in the Landtag to a tiny, embattled minority (see table 7.1). Liberal victories were also impressive in a number of the smaller German states. In the sixties, as in Vormärz, Baden remained a liberal stronghold among the south German *Mittelstaaten*; by 1861 forty-eight of sixty-three seats in the Badenese parliament were occupied by liberal delegates.[3] Liberals also made impressive gains in Hesse, Hesse-Darmstadt, Nassau, Hamburg, and Hanover. In Württemberg liberals and democrats dominated the Landtag. Even in states like Saxony and Bavaria, where antiliberal forces remained strong, the movement was powerful enough to return a vigorous and articulate *Fraktion* to the parliament.[4]

The liberals' electoral vitality was sustained by a widespread and varied set of institutions. Liberals dominated local government in most major cities.[5] They often controlled economic bodies like Chambers of Commerce, as well as professional societies, academic associations, recreational clubs, and sometimes the corporate life of the universities. Popular periodicals provided forums for liberal ideas, many influential newspapers expressed the movement's goals, and even some scholarly journals lent themselves to the liberal cause. To those contemporaries who were drawn to the movement, therefore, it seemed as though the most creative and dynamic elements in German society—scholars and businessmen, publicists and officials, local notables and national elites—were identified with the liberal "party of movement." These men could hope that the revolution's failure had been overcome and that the ascending curve of liberalism's strength guaranteed a liberal future in Germany.

Table 7.1   **The Political Composition of the Prussian Chamber of Deputies, 1858–63**

Party	1858 No. (%)	1861 No. (%)	1862 No. (%)	1863 No. (%)
Conservatives	47 (13)	14 (4)	11 (3)	35 (10)
Fortschrittspartei	—	104 (29.5)	133 (38)	141 (40)
Other Liberals				
Vincke, Mathis	195 (55)			
Grambow		91 (26)		
Constitutionalists			19 (5)	
Left-Center		48 (14)	96 (27)	106 (30)
Catholics	57 (16)	54 (15)	28 (8)	26 (7)
Poles	18 (5)	23 (6.5)	22 (6)	26 (7)
No Fraktion	35 (10)	18 (5)	43 (12)	18 (5)
Total	352	352	352	352

SOURCE: Vogel et al., *Wahlen* (1971), p. 287.

In one sense, those who derived hope from these signs of liberal strength were correct: in the 1860s liberalism was without doubt the most energetic and popular vehicle for political participation. But it is clear enough in retrospect, as it was clear to some men at the time, that despite the movement's apparent strength liberals still had to resolve formidable problems before they could become strong enough to defeat their enemies. First of all, liberals had to find the conceptual and institutional means of managing the conflicts within their own ranks and of coordinating their efforts on a national plane. Second, liberals had to develop programs and organizations which would enable them to sink the roots of their movement deep within the masses of the German people. In short, those who sought to build a liberal Germany first had to build a liberal movement based on the support of a liberal *Volk*. And to do this they had to struggle against and within a political culture which retained many of the characteristic problems created by long-standing institutional fragmentation and popular apathy.

From the very beginning of the "new era," some liberals tried to construct institutions with national scope and focus. The Kongress deutscher Volks-wirte, for instance, was committed to attracting men from throughout Germany.[6] Many of the same men who participated in the annual meetings of the Kongress were also involved in the formation of the Nationalverein, which was planned in 1859 and held the first of its annual gatherings the following year. The impetus for the Nationalverein came from Italy, which was just then embarked on the process of nation-building: its model was the Società nationale, which had sought to prepare Italian public opinion for national unification.[7] In addition to the Kongress and the Nationalverein, there were a number of other institutions through which Germans could move from local to national political involvement. In the early sixties, delegates to the various state parliaments gathered at the so-called Abgeordnetentag in Frankfurt where they discussed common goals and problems. Members of the Chambers of Commerce formed the German Handelstag, which held annual meetings. Local singing clubs, marksmen's associations, and gymnastic societies held national meetings that had muted but unmistakable political purposes. This was also true of the legal profession's Juristentag, which met in 1863 and concluded by expressing its members' commitment to national unity and constitutional government. That same year, Johann Bluntschli, who was active in the Juristentag, helped to establish the Deutscher Protestantenverein, which was devoted to seeking liberal and national goals from a religious perspective.[8] For Bluntschli and for many others, these groups seemed to indicate a broad wave of liberal support which was at last finding national expression:

> [These organizations] are symptoms of a political life which exists and grows in the nation. I would like to compare all of these organizations to brooks which flow toward a great river, brooks which continually grow bigger until the river embraces them and carries them away.[9]

The growth of these national organizations was enhanced by the expansion of the communications network within Germany. By 1862, there were 3,700 miles of all-season roads in Prussia alone (there had been less than 500 in 1816) and over 700 miles of railroad track. After 1850 the mail service improved greatly and the telegraph had begun to revolutionize certain kinds of communication. Commercial transactions and corporate finance also had begun to move outside of the narrow confines of a few communities as markets became larger and the first supralocal banking institutions developed. Equally important, with this increased movement of people, goods, and money went an ever greater movement of news and ideas. Publications like Schulthess' *Geschichtskalender* summarized the year's events for a national audience, while a few newspapers, especially from Berlin, began to address a national public.[10]

The growth of the communications network and other national institutions was quite impressive compared to the condition of those institutions in the first half of the century. And yet it is important to recognize that these changes touched the lives of a small number of Germans. Newspapers, for example, were expensive and their circulation remained limited—liberal newspapers in Prussia printed about a quarter of a million copies a day during the sixties. Equally important, their content and format were designed for the educated minority. Only a few Germans were able to travel widely, fewer still came into direct contact with the new banks and business enterprises. The membership of national organizations reflected the persistent thinness of this national public. Between 1858 and 1865, the Kongress was never able to attract more than 320 men to one of its meetings, and usually attendance was around 200. Despite some intensive organizational efforts, the Nationalverein numbered no more than 25,000 in 1862 and very quickly dropped to about 10,000 at the end of 1865. The singing and gymnastic societies were much larger (with about 60,000 and 170,000 members, respectively, in the mid-sixties), but even they attracted only a small part of the adult population.[11]

Despite some important steps toward a national political culture, therefore, politics for most Germans was centered in the various states or, even more likely, in particular regions and individual communities. Since institutions which could join these local bodies together were weak, liberals' values, attitudes, and behavior continued to reflect the social, political, and economic diversity which fragmented men's experience within central Europe.

In fact, some of the developments after 1850 intensified this diversity. The unevenness of social and economic change meant that whereas liberals in Baden and the Rhineland—to choose two regions where the movement was rather strong—might have been able to communicate with one another more easily after 1850, their social worlds were probably more dissimilar than they had been during the first half of the century. Participant politics also continued to be shaped by the very different institutional settings of the various states. Election laws differed widely, as did the power of representative institutions, the government's attitude toward the liberal movement, and the character of the opponents with whom liberals had to compete. This persistent fragmentation of the liberals' political experience can be seen by considering briefly the alignment of liberal groups in the various states.

In Prussia, the optimism generated by the regency of Prince William had inaugurated the "new era." Initially, a variety of elements in the opposition tried to cooperate with one another and with the government. During the elections of 1858, for example, some left-wing liberals refused to be candidates because they did not want to disturb this apparent harmony. In the new Landtag, most liberals joined a faction led by Georg von Vincke, who stood on the far right of the movement.[12] However, the hopes associated with the "new era" gradually paled as relations between liberals and government deteriorated. By early 1861, a number of liberal parliamentarians were unwilling to follow Vincke's excessively moderate lead. In June these men left his faction and formed the Deutsche Fortschrittspartei. To someone like Vincke, this new organization and its program represented dangerous interference with the individual delegate's right to follow the dictates of his own conscience. But the founders of Fortschrittspartei were convinced that the deepening constitutional crisis required better organization as well as a more clearly defined platform.[13] As the *Westfälische Zeitung* put it in 1861: "The program is the determining factor ... it must take precedence over the personal qualities of the candidate."[14] Although the Fortschrittspartei's formation helped to clarify political attitudes and to increase the level of political awareness, it should also be noted that the party's program remained vague and uncertain. Most of its formulations were very general and subject to a variety of interpretations. On the critical issue of universal suffrage, a point over which party members were deeply divided, the program remained completely silent. It is not surprising, therefore, that the *Kölner Zeitung* regarded the program as "too much like a theoretical declaration of faith" to have much practical meaning to individual candidates.[15] In fact, while the program was an improvement over the lofty abstractions current in Vormärz, it still reflected the liberals' inclination to seek refuge from internal conflicts in the ambiguous rhetoric of spiritual harmony.[16]

In Baden, the question of cooperation with the government, posed so dramatically by the constitutional conflict in Prussia, did not arise. Baden enjoyed a strong liberal tradition, a relatively mild political and social climate, and a progressive ruler. These combined to produce a decade of productive cooperation between liberals and the government which turned Badenese liberalism into what has been called the "governing party."[17] Nevertheless, Baden's liberals were also troubled by a number of divisive issues. Should Baden support a Prussian-led Germany? What was the proper extent of democratization within the state? How far should the government carry its hostility to the Catholic church? Should Baden adopt a policy of economic freedom or of qualified protectionism? At first, liberals tried to prevent these differences from hardening into permanent divisions by avoiding any programmatic commitment. In 1863, when the first state-wide meeting of liberals since 1848 took place, liberal leaders steered the discussion away from proposals for organizational improvements and programmatic precision. "This spirit [of reform] is our program," declared Johann Bluntschli in a speech which echoed the liberals' traditional habits of proclaiming spiritual harmony when faced with practical disagreements. Two years later, tensions between liberals and the government, together with a powerful counteroffensive by their Catholic opponents, forced liberals to seek a more effective organizational basis for their activity.[18] But the Fortschrittspartei in Baden, like its Prussian counterpart, tried to blur its internal divisions with a rather general program which left unmentioned those issues on which agreement seemed unlikely.

Liberals in most of the other *Mittelstaaten* also formed Fortschrittsparteien in the 1860s. As in Baden and Prussia, these parties attempted to attract a wide spectrum of supporters by avoiding specific policy commitments which could offend either the right or the left. In Bavaria, cohesion was further enhanced by reactionary pressures from the government.[19] In Hanover, leaders like Rudolf von Bennigsen and Johannes Miquel kept liberals united behind a general program linked to the Nationalverein.[20] Conflict with the government on religious issues kept liberals in Hesse together during the early sixties, although by the middle of the decade the right wing of the movement had begun to drift away from the Hessian Fortschrittspartei.[21] In parts of Hesse and Bavaria, as well as in states like Saxony and Württemberg, the liberal movement was also challenged on the left. This challenge was sharpest in those regions where different lines of cleavage ran in the same direction, that is, where differences on national issues, political ideology, and socio-economic policy tended to coincide. The best example of this pattern is Württemberg, where an antiliberal democratic group attracted those who opposed the liberals' commitment to Prussia, political "moderation," and ties to free-trade economic interests. But even in Württemberg relations between moderates and radicals were usually ill-defined: initially men from both groups participated in the Nationalverein and continued to join in opposition to the government on some issues. Moreover, a separate Volkspartei faction was not formed in the Württemberg parliament until 1868.[22]

If we compare liberalism's internal alignments and programmatic statements during the "new era" with those from the first half of the century, it is apparent that a certain amount of clarification had taken place. By the early sixties, most liberals had come to realize that the common *Gesinnung* which Ferdinand Falkson had proclaimed before 1848 concealed some important differences about both the ends and means of political action. But the degree of clarification, as well as its organizational and programmatic consequences, varied greatly from one community to another. As usual, the clearest divisions occurred at the two extremes of the movement. The far right of the old Vormärz opposition, which had swung over to the government's side as early as the summer of 1848, tended to separate itself from the more vigorous elements within the movement and to urge compromise with the *Staat* at almost any price. This group was represented by Vincke's followers in Prussia, the *Altliberalen* in Hesse, and like-minded men in other states. In some areas, there was an analogous split on the left which also tended to follow divisions apparent during the revolution. By the early sixties democratic organizations in many of the *Mittelstaaten* rejected cooperation with state institutions and based their hopes on a spontaneous movement of the *Volk*.[23] However, as we move away from the extremes of right and left we find the same diversity and fluidity which had characterized the movement before 1848.

Liberals' new images of themselves and their movement reflected this process of partial clarification. Unlike Rudolf Haym's prerevolutionary study of the United Landtag, E. Schmidt-Weissenfels' book on the Prussian Landtag of 1862 divided liberals into several categories and spent some time trying to define the differences among them.[24] A comparison of the first and third editions of the *Staatslexikon* suggests a similar awareness of internal divisions. The article on the "Party of Movement" in the first edition focused on a simple division between liberals and reactionaries, but by the 1850s it was necessary to point out differences within the "party of movement" and the need to reconcile them.[25] The fourth edition of Pierer's *Universal Lexikon*, published in 1860, also acknowledged that liberals could no longer be regarded as members of a single movement.[26] Nevertheless, most of these statements continued to underestimate both the extent and the permanence of intraparty dissensus. Schmidt-Weissenfels, for example, is impressively insightful when compared to Haym, but his understanding of the realities of Prussian liberalism is still far from complete. Like Haym, Schmidt operated within a biographical mode and emphasized the ideas and personalities of a few prominent parliamentarians. Furthermore, he seems to have been convinced that many divisions within liberalism were temporary, arising from differences over tactics rather than over final goals.[27] So too, Hermann Baumgarten in 1862 thought that the conflict between various elements within Prussian liberalism was peculiar to Berlin and had little meaning for the rest of Germany. Others saw the Fortschrittspartei as simply one faction within a larger "liberal party."[28]

Because they would not or could not confront their own diversity, many liberals believed that the main elements of the Vormärz opposition, perhaps narrowed somewhat on the far left and right, remained united in a single movement. To a liberal in Bavaria, for example, the very formation of Fortschrittsparteien in the various states was "a powerful witness for the communality of internal development and for similar views and needs which live in the south and north of the great fatherland."[29] The Nationalverein was based on a similar expectation that liberals could cooperate on the national level; its appeal was directed toward members of the "democratic and constitutional parties."[30] As long as the institutional basis of national politics remained weak, liberals could continue to enjoy the mixed blessing of these untested hopes, but they would have to pay a considerable price for their illusions when the creation of national institutions gradually brought into focus the movement's unresolved divisions.

So far our discussion has concerned the "horizontal" relationships among liberals, that is, their attempts to create a national network of institutions and to come to terms with their internal divisions. In both of these areas, some important changes took place during the "new era," but it is clear that the liberals' accomplishments remained limited in a number of significant ways. This same pattern of qualified success and piecemeal progress can be observed when we turn to the "vertical" relationships within liberalism, that is, the liberals' attempt to create a firm foundation for their movement in the German *Volk*.

Liberalism's failure in 1848 led some men in the movement to a greater appreciation for the institutional dimension of political action. When political activity resumed at the end of the fifties some liberals thought electoral agitation to be the best way to spread liberalism's message and to create a popular movement. Joseph Held, writing in 1864, argued that public life could produce a "noble self-consciousness" among Germans, while elections, "wonderfully enhanced by the rich and comfortable means of communication existing now," could create "numerous acquaintances, meetings, and ties between fellow citizens."[31]

The "new era" was marked by a number of efforts to give these insights practical meaning. The Nationalverein, for example, reflected its leaders' desire to create a firm institutional basis for political action. Membership dues were collected and meetings were open only to those who joined. Local organizations were formed throughout Germany in order to gather mass support. There was even a small professional staff hired to coordinate the Verein's activities. And yet the Nationalverein was still influenced by the ingrained habits of Vormärz. Its annual meetings preserved the convivial atmosphere and social narrowness characteristic of those quasi-political bodies that had met with increasing frequency during the years just before the revolution.[32] Some of its local organizations did try to engage in mass political agitation, but others were educational societies which preserved the traditional identification of politics and *Bildung*.[33]

A similar blend of new aspirations and old habits can be found in the Prussian Fortschrittspartei. The party was formed because a number of Prussian liberals saw the need for a radically different kind of political organization. Its leaders established a central election committee in Berlin which was designed to provide direction and assistance to local groups and to coordinate their activities. But the organizational basis of the party, like its program, was flexible enough to include many different points of view. Some elements within the Fortschrittspartei, such as the Verein deutscher Handwerker and the Volkstümlicher Verein embraced democratic principles and engaged in relatively intense political agitation. Elsewhere, however, informal organizations continued to prevail and politics remained the concern of a small group of notables. In these regions, and in a great many areas outside of Prussia, the establishment of a Fortschrittspartei affected parliamentary alignments but had only a slight impact on the institutional realities of local political life.[34]

The uneven and often rather thin basis of liberal politics was due in part to continued political repression in the fifties and sixties. Although government interference with political activity was a great deal less oppressive than it had been before 1848, the policeman and the censor continued to hinder public activity in some areas. Locally, pressure from a powerful landholder or some other representative of the traditional elite could have a chilling effect on popular participation. Equally important, the institutional setting of participatory politics continued to inhibit widespread popular mobilization. Suffrage limitations excluded large parts of the population in most states. Indirect voting set up an intermediary stage which separated the mass of voters from the final choice of a representative and reinforced the influence of locally-prominent electors (Wahlmänner) in whose hands the final decision rested.[35] Finally, the relative weakness of the communications network, the persistence of traditional values, and the influence of lingering habits of deference to social superiors combined to erect formidable barriers of ignorance and apathy between the majority of the population and electoral politics.

Table 7.2

Participation in Prussian Landtag Elections, 1855–63 (percentage of eligible voters)

Year	Voting Class			
	I	II	III	Total
1855	39.6	27.2	12.7	16.1
1858	50.2	37.1	18.5	22.6
1861	55.8	42.4	23	27.2
1862	61	48	30.5	34.3
1863	57	44	27.3	30.9

SOURCE: Hess, *Parlament* (1964), p. 23.

We do not have reliable figures on political participation in most of the states, but the data on Prussia given in table 7.2 are a striking example of how these practical and attitudinal inhibitions to political participation affected voter turnout. In assessing these figures one should bear in mind that the elections of the early sixties were carried out in a crisis atmosphere and were accompanied by what a number of contemporaries saw as intensive political agitation.

Viewed in one way, these data suggest why many liberals could afford to
ignore those who called for extensive organizational reforms within the
movement. In many parts of Germany, the low level of popular involvement
enabled liberals to win elections without generating mass support. But from
another perspective, the data indicate the extent of the movement's failure to
enlist the masses of the population in the struggle for a liberal future. In order
to understand this failure, it is necessary to examine liberals' attitudes about
political action and about the nature of the *Volk* itself.

For a number of influential liberals during the "new era," the proper end of
political action remained popular enlightenment. This was the burden of Karl
Biedermann's statement in the edition of the *Staatslexikon* published during
the early sixties:

> A strong, influential public opinion is not created by individuals nor by
> artificial coteries with their equally artificial influences but rather by the
> persistent and irresistible power of ideas . . . . Therefore, whoever wants
> influence on public opinion, and whoever wants to use this opinion to
> influence events, should place himself in the service of an idea. The
> greater, the freer, the more natural and healthy the idea which he serves,
> the greater will be his influence on public opinion and through that on
> public life.[36]

The continued influence of educated men on liberal politics, the persistent
popularity of educational societies, the scholarly tone and content of many
liberal publications all reflected some measure of agreement with Biedermann's restatement of the Vormärz conviction that politics was spiritual in
content and educational in practice. Even some of those who saw the limits of
this view did not abandon the notion that ideas were the moving force behind
politics. L. A. von Rochau, for one, knew that ideas did not triumph because
of their inherent "greatness" or "health," but that did not prevent him from
believing that "an idea, whether it be true or false, which can permeate a
whole *Volk* or age is the most real of all political powers."[37] In this regard, as
in many others, the author of *Realpolitik* represents his time not because his
thought is a radical break with the past but because it combines in characteristic fashion old habits and an attempt to understand new forces at work.

One reason why this "spiritualization" of politics lingered was that many
liberals continued to resist the kind of commitment which membership in a
political organization involved. We have already seen how a right-wing liberal
like Georg von Vincke refused to sacrifice his "independence" by supporting
a specific program. Vincke was proud that he had never actively sought
election or communicated in any way with his voters.[38] Traces of this hostility
to organized action can be found even among those who were much more

committed to political opposition than Vincke. Karl Twesten, for example, declared in 1859 that "we are tired of phrases" and called for a commitment to concrete goals. Nevertheless, four years later Twesten decided not to join a liberal faction in the Prussian parliament because, as he wrote to a friend, he saw no great disadvantages in being isolated. Some of those who joined a party did so with regret and uneasiness. Friedrich Hammacher had a long and active career in local government, which he greatly enjoyed, but he found the activities of the party dull and unpleasant. Georg von Bunsen had even stronger views on the subject: "I feel totally antipathetic to the idea of a faction," he wrote in 1862, "as well as to the whole sophomoric tone of the majority and the endless gabbing about formulas and party questions."[39]

In their relationship to their constituents, many liberals remained committed to the personal and informal style of political life that had been characteristic of Vormärz. Consider, for example, Eduard von Simson's lament for a passing political era which was evoked by his defeat by Schulze-Delitzsch in 1861: "I regarded the outcome of the election in Königsberg as a personal insult—to lose to a stranger whom scarcely one-fourth of the electors [Wahlmänner] had ever laid eyes on."[40] In Simson's mind, his position as a local notable with deep personal ties in the community should have taken precedence for the voters over Schulze's more vigorous liberal position. Simson's kind of politics was on the decline in cities like Königsberg, but in other places liberals could still see political office as the product of local prestige rather than political agitation. When Leopold Freiherr von Hoverbeck began his political career in 1858, his father wrote to him that "It wasn't necessary for you to tell me that you had not solicited votes, I knew that at once because you are my son."[41]

Debates among liberals about whether or not they should form parties and engage in active electoral agitation reflected their doubts about the proper role of the *Volk* in political life. Characteristically, these doubts came to the surface when liberals had to face the problem of suffrage regulations. As in the first half of the century, the question of who should be able to vote forced liberals to consider the relationship between the "real" *Volk* of enlightened men and the actual population of the German states.[42] Throughout the new era there were men on the left of the movement who unambiguously endorsed democratic suffrage. Schulze-Delitzsch urged the Prussian Fortschrittspartei to adopt this position as part of an effort to mobilize mass support for liberalism. Liberals can only benefit from democracy, Schulze assured his colleagues, because voters will continue to select men with property and education to represent them. Theodor Welcker agreed. In the third edition of the *Staatslexikon* he revised Rotteck's original article on voting, omitting the arguments in favor of restrictions and offering a rather high age-qualification (thirty or thirty-two) as an appropriate substitute. Like Schulze, Welcker seems to have felt that there was not much chance the lower orders would choose one of their own to represent them.[43] But many other liberals were not so sure. In 1864, Waldeck, one of the leaders of the Prussian left, was so frightened by Lassalle's agitation that he decided "evidently now is not the time" to fight for democratic voting rights.[44] Other liberals doubted both the long- and short-run benefits of democratic voting. In his *Staatswörterbuch*, J. C. Bluntschli maintained that "the arithmetical system of equal suffrage for all is certainly not the way to full representation." A few years earlier he had sent the king of Bavaria a suffrage scheme which made sure that the lower classes would be represented by what he called "patrons of the workers" rather than by men of their own choosing.[45] Heinrich von Sybel believed that democracy violated the very purpose of the state: he saw no advantage in a situation where "the uneducated, immoral, and unreliable man would have as much influence as someone who is wise, industrious, and patriotic."[46] But as in Vormärz, the opponents of democracy had a great deal of trouble agreeing about the precise limitations which should be imposed. A class system such as existed in Prussia, property requirements, the old notion of "independence"—all of these continued to find support. Disagreement about the actual dimensions of the electorate, together with pressure from the left of the movement and tactical considerations, made many liberals reluctant to take a clear programmatic stand on the suffrage question. The result was a certain faltering vacuity which is to be found in many of their public statements about this issue.[47]

Although liberals were often reluctant to commit themselves to a specific form of limited suffrage, there was a clear inclination within the movement to emphasize the elitist character of political enlightenment. This can be seen by considering liberals' views on "public opinion," which had always been a central category in their political thought. During Vormärz liberals usually defined public opinion in normative terms, the body of enlightened sentiment in the nation which would, more or less by definition, serve as the public expression of the liberal movement. In the fifties and sixties, however, this formulation tended to give way to a rather more limited one. Some liberals began to stress the potential for error in the public. Bluntschli wrote in 1862 that "public opinion can be deluded by the momentary passions of the mob . . . . A single individual can see clearly while everyone around him is mistaken."[48] Others emphasized the inevitably elitist character of enlightened opinion. An article in the *Grenzboten* continued to use the term as a moral category but pointed out that it was always "the judgment of a hundred thousand educated men." Karl Biedermann made much the same point when he urged that the political organizations should not be judged by their size but by "the degree of their [members'] education and the maturity of their political judgments."[49]

These internal divisions among liberals on political organization, on the problem of suffrage regulations, and on the reliability of public opinion resulted from their continued uncertainty about the nature of the *Volk*. Was the *Volk* becoming more "independent," prosperous, and reliable? Some liberals seemed to think that it was, and they could point to the movement's electoral success as clear evidence for this conviction.[50] Others in the movement were not at all sure this was the case. To them, the experience of the revolution had demonstrated the "inconstancy and unreliability of the masses."[51] Moreover, they recognized that behind the thin layer of politically active and liberally inclined voters lay the uncommitted majority of the nation. To these men the *Volk* came more and more to be what the tenth edition of Brockhaus' dictionary defined as "the raw, uneducated mob, the *Pöbel*."[52] In the "new era," therefore, the liberals' position on the central questions of political thought and action continued to be ambivalent, a complex blend of confidence in progress and anxiety about its implications. Its source was a set of lingering doubts about the relationship between the "real" *Volk* of enlightened and liberal men and the masses of the German nation.

The experience of the "new era" and the memories of the revolution worked in different ways on the men who sought to shape the liberal movement in the late 1850s and early 1860s. Some of them tried to create national organizations, to clarify liberalism's internal alignments, and to deepen its resonance within the *Volk*. And these efforts met with some success. Liberals did move toward a more powerful national network of institutions, a clearer sense of their internal alignments, and a broader base of participatory organizations. Nevertheless, any final statement on the search for a liberal *Volk* between the revolution and the *Reichsgründung* must emphasize the problems which liberals continued to confront. In 1866 liberalism was still far from being the national, cohesive, and popular movement which its rhetoric so often proclaimed. There were many reasons for this, but none was more significant than the limitations imposed by the legacies of Vormärz. The force of these legacies came not simply from the way in which they persisted in the external realities of the liberals' world, but also from the way in which they continued to influence the liberals' own conception of political and social life.

8

The Search for a Liberal *Staat*

The future of constitutionalism in Germany will be just like its past.

L. A. von Rochau (1853)[1]

After 1850 the search for a liberal state continued to be intertwined with the movement's search for a liberal *Volk*. As in Vormärz, liberals' values and expectations, ideology and tactics depended on their assessment of both of these key elements in the political equation. To many on the far right of the movement, fear of the masses encouraged clear-cut affirmation of the state's ultimate authority. This was the lesson Friedrich Dahlmann learned from the revolution, a lesson which was in line with his ideas before 1848: "If the authority of the state and popular freedom cannot be simultaneously possessed, [then] the authority of the state takes precedence in every way."[2] On the movement's left wing, the failure of the revolution, the resurgence of reaction during the fifties, and the political conflicts of the early sixties produced an affirmation of the *Volk* as the primary instrument for political change. Hans Viktor von Unruh, for example, temporarily rejected constitutional dualism between monarch and *Volk* and advocated popular sovereignty.[3] On the far left of the various Fortschrittsparteien and among the democratic groups in the south and west, a number of men argued that only popular political action could bring into being the free society for which they fought.

Despite these pulls to the right and left, most liberals continued to avoid an unequivocal commitment to either extreme. The majority of those in the movement remained uncertain and ambivalent about both state power and popular sovereignty. In fact, a number of liberals regarded their ambivalence as a source of strength and vitality. One writer in the third edition of the *Staatslexikon*, for example, praised the movement for defending freedom "against limitations imposed either by the government or by the violence of the masses." Joseph Held made the same point by saying that liberals wanted both freedom and order, "since where there is order without freedom, it is dead and deadly, but where there is freedom without order, it is unproductive if not actively destructive."[4] This effort to avoid the extremes of statism and democracy was one reason for the programmatic fluidity which was described in the last chapter. It was also the source of the practical and theoretical difficulties with which this present chapter is concerned.

Many liberals were reluctant to embrace the authority of the state in the years after 1850. In the first place, this was because a number of them blamed the states' reactionary policies for provoking the radical violence in 1848 and for the liberal experiment's ultimate failure. Second, during the fifties liberals once again felt the sting of repression and had to endure a renewal of censorship and other forms of state interference with their political rights. In some states these reactionary inclinations of the bureaucracy eased after 1858, but in others they remained very much a part of liberals' experience. Throughout the period between 1850 and 1866, therefore, liberals frequently reasserted their familiar complaints about bureaucratic excess. Rudolf von Bennigsen, who had had some unfortunate experiences with the Hanoverian administration, wrote in 1859 that "the bureaucracy and its counterpart, the lack of self-government and the inhibited freedom of labor and laborers, is deadly for us Germans." Similarly, Rochau condemned what he called "absolutism," which stood against all the forces providing "the greatness of the nation— patriotism, nationalism, lawful ambition, manly and civic pride, the spirit of enterprise, self-confidence, strength of character, and prosperity."[5]

In economic life, the everyday relationships between bureaucrats and businessmen were often troubled and tense. Some officials were openly hostile to industrialization, others favored one kind of enterprise over another, and a few wanted more rapid economic growth than did many entrepreneurs. These divided and often contradictory policies provided many occasions for mutual antagonism and irritation. As businessmen became more and more conscious of their economic power and social significance, they became less and less willing to accept the state's tutelage. And of course the growing popularity of economic liberalism provided the ideological basis from which the state could be criticized and its role in social life called into question.

The single most important instance of the liberals' persistent antagonism toward the state after 1858 was the constitutional conflict in Prussia, which began when liberal parliamentarians refused to accept the government's plans for military reform.[6] The army was a sensitive issue for Prussian liberals: politically, it was the traditional instrument of reaction whose repressive role in 1848–49 had not been forgotten; socially, it represented the continued power and prestige of the Prussian nobility and thus could serve as a focus for the liberals' deeply felt antagonism toward this social group; economically, the army seemed like an unwholesome and unwarranted burden on the taxpayers, and imposition by the state on the "productive" sectors of society.[7] When the king refused to fashion his military policy to the parliament's demands, these practical and symbolic issues fused with questions of parliamentary rights and constitutional legality. The result was a stalemate between king and Landtag which eventually brought Otto von Bismarck to the position of minister-president in September of 1862. Bismarck disturbed the liberals' political and social consciousness in a number of ways.[8] His background, manner, and appearance personified the Junker elite and thus deepened the sense many liberals had that their struggle transcended the immediate issue at hand and involved a basic confrontation between *Bürgertum* and aristocracy.[9] His arrogant defiance of the constitution violated the liberals' deeply felt commitment to the rule of law. His policies of repression against liberal officials, his efforts at censorship of the press, and his use of the governmental apparatus for an antiliberal counteroffensive recalled the worst abuses perpetrated during the era of bureaucratic absolutism. This tangle of immediate and long-term, practical and symbolic antagonisms strengthened the willingness of Prussian liberals to oppose the state and thus created a crisis which was reminiscent of the late 1840s in both its breadth and intensity.

Despite the persistence and even the intensification of this opposition, the hostility of liberals to the state and their ability to define clear alternatives to state authority were still qualified in a number of important ways. As we know, in many areas the leadership of the movement continued to be drawn from men in government service: administrators, judges, professors. The practical difficulties these men faced when they tried to combine government employment with political opposition increased significantly after 1850 because the various bureaucratic establishments became less tolerant of dissent within their own ranks. Perhaps more important than these external pressures for conformity were the psychological inhibitions imposed upon those whose training and careers were embedded in the state's apparatus. State service tended to engender habits of mind and behavior which were in some ways incompatible with the requirements of political leadership. Most officials did not find it easy to engage in the kind of organized activities and agitation necessary to build a popular movement. At the same time, their attitudes toward political issues were inevitably colored by what one contemporary called the "juridical perspective" that he observed in bodies like the Prussian Landtag.[10] The influence of the values, role conceptions, and behavior patterns associated with bureaucratic institutions continued, therefore, to have an impact on the liberal elite and to undermine their efforts to stand up against the *Staat*, both in theory and in practice.

As in Vormärz, liberals' hostility to the state was also qualified by their desire to cooperate with it on a number of practical issues. The attitudes of liberals toward religious and educational policy, for instance, suggested the degree to which they were willing to use bureaucratic institutions against what they saw as unhealthy sources of power and influence. The best example of this inclination can be found in Baden where, after 1860, liberals affirmed the importance of the state's power in their struggle against the Catholic church. Roggenbach's liberal program of 1860 recognized the church's independence but made clear that in areas such as education, where religious influence might run counter to the interests of the polity, the state had to prevail: "The state's greatest possible freedom [to administer its internal affairs] must lead it to create its own institutions for all of those aspects of civil life in whose orderly conduct it has an interest."[11] To Roggenbach and most of his colleagues, this meant state sponsorship and control of the schools. A Rhenish liberal like Heinrich von Sybel, who was equally concerned with the need to fight against the church, agreed. In 1862, when the constitutional conflict in Prussia was already well underway, Sybel declared that

> Whoever has the schools, has control over the future and the world. My convictions lead me to hope that the state will possess the schools ... and with them authority over the spirit and over the future.[12]

Liberals like Roggenbach and Sybel saw no conflict here between freedom and state power because, when they spoke in terms of state control, they had in mind a liberal state. But the theoretical and practical implications of their position seem unmistakable: in dealing with an enemy like the Catholic church, it was impossible to rely upon the free interplay of conflicting institutions; the power of the state had to impose the conditions under which freedom might eventually prosper.

Just as the liberals' support for freedom of expression did not prevent them from advocating certain limitations on the rights of their opponents, so their increasing commitment to economic freedom did not stand in the way of their embracing state power when it suited their interests. In 1857, for example, a Silesian manufacturer named Reichenheim, who would later become a leading member of the Prussian Fortschrittspartei, tried to get the local Landrat to use his power to break a strike that was disrupting Reichenheim's textile business.[13] That same year a sharp downturn in the economy led many other businessmen to turn to the state for help. The Handelskammer of Barmen-Elberfeld expressed the hope that the state would not "forgo the right and duty to protect civil society from its own abuses and excesses."[14] Moreover, in a number of states, entrepreneurs' frustration with bureaucratic interference was attenuated by the willingness to cooperate that they found in other sectors of the administration. In Prussia, laws governing the mining industry, the formation of corporations, investment procedures, and fiscal policy were altered to meet the interests of the business community.[15]

Even when political conflicts were at their height, Prussian liberals and the government were able to cooperate on economic policies. Indeed, some businessmen were sufficiently confident about the state's economic judgments that they were eager to see the bureaucracy take an active role in the formulation of legislation on industrial and commercial affairs.[16] Furthermore, in 1862 most liberals interrupted their political campaign against the government to agitate in favor of the ministry's trade policy by way of support for the commercial treaty with France.

The effect of this economic cooperation on liberals varied. A few began to wonder if it might not be better to dampen their political efforts and concentrate instead on the progressive impetus to be gained from a successful liberal economic policy. Others were reluctant to push political opposition too far because they did not want to endanger their cooperation with the state on these material issues and undermine the prosperity which they enjoyed. And even those at the very center of the opposition were subtly and indirectly restrained by their economic ties to the government.[17]

The clearest and ultimately the most consequential expression of liberals' continued ambivalence toward the state can be found in their views on the problem of national unification. As we know, the Frankfurt parliament's effort to confront the question of German unity made liberals aware of the difficulties of nation building. Moreover, in Rochau's words, "the great result of 1848 is that the idea of unity has become historical."[18] After 1850 this idea occupied a prominent place in most liberals' thinking about both the means and ends of political action.

For most liberals, the desire for national unity was an important source of dissatisfaction with the existing political system. Liberals who lived in small reactionary states saw unification as a means of escaping the narrow realities of their immediate environment. To liberals in Prussia, as well as to those who looked upon Prussia for leadership in solving the "German question," the desire for national unification also seemed inseparable from their desire for domestic reform. The king's failure to accept the German crown in 1849, the humiliation by the Austrians at Olmütz in 1850, and the passivity of Prussian foreign policy in the fifties all deepened liberals' dissatisfaction with the way the Prussian state was governed. They saw domestic reform as the necessary precondition for a more vigorous foreign policy. Rudolf Haym wrote in 1858 that diplomatic initiatives would come to nothing "if the power of the Prussian *Volk* is not won over again and reconciled to the foreign interests of the state."[19] Even when Bismarck seemed to be pursuing a vigorous foreign policy, most liberals continued to be convinced that success abroad would require reform at home. This was the apparently unmistakable lesson they learned from the story of the wars of liberation against Napoleon, a lesson that seemed to be reaffirmed by the process of national unification in Italy, a process which German liberals watched carefully.[20]

Although liberals were sharply critical of official diplomacy, their attitudes toward foreign policy also suggest some of the limitations on their willingness and ability to resist the state. Most of them acknowledged that state power would have to be the essential instrument in the struggle for nationhood; few believed that an autonomous popular uprising or a citizen army would be able to overcome the foreign and domestic opposition to a united Germany.[21] In other words, part of their frustration with the course of German foreign policy came from their belief that the state was not doing what had to be done and what they felt they themselves could never do alone. Furthermore, when Bismarck began his foreign political offensive in 1864 many liberals continued to attack his policies but very few of them had alternatives to offer.[22]

Once Prussian policy showed some signs of success, an influential minority of liberals argued that it might be necessary to subordinate domestic to foreign political goals. The root of this position is to be found in the early fifties when men like Rochau had begun to emphasize the centrality of state power in the achievement of unification.[23] By 1863, members of the opposition such as Karl Twesten were prepared to acknowledge the priority of national issues: "If I had to decide whether the Bismarck ministry would last some time longer or if the duchies of Schleswig and Holstein were to be lost forever, I would not hesitate for a moment in choosing the first alternative." When the duchies were won through Prussia's and Austria's rapid victory over Denmark in 1864, Twesten's position picked up additional support. From Bremen, Viktor Böhmert wrote that "German unity is more important to me than a few paragraphs of the Prussian constitution, over which a German parliament will in the end decide anyway." By the summer of 1865, the *Nationalzeitung* had decided that "From unity to freedom—that is our party's way."[24] As these remarks make clear, Twesten and Böhmert did not deny that unity and freedom were inseparable, but their willingness to reverse the order of their attainment helped to erode the will to resist the state in the critical years before the final victory of Prussian power, just as it foreshadowed the course taken by a majority of the movement after 1866.

The continued dependence of the liberals on the state in the realm of religious, economic, and national policy reveal some cracks in the foundation of their opposition. Their attitudes about the *Volk* point to its basic structural flaw.

A good place to begin considering this problem is with the deep uncertainty and inconsistency that inform the tactical pronouncements of many prominent liberals during the period when they were chafing at the persistent illiberalism of the German states, especially Prussia. A number of private and public

statements from the late fifties and early sixties reflect the liberals' commitment to action, to abandoning the empty phrases of the past, to mobilizing the
masses behind a powerful liberal movement. Johannes Miquel, for example,
insisted that the Nationalverein should be what he called a "political organization." He did not want its members to waste their time debating general
theories since that would prevent them from being "men of action standing in
the midst of the *Volk*." Treitschke wrote in the *Preussische Jahrbücher* that
"the political ideals [of our era] can only be achieved with mass movements." Sybel took the same position when he argued that "scholarship
must become popular or it will lose its own most powerful source of vitality."
And finally, Bluntschli wrote to Sybel in 1863 that "it takes some convincing
before one can turn to the masses, but the way things are only the masses will
be able to help."[25] It is also clear, however, that these liberals had grave
doubts about what mass action should entail and what it could accomplish.
Miquel had hoped for "action-oriented men" in the Nationalverein, but he
also recognized that "we are not diplomats or statesmen, we represent the
views of the nation and therefore it is enough for us to speak the truth."
Treitschke may have wanted to see his ideals joined to a mass movement, but
neither the style nor the content of his *Preussische Jahrbücher* was designed
to appeal to a mass following. Sybel, who wanted scholarship to become
popular, nevertheless realized that a gap between scholarship and political
action remained: "Politics which fulfill their function will never be read or
written. The statesmen who can act will not study, but will rule." And finally,
as we saw in the last chapter, a short time before Bluntschli made the call for
mass action just quoted, he had urged Badenese liberals not to extend their
political organization.[26]

In the tense atmosphere of the Prussian constitutional conflict, liberals'
uncertainty about the *Volk* proved to be especially debilitating. Both publicly
and privately, Prussian liberals spoke of the support their movement derived
from the "nation." In its electoral statement of September 1861, for example,
the Fortschrittspartei referred to what it called "the great liberal majority of
the country."[27] But paralleling such proclamations are an equally striking set
of complaints about the "unpolitical masses," the apathetic *Bürgertum*, or the
immovable peasantry.[28] As we know, these inconsistencies reflected the
mixed realities of a situation in which liberals constituted a clear majority of
the small minority participating in political life. Without an unqualified conviction that they stood for the *Volk*, liberals had no chance to challenge
effectively the government and to overcome Bismarck's arrogant willingness
to run the business of the state without parliamentary approval. To be sure, as
the hostility between crown and parliament worsened, some liberals toyed
with the idea of a popular upheaval, a democratic offensive against the gov-

ernment. In 1863, Rochau suggested that, if Bismarck could not be forced
from office, "the key to the solution of the German question is to be found in
events which will lead to the fall of Prussia." Others also spoke of the possibility of military defeat and an attendant uprising of the *Volk*.[29] But in practice,
few liberals were willing to go beyond these dark hints. They could not overcome their doubts about the depth of their support in the *Volk*. As one of them
wrote during the height of the conflict: "Those who work for freedom have no
solid basis on which to stand."[30] Moreover, they feared (and rightly so, one
must admit) that any effort at illegal action would be immediately crushed:
"Whoever can maintain a disciplined army of 200,000 men will never be overcome by force from the *Volk*."[31] Is it any wonder that many of those who
watched events in Prussia with anxious attention quickly gained the impression that the liberal opposition lacked a sense of clear purpose and direction:
"There is plenty of good will," reported Bennigsen from Berlin in 1861, "but
there is also unparalleled insecurity and confusion about the ends and means of
political action."[32]

The same self-doubts which limited the effectiveness of democratic political action also inhibited the liberals' efforts to define clear theoretical alternatives to the state. Although liberal constitutional thought continued to emphasize the value and importance of representative institutions and constitutional guarantees, most liberals continued to posit a dualism between parliament and monarch which reflected their ambivalence about *Volk* and *Staat* and
their reluctance to challenge the latter's ultimate authority in political life.[33]
Here, as in many other aspects of the movement's thought and action, the
rhetoric and the essential problems of Vormärz had survived the revolution.
This can be seen, for example, in Joseph Held's formulation of the problem
which was published in the third edition of the *Staatslexikon*. Held believed in
representative institutions, he wanted a legal definition of ministerial responsibility which would enable the parliament to impeach a minister for unconstitutional action, but he also maintained that in Germany "the unity of the
government and the power of the administration" was not to be weakened by
"party intrigues." The *Volk* should have ways to express its opinion, the rule
of law should be guaranteed, but the state's ultimate authority had to be
maintained. This would be possible, Held argued, because of the particular
virtues of the "German character," a position which foreshadowed later
efforts to defuse political reform by pointing to the peculiar needs and nature
of the German situation.[34]

Even the traumatic experience of the constitutional conflict in Prussia was
not enough to dissolve the endemic indecision most liberals felt about the
proper location of political power.[35] During the struggle with the government
over army reform and the military budget, Prussian liberals were extremely

eloquent in their defense of parliamentary power, but there is no evidence that they wanted to create a parliamentary regime on the English model.[36] Throughout the sixties they continued to demand what they had wanted since the beginning of the new era: not the right to dominate the government, but control over the budget, legal guarantees, and the right to present the views of the nation in the parliament. Even though Sybel was pushed to the left in the course of the conflict, he continued to maintain that "in Prussia the only possible form of a developed political life is now parliamentary rule under the leadership of an understanding monarch."[37] Neither one without the other could provide the necessary direction. Those further to the left than Sybel shared his reluctance to choose between king and parliament. Schulze-Delitzsch, for example, resolutely confronted the question of who should rule, then sidestepped an institutional answer with a rhetorical flourish that recalled the liberals' longstanding disinclination to deal with questions of power: "Who should rule?" Schulze asked, and answered: "Legality, the law, and the king as the law's guardian and fulfillment." Like Schulze, the young Eduard Lasker in his statements on constitutional issues concealed behind vague pronouncements about the triumph of liberal ideals an unwillingness to deal with the actual source of power.[38] At the root of these obscurities was that characteristic doubt about themselves which we have seen in liberalism since the movement's beginning: "Liberalism," wrote Sybel in 1864, "is not well-equipped to build a strong government or to provide the long-term basis for a ministry."[39]

Robert von Mohl was one of the few liberals who tried to defend the need for a parliamentary form of government. In an essay first published in 1852 and then reprinted in 1860, Mohl wrote that he had come to reject the dualism between *Volk* and *Staat* "against my will and at first almost with a bad conscience." He felt there was no alternative but to create a system like England's in which ministers would come from and depend upon a parliamentary majority. The monarch would remain "the proprietor of state power," but he would be expected to reign in accord with the majority. Despite this apparent break with liberal traditions, Mohl's essay still carried the mark of the movement's reluctance to accept the *Volk* as the primary source of legitimacy and power. This can be seen in the qualifications which he immediately began to impose upon his defense of parliamentary institutions. First, he argued that an undemocratic electoral system was an essential precondition for a parliamentary regime. Because universal suffrage opened the way for demagogues and an unhealthy multiplication of elections, parliament had to be elected by those with legitimate rights and interests, whose representation would depend upon their social and political importance. Second, a number of passages in Mohl's article suggest that he never entirely accepted a subordination of the state to representative institutions. At one point, for example, he seems ready to take back the power he intended to confer on the legislature; since unity must always have a veto over politics, he wrote, "the idea of the state must always have the last word." Finally, Mohl maintained that his system depended upon a transformation in the existing party structure. That is, the practical implications of his theory were limited by his assertion that no existing party was a suitable basis for the kind of government he had in mind. How, then, was his system to come into existence? Mohl is not very clear on this point, but he seems to imply that if the state created a parliament arranged along the lines he proposed, this would produce the required constellation of parties. In essence, therefore, Mohl's defense of parliamentary forms is less a call for vigorous opposition than the expression of a rather plaintive hope that the state would create the instrument of its own domination.[40]

Mohl's hope that the conditions for reform would be created from above were shared by a number of liberal thinkers. For some of them, this hope took the form of a longing for a great man, a Caesar who might personify and implement a reconciliation of the *Volk* and the state. Such longings almost certainly helped to shape Theodor Mommsen's famous account in the third volume of his Roman history, written during the fifties, which emphasized the way in which Caesar brought together monarchy and democracy, raising each to its "highest and final expression."[41] Karl Bollmann used a mixture of biblical images to express the same desires: Germany, he claimed, needed an "armed redeemer who will lead it to the promised land of national unity and independence, even if we must go through the Red Sea of an all-out war." At about the same time, Max Duncker called for a liberal dictator, and Unruh's deep disappointment with the *Volk* led him to the belief that "all danger would be over and the future would be secured if we had one decisive man at the top in Prussia."[42]

As the political impasse continued, these longings grew more intense and widespread. Franz Ziegler, for example, who stood well to the left in the Prussian opposition, became increasingly disenchanted with the unproductive course of liberal politics during the early sixties. Liberals, he believed, had lost their concept of the state. His solution? "One would like to go with a Caesar, if we had one." By 1866, Ziegler was ready to see foreign political triumphs as a way to escape from the inconsequential course of domestic affairs. "The heart of democracy," he told his voters in Breslau, "is always where the flags wave."[43] Significantly, there are analogues to Ziegler's position among those left-wing liberals in the south who feared the consequences of a Prussian victory. In June 1866, August Röckel argued that the democratic opponents of Prussia had to cooperate with the rulers of the smaller states in order to stop the forcible imposition of a *kleindeutsch* nation:

> However hard it may be for us to believe, we must learn to see that as
> long as we have princes and must act with them, we will only be able to
> act through them. At present, democracy can only enlighten and work
> below the surface, it still has not the power to take Germany's fate in its
> hands and shape it.[44]

Like many of his north German contemporaries, Röckel hoped this dependence on the state would be temporary. He wanted a postponement, not an
abdication, of his domestic goals. But like the others, he came to realize that,
given the existing political constellation, the choice was between an unequal
alliance with the state's power or passivity and defeat.

It is uncertain how many liberals in 1866 were prepared to abandon or
postpone their political goals and join in an alliance with the state. It is clear,
however, that by 1866 the increasingly bitter and inconclusive conflict in
Prussia, together with a marked downturn in the economy and the growing
danger of war between Austria and Prussia had produced a widespread sense
of impending crisis. Many shared the fears expressed by Rudolf Haym in the
spring of 1866 that Germany was entering a tragic era.[45] But what were
liberals to do? Bennigsen called on Prussian parliamentarians to decide once
and for all if they were going to support Bismarck or do battle with him—
either alternative would be better than the passivity which he found in this
"age of infantile diseases besetting Prussian political life."[46] But in fact
Bennigsen himself was reluctant to choose between reconciliation with the
state and all-out opposition. Because he did not trust Bismarck, but could not
and would not mobilize the *Volk*, he was left without a political strategy to
recommend. A similar uncertainty, extending to near paralysis, can be found
throughout the movement. At the meeting of the Nationalverein held in 1866,
a majority of participants continued to declare their opposition to Bismarck
even though they could not agree on a means to act without or against him.[47]
In the smaller states—Hanover, Baden, Bavaria—Prussia's enemies on the
left had to join an anti-Prussian coalition with their reactionary opponents,
while Prussia's liberal supporters had to defend policies in Berlin much like
the ones they were attacking in their own state.[48] In Prussia itself, the conflict
dragged on, apparently no closer to resolution than it had been four years
earlier.[49]

1866 is not a natural watershed for the development of liberalism as a social
movement or for the evolution of liberal institutions. At that historical moment, liberals were still in the process of coming to terms with the opportunities of the postrevolutionary age, still trying to put together the legacy of
Vormärz with the experiences of their own time. Politically, however, liberals
had reached an impasse by the mid-sixties. In many regions, they remained

caught in the tight net of *Kleinstaaterei*. Even in parts of the south and west where they had won some striking victories, they were no closer to the nation for which they yearned. In Prussia, which many contemporaries saw as the key to the national question, the liberal opposition had been unable to find a way of converting its electoral support into an effective political strategy. On the eve of the German civil war, therefore, a great many liberals had begun to feel that they had played all of their cards without winning the game.

IV

The "Liberal Era" 1866–77

On June 6, 1866, the tension which had been building between Prussia and Austria finally found release in war. While the leaders of the other European states watched in amazement, the Prussian armies won a series of extraordinarily swift and decisive victories. After easily subduing the south German *Mittelstaaten* allied with Austria, they routed the main Austrian force near Königgrätz on July 3. A peace was signed three weeks later which left Bismarck free to implement his plans for the reorganization of central Europe. Prussia annexed some German states north of the Main River (Hanover, Hesse-Cassel, Nassau, and the city of Frankfurt); the rest were gathered into a confederation whose constitution was passed by a constituent parliament in 1867. The defeated states south of the Main (Baden, Württemberg, Bavaria, and the rest of Hesse) were linked to the confederation by a series of treaties which guaranteed close military cooperation. After the victory of Prussia and her allies over France in 1870, these states became part of the German Empire.

The impact of these great events on the liberal movement must be seen against the backdrop of the liberals' own theoretical uncertainty and tactical paralysis. Suddenly, the victory of Prussian arms and Bismarckian statecraft seemed to make possible what liberals themselves had failed to attain: a united nation, a constitutional system, and a set of uniform laws governing social and economic life. Is it surprising that many liberals wanted to believe that a new political age had dawned, an age in which the goals of a liberal society, *Volk*, and *Staat* might be successfully pursued? Once again, as in the spring of 1848 and the first years of the "new era," men basked in the warm promise of a liberal future.

But the basic problems confronting German liberalism did not disappear in 1866 any more than they had in 1848 or in 1858. After the *Reichsgründung*, the relationship of liberals to the state continued to be characterized by a complex blend of compromise and opposition. Indeed, by the middle of the 1870s this blend had become increasingly unstable and divisive. Similarly, the creation of national political institutions did not dissolve the difficulties liberals faced in their efforts to build a popular base; instead, these difficulties were at once reflected and reaffirmed by the parties' declining electoral fortunes. Finally, the apparent triumph of liberal social and economic policies after 1866 was followed by a series of upheavals which further narrowed liberalism's popular support and deepened the divisions within its own ranks.

9

"Turning the Corner" Liberalism and the Bismarckian State

It is a wonderful feeling to be present when world history turns a corner. It is no longer a hope but a fact that Germany has a future and that the future will be determined by Prussia.

Theodor Mommsen (1866)[1]

The victory of the Prussian army during the summer of 1866 called into question the assumptions upon which Prussian liberals had based their opposition to the government. Bismarck, the man whom they had vilified as a hopeless reactionary, suddenly emerged as one of Europe's most creative statesmen. The army, which they had criticized as an instrument of repression, revealed itself as the instrument of nationhood. And on the very day that the war was decided at Königgrätz liberal losses in the Landtag elections made clear that their hold on the *Volk* was even less secure than it had seemed just a few months earlier.[2] When the Prussian parliament gathered again in the autumn, Bismarck tried to take advantage of the new situation by offering liberals an indemnity bill which was supposed to provide the basis for co-operation between the government and the Landtag by retroactively legalizing the unconstitutional budgets of the preceding years.[3]

Support for Bismarck's proposals came at once from Prussian liberalism's right wing. Some of these men had been uneasy about the constitutional conflict from the beginning. Now they rejoiced that the revolution of 1866 had been led "from above, by the monarchy, not from below, by the unorganized masses."[4] Others had supported the opposition only as long as they believed Bismarck would not achieve foreign political successes; now they embraced his policies without qualification. There were, of course, some converts to the right, men whose political views had suddenly been transformed by the wonderful news from the front. But most champions of Bismarck in the late sixties—Treitschke, Haym, Sybel, Baumgarten, and Rochau—had been persistent exponents of a "new realism" and had often expressed their willingness to accept national unity from any source. The "moral force of facts" in 1866 convinced them that they had been right all along. Their public statements in the years after 1866, therefore, usually built upon and extended views they had held since mid-century. This can be seen, for example, by comparing the first and second editions of von Rochau's *Realpolitik*. In the version published in 1869, the emphasis on power, on the creative role of the authoritarian state, and on the central importance of success was much greater. The qualifications of the earlier edition had become more muted, the echoes of Vormärz were fainter, but the direction of Rochau's thinking had not changed.[5]

The influence of the liberal right grew over the next decade. In the immediate aftermath of the war, however, many liberals were still uncertain about the effect of the great events of 1866 on their long-term goals. One observer of the Prussian Landtag's opening meeting after the war recorded this uncertainty when he wrote that "every speaker anxiously expresses his personal views, doubting if in the whole chamber there is one other man who agrees with him."[6] During the next few weeks, the debate on the indemnity bill produced a partial clarification of alignments. A number of moderate liberals decided to support Bismarck, not necessarily because they were willing to abandon their political goals, but because they saw no purpose in remaining in opposition. After all, these men argued, if an overwhelming liberal majority had been unable to impose its will on the government during the early sixties, what chance did a diminished liberal faction have against a regime which had just been crowned with the laurels of success? Moreover, some moderates maintained that even if the victories of 1866 had not been achieved by liberal means, they would still serve liberal ends. "Isn't unity itself," asked Ludwig Bamberger, "a piece of freedom?" Now that nationhood was attained, would not liberal reform almost certainly have to follow?[7] By accepting Bismarck's offer to end the conflict, the moderates hoped that they could abandon fruitless opposition and pursue their political objectives with, rather than against, the government. Essentially, men like Bamberger seemed to believe that the new situation provided a chance to recreate the old dualism between *Staat* and *Volk* that had always been at the center of moderate liberal politics.

A number of those in the Prussian Fortschrittspartei found Bismarck's indemnity bill unacceptable. To them, it merely legalized the "gap theory," which had allowed the minister-president to defy the parliament and did not offer any guarantees that this would not happen again. They responded by restating their party program of 1861 and by declaring their reluctance to abandon the opposition upon which the party had originally been based. But the opponents of the indemnity bill, like the liberal opposition before 1866, still had trouble establishing clear-cut alternatives to the government. Almost all of them, for example, supported Bismarck's foreign policy and were pleased with the victory of Prussian power.[8] Furthermore, the debates in the fall of 1866 showed that most of those on the liberal left did not really have a clearly defined constitutional program. They differed from their moderate colleagues not on the question of "unity versus freedom" but rather on the question of whether Bismarck's proposals offered a chance to return to constitutional government. Like those who voted in favor of the bill, most of those who voted against it did not reject the conventional liberal dualism of monarch and parliament.

The conflict between supporters and opponents of the indemnity bill may have been a matter of tactics and ideological emphasis, but nevertheless it generated a great deal of ill will on both sides. The bill's opponents saw its supporters as opportunists who had compromised their most sacred principles because of subservience and fear. Bismarck's erstwhile liberal allies viewed those voting against the bill as doctrinaire idealists who were willing to see liberalism sink into a barren negativism.[9] Over the next few weeks, many who had voted in favor of Bismarck's proposals resigned from the Progressive party. Initially, most of these men do not seem to have wanted to form a separate *Fraktion*, but gradually they coalesced into what would become, in June 1867, the National Liberal party. Within a year after Königgrätz, therefore, two liberal factions faced one another in both the Prussian Landtag and in the Reichstag of the North German Confederation.[10]

An important reason why the division over the indemnity bill hardened into a conflict between liberal *Fraktionen* was the influence exercised by liberals from the newly annexed Prussian territories, the states of the North German Confederation, and, after 1871, from the south German *Mittelstaaten*. Some of these men gravitated toward the Fortschrittspartei, but most of them found a more congenial base of operations among the National Liberals.[11]

Table 9.1 **Regional Distribution of Liberal Reichstag Districts, 1871 and 1874**

Region (total WKe)	National Liberals		Progressives	
	1871	1874	1871	1874
Prussia				
Eastern provinces (140)	24	48	18	23
Hanover (19)	9	13	—	—
Schleswig-Holstein (10)	1	4	4	2
Western provinces (67)	14	16	6	8
Bavaria (48)	10	10	6	5
Saxony (23)	8	7	8	4
Württemberg (17)	13	9	—	1
Baden (14)	10	11	—	—
Hesse (9)	7	7	—	—
Other states* (35/50)	28	29	4	6
Total (382/397)	124	154	46	49

SOURCE: *VSDR* 2, no. 3, pt. 2 (1875):1–154.
* Alsace-Lorraine did not elect delegates until 1874.

There were several important reasons for the regional alignments that are shown in table 9.1. First, liberals who had not been directly involved in the Prussian constitutional conflict did not share the deeply rooted hostility to Bismarck which continued to nourish the Prussian Progressives' opposition. Second, in the small states of the north and in a number of other regions, national unification was a source of emancipation from the stultifying pressures of a reactionary government. Third, in areas like Hanover and Saxony, as well as in several other *Mittelstaaten*, the *Reichsgründung* was linked in liberals' minds with the struggle against local forces of particularism and political Catholicism. In all of these regions, therefore, the relationship between nationalism and liberalism was very different from what it appeared to be in the Prussian heartland. To liberals from Hanover, Baden, Bavaria, and other states, the events of 1866–71 seemed like a triumphant chapter in the long story of liberalism's struggle against its traditional enemies, not as a serious setback in a constitutional conflict with the state.[12]

There is no doubt that the division which emerged in 1866–67 was of great importance, but historians have sometimes oversimplified the internal alignments within liberalism by overestimating the clarity and permanence of the movement's binary structure during the late 1860s. A number of profound differences among National Liberals were apparent from the start. Indeed, there was often as much conflict between the various wings of this party as there was between the party as a whole and the Fortschrittspartei.[13] It is also a mistake to assume that the constellation of liberal opinion in Berlin accurately reflected the movement in the nation. Political life in the various states continued to be shaped by forces which often had no clear counterpart on the national level, and, equally important, the formation of political opinion on the local level continued to take place within institutions which did not always conform to parliamentary alignments and alliances. To many contemporaries, who viewed events within the framework of their own local loyalties and interests, the conflict between the factions in Berlin must have seemed much less significant than it does to us.

In most states the strains produced by the dramatic events of 1866–71 did not result in a division within liberalism along Progressive-National Liberal lines. In Baden, for example, sharp divisions over both foreign and domestic policy surfaced during the late 1860s and almost produced a permanent split within the liberal camp. But the need to cooperate on religious issues helped to provide the basis for a united party.[14] Bavarian liberals were also absorbed by religious questions, which had become especially pressing after the mobilization of Bavarian Catholics in the so-called Patriot party. Confessional differences, as well as the very delicate balance of power in the Bavarian

Landtag, encouraged a broad coalition of liberals to remain within the Bavarian Fortschrittspartei, which concealed its political dissensus with programmatic generalities.[15] In Württemberg, it was national rather than religious issues which primarily determined political alignments. A heterogeneous collection of men favoring Prussia's German policy started the Deutsche Partei in the summer of 1866. As in Bavaria, party unity depended in large measure on the avoidance of concrete political goals; the members' emphasis was always on national policy, which they hoped would unite what one observer called "the different elements in the party which correspond to the Progressive, National Liberal, and Free Conservative factions in North Germany." The Deutsche Partei was opposed by a Volkspartei which stressed both democratic political goals and opposition to Prussian hegemony.[16] In Hesse and Saxony, national and political conflicts combined to produce a particularly complex and volatile set of party relationships. The Volkspartei had some support in both of these states; moreover, there was also a self-conscious right-wing group. This meant that Hessian and Saxon liberals were unable to create a state organization which reached as far to the left as the Badenese National Liberals or as far to the right as the Bavarian Fortschrittspartei. The result was considerable instability throughout the late sixties. After a brief interlude of unity in 1871, Saxon liberals finally formed National Liberal and Progressive factions in 1873.[17] In Hesse, the Fortschrittspartei gradually overcame or absorbed its enemies on the right but had to face continued pressure from the left. In national politics, the Hessian Fortschrittspartei tended to support the National Liberals.[18]

The incongruent patterns of alignment in the states reflected the variety of ways in which domestic and national issues affected the political life of those states. Because most Prussian liberals agreed on national issues, the primary source of cleavage in Prussia was conflict over domestic politics, a conflict shaped by the experience of the constitutional struggle and sharpened by the deeply rooted sociopolitical strains present in Prussia. In no other state did political issues present themselves in quite this fashion. The relationship between liberals and the state in Baden and Bavaria was very different from what it had been in Prussia; equally important, in Karlsruhe and Munich religious matters provided a source of cohesion among liberals that had no clear counterpart in Berlin. In Stuttgart, domestic differences among liberals were softened by a common desire to identify with Prussian leadership in the German question, as well as by the long-standing conflict between liberals and a democratically inclined, anti-Prussian Volkspartei. Another reason for the centrality of this division was the absence in Württemberg of religious issues comparable to those in the other two south German *Mittelstaaten*. Hesse and

Saxony were like Württemberg in that their liberals had to face a democratic alternative, but in these two states conservative elements also provided opposition from the right.[19]

The picture of alignments within the liberal camp becomes even more complex when we consider the local organizations in which liberals defined their views and selected their leaders. As late as 1876, Eduard Lasker could claim that "Unlike liberal parliamentarians, the liberal party in the country is not split into *Fraktionen*. Rather it is a great unity, within which there are a variety of opinions (as is always the case with a great political community), but it remains fully unified about its larger goals."[20] There is no doubt that by the time Lasker made this remark his assessment was incorrect for some parts of the Reich. By the mid-seventies, Progressives and National Liberals had come to dominate a number of local organizations. Characteristically, however, local political institutions remained rather loose and undifferentiated. The typical organization was the electoral committee, created by the leading men in the community on the eve of an election campaign. Local divisions did, of course, exist, but they were as often tied to personal and regional conflicts as they were to the programmatic divisions between the parliamentary factions. Moreover, even where there were local factions, the need to cooperate against a common enemy encouraged a unified front at election time.[21]

The links between local and national political life continued to be uneven, informal, and personal. In part this was due to the persistence of those structural characteristics of the German political system which have often been mentioned: the relative weakness of the communications network, the absence of a nationally recognized political elite, the fragmentation of political traditions and experience, and the continued vitality of local loyalties and interests. Legal restrictions on political activity also continued to inhibit the development of sustained institutional contact between the community and national organizations.[22]

As in the period before 1866, these structural characteristics affected the way liberals perceived the nature and purpose of organized political action. To a surprising degree, liberals continued to view their party as an ideological community without a clear institutional location. For instance, the first paragraph of the National Liberals' program of June 1867 speaks of the need to create a "National Liberal party," which presumably implied a parliamentary faction with ties to other kinds of political organizations; but the final paragraph of the program refers to "the other *Fraktionen* of the Liberal party ... with which we feel ourselves united in the service of freedom."[23] As is almost always the case, terminological ambiguity points to practical uncertainty: a number of liberals were still not sure what membership in either a *party* or a *Fraktion* meant. As one of them wrote in 1872, "For me, the National Liberal party is still a political fluidity and the faction is a shadow." A year later, Georg von Siemens illustrated this point even more forcefully when he reported the following exchange:

> Yesterday there was a National Liberal meeting. An acquaintance asked me if I was sure that I was a National Liberal. He was unable to answer me when I asked him for a definition of this, so I couldn't find out whether or not I really am a National Liberal.[24]

Another indication that liberals were uncertain about the meaning of their internal divisions after 1866 is the fact that many of them continued to look forward to the creation of a united movement. In the fall of 1871, for example, Forckenbeck wrote to Lasker that a "firm and great-hearted Liberal party" would be able to dominate events and "create a real political life in which the entire nation would participate." Three years later Franz von Stauffenberg expressed the same hope.[25] Forckenbeck, Lasker, and Stauffenberg retained this goal well into the seventies, as did many of those on the National Liberal left who tended to see themselves as providing a bridge between the movement's two extremes. Other liberals shared these hopes during the first decade after the formation of the Reich. Julius Hölder, for instance, seems to have believed in early 1873 that the existing structure of parties was about to be replaced by a conservative and a liberal bloc.[26] Four years later, when conflicts among liberals had reached an incendiary level, there were still those who urged that the parliamentarians abandon their *Fraktionsgezänk* and join in a common struggle for the liberal cause.[27]

At least until the mid-seventies, the ability of local liberal organizations to avoid becoming clearly identified with either national *Fraktion* was enhanced by the fact that Progressives and National Liberals cooperated on a number of important issues. From 1867 until about 1875, the two North German factions supported the government's foreign policy, social and economic program, and campaign against the Catholic church. At the same time, men from both factions joined to oppose the government's efforts to undermine the Reichstag's constitutional position. The fluidity of alignments within liberalism, therefore, was sustained by a certain fluidity in the relationship between the factions and between liberalism and the state.[28] When it became impossible for the factions to keep up this combined policy of cooperation with and opposition to the state, the pressures dividing the liberal left and right became increasingly difficult to ignore.

The combination of conflict and accommodation—both among liberals and between liberals and the government—clearly emerged during the debate over the new constitution which took place in the constituent Reichstag elected by the North German Confederation in February 1867. Except for some men on the far left of the Fortschrittspartei, most liberals wanted to work with Bismarck, not simply because they acknowledged his achievements but also because they hoped to use his power for their own purposes. Bismarck, in turn, wanted to use the liberals for his own ends: he needed their support not only to ensure the passage of his constitution but also to combat those who challenged his solution to the problem of national identity. But in 1867, as in the debate over the indemnity bill a year earlier, Bismarck wanted to be sure that cooperation with the liberals was carried out on his own terms. From the outset, he endeavored to retain the initiative during the constitutional debate. In contrast to the situation in 1848, the parliament was not expected to draft a constitution but rather to respond to a document which Bismarck and his advisers had already prepared. To gain majority support, the minister-president exploited fully the prestige he acquired from the victories of 1866. He dropped broad hints about future foreign political dangers and opportunities and let it be known that, if the parliament did not fulfill its functions correctly, he was ready to issue the constitution by decree. Government initiative, the domestic manipulation of foreign policy, and the distant but still real threat of a coup—all of these familiar elements of the mature Bismarckian system could be seen during the first months of the new Germany's existence.[29]

In the constitutional draft presented to the Reichstag, the relationship between the *Staat* and the *Volk* followed the pattern of "constitutional monarchism" which had characterized German political practice since the first decades of the nineteenth century.[30] The existence of the parliament was guaranteed and its legislative competence was recognized, but the real focal point of the system remained the hereditary president of the confederation (after 1871, the German emperor), a position to be held by the king of Prussia. The president controlled the basic instruments of military and political power and had ample emergency authority to be used if necessary. Bismarck also attempted to narrow further the parliament's ability to influence the course of political life. The national parliament's budgetary powers were to be limited and vague. The military budget, for example, was within the jurisdiction of the Reichstag but was to be funded according to a permanently fixed formula; in this way, the state parliaments (especially the Prussian Landtag) were deprived of powers which somehow disappeared in the process of being transferred to the Reichstag. Bismarck's draft also failed to mention a national executive. Presumably, the administrative work was to be done under the auspices of the Bundesrat, a kind of upper chamber composed of representatives appointed by the various states. This meant that there would be no

individual or clearly defined set of offices which the Reichstag could attempt
to hold responsible for the government's policies.

Much of the debate in the constituent Reichstag was produced by the
liberals' efforts to overcome these limitations on parliamentary power. They
had some success on the issue of the budget. In its final form, the constitution
provided for complete parliamentary control over annual government expendi-
ture, although a compromise settlement did guarantee funds for the army until
1871. The question of a national executive proved to be much more difficult.
Bismarck resisted liberal demands on this matter because he feared parliamentary interference in the affairs of the state and because he did not want to
establish a ministerial system for the Reich similar to the one with which he
had had so much trouble in Prussia. Liberals, on the other hand, saw that
some kind of constitutionally defined executive was necessary if the Reichstag
was ever going to be able to hold the government responsible for its actions.
As in earlier debates about this problem, most liberals defined "responsibility" in a legal and constitutional sense, not as a lever with which to insure
parliamentary hegemony. They were still willing, in other words, to live with
a dualism between the *Staat* and the *Volk*, but they did not want to eschew all
parliamentary influence on the government.[31] In the end, the liberals had to
settle for a good deal less than most of them wanted. Article 17 of the
constitution established the office of chancellor, who was to assume "responsibility" for legislation by cosigning laws with the president. But Article 17
did not say to whom the chancellor was responsible or how this responsibility
was to be enforced.[32]

The members of the Fortschrittspartei were sufficiently hostile to the final
version of the constitution that they voted against it.[33] Many on the left wing
of the National Liberal party were equally disappointed, but because they did
not wish to jeopardize the constitution as a whole, they joined the majority
which voted for the final draft in April 1867. It passed by a vote of 230 to 53.
Despite their opposing votes on the constitution, the two liberal factions
frequently acted in concert in the years after 1867. The Progressives found
themselves allied with the National Liberals and the government on a wide
range of social, economic, and religious issues. Similarly, the National Liberals' support for the constitution did not prevent them from joining with the
Progressives in a series of attempts to improve the position of the parliament
within the political system.

The Reichstag's control over the budget was the liberals' most effective
weapon in their struggle for greater parliamentary influence.[34] The right to
raise questions about expenditures gave men such as Lasker and Eugen Richter the opportunity to examine critically government policies on various

domestic and foreign issues. The government's need for parliamentary approval also gave liberals considerable leverage during the early seventies. Bismarck persistently tried to diminish this leverage by removing military expenses from the Reichstag's control. As in 1867, he sought to take military expenses out of the annual budgetary process by establishing a permanent level of funding. Since the military budget made up a large part of the total (in 1874, 288 million out of a total budget of 344 million marks), the political implications of such a move were unmistakable. When the compromise achieved in 1867 ran out in 1871, there was a sharp debate in which left-wing National Liberals joined with the Progressives in opposition to a permanent military fund.[35] The issue was settled by another four-year compromise but returned with even greater force in 1874. This time the lines of conflict ran within as well as between the two liberal *Fraktionen*. Fourteen Progressives broke with their party to support Bismarck's final offer of a seven-year budget, while the whole matter brought the National Liberals to the edge of disintegration. The final compromise, which was only another postponement of the basic issue, left a legacy of bitterness, both among the liberals themselves and between the liberals and Bismarck.[36]

Besides trying to defend the Reichstag's budgetary powers, liberals also attempted to reopen the question of a responsible imperial executive. In 1868, Karl Twesten presented a bill to establish an imperial ministry. It was rejected by Bismarck. The matter was raised again in 1870 and in 1874, but each time the government remained firm, despite the widespread support such a move had among liberals. Other efforts to improve the parliament's constitutional position were no more successful than the attempts to extend Article 17. Liberals were unable, for instance, to get financial compensation for Reichstag delegates. Nor were they able to influence the selection of high-level administrators, except of course when Bismarck's intentions happened to coincide with their own choices.[37]

All in all, the liberals' efforts at constitutional reform during the late sixties and early seventies had very limited results. At best, they had been able to prevent Bismarck from further weakening the Reichstag's authority, but otherwise they had little to show for a decade of struggles in which they represented the largest group and sometimes the majority in both the German and Prussian parliaments.

One reason for this lack of success was the opposition to political reform within the liberal movement itself. Liberals like Treitschke believed that the foundation of the Reich in 1871 had "fulfilled the liberal program." In the years thereafter, his increasing disenchantment with the Reichstag made him unwilling to support any efforts to define its power more clearly. Robert von Mohl, whose reluctant and ambivalent advocacy of parliamentary rule has

already been mentioned, soon began to question the desirability of transfer-
ring English institutions to German soil.[38] This point of view was supported
by historians like Sybel and political leaders like Julius Jolly, whose criticism
of British parliamentarianism was linked with a defense of the German status
quo.[39] In states where the mobilization of liberalism's enemies threatened the
movement, liberals' distrust of parliamentary power was especially apparent.
Thus, in 1872, a Bavarian liberal observed that it was fortunate that a republic
did not exist in that state because, if it did, the recent electoral success of the
Catholic party would have led to profound changes within the government.[40]
These men, most of whom had ties to the right wing of the National Liberal
party, sought to undermine or deflect the struggle to move the constitution in a
more progressive direction. Instead, they urged an acceptance of the status
quo and a more or less unqualified support for Bismarck, upon whom they
believed Germany's future ultimately would depend.[41]

Efforts at constitutional reform were also hampered by the disagreements
and uncertainties existing among moderate and left-wing liberals. Although
many National Liberals were willing to join with the Progressives on issues
which concerned constitutional change, sustained cooperation was inhibited
by intermittent bickering and rivalries. Even more important was the reformers' failure to provide an alternative vision of constitutional reality or an
effective strategy for achieving constitutional change. The liberals' characteristic imprecision about the political implications of "responsibility" continued after 1871. Their programmatic statements retained a vagueness which
reflected their own indecision and did little to create a well-informed political
public. Consider, for instance, the way constitutional matters were treated in
the Fortschrittspartei's electoral statement of March 1873: "Long and committed labor will be necessary in order to complete the constitution and the
legislative system of the Reich in a truly constitutional fashion." Did this
mean setting up a parliamentary government? Some historians have argued
that it did, but there is little evidence that most reformers advocated such a
goal. Basically, most moderate and left-wing liberals seemed to have wanted
the government to be more *responsive* to their influence and to the power of
the parliament. They did not want to dissolve the dualism between the parliament and *Staat* by making the latter directly *responsible* to, and politically
dependent upon, the former.[42]

The practical expression of this theoretical uncertainty was the reformers'
attempt to increase the power of the parliament without questioning Bismarck's right to remain in office. At least until the mid-seventies, most
liberals tried to influence rather than to eject the chancellor. In part this was
due to the remarkable hold on contemporaries' imaginations which Bismarck
acquired in the years immediately following his brilliant foreign political

triumphs.[43] Moreover, as we know, the possibility of working with Bismarck had been the essential point of departure for those who had voted for the indemnity bill and the constitution. In Ludwig Bamberger's words: "The existence of the National Liberal party depended not only on the representation of a particular opinion but on a particular relationship to the government which was in harmony with this opinion."[44] To a surprising degree this position was shared by Bismarck's critics in the Fortschrittspartei. For instance, when Bismarck threatened to resign in 1877, a leading left-wing liberal, Albert Hänel, declared that there could be no "more unhappy hour" for Germany.[45] Certainly a good many Progressives did not agree with this, but few of them were willing to try to force the chancellor from office in order to replace him with someone from the liberals' own ranks.

In the 1870s, as so often in their past, liberals' relationship with the state continued to be shaped by two conflicting sets of pressures: on the one hand, their desire to represent the *Volk* and to broaden the influence of this representation; and on the other hand, their desire to ally with the state against those forces in society which they considered dangerous. During the "liberal era," therefore, the movement's ability to oppose the state and to change the existing political system continued to be qualified—both in theory and in practice—by its willingness to grant the state a central role in German life.

An obvious example of this process at work was the liberal attitude toward military and foreign policy. As we know, the military budget provided the occasion for some of the most bitter conflicts between liberal parliamentarians and the government. Most moderate and left-wing liberals wanted to retain some measure of parliamentary control over expenditures for the army and to use their budgetary power to influence military affairs. But the liberals' ability to mount an effective campaign on the issue of the military budget was seriously compromised by their unwillingness to question the main lines of German foreign policy. Both the liberal *Fraktionen* in Berlin celebrated the triumph of Prussian power in the *Reichsgründung* and both were reluctant to challenge Bismarck's conduct of German foreign affairs after 1871. This affected their political position in at least two important ways. First, it made them quite vulnerable to Bismarck's manipulation of foreign political issues for domestic political purposes, a technique the chancellor employed with considerable success when he faced a parliamentary campaign for control over military spending. Second, the liberals' self-identification with the *kleindeutsch* Reich cut them off from a number of potential allies, especially in the south and southwest, who might otherwise have joined them in a common political struggle.[46]

Liberals not only supported the Bismarckian state as the instrument and guardian of national unity, they also joined with it in a series of measures designed to create a unified social and economic system within the new nation.[47] In the late sixties and early seventies, both liberal *Fraktionen* provided the parliamentary basis for legislation which reduced or destroyed the remaining restrictions on social mobility and economic activity. Restrictions on Germans' freedom of residence were removed by a *Freizügigkeitsgesetz* (November 1867), limitations on the right to marry were abrogated (May 1868), and liberal trade regulations were established by a new *Gewerbeordnung* (June 1869). At the same time, a number of laws were passed which removed economic barriers between the various German states, unified the currency, and liberalized commercial relations which other nations. As in the early sixties, this cooperation between the government and the liberals on social and economic issues helped to dampen the political conflicts generated by differences over the constitution. Moreover, by dismantling local and regional authority over social and economic life, the liberal legislation provided the basis for an extension of the state's regulatory power. Once again, the emancipation of society and the power of the state were inexorably linked. During the "liberal era" this linkage was personified by Rudolf Delbrück, the chief architect of government economic policy from 1867 to 1876, who was committed to social and economic freedom because he saw it as the result and the reaffirmation of the state's power in German life.[48]

Liberal reforms and a reaffirmation of state power were also joined in the legislation which revised Prussian local government in 1872 and 1876. Liberals had advocated changes in Prussia's local institutions for a long time, in part because they hoped that popular involvement in local affairs would increase their own influence in the state as a whole.[49] But there had always been a certain ambiguity in the liberals' attitudes toward *Selbstverwaltung*; even the term "self-administration" suggests an inclination to see local government as an administrative rather than a representative function. After 1866 this inclination grew more pronounced as some liberal spokesmen began to downplay the democratic and participatory ingredients in the struggle for *Selbstverwaltung*. A number of men on the movement's right wing viewed local government as a way of absorbing citizens into the administrative apparatus, not as a way of creating greater opportunities for autonomous political action. In its final form, the legislation of 1872 and 1876 limited aristocratic power and provided some avenues for popular participation, but the most important effect of these laws was to increase the bureaucratization of local institutions. As time went on, ties between the landed elite and the administration helped to preserve much of the influence over local life that the Prussian nobility initially feared had been lost.[50]

The most characteristic and in many ways the most significant expression of liberalism's alliance with the Bismarckian state was the so-called *Kulturkampf* between liberalism and Catholicism. This struggle, which brought long-standing antagonisms between Catholics and liberals to a new level of intensity, was the result of a number of developments in the late sixties and seventies. As might be expected, the formation of a Prussian-led and therefore Protestant-dominated Germany heightened Catholics' anxieties at the same time that it encouraged liberals' willingness to use the state against the church. Moreover, the Vatican's new round of attacks on the modern world through such means as the Syllabus of Errors and the proclamation of papal infallibility confirmed the liberals' darkest suspicions about clerical obscurantism and authoritarianism. Finally, deeply rooted local conflicts between liberals and Catholics were aggravated in regions where the church was identified with those groups most opposed to the socioeconomic aspects of the "liberal era."[51]

Things came to a head in the early 1870s when a series of electoral victories by the Catholics provoked liberal demands for a "cultural struggle" against the church. "Now," wrote Sybel in the spring of 1871, "we must do to the clericals in cassocks what we have done to clericals in white officers' uniforms."[52] Bismarck was willing to join the liberals' anti-Catholic activities, not because he had any great interest in the ideological aspects of the conflict, but because he viewed the new Catholic party as a potential rallying point for all of the dissident elements in the new Reich: Guelphs from Hanover, Catholics from the south, Poles from the eastern provinces of Prussia, and the French from Alsace and Lorraine. Like the liberals, the chancellor was shocked by the swiftness of the Catholics' electoral success and sought to find ways of limiting their political influence.[53] The result was a series of laws which were passed in three stages: the first centered on education, that traditional battleground for the church, liberalism, and the state; the second, which culminated in the famous Prussian May Laws of 1873, tightened the state's control over various aspects of the church's activity, especially with regard to the training, appointment, and disciplining of the clergy; the third stage involved laws which attempted to punish clergymen who refused to go along with the earlier legislation.[54]

The liberals' alliance with the government in the *Kulturkampf*, like their support for Bismarck's foreign policy and for Delbrück's socioeconomic program, tended to undermine their ability to mount a sustained drive for political reform. In 1871, for example, a good deal of the energy generated by the conflict over the military budget was dissipated by the intrusion of the religious issue. A year later, liberals' constitutional concerns had begun to gather momentum in the course of the debate over Prussian local government, but this was broken by the need to cooperate with the chancellor on what would become the May Laws of 1873. Finally, the deep-seated hostility toward the state which arose during the military budget crisis of 1874 was deflected by the government's manipulation of the religious issue. On all these occasions, the outcome was not simply due to Bismarck's skill but also to the persistence of the liberals' long-term inclination to believe that the struggle *against* the state had to be deferred or subordinated to an alliance *with* the state against the liberals' enemies in society.[55] The struggle against the church was carried on in the name of emancipation but ultimately served to strengthen the influence of the bureaucratic state over German life.[56]

In the mid-seventies, the relationships between liberalism and the Bismarckian state were disrupted by several developments. First of all, by 1875 there were a number of signs that Bismarck was in the process of revising his view of the political problems confronting the Reich. The chancellor was irritated by the continued demands for constitutional change from moderate and left-wing liberals; the increasingly difficult problem of imperial finances made the budgetary dimension of these demands particularly troublesome. Bismarck was also disturbed by the liberal majority's unwillingness to pass the legislation necessary for tougher legal controls on political radicalism, especially in the growing labor movement.[57] At the same time, he began to realize that the Kulturkampf had run its course; the resistance of German Catholics remained unbroken and, with the passage of time, their agitation seemed less dangerous than it had just after the *Reichsgründung*.[58] Furthermore, after a bitter confrontation between Bismarck and the Conservatives early in 1876, the antagonism between them began to dissipate; by spring the semiofficial press stepped up its attacks on the Progressives and expressed its support for the newly constituted German Conservative party.[59] Finally, the social and economic dislocations produced by the depression following the crisis of 1873 caused Bismarck to reconsider his earlier acquiescence in Delbrück's liberal economic policies. Delbrück's resignation in April 1876 produced rumors that Bismarck would turn to the right and led some contemporaries to expect that a new course in domestic political life was about to begin.[60]

The fading of the chancellor's enthusiasm for the "liberal era" was closely tied to a hardening of political opposition on the left of the liberal movement. The key figure in this process was Eugen Richter, whose influence in the Fortschrittspartei was significantly increased by the defection of the party's right wing in 1874 and by the death of Hoverbeck, a moderate spokesman, the following year. Richter was a long-time opponent of Bismarck, a tough parliamentary critic, a totally partisan man. He had never been especially happy with the Kulturkampf and therefore, unlike some of his party colleagues, had never been caught in the bonds it had created between liberalism and the government. Richter's loyalties were directed toward his *Fraktion*; he was a

Progressive first, a liberal second. This meant that his hostility to the government could easily be joined to a hostility to the National Liberals.[61] By 1875, Richter was in a position to encourage and articulate the cumulative dissatisfaction many Progressives felt about the outcome of the constitutional conflict, the subsequent failures of political reform, and finally, the one-sided compromise imposed during the military budget crisis of 1874. In 1876 he led his *Fraktion* into opposition on a number of important issues. In two of them, the Imperial Railroad Bill and the final draft of the new legal code, the Progressives voted against both the government and the National Liberals.[62] At the same time, the party's political program was given a somewhat sharper formulation. It still refrained from demands for Bismarck's resignation and the formation of a liberal ministry, but the notion of governmental responsibility to the parliament was considerably strengthened: the electoral statement issued in December 1876 called for "an imperial ministry which would be politically and legally responsible to the Reichstag for legislation and administration."[63]

The intensification of opposition on the left was matched by the growth of progovernmental pressures from the right wing. For example, while the Progressives bitterly attacked the National Liberals' compromise on the legal code, the right-wing liberals complained about the party's refusal to accept Bismarck's proposals for criminal sanctions against political radicalism. At the same time, these men stepped up their attacks on the Progressives, whom they listed with Social Democrats and other political untouchables as *Reichsfeinde*, totally unacceptable as allies for a National Liberal party whose main anchor was to be the chancellor's confidence and support.[64] Bismarck, acting through the semiofficial press, did his best to encourage and solidify these divisions in the liberal camp.

The reciprocally reinforcing antagonisms between the left and right affected alignments in the various states in different ways. In Bavaria, liberals maintained their common front in the Landtag elections of 1875 and continued to obscure their differences with programmatic vagueness. In some smaller states, Lippe-Detmold for instance, National Liberals joined in an alliance with the Conservatives against the Fortschrittspartei. In Saxony, relations between the two groups also deteriorated. They found it impossible to cooperate in the Landtag elections held in September 1875; when the new parliament met, left-wing liberals joined with the Conservatives in order to block the election of National Liberals as the presiding officers of the chamber.[65] Conflicts between the two *Fraktionen* were also intensified in Berlin. After some hesitation on both sides, National Liberals and Progressives finally agreed to support one another during the Landtag elections held in the summer of 1876. But by the end of the year, the conflict over the legal code had brought relations between them to the breaking point.[66] After the final vote on the code, the Fortschrittspartei formally condemned the National Liberals and announced their unwillingness to cooperate with them during the Reichstag election scheduled for January 1877. This formal decision by the *Fraktion* did not have universal support in local party organizations, but it did deepen the divisions between the two wings of the movement in a number of electoral districts.[67] After the elections these divisions were dramatized when the National Liberals refused to support a Progressive candidate for vice-president of the Reichstag. In the "liberal era," the selection of presiding officers had reflected the cooperation of the two *Fraktionen*; now the National Liberals turned to the right and helped to elect a representative of the Free Conservative party.[68]

The events of 1875 and 1876 were most painful to those on the left wing of the National Liberal party. As the chief advocates of a combined strategy of cooperation with Bismarck and the continued pursuit of political reform, these men were bound to suffer most when this strategy began to break down. Furthermore, since they had hoped that they could help create a united liberal movement by bringing together its right and left wings, the increasing conflict within liberalism affected them most deeply. In public, spokesmen for the National Liberal left continued to call for a common front between the two *Fraktionen*. But in private many of them were deeply disturbed by changes they saw taking place in German political life. As early as January 1875, Friedrich Kapp wrote that "A fragmentation of the old parties is taking place and I think it may occur during the coming year. The National Liberal party, which is numerically the most powerful, is such a catchall of different and in part irreconcilable desires, attitudes, and goals that it must come unglued."[69] Lasker was equally distressed. After the grueling struggle over the legal code, he felt that relations among liberals were the worst they had been since the constitutional debate in 1867. He lamented the "vulgar ideas and egotistical calculations which have recently expressed themselves behind a liberal mask." His assessment of the Reichstag election in January 1877 convinced him that National Liberals were no longer willing to compromise with Progressives and should now endeavor to force them to act in a more reasonable fashion.[70]

The Progressives, for their part, were in no mood to cooperate. Richter had become increasingly convinced that the National Liberals were no longer (if they had ever been) a genuinely liberal party. He was confident that the left wing of National Liberals would have to break with the majority and be absorbed into the Fortschrittspartei. This was the lesson which the Progressives' Reichstag delegation drew from the elections of 1877:

> The National Liberal party has emerged from this campaign with the liberal quality of its members significantly weakened . . . . Whatever is still liberal in the party will soon be forced to break decisively with the party . . . . Our prospects will be substantially improved when that happens.[71]

By early 1877, therefore, the political pattern of the "liberal era" had begun to unravel. The intersection of antagonisms within liberalism and between liberals and the government produced a growing sense of political crisis among many of those who once had looked upon the liberal era with such hope and enthusiasm. Before we can follow the development of this crisis, it is necessary to examine two other themes with which it would eventually be joined: the changing relationship of the liberal movement with the German *Volk* and the emergence of severe socioeconomic conflicts within the liberal camp itself.

The Challenge
of Democratization

Everywhere we see the old ideals realized
and the parties' passions satisfied. And
everywhere, even if they don't yet admit
it, men look upon this reality with dread.

Bodo von Hodenberg (1870)[1]

The most extraordinary ingredient in the German constitution of 1867 was the provision which gave the vote to all adult males. By opening the way for the German masses to enter the world of participant politics, the democratic suffrage helped to pose Imperial Germany's central political question: how were the changing needs of a modern, dynamic society to be reconciled with the continued power of established elites? Liberals proved to be especially vulnerable to the dangers of democratization, a process which eventually revealed their estrangement from the *Volk* with painful clarity.

The new suffrage law provided a prerequisite for democratic politics, but before Germans could take full advantage of their new opportunities two further conditions had to be met. First, large sectors of the population had to become convinced that participation in electoral politics had some connection with their lives. This meant that there had to be a communications network through which Germans could learn about public life and be persuaded that it touched them in some significant way. Second, Germans had to develop political loyalties and habits which would direct their participation and sustain it over time. This meant that there had to be an institutional network through which participation could be encouraged and channeled.[2] These preconditions for participatory politics had been developing slowly for decades, but they were still weak at the time of the *Reichsgründung*. As we have seen, even during crises such as the revolution of 1848 or the Prussian constitutional conflict a great many voters, probably a majority, did not go to the polls at all. Before 1867 no political organization had been able to acquire a deep and lasting hold on the masses of the nation. Although the process of political mobilization spread slowly and unevenly, by the late 1870s the implications of democratization had become unmistakable, both for the political system and for the liberal movement.[3]

Some Germans entered participant politics through the mobilization of a preexisting community. This was true, for example, in the case of political Catholicism. In the late sixties and early seventies, as Catholic leaders began to feel increasingly threatened by the new political situation, they used the church's dense organizational network to mold their coreligionists into an electoral movement. Simultaneously, they began to establish newspapers, organize voters, and form groups which could supplement the sources of cohesion already available in the church. As the result of what one shocked contemporary called "permanent electioneering," the Catholics' Center Party was able to establish itself with extraordinary speed. Unlike earlier, episodic expressions of Catholic political opinion—during the 1830s and 1840s, for example—the Center was able to retain its base of support even when the immediate crisis faded.[4] In addition to the Catholics, several other threatened communities used the ballot box to defend themselves against what they took to be the hostile forces at work in the new Reich: Poles in the Prussian east, Danes in northern Schleswig, the French in Alsace and Lorraine, as well as particularists such as the Hanoverian "Guelphs," whose allegiance was to a specific region or dynasty.[5] The mobilization of all these groups was facilitated and shaped by the existence of established sources of identity, recognized leaders, and usually some kind of institution which could serve as the foundation for collective political action. By the mid-seventies, Catholics and these other embattled communities held about one-fourth of the Reichstag's electoral districts.

In some regions, voters were mobilized within a deference community. Deference, which can be defined as an unstable blend of acknowledged prestige and overt or implicit coercion, was important where there was an established Catholic or Polish aristocracy, as well as in many of the districts which elected a representative of one of the two conservative parties. In these areas, the traditional elite could use its social position to elicit electoral support from the population. In the long run, deference worked best when it could be combined with other kinds of loyalties or interests, as was the case with Catholics and Poles. Thus while both conservative parties did rather well in the first national elections, they proved to be very vulnerable to opposition from the other parties. In many ways, the Free Conservatives, who depended almost exclusively on deference, never really recovered from the gradual democratization of the political system. The Prussian Conservatives began to establish a reliable basis of support in the late seventies when they reinforced their traditional prestige with appeals based on common interests and ideology and with the active assistance of the state.[6]

New voters also entered the imperial political system under the banners of the Socialist labor movement. We have already seen how Ferdinand Lassalle's efforts to separate workers from liberalism in 1863 marked an important milestone in the evolution of an independent working-class party. An equally important step was taken in the late sixties when several labor leaders broke from the liberal or democratic parties with which they had been allied. In part, this split was caused by their growing discontent with liberal and democratic political organizations' reluctance to acknowledge the validity of workers' particular social and economic interests. In some areas, labor leaders objected to liberals' support for the *kleindeutsch* Reich; elsewhere political differences, especially with regard to the suffrage, played a role. Some of these men must also have seen that liberal political strategy had been bankrupted by Bismarck's triumph in 1866. In the light of liberalism's increasingly difficult relationship with the state after the *Reichsgründung*, it is hardly surprising that some Germans chose to link their hopes for reform with the inexorable unfolding of socioeconomic forces as described by Karl Marx. Finally, by the end of the sixties, men such as August Bebel realized that they would always be second-class citizens within the liberal movement. An independent workers' party offered them a chance to act on their own, to use their energies and abilities without the sometimes sympathetic but usually condescending guidance of liberal elites.[7]

In the long run, the divisions between liberalism and labor in the 1860s would have momentous consequences for both movements. But their immediate impact was uneven and incomplete. It is extremely misleading, therefore, to speak of a "separation of proletarian and bourgeois democracy" after 1866.[8] In the first place, some workers remained within the liberal camp throughout the seventies. Second and more important, the "proletariat" which would form the basis for German Social Democracy did not yet exist. Unlike the Catholics and the national minorities, the labor movement could not simply mobilize preexisting groups for electoral purposes because its constituency was still in the process of being formed. Before the labor movement could emerge as a powerful national force, industrial enterprises had to grow in size and quantity, more and more Germans had to move into urban settings, and a very diverse set of social groups had to develop a sense of common identity and collective interests. It took time for men in steel mills and machine shops, dockers and miners, textile workers and cigarmakers to feel that they were all *Arbeiter* with common enemies and similar goals.[9] Social Democracy, therefore, grew slowly in the first decade of the new Reich.[10]

Whatever form political mobilization took after 1867, a great deal of it was directed against liberalism. Catholics, national minorities, particularists, and Social Democrats all entered the realm of electoral politics in movements overtly opposed to liberal policies and programs. This marked a very significant shift in liberalism's historical position. Before the *Reichsgründung*, liberals had usually been in opposition and had frequently benefited from the support of others dissatisfied with the status quo; after 1867, however, many Germans began to look upon them as the governing party. Liberals, therefore, had to bear responsibility for what various groups did not like about the contemporary world: secularization, national unification, socioeconomic freedom.[11] In the late sixties and early seventies, as during the revolution of 1848, the apparent triumph of certain liberal ideals underscored the fact that what seemed like liberty to liberals often seemed like compulsion to others. Catholics did not see laws limiting the power of the church as an emancipation from superstition but as willful interference with their sacred beliefs and institutions. Hanoverians and Bavarians did not see the events of 1866–71 as creating the opportunity to become Germans but as the destruction of important loyalties. Some shopkeepers and craftsmen did not see liberal economic and social legislation as bringing the blessings of freedom but as exposing them to the dangers of unrestricted and unfair competition.

In order to understand the breadth and intensity of this antiliberal feeling, it is important to note that the sources of opposition to liberal policies often coincided and reinforced one another. This is most obvious in the case of religious opposition to the Kulturkampf and regional hostility to the *klein-deutsch* Reich. The centers of political Catholicism—in the Rhineland and in parts of Bavaria, for example—were areas where men objected both to Prussian hegemony and to liberal Protestantism.[12] Moreover, regional and religious antagonisms were often deepened by social and economic issues: in Hanover and Bavaria, two centers of opposition to the new Reich, the final imposition of socioeconomic liberalism had not come until the late sixties; in both regions, those who suffered (or thought that they would suffer) from these laws associated them with the other changes going on in German political life.[13] Similarly, the leaders of the Center party quickly realized that their appeals to German Catholics could be amplified if calls for a defense of the church were joined with calls for a defense of traditional social and economic groups.[14] Both the remarkable economic growth preceding 1873 and the sharp downturn in the economy which occurred thereafter produced dislocations in German society which gave added force to these attacks on the liberal economic and social policies.[15]

The leaders of antiliberal movements also benefited from the fact that they could link differences over national political issues with conflicts already existing on the local level: conflicts between Protestants and Catholics, between small businessmen and large, between employers and employees, between outsiders and those tied to the local community. Political mobilization, therefore, could be directed against the unhealthy but distant machinations of parliamentarians and bureaucrats in Berlin and against their allies closer to home: exclusive and disdainful Protestant elites, officials and educators sent into the community from the outside, entrepreneurs who seemed prepared to sacrifice local interests for the profits available in national and international markets. This fusion of local and national cleavages, like the fusion of regional, religious, and socioeconomic antagonisms, provided the basis for the alienation of the liberal movement from large sectors of the German electorate.

Neither Bismarck nor the liberals foresaw these developments when the constituent Reichstag debated the suffrage issue in 1867. Bismarck believed that unequal voting laws, such as the Prussian three-class system, merely strengthened the hand of the opposition. He wanted a democratic suffrage because he was convinced that the majority of Germans could be counted upon to elect a cooperative parliamentary elite. In order to ensure that this would happen, the chancellor wanted to combine universal male suffrage with three other provisions: public voting, the exclusion of government employees from the parliament, and the insistence that delegates not receive any compensation for their service. Taken together, these regulations were designed to produce what would remain Bismarck's ideal representative body: a group of propertied men, drawn from landed and business elites, whose practical experience would make them immune to the "doctrinaire" opposition so rampant among the liberal *Gebildeten* and whose economic interests would make them susceptible to governmental pressures.[16]

During the discussion of these proposals, a few liberals expressed their complete and unequivocal opposition to universal suffrage: Heinrich von Sybel, for example, saw it as "the beginning of the end" of parliamentary institutions.[17] Most liberal delegates, however, focused their attention on the other aspects of the voting law. After considerable debate, liberals were able to extract two concessions from Bismarck: voting for the Reichstag was to be secret and the statutory ban on the election of officials was dropped. The chancellor would not retreat from his insistence that parliamentarians not be paid. In his opinion, compensation for delegates would have helped to create a cadre of professional politicians, which he wanted to avoid at all costs.[18]

The reticence of most liberals during the constitutional debate over the suffrage probably came from a number of tactical considerations, but it also reflected their initial uncertainty about what democratization would mean for the German political system. On the eve of the first Reichstag election, Eduard Lasker wondered if the new electoral law would bring about "an emancipation of the *Volk*" or if it would encourage "the mob's opposition to the maturer judgments of their betters?"[19] This was, of course, a question which liberals had always asked themselves about the German *Volk*: would it behave like the enlightened "real" *Volk* or would it become a powerful and threatening mob without reason and restraint? Would it join the liberal movement or fall victim to those demagogues who wished to use the masses against their own real interests? To understand the liberals' response to the challenge of democratization, it is necessary to consider the development of political participation as it must have appeared to observers in the years immediately following the *Reichsgründung*.

We have already seen that liberals suffered a serious setback in the elections held for the Prussian Landtag in the summer of 1866.[20] These were followed by a number of defeats in some of the *Mittelstaaten* and by the rather disappointing outcome of the voting for the two North German Reichstage in 1867 and for the so-called Zollparlament in 1868.[21] However, this downturn was reversed during the early seventies. In the Reichstag elections of 1871 and 1874, the two liberal parties' share of the popular vote remained fairly constant, but the number of their delegates increased dramatically (see table 10.1). In 1874, they were able to take advantage of serious problems within the Conservative party and win some closely fought contests in Prussian districts. These victories gave them a slim majority in the national parliament. Viewed from the perspective of the mid-seventies, therefore, the direction of liberal electoral fortunes seemed to be a favorable one.

Table 10.1   **The Political Composition of the German Reichstag, 1867–74**

Party	1867 (1) No. (%)	1867 (2) No. (%)	1871 No. (%)	1874 No. (%)
Altliberale, Liberale Vereinigung, Freie Vereinigung	41 (13.8)	28 (9.4)	30 (7.8)	3
National Liberals	80 (26.9)	78 (26.2)	125 (32.7)	155 (39)
Progressives	19 (6.4)	29 (9.8)	46 (12)	49 (12.3)
Volkspartei		4 (1.4)		
Conservatives	59 (19.8)	64 (21.5)	57 (15)	22 (5.5)
Free Conservatives (Reichspartei)	39 (13.2)	34 (11.6)	37 (9.6)	33 (8.3)
Konstitutionelle Vereinigung	18 (6.1)	21 (7)		
Center			61 (16)	91 (23)
Poles, Danes, Alsatians*	15 (5.1)	12 (4.1)	23 (6)	34 (8.6)
SPD	1	3	2	9 (2.3)
No Fraktion	25 (8.4)	24 (8)		
Total	297	297	382	397

SOURCE: Vogel et al. *Wahlen* (1971), pp. 288, 290.
* Alsace-Lorraine voted for the first time in 1874.

A similar trend could be observed in Prussia (see table 10.2). After a dismal showing during the wartime elections of 1870, liberals gained steadily over their conservative rivals in the eastern provinces.[22] These gains, together with liberal support in newly annexed territories, gave the two *Fraktionen* a majority of seats in the elections of 1873 and 1876. By the fall of 1876, the

Table 10.6   **The Political Composition of the Chamber of Deputies in Baden, 1867–77**

Party	1867 No. (%)	1869 No. (%)	1871 No. (%)	1873 No. (%)	1875 No. (%)	1877 No. (%)
National Liberals	57 (90)	55 (89)	51 (81)	50 (79)	47 (75)	48 (76)
Democrats	3 (5)	2 (3)	3 (5)	3 (5)	3 (5)	3 (5)
Catholics	2 (3)	5 (8)	9 (14)	10 (16)	13 (20.6)	12 (19)
Conservatives	1					
Total	63	62	63	63	63	63

SOURCE: Gall, *Liberalismus* (1968), p. 61, n. 8, for 1867 and 1869; Rapp, *Landtagsabgeordneten* (1929), p. 105, for 1871–77. The Badenese chamber was renewed every other year when one-fourth of its membership had to stand for election.

Table 10.7   **The Political Composition of the Bavarian Chamber of Deputies, 1869–75**

Party	1869 No. (%)	1875 No. (%)
Bavarian Partriots	80 (52)	79 (51)
Fortschrittspartei	63 (41)	—
Liberale Mittelpartei	6 (4)	—
Others (mostly liberals)	5 (3)	—
United Liberals	—	76 (49)
Total	154	155

SOURCE: Petermeier, "Daller" (1956), Appendix A, pp. 2, 4. The figures for 1869 give the results of the second election held that year; the first one ended in a 71–71 tie between liberals and Patriots.

persistent allegiance to liberalism among important urban groups.[26]

Despite this record of electoral successes, a few liberals recognized that the political system created in 1867 confronted them with radically new dangers and opportunities. Very early on, therefore, some called for a restructuring of liberal institutions in order to meet this new situation. In 1868, for example, Forckenbeck urged liberals to build organizations to mobilize a broad basis of support.[27] Exhortations like this became more insistent as the power of the liberals' enemies became more apparent. In 1874 a liberal newspaper in Trier complained that with regard to political agitation "we are still infants in comparison with the ultramontanes ... the organization of their [Center] party should provide us with a model."[28] By that time Eugen Richter was engaged in trying to build an institutional base for his Progressives. Three years later the leadership of the National Liberal party circulated a memorandum which ascribed "the weakness of the liberal, patriotic majority" to the fact that its components were "insufficiently linked with one another."[29]

These calls for a more vigorous approach to political activity did not go completely unheeded. In some regions, liberals' informal election committees gave way to more stable and well-organized leadership groups. The number of liberal Vereine increased and their agitational efforts became more intense. In districts where the lines of political conflict were sharply drawn, there were often election campaigns in what Friedrich Kapp called "the American style."[30] In the Rhineland, the Deutscher Verein was formed to mobilize and coordinate liberals' campaign against political Catholicism.[31] Moreover, by the mid-seventies we can find some efforts to provide greater direction and control from Berlin. Eugen Richter was eager to centralize authority over Progressive organizations, and by 1877 even the National Liberals had begun to collect funds for a central office with a permanent full-time staff.[32]

The scarcity of evidence about the variety of local political life makes it impossible to determine the success of these efforts to reform the style and institutional arrangement of liberal political action. There is reason to believe, however, that the impact of these efforts was severely limited. *Honoratioren* politics survived, even in the face of exhortations from within the movement and challenges from liberals' enemies.[33] The liberal press continued to address its readers in long columns filled with drab and complicated prose. Attempts at institutional innovation often succumbed to the powerful inertia of old habits and presuppositions. The Deutscher Verein, for instance, which Sybel heralded as an attempt at "intensive personal engagement with the masses of the *Volk*," remained academic in tone and limited in appeal. The same thing happened to liberal efforts at revitalization in Baden. In the words of one observer, these efforts came to nothing "because they are led by exactly the same influential men who control political affairs by virtue of their social position, intelligence and long tradition."[34]

A number of established liberal leaders actively opposed suggestions that they change their habitual approach to politics. "The representation of the *Volk*," declared one candidate in 1867, "is and should be a basically aristocratic calling. It is and should be in the hands of an intellectual aristocracy."[35] The following year a Badenese liberal remarked that "a party like the present National Liberals which rests merely on numbers" is "an absurdity."[36] In his widely read work on political parties, Johann Bluntschli did not go quite that far, but he did make clear his distaste for the restraints which parties might impose on an individual's freedom of action. "Parties," Bluntschli recognized, were inevitable, but it was important to avoid their degeneration into "factions" which rested on special interests rather than a common *Gesinnung*. As time went on, these objections to the realities of organized politics increased.[37] Johannes Miquel, for example, pointed to his disaffection with parliamentary life as one reason why he decided to accept the position of mayor of Osnabrück in 1876. And Gustav Freytag deplored what he called the rise of "parliamentary vanity . . . the ugliest and certainly the most harmful kind of vanity in the world."[38] Liberal intellectuals were particularly outspoken in their dislike for new forms of political activity. Men who had once declared that science and politics should have a common end now began to argue that the two were incompatible. Gustav Schmoller, for instance, held that the search for truth simply could not be joined with political commitment.[39] In the years after 1867, the resistance to political agitation and party organization, which had always been a leitmotif in liberal thought, became increasingly prominent and helped to limit liberals' ability to respond to the new world in which they found themselves.[40]

Why were liberals unable and often unwilling to develop the kind of institutions which might have enabled them to compete more effectively for the support of the newly enfranchised masses during this critical decade in the evolution of participatory politics in Germany?[41] One answer is that in some places such institutions did not seem to be necessary. As Treitschke put it in 1879, "many liberal delegates owe their election only to personal prestige, old habits, or the difficulties new parties face."[42] Throughout the Reich, there were electoral districts where "political life was still at the primitive level of personal trust and naive faith" and where it was often possible to assume that "every man who counted would belong to the liberal party."[43] Furthermore, even when the democratic suffrage significantly reduced the power and influence of the men "who counted" in a community, old habits and procedures were still effective in local elections. Unequal suffrage laws and the mechanism of indirect elections helped to keep the style and substance of *Honoratioren* politics and thus to blunt the full impact of democratization.[44]

In order to understand the persistence of liberal habits, it is also necessary to realize that these habits were part of a much wider web of relationships. The form and content of liberal politics resisted change because they had been shaped by, and were entwined with, other aspects of liberals' lives. The informal, discontinuous, and personal quality of liberal political institutions reflected the particular needs and experiences of those who set the tone for the movement, men who usually knew one another rather well, had gone to the same schools, belonged to the same clubs, participated in the same charitable, religious, and recreational associations, and ate in the same restaurants. When liberals began to build organizations outside of their own community—at Frankfurt in 1848, in the Kongress and Nationalverein a decade later—the style and texture of these institutions resembled local modes of interaction. Similarly, liberal newspapers were designed to appeal to a particular set of social groups; their tone and format addressed liberals in a language which they understood but which must have seemed impenetrable to large parts of the electorate. To reach out and communicate with the newly enfranchised masses, therefore, required not simply new kinds of organizations and propaganda but also a redefinition of the liberals' social world. This was something few were willing or able to do.

When liberals did seek to broaden their support, they tended to turn to those groups upon whom their hopes had long been based: ambitious, upwardly mobile members of what they called the *Mittelstand*. These men were eager to improve their lives, willing to accept the condescending solicitude which pervaded many liberal organizations, and mixed happily with those to whose attainments they aspired. As in the years before 1866, the ties between liberals and their constituencies were often educational since many liberals continued to see political action in terms of spiritual enlightenment. As the *Volksbildungsverein* of Bremen (where Socialist organizations had developed rather early) expressed it in 1874: "Party discipline, money, or even the power of the government will never be enough to conquer ignorance and brutality: education is the only weapon."[45] In the long run, this kind of approach to politics was insufficient to meet the needs and serve the interests of large sectors of the electorate.

Liberals also had trouble understanding the scope and source of their opponents' strength because they continued to see themselves as the only legitimate party, the only political alternative for reasonable, enlightened men. Liberals, therefore, were persistently reluctant to acknowledge that antiliberal movements might represent legitimate interests or reasonable alternatives. Instead they were inclined to believe that these groups were the work of a few agitators, demagogues, or reactionaries.[46] This was the way, for example, that Badenese liberals sought to explain political Catholicism when it first emerged in the mid-sixties. Catholics, they believed, were moved to oppose liberal reforms because they were confused and seduced by their priests; if these evil influences could be removed, Catholics would become truly "independent" and thus free to join with the rest of the enlightened *Volk*.[47] This perception formed the strategic assumptions for the first round of anti-Catholic legislation, which, as we know, was intended to break the political influence of the clergy and thereby open the way for political and cultural progress.[48]

A majority of liberals also had trouble grasping the significance of the emerging labor movement. One reason for this was Social Democracy's relative weakness in the years immediately after 1867. In 1868, for example, Schulthess' *Geschichtskalender* could point with pride to two meetings held that August: in Hamburg 38 men gathered to represent some 7,000 members of the Lassallean branch of socialism while in Leipzig 160 liberals were meeting to represent 220,000 members of Schulze-Delitzsch's cooperatives.[49] Many liberals who were concerned about the Socialists did not believe much could be done to help ease the discontents of the workingman because they remained convinced that the laws of the market precluded an active *Sozial-politik*. Social progress, these men believed, would occur only if the economy was allowed to grow and the ranks of the *Mittelstand* to expand. As one liberal newspaper put it in 1867, "A worker who attacks the *Bürgertum* attacks the group which he and his children must seek to enter."[50] The best way into these hallowed ranks was for workers to "gather their moral purpose, will power, and spiritual potential and say: 'I will help myself.' "[51]

In the early seventies, however, the continued, albeit slow growth of Social Democracy, the frightening example of the Paris Commune, and the sense of social dynamism created by rapid economic growth combined to convince some Germans that the solution to the national question should be followed by a solution to the "social question."[52]

A few liberals, mostly on the left, argued that labor unions were the best way for workers to find a place in existing society. Max Hirsch tried to build unions from a political base within the Progressive party, while scholars such as Lujo Brentano set out to demonstrate that unionism was not incompatible with a free economic system. In essence, liberal support for unionism was based upon the same assumptions as their support for cooperatives before 1866; unions would give workers a stake in the status quo and a source of identity and security without threatening the basic assumptions of the liberal social order.[53] At the same time, other liberals began to realize that some measure of state action was necessary in order to protect workers from the worst abuses of industrial society. Gustav Schmoller, for example, repeated an argument often made in Vormärz when he wrote that the state, "as the bearer of the whole nation's moral future" must act to defend the interest of the community as a whole.[54] Brentano and Schmoller were the leading representatives of a group of economists and politicians who met in 1872 to form what came to be called the Verein für Sozialpolitik. For a time, the Verein seemed about to provide that "basis for a reform of our social conditions" which its founders sought. But within a few years its original impetus had been lost and it turned into an academic organization devoted to scholarly debate rather than the direct formation of public opinion.[55]

The main reason why the reform impulses apparent in the early seventies dissipated so quickly was the resistance they met throughout the liberal movement as a whole. Max Hirsch found even less support for his unions within the Progressive party than Schulze had for his cooperatives. A series of strikes in the late sixties and seventies weakened Hirsch's organizations and helped to convince many Progessives that unions were both ineffective and disruptive.[56] The officials, businessmen, farmers, and merchants who set the tone for the party in both national and local affairs had little reason to accept or to understand the interest of industrial workers. This meant that even if the party leadership had been more sympathetic to the workers' cause, they would have found it difficult to persuade the rest of their constituency to share this sympathy. Like most politicians, Progressive leaders were unwilling to risk support they already had in return for support they might or might not attain.[57]

Social reformers also came under fire from men on the left wing of the National Liberals. H. B. Oppenheim set the tone for this attack in an article which called the reformers Kathedersozialisten, "academic socialists." Socialists, Oppenheim maintained, included everyone who wanted to use state action to solve the social question. In this respect, a man like Schmoller was not significantly different from the "beer-hall socialists" on the extreme left. In the words of another liberal spokesman, "They lack only courage to be like Bebel and Liebkneckt." The vigor of these criticisms came in part from their authors' doctrinaire commitment to classical economics, in part from their association with those economic interests most opposed to trade unions and the government regulation of business. Oppenheim, Bamberger, and many other left-wing National Liberals also seemed to have been convinced that the Kathedersozialisten represented a right-wing effort to win over the workers to an antiliberal alliance.[58] Whatever its motivation, the extensive campaign against the social reformers is another example of the myopia which clouded so many liberals' view of their social and political world. What else is one to make of their unwillingness even to consider social problems ("I myself," wrote Oppenheim in 1872, "am not prepared to admit without qualification that a 'social question' or even a 'housing question' actually exists") or their hysterical rejection of quite moderate proposals for change (Bamberger, for instance, called Brentano's book on the unions "pure class-hate propaganda")?[59]

For Bamberger and Oppenheim, the work of the Kathedersozialisten was dangerous because it seemed to threaten social and economic freedom. For many right-wing liberals, social reform was useless because it overlooked the essentially hierarchical nature of the social order. This was the burden of Treitschke's essay "Socialism and Its Patrons," which was published in 1874.[60] Treitschke acknowledged that there was a current of unrest in German society, although he hoped that the continued social significance of peasants and artisans might enable Germany to avoid being polarized into the very rich and very poor. But whatever the future might bring, Treitschke did not believe that social reform could reduce the fundamental inequalities within society: "class domination—or more accurately, the class order—is as necessary a part of society as the contrast between rulers and ruled is a natural part of the state.'' It was unfortunate but nonetheless certain that the masses must labor so that a minority could engage in creative cultural and political activities. In the face of these facts, liberal efforts at social amelioration were useless and dangerous. Attempts to spread education, for example, merely increased the masses' discontent since most people lacked the material and spiritual resources necessary to enjoy the fruits of learning. Nor could the state do much to improve its citizens' social condition; at most, the state could protect the social order and serve as a mediator between conflicting interests. The only real help for the poor was in the realm of the spirit, where religious faith could give them consolation and the hope for a better life in the world to come. Treitschke's argument, therefore, by maintaining that the *Mittelstand* was not the growing foundation of the common good but an elite which had to be preserved from an inevitably inferior majority, called into question the assumptions upon which liberal social reform had always rested.

Treitschke's defense of social inequality was part of a widespread hardening of attitudes on the liberal movement's right wing. By the mid-seventies, an increasing number of liberals felt threatened by the consolidation of political Catholicism, the steady growth of Social Democracy, and a variety of other changes in the style and substance of German political life. More and more of them were convinced that "public opinion" was not the expression of enlightened views but a chaotic chorus of different demands and that the actual *Volk* was not *das eigentliche Volk* of the liberal imagination but an alien and uncontrollable mass.[61] These anxieties were not new, but they found broader support in the liberal movement during the 1870s.

As in the past, liberals' view of the suffrage was a good barometer of their attitudes toward the *Volk*. In 1867, as we know, most liberals had accepted universal suffrage for the Reichstag and many seemed to assume that democratic voting would also be introduced on the state and local levels. In 1869, for example, Treitschke wrote that the three-class system for the Prussian Landtag should be replaced by a democratic franchise. That same year, Bluntschli's work on political parties called the new suffrage "progress of a powerful and genuinely liberal sort," even though popular sovereignty was dismissed as "a dangerously radical illusion."[62] Within a short time, however, opponents of democratic suffrage in the movement became more numerous and outspoken. In the early seventies, several liberal elders—Mohl, Gagern, and Prince Smith—called attention to the dangers of the new law.[63] By 1874, Treitschke had decided that universal suffrage was "organized indiscipline, the recognized hegemony of the irrational, the superiority of soldiers over their officers, of apprentices over their masters, of workers over employers." Three years later, Rudolph Haym argued that Germany had to get rid of this suffrage or go under. It was, he told his voters, like the gap in the wall of a beseiged city.[64] Haym's image is a particularly telling one since it captures the seige mentality spreading among men who saw their values and material interests coming under attack from a horde of alien invaders.

This seige mentality increased the liberals' dependence upon the state, that traditional bulwark behind which they had so often sought refuge from the dangers of democratization. As early as the spring of 1872, Julius Wiggers was struck by the way in which fear of the *Volk* inclined some liberals toward tighter regulation by the state. "In previous years," he wrote, "the call was for unity and then freedom ... now the word is no freedom, the Social Democrats and Ultramontanes are coming."[65] That same year, Rudolf Gneist's book, *Der Rechtsstaat*, gave this response a familiar and powerful theoretical base: "Society can find personal freedom, the moral and spiritual development of the individual only in permanent subordination to a constant higher power."[66] Treitschke and Schmoller may have differed sharply over *Sozialpolitik*, but the two agreed on the need for a strong state to withstand the potential for disorder in society; indeed as time went on, the liberal ingredients in Schmoller's thought diminished and his regard for state intervention grew.[67] This same inclination can be seen among those who began to realize that the Kulturkampf had failed to break the political power of the church. His experiences while living among Catholics in the Rhineland, Sybel wrote to a colleague in 1875, had convinced him that the state must retain its control over the police, the administration, and schools. Without these sources of power, the western provinces could only be controlled with violence and, in a few years, not even with military force. This same line of reasoning led a number of prominent liberals to support Bismarck's demands for limitation on freedom of the press and for strong measures against the socialists.[68]

It is difficult to assess the impact of these views on the liberal movement as a whole. We can, for example, observe a growing disquiet about the democratic suffrage, but neither liberal party was prepared to advocate officially that voting regulations for the Reichstag should be altered. In 1873, when Friedrich Kapp brought this up at a meeting of the National Liberal *Fraktion*, he found only a handful of supporters.[69] In part this reluctance to tamper with the Reichstag suffrage came from tactical considerations, in part from the familiar problem of agreeing upon alternatives, and in part from some liberals' unwillingness to jetison their hopes that they did indeed speak for the majority of the *Volk*. But liberals, especially those active in state or city government, could not mistake the fact that, as their enemies mobilized, it was only the persistence of unequal voting laws which enabled them to survive. As this sense of danger spread, liberals' commitment to spreading universal suffrage to local elections waned, even though both *Fraktionen* refrained from accepting the demands of those who wished a direct assault on the national suffrage law.[70] Similarly, liberals' anxiety about Social Democracy certainly increased in the seventies, but before 1878 a majority of liberal parliamentarians refused to support government demands for extraordinary legislation against the labor movement.

But if the right wing did not dominate liberalism, its consolidation did have some profoundly important effects on the movement. First, it helped to weaken liberal support for political reform and to strengthen animosities within and between the liberal *Fraktionen*. Second, the fears and antagonisms articulated by the right helped to undermine the movement's collective self-confidence and thereby limit its ability to respond to the problems of democratization in a positive manner. Even some liberals who would not embrace the policies advocated by men like Treitschke began to share his distrust of the *Volk*. This disenchantment with democracy had a particularly unfortunate impact on those moderate and left-wing liberals who began to feel equally uneasy about their cooperation with the Bismarckian state. In their support of the state against the *Volk*, right-wing liberals at least could enjoy the virtue of consistency. But their colleagues on the left had to find a course of action which did not rest upon either of the two sources of power in the German political system. It was along this steep and narrow path between *Volk* and *Staat* that many liberals would have to journey throughout the rest of the imperial era.

The outlines of this painful condition began to emerge with renewed clarity in the first weeks of 1877. As we know, in the course of 1876 the relationship between some liberals and the government had started to deteriorate. In January 1877 the results of the Reichstag elections suggested the problems liberals confronted in their relationship with the *Volk*. As can be seen in table 10.8, the liberal share of the popular vote changed very little, but the number of districts in which a liberal candidate was elected decreased enough to erase the factions' narrow majority. Liberal losses were caused by changes at either end of the political spectrum. On the right, the Conservatives' position was strengthened, in part because they had begun to overcome their internal divisions, in part because their improved relations with the government had brought them badly needed electoral assistance from the administration. On the left, the Social Democrats had clearly entered a new phase in their development: they were able to mount a campaign in two hundred districts and to win almost 10 percent of the popular vote, some of it in urban *Wahlkreise* which had once been dominated by the liberals.[71]

The election returns sent a shudder of anxiety through the movement. Eugen Richter expressed his concern about the Conservative revival in the east and the Socialist threat in the Progressives' urban strongholds.[72] From

Table 10.8   **The Reichstag Election of 1877**

	Votes			WKe		
Party	Total (in 1,000s)	% of eligible voters	Change from 1874 (in 1,000s)	No.	% of all WKe	Change from 1874
National Liberals	1,604.3	29.7	+ 61.8	141	35.5	− 14
Progressives	417.8	7.8	− 29.7	35	8.8	− 14
Volkspartei	44.9	.8	+ 23.7	4	1	+ 3
Conservatives	526	9.8	+ 166	40	10.1	+ 18
Free Conservatives	426.6	7.9	+ 51.5	38	9.6	+ 5
Center	1,341.3	24.8	− 104.7	93	23.4	+ 2
Poles, Danes, Alsatians, Guelphs	530.7	9.8	−14.2	34	8.6	—
SPD	493.3	9.1	+141.3	12	3	+3
Total	5,422.6	61.6	+202.7			

SOURCE: Vogel et al., *Wahlen* (1971), p. 291.

Baden, one liberal leader decried the way his party had become the focus for social and political discontents: "The working classes have begun to join the crowd of dissatisfied voters and have blamed the ruling party for its lack of accomplishments."[73] Otto Elben called the election in Württemberg "the saddest of all: Educated and independent men were defeated, while the discontented, the bureaucrats, and the masses triumphed."[74] On the eve of the liberals' crucial confrontation with the Bismarckian *Staat*, therefore, a number of them were becoming increasingly aware of the deeply rooted weaknesses in their relationship with the German *Volk*.

11

The Liberal Constituency
and the Rise
of Interest Politics

Some of the purely political questions
which were paramount in 1866 have been
solved since 1871, and some will solve
themselves as time goes on. Economic
questions have now taken their place and
have pushed into the foreground with
increasing insistence. It is very probable
—because of an intrinsic necessity—that
these questions will lead to a fragmentation of the existing parties; indeed this
has already begun to take place.

Felix Freiherr von Stein (1876)[1]

Liberalism, wrote Josef Edmund Jörg in 1867, is the "natural son of the new
economics," it is no longer part of a struggle for political liberty but rather
"the dogma of the social class created by the modern economy."[2] With this
formulation, Jörg, a well-known Catholic publicist during the era of
Reichsgründung, contributed to an antiliberal stereotype whose popularity
increased as the ranks of liberalism's enemies expanded. At the core of this
stereotype was an identification of liberalism with "Manchester economics"
and the capitalist bourgeoisie, an identification made by Catholics like Jörg,
conservatives like Rudolf Meyer, as well as Socialists like Marx and Lassalle.
All of these men saw liberalism as the ideological facade behind which selfish
interests sought their own enrichment. In this way, liberalism could be associated with all of those ominous social and economic processes which seemed to
threaten the lives of many Germans.[3]

In its most extreme formulation, the antiliberal stereotype became linked
with a new sort of anti-Semitism which appeared during the 1870s.[4] To a
number of contemporaries, Jews and liberals were joined at the source of their
era's discontents. Otto Glagau, for example, believed that "Jewry is applied
Manchestertum carried to its logical extreme."[5] Jews and liberals were the
purveyors of an alien ideology, engaged in a conspiratorial assault on those
social groups which personified the moral and material well-being of German
society. Similar refrains, delivered with varying degrees of intensity, can be
found in the Conservatives' *Kreuzzeitung* and in a number of prominent
Catholic publications. By the mid-seventies they had even begun to seep into
the writings of right-wing liberals such as Treitschke.[6] Amid the conflicts and
anxieties generated during the "liberal era," therefore, we can find the roots
of the unwholesome blend of antiliberalism and anti-Semitism which would
remain a feature of German political life for another seven decades.

As is almost always the case with stereotypes, the antiliberal image contained some elements of truth—even if it was the truth of a caricature rather
than a portrait. A large number of German Jews, for instance, had supported

the liberal movement because they viewed it as the political instrument for their own emancipation. A number of liberals did accept the main lines of classical economics and did defend financial, commercial, and industrial interests. But it is obviously nonsense to regard German liberalism as "Jewish" and only slightly less misleading to identify it with any single social class such as the "bourgeoisie." After 1866, as before, liberalism drew its national leadership from educated elites and its constituency from a fairly broad range of groups within the "middle strata" of society.

A brief look at tables 11.1 and 11.2, which give the occupational makeup of the National Liberal *Fraktionen* in Berlin, is enough to show the lines of continuity in parliamentary leadership and continued prominence of the *Gebildeten*.[7] A majority of delegates continued to be in some form of state service; the number of those who can be regarded as actively engaged in the direction of a business was rather small. The surprisingly large number of agriculturists, including owners of *Rittergüter*, reflected the way Conservative weakness in East Elbia worked to the electoral advantage of liberals even among the landed elite; by 1877, as can be seen, this advantage had begun to fade.[8]

Gebildete also formed a majority of the Progressive *Fraktion* in the Reichstag, although governmental pressures and personal inclination made civil servants a good deal rarer in the Progressives' ranks. In fact, except for a few judicial officials, those bureaucrats who belonged to the left-liberal fac-

Table 11.1   **The Social Composition of the National Liberal Delegation in the Reichstag, 1871–77**

	1871 No. (%)	1874 No. (%)	1877 No. (%)
Officials			
Administrative	15 (12.2)	22 (14)	17 (13.2)
Judicial	21 (17.2)	22 (14)	27 (21)
Local	8 (6.5)	10 (6.3)	7 (5.4)
Professors, teachers	16 (13)	17 (10.8)	10 (7.8)
Lawyers	17 (13.9)	19 (12)	12 (9.3)
Physicians and other academics	1	1	3 (2.8)
Writers and editors	5 (4)	4 (2.5)	1
Businessmen	15 (12.2)	18 (11.4)	17 (13.2)
Rentier	7 (5.7)	7 (4.4)	8 (6.2)
Agricultural occupations			
Rittergutsbesitzer	8 (6.5)	16 (10.1)	9 (7)
Other	9 (7.3)	19 (12)	17 (13.2)
Miscellaneous and unknown	—	2 (1.2)	—
Total	122	157	128

SOURCE: Kremer, *Aufbau* (1934), pp. 13–14.

Table 11.2   **The Social Composition of the National
Liberal Delegation in the Prussian
Chamber of Deputies, 1866–79**

	1866–67 No. (%)	1870–73 No. (%)	1877–79 No. (%)
Officials			
Administrative	4 (11)	17 (12.6)	18 (9.6)
Judicial	8 (22)	34 (25)	51 (27.4)
Local	3 (8)	13 (9.7)	15 (8)
Professors, teachers	2 (5.5)	9 (6.6)	12 (6.4)
Lawyers	2 (5.5)	4 (3)	3 (1.6)
Physicians and other academics	3 (8)	2 (1.4)	10 (5)
Writers and editors	—	—	2 (1)
Businessmen and rentier	7 (19)	23 (17)	36 (19)
Agricultural occupations			
Rittergutsbesitzer	3 (8)	15 (11)	21 (11)
Other	2 (5)	16 (12)	16 (8.6)
Miscellaneous and unknown	2 (5)	1 (.7)	2 (1)
Total	36	134	186

SOURCE: Kalkoff, *Fraktion* (1913).
NOTE: The figures include all of those elected during these legislative periods.

tion did so only after their retirement from active state service. Overall, however, the difference between the two liberal parties was one of degree. Progressives, like National Liberals, depended on notables, of whom only a relatively small number were directly engaged in a commercial or industrial enterprise (see table 11.3).

Despite the importance of educated men in both liberal *Fraktionen*, the number of delegates with direct ties to the business community did increase, at least if the two Berlin parliaments are compared with the Frankfurt assembly of 1848 and the Prussian Landtag of the early 1860s. Some serious problems—such as the lack of prestige in many regions and the continued difficulties of *Abkömmlichkeit*—remained, but German commercial and industrial groups had become powerful enough to send more representatives to Berlin than had been possible a decade earlier.[9] Furthermore, the influence of men with business connections probably increased in ways which are not clearly displayed in the statistics. Throughout the seventies, the *Gebildete* began to develop closer ties to commercial and industrial interests: leading National Liberals such as Miquel and Bennigsen were either directly involved with business activity or served on corporate boards.[10]

Another change not clearly reflected in the quantitative evidence is the increasing importance of men who lived in Berlin and could devote most of their time to political activity. This point can be illustrated by comparing the

Table 11.3   **The Social Composition of the Progres-
                                       sive Delegation to the Reichstag,
                                       1871–77**

	1871 No. (%)	1874 No. (%)	1877* No. (%)
Officials			
Administrative (retired)	1 (2)	2 (3.7)	1 (2)
Judicial	4 (9)	6 (11)	3 (7)
Local	4 (9)	3 (5.6)	2 (4.6)
Professors and teachers	6 (13)	5 (9)	5 (11.6)
Lawyers	7 (15.5)	8 (15)	6 (14)
Physicians and other academics	3 (7)	3 (5.6)	—
Writers and editors	3 (7)	4 (7.5)	4 (9)
Businessmen	10 (22)	10 (19)	10 (23)
Agricultural occupations			
Rittergutsbesitzer	3 (7)	5 (9)	5 (11.6)
Other	4 (9)	7 (13)	7 (16)
Miscellaneous and unknown	—	—	—
Total	45	53	43

SOURCE: Kremer, *Aufbau* (1934), pp. 46–47.
* Excludes those who resigned in 1874.

careers of Albert Hänel and Eugen Richter, two men who engaged in a prolonged intramural struggle for influence in the Fortschrittspartei.[11] Hänel had unimpeachable credentials as a liberal notable. His family had textile interests in Leipzig, and his stepfather was Heinrich Laube, a well-known liberal spokesman. Hänel himself studied law, taught at the University of Kiel and served in the city council, the provincial and Prussian Landtage, as well as in the Reichstag. Richter, the son of an army doctor, came from a much more modest background. He also studied law but found his career in government service blocked because of his political activity. From the mid-sixties on, he lived in Berlin, ran the Progressives' organization, and supervised their publications. In Max Weber's terms, he lived both for and from politics. Hänel remained a very important figure in the party, but when he competed with Richter the latter almost always prevailed because the depth and persistence of his commitment could not easily be matched on a part-time basis. The same kind of commitment helps to explain Eduard Lasker's influence over the left wing of the National Liberal party.[12] The need to stay at the center of events often made if difficult to combine local and national offices. In 1876, for example, Forckenbeck complained that his duties as mayor inhibited his ability to play a leading role in national party politics.[13]

In the various German states, differing suffrage laws, regional variations in social and economic development, and the persistent strength of political traditions continued to produce considerable variety in the composition of liberal

Landtag delegations. In Saxony, for example, there seems to have been relatively little liberal sentiment in the state bureaucracy, and therefore liberal
leaders were most often businessmen, lawyers, and landholders—a fact which
some Saxon liberals regarded as a great misfortune.[14] In Baden and Bavaria,
on the other hand, there was a tradition of cooperation between liberals and
the state which encouraged administrative and judicial officials to play an
active role in parliamentary politics (see tables 11.4 and 11.5). In both Landtage, however, liberal delegations were more heterogeneous than in either of
the Berlin parliaments. Obviously it was a good deal easier for a small
businessman or innkeeper to accept a post in Karlsruhe or Munich than it was
for him to seek election to the Reichstag in far-off Berlin. Hessian liberal parlia-

Table 11.4	The Social Composition of the Badenese Chamber, 1867–73	
	1867 No. (%)	1873 No. (%)
Officials		
Administrative	15 (23.8)	9 (14.2)
Judicial	5 (7.9)	9 (14.2)
Local*	10 (15.8)	10 (15.8)
Professors and		
teachers	3 (4.7)	5 (7.9)
Lawyers	4 (6.3)	5 (7.9)
Clergy	1	3 (4.7)
Physicians and		
pharmacists	4 (6.3)	5 (7.9)
Writers and editors	—	—
Businessmen and		
rentier	17 (26.9)	10 (15.8)
Craftsmen and		
innkeepers	4 (6.3)	3 (4.7)
Agricultural		
occupations	—	—
Miscellaneous and		
unknown	—	4 (6.3)
Total	63	63

SOURCE: Baden, *Verhandlungen* (1868 and
1874).
NOTE: I was unable to locate a list of liberals
in the Badenese Landtag, so these figures are
for the entire chamber. However, since an
overwhelming majority of the delegates
thought of themselves as liberals (90% in 1867
and 80% in 1873), a rough estimate of the
liberals' social character is possible.
* Most of these men would have had an
additional occupation.

Table 11.5   **The Social Composition of the Liberal
                                               Delegations in the Bavarian Chamber,
                                               1869–77**

	No. (%)
Officials	
Administrative	8 (6.3)
Judicial	18 (14.3)
Local*	22 (17.4)
Professors and teachers	10 (7.8)
Lawyers	14 (11.1)
Clergy	4 (3.1)
Physicians and pharmacists	2 (1.5)
Businessmen	33 (26.1)
Artisans, innkeepers	6 (4.7)
Agricultural occupations	9 (7.1)
Total	126

SOURCE: Computed from Petermeier,
"Daller," (1956), Appendix.
* Most of these men (21) were small town
Bürgermeister and therefore had an additional
occupation.

mentarians also came from a variety of backgrounds although here, as in
Saxony, there does not seem to have been any strong ties between administrators
and the local parliamentary delegations.[15] This was not the case for the Deutsche
Partei in Württemberg, largely because it was a nationally oriented group
which included a rather wide range of political opinion. In contrast to the Volkspartei, the Deutsche Partei included some rather highly placed officials and judges
as well as a range of other elements from the middle strata (see table 11.6).

The range and variety of liberal support become increasingly apparent the
closer one gets to local political life. Liberal opinion leaders in most communities seemed to have belonged to relatively prestigious social groups, but
their particular character differed from one place to another. In a town like
Krefeld, for instance, L. F. Seyffardt's long experience as a political leader,
his close ties to the commercial elite, and his prominent role in local institutions provided the basis for his influence as a liberal spokesman. In Essen,
where the local elite was less well-established, leadership was in the hands of
a somewhat more mixed group of men. In Kiel, academicians like Hänel,
together with a locally prominent editor and a few businessmen, set the tone
for liberal politics.[16] In some towns, the mayor played a key role, especially if
he was a man with an outstanding record of political activism such as Breslau's Forckenbeck or Dortmund's Becker.[17] Elsewhere, journalists and
lawyers could be very important. And in rural areas, where traditional status

Table 11.6   **The Social Composition of the Liberal**
                                            Factions and the Volkspartei in the
                                            Württemberg Chamber of Deputies,
                                            1868–82

	Liberals* No. (%)	Volkspartei No. (%)
Officials		
Administrative	8 (13)	
Judicial	8 (13)	
Local**	15 (24.5)	8 (21.6)
Professors and		
teachers	3 (5)	2 (5.4)
Lawyers and		
notaries	10 (16)	7 (19)
Writers and editors	1 (1.6)	2 (5.4)
Businessmen	9 (14.7)	7 (19)
Craftsmen and		
innkeepers	2 (3.2)	4 (10.8)
Agricultural		
occupations	4 (6.5)	7 (19)
Miscellaneous and		
unknown	1 (1.6)	
Total	61	37

SOURCE: Computed from data supplied to me
by Folkert Nanninga of the University of Kiel.
* Includes Fortschrittspartei and Deutsche
Partei.
** Most of these men would have had another
occupation in addition to their service in local
government.

tended to retain considerable significance, landowners and officials could
exert decisive political influence. Wilhelm Kulemann, for example, records in
his memoirs how his position as a judge in the small town of Gandersheim
established him as a source of advice on a wide range of subjects, including
politics.[18] Just below this stratum of local leaders was a broader and yet more
diverse collection of men who were actively involved in liberal political
efforts as local officeholders, candidates for the electoral college in indirect
elections, and public sponsors of liberal candidates.[19]

In some areas, social distinctions seem to have existed between the local
leaders and active supporters of the National Liberal and Progressive parties.
It appears that the former was more apt to draw local support from the wealthier and more prestigious sectors of the middle strata, from the higher ranks of
the civil service, the academic community, and the world of business and finance. The Progressives' active support, on the other hand, had its center of

social gravity somewhat lower in the class and status hierarchy, among small businessmen, teachers, lower-grade officials, and artisans. These differences show up in areas where the two liberal groups contested Landtag elections with a class-voting system: in the Prussian parliamentary elections held in Bielefeld in 1867 the National Liberals outpolled the Progressives 13 to 7 in the first class (which represented the highest income groups), but lost to them 14 to 6 and 0 to 18 in the other two.[20] A similar impression comes from the data on the composition of Progressive organizations in cities such as Berlin and Kiel, which show men from what might be called the *Kleinbürgertum* as being the most numerous.[21] Nevertheless, in local as in national party politics, the differences between the two wings of the movement were differences of degree, not of kind. Even if they had wanted to, National Liberals could not have limited themselves to the elites of *Bildung* and *Besitz*. Like the Progressives, they had to try to recruit their active supporters from a wide range of groups within the middle strata, or risk electoral extinction.[22]

Statistics on the Reichstag elections allow us to look beyond the ranks of liberal leaders and active supporters and examine the movement's electoral basis. It is important to recognize that this involves not only a shift in the kind of evidence available but also in the subject being studied. Electoral data do not simply tell us more about liberal supporters, they tell us something about people whose only tie to the movement may have been a single decision to vote for a liberal candidate. It cannot be assumed that these voters accepted all or even most of the liberal program. They may have been expressing their confidence in a prominent individual (a local landowner, or a distant figure like cultural minister Falk, who had probably never been in the districts which voted for him throughout the seventies). They may have been registering support for national unity (as did National Liberal voters in Hanover) or against excessive centralization (as did left-liberal voters in Schleswig-Holstein). Finally and perhaps most important of all, liberal voters may have been choosing the least unattractive alternative open to them; they might not have been voting *for* liberalism at all, but *against* political Catholicism, regionalism, conservatism, and so on.[23]

It is also important to bear in mind that there are weaknesses in the data that limit their usefulness. The published statistics are given only for electoral districts; since these districts were rather large and were not congruent with other administrative units, one cannot establish correlations between voting behavior and most social or economic variables. Usually one must be content with those characteristics which can be defined for the *Wahlkreis* as a whole: religion, regional traditions, and urban-rural makeup. Even with these variables, it is impossible to avoid the "ecological fallacy" and to uncover the social dimensions of political choice. The situation is slightly improved by combing the results of local studies, but this does no more than allow one to suggest hypotheses and illustrate lines of interpretation.[24]

As we should expect, data on the relationship between liberal voting strength and religious affiliation reveal the alignments produced by the Kulturkampf. While it cannot be proven that most liberal voters were Protestants, it is clear that liberal candidates did significantly better in *Wahlkreise* with a Protestant majority. Local and regional studies confirm the impression given by the numbers in table 11.7. As early as the Zollparlament elections of 1868, for example, Bavarian districts split along religious lines, with Catholic districts in Altbayern and Unterfranken electing "particularists" and the Protestant regions of Mittel- and Oberfranken electing liberals.[25] Alfred Kurt's study of a single district shows the same trend: in the Fifth Hessian *Wahlkreis* (Offenbach-Dieburg), the Reichstag election of 1877 produced large liberal majorities in Protestant areas, while the Catholic sectors in the eastern half of the district tended to vote for Center or Social Democratic candidates.[26] In a number of regions, therefore, liberals seem to have become the chief alternative to political Catholicism. This enabled them to gather into their ranks men who did not necessarily support the political, social, or economic aspects of the liberal program. In the words of one government official from Essen, the Landtag election of 1870 was determined "less by political than by religious considerations ... all of the parties, from the most extreme Progessive to the most moderate Old Liberal (indeed even some individuals who had once supported the conservatives) have joined in one 'liberal' party in order to win this battle."[27]

The liberal constituency can also be defined in terms of regional political traditions. By and large, liberals did well in areas where dynastic loyalties were weak. They were successful, therefore, in many of the regions which had been shifted around after the Napoleonic conquest, since here the population did not develop close ties to a dynasty under which they had arbitrarily been placed. This was true, for example, in parts of the Rhineland and Westphalia. It is even more apparent in states where the tension between nationalist and particularist forces was high. In Hanover, the inhabitants of Ostfriesland (WKe 1 and 2) did not identify with the Guelph dynasty, which had ruled them only since 1815; these districts voted liberal. But areas which had once made up the core of the Hanoverian kingdom, such as Lüneburg (WKe 14, 15, and 16), tended to support the Guelph particularists.[28] A somewhat similar pattern existed in Hesse and Bavaria.[29] Dynastic loyalties were also weak in the reactionary *Kleinstaaten* whose politically conscious inhabitants customarily saw the *Reichsgründung* as a liberation from the narrow confines of their political worlds; a majority of them supported liberal candidates throughout the seventies.[30]

Table 11.7   **Liberal Strength and the Religious**
Composition of Reichstag Districts,
1871–77

| | National Liberals | | | | | |
| | 1871 | | 1874 | | 1877 | |
	% of total vote	%of WKe	% of total vote	% of WKe	% of total vote	% of WKe
All WKe	28.5	31.5	29.7	39	29.7	35.5
Protestant WKe						
By over 75%	35.4	38.7	40.6	54.8	35.9	46.2
By less than 75%	38.2	47.1	35.1	52.8	39	62.2
Catholic WKe						
By over 75%	15.2	7.2	13.2	5.2	15.6	5.2
By less than 75%	24.2	33.3	26.2	27.1	25.6	22.9
	Progressives					
All WKe	8.3	11.6	8.6	12.3	7.8	8.8
Protestant WKe						
By over 75%	14	17.6	13.9	18.6	13	15.1
By less than 75%	8.7	13.2	13.7	20.8	6	7.6
Catholic WKe						
By over 75%	1.4	1	1.1	—	2.3	—
By less than 75%	4.7	6.3	3.7	2.1	2.9	2.1

SOURCE: Germany, *StJb* (1886), 7:164–65, 167.

Because they were closely identified with the formation of a Protestant, *kleindeutsch* Reich, the National Liberals were the chief beneficiaries of these religious and regional patterns. Their candidates were able to provide an alternative for anti-Catholic and/or antiparticularist groups in the *Kleinstaaten*, the newly-annexed areas of Prussia, and much of the south and southwest. This was an important reason for the breadth of the National Liberals' support in the seventies, when they were able to mount an effective campaign in more districts than could any other party.[31] The Progressives, on the other hand, drew their electoral support from a much narrower geographical area. Until the end of the seventies, they were usually unable to elect a candidate or even run a significant campaign in districts outside of the territory which had been part of the Prussian monarchy before 1866.[32]

National Liberal voters tended to be rather evenly distributed between urban and rural areas (see table 11.8). In parts of the Reich—most of Prussia, for example—National Liberals did much better in the cities than in the countryside. This was becaue they were better organized in the cities, because urban areas often had a somewhat larger Protestant population, and, most important, because their enemies initially had more trouble mobilizing their followers in an urban setting. A Prussian like Friedrich Kapp, for instance, believed as late as 1878 that "the cities will remain faithful to us, but the countryside will leave us in the lurch."[33] Elsewhere in Germany, however, National Liberal voters were predominately rural. This was especially true in Protestant parts of the south and southwest, where agriculture was in the hands of small proprietors rather than large estates.[34] The Progressives' constituencies were usually more exclusively urban. They did have some scattered success in rural areas, but the backbone of their strength came from the central districts of large Prussian cities—Berlin, Königsberg, Stettin—or from smaller commercial and administrative centers.

Table 11.8 **Urban-Rural Distribution of Liberal Reichstag Districts, 1871–77**

	1871			1874			1877		
	No.	% NL	% Prog.	No.	% NL	% Prog.	No.	% NL	% Prog.
All WKe	382	31.5	11.6	397	39	12.3	397	35.5	8.8
Urban WKe	21	19.1	57.1	21	28.5	52.4	21	42.8	28.6
WKe with cities	68	36.7	16.2	68	38.2	17.6	81	43.2	12.3
WKe without large cities	308	31.2	7.5	308	39.9	8.4	295	32.9	6.4

SOURCE: Germany, *StJb* (1886), 7:166.

In retrospect, it is clear that the liberals' major weakness was the thinness of their electoral base. On the national level, this thinness was concealed by the low level of electoral participation in the first few Reichstag elections. In state and local elections, public apathy was supplemented (and encouraged) by restrictions on who could vote or how much each vote might count. Gradually, however, liberalism's enemies began to make noticeable inroads among those previously uninvolved in national politics. The percentage of those voting in Reichstag elections increased, especially in urban districts where electoral participation had been disproportionately low.[35] At the same time, in some Prussian Landtag districts, liberals were forced out of the third voting class and challenged in the second.[36] Elsewhere, organized opposition to liberal power also began to break out of limitations imposed by suffrage inequality. By 1877, therefore, there were signs that liberals would have trouble withstanding the onslaught of their enemies. The danger of these external threats was increased by the deep divisions which began to appear within the ranks of the liberals' own constituency, those elements in Protestant middle strata upon which they had traditionally depended.

After 1866, the nature of the middle strata and the relationships among them continued to change along the lines already apparent in the 1850s. The wealthiest and most powerful elements increasingly came to view themselves as a propertied elite, self-consciously different from the majority of the middle strata. Data on tax payments suggest that the position of those at the top of the income pyramid was strengthened as the economy expanded.[37] Moreover, the number of large enterprises increased. In 1882, a majority of the industrial work force was still employed in enterprises with fewer than six employees, but 11 percent worked in enterprises with between 51 and 200 and another 11 percent in even larger firms.[38] These figures reflect important changes in men's work experience, life-style, and life chances. At one time, the successful entrepreneur and prosperous craftsman had shared a great deal: perhaps common origins, certainly the common experience of working in enterprises with similar organizations and procedures. But as large firms became bureaucratically organized and technically oriented, these similarities faded. The entrepreneurial elite became increasingly self-recruiting, its ranks filled by men with a university education or by the sons of the firm's founder. At the same time, this entrepreneurial elite began to live in a different, separate world from that of the shopkeeper and artisan: a world of conspicuous consumption, suburban villas, summer homes, and private carriages.[39] More and more, the distinctions in degree which had always separated elements in the middle strata were turning into distinctions in kind.

As men of property began to draw away from the rest of the middle strata, they tended to associate and identify with the other elites in German society: the highest ranks of the administration, the academic community, and the landed nobility. In the years after 1866, therefore, the elites of *Bildung* and *Besitz* began to establish closer ties to one another and to the traditional aristocracy. They sought patents of nobility or one of the many titles and honors which the state could grant; they purchased estates and adopted those forms of recreation which brought them into contact with noblemen; their sons sought positions in prestigious regiments, high-status government posts, and brides from among the daughters of titled families. This merger of elites was a slow and uneven process; it took time and considerable effort. But by the mid-seventies, it was clearly underway. A number of Germans had begun to see success in business, the civil service, or the university as a prelude to joining those whose position in society rested upon traditional values. No longer was success to be seen as a contribution to the advancement of the progressive trends which the middle strata embodied. When the upper ranks of the *Bürgertum* became—in Robert Michels' phrase—"the vestibule to the aristocracy," its members stopped being the vanguard for the *Mittelstand*'s emancipation.[40]

It is more difficult to generalize about the economic and social condition of those below this small stratum of propertied and educated men. There were sectors of the middle strata—professional men, the owners of small and

medium-sized enterprises, the middle ranks of civil servants and managers—
that prospered after 1866 and remained relatively stable and secure. We know
very little about their values and life-style, although it is clear enough that
they lacked the resources to finance that expensive journey into the aristocracy. The picture is even more complicated when the lower fringes of the
middle strata are considered: small shopkeepers, craftsmen, small farmers,
minor civil servants, foremen, and clerks. In the period after 1866 some
members of these groups joined the continued flow of emigrants who left
Germany in search for a stable future in the New World. Others lost their
social identity because of social and economic developments. Even those who
survived were usually fearful and insecure, worried that they would not be
able to defend their claim to be "independent men," separated from the
masses of workers, landless laborers, and employees without rank or
privilege.[41]

In addition to these vertical differences in wealth and status within the
middle strata, there was also a complex web of lateral distinctions. Some of
them were regional, between, for example, craftsmen in Prussia and in a
southern or western state where the memories of guild privileges were much
fresher. Others were between men with similar status but different relationships to the market: shopkeepers and farmers. And still others came from the
different needs and conditions of various trades and branches of industry:
mining and manufacturing, exporters and importers, the producers of raw
materials and of finished goods, and so on.

Both the vertical and lateral differences within the middle strata were
deepened by the turbulent course of German economic development after
1866. The Austro-Prussian War caused a brief crisis in the economy, but this
was quickly overcome in most regions. There followed a short period of
extremely rapid growth, accelerated by Prussia's swift victory over France in
1870. Industrial output increased; new firms proliferated; and investment
patterns were reshaped by a wave of speculation. These were the so-called
Gründerjahre, which recall those years just before 1929 in the United States
when many Americans believed in limitless prosperity. But the economic
dynamism of Germany's *Gründerjahre* did not benefit everyone. In some
places, the pace of change threatened and even destroyed existing institutions.
Moreover, since the fruits of growth were distributed unevenly, these years
witnessed widespread frustration among those who felt they were not getting
their fair share of the new prosperity.[42]

In 1873, a crisis gripped the financial community and then spread into the
economic system as a whole, touching off what some economic historians
have called "the Great Depression."[43] In terms of its measurable impact, the
depression was extremely uneven: periods of retraction and recovery alter-

nated until the mid-nineties when a new boom seems to have begun. To many contemporaries, however, the sudden break in the upward direction of growth seemed almost impossible to mend. Rudolph Gneist, for instance, spoke of this period as a time of "universal discontent," in which pessimism became the established mode of cultural expression.[44] The Handelskammer in Aachen did not hesitate to compare the depression with the dislocations caused by the Thirty Years' War; its report for 1876 concluded with the somber remark that "one does not know if things will ever get any better."[45] The psychological effects of the depression were compounded by the fact that it touched different sectors of society in very different ways. Some branches and firms were very hard hit; others suffered a mild contraction. Some people, for example those living on fixed incomes, even benefited from the deflationary effects of the economic decline. Those groups and regions which felt they were suffering most were inclined to turn against those who seemed to be less severely affected by the situation.

One indication of the increasing political significance of social and economic conflict during the 1870s was a change in the scope, scale, and structure of institutions designed to represent economic interests.[46] The best example of this was the Centralverband deutscher Industrieller founded in 1875. The Centralverband differed from earlier organizations in several important ways. First, it tried to bring together similarly inclined men from throughout German industry, not just those from a particular branch or region. Second, the Centralverband attempted to create a tightly knit organization with a full-time staff and a large budget. Finally, it became engaged with political decision-making on specific issues (tariff policy, for example) the outcome of which it tried to influence through public debate, "lobbying" with parliamentarians and administrators, and electoral activities. The Centralverband, therefore, attempted to transcend the limitations of regionally based special-interest groups; it was far tougher and more vigorous than the Handelskammer; and it differed from organizations like the Kongress Deutscher Volkswirte by seeking to influence policy decisions directly rather than by just spreading enlightenment through debate and scholarly research.[47]

The emergence of new-style interest groups created problems for all of the political parties and especially for the liberals. Liberals, as we know, customarily tried to obscure or absorb their conflicts over economic issues by defining themselves in terms of common attitudes and by insisting that whatever interests were present in their ranks were identical with the properly understood interests of society as a whole. This mode of self-definition could survive as long as constitutional, national, and cultural concerns provided the focus for liberal politics. By 1866, it had already begun to wear a little thin, and in the years thereafter the rising importance of special interests made it increasingly difficult to sustain.

Some liberals—especially those educated elites who continued to play key roles in party affairs—responded to this situation by reasserting their old views with new insistence.[48] In 1873, for example, a contributor to the *Nationalzeitung* surveyed liberalism's ranks and concluded that "Occupation and economic style, domestic life, the love of learning, and the attitude to religion and the church—all can be found with the same shape and variety in both the liberal parties."[49] That same year, the *Kieler Zeitung* maintained that "every occupational class in the nation now has a common goal, the development of the state in the direction of freedom."[50] Other liberals explicitly rejected efforts to engage their parties in the pursuit of specific economic objectives. Treitschke dismissed calls for protective tariffs as a scramble for higher profits; what Germany needed, he thought, was "moral betterment and a return to our old commercial customs." Albert Hänel was also worried about a "fragmentation of our political parties into pure interest associations."[51] Men like Treitschke and Hänel regarded with distrust those in their parties who seemed too close to "special interests." This was one of the grounds for the Progressives' hostility to the trade unions espoused by Max Hirsch. Similarly, Johannes Miquel was criticized for his ties to big business, and Ludwig Bamberger felt obliged to resign as a director of the Deutsche Bank because he feared that this position was not compatible with his parliamentary mandate.[52]

Despite the antipathy which some felt toward "special interests," the intrusion of economic concerns into liberal party life was impossible to stop. Debates over state finances and tariff policy in 1873 and 1875 foreshadowed the disruptive potential in these issues.[53] In February 1876, Heinrich Schulthess noted uneasily that economic debates had become increasingly important during the Reichstag session concluded that month.[54] The immediate impetus for these debates was the growing demands for changes in Germany's commercial and fiscal policies by those who wanted tariff protection and new sources of tax revenue. These demands were opposed by commercial groups that depended on exports and feared the results of higher tariff barriers, as well as by many consumers and small businessmen who opposed any increase in prices or indirect taxes. Tariff and taxation policy, therefore, directly touched the lives of a great many men in the liberal constituency.[55] Equally important, these issues were related to conflicting conceptions of the social and political order. On all sides of the debate, men presented their positions on specific economic policy in terms of the national interest; everyone proclaimed that his position was the one most in tune with the real meaning of liberalism and with the interests of society as a whole. In this way, the liberals' traditional mode of self-definition lived on. However, rather than defusing interest conflicts as some hoped, this self-image helped to convert disagreements over economic policy into debates over *Gesinnung* and to give these debates an ideological resonance which inhibited compromise and encouraged lasting dissensus.[56]

The Fortschrittspartei opposed new taxes and higher tariffs, a position which reflected the needs of its constituents: sectors of the financial community, manufacturers with close ties to foreign markets, farmers dependent on low-cost fodder, and especially urban consumers who opposed any measures which would raise retail prices. But the party did not present its economic policies in terms of these interests. Instead, it stressed the connection between its hostility to protectionism and its growing opposition to other aspects of the Bismarckian state. In fact, the Progressives were reluctant to acknowledge that their position had anything to do with interests. Their electoral statement published in December 1876, for instance, declared their opposition to "efforts to divide the population into interest groups and to abandon the tried and true principles of our commercial and trade policies."[57] As this formulation suggests, Progressives claimed that they were defending principles, not material interests; they represented the good of the whole, as liberals had always done, while the advocates of protectionism were prepared to sacrifice the common good for the betterment of a selfish few.

This blend of economic interests and ideological justification was shared by a number of National Liberals. Like the Progressives, these men based a defense of their own interests on time-honored ideals and on the conviction that somehow they stood for the interests of society at large. The chief exponents of this view were men such as Ludwig Bamberger, who objected strenuously to any intervention of the state in social and economic life. Bamberger and a number of his colleagues, especially in the Prussian wing of the party, continued to defend orthodox liberal economics throughout the seventies, clinging with desperate determination to the belief that prosperity and progress were only possible in a society which allowed the laws of the market to operate freely. It was not a coincidence that these ideas found support among those elements in the party whose material well-being seemed tied to liberal commercial policies.

But this point of view did not dominate National Liberalism. Because the party's constituency was larger and more diverse than the Progressives', it contained a much more complex blend of specific needs and ideological assumptions. By the mid-seventies, a number of National Liberals had begun to doubt the wisdom of free trade. The impact of the depression convinced some businessmen and certain sectors of German agriculture that their goods

had to have a protected market at home. Initially at least, advocates of this
view were especially prominent among industrialists in Prussia's western
provinces and in parts of the south, that is, in areas where National Liberalism
had traditionally been the accepted vehicle for liberal political action on the
national level.[58]

Like the free traders, protectionists tried to express their interests in terms
of larger political and social issues. In this endeavor, the protectionists were
often joined by those National Liberal intellectuals who began to regard an
unregulated economy with growing apprehension. Distrust for unrestrained
economic development was, of course, a persistent leitmotif in liberal
thought. It had been prominent during Vormärz and continued, albeit in
somewhat weaker form, during the heyday of classical liberalism after 1850.
The accelerated rate of economic and social change after 1866 evoked new
formulations of these old anxieties. In 1872, for example, Alfred Dove wrote:

> I deeply regret the changes which have occurred in the past years.
> Capitalism's juridical personality is certainly progressive economically,
> but not morally. The last ties which have benevolently linked men, which
> have united employer and employee, have been carelessly ripped asunder.
> Mass faces mass, and thus can the battle of the masses begin.[59]

Just a few months earlier, the Paris Commune had given men like Dove a
vivid image of what such a *Massenschlacht* might look like. After 1873, the
depression slowed the pace of growth but brought new sources of anxiety.
Now men feared that the overproduction of goods would produce bank-
ruptcies, mass unemployment, and a growing body of rootless men prepared
for an assault on the established order.[60]

Some of this same imagery was used by those who demanded state help for
craftsmen in the 1870s. In many trades, the depression of 1873 had deepened
the difficulties already produced by industrial competition and other structural
changes in German economic life. Faced with the dangerous failure of liberal
economics, artisans demanded state help, a strengthening of their own rights
of self-administration, and other limitations on free competition. This desire to
return to the protective confines of the guilds led some craftsmen to a conservative party; others remained within liberal organizations and added their
voices to the growing chorus of dissatisfaction with economic freedom on the
movement's right wing.[61]

In a sense, industrialists eager to defend their factories, intellectuals worried about the social impact of modern economics, and craftsmen anxious
about their livelihood were unlikely allies. But they were drawn together by
their common distrust of freedom. Like those liberals who opposed political
reform and feared the results of democratization, these men did not believe

that the free operation of autonomous forces could preserve the social order.
This is why they all wanted protection of some sort, protection from the *Volk*,
protection from foreign competition, protection from the dangers of a free
market economy.

The crisis of confidence which spread throughout the movement in the seventies encouraged some liberals to reassess their relationship to the parties on
their right. In 1874, for example, Hans Blum cautioned his readers against
deriving too much satisfaction from the defeat just suffered by the Conservatives in the Prussian Landtag elections. Blum was not an admirerer of the
"fanatical *Kreuzzeitung* party," but he did see the need for a moderate party
on the right: "A state which destroys its conservative elements is at the start of
a slippery slide, at the end of which stand the Social Democrats and all the
other enemies of the modern political order."[62] In Saxony and other areas
where the Socialists' strength became apparent early in the seventies,
similar sentiments often led to tentative alliances between liberals and
conservatives.[63]

Paralleling this political assessment of the right was a gradual shift in some
liberals' attitudes toward the Prussian aristocracy. Before 1866, most liberals
had seen the Junker as the personification of the social values which they
wanted to destroy—values which sustained Bismarck's defiance of the constitution, fed the arrogance of the officer corps, and kept alive the oppressive
institutions of the East Elbian estates. During the exciting weeks after Königgrätz, Hermann Baumgarten wrote one of the first and most influential challenges to this traditional conception. In an essay entitled "Liberalism: A
Self-Criticism," Baumgarten declared that the nobility was an "irreplaceable
element in a monarchical state." As the war made clear, "the much despised
Junker knows how to fight and die for the fatherland." Liberals, therefore,
must modify their prejudices a little and "accept an honorable position next to
the nobility." Baumgarten's reassessment of the Junker was linked to his
conviction that liberalism's "extraordinary ineptitude" proved that the *Mittelstand* was "little suited for real political action.... The middle class
individual is, by virtue of his social position and life-style, character and
intellect, only in exceptional cases able to participate in great political
endeavors with success." At the heart of Baumgarten's argument, therefore,
was not just a call for a new attitude toward the Junkers but also a fundamental
challenge to the social values and assumptions upon which liberal politics had
always been based.[64]

Like the other lessons of the *Reichsgründung*, Baumgarten's "self-
criticism" was absorbed within the movement slowly and unevenly. When his
essay first appeared, it was rejected by a great many liberals who refused to

abandon their hopes and expectations.[65] But in the years after 1866, the attitudes Baumgarten expressed found an ever greater audience; by the 1890s one young man could report that his contemporaries had read the essay over and over again, adopting it as the foundation for their political opinions.[66] The influence of Baumgarten's ideas spread because they conformed to a number of those developments which have occupied our attention in these chapters on the ''liberal era.'' Politically, a reevaluation of the aristocracy was nourished by desires for an alliance with the conservatives against the left; socially, by the ambitions of propertied and educated elites for aristocratic status; economically, by a growing communality of interests between protectionists in industry and agriculture. Each of these positions reflected one facet of liberalism's larger failure to shape German politics and society.

As late as 1876, those who held these views were still a minority within the National Liberal party: in September of that year, the party officially rejected ''political and economic reaction, the representation of material interests, the mixture of Junkerism, guildism, and protectionism.''[67] But the process through which important elements in liberalism were pulled toward the right had begun. In the course of the next two years the significance of this process for liberalism's future became clear as the government set out to shatter the movement and absorb its right wing into a new basis for the Reich.

V   Division and Decline
1877–90

In March 1877, Bismarck provoked a crisis. The immediate cause was a conflict with General von Stosch, chief of the Imperial Naval Office and an associate of some of the chancellor's rivals at court. After delivering a sudden and bitter attack on Stosch in the Reichstag, Bismarck threatened to resign and, as soon as he had made sure that the emperor would never consent to his resignation, withdrew to his estates where he remained for the next eleven months.[1] Many well-informed contemporaries realized that there was more at stake than Bismarck's hatred for Stosch. Rudolf Haym, for example, believed that Bismarck intended either to resign and take care of his health or "to change the situation so basically that it would be worth the devotion of his last strength."[2] One may suspect that Haym overestimated Bismarck's willingness to surrender his offices, but the events of the next two years left little doubt about his commitment to seeking a new political direction for Germany. In 1878 and 1879, Bismarck made a series of important changes in the bureaucracy, began a repressive campaign against the labor movement, and introduced a cluster of new fiscal and commercial policies.[3]

The "Second *Reichsgründung*" of 1878–79 brought the liberal era to an end. As the possibility of cooperation with the state waned and the liberals' position in the *Volk* deteriorated, the movement was forced to confront deep divisions within its own ranks. In the following chapters, our first task will be to examine the immediate impact of the dramatic events of 1878 and 1879. Then we can trace the painful process of self-doubt and mutual recrimination which attended the liberals' desperate search for new goals and alternative strategies.

The "Second Reichsgründung"

> The Bismarckian system has developed
> with terrifying swiftness, as I have
> always feared it would. Conscription,
> unrestricted and extensive indirect taxes,
> a disciplined and degenerate Reichstag,
> public opinion which has been corrupted
> and rendered impotent by the conflict of
> material interests—this is the politics of
> a powerless *Volk*, of declining constitu-
> tional freedom, of terrible dangers for
> Germany and the young empire.
>
> Max von Forckenbeck
> (January 19, 1879)[1]

By the early spring of 1877, a number of considerations seemed to have convinced Bismarck that a basic shift in German politics was necessary. For one thing, he continued to be vexed by the efforts of some parliamentarians to interfere with the power of the executive. This also made him anxious to find a way of solving the Reich's financial difficulties without increasing the Reichstag's budgetary powers. One way to do this, he had come to believe, would be a system of protective tariffs and state monopolies. These measures would also help to stabilize the economy and thus combat the dangers inherent in the steady expansion of Social Democracy.[2]

Behind these perceptions of the situation in the spring of 1877 was the long-range goal which Bismarck had pursued since he became Prussian minister-president fifteen years earlier: the creation of a parliament of proper-tied men firmly tied to the established order and dependent on the state. In 1867, he had hoped that universal suffrage and the absence of compensation for delegates would encourage the growth of such a parliamentary elite. But old enemies like Lasker, as well as new antagonists like Windthorst and Bebel, continually drove home the fact that these hopes had not been realized. His efforts in 1877–79, therefore, were a new attempt to attain what he had failed to get a decade before. The "Second *Reichsgründung*" was a search for goals left unfulfilled after the first.

Bismarck's long- and short-run goals required that he remove the possibility of a liberal Reichstag. The elections of 1877 had erased the liberals' thin majority, but the two *Fraktionen* still held the largest bloc of seats. During the first months of 1877, they had continued to oppose the chancellor on a number of key issues. Bismarck decided, therefore, to divide the liberal movement, isolate its left wing, and draw the moderate and right-wing elements into a firm alliance with the government. He first attempted to do this by placing a wedge at the place occupied in National Liberalism by Rudolf von Bennigsen, the Hanoverian aristocrat who was one of the party's leading moderates and an important conciliatory force within the Reichstag *Fraktion*. In April 1877, Bismarck tried to dislodge Bennigsen from his party by offering him a position in the government. Bennigsen, however, did not respond as Bismarck had wished. After consulting with his colleagues, he asked for some constitutional changes and two additional ministerial posts for members of the party, hoping thereby to establish that reconciliation between liberalism and the *Staat* for which liberals had always yearned. This was the last thing Bismarck wanted. Although negotiations between the two men dragged until February 1878, they were bound to come to nothing.[3]

The Bennigsen candidacy showed that a great many National Liberals were still inclined to put limitations on their willingness to cooperate with the government. The pull of the *Staat* was strong but not yet irresistible. At the same time, however, their willingness to mount a vigorous campaign against Bismarck was also extremely limited. This became clear in the spring of 1878 during the Reichstag's debate over Bismarck's proposals for reform in the imperial administration. As we know, many liberals wanted a revision of the constitution which would establish "responsible" officials for the Reich in addition to the chancellor. Early in March 1878, Bismarck seemed to respond to this with a proposal that a deputy, a *Stellvertreter*, be designated. However, his proposals made no mention of this officer's "responsibility"; in fact, the bill simply reaffirmed the chancellor's own authority to select and control his subordinates. The Progressives condemned this proposal, as did Eduard Lasker and others on the National Liberal left. But in the end, the National Liberals joined with the Conservatives to vote for the law, thereby signalling once again their reluctance to engage in a sustained drive for political reform.[4]

Bismarck emerged from the Reichstag debates of February and March 1878 more convinced than ever that a new political alignment was necessary. He still did not have a majority for his economic policies, and the continued importance of men like Lasker helped to keep alive the parliament's political ambitions. On March 10, Bismarck unveiled the next step in his antiliberal campaign by sending a program to the Bundesrat which called for fiscal reform and a tobacco monopoly. He hoped these measures would provide revenue without parliamentary interference and also would dismember the liberal movement by activating its deeply rooted socioeconomic dissensus. In the next elections, Bismarck promised, public opinion would turn from political to economic issues. This would disrupt the existing *Fraktionen* and "diminish the excessive number of doctrinaires within the parliament."[5]

Bismarck did not have to wait for the next scheduled elections in order to strike out against the liberal "doctrinaires." On May 11, an attempt was made on the life of the emperor. William was not hurt, but Bismarck seized the opportunity to introduce new legislation against the Social Democrats. As he recognized at once, the liberals' persistent divisions about the danger of revolution might be as disruptive as their differences over economic policy. However, the government's hastily written and badly presented bill was rejected by both the Progressives and a majority of National Liberals. The National Liberal right was deeply annoyed by the outcome of this vote, but the *Fraktion* remained intact. Then, just eight days after the government's bill was defeated, another assassin struck. This time the emperor's wound was serious. Without hesitation, Bismarck dissolved the Reichstag and called for new elections. "Now I've got them," he is supposed to have said. "The Social Democrats?" he was asked. "No, the National Liberals!"[6]

The election campaign, which lasted from mid-June until the end of July, was conducted in an atmosphere of carefully orchestrated crisis. The government exploited and encouraged the public outrage over the emperor's injuries. The responsibility for the *Attentat* was placed on the Social Democrats, as well as on their "fellow travellers" in the Fortschrittspartei and those sectors of the National Liberal party which pursued Progressive policies "behind a National Liberal mask."[7] Special detachments of troops were deployed in the capital to emphasize the supposed danger of unrest. The administrative apparatus in the countryside was mobilized behind the progovernment parties. Bismarck, basking in the prestige he gained from presiding over the Berlin Congress (which met earlier that summer), made clear that the government would not shrink from radical measures if the electorate should fail to do its duty. Thus the campaign revealed the full array of weapons with which Bismarck sought to impose his will: a manipulated fear of revolution, the exploitation of diplomacy for domestic ends, the use of the bureaucracy as an electoral instrument, and the threat of a coup should all else fail. The fact that Bismarck felt obliged to employ these extraordinary measures just to gain a parliamentary majority for his program was at once a symptom of and a contribution to the climate of crisis which would never again be completely absent from the Reich.

The campaign posed serious problems for both liberal *Fraktionen*. The Progressives tried to sustain their opposition to the Socialists and to the government's anti-Socialist measures—a perilous enterprise at best. The National Liberals had to find some formula which would obscure their own divisions on the subject of repressive legislation. They also had to contend with their differences on social and economic issues. With regard to tariff and taxation policies, the best their electoral statement could do was to promise that the party would seek to defend the interests of the nation as a whole.[8] Most liberal leaders knew that these measures would not be enough. They sensed a rising tide of antiliberal sentiment which made their movement a focus for the nation's discontents and anxieties.[9] The results of the elections confirmed their worst fears. A liberal majority, which had seemed such a strong possibility just a few months before, was now shattered by what Lud-

Table 12.1   **The Reichstag Election of 1878**

	Votes			WKe		
	Total (in 1,000s)	% of eligible voters	Change from 1877 in 1,000s	No.	%	Change from 1877
National Liberals	1,486.8	25.8	− 117.5	109	27.3	− 32
Progressives	385.1	6.7	− 32.7	26	6.5	− 9
Volkspartei	66.1	1.1	+ 21.2	3	.8	− 1
Conservatives	749.5	13	+ 223.5	59	14.9	+ 19
Free Conservatives	785.8	13.6	+ 359.2	57	14.4	+ 19
Center	1,328.1	23.1	− 13.2	94	23.7	+ 1
Poles, etc.	507.7	8.8	− 23	40	10.1	+ 6
SPD	437.1	7.6	− 56.2	9	2.3	− 3
Total	5,780.9	63.4	+ 358.3			

SOURCE: Vogel et al., *Wahlen* (1971), p. 291.

wig Bamberger called that "ruinous combination . . . Bismarck's drive for mastery and the selfishness of all Germany's vulgar urges."[10]

As the data in table 12.1 suggest, the liberals' decline was accompanied by a significant shift to the right. Part of this was due to the continued resurgence of the Conservatives in eastern Prussia, a process which had already been apparent during the elections of 1877. The Progressives were especially hard hit by this development, which characteristically involved a defection of liberal supporters and the mobilization of new voters by the antiliberal forces. In Gumbinnen-Insterburg (Gumbinnen *WK* 3), for instance, the Progressives had outpolled the Conservatives by two thousand votes in 1877 (59 percent to 40 percent, with 48 percent of those eligible voting), but lost by over seven thousand votes in 1878 (26 percent to 71 percent, with 74 percent voting). National Liberals also lost heavily in the eastern parts of Prussia, sometimes to Conservatives, sometimes to Free Conservatives. Electoral District 5 in Merseburg provides a particularly striking example of this: in 1877, a deeply divided Conservative party had been able to win only 285 votes, thereby insuring an easy victory for the National Liberals; in 1878, electoral participation doubled (from 28 percent to 57 percent) and a Free Conservative candidate won easily with a total of 8,108 votes. Table 12.2 suggests the dimensions of the liberals' losses in the Prussian east. In almost every administrative district, the level of participation increased while the absolute number of liberal voters declined. Significantly, the three exceptions to this pattern were urban districts in which liberal voters resisted the overall trend to the right.

Conservative gains were not confined to eastern Prussia. In Schleswig-Holstein (WK 2), Kassel (WK 6), Saxony (WK 2), Württemberg (WKe 5, 6, and 8), Baden (WK 10), Mecklenburg-Schwerin (WK 4), Saxony-Weimar (WK 1), Saxony-Altenburg, and Schwarzburg-Sonderhausen, a shift to the right among liberal supporters and an increase in conservative strength from

Table 12.2   **The Reichstag Elections of 1877 and 1878: Liberal and Conservative Votes in Administrative Districts of Eastern Prussia (Excluding Berlin)**

	First-ballot votes (seats won)					
	Conservatives		Liberals		Participation (% of eligible voters)	
District	1877	1878	1877	1878	1877	1878
Königsberg	32,331 (5)	55,716 (8)	40,810 (3)	31,916	48	54
Gumbinnen	31,065 (2)	59,270 (7)	33,084 (5)	26,279	47.9	59
Danzig	9,059	18,556 (1)	18,529 (3)	17,257 (1)	60.7	65
Marienwerder	22,460 (3)	33,998 (5)	33,403 (4)	23,962 (1)	75	74
Potsdam	53,026 (5)	66,004 (6)	40,213 (5)	56,343 (4)	45	56
Frankfurt	51,000 (7)	69,903 (9)	43,423 (3)	40,707 (1)	48	57
Stettin	27,537 (4)	43,454 (6)	27,449 (3)	22,394 (1)	43	49
Köslin	44,601 (5)	46,594 (5)	4,429	3,839	49	49
Stralsund	8,682 (1)	14,955 (2)	12,168 (1)	5,167	48	47
Posen	19,935 (1)	41,102 (1)	26,499 (1)	12,981 (1)	74	74
Bromberg	25,580 (1)	34,153 (3)	8,502 (1)	3,235	74	76
Breslau	61,947 (6)	88,619 (7)	44,147 (4)	36,303 (3)	55	61
Liegnitz	37,466 (3)	67,909 (4)	45,727 (7)	45,295 (6)	45	58
Oppeln	41,862 (1)	72,738 (2)	18,121	—	69	74
Magdeburg	25,411 (2)	39,214 (2)	47,442 (6)	70,767 (6)	42	61
Merseburg	30,509 (3)	52,733 (5)	39,493 (5)	53,378 (3)	40	57
Erfurt	18,586 (2)	27,589 (2)	6,134 (1)	5,861 (1)	47	54

SOURCE: *SDR* 27, no. 6 (1879): 40–86.

new voters combined to produce electoral victories for one of the two conservative parties.[11] Liberals also lost some seats to their other enemies. Catholics, particularists, and even the beleaguered Social Democrats were able to take advantage of the liberals' disarray and defeat them in a number of closely fought contests. Unlike their losses to the conservatives, these defeats did not usually come from a defection of liberal voters to their opponents but rather were caused by the liberals' inability to get their supporters to the polls.[12] In the summer of 1878, therefore, the sources of liberalism's decline became apparent: division and uncertainty in their own ranks coincided with growing vitality of their opponents to mark a downward trend which would eventually reduce the liberal movement to a permanent minority.[13]

The immediate result of the election was to ensure the passage of a bill against the Socialists. There were still those on the National Liberal left who opposed the government's draft, but they could not withstand the pressure from the party's right wing which now had the support of moderates like Bennigsen.[14] After some compromises between National Liberals and Conservatives, the anti-Socialist law was accepted on October 19. The discipline

of the *Fraktionen* held unusually firm: the National Liberals and the two
conservative parties voted for the law, while the Progressives, Center, Social
Democrats, and national minorities voted against it.[15] Although the entire
Fraktion supported the law, the debate aggravated the National Liberals'
internal conflicts. The right was incensed by the continued reservations of the
left, whereas Lasker and his allies were embittered by the enthusiasm shown
by some in the party for an alliance between the liberal movement and the two
conservative parties.

These wounds had no time to heal because the debate on the anti-Socialist
bill was followed at once by a prolonged conflict over tariff policies. As
Eugen Richter astutely noted at the time, the Socialist controversy was merely
a prelude to this issue, which he recognized as the government's most
important attempt to effect a reorientation of German politics.[16] On the
day the Reichstag passed the Socialist Law, a group calling itself the
Volkswirtschaftliche Vereinigung issued a declaration calling for a revision
of the Reich's economic legislation. The declaration was cautiously worded
(in large measure because most agricultural interests were still uncertain about
the advantages of protective tariffs), but it did mark a clear break with the economic assumptions of the "liberal era." Almost one-third of the National
Liberal *Fraktion* joined with men from the conservative parties and the Center
in support of this statement.[17] Two weeks later, the Handelstag, an organization representing German Chambers of Commerce, met in Berlin. After an
acrimonious debate, the advocates of free trade were defeated.[18]

On December 15, the semiofficial *Norddeutsche Allgemeine Zeitung* published the government's program for economic reform. This program sought
to consolidate the protectionists' position by weaving together tariff and taxation policies, as well as by trying to combine the special interests of industry
and agriculture.[19] The program of December 15 marked another step in Bismarck's attempt to split liberalism and to create that combination of propertied
men upon whom the government might depend. In the spring of 1879, as the
parliamentary debate itself got underway, Bismarck stepped up his attack on
the liberal left. On May 8, for example, he delivered a bitter attack on those
"whom our sun does not warm, nor our rains make wet, who neither farm,
nor produce, nor own an enterprise."[20] This stereotype of the liberal "doctrinaire,"which often appeared in the chancellor's statements from this
period, designated the enemy against which a new parliamentary elite was to
be directed.

The supporters of free trade tried to answer this assault on liberal economics
with the arguments they had always used. Protectionism, they claimed, sac-
rificed the good of the nation as a whole to the interests of a minority;
economic freedom was inexorably tied to political freedom; the laws of the

market could not be broken without damaging the economy and inhibiting social progress.[21] The free traders' counterattack reached a high point on May 17, 1879, when representatives of seventy-two German cities met in Berlin and voted overwhelmingly to oppose any tariff on foodstuffs. That evening a banquet was held in which these representatives were joined by free-trade advocates from all sectors of the liberal movement. The keynote speech was delivered by Max von Forckenbeck, lord mayor of Berlin and president of the Reichstag. To the resounding cheers of the assembled notables, Forckenbeck called for a new liberal party which would rally the free *Bürgertum* and unite them in a single political movement devoted to social, economic, and political liberty.[22] Perhaps, for a moment at least, there were those who believed that a new political force had been born that night in the Zoological Gardens' banquet hall. But as the events of the next few months would show, this new version of an old liberal dream was unable to change the course of German politics. As had happened so often in the movement's past, liberals' hopes for a united *Bürgertum* shattered as they met the hard realities of German life.

The preliminary voting on the tariff law made clear that an unbridgeable gap existed within the National Liberal *Fraktion*.[23] As the day of the final vote approached, Bennigsen made a last, desperate attempt to hold his party together. He tried to get Bismarck to agree to an arrangement in which the National Liberals' support for the tariff might be compensated by some constitutional guarantees protecting the Reichstag's authority.[24] Bismarck, however, had no desire to make things easier for the liberals. He refused Bennigsen's offer and instead struck a bargain with the Center which involved concessions to the individual states in the so-called Franckenstein amendment. This pact with the liberals' old enemies showed the degree to which the chancellor's political priorities had shifted since the days of the Kulturkampf.[25] Reluctantly, moderate National Liberals joined the Progressives in voting against the tariff, which was passed by a majority of Conservatives and Centrists. On July 15, the day the tariff law went into effect, fifteen members of the National Liberal right formally resigned from the party.[26] But this did little to ease the National Liberals' internal divisions. The left was outraged by the party's indecision and by the moderates' failure to take a clear and effective stand in defense of liberal economics. This failure, compounded by the bitterness generated in a whole series of intramural conflicts, convinced men like Forckenbeck and Lasker that their days in the party were limited. As early as June 9, Forckenbeck had written that "a division of the Party is ... unavoidable; whether it happens today, in a few weeks, or at the end of the Reichstag session is only a question of tactics." Lasker agreed. On June 29, he wrote that the party was not merely divided by "particular votes," but by "basic differences of values and opinions."[27]

The abandonment of free trade was just the first in a series of revisions in the government's economic and social policy. New tax laws, efforts at creating state monopolies, and an ambitious system of social insurance all deviated from the ideal of liberal-state cooperation pursued in the Delbrück era. At the same time, the consensus between the state and liberalism on religious policy disappeared. Some of the measures adopted during the Kulturkampf were abandoned, others simply were not enforced. Moreover, the bureaucracy showed a renewed willingness to support and encourage religious orthodoxy.[28]

These changes in policy were accompanied by important changes in personnel. In 1879 half of the Prussian ministry was replaced, usually with men farther to the right politically. In both Prussia and the Reich, the administrative machine as a whole began to be permeated by a new set of values. Under Bismarck's direction, efforts were made to remove the residues of bureaucratic liberalism. The appointment process was arranged to inhibit the movement of "unreliable" men into politically sensitive posts. Gradually, the carriers of the tradition of bureaucratic reform were replaced by men willing to conform, to obey orders, to defend the status quo without demur.[29] In 1882, one well-placed observer complained that "officials who are true to their own convictions are now being hunted down."[30] That same year, Georg von Bunsen recorded his own disillusionment in words which are an appropriate epitaph for the "liberal era":

> The purpose of my life, which was to help establish a progressive
> bureaucracy in Prussia . . . has been shattered, destroyed, dissolved by
> Bismarck's statism and by the disrepute he has brought to every free
> activity.[31]

The events of 1878–79 left German liberalism seriously weakened. The elections of 1878 revealed the fragility of the liberals' hold upon the *Volk*. The debate on the tariff displayed the deep social and economic conflicts within their constituency and, when combined with the other equally divisive issues, set into motion a process of disintegration which would eventually banish forever the possibility of a united movement. Finally, changes in both the policies and personnel of the Bismarckian state brought to an end the last of a series of alliances between liberalism and bureaucratic power. After 1879, few liberals could hope that the state might be joined with the movement in a common quest for social and political emancipation.

13 National Liberalism Moves to the Right

> We no longer recognize that kind of
> liberalism which defines progress as the
> diminution of the state's role, an exclu-
> sive reliance on self-help, and the rejec-
> tion of all public social and economic
> organizations; which identifies free trade
> with political freedom; and which will
> not let the state do anything in economic
> affairs because the state cannot do
> everything.
> Johannes Miquel (May 1884)[1]

By the summer of 1879, two years of electoral defeat and parliamentary
conflict had made National Liberals painfully aware of their own disagreements. Those whose image of political life still emphasized liberalism's
spiritual mission of enlightenment looked with dismay on the rise of material
interests and of a "politics which is no longer political." Business leaders and
others who prided themselves on being "practical" decried the persistent
influence of men whom they regarded as doctrinaire idealists. The left viewed
support for the government's antiliberal course as a betrayal of its most
cherished goals, while the right regarded Bismarck's critics within the party as
secret allies of the Progressives, or worse. There were, of course, still those
who called for a revitalization of liberalism and held on to the promise of its
eventual triumph, but these voices found little support. The letters of the
liberal elite from this period are filled with uncertainty and despair. Once
again, men began to raise the question which had always been just below the
surface of liberals' public image: "Does a liberal party actually exist or is
there in fact only a certain number of individuals whose ideas are more or less
liberal?"[2]

That fall, the party's preparations for the Prussian Landtag elections were
undermined by a mood of resignation and a sense of inevitable decline. In a
number of districts, incumbent delegates decided not to run and the party had
difficulty finding candidates to replace them—always a sign of trouble at the
grass roots.[3] In Sieg-Mülheim-Wipperfürth, for example, local liberals met
on September 7 but failed to decide upon a candidate. They were forced to
promise their voters that they would come up with a suitable individual after
the popular voting had taken place.[4] This might have worked a decade or two
earlier, but it was not an appropriate response to the political demands of the
late seventies. At the center of political life things were no better. Bennigsen
decided not to run for the Landtag, largely because he was convinced that the
party's present course was doomed to failure. Lasker allowed himself to be
nominated, but did not campaign. After some delay, the party leadership
issued a rather colorless electoral statement, but did little else to rally their

supporters.[5] Even an increase in Conservative and Socialist strength in the elections to the Saxon Landtag held early that September had little impact; indeed, the *Nationalzeitung* pointed out how little attention was paid to this election.[6] "On the whole," wrote H. B. Oppenheim in August, "I don't find it unfortunate that the party is still silent and apathetic . . . . It will have to accept the disadvantageous consequences of its own virtues and mistakes. The magic is now gone."[7]

The Prussian elections turned out to be a disaster for both liberal parties. As table 13.1 suggests, the liberal defeat was again connected to a resurgence of Conservative strength already apparent in the Reichstag elections of 1878.

Table 13.1   **The Political Composition of the Prussian Chamber of Deputies, 1876 and 1879**

	1876 No. (%)	1879 No. (%)
National Liberals	169 (39)	104 (24)
Progressives	63 (14.5)	38 (8.7)
Conservatives	41 (9.4)	110 (25.4)
Free Conservatives	35 (8)	51 (11.7)
Center	89 (20.5)	97 (22.4)
Poles	15 (3.4)	19 (4.3)
No Fraktion	21 (4.8)	14 (3.2)
Total	433	433

SOURCE: Vogel et al., *Wahlen* (1971), p. 287.

Certainly one reason for this was the electoral activity of the bureaucracy, whose influence was especially powerful because of the public and indirect voting procedures for the Landtag. At the same time, however, the ability of Conservative elites to gather a reliable set of electors had also significantly increased: by 1879 they had made substantial gains among those urban and rural members of the middle strata upon whose support liberalism had traditionally depended.[8] In addition to these losses to the right, liberals also suffered at the hands of their other opponents, especially the Center. The liberals' disarray at both the national and local level made it difficult for them to resist the well-disciplined efforts of the Center, which was able to elect its candidates in some districts where Catholics made up only about one-third of the population.[9] Liberals were shaken by the magnitude of their defeat, which demonstrated that they were as vulnerable in elections held under an indirect and unequal suffrage as they had been in the direct and democratic elections to the Reichstag. "We lost a good deal because of our organizational weak-

ness," concluded the *Nationalzeitung*, "but we were also beaten because of
our program."[10]

The big loser in 1879 was National Liberalism's left wing, which was
significantly diminished in size and greatly weakened by the defeat of its most
effective leader, Eduard Lasker. The left's electoral setbacks were reaffirmed
when only one of its followers was chosen as a member of the *Fraktion*'s
executive committee.[11] At the same time, the elections improved the relative
position of National Liberalism's right wing in two important ways. First, the
distribution of parties in the new Landtag created the possibility of a
conservative-Center majority. This meant that those who advocated a liberal
alliance with the conservatives could argue that this was the only real alternative to a "blue-black" coalition which would dismantle the Kulturkampf.[12]
Second, the elections provided further evidence for the right wing's conviction that the *Volk* would not support a policy of opposition to the government.
The defeats of 1879, like those in the Reichstag elections a year earlier,
seemed to demonstrate that no matter how difficult the party's relationship
with the government might be, liberals were better off trying to find a mode of
cooperation with Bismarck than attempting to mount a popularly based drive
against government policy. As always, the attraction of an alliance with the
Staat was intimately connected with liberals' perceptions of the *Volk*.

As the party moved to the right, the position of the left became increasingly
untenable. Despite Bennigsen's efforts to qualify the National Liberals' growing subservience to Bismarck by the retention of a few liberal goals, the left
wing's leaders recognized that the chancellor was no longer interested in the
kind of cooperation which had occurred in the early seventies.[13] By the end of
1879, some members of the left had stopped participating in the *Fraktion*'s
deliberations. It was now no longer a question of whether they would leave,
but when.

Lasker was the first to move. In mid-March 1880 he formally resigned from
the National Liberal Reichstag *Fraktion* and thereby abandoned an enterprise
to which he had devoted his time and energy for the previous thirteen years. In
an explanatory statement to his voters, Lasker made two points which were to
appear again and again in the public and private remarks of the National
Liberal left. First, Lasker argued that the *Fraktion*'s present course was incompatible with liberal goals and dangerous for liberalism's future. By giving
in to the prevailing conservative mood, liberals were weakening their ability
to respond when this mood changed. Whatever the pressures of the present,
Lasker believed that liberal strategy should look to the future. Second, he
emphasized that he was leaving the National Liberal *Fraktion* but not the

liberal "party." This reassertion of the old distinction between party and *Fraktion* allowed Lasker to reaffirm his membership in a broad ideological community of liberals and to present his move as a contribution to liberal unity, to the formation of a "great liberal party" which would gather together all the friends of liberty within the German *Volk*.[14]

The left wing's willingness to follow Lasker increased that spring and summer as Bismarck relentlessly raised the price of his cooperation with the liberals.[15] Finally, when party moderates felt obliged to accept a school bill which significantly favored the Center, many on the left decided that the opportune moment had arrived. On August 19, Heinrich Rickert delivered a widely quoted speech to a liberal organization in Danzig which called for the creation of a united liberal movement based on the policies of Falk and Delbrück.[16] A few days later, twenty-seven National Liberal delegates from the Reichstag and Landtag *Fraktionen* issued a formal statement which declared that "the experience of the past two years" had revealed National Liberalism's basic disunity. The statement went on to propose that the "whole liberal party" rededicate itself to "a defense of political and economic freedom (with which political freedom is intimately tied), tax reform, and the predominance of the state over the church."[17]

Among the original leaders of the Sezession were several of those men "without interests" against whom so much of Bismarck's rhetorical venom had been directed: lawyers, local government officials, and men living from their investments. In addition to some landowners and businessmen, there were also a number of men with ties to the banking community.[18] Regionally, the Sezession was centered in eastern Prussia, although there were also a few representatives from other parts of the Reich. Generally speaking, therefore, the National Liberal left drew its strength from a cross section of those who supported free trade, men who did not have strong ties to either the industrial or the bureaucratic elites and whose regional base was usually in districts where the liberals' main opposition was some form of conservatism. These impressions are confirmed by evidence on the social composition and regional distribution of delegates elected by the Liberale Vereinigung in 1881, the only national election in which the Sezession ran as a separate party. As tables 13.2 and 13.3 suggest, industrialists, ranking administrative officials, and landowners were underrepresented, as were delegates from Hanover and Prussia's western provinces, most of the *Mittelstaaten*, and the Hansa cities.

In essence, the split in National Liberalism at the end of the "Second *Reichsgründung*" replicated the division of the liberal movement which had occurred following the formation of the Reich thirteen years before. In 1880, as in 1867, some liberals decided that the price of continued cooperation with the government was too high. But the National Liberal left, like those who

Table 13.2   **The Reichstag Delegation of the
                               Liberale Vereinigung, 1881 (Social
                               Composition)**

	No. (%)
Officials	
Administrative	5 (10)
Judicial	2 (4)
Local	5 (10)
Teachers, professors	3 (6)
Lawyers	8 (16)
Other academics	3 (6)
Businessmen	13 (26.5)
Rentier	2 (4)
Agricultural occupations	
Rittergutsbesitzer	2 (4)
Others	6 (12)
Total	49

SOURCE: Kremer, *Aufbau* (1934), pp. 25–26.

Table 13.3   **The Reichstag Delegation of the
                               Liberale Vereinigung, 1881 (Regional
                               Distribution)**

Region	WKe Represented
Prussia	
Eastern provinces	24
Schleswig-Holstein	2
Hanover	—
Western provinces	1
Bavaria	4
Saxony	1
Württemberg	—
Baden	1
Hesse	5
Small states	8
Hansa Cities	—
Alsace-Lorraine	—
Total	46

SOURCE: *SDR* 53, no. 3 (1882): 1–50.

remained in the Fortschrittspartei after Königgrätz, put some significant qualifications on their willingness to oppose the government. In his speech of August 19, for example, Rickert made clear that he would continue to support the chancellor's foreign policy, a position which had been anticipated a few weeks earlier when only a handful of National Liberals voted against the government's new military budget.[19] Furthermore, the Sezession was silent on a great many political issues: its speeches and joint statements contained no mention of basic constitutional goals such as a parliamentarization of the Reich. With this familiar ambivalence about the state went a deep uncertainty about the *Volk*. The left's public statements were filled with hope for a liberal future, but in private its members lamented their lack of support in the public at large. Early in 1880, for instance, Rickert wrote that "everything is lifeless in the nation," and a few weeks later Stauffenberg complained about the deep political apathy he found in the south. "What is known as the liberal party," he lamented, "leads a shadowy existence . . . . our role seems to have been played out."[20] Surely this sense that the basis of their support was thin is one reason why the left waited so long to make a final break with the National Liberal *Fraktion*. It must have been difficult to abandon once and for all the empty dream of cooperation with the *Staat* when there was so little hope that an alternative source of influence might be available in the *Volk*.

The clearest expression of the Sezession's continued ambivalence about both the *Staat* and the *Volk* can be found in Ludwig Bamberger's pamphlet *Die Sezession*, which was written in the late summer of 1880 and went through four editions during the next few months.[21] Bamberger began by emphasizing that the new group had been formed because of the government's unwillingness to cooperate with the liberals. In contrast to the mutual accommodation of the "liberal era," after 1878 the government had tried to extract collaboration on its own terms. It had demanded "the old dependence without compensation"; it wanted support even after it had abandoned liberal goals. At the root of this problem was the unhealthy position occupied by Bismarck, whose power was supposed to remain constant while the parties changed around him. This situation was ruinous to the parties and produced deep confusion in the nation at large. The only possible answer was "complete independence" through a reassertion of the liberal party's own principles. But what exactly did this independence mean for the distribution of power in the Reich? Was an independent liberal party to become the basis for the government? Was a liberal majority to demand the removal of Bismarck and seek his replacement from its own ranks? Bamberger did not say, perhaps because he was so pessimistic about the chances of creating such a majority. He did acknowledge the need for unifying the liberal party, but it is clear that he saw this as a long and difficult task. It is not, Bamberger acknowledged, Bismarck's fault that he seems to be indispensable: the blame rests with the nation itself and with the widespread feeling that Germany was "helpless and at sea without him." This sense of the *Volk*'s weakness is the real burden of Bamberger's argument. It emerges with particular clarity in the concluding section:

Among all the civilized nations [*Kulturländern*], Germany has experienced least the political power of its *Bürgertum*. This means that feudal
ideas have remained stronger here and that Socialist ideas have . . . .
gained more and more power.

For this reason, Germany will be the natural battleground for Socialists'
assault on the *Bürgertum*, just as eighteenth-century France had been the
battleground for the attack of the middle class on the aristocracy. The best defense
against this assault, Bamberger concluded, was the army, which was the
foundation of the existing social order and must at all costs be kept free from
Socialist influence. What an extraordinary ending for a pamphlet written to
explain why the National Liberal left had decided to cut its ties with those who
wished to support the government!

Bamberger's analysis captures the mood of the Sezession much better than
the rhetorical calls for liberal unity which filled the public pronouncements of
men like Lasker and Rickert. His sense of discouragement and decline, which
is linked to a negative assessment of liberalism's social foundation in Germany, recalls Baumgarten's "Selbstkritik" of 1866. Like Baumgarten's essay, Bamberger's bleak assessment of German liberalism deserves a place as
an important milestone in the movement's long downhill journey through the
imperial era.

Many of the same attitudes about the *Volk* that shadowed the National Liberal
left's decision to enter the ranks of the opposition helped to strengthen the
right wing's conviction that conservative elements in Germany should stand
together in defense of the existing social and political order. In the late
seventies and early eighties, the conflicts generated during the "Second
Reichsgründung" produced a series of influential statements from the liberal
right which amplified and hardened the views which had begun to surface in
this part of the movement after 1871.

One vehicle for this process of ideological mobilization on the right was the
Grenzboten, a periodical whose founding in the 1840s had been one sign of
the liberal movement's original vitality. By the end of the seventies, the
Grenzboten had swung over to supporting Bismarck without qualification. Its
pages were filled with attacks on those who opposed the anti-Socialist laws
and on the "Manchesterites" within liberalism whose selfish cosmopolitanism reflected Semitic influences. Contributors to the *Grenzboten*
argued that the old divisions between conservatives and liberals were anachronistic. The *Bürgertum* had to realize that the "natural grouping" of
parties was an alliance of all the conservative forces in society against the
radicals, by which was meant an alliance of conservatives and nationally

oriented liberals against the Catholics, the Progressives, and the Social
Democrats. In order for this alliance to be formed, liberals would have to give
up some of the illusions which had been part of their world view for decades:
one of these was the belief that the "vast majority of the *Volk*" was
interested in political ideas; another was that "the national state can rest upon
civil society." Germany was too divided, its population too unruly and unreliable to support a system of parliamentary government. Instead, the goal of a
truly "national party" should be "to lead the educatable part of the German
Bürgertum to the recognition that the living roots of German unity must be
found somewhere besides in the sovereignty of a parliament which for a long
period can only be the mirror of a fragmented nation."[22]

The themes articulated by the *Grenzboten* can be found in a number of
books and magazines during this period. In 1880, for example, Julius Jolly
published a widely cited study of *Der Reichstag und die Parteien*. Jolly was by
no means hostile to representative institutions, indeed his opening chapters are
filled with accolades to the Reichstag's accomplishments during the "liberal
era." But the purpose of his book was less to praise past accomplishments
than to warn of future dangers. Jolly regarded the Socialists as a menace, a
"sickness ... which can only serve as an impediment to German political
development." The Center party was also basically at odds with the principles
of German life. The other parties, despite their various virtues, were all
incapable of being a "governing party"; this meant that the parliamentary
system was impossible in Germany.[23] These same arguments were repeated
in influential journals like the *Preussische Jahrbücher* and *Im neuen Reich*,
both of which carried articles demonstrating that the "English system" was
not appropriate to the German situation.[24] The practical implication of these
arguments was clear: given the unfortunate tendencies present in German
party development, the state would have to remain the guardian of the common good. As one author put it, "Thank God Bismarck is around to pursue
the national interest."[25]

For some on the liberal right, disaffection with party life called into question the democratic franchise. It is impossible to know how many liberals
would have been willing to see the Reichstag suffrage changed, but there are
strong indications that more and more of them had begun to share Rudolf
Haym's conviction that in the long run the state could not survive with such a
law.[26]

As had always been the case, the liberals' uneasiness about the political
implications of parliamentary power and democratic participation was linked
to their fear of social forces in Germany. During the late 1870s, these social
anxieties also found greater resonance. Indeed, the sharp increase in concern
about social unrest calls to mind the prevailing mood of the troubled years just

before 1848. The intensification of these fears about modernity among the
liberal middle strata is yet another sign that the "liberal era" was over. From
this time on, the relatively optimistic views of social change which had tended
to predominate after mid-century gradually gave way to an antimodernism
which helped to dissolve many liberals' commitment to political reform.

A striking example of this process can be found in the works of Gustav
Rümelin, a longtime liberal and a careful observer of social developments.[27]
At the end of 1879, Rümelin summarized the recent evolution of his thought
in the following fashion:

> All my life I have been optimistically inclined, but now, either because of
> the weakness of old age or with good reason, Germany's future looks
> bleak to me. I have become a kind of Malthusian and I see in the abnor-
> mally rapid growth of our population ... the greatest danger and the real,
> decisive source of our social and economic difficulties.[28]

Rümelin first expressed his new position in a series of articles published by the
Allgemeine Zeitung in January 1878; these were reprinted in 1881 with the title
"The Problem of Overpopulation." Rümelin's essay reflected the depression
psychology which permeated so much of German social thought after 1873.
But like many others, his analysis transcended the particular problems facing
the German economy and called into question the basic direction of social
change. Under the impact of the depression, Rümelin revised his positive
opinion of urban life and industrial development. In a desperate search for a
source of stability, he called for the protection of German agriculture, that
"most solid pillar of the state and society." Moreover, like Robert von Mohl
four decades earlier, he wanted limitations on the poorer classes' right to
marry and other measures designed to prevent the growth of a proletariat.[29]
Rümelin spelled out the political implications of his new position in a series of
essays written during the 1880s. In a long discussion of the Reichstag suffrage, he rehearsed the usual arguments against a democratic franchise (the
absence of a unified political elite, the peculiarly German inclination to dissensus and fragmentation, the basic unreliability of the masses) and urged that
the existing suffrage system be replaced by one in which Reichstag delegates
would be chosen by the state Landtage (he meant here both the upper and
lower chambers). He felt this would encourage the evolution of an acceptable
elite without surrendering the advantages of representative institutions. Eight
years later, in a work entitled "The Concept of Society," Rümelin restated
that tension between the state and society which had been a persistent ingredient in German thought at least since Hegel: society was an important source
of creative energy, but without the stabilizing influence of the state it would
sink into chaos or anarchy.[30]

After 1880, a number of factors helped to increase the influence of the
National Liberal right within the party as a whole. The defection of the left not
only removed a large number of those whose views had always counter-
balanced those of the right, it also produced a shift in the social composition
of the party elite. Between 1877 and 1887 the number of businessmen in the
National Liberal Reichstag faction increased from 17 (13 percent) to 33 (32
percent), while those who might be classified as *Gebildete* decreased from 77
to 47 (60 percent to 45 percent). Thus the persistence in leadership which
helped to keep liberal traditions alive during the first decade after 1867 was
gradually weakened.[31] More significant than these changes was the growing
importance within the party of those areas which tended to favor protectionism and in which National Liberalism had become (or sought to become) a
governmental party directed against the Catholics and the left rather than a
middle party directed against the right.[32]

At the same time that the social and regional character of National
Liberalism's national leadership shifted, there were some important political
changes in the various states.[33] In Baden, for example, the liberals' unques-
tioned hegemony in the Landtag was threatened by Catholic victories in the
elections of 1879 and 1881. Even in this traditional center of liberal
strength, therefore, the "liberal era" seemed to be coming to an end. In
Bavaria, where liberalism had never been as robust, liberals continued to
retreat in the face of steady gains by political Catholicism. The main challenge
to Saxon liberalism came from the Conservatives, who were able to score
telling victories in 1879 and 1881.[34] There was also a shift to the right in
Hesse, although there it tended to take place within liberalism itself; after
1881, the influence of more conservative elements within the Hessian party
grew markedly as did the power of right-wing leaders such as Freiherr von
Heyl.[35]

In all of these states, as well as in a number of other parts of the Reich,
some liberals began to argue that the best way to defend their position was to
secure their right flank and broaden the basis of cooperation with progovernmental groups of all kinds, especially with the Free Conservatives.
This same sentiment was matched in places like Hanover and Württemberg
where the chief enemy remained some form of local particularism. As one
leader from the latter state put it in 1881: "To us ... Bismarck is the most
powerful protection against the new threat of the old particularism. Because of
this, we are willing to overlook the issues which displease us."[36]

Under Bennigsen's leadership, the moderate elements within National
Liberalism tried to contain these growing pressures from the right. In the
period immediately after the Sezession, Bennigsen continued to steer that
difficult course between opposition and complete collaboration. The party

program of May 1881 was designed to support this position by attempting to
satisfy the right without encouraging further defections on the left. The program began by acknowledging that the relationship between the party and the
state had entered a new and more difficult phase, but it promised that the party
would examine carefully the government's proposals and support those it
found worthwhile. On economic matters, the program was no less ambiguous:

> We are determined to defend the existing industrial legislation and the
> economic freedom upon which it rests from reactionary attacks, but we
> are convinced that conflicting opinions on the tariff issue should not be
> made the basis for a political party. . . . There should be room for dif-
> ferences on tariff policy within our party. To abandon this freedom of
> opinion would make it impossible to have a National Liberal party which
> could exist throughout all of Germany.

Nor did the program clarify the party's relationship with other liberal groups:
it condemned radicalism of both the left and right, but promised to cooperate
with those who pursued "the same or similar goals." The program was a
masterful display of rhetorical evasion which could be read in very different
ways by various elements within the party.[37] But for those who wanted a
clear-cut commitment to the new Bismarckian state in all of its manifesta-
tions, this kind of rhetoric was not enough. By the spring of 1883, Bennigsen
was sufficiently discouraged by the failure of his efforts to keep National
Liberalism as a "middle party" that he resigned from the parliament.[38]

   Bennigsen's departure opened the way for men such as Johannes Miquel,
who wanted to see National Liberalism as a bulwark for the protectionist
state.[39] In March 1884, the efforts of the right to move the party in this
direction gathered momentum when forty members of the "national and liberal" parties from Baden, Württemberg, Bavaria, and Hesse gathered in
Heidelberg. The "Heidelberg Declaration," drafted by Miquel and formally
ratified at this meeting, reflected the changes which had taken place within
National Liberalism over the past few years.[40] In the first place, the declaration advocated what the party had tried to resist for so long: a clear-cut
position on tariff questions. The men at Heidelberg believed that any efforts to
change the existing policy of protectionism would be "harmful and dangerous." They also supported Bismarck's social insurance scheme and his efforts
to reform the tax system. Furthermore, in a move which acknowledged the
growing importance of rural interests in the south and southwest, the declaration emphasized the essential role played by agriculture in German economic
life. There was also a political dimension to the declaration's support of the
government: after a few brief remarks on the need to defend parliamentary
rights, the Heidelberg meeting emphasized the need to cooperate with Bis-

marck's policies, especially with his efforts to maintain a strong army to
defend the existing order.from the dangers of revolution. Finally, the declaration renounced efforts at unity with other elements within liberalism, thereby
confirming the bifurcation of liberalism which had begun a few weeks earlier
when the Sezession and the Fortschrittspartei agreed to merge.

Shortly after the Heidelberg meeting, Miquel underscored the basic division between the liberal left and right when he told a group of National
Liberal leaders in Neustadt that the two wings of the movement had totally
different views on the "duties, rights, and functions of the modern state."
This remark captures the essence of the position Miquel was seeking to have
his party accept: full support for the Bismarckian state as it had emerged from
the "Second *Reichsgründung*."

The Neustadt meeting, attended by delegates from throughout the south and
southwest, proved to be a great triumph for Miquel and his associates.[41] Most
of those present accepted the Heidelberg Declaration as a useful way of
drawing the various state parties into a closer relationship with National
Liberalism. Now the question was how this would be viewed in Prussia
where, as Miquel acknowledged, "the situation ... is somewhat different."[42] There were a number of reasons to be aware of these differences in
the spring of 1884. On March 6, for instance, the *Nationalzeitung*, which
continued to speak for the Prussian left within National Liberalism, had sym-
pathetically discussed the merger of the two left liberal groups and had declared that there was nothing in their program with which liberals could not all
agree. The party's official *Korrespondenz* did not take as positive a view, but
its response to the new *Deutsche Freisinnige Partei* was a good deal more
restrained than the outright rejection expressed at Heidelberg.[43] The North
Germans realized that in a number of districts men from both wings of
liberalism would have to work together or be defeated separately. Moreover,
there was still enough support for free trade in the north to make many
Prussians reluctant to go on record in favor of protectionism or indeed of any
specific economic program. Just a week after the Heidelberg meeting, a
Prussian Landtag delegate had reaffirmed that it was similarities in "*Gesinnung* and *Denkweise*," not shared economic interests, which held the party
together.[44]

The party leadership in Berlin delayed for more than a month before responding to the new developments in the south. Finally, at the beginning of
May, the Reichstag and Landtag *Fraktionen* met and issued a statement which
expressed admiration for the Heidelberg Declaration, acknowledged the declaration's formal and not entirely consistent support for the party program of
1881, and simply ignored the important differences between the declaration
and the program.[45] On May 18, an official convention attended by over five

hundred National Liberals met in Berlin and produced a carefully worded statement which tried to take advantage of the new energies apparent in the south without making it impossible for the northern wing to remain in the party. The convention did emphasize the need for cooperation with the government and, following Miquel's lead, excluded the possibility of a merger with the left. However, the meeting did not endorse protectionism nor did it accept the Heidelberg Declaration's remarks on the central importance of agriculture.[46]

Despite the continued divisions apparent at the Berlin convention, there is little doubt that 1884 marked a clear movement to the right for the party as a whole. Miquel's position in the national leadership was strengthened and, equally important, right-wing elements became more deeply entrenched in a number of regions. In Hanover and Prussia's western provinces, support for the Heidelberg position was considerable.[47] And in parts of the south and southwest, candidates had to accept this program if they wanted support from local organizations.[48]

The strength of right-wing liberalism in 1884 was enhanced by Bismarck's dramatic decision to support the acquisition of overseas possessions. For the chancellor, imperialism—like his tax and tariff policies, his insurance scheme, and a variety of other issues which he raised after 1878—was an attempt to isolate enemies and rally friends, to build a basis of support and thus ease the tensions within the imperial system.[49] For many liberals, imperialism was a way of integrating a wide range of values and interests. In the first place, imperial expansion had long been advocated by a number of those leaders of commerce and industry who were to be found on the liberal right. These men saw the acquisition of colonies as a necessary response to the problems of the depression since they believed that colonies could be turned into secure markets and a profitable source of raw materials. Equally important, overseas expansion was seen by many as a way of consolidating the domestic order. This position, which merely extended arguments made by Treitschke and others well before 1884, emphasized the use of foreign political triumphs to rekindle a sense of national purpose. Finally, imperialism gave many liberals the sort of issue with which they had traditionally been most comfortable. Unlike social and economic matters or questions of domestic politics, a belief in the need to expand national power was something most of them shared, and it thus provided a particularly effective issue for the upcoming Reichstag elections. The cohesive influence of imperialism was particularly attractive to those who wished closer ties with other right-wing parties, especially with the Free Conservatives. In fact, National Liberals and Free Conservatives often served together in proimperialist organizations, thereby reinforcing personal and political alliances.[50]

The elections of 1884 were not a major triumph for the National Liberals, but the party did manage to stage a modest comeback. In a few districts, National Liberals were able to regain some of the ground lost to the left three years before. Elsewhere, the party benefited from the support of those who had previously voted for a conservative party. This was especially true outside of pre-1866 Prussia, where the Heidelberg Declaration facilitated the National Liberals' presentation of themselves as a governmental party.[51] At the same time, the number of electoral contests between the two wings of the liberal movement increased rather sharply, while the number of confrontations between National Liberals and one of the conservative parties declined.[52]

These developments were formalized during the election of 1887. In January of that year Bismarck dissolved the Reichstag when the Center and the left liberals combined to defeat his efforts to gain a new seven-year military budget.[53] The National Liberals and the two conservative parties, which had all supported the government, formed an electoral alliance. Each party agreed not to contest districts held by one of its allies; elsewhere they promised to seek a compromise candidate pledged to support the seven-year budget. The campaign was carried on within an atmosphere of foreign-political crisis which many believed would culminate in a war with France. As usual, the government did its best to exploit this situation by trying to link the domestic opponents of the army bill with the Reich's foreign enemies. The National Liberals were once again able to wage what Miquel called "a purely national battle" in which their own differences, as well as their disagreements with the conservatives, were hidden behind the banners of patriotism.[54] This enabled them to appeal to "all Germans ... who put the security and independence of the German Empire above the relentless assertion of party programs."[55] In fact, "all Germans" did not respond: the Social Democrats and the Center, for example, were both able to hang on to their electorates. But a large number of new voters did appear at the polls, and these men, together with a number of voters who defected from left-wing liberalism, gave the Kartell a significant electoral victory.[56]

The elections of 1887 were the culmination of National Liberalism's rightward shift in the eighties. But the Kartell Reichstag also showed the limitations of the right wing's ability to dominate the party. After 1887, a number of National Liberals found it impossible to convert their electoral cooperation with Bismarck and the two conservative parties into a productive political alliance. It turned out to be increasingly difficult for them to work with the Prussian Conservatives; moreover, by 1890 some liberals had begun to have grave doubts about Bismarck's domestic policies, especially those directed against Social Democracy. The National Liberals' restlessness in the Kartell was matched by the chancellor's own search for new political alignments.

During the election of 1890 he did little to support the Kartell and seems to
have been considering either a clerical-conservative alliance or a basic change
in the constitutional system which would alter the character and function of
the Reichstag.[57]

As important as these tensions within the parliament was the persistent
influence of regional diversity on National Liberalism. In parts of Prussia, for
example, National Liberal hostility to the Conservatives continued. During
the Landtag elections of 1885 and 1888, Conservative and National Liberal
candidates continued to confront one another in a number of eastern districts,
thus making a Prussian version of the Kartell extremely difficult to achieve.[58]
Moreover, despite the initial support for the Heidelberg program in parts of
Baden and Bavaria, the centrality of religious conflict in these states continued
to encourage cooperation among a variety of liberals, thereby creating a
situation quite different from that existing in states like Hesse, Württemberg or
Saxony.[59] Regional diversity was both reflected and reinforced by the National Liberals' loose organizational structure which inhibited the imposition
of any centralized and consistent policy on the party as a whole. Taken
together, these factors limited the right-wing's ability to move from its victories in 1884 and 1887 to a lasting position of unchallenged control over
party life. The movement to the right in the 1880s had produced a shift in the
party's center of gravity, but it did not enable National Liberals to pursue a
consistent and coherent set of political goals.

The Liberal Left and the Burdens of Opposition

> Our entire party life is in the process
> of dissolution. Bismarck is a consum-
> mate master of the art of destruction.
> One can only shudder at the thought of
> his political heritage's final liquidation.
>
> Theodor Barth (1887)[1]

Although the Progressives suffered severe losses in the Reichstag election of 1878 and the Prussian Landtag election of 1879, they did not experience the traumatic intraparty divisions which beset the National Liberals. Because they appealed to a relatively narrow range of socioeconomic groups, centered in Prussia, Progressives did not confront the diverse views on tax and tariff policy which confounded the larger liberal *Fraktion*. Moreover, the break-down of the "liberal era" was much less unsettling for the Fortschrittspartei. After all, it had begun as a party of opposition whereas the National Liberals' formative assumption had been that some measure of cooperation with the government was possible. It was almost with a sense of relief, therefore, that Richter announced Bismarck's return to the reactionary policies of the *Konfliktzeit*. He believed that resistance to the government would bring cohesion to the Progressives' ranks just as the opportunity for collaboration had divided them, first in 1867 and then again in 1874.[2] Another reason for the Progressives' solidarity was Richter himself: alone among liberal leaders of the 1870s, he had the energy, will, and organizational ability to create and manipulate a political movement in accord with his own strategic and ideological vision.

Richter's notion of what the Fortschrittspartei should be dominated the party's first national convention, held in Berlin during November 1878. This convention represented the Progressives' attempt to bring their program and organization up to date so that they could respond to the new turn in government policy and to the growth of their opponents on both the right and the left.[3]

The party program, eventually accepted by a majority of the convention delegates, began with a restatement of the party's original goals: the defense of constitutional rights and civil liberties and the advancement of the nation's material and moral well-being. The program went on to advocate the "development of a parliamentary constitution, with increased rights for the Reichstag and an imperial ministry responsible to it."[4] Although this statement was a great deal more specific than the vague references to parliamentary

power common in the sixties, the party stopped short of saying how the
"development of parliamentary government" was to take place. Nowhere do
we find a call for Bismarck's removal from office or the demand that he be
replaced by a ministry based on a parliamentary majority. Indeed, men like
Albert Hänel, who was one of the Progressives' most distinguished students
of constitutional affairs, continued to emphasize the importance of balancing
parliamentary power with a strong and independent state.[5]

The party was even more cautious in dealing with the issue of popular
participation. As one delegate pointed out, Progressives opposed both the
government and "the masses which threaten society." This attitude was
reflected in the party's position on the suffrage: the program defended an
unrestricted franchise for the Reichstag, but refrained from advocating its
extension to state and local elections. The qualifications which Progressives
placed on their support for democracy were even more clearly expressed in the
convention's rejection of demands by certain left-wing groups that the party
be reconstituted as a democratic organization pledged to the formation of a
broad antireactionary coalition. Richter emphasized that the Fortschrittspartei
of 1878 was the heir of the compromise between moderates and democrats
achieved in 1861 and not of the democratic forces of 1848. This meant that
other left-wing groups, such as the South German Volkspartei, would be
welcome allies only if they accepted the Progressives' position. As for the
Social Democrats, most delegates agreed with Rudolf Virchow's assertion
that they "are even more our enemies than the Conservatives." Officially, the
party continued to oppose special legislation against the Socialists, but in
1884 enough of them—apparently with Richter's tacit approval—voted for a
renewal of the anti-Socialist law to ensure that it would pass.[6]

A majority of the convention rejected amendments calling for a programmatic commitment to social reform. When Richter was reproached for
not taking an active interest in the "social question," he replied by invoking
the spirit of Schulze-Delitzsch. Social problems, he maintained, were basically cultural problems, best solved by education and self-help.[7] On this
crucial issue, therefore, the convention of 1878 showed no significant change
from the 1860s. Despite the massive changes which were transforming German society, the Progressives' answer to industrial workers and the urban
poor was what it had always been: become like us.

The political and social dimensions of the Progressives' program reflected
the values of those to whom the party had always looked for support: "the
independent, industrious, propertied elements in the middle of the good old
German Bürgertum." Table 14.1 makes clear the social groups which dominated the convention and provided the local notables who led the party in
cities and towns throughout Prussia: judges, city employees, teachers,

lawyers, journalists, businessmen (many of them with rather modest enterprises), a few artisans, and a great many farmers.[8]

Table 14.1   **The Social Composition of the Progressive Party Convention, 1878**

	No. (%)
Officials	
Administrative	1
Judicial	13 (4)
Local	21 (7)
Professors, teachers	13 (4)
Lawyers	30 (10)
Physicians and other academics	23 (8)
Writers, editors, journalists	36 (12)
Businessmen	76 (26)
Rentier	6 (2)
Craftsmen, innkeepers	11 (4)
Agricultural occupations	
Rittergutsbesitzer	1 —
Other	33 (11)
Miscellaneous and unknown	26 (9)
Total	290

SOURCE: Fortschrittspartei, *Parteitag* (1879), pp. 5 ff.

These men did not like the reactionary state but they also feared the implications of democracy. They knew they were vulnerable to the pressures of the administrative apparatus, but they also recognized that the Catholic and Socialist masses could sweep them out of office, both in national and local elections. As members of the middle strata, acutely conscious of their status as "independent" men, few of these individuals had much sympathy for the problems of industrial workers. They saw little reason to pay higher taxes in order to support state help for the dispossessed. Eugen Richter's power in the party was based on his ability to speak to and for these groups.

Richter's strategy for expanding his party's electoral base was to organize the German middle strata more effectively rather than to add new social groups to the Progressives' constituency. These organizational efforts were a major concern for the convention and dominated party activity during the years thereafter.[9] Under Richter's leadership, Progressives tried to form organizations throughout the Reich. In a large number of states, local Vereine were created and regional conventions were held. But at the same time, control over the party's program and tactics remained in Berlin. Policy-making power was in the hands of an executive committee composed of men from the two parliaments which met in the capital. In fact, Richter himself

dominated party life because of his key position on this committee and his
influence over the publications which transmitted information and decisions to
the local organizations. Like the party program, these local organizations
were primarily directed toward the middle strata. They sought to mobilize
men throughout the Reich who opposed both the reactionary state and the
radical left. In Richter's mind, the ideal local leader was not a charismatic
agitator but an efficient and obedient administrator who, like the stereotype of
a Prussian *Beamter*, would follow the policy formulated in Berlin.[10] In this
way, Richter, like so many other German liberals who tried to organize
resistance to the *Staat*, remained influenced by its values and procedures.

The program adopted by the Progressives' convention in 1878 and the
party's organizational activity reflected Richter's conviction that the
Fortschrittspartei was the only legitimate carrier of the liberal tradition and the
only real hope for liberalism's future. Because he was not willing to see his
organization absorbed into the "great liberal party" which was so important
in the rhetoric of the National Liberal left, he looked upon the Sezession
without much enthusiasm. The Progressives' official response to the defection
of the National Liberal left was formulated at a meeting of the executive
committee in early September 1880. The committee's statement acknowledged the Sezession as a "favorable event for the common liberal cause" but
emphasized that there were still a great many important differences between
the Sezession and the Fortschrittspartei. It would, therefore, be necessary "to
wait and see if it will be possible to reach an agreement about these differences and also to create sharper lines of demarcation from the other parties."[11] The implication of these remarks was clear enough: the members of
the Sezession would be welcome in the Progressive party if they accepted its
program and cut their own ties with the National Liberals.

Most of the secessionists were unwilling and unable to do this. In the first
place, they disliked and distrusted Richter. They found him personally obnoxious and looked upon his disciplined network of followers as authoritarianism
in liberal disguise.[12] They remained much more comfortable with the *Honoratioren* style, in which local notables cooperated through a loose set of
personal and informal organizations. Furthermore, the disengagement of the
Sezession from National Liberalism was a very complex process. It had been
simple enough for a few parliamentarians to leave the Berlin factions, but it
was extremely difficult to know what this would mean on the local level. Few
secessionists were so confident about their constituencies that they were prepared to engage in an all-out assault on their former colleagues. In public,
therefore, the secessionists and the National Liberals treated each other with
considerable caution as they tried to test and secure the loyalties of local

leaders and organizations. In some places, where the lines of political conflict were clearly drawn, this did not take long. Elsewhere, however, relationships between the two groups remained unsettled for quite some time.[13]

The final reason why the secessionists responded coolly to Richter was their continued hope for a unified movement in which they would provide the link between moderate men in both the Progressive and National Liberal parties.[14] In the spring and summer of 1881, therefore, the leaders of the Sezession tried to get the other liberal *Fraktionen* to join them in an electoral alliance.[15] They failed. Although National Liberals and Progressives did work together in some areas, neither party was willing to accept a nationwide agreement with the other. Instead Progressives and National Liberals ran against one another in forty-four districts during the Reichstag elections of 1881. The secessionists, on the other hand, challenged the National Liberals in only twelve districts and the Progressives in only two.[16]

One reason why Richter wanted no part of an alliance with the National Liberals was his belief that the tide of public opinion had turned in the Progressives' favor. As early as June 1880, he predicted a liberal victory comparable to the one in England which had swept Gladstone into office.[17] In fact, during 1880 and 1881, a new surge of energy was apparent throughout the Fortschrittspartei. The number of local Vereine doubled in this period (from forty to eighty-three), and nine regional conventions were held to coordinate further agitation. Some startling successes in Reichstag by-elections encouraged those who hoped for a major victory in the national elections scheduled for 1881.[18] Richter himself concentrated all of his formidable energies on this campaign. In speech after speech, he emphasized the Progressives' opposition to the government's political and economic program. He condemned Bismarck's efforts to diminish the Reichstag's authority and denounced those fiscal and tariff policies which hurt the consumer and middle-income taxpayer. He did not, however, demand Bismarck's resignation since he did not want to risk pitting his party against the chancellor's personal position. The issue, he insisted, was the system, not the man.[19]

The revitalization of the liberal left was part of a widespread mood of dissatisfaction which existed in many sectors of German society around 1880. In Hamburg, opposition to the imperial government helped to give the Socialists a victory in a Reichstag by-election held during the spring of 1880.[20] Elsewhere, there was a sharp increase in anti-Semitic agitation which turned social and economic frustrations against both the government and its supposedly "liberal" allies. After 1879, for example, Adolf Stoecker's *Berliner Bewegung* sought to use anti-Jewish feelings as a weapon against the Progressives; in the summer of 1881 there were scattered outbreaks of anti-Semitic violence in several Prussian cities.[21] During the summer and fall of

1881, while the Reichstag campaign was already underway, Landtag elections were held in Saxony, Baden, and Bavaria. In all three states those most closely associated with the imperial government's policies lost ground, in Saxony to the right, in the other two states to the Catholics.[22]

Opposition to the government also determined the outcome of the Reichstag elections. As Richter had hoped, the liberal left proved to be the chief beneficiary of this trend. The election results convinced Richter that a new liberal era was at hand. "The Conservatives," he confidently predicted, "have no future." Even Eduard Lasker, who had been so pessimistic about Germany's prospects just two years earlier, now believed that if only liberals could work together the next Reichstag elections might bring them a new majority.[23]

Table 14.2   **The Reichstag Election of 1881**

	Votes				WKe	
	Total (in 1,000s)	% of eligible voters	Change from 1878 (in 1,000s)	No.	% of all WKe	Change from 1878
National Liberals*	746.6	14.6	} −311	47	11.8	} −15
Liberale Vereinigung*	429.2	8.4		46	11.6	
Progressives	649.3	12.8	+ 264.2	60	15.1	+34
Volkspartei	103.4	2	+ 37.3	9	2.3	+6
Conservatives	830.8	16.3	+ 81.3	50	12.6	−9
Free Conservatives	379.3	7.5	−406.5	28	7.1	−29
Center	1,182.9	23.2	−145.2	100	25.2	+6
Poles, etc.	449	8.8	− 58.7	45	11.3	+5
SPD	312	6.1	−125.1	12	3	+3
Total	5,118.4	56.3	−662.5			

SOURCE: Vogel et al., *Wahlen* (1971), p. 291.
* Since these two parties did not run separately in 1878, the figures on their changes in strength have only limited meaning.

As even a cursory look at table 14.2 suggests, the elections of 1881 were not really a victory for liberalism as a whole, whose vote did not increase. The most significant shifts came *within* liberalism as the movement's left wing scored some impressive victories against the right. The two left-wing liberal parties took seats away from the National Liberals in different ways: the Progressives engaged them in direct electoral confrontations, whereas the Liberale Vereinigung most often won by securing the allegiance of candidates and local organizations before the voting began. The two conservative parties did suffer some significant setbacks in 1881. Among the seats newly acquired by one of the left liberal parties, at least thirty-two had been occupied by a Conservative or Free Conservative in 1878. Twenty-three of these were in eastern Prussia, where the liberal left was able to regain a

number of seats that had been lost to the Conservatives three years before. In
some districts, this happened because revitalized Progressive organizations
(especially in towns and cities) mobilized enough voters to win narrow victories. Elsewhere, however, there was a shift of voters to the left as striking as
the rightward shift which had occurred in 1878. The returns from Stettin-
Ueckermunde (Stettin WK 2) provide a vivid example: in 1877, with only 31
percent of those eligible voting, the National Liberals won over the Conservatives with 57 percent of the votes cast; in 1878, 49 percent participated and the
Conservatives won 71 percent of the vote; in 1881, 67 percent participated
and the Liberale Vereinigung won with 59 percent of the total. Left liberals
also made some gains outside of Prussia: in Württemberg, the Volkspartei
picked up three seats previously held by the Free Conservatives, who also
lost seats in Saxony, Hesse, and Schwarzburg. Throughout the Reich, the
Free Conservatives proved to be particularly vulnerable to the left's
attacks, probably because of their close identification with the government
and their customary disdain for political organizations and electoral agitation. The Conservatives, on the other hand, lost mandates but not voters.
Indeed, the fact that their total popular vote increased despite an overall
decline in participation indicates that Richter's obituary for German
conservatism was somewhat premature.

There is no doubt that the liberal left did extremely well in 1881; the
important question is, Why? Was their victory a sign that German voters were
opposed to the reactionary policies emanating from Berlin, to Bismarck's
purge of the administration and threats against the Reichstag? Richter thought
so. And if he was right, then he bears a great deal of responsibility for
allowing these political energies to dissipate so swiftly after 1881.[24] But it
seems likely that political motives played a smaller role in the minds of the
electorate than Richter believed and hoped. If one views the election within
the context of voting behavior before and after 1881, the leftward shift seems
to have come from social and economic discontents. A rise in retail prices, for
example, may well have been the most important reason for the Progressives'
success in Prussian cities and towns, whose inhabitants were looking for a
way to register their dislike of protective tariffs.[25] Elsewhere, government
support for a tobacco monopoly generated a great deal of antipathy among
those who would be directly affected by such a step. These issues, set within a
still fluid pattern of political alignments and a diffuse mood of unrest, were the
most important reason why so many Germans decided to vote for the liberal
left. The Progressives and secessionists, therefore, gained supporters in 1881
because they were able to convince them that voting for a left liberal was a
way of indicating their opposition to certain specific issues as well as their
general frustration with the status quo.[26] However, as would quickly become

apparent, liberals were not able to build on this support because they could not
find a way to absorb these voters into a sustained and cohesive drive for
political reform.

The years immediately following the elections of 1881 were difficult ones
for the leaders of all three liberal parties. As we have seen, it proved impossible for Bennigsen to steer a middle course against the prevailing winds from
the right wing of National Liberalism. And, as the National Liberals moved
right, the hopes of the Sezession for liberal unity had to fade. Despite some
support from within the Fortschrittspartei (but not, it should be noted, from
Richter), the secessionists were unable to get anything more than a highly
qualified arrangement among liberals for the Prussian Landtag election of
1882.[27] Finally, the results of this election made it painfully apparent that
Richter's hopes for a new liberal era had no firm foundations.

Table 14.3 summarizes the overall changes in the Landtag's composition
produced by the elections. As these data indicate, the decline of liberal
strength which began in 1879 continued. The record of seats won and lost in
each province, given in table 14.4, shows that the Progressives' losses to the
Conservatives were much more substantial than the total vote would indicate.
The Conservatives' increasing domination of the countryside, together with
the effects of unequal, indirect, and public voting, seem to have prevented the
radical shifts in voter preference which had occurred in the Reichstag elections of 1881. Once the *Wahlmänner* in rural areas and in the villages and
towns dependent on these areas shifted to the right, they tended to stay there.
The left was able to compensate for these losses to the Conservatives by
taking seats from the National Liberals; as in 1881, the liberal electorate

Table 14.3	The Political Composition of the Prussian Chamber of Deputies, 1882	
	Before election No. (%)	After election No. (%)
National Liberals	87 (20)	68 (16)
Liberale		
Vereinigung	20 (4.6)	20 (4.6)
Progressives	40 (9)	39 (9)
All liberals	*147 (34)*	*127 (29)*
Conservatives	113 (26)	136 (31)
Free Conservatives	53 (12)	50 (11.5)
Center	99 (23)	100 (23)
Poles, etc.	21 (5)	20 (4.6)
Total	433	433

SOURCE: *EGK 1882*, p. 187.

Table 14.4   **The Impact of the Landtag Elections
of 1882 by Province**

	National Liberals	Lib. Vereinigung	Prog.	Cons.	Free Cons.	Center	Poles, etc.
	No. of seats won (net change)						
Province	National Liberals	Lib. Vereinigung	Prog.	Cons.	Free Cons.	Center	Poles, etc.
Ostpreussen	1 (+1)	1 (−1)	2 (−10)	21 (+9)	3 (+1)	4	—
Westpreussen	4	3	3 (−1)	3 (+1)	4 (−1)	1 (+1)	4
Brandenburg	(−2)	2 (+1)	9 (−2)	27 (+2)	7 (+1)	—	—
Pommern	—	1	—	23	2	—	—
Posen	1 (−2)	—	3 (+2)	7	4 (+1)	—	14 (−1)
Silesia	2 (−9)	6	3 (+3)	24 (+5)	5 (−2)	25 (+3)	
Saxony	6 (−5)	3	1 (+1)	13	13 (+4)	2	—
Schleswig-Holstein	7	1	6 (+2)	1	2 (−2)	—	2
Hanover	27	—	—	—	5	4	—
Westphalia	5 (−2)	—	4 (+2)	6 (+1)	1	15 (−1)	—
Hesse-Nassau	4 (−2)	2 (−1)	7 (+2)	9 (+1)	1	3	—
Rhineland	11 (+2)	1	1	2	3 (−1)	46 (−1)	—
Total	68	20	39	136	50	100	20

SOURCE: *EGK 1882*, pp. 186–90.

(presumably concentrated in the cities) tended to vote for a candidate associated with liberalism's left wing.[28]

The Progressives' defeats in the elections of 1882 were accompanied by other symptoms of diminished energy within the party. Fund raising became more difficult, qualified candidates became hard to find, and there was an overall decline in the level of party activity throughout the Reich. These problems weakened the force of Richter's main objection to closer ties with the Sezession since they raised doubts about the Progressives' autonomous ability to renew the liberal movement. By the beginning of 1884, therefore, Richter was prepared to listen to those who had always been sympathetic to a fusion of the two left-liberal groups. Meanwhile, a willingness to join with the Progressives increased within the Sezession: the National Liberals' shift to the right, together with the government's increasingly reactionary course, underscored the need for sustained cooperation before the national elections scheduled for 1884. Moreover, a few members of the Sezession wanted to construct as broad a political base as possible for what they hoped would be a liberal regime under the leadership of Crown Prince Frederick William.[29]

Formal negotiations between the two liberal parties began in January 1884. There were some doubts and disagreements on both sides, but in the end the two merged into what was called the Deutsche Freisinnige Partei. A program was published on March 5 and ratified in separate conventions held a few days later.[30] In part, the program represented a compromise between the two parties: for example, it began with a call for parliamentary government, despite Ludwig Bamberger's conviction that this "old war horse" would be better left unmentioned, but the Progressives' insistence on an annual military budget was replaced by the demand for a budget to be determined within each Reichstag period, in other words, every three years. Most of the rest of the program merely restated in general terms the familiar demands and dissatisfactions of the liberal left: defense of the Reichstag suffrage (but no call for its extension to other elections), opposition to "state socialism" (Bismarck's welfare legislation), condemnation of tariff policies based on special interests (protectionism), and so on.

The Freisinnige program was another example of the liberals' ability to reconcile diverse views rhetorically. But as the basis for a counteroffensive against the Bismarckian system, the program left a great deal to be desired. The two central political questions facing the Reich—suffrage inequalities in state and local elections and the position of Bismarck—were scrupulously avoided. Equally important, the material needs of large sectors of the population were ignored. It may well have been that a vigorous and consistent campaign against the chancellor would not have succeeded; perhaps even the attempt to mount such a campaign would have cost the liberal left a large part of its support among the middle strata without enabling it to gain ground among workers and other lower class and status groups. But whatever the outcome might have been, the program of 1884 made clear that the leaders of left-wing liberalism were not prepared to embark upon the perilous road of mass-based opposition. They chose instead to continue on the more familiar, but in the end no less difficult, path of qualified resistance to both reaction and democracy.

The liberal left's ability to oppose the state was also limited by the fact that behind the near unanimous approval of their common program a great deal of the antagonism between the two parties remained. Although the statutes of the Freisinnige Partei called for an institutional fusion of the two groups, the Progressives' organizational network continued to be in Richter's hands and was still largely dependent for its support on the urban middle strata of Prussia. The Sezession leaders, on the other hand, tried to maintain the *Honoratioren* style with which they were most comfortable and continued to do best in some scattered districts with rural or small-town constituencies.[31] Moreover, some substantive issues remained, especially military and foreign policy, because here the old National Liberal left retained a somewhat greater willingness to defer to the government. Considering these differences—

personal, organizational, and ideological—it is hardly surprising that the unity achieved in 1884 was frequently strained and eventually broken by the vicissitudes which the left had to suffer in the years thereafter.[32]

The Reichstag elections of 1884 brought the shape of these vicissitudes into somewhat sharper focus.[33] As table 14.5 shows, the liberal left was the only group to lose voters in an election which saw a sharp rise in participation; as a result it had to relinquish a number of mandates conquered in 1881. The greatest concentration of losses by the Freisinnigen were in Altpreussen, where the Conservatives won back seventeen districts; all but three of these were in predominately rural, eastern areas. One cannot know with certainty if these victories came from a defection of formerly liberal voters, but in most districts the Conservatives' total vote increased while the liberals' declined. It is likely, therefore, that a rightward shift did take place, although in some areas liberal voters may have simply dropped out of electoral politics in the face of mounting Conservative pressures. The returns from Stettin's Wahlkreis 2 reflects the instability in voting behavior which continued in many Prussian districts: in 1881, with 67 percent of those eligible voting, the Liberale Vereinigung had received 59 percent of the vote, the Conservatives 40 percent; in 1884, with 58 percent voting, the Conservatives won 62 percent and the Freisinnige Partei 36 percent.[34] In eight of the districts won by the Conservatives, voter preferences seem to have stabilized in 1884; these districts remained Conservative through the rest of the imperial period.

Table 14.5   **The Reichstag Election of 1884**

| | Votes | | | | WKe | |
| | Total (in 1,000s) | % of eligible voters | Change from 1881 (in 1,000s) | No. | % of all WKe | Change from 1881 |
Party						
National Liberals	997	17.6	+250.4	51	12.8	+4
Freisinnige Partei	997	17.6	−81.5*	67	16.9	−37
Volkspartei	95.9	1.7	−7.5	7	1.8	−2
Conservatives	861.1	15.2	+30.3	78	19.6	+28
Free Conservatives	387.7	6.9	+8.4	28	7.1	—
Center	1,282	22.6	+99.1	99	24.9	−1
Poles, etc.	479.6	8.5	+30.6	43	10.9	−2
SPD	550	9.7	+238	24	6	+2
Total	5,681.7	60.5	+563.3			

SOURCE: Vogel et al., *Wahlen* (1971), p. 291.
* This was computed by subtracting the 1884 total from the combined total vote of the Progressives and the Liberale Vereinigung in 1881.

The left liberals also lost eight *Wahlkreise* to the Free Conservatives. In five of these, the Free Conservatives provided a compromise candidate who united conservative and right-wing liberal voters. This was the case, for instance, in Saxony's *Wahlkreis* 20 where the Free Conservatives were able to win a first-ballot victory with 70 percent of the vote; three years earlier a second-ballot alliance between Progressives and Socialists had defeated the Conservatives by a two-to-one margin. Despite their successes in 1884, however, the Free Conservatives were unable to consolidate their support; none of the districts they won remained in their hands permanently. As was pointed out in the last chapter, the election of 1884 also produced a shift to the right within liberalism: the National Liberals gained mandates and voters, sometimes because of defections from the left, sometimes because of newly won support from nonvoters or former supporters of a right-wing party.

An equally dangerous portent of left liberalism's future was the number of seats lost to the Social Democrats: seven previously held by the Progressives, two by the Liberale Vereinigung, and one by the Volkspartei. Eight of these were in large cities; six had returned a liberal representative since the beginning of the Reich. As was the case with the Conservatives, the Socialists' success seems to have come in part from their ability to attract liberal voters: in all of the districts where they won, the Socialist vote increased while the left liberals' declined.[35] In most areas, however, the principal reason for the Socialists' success was the way in which they could encourage and contain large numbers of new voters. This was especially true in rapidly expanding urban and industrial districts such as the two Berlin *Wahlkreise* which the SPD took from the Progressives, where the total number of eligible voters increased from fifty to seventy thousand between 1881 and 1884. Finally, in three districts the left liberals' defeat by the Socialists was facilitated by the liberals' simultaneous loss of support to the right. These areas reproduced in microcosm the overall trend of the election in the Reich as a whole.

The unfortunate outcome of the elections in 1884 was repeated three years later.[36] As can be seen in table 14.6, despite a massive increase in the number of Germans who went to the polls, the total popular vote for the left liberals decreased—the only group for which this was the case. The left liberals' weakness in 1887 was also demonstrated by their inability to elect a candidate on the first ballot in more than ten districts. In sixteen others, that is, half their eventual total, they owed their second-ballot success to the Socialists' willingness to vote for a left liberal rather than for a candidate from a right-wing party. Without this support, it is possible that left-wing liberalism might have disappeared from the national scene. Eugen Richter's expectations about a liberal majority based on the Fortschrittspartei, which had seemed possible

Division and Decline
1877–90

Table 14.6   **The Reichstag Election of 1887**

Party	Votes			WKe		
	Total (in 1,000s)	% of eligible voters	Change from 1884 (in 1,000s)	No.	% of all WKe	Change from 1884
National Liberals	1,678	22.2	+681	99	24.9	+48
Freisinnige Partei	973.1	12.9	−23.9	32	8.1	−35
Volkspartei	88.8	1.2	−7.1	—	—	−7
Conservatives	1,147.2	15.2	+286.1	80	20.2	+2
Free Conservatives	736.4	9.8	+348.7	41	10.3	+13
Center	1,516.2	20.1	+234.2	98	24.7	−1
Poles, etc.	578.9	7.5	+99.3	33	8.3	−10
SPD	763.1	10.1	+213.1	11	2.8	−13
Anti-Semites	11.6	.2	—	1	.2	+1
Total	7,570.7	77.5	+1,889			

SOURCE: Vogel et al., *Wahlen* (1971), p. 291.

just six years earlier, were now shattered. As Ludwig Bamberger bitterly observed:

> The elections of 1887 ... were a true expression of German public opinion: Junkers and Catholics, who both see clearly what they want, and a naive, childish *Bürgertum*, which is politically inept and desires neither freedom nor justice.[37]

German electoral development from 1877 to 1887 vividly illustrates the double bind in which the liberal left found itself. First of all, the steady growth of Conservatives in the Progressives' old bastions of eastern Prussia reflected the new electoral vitality of the liberals' enemies on the right. This vitality was partly due to the support Conservatives gained from the bureaucratic establishment, but it also came from that party's ability to mobilize rural voters by appealing to their common economic interests, especially the need for protective tariffs. The Progressives' strong ties to the urban groups which supported free trade made them unwilling and unable to counter this appeal. Second, the elections of 1878, 1884, and 1887 showed that an important sector of the left's constituency was susceptible to certain kinds of appeals by the government and its political supporters: when opposition to Socialism, support for imperialism, or military policy provided the focus for an election campaign, the left found itself deserted by an important number of former supporters and opposed by many new voters attracted by the government's propaganda. To counter these currents would not only have gone against left-wing liberals' principles, it would also have increased the already danger-ous erosion of part of their constituency to the Socialists.

If the election of 1887 demolished Richter's hopes for a liberal *Volk*, the events of 1888 destroyed the hopes of those who looked to Crown Prince Frederick William as the leader of a new liberal era. For some time, a few men associated with the old National Liberal left had had contracts with Frederick William's court. These men hoped that when the prince became emperor, his progressive impulses would create a new political climate in the Reich. This turned out to be the most pathetic instance of the liberals' persistent belief that an intervention from above could save them from the results of their own failures. It was pathetic not only because the crown prince was terminally ill by the time his father died, but also because there was so little in his character and conduct upon which to base optimistic expectations about a liberal reign. The second empire's "liberal" emperor did not alter the system he inherited; he ruled, in silence, for just ninety-nine days.[38]

The Kartell's victory in 1887 and the short, sterile reign of Frederick III were both apparent victories for Bismarck. But neither the new Reichstag nor the new emperor, Frederick's son William, turned out to be a reliable basis for the chancellor's power. By 1890, Bismarck again embarked on a search for ways to stabilize the Reich—a sure sign that many of the "Second *Reichsgründung*'s" goals were still unrealized. The collapse of the Kartell demonstrated that efforts to create a conservative elite of propertied men within the parliament had failed. The Reichstag's continued concern for political issues showed that Bismarck had not been able to displace political awareness with economic interests; in fact, by encouraging the penetration of economic interests into party life, he had inadvertently linked political conflicts with the struggle between interest groups.[39] Finally, those whom Bismarck had designated as *Reichsfeinde* continued to flourish: the national minorities, the Catholics, and especially the Social Democrats, who, after twelve years of repression, now showed signs of unprecedented vitality. Is it any wonder, therefore, that as the Bismarckian era drew to a close, the chancellor's thoughts turned to violence, to a *Staatsstreich* which would banish once and for all the unresolved conflicts which flawed the Reich?[40]

One goal of the "Second *Reichsgründung*," however, had been achieved: the "liberal era" was over. By 1890, liberal sentiments within the administration had been significantly reduced. Furthermore, key elements within German society—business groups and academics, farmers and craftsmen—had begun to abandon their allegiance to liberal goals even if many of them continued to vote for a liberal party. In the Reichstag and in a number of state parliaments, the liberal movement had been reduced to an uncertain and deeply divided minority.

By the end of the 1880s, many of those who had guided liberalism since the

Reichsgründung had given up politics. Some had died, others retired, still others watched from the sidelines while their dreams dissolved.[41] Friedrich Kapp, for example, who had returned from America to bask in the warmth of the liberal era, withdrew from political life because he could not stand the new demands placed upon those seeking electoral office. Kapp prided himself on being an "independent man" without special interests, whereas the new politician had "to want something for himself" and had become, without knowing it, "part of the herd [*Herdenvieh*]."[42] This sense that the tone and style of political activity were no longer compatible with an individual's personal and public ideals had always troubled some liberals and it troubled a great many more after 1880. Some responded by withdrawing into the more comfortable confines of local government or turning to the immediate pleasures of private life. In both liberal parties, it was often difficult to find men willing to run for office and to assume positions of responsibility in political affairs.[43] The belief that politics was no longer the proper task for a respectable member of the *Bürgertum* was yet another sign that the foundations of liberalism were eroding.

Those who remained politically active were often conscious that their day had passed. Even Eugen Richter was forced to retreat somewhat from an increasingly empty optimism. In a book published in 1881, Richter had predicted a parliamentary government for the Reich in the "near future," but in the 1889 edition the word "near" was quietly dropped.[44] Others were much less restrained in expressing their discomfort with the direction of events. By 1885, Georg von Siemens had decided that "parliamentarism" throughout Europe had become "a rather questionable form of government." After all, Siemens asked, "What is the majority? The majority is irrational; understanding is always to be found only in a few men." Two years later, having tasted the bitter defeat of 1887, Ludwig Bamberger wrote, "German parliamentarism was only an episode . . . . Never mind." And finally, Hermann Baumgarten, whose critique of liberalism in 1866 foreshadowed so much of what was to follow, lamented to his colleague Sybel in 1890 that "the time in which our ideals had power is gone, perhaps forever."[45]

VI

The Wilhelmine Age
1890–1914

In March 1890, the young emperor William II forced Bismarck to resign.[1] The first chancellor's fall from power soon became a line of demarcation for contemporaries, and it has remained one of those "turning points" with which historians punctuate their narratives. Although this convention is followed here, it should be emphasized that the most significant changes taking place in late nineteenth-century Germany cannot be reduced to a discrete chronological point and were not tied to the career of a single man. These changes had been building for decades and eventually they touched the lives of almost every German. They include a dramatic increase in population, massive movements of men and women into new environments, the growth of new sorts of occupations, the dissolution of old patterns of social interaction, and the slow emergence of new kinds of relationships and values.[2] To follow the course of German history after 1890, therefore, one must look beyond the events which brought a new tenant to the chancellor's office on Berlin's Wilhelmstrasse. Of course Bismarck's dismissal was important, but the end of the social world upon which his policies had been based was far more critical, both for Germany and for liberalism.

The following chapters examine the development of the liberal parties in what might be called the "postliberal" age. First, it will be necessary to draw the dimensions of the movement and to show the institutional nexus which united (and divided) its supporters. Then the social location of the movement can be defined by establishing the nature and relationship of the groups which remained part of the liberal constituency. Finally, an old problem will be viewed in its new setting: the long-standing conflict within liberalism between left and right, between the advocates of freedom and order, the *Volk* and the *Staat*.

15 From Movement to Minority

"We have become millions—that is the basic political principle of an industrial nation."

Friedrich Naumann (1900)[1]

Between 1871 and 1912, the years of the first and the last imperial election, the size of the German electorate doubled, while the number of those actually going to the polls tripled.[2] The liberals' failure to attract their share of these new voters reduced them to the status of a permanent minority. The graphs in figures 15.1, 15.2, and 15.3 trace the dimensions of this failure: the deterioration of the liberal parties' *relative* electoral strength and the rather more dramatic decline in the number of districts which they were able to win. As these graphs suggest, the liberals' decline was matched by the Social Democrats' advance. By 1912, the Socialists were able to win or at least reach the second ballot in two-thirds of all *Wahlkreise* with a Protestant majority. They had, in other words, been able to gain the lion's share of those voters—or more precisely, those Protestant voters—who had entered participatory politics after 1890.[3] Unfortunately for the liberals, they were unable to balance losses to the Social Democrats with victories over the Center party or over the representatives of a national minority. Despite a significant erosion of Catholics from its ranks, the Center held on to eighty-one districts throughout the Wilhelmine period.[4] In addition, some twenty other districts returned a Polish, Alsatian, or Danish delegate. This meant that besides the mandates lost to the SPD, about one hundred others—one-fourth of the total—were permanently closed to a liberal candidate.

Whereas the liberals' electorate was usually divided from that of the Socialists and Catholics by relatively clear-cut barriers, liberals, conservatives, and radical right-wing groups tended to compete for the same kind of voters, those belonging to the Protestant "middle strata." This means that the relationship between liberals' electoral fortunes and those of the right-wing parties was extremely complex. In some areas, there was a marked instability in voter alignment and rapid movements from one of these parties to another. Elsewhere, the parties combined or entered into close alliances.

As the overall position of the liberals deteriorated, the relative position of the two wings of the movement tended to equalize (see figures 15.4 and 15.5).

In 1890, conditions favorable to the left (high food prices, widespread dis-satisfaction with the government) produced a series of Progressive victories, many of them at the expense of National Liberalism.[5] But if the electlon of 1890 resembled that of 1881, the election of 1893 was like that of 1884 or of 1887 because in 1893 a controversy over military spending enabled the Na-tional Liberals to mobilize patriotic voters and regain some of the districts they had lost three years earlier. Thereafter, the number of districts exchanged between left- and right-wing liberals decreased and active conflict between them became confined to a few regions. Gradually, the right and left became roughly the same size, until by 1912 each accounted for about half of the movement's total strength.[6]

Although the decline of liberalism in national elections can also be seen in the data on state and local representative institutions, the timing and mag-nitude of this decline differed from one region to another. These differences were shaped by the persistence of regional diversity within the Reich and, more directly, by the variety of suffrage systems which provided a constitu-tional basis for the incongruence between national and local politics.[7]

The best examples of this incongruence were the two parliaments which met in Berlin. Despite some fitful efforts at reform, the three-class suffrage system for the Prussian Landtag survived until 1918 and thereby blocked the democratic pressures which had transformed the Reichstag. In the Prussian chamber, therefore, the pattern of political alignments which emerged in the late seventies remained virtually intact: the liberal majority destroyed by the resurgence of the right in 1879 never reappeared; the Center held on to about 100 seats, the two conservative parties about 200, and the two liberal parties about 110 (see table 15.1).[8]

Unlike the situation in Prussia, the political composition of the Saxon Landtag, which is given in table 15.2, changed rather dramatically in the course of the Wilhelmine period. There was no region in Saxony comparable to East Elbian Prussia, where an entrenched Conservative party could win every election. Moreover, political Catholicism was weak and thus did not dominate a fairly stable number of districts as it did in both Prussia and the Reich. Finally, two significant changes in the election laws had an immediate impact on the political fortunes of the parties. In 1896, Conservatives and National Liberals became alarmed by the Socialists' increasing strength in the Landtag and pushed through a law establishing a three-class suffrage system. A decade of right-wing hegemony followed. In 1909 liberals supported a highly complicated system of weighted voting that more clearly reflected the social and political character of the Saxon population. This resulted in a shift to the left and a correspondingly rapid decline in Conservative strength.[9]

The sharp conflicts between left and right that shaped the course of Saxon

Fig. 15.1.   **Reichstag elections, 1890–1912 (total vote, first ballot)**

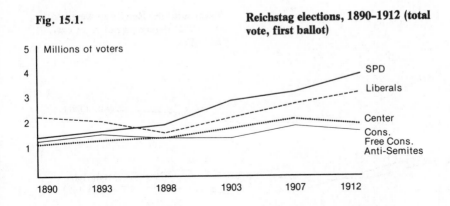

Fig. 15.2.   **Reichstag elections, 1890–1912 (percentage of votes cast, first ballot)**

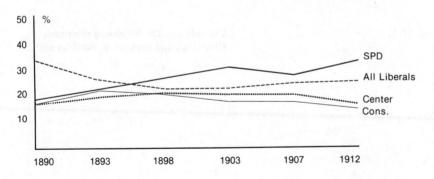

Fig. 15.3.   **Reichstag elections, 1890–1912 (percentage of districts won)**

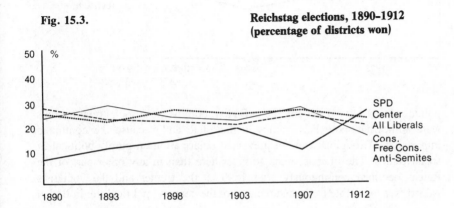

Fig. 15.4.   **Liberals and the Reichstag elections,
                                        1890–1912 (percentage of votes cast,
                                        first ballot)**

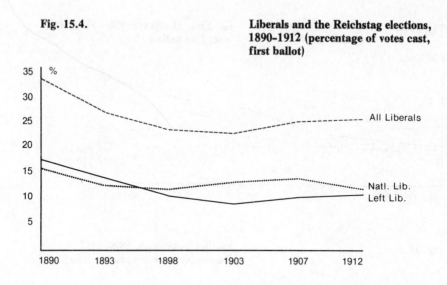

Fig. 15.5   **Liberals and the Reichstag elections,
                                        1890–1920 (percentage of districts won)**

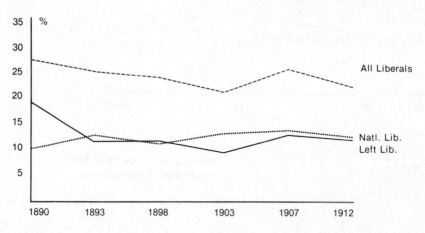

politics after 1890 did not emerge in Baden, both because social relationships
were somewhat more harmonious in that state and because the continued
importance of religious conflict prevented polarization on purely political or
social issues. The liberals, once stronger here than in any other part of the
Reich, declined continuously after 1890 as the Center and the Socialists
gained (see table 15.3). Around the turn of the century, political life in Baden

was dominated by a tripartite relationship among these three groups, with liberals and Catholics more or less evenly divided and the Social Democrats allying with one side or the other depending on the issue at stake. A turning point came in 1905 when the introduction of direct voting further undermined the liberals' position and threatened to produce a Center majority. This threat provided the basis for an alliance between liberals and Socialists which halted the Center's advance but greatly strengthened the Socialists' position. Just before the war, the Center and the National Liberals moved toward an alliance against the Socialists. But by this time, the best liberals could do was to prevent either of their opponents from dominating; the days of their own hegemony were clearly gone forever.[10]

In Bavaria, as in Baden, the growth of Social Democracy produced changes in the long-standing battle between liberals and Catholics. But whereas Badenese liberals and Socialists joined to prevent a Catholic majority, Bavarian Socialists and Catholics united against the liberals, largely because of liberal resistance to electoral reform. As a result, the liberals' parliamentary decline was accelerated. As can be seen in table 15.4, the elections of 1899 and 1905 cost liberals over forty seats. In 1912, under the new suffrage law which they had opposed for so long, agreements with the Socialists enabled liberals to make a slight recovery. Nevertheless, the formation of the Hertling ministry that year underscored the fact that liberalism, both in the Landtag and in the government, had ceased to be a powerful influence on Bavarian political life.[11]

Unlike in Bavaria and Baden, party alignments in Württemberg had originally been formed by national rather than religious conflicts. In the 1890s, however, the social and political forces at work throughout Germany began to disrupt the configuration of parties created during the *Reichsgründung*. In the state elections of 1895, the Deutsche Partei, which had originated as a pro-Prussian coalition of liberals and moderate conservatives, began to lose its constituency to the left and the right (see table 15.5). At the same time, the Center, which had been organized in Württemberg only the year before, made a dramatic electoral debut by winning twenty Landtag seats. Finally, the Volkspartei, whose core was made up of those who had once opposed the Bismarckian Reich, now began to pick up support from left-wing liberals throughout the state. The ascendancy of the Volkspartei lasted until the turn of the century when its position on the left was challenged by the growing strength of Social Democracy. Both the Socialists and the right wing benefited from a constitutional reform in 1906 which increased the number of delegates elected by popular voting. In the last prewar election, therefore, the Volkspartei found itself caught between an increasingly powerful labor movement and a right-wing coalition of Catholics and Conservatives.[12]

In Hesse, the Wilhelmine era opened with the National Liberals in firm contol of the Landtag. The absence of an independent conservative party, the relatively small number of Catholics, limitations on the suffrage, and widespread voter apathy all played into the liberals' hands. But here, as in the other *Mittelstaaten,* liberals proved unable to contain the growing pressure of economic, social, and political conflict. The most dangerous source of this pressure was the radical right, whose strength made Hesse the heartland of prewar anti-Semitism. A great many of the right-wing's supporters were men who had formerly voted for the National Liberals. This shift to the right, together with small gains by the left liberals, Center, and Social Democrats, effectively destroyed the liberal majority (see table 15.6).[13]

The incongruence which persisted between national and state politics was even more pronounced in the composition of urban representative institutions. In Hamburg, which was both an important urban center and one of the empire's twenty-six states, local government remained in the hands of a patrician

Table 15.1   **The Political Composition of the Prussian Chamber of Deputies, 1879–1913**

Party	1879 No. (%)	1882 No. (%)	1885 No. (%)	1888 No. (%)	1893 No. (%)	1898 No. (%)	1903 No. (%)	1908 No. (%)	1913 No. (%)
National Liberals	104 (24)	66 (15)	72 (16)	86 (20)	84 (19)	75 (17)	79 (18)	65 (14)	71 (16)
Left Liberals*	38 (9)	53 (12)	40 (9)	29 (6.6)	20 (4.6)	36 (8)	32 (7)	36 (8)	40 (9)
Conservatives	110 (25)	122 (28)	133 (31)	129 (30)	144 (33)	144 (33)	143 (33)	152 (34)	148 (33.8)
Free Conservatives	51 (12)	57 (13)	62 (14)	64 (15)	65 (15)	58 (13)	59 (13.6)	60 (13.5)	54 (12)
Center	97 (22)	99 (23)	98 (22.6)	98 (22.6)	95 (22)	100 (23)	97 (22.4)	104 (23)	102 (23)
Poles	19 (4)	18 (4)	15 (3)	15 (3)	17 (4)	13 (3)	13 (3)	15 (3)	12 (3)
SPD	—	—	—	—	—	—	—	7 (1.5)	10 (2)
No Fraktion	14 (3)	18 (4)	13 (3)	12 (3)	8 (2)	7 (1.6)	10 (2)	4	3
Total	433	433	433	433	433	433	433	443	440

SOURCE: Vogel et al., *Wahlen* (1971), p. 287.
* Includes the Fortschrittspartei in 1879, the Fortschrittspartei and the Liberale Vereinigung in 1882, the Deutsche Freisinnige in 1885 and 1888, the Freisinnige Vereinigung and the Freisinnige Volkspartei from 1893 to 1908, and the Fortschrittliche Volkspartei in 1913.

Table 15.2   **The Political Composition of the Saxon Chamber of Deputies, 1881–1913**

Party	1881 No. (%)	1885 No. (%)	1889 No. (%)	1893 No. (%)	1897 No. (%)	1901 No. (%)	1905 No. (%)	1909 No. (%)	1913 No. (%)
National Liberals*	16 (20)	14 (17.5)	13 (16)	14 (17)	21 (25)	22 (27)	24 (29)	28 (31)	29 (32)
Left Liberals**	15 (19)	14 (17.5)	12 (15)	9 (11)	3 (3.6)	2 (2)	2 (2)	8 (9)	8 (9)
Conservatives	45 (56)	47 (59)	48 (60)	43 (52)	50 (61)	58 (71)	54 (66)	23 (25)	29 (32)
Free Conservatives	—	—	—	—	—	—	—	1	—
Radical Right	—	—	—	2 (2)	—	—	1	6 (6.5)	—
SPD	4 (5)	5 (6)	7 (9)	14 (17)	8 (10)	—	1	25 (27)	25 (27)
Total	80	80	80	82	82	82	82	91	91

SOURCE: Saxony, *StJb* (1912), p. 18, for 1881–1909; Kalkoff, *Parlamentarier* (1917), p. 303, for 1913.
NOTE: In Saxony part of the Chamber was elected every two years; this table gives the composition at the end of every other election.
* Included here are also those who simply give their party as *liberal*.
** Includes Fortschrittspartei and Freisinnige Partei.

Table 15.3   **The Political Composition of the Badenese Chamber of Deputies, 1881–1913**

Party	1881 No. (%)	1885 No. (%)	1889 No. (%)	1893 No. (%)	1897 No. (%)	1901 No. (%)	1905 No. (%)	1909 No. (%)	1913 No. (%)
National Liberals	31 (50)	43 (69)	47 (74)	30 (47)	25 (40)	24 (38)	23 (31)	17 (23)	20 (27)
Left Liberals*	5 (8)	5 (8)	2 (3)	5 (8)	7 (11)	7 (11)	6 (8)	7 (9.5)	6 (8)
Conservatives	3 (5)	1	1	2 (3)	2 (3)	1	3 (4)	2 (3)	5 (7)
Radical Right	—	—	—	—	2 (3)	2 (3)	1	1	—
Center	23 (37)	14 (22.5)	13 (20.6)	23 (36)	21 (34)	23 (36.5)	28 (38)	26 (35)	29 (40)
SPD	—	—	—	3 (4.6)	5 (8)	6 (9.5)	12 (16)	20 (27)	13 (18)
No Fraktion	—	—	—	1	—	—	—	—	—
Total	62	62	63	64	62	63	73	73	73

SOURCE: Kalkoff, *Parlamentarier* (1917), p. 371.
NOTE: The chamber was partially renewed every two years. This table, therefore, gives the composition of the chamber at the end of every other election.
* Democrats, Fortschrittspartei, and Freisinnige Partei.

Table 15.4   **The Political Composition of the
                                        Bavarian Chamber of Deputies,
                                        1881–1912**

Party	1881 No. (%)	1887 No. (%)	1893 No. (%)	1899 No. (%)	1905 No. (%)	1907 No. (%)	1912 No. (%)
Patriots/Center	89 (55.9)	79 (50)	74 (46.5)	83 (52.2)	102 (64)	98 (60)	87 (53.3)
Liberals*	70 (44)	70 (44)	67 (42)	44 (27.6)	22 (13.8)	25 (15.3)	30 (18.4)
Volkspartei	—	1	1	1	2 (1.2)	—	—
Conservatives, etc.	—	5 (3.1)	3 (1.8)	6 (3.7)	4 (2.5)	6 (3.6)	7 (4.2)
Bavarian Bauernbund, etc.	—	—	9 (5.6)	12 (7.5)	15 (9.4)	13 (8)	8 (4.9)
SPD	—	—	5 (3.1)	11 (6.9)	12 (7.5)	20 (12.2)	30 (18.4)
Miscellaneous and unknown	—	4 (2.5)	—	2 (1.2)	2 (1.2)	1	1
Total	159	159	159	159	159	163	163

SOURCE: Möckl, *Prinzregentenzeit* (1972), pp. 213, 461, 488, 532, 541, 546.
* Party labels vary; these figures include those listed as "Liberal" as well as "Freisinnige," etc.

Table 15.5   **The Political Composition of the
                                        Württemberg Chamber of Deputies,
                                        1895–1912**

Party	1895 No. (%)	1900 No. (%)	1906 No. (%)	1912 No. (%)
Deutsche Partei/National Liberals	10 (14)	12 (17)	13 (14)	10 (11)
Volkspartei	31 (44)	28 (40)	23 (25)	19 (20.6)
Conservatives and other right-wing groups	1	6 (8.5)	15 (16)	20 (21)
Center	18 (26)	18 (26)	25 (27)	26 (28)
SPD	2 (3)	5 (7)	16 (17)	17 (18)
No Fraktion or unknown	8 (11)	1	—	—
Total	70	70	92	92

SOURCE: Schlemmer, "Rolle" (1953), p. viii.
NOTE: This table does not include the twenty-three members of the chamber who were not elected by popular vote before the reform of 1906.

Table 15.6   **The Political Composition of the**
Hessian Chamber of Deputies,
1878–1914

Party	1878–81 No. (%)	1884–87 No. (%)	1890–93 No. (%)	1893–96 No. (%)	1900–1902 No. (%)	1905–8 No. (%)	1911–14 No. (%)
National Liberals	40 (80)	37 (74)	37 (74)	32 (64)	22 (44)	18 (36)	17 (29)
Left Liberals	1	4 (8)	5 (10)	5 (10)	2 (4)	3 (6)	8 (14)
Conservatives	1	1	1	—	—	—	—
Radical Right	—	—	—	4 (8)	—	—	—
Bauernbund	—	—	—	—	—	13 (26)	15 (26)
Center	8 (16)	6 (12)	4 (8)	5 (10)	7 (14)	7 (14)	9 (15)
SPD	—	2 (4)	3 (6)	4 (8)	6 (12)	7 (14)	8 (14)
No Fraktion	—	—	—	—	13 (26)	2 (4)	1
Total	50	50	50	50	50	50	58

SOURCE: Kalkoff, *Parlamentarier* (1917), p. 405. The shift in the total for the 1911 period probably comes from the fact that Kalkoff included those elected in special elections.

elite, whose position was protected by a highly unequal suffrage for both houses of the city parliament. Although the SPD held Hamburg's three Reichstag districts from the 1880s on, a Socialist did not enter the lower house of the city parliament, the Bürgerschaft, until 1901. When twelve Socialists were elected three years later, the city fathers decided to do something about it. In 1906, they revised the suffrage in order to limit Socialist influence. This move prevented the SPD from dominating the Bürgerschaft (in 1913 they held only 20 of that body's 160 seats). However, the debate over the suffrage increased the level of ideological cleavage as the factions in the Bürgerschaft became identified with political programs, and the influence of national alignments became more pronounced. Local politics still did not conform to the configuration of parties or to the political style present in the Reichstag, but by 1914 the Bürgerschaft was very different from the informal and elitist assembly it had once been.[14]

In a significant number of German cities, established elites, many of them identified with some form of liberalism, also used unequal suffrage systems to deflect the impact of mass-based political movements. In some places, such as the other two Hansa cities (Bremen and Lübeck), cities in Saxony, and in a number of the smaller states, this involved changing the voting laws in order to limit the influence of Social Democracy. In most of Prussia (except for Frankfurt and cities in Hanover and Schleswig-Holstein), some variant of the three-class suffrage was maintained. Elsewhere, election to local office was limited by some kind of property restriction. Even where efforts were made to reform the suffrage, other measures were employed in order to limit the full impact of democratization.[15]

Suffrage inequality, often accompanied by widespread voter apathy, helped

to produce a significant disjunction between the distribution of political power
in the community and at the national level. In Trier, for example, the Center
party dominated Reichstag elections from the mid-1870s on, but was not able
to win a majority in the city council until 1911.[16] The Socialists were in an
even less favorable position: by 1912, when they were able to elect candidates
in a majority of urban Reichstag districts, they remained a small minority in
most councils and were able to win a majority of seats in only a few,
relatively unimportant, cities and towns.[17]

Table 15.7   **The Political Composition of Fifteen
                                         Municipal Councils, 1910–14**

City (election date)	Liberals	SPD	Center	Conservatives/ Right-wing	Unknown	Source
Augsburg (1911)	35	3	8		2	*KPB*, 2:359
Barmen (1911)	18		2	10	1	*KPB*, 2:357
Berlin (1914)	98	44				Grassmann, p. 10*
Bochum (1911)	38		10			*KPB*, 2:363
Breslau (1910)	57	12		33		*KPB*, 1:376
Cologne (1911)	19		32			*KPB*, 2:355
Düsseldorf (1911)	37		20			*KPB*, 2:357
Frankfurt (1912)	44	23	1	3		*KPB*, 4:18
Karlsruhe (1911)	48	30	16	2		*KP*, 11:899
Königsberg (1913)	c. 83	19				*KP*, 13:1643
Mannheim (1911)	42	40	12	2		*KP*, 11:1510
Munich (1911)	30	14	14	2		*KPB*, 2:277
Nuremberg (1911)	42	10		7	1	*KPB*, 2:278
Stuttgart (1913)	16	14	2	3		Kohlhass, p. 39**
Würzburg (1911)	15	2	15	9		*KPB*, 2:279

* S. Grassmann, *Hugo Preuss und die deutsche Selbstverwaltung* (Lübeck and Hamburg, 1965).
** W. Kohlhass, *Chronik der Stadt Stuttgart, 1913–1918* (Stuttgart, 1967).

As the data in table 15.7 suggest, the city councils tended to be the last
bastions of liberalism in the Reich. Even in the city councils, however,
liberals were under strong attack, from Catholics in the Rhineland and the
south, from Socialists in almost every major city, and from radical right-wing
splinter groups in Saxony, Hesse, and a few eastern cities such as Breslau.
These parties not only won a steadily increasing share of council seats, they
also injected into municipal affairs a mode of political action which threatened
the liberals' cherished assumptions about how local politics should be conducted. Nevertheless, the councils were the only representative bodies in
which traces of the "liberal era" remained more than the memory of a lost
world.[18]

Changes in the parties' electoral strength were closely tied to alterations in the scale, style, and substance of participatory institutions. In the late nineteenth and early twentieth centuries, party and pressure-group organizations expanded in size and in the range of their activities; the volume of political publications, pamphlets, and newspapers increased; election campaigns became more expensive, better organized, and often more bitterly contested. Of course these developments were unevenly distributed throughout the Reich; even in 1914 there were a few districts where the level of political involvement was very low. But overall, participatory politics had begun to touch the lives of most Germans, to whom organized political groups promised new sources of identity, a way of defending special interests, and assistance in dealing with the expanding bureaucratic apparatus.[19]

The paradigmatic expression of this process was Social Democracy, which became the most dynamic force on the German political scene soon after the antisocialist laws lapsed in 1890. The foundation of socialism's extraordinary growth was a widespread and tightly woven network of institutions: trade unions which represented the economic interests of workers; electoral organizations which gave them political direction; newspapers, libraries, and educational societies which provided them with information and cultural enrichment; and clubs, athletic groups, and other associations which met their recreational needs.

To some extent, every party was affected by similar developments: "Organization! [wrote one politician in 1911] That is the cry one hears today in every corner of public life ... Everywhere it is recognized that only firm, well-ordered collective action can produce influence and success."[20] Within the non-Socialist parties, new forms of institutionalized political action usually coexisted with traditional loyalties, styles, and elites. In the Center party, for example, the importance of parish organizations, religious belief, and clerical leadership was qualified but not destroyed. Similarly, the power of landed elites in the Conservative party was not dissolved. But all along the political spectrum efforts were made to create institutions that would facilitate the mobilization and control of a mass electorate. The Center party sponsored trade unions and agrarian associations; the Conservatives helped to establish the Bund der Landwirte in an effort to defend themselves in the new political game. In every party, the interaction of old and new elites and institutions produced some friction. But nowhere was the challenge of Wilhelmine politics as painful and provocative as it was among liberals.

After 1890 a number of liberal leaders recognized the increasing importance of political organization, produced some impressive analyses of mass politics, and urged their colleagues to confront the demands of the new age. This was the message which appeared again and again in the writings of a man

like Friedrich Naumann who called upon liberals to jettison their commitment
to individualistic, informal patterns of political action:

> The old liberal slogans about the individual compare to contemporary
> economic life like the old-fashioned Hamburg storerooms compare to the
> giant warehouses on Kaiser-Wilhelm Quai. What can the individual with
> his small boat do on the great ocean? Community, cooperation is
> everything.[21]

Even many of those who did not embrace these ideas with Naumann's
eloquent fervor recognized that liberals had to win the masses if their movement was to survive. In the capital and in local electoral districts, liberals
began to alter their institutions in order to take into account the changing scale
and substance of political life.

Between 1890 and 1914, the number of local associations allied with the
National Liberal party increased from about 300 to 2,207. These were coordi-
nated by organizations at the provincial and state level. As the need to have
party policies legitimated by the membership grew, National Liberal leaders
felt obliged to call conventions, which were run according to procedures
formalized by statute and had a composition designed to represent various
regions and elements with the party. Twelve such *Parteitage* were held after
1890 with a steadily increasing level of attendance. At the same time, the
volume of party publications increased, as did efforts to enroll members and
communicate with as many voters as possible. All of this required a full-time
staff. By 1902, the party's central office in Berlin employed a general secre-
tary and three officials; five years later the number of employees had grown to
seventeen. Compared with that of the Social Democrats, this apparatus was
modest, but compared with the mode of liberal activity a few years earlier, it
reflected significant progress.[22]

As we know, men on the liberal left such as Eugen Richter had been
advocates of intensive party organizations since the late 1870s. After the
division between Richter's followers and the old Sezession in 1893, the
former retained control of the institutional base and continued to use it to hold
on to the core of support within the Prussian middle strata.[23] After the turn of
the century, especially in the south and west, left liberals' organizational
efforts increased. When a unified left-liberal party was formed in 1910, these
activities intensified throughout much of the Reich: in 1912 alone, local
Vereine increased from 1,452 to 1,680 and could be found in 129 Reichstag
districts. As was the case with the National Liberals, an increase in the
number of associations was accompanied by the growth of a full-time staff
and the use of party conventions to sample and influence the membership's
opinions.[24]

Despite some important innovations, however, the advocates of institutional reform in both wings of the movement had only limited success. As late as 1902, for example, National Liberals had to be reminded to select candidates for the upcoming Reichstag elections more than a month in advance.[25] Five years later, one local official noted that "the National Liberal party is formally organized through an electoral committee in Neuwied and through party agents in the large localities. This organization, however, exists for the most part on paper."[26] Even in 1912, only 11.4 percent of the National Liberals' Reichstag electorate belonged to some kind of party organization. Moreover, a number of these organizations were still shaped by traditional elites and practices. The old *Honoratioren* dominated local politics in many regions, while the direction of national policy rested in the hands of the parliamentary factions, not with the full-time staff or the convention delegates.[27]

Although left-wing liberals were more ideologically committed to democratic political action than most National Liberals, their institutional development was also uneven and incomplete. Indeed, the ratio of party members to voters on the liberal left was even more unfavorable than on the right: in 1912 just 8 percent of its Reichstag electorate belonged to a party organization.[28] The majority of these members came from the same sectors of the middle strata upon which left liberalism had always depended, a characteristic social limitation which was not transcended even in those regions where the left was especially active during the years just before 1914. The same was true of the south German Volkspartei. Despite some attempt to create a mass-based party organization, the Volkspartei experienced the same problems as the other liberal factions; its organizations were as limited in their appeal, its constituency as volatile and inconstant.[29]

The relative weakness of liberal institutions played an important role in the movement's decline after 1890. The inability of either liberal party to attract the masses of new voters who came into the political system after 1890 was partly due to the failure of liberal organizations to provide these groups with satisfactory sources of information, cohesion, and direction. Equally important, the low level of commitment present within the liberal constituency itself was connected to the shallowness of the parties' institutional roots. But to say that liberalism declined because of its institutional failings only suggests another, more basic question: Why did liberals have such limited success in creating organizations which might have allowed them to attain a broader and more reliable constituency? Part of the answer to this question can be found in the attitude about party politics and the patterns of affiliation prevalent among those to whom German liberals had traditionally looked for support.

As we know, a certain distaste for party organization and electoral agitation had always been present in German liberalism, even at the crest of the movement's popularity. After 1890, as the style and substance of political life was transformed by the growth of the electorate and the intensification of political conflict, this distaste often hardened into animosity and rejection. Members of the established liberal elite frequently looked upon advocates of organizational reform within the movement as unpleasant young men on the make, "professional politicians" who lacked the standing and style traditionally associated with a leadership role.[30] To many liberals, the necessity of addressing large meetings or participating in the mundane business of local organization rendered the whole enterprise of party politics something a "respectable" paragon of the *Bürgertum* ought to ignore.[31]

Many members of those social groups and institutions which once had sustained the liberal cause now turned away from active involvement in political life. This process can be seen most clearly in the academic community. In the middle decades of the century, liberal professors had spoken of the need to combine scholarship and political commitment, but now—in the words of one spokesman for the academic establishment—most believed that "whoever is devoted to the quest for truth cannot be a party man."[32] If a professor spoke out on public issues, it should be as an objective, neutral observer, as the opponent of "the vulgar opinions of the day" and of "one-sided class interests."[33] In this view, the scholar's role was not to make or guide public opinion, but rather to serve as an antidote to its unhealthy influence.

This "depoliticization" of the academic profession influenced the method and content of a number of scholarly disciplines. Jurisprudence, for example, became dominated by a legal positivism which deemphasized the political implications of the law, removed the critical impulse from the concept of the *Rechtsstaat,* and turned legal theory into an uncritical defense of the status quo.[34] Economics suffered from a marked decline in concern for the immediate problems of industrial society and a growing inclination among economists to see their discipline as providing advice for the administration.[35] Modern historians, for their part, paid little attention to the evolution of participatory politics and instead studied intellectual or diplomatic history, with particular emphasis on the triumphant emergence of the Bismarckian Reich.[36]

At many universities, the tone for student life was set by fraternities which combined uncritical patriotism, feudal residues like dueling, and pragmatic careerism. Even those students who did not belong to fraternities displayed little interest in parties and elections. A survey of student periodicals in 1904, for example, indicated that only fifteen out of forty treated political affairs at all and these did so in a casual way.[37] In 1907, when a French visitor tried to draw German students into a political discussion, he found "their ignorance touching and their indifference depressing."[38]

Ignorance and indifference seem to have persisted among many educated Germans after they left the university. Just as professors celebrated the separation of scholarship and politics, so officials tried to maintain a distinction between "administration" and "politics."[39] Governmental pressures for conformity played an important part in this, but even among municipal officials, where these pressures were less potent, similar attitudes can be found. By the 1890s, the great age of the politically engaged Bürgermeister like Forckenbeck and Becker had passed and in their places we find big-city mayors such as Franz Adickes of Frankfurt, who was vaguely liberal in his sympathies but regarded active participation in party affairs as incompatible with his duties and self-image as a *Beamter*.[40] The national importance of many of these mayors during the 1920s suggests the degree to which Germans continued to search for "neutral" and "objective" leaders, those whom Hans Luther proudly called "politicians without a party."[41]

The negative attitude about party politics in the *Bildungsbürgertum* exerted an influence on German life which extended well beyond the small sector of society directly touched by higher education. These attitudes, for instance, filtered into the textbooks used in German grammar schools from which students learned that after the 1870s "the nationally oriented Reichstag was replaced by parliaments in which factionalism and negativism produced opposition to every government proposal."[42] A similar point of view can be found in many of the periodicals which were directed toward the middle strata. Most of these magazines either ignored parties and representative institutions or published laments about their unhealthy influence.[43] The cult of Bismarck, whose great deeds provided one of the most popular themes for these periodicals, emphasized the negative influence of the parties against which the "Iron Chancellor" had had to struggle.[44]

Even those who continued to participate in party affairs often tried to maintain that what they were doing was not really "political." Arnold Brecht, for example, recalls that his father, a railroad official in Lübeck, supported the liberals but regarded his own views as "objective, reasonable, unpolitical. Everyone who stood either to his right or left—these were the politicians."[45] There were, of course, many who threw themselves into the world of participant politics and cared deeply about constitutional issues and parliamentary affairs. But the evidence suggests that a significant sector of the liberal constituency voted for a liberal candidate without further participation in party activities. "My political views," wrote Theodor Fontane, "which were always of a shaky sort, usually coincided with the National Liberals ...

even though I never had close ties to them. I was, therefore, a typical National Liberal."[46]

A reluctance to be involved in party organizations was often accompanied by a tendency to reduce liberal programs to a set of empty slogans or, more characteristically, to regard liberalism as a negative response to political Catholicism, Social Democracy, or a national minority. "Liberal," noted the liberal electoral committee in Trier, "is the name for everyone who is not clerical."[47] Similarly, young Otto Baumgarten defined his political position in terms of his opposition to "the Catholic tendencies of the conservative · church and the antinational tendencies of the Socialists."[48] When they sought to define what they were for, rather than what they were against, many liberals retreated into the realm of vague generalities or opaque references to the "nation," "tolerance," and "freedom." Consider, for instance, the views of Otto Heinemann, a minor executive in the Krupp organization whose autobiography was published when his son became president of the Federal Republic. The elder Heinemann voted Progressive because he disliked William II, but his political "declaration of faith" lacks both ideological depth and practical implication: "To be German and to be a nationalist, my fatherland above all else; to be socially conscious in my feelings, thought and action; to insure equal rights and duties for everyone."[49]

The fragile bonds between the liberal parties and their constituencies, therefore, were the result of a widespread uncertainty about the meaning and significance of party politics. But this disenchantment with "politics" did not prevent members of the middle strata from participating in public life. The so-called "unpolitical German" did not withdraw into a private world. He was not an isolated member of an atomized "mass society."[50] Members of the middle strata may have looked with disdain on parties and elections, but they participated with extraordinary vigor in a dense network of other institutions through which they sought political influence, social identity, and economic advantage.

German professors sought to shape the course of public policy in organizations such as the Verein für Sozialpolitik, which was supposed to be without party affiliation and thus in harmony with the "neutrality" of scholarship. Moreover, the Verein's educational goals and convivial atmosphere separated it from the democratic world of electoral strife.[51] During the nineties, some progressively inclined academicians hoped that Friedrich Naumann's National Social Association could provide them with a suitable forum, but many of them turned away from Naumann after he joined a party, got elected to the Reichstag, and became—in the words of one former admirer—a "parliamentarian just like any other."[52] Professors and other members of the educated elite were also active in various patriotic associations and in a wide variety of organizations which tried to find a way of reforming German society without becoming enmeshed in party politics. This was also the aim of the Youth movement, to which many young people from the upper ranks of the middle strata flocked around the turn of the century.[53] Businessmen hoped that interest groups might free them from the need for party affiliation and sometimes longed for corporate organizations that would replace the parliaments with "unpolitical" representation.[54] Even Jews, who had traditionally viewed the liberal parties as the best defense for their civil rights, began to seek new paths to power with institutions such as Centralverein deutscher Staatsbürger Jüdischen Glaubens (1893), or the Verband deutscher Juden (1904).[55]

Local government provided another refuge for those excluded or alienated from national party politics. Here liberals could still be *unter sich*. They lost no opportunity to emphasize the value of these experiences and to contrast them with the unfortunate tendencies at work in the rest of the political system. In the words of Arthur Hobrecht, a National Liberal parliamentarian and former mayor of Berlin: "The citizenship which is derived from common endeavors in the organs of local government becomes increasingly valuable for us the more the conflict of material interests fragments contemporary society as a whole."[56] In addition to the city councils, most German communities had a large number of other organizations in which members of the middle strata could enjoy the company of men like themselves. In Merseberg, for example, there were well over fifty recreational and cultural associations by the end of the 1870s; in a smaller city such as Naumberg, there were over a hundred such *Vereine* at the turn of the century.[57] These organizations were so numerous and popular that contemporaries talked about the *Vereinsmeierei* which beset their society and joked that whenever three or more Germans gathered they were likely to formulate statutes and constitute themselves as an association.[58]

The relationship between these various organizations and the liberal parties was always tense and unstable. At times, interest groups and patriotic associations, city councils and local *Vereine* could not resist being drawn into electoral politics. In some areas, they played an indispensable role in the political process as forums for the selection of leaders and as instruments for the mobilization of popular support. Nevertheless, most of them preserved their independence from the parties and nourished the often illusory conviction that they were "unpolitical." The liberals, unlike the Catholics, Social Democrats, or even the Conservatives, were usually unable to absorb these institutions into a cohesive political movement. Instead, the complex pattern of affiliation within the "social milieu" of liberal voters set significant limits on the parties' ability to construct a political movement from their constituents' diverse loyalties and interests. The various organizations to which

members of the Protestant middle strata belonged, therefore, helped to
deepen the divisions within their ranks and furthered the debilitating fragmentation of liberalism's social base.[59]

The Fragmentation of the Middle Strata

The break with the liberal era is obvious. Wherever one looks, the old liberalism of the preachers of freedom of movement, the natural harmony of interests, limitation of state power, and all the moral and political ideals that are associated with these things, is being pushed back by a national closing off against the outside and a tightening up within. The world has become harder, more warlike, more exclusive.

Erich Marcks (1903)[1]

Despite the massive changes which occurred in the world of participatory politics, many of the most prominent spokesmen for the liberal movement after 1890 continued to come from the elites of property and education. The social composition of the National Liberals' Reichstag faction clearly reflects this continuity (see table 16.1). The importance of businessmen had increased until the turn of the century and then began to decline. Officials never recovered the role they had played during the "liberal era," but the position of lawyers, that sector of the *Bildungsbürgertum* best suited to full-time political activity, steadily improved. Since the National Liberals found themselves more and more dependent upon rural *Wahlkreise*, the relative significance of farmers and landowners also grew. Finally, the *Fraktion* elected in 1912 contained a few faint signs of "democratization." The presence of three workers and artisans, as well as a number of white-collar employees, was the result of the party's somewhat desultory attempts to broaden its social base.[2]

After 1890, as before, the particular blend of elites within liberal parliamentary leadership varied from state to state. In Prussia, for example, the National Liberal Landtag faction was dominated by a combination of officials and businessmen, with the latter, most of whom were industrialists from the western provinces, able to play a far greater role than at the national level.[3] Industrialists were also very well represented in Saxony, while in Bavaria government employees remained the single largest group in the liberal delegation.[4]

The direction of local party affairs was also usually in the hands of those with *Bildung* or *Besitz*. Sometimes, as in Hesse, an aggressive entrepreneur like Freiherr von Heyl set the tone. Elsewhere administrative officials or perhaps the mayor provided leadership for electoral activities even though such men were not usually candidates themselves. Data on eminent National Liberals in Braunschweig reveal the importance of local officials, teachers, professional people, and businessmen.[5] This collection of social groups also dominated the party's *Vorstand* at the end of the imperial period, as is demonstrated by the material summarized in table 16.2. Data on regional organiza-

Table 16.1   **The Social Composition of the National
                                        Liberal Reichstag Delegation,
                                        1890–1912**

	1890 No. (%)	1893 No. (%)	1898 No. (%)	1903 No. (%)	1907 No. (%)	1912 No. (%)
Officials						
Administrative	2 (5)	2 (4)	2 (4)	3 (6)	4 (7)	4 (9)
Judicial	4 (9.5)	4 (7)	3 (6)	2 (4)	3 (5)	2 (4)
Local	2 (5)	2 (4)	3 (6)	1 (2)	3 (5)	1 (2)
Professors and teachers	2 (5)	7 (13)	4 (8)	3 (6)	7 (13)	4 (9)
Lawyers	2 (5)	4 (7)	3 (6)	2 (4)	6 (11)	9 (20)
Physicians and other						
academics	—	2 (4)	2 (4)	1 (2)	2 (3.6)	1 (2)
Writers	1 (2)	1 (2)	—	1 (2)	—	2 (4)
Interest-group employees	—	—	1 (2)	—	1	1 (2)
Businessmen	17 (40)	14 (26)	10 (20)	14 (29)	9 (16)	6 (13)
Rentier	1 (2)	1 (2)	2 (4)	1 (2)	2 (3.6)	1 (2)
Agricultural occupations						
Rittergutsbesitzer	4 (9.5)	2 (4)	6 (12)	6 (12.5)	7 (13)	3 (6.6)
Others	7 (16.6)	14 (26)	12 (24)	11 (23)	8 (14.5)	8 (18)
Craftsmen and workers	—	—	—	—	—	3 (6)
Miscellaneous and						
unknown	—	1 (2)	1 (2)	1 (2)	2 (3.6)	—
Total	42	54	50	48	55	45

SOURCE: Kremer, *Aufbau* (1934), pp. 13–14.

Table 16.2   **The Social Composition of the National
                                        Liberal *Vorstand*, 1913–17**

	No. (%)
Officials	
Administrative	20 (8)
Judicial	25 (10)
Local	10 (4)
Professors, teachers, pastors	30 (12)
Lawyers	48 (20)
Other professionals	6 (2)
Editors and writers	8 (3)
Businessmen	65 (27)
Craftsmen	1
Agricultural occupations	15 (6)
Private employees	10 (4)
Miscellaneous and unknown	6 (2)
Total	244

SOURCE: Reiss, *Bassermann* (1967),
pp. 66–80.

tions and local officeholders reveal a broader spectrum of social groups including minor officials, white-collar workers, artisans, and farmers. But it was unusual for someone with one of these occupations to be given an important position in the party.[6] All in all, the evidence confirms Erich Dombrowski's contemporary assessment that "probably in no other party are ... the socially respectable classes so numerous in local organizations or so exclusively represented in the central leadership as in National Liberalism."[7]

Ernst Müller-Meiningen, a left liberal from south Germany, once contrasted his faction with the National Liberals by recalling that he and his colleagues went to the Reichstag canteen and ate dinner while the National Liberals "dined out" at restaurants where meals cost twice as much.[8] The difference Müller tried to summarize with this remark was a very real one: right-wing liberals were usually wealthier and more prestigious than their counterparts on the left. Nevertheless, as table 16.3 suggests, left-wing liberalism's Reichstag faction was also composed of men who could qualify for membership in the elites of *Bildung* and *Besitz*. Moreover, some of the changes within the two liberal parties were rather similar: during the nineties, the left was also represented by a fairly large number of businessmen, many of

Table 16.3   **The Social Composition of the Left-Liberal Reichstag Delegations, 1890–1912**

	1890 No. (%)	1893 No. (%)	1898 No. (%)	1903 No. (%)	1907 No. (%)	1912 No. (%)
Officials						
Administrative	5 (7.4)	1 (2.8)	1 (2)	—	—	—
Judicial	3 (4.4)	3 (8.5)	5 (11.9)	2 (6.6)	2 (4.7)	1 (2.4)
Local	4 (6)	—	—	1 (3.3)	4 (9.5)	1 (2.4)
Professors and teachers	6 (8.9)	2 (5.7)	6 (14.2)	3 (10)	10 (23.8)	8 (19.5)
Lawyers	7 (10.4)	6 (17)	7 (16.6)	5 (16.6)	4 (9.5)	12 (29)
Physicians and pastors	2 (3)	—	2 (4.7)	3 (10)	4 (9.5)	2 (4.8)
Writers	5 (7.4)	4 (11.4)	5 (11.9)	4 (13.3)	1 (2)	3 (7.3)
Interest-group and						
party employees	3 (4.4)	1 (2.8)	1 (2)	4 (13.3)	4 (9.5)	4 (9.7)
Businessmen	18 (26.8)	8 (22.8)	8 (19)	6 (20)	11 (26)	3 (7.3)
Rentier	4 (6)	—	1 (2)	—	1 (2)	1 (2.4)
Agricultural occupations						
Rittergutsbesitzer	1	2 (5.7)	—	—	1 (2)	1 (2.4)
Others	8 (11.9)	8 (22.8)	6 (14.2)	2 (6.6)	—	3 (7.3)
Craftsmen and innkeepers	—	—	—	—	—	2 (4.8)
Miscellaneous and						
unknown	1	—	—	—	—	—
Total	67	35	42	30	42	41

SOURCE: Kremer, *Aufbau* (1934), pp. 46–47.
NOTE: *Volkspartei* members are not included in this table.

whom were to be found in the Freisinnige Vereinigung (the heirs of the old Sezession, which split from Richter's Freisinnige Volkspartei in 1893).[9] After 1900, however, economic elites became less significant, and on the left, as on the right, some of their places in the Reichstag were taken by lawyers. The major differences between the two groups were the absence of administrative officials on the left, the smaller role of those from agricultural occupations, and the rather larger part played by journalists and interest-group employees. It was this last group, rather than the tiny number of artisans, which reflected left liberal efforts at "democratization."[10]

Differences between the Reichstag factions of right and left prepare us for the differences to be found in their local leadership. Unlike the National Liberals, the Progressives could not count on the electoral support and direction of the administration, nor can one find many wealthy industrialists on the left comparable to the National Liberal elite in the western provinces of Prussia. Nevertheless, the Progressives' local leadership was most often made up of men with established positions in society: judicial officials, lawyers, teachers, members of the financial community, small manufacturers, merchants, and *Rentier*. In Berlin, for example, the city council, long a Progressive stronghold, was run by part of the business elite. In the small Silesian town where Willy Hellpach grew up, judges, merchants, pharmacists, and physicians provided the left-liberal leadership during the nineties. In parts of the south, party life was dominated by lawyers and judges.[11] This mix also dominated the executive committee of the Volkspartei in Württemberg.[12] At the lowers levels of organized party activity, the Progressives' social composition was more diversified and "democratic" than that of the National Liberals.[13] However, even here the main differences were of degree, not kind, as is suggested by the data in table 16.4 on those attending the parties' conventions in 1911 and 1912.

Religious affiliation remained the single most important factor in determining which sectors of the middle strata voted liberal. As in our earlier discussion, there is no way to avoid the so-called "ecological fallacy" when trying to demonstrate this with national returns, but these data do illustrate the connection between religion and political alignment: in 1912, the population of *Wahlkreise* in which liberals were successful was usually about 75 percent Protestant and sometimes much more than that; furthermore, left liberals were able to elect a delegate in only three districts with a Catholic majority (all of them in the central sections of cities—Danzig, Munich, and Freiburg), the National Liberals in only seven.[14] The relationships suggested by these data are confirmed if one examines various local studies which make clear that most liberal voters were Protestants.[15]

Table 16.4   **The Social Composition of Two
Liberal Party Conventions, 1911–12**

	National Liberals, 1911 No. (%)	Fortschrittliche Volkspartei, 1912 No. (%)
Judicial Officials	95 (12.3)	18 (4)
Professors, teachers, and pastors	115 (14.9)	58 (14.6)
Lawyers and other professionals	123 (16.1)	78 (19.6)
Private and public employees*	75 (10.2)	48 (12)
Journalists and party employees	84 (10.9)	47 (11.8)
Businessmen	197 (25.5)	92 (22.8)
Craftsmen	16 (2.1)	10 (2.5)
Workers**	12 (1.6)	4 (1)
Agricultural occupations	22 (2.9)	16 (4)
Miscellaneous and unknown	33	26
Totals	772	397

SOURCE: Nipperdey, *Organisation* (1961), p. 105, for the National Liberals; Reimann, *Müller-Meiningen* (1968), p. 82, for the Fortschrittliche Volkspartei.
* Included are 33 local officials among the National Liberals and an unknown number on the left.
** Included are minor officials among the National Liberals.

Regional traditions continued to influence liberal voters in some parts of the Reich. This was true, for example, in sections of Silesia, Schleswig-Holstein, Württemberg, Hanover, the western provinces of Prussia, and some of the *Kleinstaaten*.[16] However, traditional centers of liberal support were often inundated by an influx of new voters. This happened, for example, in the Palatinate, where the Social Democrats eventually mobilized enough voters to overwhelm the townsmen and farmers who had once been able to send a liberal to the Reichstag.[17]

This process was also at work in most German cities. By 1912, the two liberal parties could win only eight of the forty-seven *Wahlkreise* in cities of over a hundred thousand; the Social Democrats won thirty-six. Increasingly, therefore, the national representatives of the liberal movement came to be drawn from districts dominated by small cities, towns, or agricultural villages.[18] However, if we look at the liberal electorate rather than at the districts which liberals were able to win, a very different picture emerges. The voters for National Liberals were more or less evenly distributed among communities of various sizes, whereas the left liberals tended to do better in larger communities than in smaller ones (see table 16.5). These averages conceal important regional differences: in Hanover and Hesse, for instance, National Liberals did better in the countryside, which they could mobilize in opposition to the Socialist cities; in eastern Prussia, on the other hand, National Liberals and especially the Progressives tended to represent townsmen in opposition to the conservative countryside.[19] The same thing happened in Baden, where liberals usually did better in urban districts than in the Center-dominated rural regions.[20]

Table 16.5   **The Distribution of Liberal Voters by Community-Size, Reichstag Elections, 1903 and 1912**
                                        (percentage of votes cast)

	National Liberals		Left Liberals	
Size of Community	1903	1912	1903	1912
Under 2,000	10.4	12.8	7.1	8.8
From 2,000 to 10,000	12.2	15	9.2	12.1
Over 10,000	18.6	13.8	11.8	15.6
Reich	13.9	13.6	9.9	12.3

SOURCE: Bertram, *Wahlen* (1964), p. 218.

As usual, it is impossible to be very precise about the urban social groups upon which liberalism's strength depended. It seems likely, however, that both parties drew their support from a fairly diverse group within the middle strata.[21] Despite the diversity of their support, liberals tended to do disproportionately well among higher-income groups. This is suggested by the evidence on Prussian state elections, which divided voters into classes based on their share of the tax burden. As table 16.6 shows, the National Liberals consistently did better in the first and second class than in the third; this became true for the Progressives when the Socialists began to capture voters in the third class after the turn of the century. Material on voting patterns in municipal elections yields similar results, as can be seen from the data in table 16.7 on four Rhenish cities of different sizes in 1909 and 1910.

In most rural regions, liberalism's constituency was composed of groups comparable to those in the urban middle strata. Rudolph Heberle's study of Schleswig-Holstein, for instance, showed that the core of left-wing liberal

Table 16.6   **The Distribution of Liberal Voters in
                                         Urban Areas by Voting Class,
                                         Prussian Landtag Elections, 1898–
                                         1913 (percentage of votes cast)**

	1898		1903		1908		1913	
Class	NL	Left Lib.	NL	Left Lib.	NL	Left Lib.	NL	Left Lib.
I	26.6	20.6	30.9	19.4	29.1	17.5	27.6	17.7
II	23.5	20.4	27.3	16.5	21.2	12.6	20	13.6
III	16.8	20.9	15.4	5.1	12.3	5.5	12.8	7.6

SOURCE: Evert, "Landtagswahlen" (1905) and (1909) and Höpker, "Landtagswahlen" (1916).

support was in areas dominated by small farms; large landowners tended to
vote for a right-wing party, while the Socialists had made some inroads
among agricultural laborers. By and large, this pattern was repeated throughout the Reich. In east Elbia, liberals did best in a region such as Liegnitz,
which had an unusually large number of small and medium-sized agricultural
enterprises. They also did rather well among small producers (animal raisers,
vineyard owners, dairy farmers) in Hanover, parts of the Rhineland, Hesse,
and Baden.[22]

Only in a few areas is it possible to define the differences between the social
character of the two wings of liberalism. In Oldenburg's second district, for
example, the two parties competed for an essentially rural constituency; here
the owners of large farms, who were in favor of protective tariffs, voted

Table 16.7   **Local Elections in Four Cities,
                                         1909–10**

Voting Class	Eligible Voters	Liberals	Center	SPD	Conservatives
		Cologne (population = 516,527) 1909			
I	875	364	52	—	—
II	11,272	4,349	4,807	—	48
III	78,682	4,310	25,019	12,980	—
		Krefeld (population = 129,412) 1909			
I	245	148	—	—	—
II	1,950	756	541	—	—
III	20,790	1,886	4,875	2,260	—
		Düren (population = 32,460) 1910			
I	18	8	—	—	—
II	356	149	90	—	—
III	5,077	—	1,916	55	—
		Dülken (population = 10,518) 1910			
I	42	20	—	—	—
II	213	93	116	—	1
III	1,447	409	609	—	—

SOURCE: *KPB* (1911), nos. 11–12, pp. 324 ff.

National Liberal while the free-trade-oriented small farmers and animal raisers tended to vote Progressive.[23] In Württemberg, where there was a long-
established conflict between left and right, the *Kleinbürgertum* inclined
toward the former and the more prestigious and prosperous elements in society toward the latter.[24] In most places, however, the line is more difficult to
draw: sometimes because the two parties did not compete, sometimes because
the evidence is insufficient, and sometimes because the relationship between
the two groups was fluid and unstable. Generally speaking, however, differences within the liberal electorate more or less paralleled the differences in
their leadership. Usually these were differences in degree, with the better-
placed sectors of the middle strata leaning to the right and the lower economic
and status groups leaning to the left.[25]

The typical liberal voter, therefore, was a Protestant who belonged somewhere in the middle range of the class and status hierarchies. It was from these
groups that the bulk of the two parties' 3.15 million voters came in the
elections of 1912. And it was districts where these groups were best
represented which elected a majority of the liberals' eighty-seven delegates.
In size and social composition, these districts tended to fall in between the
small, agrarian *Wahlkreise* dominated by the Conservatives and the huge,
urban, and/or industrial districts controlled by the SPD. Characteristically, the
liberals' districts were touched but not transformed by the social, economic,
and cultural changes at work in German society. They were composed of
small and medium-sized towns, not great cities or distended industrial sub-
urbs; when liberals did win in large cities, it was most often in the relatively
stable central districts where the urban middle strata still predominated. Similarly, their rural support came in places where agriculture was carried on by a
large number of proprietors, not by a few big landowners.

Although some districts offered liberals a better chance for success than
others, neither party had a cluster of "safe districts," *Wahlkreise* in which
party leaders could count on being elected while they concentrated on more
hotly contested races. After 1890 the liberals' ability to gain a first-ballot
victory steadily decreased, until by 1912 only four candidates (all of them
National Liberals) could be elected without a *Stichwahl*. This meant that both
liberal parties owed their existence on the national level to a tangled and often
contradictory set of alliances with other political parties.

An important reason for this situation was the fact that the liberal electorate
was nationally extended but relatively shallow. Unlike the Catholics, the
Social Democrats, and to a lesser extent the Conservatives, liberal voters were
not concentrated heavily in a few areas.[26] Furthermore, the liberal electorate
was not only thinly spread, it was also volatile and susceptible to appeals from
a variety of other groups. Liberals, therefore, not only had to engage in an

unusually complex set of alliances with other parties, they also had to defend their electoral base from an unusually varied set of competitors.

In some areas and at certain times, liberal voters shifted their allegiance to the Social Democrats. Often, this was temporary: in 1903, for example, a number of discontents produced a swing to the left among Saxon craftsmen and shopkeepers, most of whom did not remain in the Socialist camp.[27] As the labor movement gradually established itself as the most prominent and effective spokesman for the urban lower classes, some skilled workers, minor officials, and craftsmen permanently switched to the SPD. The liberals' support often was so thin that these defections could tip the balance in a few districts; overall, however, the main reason why liberals lost ground to the SPD was not the defection of their supporters but rather the Socialists' greater ability to win over newly active voters.[28]

There was more movement back and forth between the liberal and right-wing parties. In both urban and rural areas, these parties competed for the same social groups: Protestant members of the middle strata, who were unwilling or unable to join either the Socialists or the Center. Although each of the liberal and conservative parties was able to attract a certain number of these voters and build them into a core of support, most of them were not strongly attached to any one party.[29] After 1890, therefore, the movement of voters between liberals and conservatives in the Prussian east continued just as it had during the seventies.[30] Radical right-wing groups, many of them committed to a form of racial nationalism, also began to provide serious competition for liberals in certain areas. In some elections, liberal voters chose a radical candidate as a way of expressing their resentment about a particular policy or situation; elsewhere, however, there were more profound and lasting shifts among peasants, craftsmen, and white-collar workers who found that traditional liberalism no longer offered them a meaningful source of political identification. There were also some liberal supporters who moved to the right en masse behind a candidate who may have continued to run under a liberal lable but who was, in fact, closely identified with a right-wing group such as the Bund der Landwirte.[31]

The instability of political commitments among the Protestant middle strata can also be seen in their movement in and out of what some scholars have called the "party of nonvoters." In Reichstag elections, this "party" was not very large, but after 1890 it does seem to have contained a significant number of potentially liberal voters, who could only be mobilized by patriotic appeals. This is apparently what happened in the elections of 1887 and 1907.[32] In state and local elections, the number of nonvoters was often quite substantial. In the Prussian Landtag elections, for example, participation was always well below the national level, even among those who would have been advantaged by the three-class system. Here again we find evidence of the liberals' failure to mobilize their constituencies in a sustained and effective manner.

Although there was considerable continuity in the movement's social composition, the nature and relationship of the groups supporting liberalism changed significantly during the Wilhelmine era. The main force behind these changes was a process of economic development which was at once very rapid and highly uneven. After 1890, and especially after 1896, every indicator—overall production, production per capita, national income, income per capita—moved upward. But this growth was unequally distributed. The industrial sector grew faster than the agricultural, some industries (chemical, electrical, metalworking) grew faster than others (textiles and mining), larger firms grew faster than smaller ones. Nor did prosperity bestow its blessings equally. A significant number of Germans found that "progress" was full of perils, and even many of those whose economic position did improve were convinced that their share of economic growth was too small and insufficiently secure.[33]

The unevenness of economic growth and prosperity led many contemporaries to fear that the old German *Mittelstand* was being destroyed.[34] Again and again we find images of the craftsman ground to dust by an industrial giant or of the shopkeeper forced into bankruptcy by a department store. And of course, these things did happen. But many small enterprises (saloons, barbershops, shoe repair shops) did not face serious competition from larger firms, while others (certain kinds of precision instrument and machine shops, for example) actually benefited from the expansion of a technologically oriented industrial economy. Thus in 1907, well over three million Germans, roughly one-third of those engaged in mining and manufacturing, were either self-employed or worked in firms with five or fewer employees. Retail trade and the service sector continued to be dominated by small establishments.[35] The evidence on agricultural holdings also points to the persistence and perhaps even the relative growth of small and middle-sized farms.[36] In addition to these groups within the proprietary urban and rural *Mittelstand*, the middle ranks of society were increased after 1890 by the growing number of white-collar workers and government employees. Between 1882 and 1907, the number of *Angestellten* (a category which included managerial personnel as well as clerks and salesmen) increased from about five hundred thousand to two million. By 1907 there were also about one million government employees who considered themselves *Beamte* (administrative and judicial officials, teachers, postal and railway employees, municipal employees, and so on), most of whom, in terms of income and status, would qualify as members of the middle strata.[37]

While the Wilhelmine period did not produce a bifurcation of German
society into rich and poor, economic development and social change did result
in a pattern of fissures and strains throughout the social structure and particularly among those who occupied its middle ranks. There were, first of all, a set
of deeply rooted horizontal conflicts between the beneficiaries and victims of
progress, owners of large enterprises and owners of smaller ones, managers
and employees, university professors and grammar school teachers. Superim-
posed upon these conflicts was a pattern of vertical antagonisms which often
involved men with roughly similar incomes: industrialists and landowners,
commercial and manufacturing groups, heavy and light industry, producers
and consumers, city dwellers and farmers. These antagonisms, which had
been present in German society for decades, were aggravated after 1890 by
growing inequalities of wealth and by differences among the middle strata's
life-styles and life chances.[38]

Conflicts among the middle strata found expression in an expanding network of pressure groups designed to reinforce men's social identity, inform
them about their common economic interests, and channel their energies
toward collective action.[39] As these needs increased, both in variety and
intensity, the nature of interest-group activity began to be transformed.

In the first place, a process of "lateral differentiation" occurred whenever
more narrowly defined social or economic groups formed their own particular
organizations. In the words of one contemporary, "a new organization was
created for every purpose."[40] Sometimes this caused divisions in existing
institutions: the chemical industry, for example, left the Zentralverband
deutscher Industrieller because its leaders did not feel their own needs were
served by an organization dominated by representatives of iron, coal, and
steel producers. More often, lateral differentiation encouraged the formation
of new groups of manufacturers and retailers, officials and teachers, farmers
and workers, white-collar employees and shopkeepers. The picture was
further complicated by regional variations and by the existence of some
organizations, such as the Arbeitgeberverbände which cut across both
regional and branch lines, thereby adding yet another thread to the complex
pattern of organizational life.[41] And of course older economic organizations,
such as the Handelskammer, continued to exist and adapted with varying
degrees of success to the new situation.[42]

Second, a process of democratization significantly deepened the roots of
interest groups in German society. Trade unions were the most impressive
instance of this: by 1912 the Socialists' Free Union movement had over two
and a half million workers in its ranks, another 344,000 belonged to the
Catholic unions and 109,000 to the liberal Hirsch-Duncker Vereine. The
Bund der Landwirte, formed in 1893, represented almost a third of a million

farmers by 1910, a figure that seems all the more impressive when we consider that the Bund's predecessor, the Deutscher Bauernbund, had been able to organize only about 35,000 in the late 1880s. Over a half a million white-collar workers belonged to the eleven major Angestelltenverbände in 1911 and about 700,000 government employees were members of some kind of Beamtenverein. Finally, there was a wide range of national and local organizations which included in their ranks a growing number of small manufacturers, store owners, and other elements in the middle strata.[43]

Both lateral differentiation and democratization had profound effects on the relationship between interest groups and parties. Differentiation presented almost every party with a competing set of organized groups within its own ranks, groups which were often frustrated by what they regarded as the party's failure to respond to their own special needs. At the same time, democratization enabled some interest organizations to play a direct and autonomous role in electoral politics and thus to compete with the parties on their own ground. To some contemporaries, these trends seemed to signal the eventual displacement of political concerns by socioeconomic ones. In 1912, for example, Emil Lederer predicted that "Modern economic development, which activates all classes and brings to life all previously passive interests, will have to transform the ideological and principled parties and parliaments ... and must replace political ideas with economic interests."[44] In fact, Lederer's expectations were never fully realized. Political loyalties and institutions were much too deeply enmeshed in German life; they might be penetrated and reshaped by social and economic alignments but they could not be displaced. Nevertheless, in every German party the growing significance of social and economic interests created intense internal difficulties.[45] After 1890, as before, these difficulties were most keenly felt by the liberals.

The intensification of interest-group activity aggravated long-standing and deeply rooted socioeconomic divisions within the liberal constituencies. National Liberalism, for example, is often depicted as the party of big business and not, of course, without reason. But a significant number of entrepreneurs felt that the National Liberal party was not a reliable vehicle for their interests because it was obligated to so many other competing social and economic groups.[46] At one time or another, this same feeling was shared by farmers, members of the proprietary and white-collar *Mittelstand*, and numerous other sectors of the party's heterogeneous electorate. But interest groups did more than just generate internal discord; they also established forms of collective identity which cut across and sometimes through existing political alignments. The leader of a *Mittelstand* organization who proclaimed in 1911 that his membership belonged to all the *bürgerliche* parties could have been speaking for any one of a number of interest groups which sought to represent the middle strata.[47] Sometimes this incongruence between political and socio-economic institutions could lead to a change in voting behavior; even when it did not, it usually weakened the internal cohesion of the liberal parties by lowering the level of political commitment.

In both liberal parties, the leaders' response to these problems was inhibited by the fact that they often did not share their voters' economic interests or social identity. These differences between the social character of the liberal elite and the liberal electorate obviously became more significant for liberal politics as the electorate's social self-consciousness grew. National Liberal parliamentarians, for instance, were much more apt to live in a city than National Liberal voters. This was one reason for the successful inroads which the Bund der Landwirte was able to make in some traditionally liberal districts.[48] A considerable social distance also separated left-liberal lawyers, journalists, and full-time organizers from the men upon whom they depended for votes. The effects of this social distance were sometimes aggravated by geographical distance: in 1912, a significant number of liberal parliamentarians did not reside in their *Wahlkreise* and a surprisingly large number lived in the capital, where they could spend almost all of their time on political activities.[49] Like the differences within the liberal electorate, this distance between leaders and followers limited the parties' ability to communicate with and mobilize their supporters.

The liberal parties responded to the increase of internal social conflict with an unstable blend of compromise, evasion, and rhetorical reconciliation. The National Liberals, for example, never tired of proclaiming that their common allegiance to the general welfare was far more significant than their "minor differences of opinion and interest conflicts."[50] In their more candid moments, however, some National Liberals acknowledged that these differences were far from minor and that social and economic matters could be profoundly debilitating. As Arthur Hobrecht pointed out in 1897:

> We are not the representatives of a class or a stratum; it is just an oratorical expression, which is perhaps sometimes useful, that we are the true representatives of the educated *Mittelstand*—I myself have never been able to think anything like that. The so-called middle classes are too indefinite and diverse a substance on which to build a firm foundation, and the German *Bürgertum* is too German to be especially unified or cohesive.[51]

A few years later, Ernst Bassermann made the same point when he refused to tie the party more closely to various social and economic interests: "We are a middle party which includes all occupational groups, and therefore we must hold to a middle line. For this reason it will never be possible for us to take the lead in any kind of class-based movement."[52] When the National Liberals did take a programmatic stand on social and economic issues, it was usually done in the vaguest and most ambiguous way possible. The program of 1907, for instance, carefully balanced the competing elements within the party and presented a set of recommendations which could be understood in a variety of ways.[53] It is hardly surprising that this kind of rhetorical cosmetic did little to conceal, let alone to heal, the disruptions caused by severe social and economic differences.

As had usually been the case, the left liberals' somewhat narrower social and regional base made it easier for them to handle intramural conflicts over material interests. By stressing their constituency's common interests as consumers and taxpayers rather than their diverse interests as producers or employees, the Progressives were able to avoid some of the discord which persisted within National Liberalism. Nevertheless, the liberal left was also divided, and in many ways their social rhetoric was as threadbare as the right's. In 1900, Eugen Richter was still announcing that "we are certainly not the representatives of a single *Stand*, but of the entire *Volk* ... our core is the middle classes of society."[54] By then, of course, it was painfully obvious that the interests of the *Volk* and "middle classes" were by no means identical. And it was equally clear that there was no single "middle-class" interest. In fact, Richter himself had only certain sectors of the middle strata in mind, the small proprietors, farmers, and white-collar employees upon whom his support depended. Throughout the nineties he had sought to rally these groups against those whom he condemned as the "allies of big capital" in left-wing liberalism. This rivalry, which helped to feed the conflict between Richter's Freisinnige Volkspartei and the Freisinnige Vereinigung, set up a persistent source of strain within the liberal left.[55]

Some Progressives, like some National Liberals, wanted to break through the old rhetoric and create a political movement directly dependent on class interests. Friedrich Naumann, for example, argued that the drive for domestic reform has to be based on class solidarity: "Only through the rule of a class that has material interests of its own in democracy will the democratic spirit triumph in the life of any state. A liberal era will not dawn unless a new class throws an old one out of the saddle."[56] But by 1912, Naumann's perceptions seem to have changed: "We are pledged," he told a gathering that year, "to a party which knows no class differences; in the city and the country, workers and management are brothers together."[57] Naumann evidently had learned what many liberal leaders knew all along: liberalism could not be based on class interests because there was no single "class" to which the liberal electorate belonged, no coherent set of material interests behind which all liberals could be rallied.

The fragmentation of the liberals' social base can be vividly illustrated by examining the fate of the term *Mittelstand*, which they had once used to describe their social location and proclaim their moral identification with the common good. The program published by the Fortschrittliche Volkspartei in 1910 did not use this term at all. In the preamble there was a brief reference to the *Bürgertum* ("which is essential for the good of the whole"), but in the social and economic sections of the program no attempt was made to give the *Bürgertum* a single set of interests or goals. Instead, the program listed a variety of social and economic groups, each of which was promised support insofar as its needs were compatible with the party's commitments to economic freedom and the common good. The National Liberals' electoral statement of 1911 did call for a strengthening of the *Mittelstand*, but the word was used to refer to small proprietors, who were listed together with farmers, officials, and white-collar workers as groups whose particular interests the party wished to represent.[58]

The liberal parties' inability to maintain the traditional centrality of the *Mittelstand* reflected a growing discomfort with the term among social theorists. In 1897, for example, Gustav Schmoller published a pamphlet whose title asked: "What do we mean by *Mittelstand*?" Schmoller was forced to admit that, after a lifetime spent studying the subject, he was no longer sure. A variety of social developments, including the growing number of employees and officials, had given the middle strata of society "a whole series of different aspects and characteristics." Schmoller tried to preserve the *Mittelstand*'s conceptual integrity by finding some source of common values or moral attainment for all of its components. But in the end he was left with income as the surest boundary separating the middle strata from the rest of society. The *Mittelstand*, he argued, was composed of those who earned between 1,800 and 8,000 marks per year and whose total wealth amounted to less than 100,000 marks.[59] Leo Müffelmann came to much the same conclusion in 1913. After trying a variety of definitions, he chose income as the best designation of *Mittelstand*. Even J. Wernicke, perhaps the most astute analyst of this problem after the turn of the century, could do no better. In the course of a monumental work on the subject, Wernicke defined *Mittelstand* as all of those who "are above the masses of workers because of their skills, education or property, but do not have a high enough income to join the capitalist or propertied classes." Wernicke knew that this definition left him with an extremely heterogeneous mixture. "The so-called *Mittelstand*," he admitted, "includes the most diversified collection of propertied, educational, and occupational elements."[60]

As the social meaning of *Mittelstand* became more diffuse, its usefulness as a progressive moral category diminished. Increasingly, the presentation of the *Mittelstand* as the source of certain moral virtues came from the right of the political spectrum, from conservatives, anti-Semites, and right-wing National Liberals. These groups argued that the *Mittelstand* personified German virtues because it was "the best and strongest bulwark against the red flood."[61] This formulation retained the moral overtones of the concept without its progressive connotation. To its defenders on the right, therefore, the *Mittelstand* was not the vehicle and beneficiary of progress, but rather was an embattled bastion of social stability which had to be protected from the vicissitudes of modern social and economic life.

The changing meaning of *Mittelstand* was just one example of a widespread decline of the progressive impulse within German social thought at the end of the nineteenth century. Another was the growing pessimism about the German middle strata's values and political potential. There was, of course, nothing especially new or uniquely German about this; self-criticism seems to be a persistent and pervasive part of bourgeois culture. But after 1890 liberals' criticism of the "middle classes," *Mittelstand*, and *Bürgertum* became more strident and their proclamations of "middle-class" virtues became less frequent and convincing. Again and again, we find contemporary attacks on the German *Bürgertum*'s "philistinism," their obsession with monetary gain, their absorption with special interests, and their inability to generate a common set of social values and political goals.[62]

Many of these attitudes toward the *Bürgertum* can be found in Max Weber's social thought. Weber came from the very heart of the liberal establishment; his grandfather was a textile manufacturer in the west, his father a successful lawyer and National Liberal politician. Weber himself underwent the rites of passage characteristic of his social group: a law degree, membership in a dueling fraternity, a reserve officer's commission, a professor's chair. But Weber could not sustain that faith in the *Bürgertum* upon which the progressive expectations of the liberal social vision had once rested:

> I am myself [Weber wrote in 1895] a member of the *bürgerlich*
> class . . . and was raised with its attitudes and ideals . . . . When I ask
> myself if the German *Bürgertum* is today mature enough to be the political leaders of the nation, I am not able *today* to answer this question in the
> affirmative.[63]

Like many of his contemporaries, Weber believed that he belonged to an epigonic generation, doomed to live in the twilight of decline. As they looked back to the years before 1890, a number of Wilhelmine liberals seemed to see a happier, simpler, more integrated age. This, for example, was the feeling aroused in one reviewer by his reading of Joseph Hansen's biography of

Gustav Mevissen: "Doesn't something like homesickness for a lost world
creep over us when, in this age of *Realpolitik* and conflicting interests, we
read of the Vormärz liberals' burning idealism and pure selflessness?"[64] In an
essay on Alfred Dove, Friedrich Meinecke recorded a similar perception of
decline. During the years after the *Reichsgründung*, Meinecke wrote,
"classical liberalism" gradually was replaced by a new emphasis on sensual-
ity, restlessness, and pessimism. This spiritual reaction, he argued, was
closely tied to changes in the nature of German life itself, changes in which
"the internal and external worlds, society and the individual, spirit and nature
affected one another in ever darker ways."[65] The newly popular writings of
Nietzsche and Schopenhauer, novels such as Thomas Mann's *Buddenbrooks*,
and social analyses like Tönnies' *Gemeinschaft und Gesellschaft* all point to
this diffuse sense of uneasiness within German culture.[66] Even Weber, who
was much too tough-minded to embrace the fantasies sometimes provoked by
this fashionable pessimism, based his view of social change on the belief that
"rationalization," once thought to be the source of liberation and enlightenment, was in fact producing ever more restrictive limits on individual
freedom.

At the source of this growing disaffection with modernity was usually an
image of the social world threatened by disorder, beset by the evils inherent in
big-city life, strained by the pressures of an uncontrollable population growth,
and culturally blighted by an apparently irresistible decline of taste and discrimination.[67] The corporate values and social background of Germany's
educated elites may have made them particularly susceptible to this kind of
world view. Many universities were still in small towns where traditional
mores lasted, professors often came from traditional social groups without
close ties to the worlds of industry and technology, and academic values
continued to resist an acceptance of modernity.[68] Many *Gebildete*, therefore,
looked without understanding or sympathy on the transformation of German
society and presented themselves as the beleagured guardians of culture
within a hostile environment. How much of this was truly felt and how much
of it was pose, we will probably never know. Indeed, one wonders if these
men knew themselves.

Nor do we know how widespread and deeply felt these pessimistic perceptions were in the rest of German society. Certainly only the most extreme and
alienated social critics could condemn modernity with that total consistency
which is always the mixed blessing of a small minority. Furthermore, it is not
difficult to assemble counterexamples of men who celebrated the achievements of the age.[69] One suspects that most Germans (and most German
liberals) were somewhere between the extremes of unrelieved pessimism and
boundless optimism, aware of the tensions and conflicts in their society but

also proud of its achievements. These people could view with satisfaction
Germany's towering technological accomplishments, industrial strength, and
military power. But they sensed that these same developments were creating a
world filled with dangers for their own values and interests.[70]

Some Germans turned to social Darwinism as a way of reconciling their
hopes and fears about the present. The "Darwinian" view of persistent struggle, both within and among nations, accounted for the disturbing features of
the contemporary world without destroying the hope that history moved on an
upward course. After 1890, social Darwinism attracted men from a variety of
points in the liberal movement. Friedrich Naumann, for example, sought to
give it a democratic, reformist cast: he wanted, as he put it, to blend Darwin
and Rousseau. On the right, Darwinism had a harsher visage. To someone
like Alexander Tille, the "survival of the fittest" became an ideological
justification for repression at home and imperial expansion abroad; the
dangerous elements in Germany, like the lesser races in the world, had to be
mastered so that the "fittest" could win the battle for existence. In Germany
social Darwinism did not become linked with laissez-faire; both its left- and
right-wing advocates acknowledged that the state would have to play a role to
insure that the struggle for existence turned out as they thought it should.[71]

Although many liberal social thinkers did not embrace social Darwinism,
an increasing number of them did recognize that social conflict was a permanent part of the contemporary world. This increased the right wing's desire for
a strong interventionist state. And even on the left, where the progressive
impulses of liberal ideology retained some residual vitality, fewer and fewer
men believed that social conflict could be resolved or even contained by the
free flow of social and economic forces. In the face of the labor movement's
increasing power and the periodic outbreak of massive industrial disputes, it
became almost impossible to maintain that doctrinaire passivity once preached
by Prince Smith and his disciples. Many left-wing liberals, therefore, began to
think in terms of state action as one answer to the long-debated "social
question." For instance, by 1905 Lujo Brentano, who had once hoped that
trade unions could synthesize economic freedom and social progress, began to
argue that state-sponsored institutions should be established in order to help
workers and employers settle their differences. The alternatives, Brentano
feared, were either a "new serfdom" or the persistence of labor struggles like
the miners' strike which had threatened to cripple the German economy in
1905.[72]

Another example of liberals' declining faith in the free play of
socioeconomic forces can be seen in their attitudes toward cartels.[73] There
was, of course, a great deal of disagreement about cartels as they then existed.
The representatives of heavy industry argued that they were a necessary

contribution to Germany's domestic prosperity and global power; other manufacturers, such as those for whom Gustav Stresemann spoke, complained
when cartels injured their own special interests; and some maintained that they
were a conspiracy against small proprietors and consumers. Nevertheless, a
remarkable number of liberals, even on the left, accepted cartels as a fact of
economic life and believed that, if they were properly regulated, they could
make a useful contribution to the general welfare. A similar consensus about
the idea of cartels (and a similar disagreement about the specifics of their
operation) existed among professional economists. Once again, Lujo Brentano is a useful illustration of a shift away from classical economic doctrines.
In 1904, in a speech which carries the added weight of personal confession,
Brentano declared:

> We still speak as though we live in an age of economic freedom (*Gewer-
> befreiheit*) and competition. This is an example of how our past experi-
> ences hinder our perception and judgment of the world around us. Today
> economic freedom and competition belong to the past. We live in an age
> of increasingly expanding monopoly.[74]

Brentano did not like this, any more than he liked the idea of state-sponsored
Sozialpolitik. But he accepted it as an inescapable fact and was willing to
recognize that cartels were there to stay. For him and for many others, both
cartels and state action were the inevitable consequence of Germany's inability to manage the conflicts engendered within a free social and economic
system.

The fear that freedom would not lead to harmony and progress had always
been an important motif in German liberal thought. This fear deepened after
1890 as an increasing number of liberals came to realize that the free movement of social and economic forces would have to be tightly controlled if their
brittle social order was to survive.

The Liberal Parties
between Right and Left

> Our public life displays the deepest
> internal divisions and uncertainties . . .
> not only are the political movements
> splintered into innumerable small and
> powerless groups . . . but also none of
> the different parties is at peace within
> itself.
>
> Wilhelm Kulemann (1911)[1]

The preceding chapters have shown how Wilhelmine liberalism was weakened by an erosion of its electoral position and an intensification of its internal socioeconomic conflicts. But despite these problems, the liberal parties would have had enough support to play a more effective role in German public life if they could have cooperated on a coherent political program. Instead, electoral decline and social dissensus increased the political divisions within the movement. After 1890, more and more liberals began to seek allies on their right and left flanks, among the conservatives and Socialists. The logic of electoral survival seemed to require such alliances in some areas. Moreover, the need for support in struggles over social and economic policy encouraged liberals to form coalitions with those with similar interests or at least similar positions on specific issues. As they turned toward these new alliances, liberals necessarily turned against one another.

After 1890, the cleavage between the two wings of the movement remained unbridgeable and the conflicts within each of the parties increased. The result was a complex pattern of political fragmentation which overlaid and reinforced the social and economic fragmentation which has just been described. There were, of course, still those who called for a united liberalism, a single party representing all progressive elements in the middle strata. Even in its closing chapter, the story of German liberalism is not without such poignant examples of hope's triumph over experience.[2] But most liberals knew that the hour of a united *Bewegung* had long since passed. Ernst Bassermann, for instance, dismissed liberal unity as a "phantom," while Eugen Richter had become reconciled to a new ideal, which he defined as a small faction of fifteen men "with whom one can maneuver."[3]

In the years immediately following Bismarck's resignation, the rightward drift of some elements within National Liberalism gathered increased momentum. In those districts where farmers made up a large part of the National Liberals' constituency, the mobilization of German agriculture against the Caprivi government's commercial policies exerted an almost irresistible pull to the right.

In Hesse, for example, National Liberals had to make arrangements with the right-wing Bund der Landwirte or else risk losing their electoral base. A similar pull came from some craftsmen and shopkeepers, who were attracted by the call of the right-wing parties for a revision of the liberal Industrial Code. In regions such as the Ruhr, the officials and businessmen who dominated party life increasingly saw themselves as a basically conservative political force with interests and values like those of the traditional right. Agrarians, *Mittelstand*, and industrialists all identified the pursuit of their own specific interests with the defense of German society against Social Democracy. And as the Socialists' successes lengthened the shadow cast by the "red menace" over German life, the desire for a coalition of "state-affirming" forces increased. [4]

These desires for a broad, right-wing coalition were most clearly articulated in 1897 when Johannes Miquel, the author of the Heidelberg Declaration of 1884, called for a *Sammlung* of liberal and conservative politicians. [5] One impetus for the Sammlung was to come from the common economic interests of industry, agriculture, and the *Mittelstand*. Another was to be their common conviction that German society had to be defended against the dangers of democratization. [6] In a speech given in 1897, William II brought these two themes together when he promised that the "protection of the national labor of all productive strata" was to be accompanied by the "ruthless repression of all disorder, which will involve, among other things, special legislation limiting the workers' right to strike." [7]

The Sammlung was a revised version of that sociopolitical coalition which Bismarck had hoped to construct in 1866, during the "Second *Reichsgründung*" of 1878–79, and in the Kartell Reichstag of 1887. At the leadership level, it was sustained by a nexus of personal relationships and political alliances between propertied, educated, and aristocratic elites. Many of its leading advocates, like Miquel himself, had direct ties to landed aristocracy through intermarriage and personal ennoblement. [8] Regionally, the Sammlung worked best where National Liberalism had become the functional equivalent of a conservative party: Westphalia, parts of Hanover and Schleswig-Holstein, Hesse, and a few other areas in the south and west. [9]

The common interests, values, and anxieties which lay at the basis of the Sammlung were of profound importance for German political and social developments after 1890. The leadership groups directly involved formed that coalition of elites which ran the administration, the military establishment, and vital sectors of the economy. They dominated liberal politics in some state Landtage—including Prussia—and on the national level they were able to prevent National Liberalism from ever becoming part of a broad movement for political and social change.

Despite their remarkable success in inhibiting reformist impulses in National Liberalism, the advocates of the Sammlung were not able to impose their will on the party as a whole. In a number of Reichstag districts, the structure of political alternatives precluded an alliance of National Liberals and conservatives. This was the case in areas where both liberal parties joined together against the Poles or the Catholics, as well as in those districts, mainly in eastern Prussia, where liberalism continued to represent an alternative to the right. In these situations, the increasing need for *Stichwahl* support drew National Liberals toward arrangements with the Progressives and in some cases with the Social Democrats, not toward a Sammlung with the right.[10]

The problem of regional diversity was more pronounced in state and local politics. Even in Prussia, where the Sammlung was strong, there were Landtag districts in which the National Liberals continued to battle against one of the conservative parties.[11] In Baden, liberals were often pulled to the left by their hostility to the Center; from 1908 to 1913, they were allied with the SPD in the so-called *Grossblock*. Anti-Catholicism had similar implications for some other southern liberals. In Bavaria, for example, a few National Liberals joined with Progressives in 1907 to form the Nationalverein für das liberale Deutschland, which sought to provide the basis for a united liberal movement.[12] At no point in the Wilhelmine era was the central organization of the National Liberal party strong enough to counter these regionally based divisions. In fact, as the party's national position grew weaker, the relative weight of local institutions probably increased.[13]

The influence of the Sammlung on National Liberalism was also limited by the party's continuing socioeconomic diversity, which pulled elements to the left as well as to the right. The great tariff debates of the 1890s, for instance, reawakened the deep divisions within National Liberalism on the question of free trade and protectionism.[14] National Liberals were even more divided about *Sozialpolitik*. To be sure, almost all of them were opposed to Social Democracy, but they did not agree about the best means to combat it. Some party members continued to advocate social reform measures and a majority of the Reichstag faction refused to vote in favor of repressive legislation against the labor movement.[15] Differences over *Sozialpolitik* often coincided with other socioeconomic conflicts within the party, especially those between the producers of raw materials and manufacturing interests.[16] Nor was there unanimity about the demands of the so-called *Mittelstand*, especially when it came time to translate general promises of support into concrete legislative accomplishments. This became clear during the Reichstag debate on the handicrafts law of 1897. In its final form, the law accepted some of the artisans' demands for corporate institutions and legal restrictions on apprenticeship, but each local trade was allowed to decide if these were to be compulsory.[17] In

essence, the law was a complex blend of freedom and compulsion, of the
interests of consumers and craftsmen, and thus reflected the contrary impulses
within National Liberalism itself. Understandably, the law did not satisfy the
extremist elements within the *Mittelstand,* just as the final resolution of the
tariff issue in 1902 would fail to fulfill the demands of the Bund der Landwirte.

By the turn of the century, a group of moderate National Liberals had begun
self-consciously to set themselves apart from the pro-Sammlung forces. Gustav Stresemann, for example, criticized the right wing of his party because of
its ties to heavy industry, whose interests were often at odds with the manufacturers he was paid to represent. Moreover, the political dimensions of the
Sammlung did not correspond to Stresemann's experiences in Saxony where,
by 1900, the era of liberal-conservative cooperation had been replaced by an
increasingly bitter struggle for power. Of course, Stresemann was an unwav-
ering enemy of socialism and the labor movement. In 1903, he joined in the
employers' campaign to create defensive institutions against trade unions. But
he did not believe in the kind of mindless repression popular among some coal
and iron producers from the Ruhr, nor was he willing to give up the hope that
a certain amount of reform might help to moderate the Social Democrats'
political and economic demands. Similarly, Stresemann, an outspoken advocate of imperialism, believed that Germany's role as a world power required
the conciliation of domestic conflicts, and therefore he distrusted those who
argued that imperial success should be the occasion for a preventive war
against Social Democracy.[18]

Around 1900 there was also a minor resurgence of the National Liberals'
left wing. The most significant institutional expression of this was the so-
called "Young Liberal" movement which began in Cologne in 1898. By
1906, there were sixty-four local Young Liberal organizations with over ten
thousand members. The point of departure for the *Jungliberalen* was anti-
clericalism, which they soon combined with opposition to the conservative
parties, a desire to cooperate with the Progressives on domestic issues, a
commitment to moderate political reforms, and a qualified willingness to
consider accommodations with Social Democracy. Although the Young Liberals were unable to gather enough strength to elect a candidate to the
Reichstag and never had a chance to impose their views on the party as a
whole, their enemies were never able to drive them from the party. They
remained, therefore, yet another element in National Liberalism's permanent
dissensus.[19]

It is within this context of permanent dissensus that Ernst Bassermann's
role can best be understood.[20] Bassermann's rather rapid rise to party leadership and his ability to survive repeated attacks from both the right and the left

were due not only to his talent for compromise but also to the way in which his career combined the conflicting elements in his party. Bassermann was a southerner, from Baden, but he was not an advocate of the *Grossblock*. He was a local notable and city councillor from the *Honoratioren* mold of traditional liberal leadership, but he was prepared to devote full time to political activity and showed considerable understanding for the organizational ambitions of the younger men within the party. As a lawyer, he was free from total dependence on any one interest group, but he was also a director of a number of corporations and thus had close ties to the business community. A self-conscious member of the *Bürgertum*, he was critical of the traditional aristocracy but did not share the *Jungliberalen*'s total disregard for the values and ideals of the Conservative party and its Junker leadership. He was willing to consider some kinds of political reform, such as a revision of the suffrage laws, but he did not believe in full democratization. He was a critic of the incompetence and shortsightedness often shown by the emperor and his advisers, but he was

> not only a politician and a statesman, but also—from inner conviction and with full significance—a former member of a duelling fraternity and a reserve officer. He could not and would not transcend these roles, so he struck out against the walls of the existing system without having the will to break through them.[21]

Bassermann, together with a number of other National Liberals who wished to reconcile the conflicting forces within the party, had high hopes for the Bülow Bloc, the electoral alliance between the conservatives and all three liberal parties which was formed in 1906 in order to defend the government's colonial policies. Bassermann expected that an agreement with the groups on either flank would lessen the right-left tensions among National Liberals. Moreover, by focusing voters' attention on the need to support imperialism and to oppose the Catholics and the Social Democrats, the party could downplay its own socioeconomic differences. In fact, the campaign which preceded the Reichstag elections of 1907 brought greater harmony ·to the National Liberals' ranks than many would have thought possible just a few months earlier. For a moment it appeared that the party might establish itself as the central link between right and left and thus once again become the government's indispensable parliamentary ally.[22]

But the bloc did not bring about a return of the "liberal era" of the 1870s. His own self-advertisements to the contrary notwithstanding, Bülow was not Bismarck. Nor was the sociopolitical world of 1907 like that of the early seventies. As someone remarked, the bloc resembled a new orchestra which could play only the simplest of tunes—they specialized, one might add, in

patriotic melodies. From the first, the parties on the bloc's far right and left
were restive and their agitation inevitably stirred up trouble among National
Liberals. Conflicts between heavy industry and manufacturers, agrarians and
industrialists, reactionaries and moderates, the Reichstag and Prussian Landtag *Fraktionen* became increasingly disruptive as time went on. In 1909,
when the government insisted on retaining inheritance taxes in its proposals for
financial reform, the Conservatives, as well as several National Liberals
closely allied with agrarian interests, voted against the bill and brought about
a dissolution of the bloc.[23]

The disappointment produced among moderate and left-wing National Liberals by the breakup of the bloc intensified their opposition to the Sammlung.
One expression of this was the Bauernbund, formed by liberals in 1909 in
order to challenge the position of the right-wing Bund der Landwirte among
agrarian groups.[24] Another was the Hansabund, which was organized in June
1909 while the Reichstag was still debating the tax question. The purpose of
this organization, as Gustav Stresemann told a meeting in Dresden, was to
ensure that the "productive *Bürgertum*" attained the political significance its
social and economic power merited. To do this, it was necessary to have an
institution as powerful as the Bund der Landwirte or the labor movement.[25] In
fact, the Hansabund made some impressive gains during its first year of existence: by 1910 it had some five hundred local organizations with a quarter of a
million members. Equally impressive was the range of social groups the Bund
was able to attract: industrialists, bankers, interest-group representatives, as
well as white-collar workers, artisans, and small businessmen. It also contained men from both wings of the liberal movement. In 1912, for example,
twenty-one National Liberals and thirty-eight left liberals were elected to the
Reichstag with the Hansabund's support.[26]

Some enthusiasts saw the Hansabund as the foundation of a new liberal era,
a turning point in the domestic history of the Reich. In fact, the history of the
Bund illuminates the liberals' inability to create a cohesive basis for support
among the middle strata. From the beginning, the Hansabund was sorely
troubled by internal divisions which quickly sapped much of its initial vitality;
after a year of rapid growth, its membership stagnated at the level reached in
1910.[27] Nor was the Hansabund able to overcome the deep fissures within
National Liberalism: at the same time that it helped bring some liberals together on the left, it further alienated others on the right. The National Liberals' Reichstag delegation elected in 1912, therefore, contained men associated
with the Hansabund and with the heavy industrialists' Zentralverband
deutscher Industrieller, men from the Bauernbund as well as supporters of the
Bund der Landwirte, defenders of moderation and of authoritarian reaction.[28]

During the years just before the war the conflicts among these various

elements within National Liberalism intensified. The Socialists' dramatic
election victory in 1912 and a new outbreak of strikes encouraged right-wing
demands for a concerted attack on their domestic enemies. The Kartell der
schaffenden Stände, established by agrarians, *Mittelstand* groups, and industrialists in 1913, signaled the beginning of a new antidemocratic counteroffensive.[29] At the same time, liberal elites in a number of regions moved to the
right. Antagonisms between the right-wing Prussian Landtag *Fraktion* and the
national leadership grew sharper. In Baden, the *Grossblock* dissolved and thus
ended the only instance of sustained cooperation between liberals and
Socialists on the state level. In Bavaria, men from the liberal *Bürgertum*
seemed willing to join with various clerical elites against their common
enemies on the left.[30] And in parts of Hanover and Westphalia, formerly
liberal elements were won over to conservative organizations.[31]

Bassermann responded to this situation just as Bennigsen had three decades
earlier, by reasserting the party's middle position and obscuring internal differences with reaffirmations of unity. Tactically, he tried to find a way between left and right. He was willing to support ad-hoc alliances between
National Liberals and Progressives (which occurred in some districts during
the Reichstag elections of 1912, the Prussian elections of 1913, and the Saxon
elections of 1914), but he rejected any fusion of the two parties. He would not
go along with proposals for repressive action against the labor movement, but
he continued to condemn those who wanted greater accommodation and
reform.[32]

There are a number of indications that by 1914 Bassermann's ability to
keep his party together was ebbing. In 1912, 30 of the 109 voting members of
the National Liberal *Vorstand* handed in blank ballots when he was reelected
party chairman.[33] And in June 1914, just a few days before the assassination
at Sarajevo, Bassermann warned his colleagues that National Liberalism was
faced with a new *Sezession*.[34] Perhaps, if war had not come that summer, the
National Liberals would have had to face another round of those defections
which had been so devastating in the late seventies. But even if the party
remained formally united, it was apparent to many National Liberals that their
unity was shallow and without substance. As one liberal wrote at the end of
June 1914: "one gradually beholds his membership in that which one still has
the courage to call a party. . . . Brrr!"[35]

When one considers what Bassermann was up against, his ability to postpone a final split within his party is very impressive. But the price of unity was
often impotence. For example, the National Liberals were forced to adopt a
self-consciously ambiguous position with regard to suffrage reform.
Officially, the party endorsed the existing democratic suffrage for the
Reichstag (even though many on the right would have liked to see it changed)

but advocated only minor adjustments in the Prussian three-class system (even though some on the left favored more extensive reform). The result of this position was to frustrate both wings of the party and, equally important, to contribute to the parliament's failure to resolve an issue of increasing symbolic and practical importance.[36] A similar pattern emerged in the National Liberals' attitudes toward constitutional reform. Even before 1908, when William II gave his monumentally inept interview to the *Daily Telegraph*, many thoughtful Germans had begun to worry about the power given to the monarch in the imperial constitution. Bassermann shared these worries and, together with a number of moderate liberals, tried to find ways of increasing the "responsibility" of the executive. But neither Bassermann nor the majority of his colleagues was willing to consider a significant expansion of parliamentary power. As had so often happened in the past, National Liberals lacked a clear alternative to the *Staat*'s hegemony over the *Volk*. In 1913, when the inherent contradictions of the imperial system had become unmistakable, Bassermann's response was the rather pathetic hope for a great man. "In this time of epigones," he wrote, "the desire for a powerful statesman, such as Bismarck once was, is becoming stronger and stronger."[37] In the lost opportunities for reform which filled Germany's final decade of peace, we can find vivid illustrations of the liberals' persistent inability to unravel the long-standing dilemmas in their political thought and action.

The story of left-wing liberalism in the Wilhelmine period begins with a renewal of that old division between Fortschrittspartei and Sezession which had temporarily been healed in 1884. By the early nineties, the leaders of the Sezession had come to regret their decision to merge with the Progressives. They were convinced that Eugen Richter's rigid policy of opposition was preventing them from achieving a broader popular base and more fruitful participation in Chancellor Leo von Caprivi's "new course." When these frustrations came to a head during the debate over the military budget in 1893, the two groups split once again into opposing factions.[38] But the division of 1893, like the merger of 1884, was quickly followed by the destruction of the hopes upon which it had been based. The Reichstag and Landtag elections of 1893 produced smashing defeats for both left-liberal groups. A year later, Caprivi's well-intentioned but rather ineffective political career was over and with it ended the Sezession's hopes for better relations with the administration.[39]

From 1893 until just before his death in 1906, Eugen Richter dominated the Freisinnige Volkspartei. Richter seems to have become reconciled to being the leader of a permanent minority, which he kept together with a well-run organization and the force of his untiring but unchanging political rhetoric.[40]

To many leaders of the Freisinnige Vereinigung, however, this was not enough. They refused to abandon the hope that they might achieve a greater role in German political life. And to do this, they were prepared to abandon some old beliefs and habits. "The danger of becoming ossified is at hand," wrote Theodor Barth in 1893, "the party has lost its powers of attraction, it lives from old traditions.... New times create new problems."[41]

In the years after 1893, left liberals' search for new political strategies became more urgent as they became increasingly involved in struggles over economic policy. Both interest and ideology led them to defend Caprivi's tariff treaties and to oppose efforts to limit free enterprise. As we have seen, left liberalism appealed to consumers and to those occupational groups which were advantaged by free trade: some bankers and financial interests, commercial elites in coastal cities, animal raisers, some small businessmen, and so on. Most of these same groups also opposed revisions of the *Gewerbeordnung* which would restrict competition and therefore raise retail prices.[42] This defense of material interests was embedded in a matrix of spiritual values. Left liberals still saw themselves as the spokesmen for the common good against special interests; moreover, the mobilization of agrarian protectionism by the Junkers revitalized antiaristocratic sentiments and helped to convert the debate over economic issues into a struggle between "progress" and "reaction."[43]

Just as the desire for protection encouraged coalitions on the right, the struggle for economic freedom made some liberals look for allies on the left. The founders of the Handelsvertragsverein, like some advocates of the Sammlung, hoped that material interests might provide a source of cohesion for different political groups. Thus Georg von Siemens, one of the Verein's founders, argued that free trade was basically a "question of feeding the population [*Magenfrage*]" and therefore something which concerned everyone regardless of party affiliation.[44]

This search for allies led some liberals toward the Social Democrats, who had favored the Caprivi treaties and opposed their revocation. Socialists and left liberals had also voted together against proposals for new repressive legislation in 1894 and 1899 and against the handicrafts law of 1897. Equally important, a few liberal leaders were deeply impressed by the emergence of revisionism within Social Democracy. The ideas of Socialists such as Vollmar and Bernstein seemed to indicate that the SPD was ready to join in a moderate alliance in favor of economic liberalism and political reform. By the mid-nineties, Theodor Barth was calling attention to these changes in Social Democracy, and by the turn of the century he was urging electoral alliances between liberalism and the Social Democrats. Barth recognized that such an alliance would require the liberals' support for an active *Sozialpolitik*, a policy

he urged on his party colleagues with the help of such veteran social reformers
as Lujo Brentano. In 1902, Theodor Mommsen gave this strategy his blessing
in a widely read pamphlet entitled "What Can Save Us."[45]

Barth's position also found support in the National Social Association
founded by Friedrich Naumann in 1896.[46] Naumann, a Protestant clergyman
turned full-time activist, began his career in Adolf Stoecker's socially conscious but politically conservative Christian Socialist movement. In the mid-
nineties he broke with Stoecker and began to advocate a distinctive blend of
nationalism, social reform, and political democratization. Naumann and Barth
were drawn together by their common struggle against reaction and for free
trade, as well as by their desire to make the labor movement part of a
moderate reformist coalition. In 1903, after a series of election defeats,
Naumann dissolved his association and led the majority of its members into
the Freisinnige Vereinigung.[47]

Eugen Richter and his followers viewed Barth and Naumann with undis-
guised hostility. They did not like their emphasis on national power and did
not share their enthusiasm for naval expansion and *Weltpolitik*. Naumann's
grandiose plans for a broad coalition "from Bebel to Bassermann" did not
meet with much sympathy among men who had come to regard a small,
well-disciplined party of the middle strata as the best response to the problems
posed by liberalism's decline. Despite the fact that they had to make some
electoral accommodations with the SPD, the Freisinnige Volkspartei continued to oppose policies which might have made more sustained cooperation
possible. They did not, for example, press for a democratization of local
elections and they were persistently reticent on the subject of social reform
legislation. As long as Richter lived, therefore, his party continued to wage an
increasingly fruitless struggle against both the left and the right.[48] In south
Germany, the Volkspartei was much more open to political democracy than
Richter's group, but a majority of its members also resisted efforts to include a
vigorous social reform plank in their program. This lingering apathy about the
problems of industrial society helped to prevent closer cooperation between
the Volkspartei and the labor movement.[49]

There was also a good deal of resistance to Naumann and Barth in the
Freisinnige Vereinigung itself. But because the heirs of the Sezession had a
tradition of loose and decentralized political action, their ideas were tolerated
even when they were not accepted. This organizational style was one reason
why the merger of National Socials and the Vereinigung went off so
smoothly—a rather ironical situation considering Naumann's theoretical
commitment to organizational cohesion and disciplined collective action.
Moreover, some of the banking and commercial interests in the Vereinigung
realized that "an opening to the left" (or at least talk of "an opening to the

left'') might bring them valuable support in their campaign for free trade. Because they did not employ many workers, they could easily afford to support some social reforms and trade unionism. But there was never any doubt that the interests of these bankers and merchants had little in common with even the most moderate formulation of Social Democratic demands.[50]

Another limitation on the acceptance of an ''opening to the left'' among both Freisinnige factions stemmed from the conflicting electoral strategies they were forced to follow in different regions. Just as the advocates of the Sammlung were often opposed by National Liberals who needed left-wing support, so Naumann and Barth were opposed by left-wing liberals who needed assistance from the right in order to survive in certain Reichstag districts.[51] A similar situation existed in the Prussian state elections: in some Landtag districts, the liberal left served as an alternative to the SPD, elsewhere it represented the left against the right, and in a few areas it joined with right-wing parties against the Poles. In many cities and southern states, right- and left-wing liberals combined against their common enemies.[52] For the Freisinnige, as for the National Liberals, the contrary pull of left and right was not simply a matter of interests and ideology, it was built into the structure of political alternatives in various parts of the Reich.

By 1906, some of the original enthusiasm for an opening to the left had begun to ebb. Four years earlier, a new tariff law had settled the economic issues which had provided an important source of communality between liberals and labor. The Social Democrats' official rejection of revisionism, together with a rebirth of radicalism on the Socialist left, also weakened the advocates of a liberal-Socialist alliance in both parties. Finally, by 1906 a movement toward closer cooperation among the left-liberal factions was underway. Eugen Richter's death that year removed one important impediment to closer cooperation. At about the same time, the Volkspartei came under the influence of a new generation of leaders who were much less reluctant to cooperate with those whom their fathers had dismissed as ''Prussian'' Progressives.[53] Support for a fusion of the left-liberal parties significantly increased when all three factions joined in the Bülow Bloc. By bringing all the liberals together, the bloc helped to fulfill Naumann's dream of a united liberalism. But whereas Naumann had hoped this unity would spark a campaign against reaction, the unity in the bloc also involved alliances with right-wing parties (including, in some areas, radical anti-Semitic groups) and sharper opposition to Social Democracy.[54] The cost of membership in the bloc eventually proved to be too high for Barth, who defected with a small group of left liberals in 1908.[55] But Naumann, together with a majority in the other factions, stayed on until the bloc was dissolved a year later.

The distance between the liberal left and the labor movement was not

narrowed when the three left-liberal factions finally united to form the
Fortschrittliche Volkspartei in 1910.[56] Differences of ideology, material
interest, and political strategy continued to inhibit any sustained cooperation
between the new party and what Naumann referred to as "the proletarian wing
of liberalism." These inhibitions can be seen clearly in the new party's
position on the suffrage question, which many Social Democrats had come to
regard as the clearest expression of political inequality in Germany. Unlike
the National Liberals, the liberal left was prepared to advocate a democratization of the Prussian suffrage. This allowed them to reaffirm their opposition to
the Conservatives without much cost since their already fragile position in the
Landtag would probably not have suffered much from a change in the electoral laws. But the question of voting regulations for local elections was much
more difficult. In the cities, it was not Conservatives but Social Democrats
who made up the liberals' most formidable opposition; furthermore, in many
cities and towns the left liberals still had considerable influence, precisely
because the suffrage advantaged the urban middle strata from whom their
support was drawn. In these cities, local liberal leaders knew that universal
suffrage would mean political extinction. The party program, therefore, spoke
of the need to reform local election laws and even advocated the end of the
class suffrage, but it stopped short of demanding full democratization.
Equally important, left liberals in many cities continued to take advantage of
existing inequalities and even went out of their way to preserve them. Understandably enough, the Socialists looked upon this as yet another example of
liberal hypocrisy and unreliability.[57]

Conflicts between liberals and Socialists were sometimes mitigated by tactical accommodations and personal cooperation. But the evidence on local
political affairs records numerous instances of distrust and animosity between
the two movements.[58] Here, at the lowest level of political and social interaction, long-established patterns of hostility and discrimination continued to
create formidable barriers to a political alliance between the middle strata and
the working class. Professors and publicists such as Naumann, Barth, and
Mommsen might solemnly declare that the liberal left had to join with the
labor movement, but they were unable to create the climate necessary for such
cooperation in the everyday world of the liberal voter.[59]

Voting behavior during the elections of 1912 suggests that these problems
persisted throughout the prewar period. Following the first round of voting,
both the left liberals and the Socialists recognized the need for cooperation.
The leaders of the SPD wanted liberal support against the right so that they
could extend what they already foresaw as a massive victory; the left liberals,
on the other hand, had been unable to elect a single delegate in the first round
and were desperately trying to avoid total disaster. In order to win over the

liberals, the Socialists were prepared to make a number of concessions, including the surrender of a few districts where they still had a chance of
defeating the liberal candidate. The Fortschrittliche Volkspartei responded to
this offer with caution since, as usual, they faced a two-front battle and
needed right-wing support in some places, Socialist backing in others. Nevertheless, party leaders did promise to have their voters support the SPD in
thirty-one *Wahlkreise*. In some districts there was a noticeable shift to the left
among the Progressives, but elsewhere left-liberal voters were extremely reluctant to support the SPD. As Carl Schorske pointed out in his study of
German Social Democracy, the elections of 1912 demonstrated once again
that the main line of cleavage in German political life was the one separating
the labor movement from the rest of German society.[60]

As had always been the case, the liberals' relationship with the *Volk* affected their views of the *Staat*. After 1890, the liberals' estrangement from the
labor movement seriously undermined their ability to find practical or theoretical alternatives to the imperial system. Officially, the left-liberal parties were
on record as favoring greater parliamentary power. The program of the
Fortschrittliche Volkspartei drafted in 1910 contained demands for:

> The extension of constitutional freedom in the imperial system; a respon-
> sible, collegial imperial ministry; strengthening and utilization of the par-
> liament's rights and a strengthening of its initiative.[61]

But these calls for an extension of the Reichstag's authority were always
limited by the knowledge that any parliamentary system would have to favor
the right or the left, not the liberals. In practice, parliamentary rule would
require that the Progressives either abandon all hope of participating in the
government or choose to join a coalition of right or left. Because they would
not (and perhaps could not) do this, they continually backed away from
supporting an unambiguous call for parliamentary sovereignty.[62] Indeed, during the crises which punctuated the final phase of the Reich's development—
the *Daily Telegraph* affair of 1908, the Zabern debate of 1913, and the
wartime crisis which began in 1917—liberal spokesmen were always careful
to disassociate themselves from calls for a party government.[63] In comparison
to the National Liberals, the liberal left was a great deal more vigorous in its
criticism of the status quo, but, like the right wing of the movement, the left
failed to develop clear-cut alternatives to the existing system. Friedrich Payer,
who was himself deeply involved in these debates, summarized the situation
correctly when he wrote that ''the Reichstag lacked not only the power but
also the will to direct government policy.''[64]

The same weakness can be found in left-liberal political theory. Friedrich
Naumann, for instance, that self-professed apostle of liberal renewal, advo-

cated a new version of the old liberal dualism in his well-known work *Demokratie und Kaisertum*. Political reform, Naumann maintained, was to come from a conversion of the emperor to the cause of democratization.[65] Max Weber did not share this faith in the emperor's democratic potential, but he also found it impossible to accept the autonomous power of the "popular will." "It is as if one were to speak of a will of shoe consumers," he wrote in 1908, "which should determine the technology of shoemaking. Of course the consumers know where the shoe pinches, but they never know how it can be improved."[66] Eventually Naumann and Weber moved closer to an advocacy of parliamentary government. Eventually both saw that the only resolution of the conflict between *Volk* and *Staat* was some kind of popular sovereignty. But they never totally abandoned the belief that the unreliability of the *Volk* might have to be checked by strong and independent leaders. This belief influenced the left liberals' contribution to the Weimar constitution and thus enabled liberalism's long-standing ambivalence about democracy to live on, with unfortunate consequences, well after 1919.[67]

We will never know how German liberalism would have developed if the war had not broken the continuity of German political development.[68] Some historians have found signs of a new vitality on the eve of the war, especially among left-wing liberals. It also seems as if the pressure from the liberals' enemies had eased: right-wing radicalism, at least as expressed in separate parties, had ebbed; the Social Democrats may have reached the limits of their potential constituency; and liberals were able to score some modest victories over the conservatives in eastern Prussia. But despite these hopeful signs, there is little indication that the movement as a whole was about to reverse its long-term decline. Throughout the Reich, liberals continued to face dangerous competitors all along the complex frontiers of their constituencies. Equally important, conflicts within the movement remained. There is no indication in 1914 that either liberal party, not to mention liberalism as a whole, would be able to overcome its regional, social, and ideological divisions and mobilize its supporters behind a coherent political vision.

Conclusion
Liberalism, Nationalism,
and the German Question

Perhaps the best way to begin summarizing the story of liberalism's decline in Germany is to recall those hopeful expectations which once had nourished liberal thought and action. Until the last decades of the century, many liberals looked forward to the creation of a harmonious social and political world, based on a reconciliation of *Volk* and *Staat*. They saw themselves as both instrument and beneficiary of this reconciliation. As the embodiment of enlightened opinion, liberalism was the party of the real *Volk*; as the representation of the *Mittelstand*, it was the expression of the common good; as the party of movement, its triumph was assured by the direction of historical change. There were, as we know, always some liberals who did not share this optimistic vision and many more who were touched by doubts and anxieties. But for almost a century, progressive Germans drew strength and courage from the hope that the future would belong to them. My analysis has tried to show why this did not happen.

From the start, those who wanted to use liberal ideas to understand and alter German reality confronted formidable obstacles: the power of the bureaucratic state, the "backwardness" of economic development, the fragmentation and fragility of participatory institutions. These aspects of Germany's historical condition inhibited the growth of a powerful liberal movement by imposing external restrictions and by shaping the liberals' own ideas and behavior. State power, for example, frustrated liberals but also fascinated them. Both as enemy and as a potential ally, the *Staat* helped to undermine their willingness and ability to provide meaningful political alternatives. Similarly, economic backwardness weakened their social base at the same time that it heightened their uneasiness about the nature and direction of social change. Finally, restrictions on participatory politics limited liberals' organizational efforts and also encouraged them to think of political action in spiritual terms. Liberals' ambivalence—toward the state, economic development, and political participation—reflected the fact that they had to struggle both *against* and *within* their historical world.

From the 1840s until the 1870s, it frequently seemed that the liberals'

struggle would end in triumph. In the business community and the universities, in local associations and national organizations, in journalism and even
in certain sectors of the bureaucracy, most vigorous and progressive men were
identified with the liberal cause. Support from these strategic elites was reinforced by the electoral victories that liberals scored in 1848, in the "new era"
a decade later, and in the first imperial elections. Furthermore, in the mid-
seventies liberals could look with satisfaction on a number of significant
accomplishments. The nation which they had desired for so long was a reality;
most of the old restrictions on social and economic freedom had been removed; and a national political public, guaranteed by a constitution and institutionalized in a German parliament, was beginning to take shape.

But these fruits of the "liberal era" did not provide the basis for a reconciliation of *Volk, Staat,* and *Bewegung.* Instead, the Bismarckian state,
greatly strengthened by its role in the achievement of nationhood, turned
against its would-be liberal allies; the effects of social and economic freedom
deepened the divisions within the liberals' own ranks and alienated them from
other important social groups; the formation of unified representative institutions provided a forum within which Germans could express their diverse
interests and loyalties. By the 1890s, their dreams emptied by frustration,
dissension, and defeat, the liberals receded to the fringes of political life.

The decline of liberalism as a political force had some profound consequences for German history during the first half of the twentieth century. In
the first place, liberals' inability or unwillingness to work for political change
contributed to the prolonged stalemate which characterizes the Wilhelmine
era. The ideological and strategic emptiness of so much of liberal politics—as
illustrated by the Caesarist longings on both the right and left—undermined
efforts to renovate German public life. Liberals, therefore, must bear some of
the responsibility for the failure of reform before 1914, the rather desultory
efforts at parliamentary initiative during the war, and the unhappy legacy
bequeathed to the Weimar Republic.

German liberalism's failure was not only a matter of parliamentary
paralysis and ideological sterility. Equally important was the way in which the
parties' decline—both qualitative and quantitative—deprived important
groups in German society of an effective vehicle for political action. Those
whom liberalism had traditionally sought to represent, the Protestant middle
strata, had neither the institutions nor the loyalties with which to convert their
special interests and parochial commitments into a national political force. As
a result they were left without a stable political position, suspicious of party
organizations, and susceptible to mythic promises of a transpolitical community. By the turn of the century, the most potent of these promises was the one
offered by national values and institutions.

As we have seen, nationalism had always been an important part of liberalism's historical development in Germany. Liberals had been instrumental in defining national issues and in making them a central element in German political life. By setting the search for national unity within a broader ideological context, liberals had given political meaning to the concept of nationality; by mobilizing popular support for the cause of national unity, liberals had provided nationalism with an institutional base. Both ideologically and institutionally, therefore, liberalism was the means through which cultural nationalism and traditional patriotism were transformed into a political commitment to national unification. Throughout the first two-thirds of the nineteenth century, liberals disagreed among themselves about the character and relative importance of this commitment. Most liberals assumed, however, that the freedom of the German *Volk* at home was inseparable from the freedom of the German *Volk* to define itself as a nation. The struggles for nationhood and for political reform seemed to be against the same enemies and for the same goals.

After 1866, the relationship between liberalism and nationalism was fundamentally altered. The first and most obvious reason for this was the way in which the Bismarckian "revolution from above" had severed the link between foreign political success and domestic political progress. Even though some liberals tried to maintain that there was an inevitable connection between unity and freedom, the lesson taught by Bismarck's triumphs became increasingly apparent: nationalism was not an inherently liberal concept and national goals need not be part of a progressive political ideology. On a number of levels and in a variety of ways, national issues were separated from a commitment to domestic reform. In school books and public rituals, periodicals and popular literature, the nation was presented as an autonomous source of values, a preeminent focus of loyalties, a political end in itself.[1] As early as 1871 Treitschke had begun to argue that nationalism should be the primary source of cohesion in German life. "Immature youth," he wrote, "is inclined to think of parties with the idealistic enthusiasm which a grown man reserves for his country." Nationalism, not liberalism; the army, not the parliament; war, not domestic politics—these were to be the formative values, institutions, and experiences through which social solidarity and political stability could be maintained.[2]

The *Reichsgründung* also encouraged changes in German attitudes about the character and purpose of foreign policy. A concern for the role of power, especially military power, had been growing since the 1850s; this concern was substantially strengthened by the dramatic victories of the Prussian army in 1866 and 1870.[3] At the same time, the achievement of nationhood helped to produce a shift in emphasis from the right of national self-determination to the defense of national self-interest. National power and interests, moreover, came to be defined in global terms. Bismarck had encouraged this process with his colonial policies in the mid-1880s, and his successors gave even greater attention to *Weltpolitik*. By the turn of the century, a significant part of the German public was convinced that an expansion of their national power overseas was dictated by a relentless logic inherent in modern life. Population growth, industrial development, and the threat of foreign competition combined to make imperialism seem like a prerequisite for national survival.[4]

The significance of these changes in the character of German nationalism was amplified by the fact that public concern for national issues developed a powerful institutional base. Like economic interests, regional loyalties, and political ideologies, nationalism was profoundly affected by the "participation revolution." By the 1890s, there was an extensive set of organizations devoted to mobilizing popular support for a variety of foreign political goals. Some of these organizations had a specific purpose, such as the defense of German interests against the Poles in eastern Prussia or the advocacy of a powerful battle fleet. Others were devoted to more diffuse goals such as military preparedness and imperial expansion. Almost all of these organizations drew their membership from the Protestant middle strata: the educated elite, which saw itself as the ideological standard bearer for the national cause; businessmen, for whom national power was often closely linked to personal profit; and a diverse collection of schoolteachers, shopkeepers, farmers, and craftsmen, who wanted a way of expressing their own identification with the nation. These national pressure groups had a preeminent place among all of the various institutions in which Germans participated in public life. The Kriegervereine, for example, had 31,915 local branches in 1913, with a total membership of 2.8 million—only the labor unions could come anywhere near that figure. The Flottenverein had 3,878 branches and well over a million individual and corporate members—substantially more than either liberal party. And even rather small organizations, such as the Pan-German League, could acquire considerable influence because of its members' importance in the cultural, economic, or political establishments.[5]

Like the local Vereine and special-interest groups which attracted the Protestant middle strata, national organizations were often overtly hostile to the parties and sought to distinguish their activities from the demeaning and divisive character of party politics.[6] Nevertheless, the relationship between these organizations and the parties was characteristically complex and problematic. Like so many other organizations, national pressure groups could not avoid becoming involved in electoral politics. Again and again, these groups found it necessary to further their goals by supporting a sympathetic candidate or party. Parliamentarians and party leaders frequently joined these organizations and sought to use them to provide electoral support and financial resources.

The political uses of nationalism were especially apparent to men on the right wing of the liberal movement. Most of the liberal right sympathized with the goals of military preparedness and colonial expansion sponsored by organizations such as the Flottenverein and Pan-German League. Moreover, these men regarded nationalism as a means of isolating and defeating their domestic opponents, whom they saw as linked to international movements and conspiracies. In the rhetorical world of the liberal right, therefore, the image of a free *Volk* struggling to fulfill its destiny was replaced by the image of an embattled nation, threatened by foreign and domestic enemies against whom only superior power could prevail. In this view, foreign political success became an antidote to domestic reform rather than its prerequisite.

National issues and organizations also helped to pave the way for an alliance between the liberal right and other conservative elements in German society. As we know, in 1884 and 1887 national agitation had been the occasion for political agreements between National Liberals and members of the two conservative parties. Similarly, the Sammlung advocated by Miquel at the end of the nineties had a foreign political dimension. From the outset, the Sammlung and the campaign for *Weltpolitik* drew their support from many of the same sources: national pressure groups, industrial interests, and party leaders who were eager to find new ways to maintain the established order. Miquel, together with men in the government such as Bülow and Tirpitz, persistently tried to fuse the search for a new conservative coalition with efforts to expand German power in the world. The primary goal of both campaigns was the same: a defense of the status quo against the dangers of democratization.

Even National Liberals who had doubts about the Sammlung realized that nationalism was a weapon they could not do without. In the first place, foreign political issues were one of the only sources of consensus within the party. As Friedrich Meinecke pointed out in 1912, the idea of imperialism was the most effective bond holding National Liberals together.[7] Equally important, nationalism offered a way to compensate for the National Liberals' failure to develop strong ideological and organizational roots within their constituency. "Elections," noted Ernst Bassermann in 1910,

> are not decided by the organized party following. Elections are decided by the non-organized, by what we call the driftwood. This is the secret reason why at times of momentous national questions, with great agitation of the national spirit, a sharp change comes about . . . . These great power movements . . . bring the sudden transformation. At hand are these hun-

dreds of thousands of non-organized voters who shift over to the parties
which urge the affirmative.[8]

And even when there was no dramatic national issue, the National Liberals
frequently were dependent on the aid of nationalist organizations. These were
among the most important of those "parallel action groups" which, as
Anthony O'Donnell has recently demonstrated, "provided party elites with an
array of substitute, non-party structures for mobilizing a mass constituency."[9]

Traditionally, the liberal left was much less comfortable with national
issues than the National Liberals. In many areas of the south and west,
left-wing liberals represented those who had opposed Prussian militarism in
1866 and continued to look with suspicion on an aggressive foreign policy.
The north German Progressives never entirely lost the hostility to official
military policies which had led to their emergence as a party. Furthermore,
throughout the Reich left-liberal voters tended to be more conscious of the
fiscal burdens imposed by large military budgets and unprofitable colonial
adventures than of their alleged economic advantages. Nevertheless, in the
course of the 1890s left-liberal attitudes toward national questions began to
change. The generation of leaders which came of age around the turn of the
century found the lure of imperial power much more compelling than the
memory of old issues and antagonisms. These men were usually less critical
of military policy than their elders had been and much more willing to support
Weltpolitik.[10] As we know, in 1907 the left liberals' support for colonial
policy had led them to join the Bülow bloc, a move which helped to open the
way for a fusion of the three left-wing parties in 1910. It may be an exaggera-
tion to claim, as one contemporary did in 1911, that naval and colonial
policies were no longer a source of disagreement among the *bürgerlich* parties, but their sharp differences had substantially diminished.[11]

On the left, as on the right, there were those who made foreign political
considerations their ideological fulcrum. Perhaps the most prominent example
is Max Weber, whose painful search for political and social values has already
been described. Throughout his career, Weber clung to his conviction that the
struggle for national survival was the central fact of modern political life and
the most compelling reason for the necessity of reform at home.[12] Weber's
views were given effective popular expression by Friedrich Naumann, who
also combined a desire for liberal renewal with support for Germany's imperial mission. Indeed, like the advocates of the Sammlung, Naumann's call for
an "opening to the left" rested on the belief that this political alignment
would be the best basis for an expansion of national power. However, on the
left, unlike on the right, national issues tended to make cooperation more

difficult. Naumann's well-deserved reputation as an imperialist was an important reason for the suspicion which he aroused among many in the labor movement.

The growing importance of national values on both the left and right of the liberal movement suggests the degree to which nationalism had permeated the political life of Wilhelmine Germany. It also points to the fact that nationalism was not a very good guide to political action or, in the long run at least, a very effective source of cohesion. Both reactionaries and reformers, protectionists and free traders, opponents and advocates of *Sozialpolitik* could buttress their positions with appeals to the "national interest."[13] At times—the elections of 1907, for example—nationalism could provide a focus for cooperation among very diverse groups; but as soon as the crisis had passed, disagreements about the meaning and implication of the national interest reemerged. Throughout the years after 1890, therefore, nationalism was much more likely to be used as a weapon in political controversy than as a means for its resolution.

Nationalism offered no real answers to the questions which beset German political and social life. Nationalism, after all, is not an ideology, not an explanation of the present, a plan of action, a model of the future. Nationalism is a myth, the symbolic expression of deep collective longings, anxieties, and discontents. And, as Bronislav Malinowski once wrote, "myths function where there is a sociological strain ... where profound historical changes have taken place."[14]

Many strains and changes contributed to nationalism's significance in imperial Germany: the character and timing of the *Reichsgründung*, Germany's vulnerable geographical position, the unfulfilled ambitions of this recent arrival among the great powers. But for our purposes, the most significant source of nationalism's hold on the imaginations of Germans is the way in which national values and organizations helped to fill the void left by the ebbing power of liberal thought and action. This is why nationalism was so particularly appealing to the Protestant middle strata from which liberalism had traditionally drawn its support. Once the *Bewegung* had broken into warring factions, the *Partei* hopelessly alienated from the *Volk*, and the *Mittelstand* permanently fractured into competing interests, the *Nation* seemed to offer the last best hope for unity and direction.[15] Just as the search for a free and united Germany had been part of liberalism's rise, so the search for a mythic national community was closely linked to the decline of liberal ideas and institutions. Politics, like nature, abhors a vacuum.

The national myth found its apotheosis in the summer of 1914, when Germans seemed to unite in celebration of the great victories they knew would soon be theirs. "I recognize no parties," said the Emperor, "only Germans." "On

the day of mobilization," said another observer, "society ... was transformed into a community."[16] The extraordinary power which this experience
exercised on Germans' imaginations came from the way it satisfied their
longings for a source of cohesion which transcended the ordinary social and
political world, for a unity unblemished by the struggles among parties and
interests. In August 1914, the outbreak of war seemed to have made possible
an "unpolitical politics" and a "national community." As Friedrich
Meinecke put it, "by cleansing the idea of the nation of everything political
and infusing it instead with all the spiritual achievements that have been won,
the national idea was raised to the sphere of religion and the eternal."[17]
Indeed, when one reads the accounts of these wonderful "August Days," one
is reminded of that sense of common purpose which Victor Turner has found
in some religious pilgrimages, that *communitas* of men who have joined in the
quest for some transcendent ideal, that ecstasy which accompanies the belief
that myth and reality have become one.[18]

When Germans awoke from these intoxicating dreams of community they
found that the war had deepened their divisions and increased the dreadful
distance between the myth of a unified nation and the realities of German life.
Every group in Germany suffered from this, but none felt the agonies of
awakening more keenly than the Protestant middle strata upon which
liberalism depended. The political upheavals after the war threatened the
state—to which many of these groups had looked for protection—and allowed
their traditional enemies, the Catholics and the labor movement, more
influence than anyone would have thought possible just a few years earlier.
Wartime mobilization, inflation, and then "economic rationalization" deeply
wounded some elements in the middle strata and further aggravated the social
and economic divisions among them.[19] Military defeat brought national
humiliation and called into question the very existence of the nation which
many in the middle strata saw as the ultimate political value and the last hope
for political cohesion. Every political movement was severely affected by the
war, every party faced new divisions and challenges, but only the liberals
confronted the danger and eventually the fact of total disintegration.

At first, the full extent of the postwar challenge to liberalism was not
apparent. In the elections for the Republic's Constituent Assembly held in
January 1919, the left-liberal Democratic party received 5.6 million votes,
over 18 percent of the total. But in 1919, as in 1881 and 1890, the liberal left
was unable to consolidate and build upon these victories. In 1920, as in 1884
and 1893, a number of liberal voters moved to the right and cast their ballots
for members of the People's party, the National Liberals' republican suc-
cessor. The Democrats never really recovered from this setback: by 1928 they
were able to win only about 1.5 million votes, 5 percent of the total. Nor was

the People's party able to hold on to its supporters: it declined from the 4 million votes won in 1920 (14 percent) to just 2.6 million (9 percent) eight years later.[20] As one contemporary at the end of the decade put it: "The middle strata run from party to party, with the advantaged party rising like a balloon only to be deflated again in the next election."[21]

In some areas, liberal voters turned away from the established parties immediately after the war and sought some new vehicle for political action. But until the mid-twenties most of the Protestant middle strata remained committed to one of the alternatives which had existed in the empire: the liberal left, the liberal right, and the traditional right. After 1924, however, a basic change in voting patterns began to emerge as an increasing number of voters moved to one of the newly created splinter groups. By 1928, this process had affected about 18 percent of the electorate. Some of these new parties were regionally oriented, such as the Schleswig-Holstein Landespartei and the Hanoverian party; others were social and economic, such as the Wirtschaftspartei and the Bauernbund; and others were religious or ideological, such as the three Protestant parties established between 1924 and 1928.[22] To some extent, all of these new groups were protest parties which attempted to mobilize their voters against both the existing political order and traditional political organizations. All of them, moreover, tried to find a way to link national political alignments more closely to local loyalties, special interests, or ideological communities—in short, all tried to root electoral politics more firmly in the specific social milieu of their constituency.[23] On the eve of the republic's final crisis, therefore, the Protestant middle strata were represented by a variety of groups which reflected their frustration and their fragmentation, but which further weakened their ability to play a positive role in German politics.

In the elections of 1930, the alternatives facing the Protestant middle strata were again fundamentally rearranged. That year, the National Socialists emerged from the pack of splinter parties and established themselves as a major political force by winning 6.4 million votes, 18 percent of the total. Some uncertainty remains about the *relative* importance of the various groups that enabled the Nazis to win this extraordinary victory, but the identity of these groups is clear enough: in addition to their own hard-core supporters, the Nazis picked up almost half of the traditional right's 1928 electorate, a significant number of new voters, and some voters who had previously supported one of the "middle parties," especially the right-wing liberal People's party.[24] After the Nazis' initial success, they began to attract voters from both liberal parties and from all of the splinter parties. Beginning with the state and local elections of 1930 and 1931 and continuing through the national elections of 1932, the National Socialist vote grew as these other parties shrank.[25]

Among the parties of the Protestant middle strata, the only effective resistance to this process came from the traditional right, not from the liberals. After its losses in 1930, the National People's party stabilized and even increased slightly in the elections of November 1932. In that election, on the other hand, the liberal and splinter parties won about 6 percent of the vote, just one-fifth of the amount they had shared four years earlier. For the first time since the "liberal era" a half-century before, the overwhelming majority of the Protestant middle strata were gathered within a single political movement.

The shift of liberal voters into the Nazi camp has often been noted by scholars who have sought to explain the rise of fascism in Germany. Seymour Martin Lipset, for example, made this shift the central element in his interpretation of fascism as the "extremism of the middle." But Lipset, together with most of those who have sought to revise or reinforce his analysis, concentrate their attention on the last years of the Republic and do not try to see how voting behavior in these elections was related to previous electoral preferences and earlier political experience.[26] The most important exception in this respect is Rudolf Heberle's masterful study of Schleswig-Holstein which shows how the political traditions and social structure of that region influenced those who switched from the liberal parties to National Socialism. Heberle's work is in line with the studies of contemporary electoral behavior which emphasize how established habits and values influence voters' choices between particular alternatives. As the authors of one classic work in this field have put it: "any particular election is a composite of various elections and various political and social events."[27]

In what way were the elections at the end of the Weimar era a composite of earlier elections? How was the appeal of the Nazi alternative to the liberal constituency amplified by earlier attitudes and values? These are necessary questions to ask if we are to understand why former liberal voters proved to be so much more vulnerable to National Socialism than the supporters of political Catholicism, the labor movement, and even—at least after 1930—of the traditional right.

In the first place, the Nazis' rapid conquest of the liberal electorate was made possible by the relatively low level of commitment to party politics which has so often been mentioned in our discussions of the Protestant middle strata.[28] This lack of involvement with, and even animosity to, the traditional parties undermined liberal activities before 1914, prevented the consolidation of either liberal party after 1919, and benefited the splinter parties in the mid-twenties. The Nazis, therefore, extended the appeal of the splinter groups which had proliferated after 1924: like these parties, the Nazis stressed that they represented a new alternative, untainted by past failure and uncorrupted by participation in the present regime.[29]

Second, those who voted *for* the Nazis after 1930 were continuing to vote *against* their traditional enemies, political Catholicism and the parties of industrial labor. An important reason why the Nazis were an acceptable alternative to the Protestant middle strata was the fact that these parties were not such an alternative. Indeed, the social and political disorders of the early thirties convinced many in the middle strata that strong measures were necessary against these old enemies and especially against Social Democracy and Communism. National Socialists, therefore, could present themselves as the most energetic and effective guardians of what had been, at least since the 1870s, Germany's most important sociopolitical frontier, that which separated the middle strata from the working class. The importance of this threat from the left was one reason why, after the elections of 1930, the Nazis seemed a better choice than the smaller and less powerful splinter groups.

Third, the Nazis were able to build upon and extend the distrust for party politics and parliamentary rule which had long been prevalent in the liberal constituency and which was substantially strengthened by the association of the republic with the catastrophes of defeat, revolution, and economic dislocation. By 1930, doubts about "politics" had become so widespread that both liberal parties had entered into alliances with political groups which overtly rejected the existing political system and actively sought some new kind of political order.[30] The Nazis were especially skillful in their manipulation of the middle strata's deeply rooted longings for an "unpolitical politics." Their propaganda included all of the various means through which political conflict might be transcended: a strong, authoritarian state, a corporate "depoliticization" of interests, and the creation of mystical bonds of cohesion in a national community.

This appeal to nationalism, which had played such a central role in liberal rhetoric before 1914, provided the most important and powerful link between established values and Nazism's success. From the campaign against the Young Plan until the famous Potsdam ceremony in the spring of 1933—in other words from the beginning to the end of Hitler's final drive for power— national issues, symbols, and institutions were fundamental parts of Nazism's program and strategy.[31] For some of his supporters, Hitler's poisonous blend of nationalism and racism was of particular importance, but the majority of those who moved into the Nazi camp after 1930 were responding to nationalist appeals of a more traditional kind. Like the prewar parties, the Nazis used patriotic organizations to mobilize support and used national loyalties to set themselves apart from their enemies, whose primary allegiance was to red, black, or Jewish internationalism. Moreover, and here again the comparison with imperial politics is striking, the Nazis used nationalism to build coalitions with other groups, to blur ideological divisions within their own ranks, and to deflect attention away from potentially divisive social and economic concerns.

By linking Nazism with long-standing attitudes and values, I do not mean to imply that January 1933 was the culmination of German history. A concern for continuities need not lead to a rigid determinism that denies the importance of personalities, particular events, and the force of immediate circumstances. Nor should we forget that Hitler's electoral success lasted for a rather brief period. It is possible, perhaps even likely, that the National Socialists would eventually have had to confront the same centrifugal pressures which had fragmented every previous effort to unify the Protestant middle strata. Nevertheless, after all the necessary qualifications have been recorded, the fact remains that the liberal constituency proved to be especially susceptible to Nazism after 1930. This is, I think, the clearest indication of German liberalism's bankruptcy and the most consequential effect of liberalism's failure to provide the ideas and institutions with which Germans could understand and master the problems posed by their nation's long journey to modernity.[32]

Notes

A complete list of works cited in
shortened form can be found in the
bibliography. Infrequently used works
are given in full in the notes. I have used
the following abbreviations throughout.

AHR	*American Historical Review*
AJS	*American Journal of Sociology*
APSR	*American Political Science Review*
AGSA	*Archiv für die Geschichte des Sozialismus und der Arbeiterbewegung*
AfK	*Archiv für Kulturgeschichte*
ASGS	*Archiv für Soziale Gesetzgebung und Statistik*
AfS	*Archiv für Sozialgeschichte*
ASW	*Archiv für Sozialwissenschaft*
AZ	*Allgemeine Zeitung*
CEH	*Central European History*
CSSH	*Comparative Studies in Society and History*
DAZ	*Deutsche Allgemeine Zeitung*
DR	*Deutsche Revue*
DV	*Deutsche Vierteljahrs-Schrift*
EGK	*Europäische Geschichtskalender,* ed. H. Schulthess
FBPG	*Forschungen zur brandenburgischen und preussischen Geschichte*
Fricke	Fricke et al., *Die bürgerlichen Parteien in Deutschland*
GWU	*Geschichte in Wissenschaft und Unterricht*
GuG	*Geschichte und Gesellschaft*
Gb	*Grenzboten*
HW	Heyderhoff and Wentzcke, *Deutscher Liberalismus im Zeitalter Bismarcks*
HJ	*Historical Journal*
HV	*Historische Vierteljahrsschrift*

HZ	*Historische Zeitschrift*
HJb	*Historisches Jahrbuch*
Huber	E. R. Huber, *Deutsche Verfassungsgeschichte*
INR	*Im neuen Reich*
IRSH	*International Review of Social History*
JbGMO	*Jahrbuch für die Geschichte Mittel- und Ostdeutschlands*
JbG	*Jahrbuch für Geschichte*
JbS	*Jahrbuch für Sozialwissenschaft*
JbW	*Jahrbuch für Wirtschaftsgeschichte*
JbbNS	*Jahrbücher für Nationalökonomie und Statistik*
JCEA	*Journal of Central European Affairs*
JCH	*Journal of Contemporary History*
JEH	*Journal of Economic History*
JHI	*Journal of the History of Ideas*
JMH	*Journal of Modern History*
KP	*Kommunale Praxis*
KPB	*Kommunalpolitische Blätter*
MSDR	*Monatshefte zur Statistik des Deutschen Reichs*
NZ	*Nationalzeitung*
PP	*Past and Present*
PSQ	*Political Science Quarterly*
PV	*Politische Vierteljahrschrift*
PJbb	*Preussische Jahrbücher*
RP	*Review of Politics*
RV	*Rheinische Vierteljahrsblätter*
SJb	*Schmollers Jahrbuch*
StL	*Staatslexikon*
StJb	*Statistisches Jahrbuch*
SDR	*Statistik des Deutschen Reichs*
VfSP	Verein für Sozialpolitik
VfZ	*Vierteljahrshefte für Zeitgeschichte*
VSDR	*Vierteljahrshefte zur Statistik des Deutschen Reichs*
VSWG	*Vierteljahrsschrift für Sozial- und Wirtschaftsgeschichte*

VVK	*Vierteljahrsschrift für Volkswirtschaft und Kulturgeschichte*
VZ	*Volkszeitung*
WK(e)	Wahlkreis(e)
Wigard	F. Wigard, *Stenographischer Bericht über die Verhandlungen der Deutschen constituierenden National- versammlung zu Frankfurt*
ZPSB	*Zeitschrift des königlich Preussischen statistischen Bureaus*
ZBL	*Zeitschrift für Bayerische Landesgeschichte*
ZGO	*Zeitschrift für Geschichte des Oberrheins*
ZfG	*Zeitschrift für Geschichtswissenschaft*
ZfP	*Zeitschrift für Politik*
ZfGS	*Zeitschrift für die gesamte Staatswissenschaft*

Introduction

1. Clifford Geertz, "Ideology as a Cultural System," *The Interpretation of Cultures: Selected Essays* (New York, 1973), p. 218. Geertz's essay is an excellent introduction to the problem of ideology.

2. Quoted in Angermann, *Mohl* (1962), p. 28. Some other examples can be found in Engelsing, "Bildung" (1968), pp. 346 ff.; T. C. W. Blanning, *Reform and Revolution in Mainz, 1743–1803* (Cambridge, 1974), Prologue; F. Gunter Eyck, "English and French Influences in German Liberalism before 1848," *JHI* 18, no. 3 (June 1957): 313–41; J. Snell, "The World of German Democracy, 1789–1914," *The Historian*, 31, no. 4 (August 1969): 521–38.

3. Until recently, most general works on German liberalism were loose narratives about liberal leaders and their ideas. The best known of these are Klein-Hattingen (1911–12), Stillich (1911), and Sell (1953). After I had virtually finished with this manuscript, three new interpretations appeared: Faber, "Strukturprobleme" (1975); Gall, "Liberalismus" (1975); and Mommsen, "Liberalismus" (1975). *Movement* (1976), by the late John Snell, also appeared too late for me to use; Snell's book covers a broader range of groups than mine—he includes everyone judged to belong to the democratic tradition—and it places more emphasis on personalities and political narrative. Gall's collection of essays, *Liberalismus* (1976), has the best bibliographical guide to the historical literature.

Part I

1. G. de Bertier de Sauvigny, "Liberalism, Nationalism, Socialism: The Birth of Three Words," *RP*, 32, no. 2 (April 1970): 147–66, discusses the evolution of the term's uses in Europe. A good brief treatment of the problem of definition is Rosenberg, "Rationalismus" (1930), pp. 508–14. For some other examples, see: Valentin, *Geschichte* (1930–1931), 1:326–27; Brandenburg, "Parteiwesens" (1919), Hock, *Denken* (1957), p. 3.

2. Goethe is quoted in Aris, *History* (1936), p. 187; Bismarck, *Erinnerungen und Gedanke, Werke* (1923–33), 15:16. On changes in the vocabulary of politics, see Sheehan, "Partei" (1974), and the literature cited there.

3. L. Wittgenstein, *Philosophical Investigations* (Oxford, 1953), p. 32.

Chapter 1

1. A. Ruge, "Selbstkritik des Liberalismus" (1843), *Sämmtliche Werke*, 2d ed. (Mannheim, 1847), 4:80.

2. See Kant's essay of 1784, "What Is Enlightenment?" reprinted in Kant, *Writings* (1970), pp. 54 ff.

Habermas, *Strukturwandel* (1962), Reinhart Koselleck, *Kritik und Krise. Ein Beitrag zur Pathogenese der bürgerlichen Welt* (Freiburg and Munich, 1959), Vierhaus, "Bewusstsein" (1967), Hans-Jürgen Haferkorn, "Der freie Schriftsteller. Eine literatursoziologische Studie über seine Entstehung und Lage in Deutschland zwischen 1750 und 1800," *Archiv für Geschichte des Buchwesens* 5 (1964): 523–711, discuss the emergence of a German public. Irene Jentsch, *Zur Geschichte des Zeitungslesens in Deutschland am Ende des 18. Jahrhunderts. Mit besonderer Berücksichtigung der gesellschaftlichen Formen des Zeitungslesens* (Diss., Leipzig, 1937), has a good deal of information on newspapers; Gerth, *Lage* (1935), treats the social position of intellectuals.

3. Schlumbohm, *Freiheit* (1975), pp. 39 ff.

4. Early institutional expressions of political opinion are discussed in the following works: Manheim, *Träger* (1933), especially on the lodges; F. Eulen, *Vom Gewerbefleiss zur Industrie. Ein Beitrag zur Wirtschaftsgeschichte des 18. Jahrhunderts* (Berlin, 1967), pp. 180 ff., on economic improvement associations; Gerteis, "Bildung" (1971), and Epstein, *Genesis* (1966), pp. 84 ff., on the reading societies. Nipperdey's article "Verein" (1972) is the best overall introduction to the problem of organizations in this period.

5. Quoted in Schneider, *Pressefreiheit* (1966), p. 82.

6. On the impact of 1789 in Germany, see: Valjavec, *Entstehung* (1951), pp. 146 ff.; Schnabel, *Geschichte* (1949–59), vol. 1; Julku, *Bewegung* (1965–69); T. C. W. Blanning, *Reform and Revolution in Mainz. 1743–1803* (Cambridge, 1974).

7. Schwemer, *Geschichte* (1910–1918), vol. 1, on Frankfurt; and Gothein, *Wirtschaftsgeschichte* (1916), vol. 1, pt. 1, pp. 1–56, on Cologne.

8. The most convenient guide to these developments is in Huber, 1:42 ff., and the summary on pp. 315–36. There is an excellent analysis of the revolution's impact on the free cities and small states of the west in Walker, *Home Towns* (1971), chaps. 6 and 7. Rudolf Morsey, "Wirtschaftliche und soziale Auswirkungen der Säkularisation in Deutschland," *Dauer und Wandel der Geschichte*, ed. R. Vierhaus and Manfred

Botzenhart (Münster 1966), pp. 361–83, offers a stimulating interpretation of the secularization of church lands; Helmut Berding, *Napoleonische Herrschafts-und Gesellschaftspolitik im Königreich Westfalen 1807–1813* (Göttingen, 1973), describes the Napoleonic system in a "satellite state."

9. Valjavec, *Entstehung* (1951), pp. 344–45, on Rotteck. For another example, see Franz Schnabel, *Ludwig von Liebenstein. Ein Geschichtsbild aus den Anfängen des Verfassungslebens* (Karlsruhe, 1927).

10. The connection between territorial reorganization and political dissent can be seen in the following regional studies: Grösser, *Liberalismus* (1929), p. 9, on Bavaria; Heger, *Partei* (1927), p. 9, on Württemberg; Karl Kurmeier, *Die Entstehung der nationalliberalen Partei Hannovers* (Diss., Göttingen, 1923); Karl Dorn, "Die Anfänge der deutschen Fortschrittspartei in Bayern" (Unpubl. diss., Munich, 1922).

11. Quoted in A. Schlingensiepen-Pogge, *Das Sozialethos der lutherischen Aufklärungstheologie am Vorabend der Industriellen Revolution* (Göttingen, 1967), p. 21.

12. Krieger, *Idea* (1957), pp. 261 ff.; Schnabel, *Geschichte* (1949–59), vol. 1. See also W. von Groote, *Die Entstehung des Nationalbewusstseins in Nordwest-Deutschland 1790–1830* (Göttingen, 1954).

13. Krieger, *Idea* (1957), pp. 261 ff.; Huber, 1:705 ff.; Griewank, *Studenten* (1949), pp. 8 ff.; Paul Wentzcke et al., eds., *Darstellungen und Quellen zur Geschichte der deutschen Einheitsbewegung im neunzehnten und zwanzigsten Jahrhundert*, 9 vols. (Heidelberg, 1957–74). For two examples of the influence of these experiences, see Gagern, *Liberalismus* (1959), pp. 57 ff., and Pagenstecher, *Lebenserinnerungen* (1913), 1:36 ff. According to Eyck, at least 11 percent of the men elected to the Frankfurt parliament in 1848 had belonged to a *Burschenschaft*: Eyck, *Frankfurt* (1968), p. 101.

14. There is a description of one of these ceremonies in Veit Valentin, *Frankfurt-am-Main und die Revolution von 1848/49* (Stuttgart and Berlin, 1908), p. 1.

15. A guide to these institutions can be found in Huber, vol. 1. The best general analysis is Brandt, *Repräsentation* (1968). Lloyd E. Lee, "Liberal Constitutionalism as Administrative Reform: The Baden Constitution of 1818," *CEH* 7, no. 2 (June 1975): 91–112, is a concise and lucid account of constitutional developments in Baden. Herbert Obenaus, "Finanzkrise und Verfassungsgebung. Zu den sozialen Bedingungen des frühen deutschen Konstitutionalismus," in Ritter, ed., *Gesellschaft* (1974), pp. 57–76, emphasizes the importance of fiscal considerations for the official sponsors of constitutionalism.

16. The most important documents are in Christian Engeli and Wolfgang Haus, eds., *Quellen zum modernen Gemeindeverfassungsrecht in Deutschland* (Stuttgart, 1975), and August Krebsbach, *Die preussische Städteordnung von 1808* (Stuttgart and Cologne, 1957). See also Koselleck, *Preussen* (1967), pp. 341 ff., 360 ff., 570 ff.

17. On censorship, see Schneider, *Pressefreiheit* (1966). Birker, *Arbeiterbildungsverein* (1973), pp. 17 ff., has a convenient summary of the laws governing organizations during the first half of the century.

18. The best discussion of these restrictions is in Kramer, *Fraktionsbindungen* (1968), pp. 17 ff.

19. Huber, 1:165 ff. For a contemporary critique of the provincial Landtage, see Hansemann (1830), in Hansen, *Briefe* (1967), pp. 28–29.

20. The conservatives' critique of representative institutions is discussed in Brandt, *Repräsentation* (1968), pp. 47 ff.

21. Huber, 1:342, and Vogel et al., *Wahlen* (1971), pp. 66–75.

22. Valentin, *Geschichte* (1930–31), 1:182, on Nassau; and Köllmann, *Harkort* (1964), pp. 141 ff., on Westphalia.

23. Political culture is defined in G. Almond and S. Verba, *The Civic Culture: Political Attitudes and Democracy in Five Nations* (Princeton, 1963), chap. 4.

24. Huber, 1:36 ff.; Grösser, *Liberalismus* (1929), pp. 19–26, on Bavaria; Annelise Reinhardt, "Volk und Abgeordnetenkammer in Baden zur Zeit des Frühliberalismus (1819–1831)" (Unpubl. diss., Göttingen, 1952), pp. 4–36, 44 ff.

25. Adam, *Jahrhundert* (1919), p. 23.

26. Stein, *Geschichte* (1884), p. 26, on Breslau; Otto Schell, *Elberfeld im ersten Dreiteljahrhundert der Hohenzollernherrschaft 1815–1840* (Elberfeld, 1918), pp. 28 ff.; Gause, *Geschichte* (1965–68), 2:334 ff., on Königsberg; Piechowski, "Wirksamkeit" (1967), on Halle.

27. The following contain information on the impact of 1830: Krieger, *Idea* (1957), p. 280; Neumüller, *Liberalismus* (1973), pp. 111 ff.; Christern, "Dahlmanns" (1921), pp. 235, 240; Pagenstecher, *Lebenserinnerungen* (1913), 3:9 ff.; Rosenberg, *Haym* (1933), pp. 44–46; Schramm, *Hamburg* (1943), p. 276; Valentin, *Frankfurt* (1908), pp. 70 ff.; Schmidt, *Staatsreform* (1966), pp. 103 ff., on Saxony.

28. See the following regional studies for the development of liberalism in the 1830s: Wilhelm Lempfrid, *Die Anfänge des parteipolitischen Lebens und der politischen Presse in Bayern unter Ludwig I, 1825–1831* (Strassburg, 1912), on Bavaria; Rotteck, *Schriften* (1841–43), 1:413 ff., on Baden; Brandt, "Gesellschaft" (1974), pp. 101–18, and Langewiesche, *Liberalismus* (1974), pp. 77 ff., on Württemberg; Johannes Iseler, *Die Entwicklung eines öffentlichen politischen Lebens in Kurhessen in der Zeit von 1815–1848* (Diss., Marburg, 1913), and Bullik, *Staat* (1972), pp. 43 ff., on Kurhessen; Sonnemann, "Oppermann" (1922), pp. 57 ff., on Hanover. Gunther Hildebrandt, "Programm und Bewegung des süddeutschen Liberalismus nach 1830," *JbG* 9, no. 1 (1973): 7–45, and Kramer, *Fraktionsbindungen* (1968), pp. 25 ff., have general accounts of politics in the *Mittelstaaten*.

29. Huber, 2:133 ff.; Fritz Trautz, "Das Hambacher Fest und der südwestdeutsche Frühliberalismus," *Heidelberger Jahrbücher* (1958), 2:14–52; and Edgar Süss, *Pfalzer im Schwarzen Buch. Ein personengeschichtlicher Beitrag zur Geschichte des Hambacher Festes, des frühen pfälzischen und deutschen Liberalismus* (Heidelberg, 1956), all contain accounts of the Hambach events. On Frankfurt, see Schwemer, *Geschichte* (1910–18), 2:590 ff.

30. Quoted in Hansen, *Briefe* (1967), p. 205.

31. On liberalism in the forties, see: Huber, 2:448 ff.; Koselleck, *Preussen* (1967); Krieger, *Idea* (1957), pp. 282 ff.; Kramer, *Fraktionsbindungen* (1968); Heffter, *Selbstverwaltung* (1950), pp. 246 ff.

Data on book publishing is given in Gerth, *Lage* (1935), pp. 101–3; the press is discussed in Koszyk, *Geschichte* (1966), pp. 87 ff.; magazines in Joachim Kirchner, "Redaktion und Publikum. Gedanken zur Gestaltung der Massenzeitschrift im 19. Jahrhundert," *Publizistik* 5 (1960), especially pp. 463 ff. The incidence of popular disorder is measured in Richard Tilly's important article, "Disorders" (1970).

32. J. Jacoby, *Vier Fragen beantwortet von einem Ostpreussen* (Mannheim, 1841). On the context and influence of this work, see: Edmund Silberner, "Johann Jacoby, 1843–1846. Beitrag zur Geschichte des Vormärz," *IRSH* 14, no. 3 (1969): 353–411; Gause, *Geschichte* (1965–1968), 2:514 ff.; Schorn, *Lebenserinnerungen* (1898), 1:144 ff.

33. K. Rosenkranz, *Aus einem Tagebuch* (Leipzig, 1854), p. 239.

34. Piechowski, "Wirksamkeit" (1967).

35. The problem of regionalism in Germany is discussed in general terms by Heinz Gollwitzer, "Die politische Landschaft in der deutschen Geschichte des 19/20. Jahrhunderts," in *Land und Volk. Herrschaft und Staat in der Geschichte und Geschichtsforschung Bayerns* (Munich, 1964); Dietrich Gerhard, "Regionalismus und ständisches Wesen als ein Grundthema europäischer Geschichte," *HZ* 174, no. 2 (1952): 307–38; Schieder, "Partikularismus" (1962). For various dimensions of the problem, see: Sombart, *Volkswirtschaft* (1909), chap. 1, on communications; Richard Tilly, "Germany 1815–1870," in *Banking in the Early Stages of Industrialization*, ed. R. Cameron (New York, 1967), pp. 151–82; Borchardt, "Kapitalmangels" (1961), p. 414, on investment; O'Boyle, "Image" (1968), p. 302, on journalism.

36. Hans Zehntner, *Das Staatslexikon von Rotteck und Welcker. Eine Studie zur Geschichte des deutschen Frühliberalismus* (Jena, 1929), pp. 94 ff., and Robert von Mohl, "Drei deutsche Staatswörterbücher," *PJbb* 2, no. 3 (1858): 248–49.

37. On the slow development of ties among various leaders of the opposition, see: Born, *Erinnerungen* (1898), p. 34; Hansen, *Mevissen* (1906), 1:302 ff. and 495 ff.; Gagern, *Liberalismus* (1959), pp. 115 ff.; Rosskopf, "Itzstein" (1954), pp. 135 ff.; Schmidt, *Blum* (1971), pp. 58 ff.

38. Besides in Nipperdey's fine article, "Verein" (1972), organizational patterns are discussed in Meyer, *Vereinswesen* (1970); Müller, *Korporation* (1965); Friedrich Sengle, *Biedermeierzeit. Deutsche Literatur im Spannungsfeld zwischen Restauration und Revolution 1815–1848* (2 vols., Stuttgart, 1971–72).

39. Edmund Silberner, "Zur Jugendbiographie von Johann Jacoby," *AfS* 9 (1969): 60 ff.; Hans Blum, *Lebenserinnerungen*, 2 vols. (Berlin, 1907–08) 1:27; Elben, *Lebenserinnerungen* (1931), pp. 10 ff. and 54 ff., on gymnastic societies and singing clubs. Additional examples of this kind of political activity can be found in: Falkson, *Bewegung* (1888), pp. 106 ff., and Gause, *Geschichte* (1965–68) 2:359 ff., 524 ff., on Königsberg; Rosenberg, *Haym* (1933), pp. 101 ff., on Halle; Stein, *Geschichte* (1884), pp. 213–14, on Breslau; Meyer, *Leben* (1912), pp. 40 ff., on Berlin; Böttcher, *Stephani* (1887), pp. 4–5, on Leipzig; Schramm, *Hamburg* (1943), pp. 282 ff.; Krabs, "Hamm" (1964), pp. 215 ff.; Koszyk, "d'Ester" (1960), pp. 43 ff., on Cologne.

40. Gothein, *Wirtschaftsgeschichte* (1916), vol. 1, pt. 1, p. 360. Additional treatments of the Handelskammer can be found in: Hansen, *Mevissen* (1906), 1:199; Klara von Eyll, *Die Geschichte einer Handelskammer, dargestellt am Beispiel der Handelskammer Essen. 1840–1910* (Cologne, 1964); Köllmann, *Sozialgeschichte* (1960), pp. 53 ff.; Zunkel, *Unternehmer* (1962), pp. 149 ff.; Fischer, *Staat* (1962), pp. 180 ff.

41. Quoted in Thomas, *Liberalism* (1951), p. 27. Two other examples: Schmidt, *Blum* (1971), pp. 80 ff., and Schurz, *Lebenserinnerungen* (1912–30) 1:107, which both deal with religious dissent within Catholicism. For more on this problem, see the literature cited below, chap. 3, nn. 26–28.

42. On this subject, see the stimulating remarks in Nipperdey, "Grundzüge" (1965), and Rosenberg, *Haym* (1933), p. 110. The identification of politics and "education" was not confined to liberalism. For similar trends in the labor movement during its early phase, see Born, *Erinnerungen* (1898), pp. 23–24, and Schieder, *Anfänge* (1963), p. 133. On the concept of *Bildung*, see: Vierhaus' article in Brunner et al., *Grundbegriffe* (1972), pp. 508–51; Hans Weil, *Die Entstehung des deutschen Bildungsprinzips* (Bonn, 1930); Hans Speier, "Zur Soziologie der bürgerlichen Intel-

ligenz in Deutschland," *Die Gesellschaft* 6, no. 2 (1929): 58–72; and Hajo Holborn's classic article, "Der deutsche Idealismus in sozialgeschichtlicher Beleuchtung," *HZ* 174, no. 2 (1952): 359–84.

43. Habermas, *Strukturwandel* (1962), pp. 118 ff.

44. Stein is quoted in Karl Georg Faber, "Die kommunale Selbstverwaltung in der Rheinprovinz im 19. Jahrhundert," *RV* 30, no. 1 (1965): 134, and Friedrich Meinecke, *Das Zeitalter der deutschen Erhebung, 1795–1815* (Göttingen, 1957), p. 96.

45. Gervinus, *Leben* (1893), pp. 238–39.

46. Quotations are from Engelsing, "Bildung" (1968), p. 355, and Balser, *Anfänge* (1959), p. 261, n. 58. See also Birker, *Arbeiterbildungsvereine* (1973), pp. 32 ff.

47. Rudolf Stadelmann, *Das landwirtschaftliche Vereinswesen in Preussen. Seine Entwicklung, Wirksamkeit, Erfolge und weiteren Ziele* (Halle, 1874), p. 308, on agricultural organizations, and Manfred Erdmann, *Die Verfassungspolitische Funktion der Wirtschaftsverbände in Deutschland 1815–1871* (Berlin, 1968), on the Handelskammer.

48. Quoted by Griewank, *Studenten* (1949), p. 12, from the constitution of an organization of students formed in Erlangen during the early 1830s.

49. Sybel quoted in G. P. Gooch, *History and Historians in the Nineteenth Century* (Boston, 1959), p. 131. For some other examples of this view, see: Christern, "Dahlmanns" (1921), p. 332; Wilhelm Treue, "Das Verhältnis der Universitäten und ihre Bedeutung für die Wirtschaft," in Lütge, ed., *Situation* (1964), pp. 228–29, on Liebig; Biedermann, *Leben* (1886), 1:60–61; Rosenberg, *Haym* (1933), p. 29; Jörn Rüsen, "Politisches Denken und Geschichtswissenschaft bei J. G. Droysen," in Kluxen, ed., *Ideologien* (1968), pp. 171–88.

50. Falkson, *Bewegung* (1888), pp. 71–72. On the liberals' concept of party, see: Sheehan, "Partei" (1974); the essays by Schieder in *Staat* (1958); Nipperdey, "Grundzüge" (1965); Gall, "Problem" (1968) and *Constant* (1963), pp. 286 ff.; Eichmeier, *Anfänge* (1968), pp. 1 ff.

51. K. Rosenkranz, *Über den Begriff der politischen Partei* (Königsberg, 1843). See also his *Tagebuch* (1854), p. 239.

52. Letter of February 1834 reprinted in Gagern, *Liberalismus* (1959), p. 133.

53. Falkson, *Bewegung* (1888), p. 111. Compare Mittermaier's views as cited in Conze, "Spannungsfeld" (1962), p. 232, and Gagern's remarks in January 1841, cited in *Liberalismus* (1959), pp. 236–37.

54. R. Haym's *Reden und Redner des ersten Vereinigten Preussischen Landtags* (Berlin, 1847) is a good example of this. See Rosenberg, *Haym* (1933), pp. 110 ff. Sybel's *Die politischen Parteien der Rheinprovinz* (Düsseldorf, 1847) gives more specific information than Haym's book, but is still very vague and uncertain about political alignments.

55. Hansen, *Mevissen* (1906), 1:243 ff. The most recent treatment is W. Klutentreter, *Die Rheinische Zeitung*, 2 vols (Dortmund, 1966–67).

56. Johann Jacoby (1832), quoted in Adam, "Jacobys" (1930), p. 70. For two other examples, see W. T. Krug's remarks quoted in Rosenberg, "Rationalismus" (1930), p. 523, and Robert Blum, quoted in Boldt, *Anfänge* (1971), pp. 161–62.

57. *StL* (1st ed.), 9:714. See also Gall, "Opposition" (1968), pp. 168–69.

58. Mundt quoted in Ruth Horovitz, *Vom Roman des Jungen Deutschland zum Roman der Gartenlaube. Ein Beitrag zur Geschichte der deutschen Liberalismus*

(Breslau, 1937), p. 20; Pfizer, *StL* (1st ed.), 9:70. Another example: W. Bussmann, "Gustav Freytag. Massstäbe seiner Zeitkritik" *AfK*, 34, no. 3 (1952): 264 ff.

59. Pankoke has a good discussion of the term in *Bewegung* (1970), pp. 19 ff. Gall, *Constant* (1963), pp. 44 ff., describes the concept in a European perspective. For two German examples, see: Rotteck, "Bewegungspartei," *StL* (1st ed.), 2:558–65, and the anonymous article, "Eine Umschau in der Gegenwart," *DV* (1846): 67–138.

60. Benzenberg is quoted in Horovitz, *Roman*, p. 19; Rotteck, *Schriften* (1841–43), 1:157 ff. Another example in Birtsch, *Nation* (1964), p. 24, n. 47.

61. Quoted in Conze, "Spannungsfeld" (1962), p. 233.

62. Erich Ackermann, *Georg Freiherr von Vincke und die innere preussische Politik in den Jahren 1845 bis 1849* (Diss., Marburg, 1914), pp. 18, 64; anon., "Parteien in Berlin," *Gb* (1846), pp. 179–80.

63. Quoted in Gall, "Problem" (1968), pp. 162–63. See also Wilhelm, *Verfassung* (1928), pp. 164 ff., and R. Eigenbrodt, *Meine Erinnerungen aus den Jahren 1848, 1849, und 1850* (Darmstadt, 1914), p. 20.

64. Rosenberg, "Strömungen" (1929), pp. 562–63.

65. This point is developed in Schieder, *Staat* (1958), pp. 114–15; Fraenkel, *Deutschland* (1968), especially pp. 13 ff.; Nipperdey, "Grundzüge" (1965).

Chapter 2

1. Engels, "Status Quo" (1964), p. 50.

2. Schultze, *Auseinandersetzung* (1925), pp. 44, 132. Manheim, *Träger* (1933), pp. 90, 102–3.

3. Gall, *Liberalismus* (1968), pp. 22, 32–33, 43–44; Fischer, "Staat" (1962), pp. 146, 149; Reinhart, "Volk" (1952), pp. 82 ff.; Glück, *Beiträge* (1931), p. 94; Büttner, *Anfänge* (1969), pp. 108 ff.; and Eckard Heintz, *Der Beamtenabgeordnete im Bayerischen Landtag. Eine politische Studie über die Stellung des Beamtentums in der parlamentarischen Entwicklung Deutschlands* (Diss., Berlin, 1966), pp. 56 ff.

4. On bureaucratic liberalism in Prussia, see Koselleck, *Preussen* (1967), especially pp. 368 ff., 385 ff., and Gillis, *Bureaucracy* (1971). Faber, *Rheinlande* (1966), pp. 419–21, has data on Rhenish publicists which suggest the prominence of officials, educators, and lawyers.

5. See Schnabel, *Geschichte* (1949–59), 2:204 ff., on the political professors and Nipperdey, "Volksschule" (1968), on the grammar-school teachers.

6. For two examples of politically active physicians, see E. Silberner, "Zur Jugendbiographie von Johann Jacoby," *AfS* 9 (1969): 5–112, and K. Koszyk, "Carl d'Ester" (1960). The political role of pastors is discussed in Bigler, *Politics* (1972).

7. Oncken, *Bennigsen* (1910), 1:117 ff.; Matern, *Wahlen* (1959), pp. 28 ff.; Sonnemann, "Oppermann" (1922); Valentin, *Frankfurt* (1908), p. 71.

8. O'Boyle, "Image" (1968), and Engelsing, *Massenpublikum* (1966), pp. 39 ff. and 55–56. For an example of a liberal journalist in Vormärz, see Freytag, *Karl Mathy* (Leipzig, 1898).

9. Adam, "Jacoby" (1930), p. 12. Jacoby's *Briefwechsel 1816–1849*, ed. E. Silberner (Hanover, 1974), appeared too late for me to use it in this chapter; it is now the basic source for his activities in Vormärz.

10. On regional antagonisms, see Grosser, *Liberalismus* (1929), p. 9, and Heger, *Partei* (1927), p. 9. Walker's *Home Towns* (1971) has a good analysis of liberal

bureaucrats' motivation, especially in the newly-created *Mittelstaaten*.

11. Plickat estimates that in 1849 the Prussian government spent 260 times more on a Gymnasium student than on a student in the Volksschule: Hans-Heinrich Plickat, *Die Schule als Instrument des sozialen Aufstiegs* (Weinheim-Bergstrasse, 1959), pp. 30–31. On universities, see Wolfgang Zorn, "Hochschule und höhere Schule in der deutschen Sozialgeschichte der Neuzeit," *Spiegel der Geschichte: Festschrift für Max Braubach* (Münster, 1964), pp. 321–39.

12. Quoted in Gillis, *Bureaucracy* (1971), p. 41. See also O'Boyle, "Problem" (1970), and the data in Koselleck, *Preussen* (1967), pp. 438–47.

13. Valentin, *Frankfurt* (1908), pp. 71 ff. On journalists, see Engelsing, *Massenpublikum* (1966), pp. 50–51, 177 ff.

14. For an interesting example, see Freytag's description of his father's career: *Erinnerungen* (n.d.), p. 434.

15. Weber's definition of *Abkömmlichkeit* can be found in *From Max Weber*, ed. H. Gerth and C. W. Mills (N.Y., 1958), p. 85. On the legal position of officials as representatives, see Clauss, *Staatsbeamte* (1906), pp. 42 ff.

16. Köllmann, *Harkort* (1964), pp. 64 ff., 114 ff. Kocka, *Unternehmensverwaltung* (1969), pp. 78 ff., discusses the shortage of skilled labor in the first half of the century.

17. Büttner, *Anfänge* (1969), pp. 149 ff., pp. 132–33 (on the Landtag of 1826–27); Fischer, "Industrialisierung" (1972), pp. 212–13.

There is a list of deputies to the Baden Landtag in Adam Bauer, *Badens Volksvertretung in der zweiten Kammer der Landstände von 1819–1890* (Karlsruhe, 1891). Bauer gives each individual's occupation, but not his political affiliation. In the Landtag of 1831, there were twenty-four civil servants, eleven judicial officials, seven teachers and clergymen, thirteen local government officials, eight craftsmen, two innkeepers, and four manufacturers. It is likely that most if not all of the local officials had another occupation, probably either farming or trade. For an example of liberal leadership at the local level in Baden, see Paul Stemmermann, *Philip Thiebauth* (Karlsruhe, 1964). Thiebauth was an innkeeper.

18. Schramm, *Hamburg* (1943); Croon, "Städtevertretung" (1958), on Krefeld and Bochum; Gerd Filbry, "Die Einführung der revidierten Preussischen Städteordnung von 1831 in der Stadt Münster," *Westfälische Zeitschrift* 107 (1957): 169–234.

19. Huber, 1:172 ff., and Koselleck, *Preussen* (1967), pp. 560 ff., discuss the operation of municipal elections in Prussia. For some examples, see: Johannes Ziekursch, *Das Ergebnis der friderizianischen Städteordnung und die Städeordnung Steins am Beispiel der schlesischen Städte dargestellt* (Jena, 1908); Stein, *Geschichte* (1884), on Breslau; Gause, *Geschichte* (1965–68), 2:400, on Königsberg. Additional material can be found in Sheehan, "Liberalism" (1971) and "Liberalism" (1973), especially p. 589, n. 22, in the latter.

20. Schramm, *Hamburg* (1943), pp. 15 ff., 285; Gause, *Geschichte* (1965–68), 2:507 ff.; Kaelble, "Kommunalverwaltung" (1970), pp. 396 ff.; Konrad Kettig, "Gemeinsinn und Mitverantwortung. Beiträge zur Geschichte der Berliner Stadtverordnetenversammlung zugleich eine Würdigung des Stadtverordnetenvertreters Heinrich Kochhann," *Der Bär von Berlin* 12, no. 1 (1963): 7–27; Meyer, *Leben* (1912); Kochhann, *Auszüge* (1906).

21. E. Süss, *Pfalzer im Schwarzen Buch* (Heidelberg, 1956).

22. Rosenberg, "Rationalismus" (1930), p. 534.

23. Gause, *Geschichte* (1965–68), 2:520 ff., on Königsberg, and Stein, *Geschichte* (1884), pp. 213–24, on Breslau.

24. The quotations are from: Unruh, *Erinnerungen* (1895), p. 67; Born, *Erinnerungen* (1898), p. 137; Engels, *Revolutions* (1967), p. 125.
Engel's essay on the "Status Quo" (first written in 1847, reprinted 1964) reflects a significant inconsistency about the social basis of German politics. At one point he refers to the bourgeoisie as the "leading class" in Germany (pp. 46–47), but he later recognizes the complexity of class relations (see the present chapter's epigraph) and adds that the "Kleinbürgerschaft" is actually the "Normalklasse" which has infected the rest of society with its views.

25. Büttner, *Anfänge* (1969), p. 110, on Jaup; F. Schnabel, *Ludwig von Liebenstein* (Karlsruhe, 1927); Thorwart, *Schulze-Delitzsch* (1913); Koszyk, "d'Ester" (1960); Bergengruen, *David von Hansemann* (Berlin, 1901); Hansen, *Mevissen* (1906); A. Caspary, *Camphausens Leben* (Stuttgart and Berlin, 1902); A. Duckwitz, *Denkwürdigkeiten* (Bremen, 1877), pp. 20 ff.; Johann Hermann Hüffer, *Lebenserinnerungen. Briefe und Aktenstücke*, ed. W. Steffens and E. Hövel (Münster, 1952); H. Gollwitzer, *Friedrich David Bassermann* (Mannheim, 1955); Kochhann, *Auszüge* (1906); P. Stemmermann, *Philip Thiebauth* (Karlsruhe, 1964); Fontane, *Zwanzig* (1967), p. 13.

26. In Königsberg, for example, the *Bürgergesellschaft* included master artisans, but it would only accept apprentices if they were recommended by a master. Gause, *Geschichte* (1965–68), 2:520 ff. For two contemporary views on the lower limits of these organizations, see Hansen, *Briefe* (1919), p. 698, and the article on *Lesevereine* in *DV* 18, no. 1 (1839): 250–51.

27. For a different view, see Hamerow, *Restoration* (1958), especially pp. 58 ff., and O'Boyle, "Middle Class" (1966).

28. My formulation owes a great deal to Mack Walker's splendid study, *Home Towns* (1971), especially his remarks on pp. 4 ff.

29. The best way to get a sense of the social structure in Vormärz is by examining a number of regional studies; no satisfactory synthesis yet exists. See, for example: Köllmann, *Harkort* (1964), pp. 190 ff., on Westphalia; Röttges, *Wahlen* (1964), on Düsseldorf; Ayçoberry, "Probleme" (1968) and "Strukturwandel" (1975), on Cologne; Köllmann, *Sozialgeschichte* (1960), pp. 94 ff., on Barmen; Hans Mauersberg, *Wirtschafts-und Sozialgeschichte zentraleuropäischer Städte in neuer Zeit* (Göttingen, 1960); Klaus Assmann, *Zustand und Entwicklung des städtischen Handwerks in der ersten Hälfte des 19. Jahrhunderts* (Göttingen, 1971), on four Hanoverian cities.

30. There is an extremely interesting discussion of regionalism in Sidney Pollard, "Industrialization and the European Economy," *The Economic History Review*, 2d ser., 26, no. 4 (November 1973), especially pp. 640–41. For some German examples, see Wolfgang Zorn, "Eine Wirtschaftskarte Deutschlands um 1820 als Spiegel der gewerblichen Entwicklung," in F. Lütge, ed., *Wirtschaftliche und soziale Probleme der gewerblichen Entwicklung im 15./16. und 19. Jahrhundert* (Stuttgart, 1968), and "Sozialer Wandel in Mitteleuropa, 1780–1840: Eine vergleichende landesgeschichtliche Untersuchung," in Ludz, ed., *Soziologie* (1972). A. Schröter and W. Becker, *Die deutsche Maschinenbauindustrie in der industriellen Revolution* (Berlin, 1962), p. 24, have data on the regional distribution of machinery.

31. See, for example, the comparisons with England in Hoffmann, "Take-Off" (1963), p. 118. There is a good introduction to eighteenth-century economic and social developments in H. Aubin and W. Zorn, eds., *Handbuch der deutschen Wirtschafts-und Sozialgeschichte* (Stuttgart, 1971), vol. 1, chaps. 20–24. On the early nineteenth cen-

tury, see K. Borchardt, "The Industrial Revolution in Germany, 1700–1914," in C. Cipolla, ed., *The Fontane Economic History of Europe* (London and Glasgow, 1972), 4:38–63.

32. Walker, *Home Towns* (1971), pp. 329 ff.; Fischer, "Status" (1972); L. Baar, *Die Berliner Industrie* (Berlin, 1966), p. 104; Fritz Redlich, "Frühindustrielle Unternehmer und ihre Probleme im Lichte ihrer Selbstzeugnisse," in W. Fischer, ed., *Probleme* (1968), pp. 339–412; Ilja Mieck, *Preussische Gewerbepolitik in Berlin, 1806–1844. Staatshilfe und Privatinitiative zwischen Merkantilismus und Liberalismus* (Berlin, 1965), pp. 44–45; and especially the recent articles by F. Marquardt, "Class" (1974) and "Aufstieg" (1975).

33. F. Sengle, *Biedermeierzeit*, 2 vols. (Stuttgart, 1971–72); Hermann Glaser, *Kleinstadt-Ideologie zwischen Furchenglück und Sphärenflug* (Freiburg, 1969); Stadelmann and Fischer, *Bildungswelt* (1955), pp. 59–61. Walker, *Home Towns* (1971), pp. 307 ff., 322 ff., has some very interesting things to say about the "Biedermeier" style, but I think he overstates its antipathy to liberal political values. For an outsider's view, see W. Howitt, *German Experiences* (London, 1844), pp. 95–97.

34. Quoted in Percy Ernst Schramm, *Neun Generationen. Dreihundert Jahre deutscher 'Kulturgeschichte' im Licht der Schicksale einer Hamburger Bürgerfamilie* (Göttingen, 1964) 2:23. For some other examples, see: Elben, *Lebenserinnerungen* (1931), p. 5, on Stuttgart; Schorn, *Lebenserinnerungen* (1898), 1:15 ff., 53 ff., on Essen and Bonn; W. Kiesselbach, "Drei Generationen," *DV* (1860): 1–37, on Bremen; Georg Steinhausen, *Häusliches und gesellschaftliches Leben im 19. Jahrhundert* (Berlin, 1898), pp. 9 ff.

35. Henning, *Bürgertum* (1972), p. 87, cites some data which show the relatively low consumption of luxury goods during the first half of the century. Rolf Engelsing, "Lebenshaltungen und Lebenshaltungskosten im 18. und 19. Jahrhundert in den Hansestädten Bremen und Hamburg," *IRSH* 11, no. 1 (1966): 73–107, discusses styles of life in the north. See also his essay on the *Angestellten* in Engelsing, *Sozialgeschichte* (1973), especially pp. 72 ff.

36. Biedermann, *Leben* (1886), vol. 1, and Richard Bazillion, "A German Liberal's Changing Perspective on the Social Question: Karl Biedermann in the 1840's and 1890's," *Laurentian University Review* 5, no. 1 (June 1973); Wieber, *Ideen* (1913), pp. 1 ff., on Jordan; Huber, 2:137, on Siebenpfeiffer; E. Silberner, "Zur Jugendbiographie von Johann Jacoby," *AfS* 9 (1970): 5 ff.; Schramm, *Hamburg* (1943), p. 169, on Meyer; A. Caspary, *Camphausens Leben* (Stuttgart and Berlin, 1902), pp. 1 ff.; A. Bergengruen, *David Hansemann* (Berlin, 1901), pp. 1 ff.

According to Frank Eyck, almost one-fifth of the men elected to the Frankfurt parliament in 1848 had risen "from relatively humble origins to professional positions, to wealth and to higher social status" (*Frankfurt* [1968], p. 97).

37. Gillis, *Bureaucracy* (1971), p. 13, and Bigler, *Politics* (1972), pp. 58, 71 ff., have material on the backgrounds of officials and pastors. On entrepreneurs see: H. Beau, *Das Leistungswissen des frühindustriellen Unternehmertums in Rheinland-Westfalen* (Cologne, 1959); H. Wutzmer, "Die Herkunft der industriellen Bourgeoisie Preussens in den vierziger Jahren des 19. Jahrhunderts," in H. Motteck, ed., *Studien der Industriellen Revolution in Deutschland* (Berlin, 1960); Fischer, *Wirtschaft* (1972), pp. 375 ff.; H. Sachtler, *Wandlungen des industriellen Unternehmers in Deutschland seit Beginn des 19. Jahrhunderts* (Berlin, 1937).

It should be pointed out that there are some serious difficulties involved in using all of these works, the most significant of which is their terminological uncertainty.

38. Schultze, *Auseinandersetzung* (1925), pp. 85, 101 ff.; R. Pascal, *The German Sturm und Drang* (Manchester, 1953), p. 56; A. Schlingensiepen-Pogge, *Das Sozialethos der lutherischen Aufklärungstheologie* (Göttingen, 1967), pp. 40 ff., 168.

39. For some examples of liberals' views of the aristocracy, see: Christern, "Dahlmanns" (1921), p. 215; Köllmann, *Harkort* (1964), pp. 168–69, 179 ff.; Schib, *Grundlagen* (1927), pp. 65 ff., on Rotteck; and Welcker, "Adel," *StL* (1st ed.), 1:257–354.

40. Dahlmann, *Politik* (1924), p. 200. Similar statements can be found in: Hegel, *Philosophy* (1952), par. 297, pp. 193, 291; Harkort, *Schriften* (1969), p. 5; Weidemann, "Murhard" (1926), p. 238. The uses of the term in the *StL* are examined in Martin Schumacher's highly informative dissertation, "Ständebegriff" (1956), especially pp. 211 ff. See also Winkler, *Mittelstand* (1972); Faber, *Rheinlande* (1966), pp. 418–19; Marquardt, "Aufstieg" (1975), pp. 45 ff.

41. Quoted in Thomas, *Liberalism* (1951), p. 72.

42. Kant, *Rechtslehre*, par. 46, in *Werke* (Berlin, 1922), 7:120–21. See also Henning, *Bürgertum* (1972), p. 98. Two further examples, one from the left and one from the right: Schmidt, *Blum* (1971), p. 27, and David Hansemann, quoted in Hansen, *Briefe* (1967), pp. 17, 48, 53.

43. Balser, *Anfänge* (1959), pp. 100 ff.

44. See the interesting remarks on this in Mommsen, *Stein* (1954), pp. 282 ff. Additional references and analysis can be found in Sheehan, "Partei" (1974).

45. Kurt Koltzbach, *Das Eliteproblem im politischen Liberalismus. Ein Beitrag zum Staats- und Gesellschaftsbild des 19. Jahrhunderts* (Cologne and Opladen, 1966), pp. 46 ff.; Schilfert, *Sieg* (1952), pp. 12 ff.; Philippson, *Ursprung* (1913), pp. 5–26; Gall, *Constant* (1963), pp. 240 ff.; Boberach, *Wahlrechtsfrage* (1959); Rudolf Smend, "Massstäbe des parlamentarischen Wahlrechts in der deutschen Staatstheorie des 19. Jahrhunderts" (1911), in *Staatsrechtliche Abhandlungen und andere Aufsätze* (Berlin, 1955), 19–38. These difficulties were vividly expressed during the suffrage debate at Frankfurt in 1848: see above, chap. 5 and the literature cited in chap. 5, nn. 50, 51.

46. Rotteck, "Census," *StL* (1st ed.), 3:366–88, especially pp. 376, 385. See also Rosskopf, "Johann Adam von Itzstein" (1954), pp. 78–79.

47. H. von Sybel, *Die politischen Parteien der Rheinprovinz* (Düsseldorf, 1847), p. 78.

48. Quoted in Martin Schumacher, *Auslandsreisen deutscher Unternehmer 1750–1851 unter besonderer Berücksichtigung von Rheinland und Westfalen* (Cologne, 1968), p. 41. For a discussion of similar viewpoints, see Christian Hildebrand, *Der Einbuch des Wirtschaftsgeistes in das deutsche Nationalbewusstsein zwischen 1815 und 1871. Der Anteil der Wirtschaft an der Reichsgründung von 1871* (Diss., Heidelberg, 1936), pp. 5 ff., and Haferland's account of the *StL*, *Mensch* (1957), pp. 43–44.

49. Beckerath quoted in Zunkel, *Unternehmer* (1962), p. 149; Weidemann, "Murhard" (1926), pp. 242–43.

50. Brüggemann quoted in Karl Buchheim, *Die Stellung der Kölnischen Zeitung im vormärzlichen rheinischen Liberalismus* (Leipzig, 1913), p. 109; Biedermann, *Leben* (1886), 1:55–57. On the railroad as a metaphor and symbol of progress see: Schnabel, *Geschichte* (1949–59), 3:390; Pankoke, *Bewegung* (1970), pp. 23–24; and especially Manfred Riedel, "Vom Biedermeier zum Maschinenzeitalter. Zur Kulturgeschichte der ersten Eisenbahnen in Deutschland," *AfK* 43, no. 1 (1961): 100–123.

51. Schnabel, *Geschichte* (1949–59), 3:352, on List: Haferland, *Mensch* (1957),

pp. 115 f., on List and Mathy, and pp. 148–49, on Mohl. See also Angermann, *Mohl* (1962), pp. 222 ff., and Mohl's article "Über die Nachteile" (1835), reprinted in Jantke and Hilger, *Eigentumslosen* (1965), pp. 294 ff.

52. L. Caspary, *Camphausens Leben* (Stuttgart and Berlin, 1902), p. 102, and Fischer, "Mez" (1972). See also the insightful remarks contrasting English and continental entrepreneurs in Landes, *Prometheus* (1969), pp. 190–92.

53. Gertrud Milkereit, *Das Unternehmerbild im zeitkritischen Roman des Vormärz* (Cologne, 1970). Although Immermann himself was a conservative, his audience came from throughout the educated public in Germany.

54. Seidel, *Armutsproblem* (1970).

55. Julku, *Bewegung* (1965–69), 1:90. For some examples, see: Angermann, "Mathy" (1955), p. 11; Wieber, *Ideen* (1913), pp. 68 ff., on S. Jordan; Vopelius, *Ökonomen* (1968), pp. 14 ff. John Gagliardo, *From Pariah to Patriot. The Changing Image of the German Peasant, 1770–1840* (Lexington, 1969), has a useful discussion of the image of the peasant in German literature and social thought.

56. Rotteck, *Schriften* (1841–43), 2:435. Schumacher, "Ständebegriff" (1956), p. 208, has a similar quote from Welcker. Mohl, "Ackerbau," *StL* (1st ed.), 1:211–12.

57. Gagern, *Liberalismus* (1959), p. 347; Welcker, "Städte," *StL* (1st ed.), 15:104. See also Hansemann in Hansen, *Briefe* (1967), p. 54, and Harkort, *Schriften* (1969), p. 82.

58. Mohl, "Nachteile," in Jantke and Hilger, *Eigentumslosen* (1965), p. 302, and Schulz in the *StL* (1st ed.), 12:484–85. This image of the city was given a vivid literary formulation in Sue's *Mysteries of Paris*, a book which was widely read and imitated in Germany: see E. Edler, *Eugene Sue und die deutsche Mysterienliteratur* (Diss., Berlin, 1932).

59. Quoted in Schib, *Grundlagen* (1927), pp. 52–53 (see also the remarks on pp. 46 ff.).

60. Fischer, *Staat* (1962), p. 74; Gall, *Liberalismus* (1968), p. 34; Treitschke, *History* (1915–19), 3:149. There is a good summary of the uneven development of *Gewerbefreiheit* in Stadelmann and Fischer, *Bildungswelt* (1955), pp. 107–8.

61. Rosskopf, "Itzstein" (1954), p. 60. See also Rotteck's defence of free trade (1822) and his critique of the Zollverein (1835) in *Schriften* (1841–43), 3:291 ff., 321 ff. For a general discussion of the Zollverein debate, see Henderson, *Zollverein* (1939), pp. 179 ff.; Bernd Bab, *Die öffentliche Meinung über den deutschen Zollverein zur Zeit seiner Entstehung* (Diss., Berlin, 1930); and the contemporary discussion in Schüz, "Die Gegenwartige Universitäts-Doctrine in Deutschland über Handelsfreiheit und Schutz-Zölle," *ZGS* 2, no. 4 (1845): 706–43.

62. Vopelius, *Ökonomen* (1968); Wilhelm Treue, "Adam Smith in Deutschland. Zum Problem des 'politischen Professors' zwischen 1776 und 1810," in *Deutschland und Europa (Rothfels Festschrift)*, ed. W. Conze (Düsseldorf, 1951), pp. 101–34; Wilhelm Roscher, *Geschichte der Nationalökonomik in Deutschland* (Munich, 1874), pp. 821 ff.

63. Rohr, *Origins* (1963), pp. 78 ff., and Vopelius, *Ökonomen* (1968), pp. 104 ff.

64. Prince Smith's own work has been collected in *Schriften* (1877–80). On his career, see: Henderson, "Prince Smith" (1950); Rohr, *Origins* (1963), pp. 85–91; Julius P. Köhler, *Staat und Gesellschaft in den deutschen Theorien der auswärtigen Wirtschaftspolitik und des internationalen Handels von Schlettwein bis auf Friedrich List und Prince Smith* (Stuttgart, 1926), pp. 118 ff.

65. H. W. Bensen (1847), as quoted in G. Briefs, *The Proletariat* (New York, 1937), p. 65. Conze's article "Pöbel" (1966) provides a good introduction to the development of the "social question" during the forties. There is an excellent bibliography and a useful collection of contemporary materials in Jantke and Hilger, *Eigentumslosen* (1965). See also: Marquardt, "Pauperismus" (1969) and "Aufstieg" (1975); Wilhelm Abel, *Der Pauperismus in Deutschland am Vorabend der industriellen Revolution* (Dortmund, 1966), and "Der Pauperismus in Deutschland. Eine Nachlese zu Literaturberichten," in *Wirtschaft, Geschichte und Wirtschaftsgeschichte: Festschrift für F. Lütge* (Stuttgart, 1966), pp. 284–98; Pankoke, *Bewegung* (1970), especially pp. 49 ff.

66. Jantke and Hilger, *Eigentumslosen* (1965); Paul Mombert, "Aus der Literatur über die soziale Frage und die Arbeiterbewegung in Deutschland in der ersten Hälfte des 19. Jahrhunderts," *AGSA* 9, no. 1 (1921): 169–236; Kuczynski, *Literatur* (1960), all have extensive lists of contemporary works on social problems; all show a sharp increase in public attention to these issues after 1840.

On the variety of views among liberals, see: Nora Stiebel, "Der 'Zentralverein für das Wohl der arbeitenden Klasse' im vormärzlichen Preussen. Ein Beitrag zur Geschichte der sozialreformerischen Bewegung" (Unpubl. diss., Heidelberg, 1922); Köster, *Frühliberalismus* (1938), especially pp. 49–50, 59; Ernst Czobel, "Zur verbreitung der Worte Sozialist und Sozialismus in Deutschland und Ungarn," *Archiv für die Geschichte des Sozialismus* 3 (1913): 481–85; L. H. Adolf Geck, *Über das Eindringen des Wortes sozial in die deutsche Sprache* (Göttingen, 1963).

67. O. Wolff, "John Prince Smith," in Prince Smith, *Schriften* (Berlin, 1880), 3:216–17, 236–39.

68. Quoted in Seidel, *Armutsproblem* (1970), p. 17. See also Zunkel, *Unternehmer* (1962), pp. 166 ff.

69. Pankoke, *Bewegung* (1970), pp. 52 ff., and Rohr, *Origins* (1963), pp. 76–77.

70. Quoted in Koselleck, *Preussen* (1967), p. 599.

71. On the changing meaning of *Arbeiter*, see Schieder, *Anfänge* (1963), pp. 82 ff., and Marquardt, "Aufstieg" (1975).

72. Angermann, *Mohl* (1962), chap. 3, and the material by Mohl in Jantke and Hilger, *Eigentumslosen* (1965), pp. 319–37.

73. Camphausen, as quoted in G. A. Kertesz, "The German Moderate Liberals and Socialism, 1848–49," Paper from the Canberra Seminar in the History of Ideas (August, 1974), p. 3. On the various definitions offered for *Proletariat*, see: Conze, "Pöbel" (1966), pp. 117 ff.; Jantke and Hilger, *Eigentumslosen* (1965), pp. 26 ff.; Noyes, *Organizations* (1966), pp. 21–22. Three contemporary examples: H. W. Bensen (1847), reprinted in Jantke and Hilger, *Eigentumslosen* (1965), pp. 426 ff.; Mevissen (1845), reprinted in Hansen, *Mevissen* (1906), vol. 2; J. Kuranda, "Berlin und die unteren Volksklassen," *Gb* 3, no. 1 (1844): 1 ff.

74. Jantke and Hilger, *Eigentumslosen* (1965), p. 447. See also: Pankoke, *Bewegung* (1970), p. 58, and Edward Shorter, "Middle Class Anxiety in the German Revolution of 1848," *JSH* 2, no. 3 (Spring 1969): 189–216.

75. Köster, *Frühliberalismus* (1938), pp. 54 ff.

76. Hans Stein, "Pauperismus und Assoziation. Soziale Tatsachen und Ideen auf dem westeuropäischen Kontinent von Ende des 18. bis zur Mitte des 19. Jahrhunderts, unter besonderer Berücksichtigung des Rheingebiets," *IRSH* 1, no. 1 (1936): 1–20, and Stiebel, "Zentralverein" (1922), chap. 2. For some examples, see: Angermann,

"Mathy" (1955), p. 522; Schmidt, *Blum* (1971), p. 126; Hansen, *Mevissen* (1906), 1:175, 343 ff.; Johannes Fallati, "Das Vereinswesen als Mittel zur Sittigung der Fabrikarbeiter," *ZfGS* 1, no. 4 (1844): 737–91.

77. Quoted in Karl Obermann, *Die deutschen Arbeiter in der Revolution von 1848*, 2d ed. (Berlin, 1953), p. 106.

78. Quoted in Winfried Schulze, "'Sozialistische Bestrebungen in Deutschland': Bemerkungen zu einer Aufsatzfolge Karl Biedermanns (1846)," *VSWG* 57, no. 1 (April 1970): p. 101. For some other examples of liberal support for state-sponsored social reform, see Fieker, "Liberals" (1972), pp. 42 ff.

79. Hansen, *Mevissen* (1906), 1:177; Angermann, *Mohl* (1962), pp. 200–201; Meyer, *Leben* (1912), p. 38. On the problem of population pressures and possible restraints, see: Köllmann, "Bevölkerung" (1968); John Knodel, "Law, Marriage and Illegitimacy in Nineteenth Century Germany," *Population Studies*, 20, no. 3 (March 1967): 279–94; Harold Schinkel, "Armenpflege und Freizügigkeit in der preussischen Gesetzgebung vom Jahre 1842," *VSWG* 50, no. 4 (1963): 459–79.

80. *Philosophy of Right* (1952), especially par. 185 on the dangers of "civil society" and pars. 201–2 on the "universal estate."

81. Rohr, *Origins* (1963), p. 121, and Hansen, *Mevissen* (1906), 2:90 (reprints a memorandum of 1840). For another example, see Langewiesche, *Liberalismus* (1974), pp. 84 ff, especially the quotation on p. 93.

Chapter 3

1. Quoted in Gall, *Constant* (1963), p. 108.

2. Rosenberg, *Bureaucracy* (1958), and Koselleck, *Preussen* (1967), provide stimulating analyses of the role played by bureaucratic institutions in Prussian history. Eberhard Weis, *Montgelas, 1759–1799. Zwischen Revolution und Reform* (Munich, 1971), and Helen P. Liebel, *Enlightened Bureaucracy versus Enlightened Despotism in Baden, 1750–1792* (Philadelphia, 1965), discuss this process in Bavaria and Baden. For a study of the changes in language which attended bureaucratic growth, see W. Damkowski, *Die Entstehung des Verwaltungsbegriffes: Eine Wortstudie* (Cologne, 1969), and Weinacht, *Staat* (1968).

3. Huber, vol. 1, gives a summary of the most important legislation and an introduction to the leading reformers' policies and careers. In addition to the works cited in n. 2, see: Schmidt, *Staatsreform* (1966), on Saxony; Faber, *Rheinlande* (1966); Franz-Ludwig Knemeyer, *Regierungs- und Verwaltungsreformen in Deutschland zu Beginn des 19. Jahrhunderts* (Cologne and Berlin, 1970).

4. Quotes from Walker, *Home Towns* (1971), p. 201, and Weinacht, *Staat* (1968), p. 193.

5. Schneider, *Pressefreiheit* (1966), pp. 129–30, cites the most recent literature on censorship. Jaup's article, "Pressefreiheit," *StL* (1st ed.), 12:331–88, is a characteristic contemporary statement. In *Geschichte* (1948), p. 43, Rudolf Stadelmann made the interesting observation that the importance of foreign models for German political thought was increased by the censors' willingness to allow a rather uninhibited discussion of political developments outside of Germany.

6. Dahlmann, *Politik* (1924), pp. 258 ff. See also Hansemann (1830), as quoted in Hansen, *Briefe* (1967), pp. 22 ff., and the debate in the Baden Landtag of 1831 which is discussed in Gall, *Constant* (1963), pp. 86–87.

7. Quoted in Weidemann, "Murhard" (1926), p. 233. See also Welcker in *StL* (1st ed.), 3:327. The best discussion of this whole issue is J. Habermas, *Strukturwandel* (1962).

8. Treitschke, *History* (1915–19), 2:668–69. These stories may, of course, be apocryphal, but the point is that many contemporaries believed them.

9. Eyck, *Frankfurt* (1968), p. 93. For some examples, see: A. Bergengruen, *David Hansemann* (Berlin, 1901), pp. 81 ff.; Mohl, *Lebenserinnerungen* (1902), 2:3 ff.; Wieber, *Ideen* (1913), pp. 5 ff.; Weidemann, "Murhard" (1926), pp. 241, 274.

10. Schnabel, *Geschichte* (1949–59), devoted vol. 4 to religious developments. See also Engelsing, "Bildung" (1968), pp. 350 ff.; Bigler, *Politics* (1972); W. Brazill, *The Young Hegelians* (New Haven, 1970).

11. Catherine Holden, "A Decade of Dissent in Germany: An Historical Study of Protestant Friends and the German-Catholic Church, 1840–1848" (Unpubl. diss., Yale, 1954), is a good introduction to the *Lichtfreunde*. See also: Bigler, *Politics* (1972), pp. 139 ff., 187 ff.; Rosenberg, *Haym* (1933), p. 86; Renner, "Twesten" (1954), p. 15.

12. Köllmann, *Sozialgeschichte* (1960), pp. 42 ff. See also Zunkel, *Unternehmer* (1962), pp. 136 ff., and "Beamtenschaft" (1964), pp. 261 ff.

13. Hansen, *Mevissen* (1906), 1:379 ff., and A. Bergengruen, *David Hansemann* (Berlin, 1901), pp. 100 ff.

14. Gustav Croon, *Der Rheinische Provinziallandtag bis zum Jahre 1874* (Düsseldorf, 1918), pp. 101 ff.; O. Glück, *Beiträge zur Geschichte des Württembergischen Liberalismus* (Diss., Tübingen, 1931), p. 16; Jacoby, *Vier Fragen* (Mannheim, 1841), pp. 22–23.

15. Gagern, *Liberalismus* (1959), pp. 71 ff., and Oncken, *Bennigsen* (1910), 1:126 ff. On Catholics' attitudes toward the state, see Schnabel, *Geschichte* (1949–59), 4:199. Hansen's *Briefe* (1967) contains ample evidence of the animosity toward Prussian bureaucrats felt by many Rhinelanders.

16. Aris, *History* (1936), p. 156.

17. Quoted in J. Celotti, "The Political Thought and Action of Friedrich Christoph Dahlmann" (Unpubl. diss., Stanford, 1970), p. 97.

18. P. Pfizer, *Briefwechsel zweier Deutschen*, 2d ed. (1832), reprinted in *Deutsche Literaturdenkmale*, no. 144 (Berlin, 1911), pp. 113–14, 118–19. The following provide useful discussions of the problem of German attitudes toward the state in the first half of the century: Krieger, *Idea* (1957); Wilhelm, *Idee* (1933); Gall, *Constant* (1963), especially pp. 107–8; Hock, *Denken* (1957), pp. 63 ff., 121.

19. Welcker quoted in Angermann, *Mohl* (1962), p. 115, Mathy in Angermann, "Mathy" (1955), p. 509. See also Welcker's article "Staatsdienst," *StL* (1st ed.), 14:727–63. For an analysis of the ideas expressed in the *StL*, see Schumacher, "Ständebegriff" (1956), and Haferland, *Mensch* (1957), especially pp. 56, 65 ff.

20. Reprinted in Mohl, *Schriften* (1966), pp. 276–310. See Wilhelm, *Idee* (1933), p. 14, and Angermann, *Mohl* (1962). For a similar view, see anon., "Staatsdiener," *DV* 25, no. 3 (1846): 130 ff.

21. Camphausen (1843) quoted in Kurt Utermann, *Der Kampf um die preussische Selbstverwaltung im Jahre 1848* (Berlin, 1937), p. 16; Droysen, *Schriften* (1933), pp. 28–29.

22. Diesterweg quoted in Nipperdey, "Volksschule" (1968), p. 136. Nipperdey's essay is the best general introduction to the problem of education and society in Vormärz. See also Eugene N. Anderson, "The Prussian *Volksschule* in the Nineteenth

Century," in *Enstehung und Wandel der modernen Gesellschaft. Festschrift für Hans Rosenberg*, ed. G. A. Ritter (Berlin, 1970); Blättner, *Gymnasium* (1960); Huber, 1:260 ff.; Peter Lundgreen, "Industrialization and the Educational Formation of Manpower in Germany," *JSH* 9, no. 1 (Fall 1975): 64–80; Flitner, *Erziehung* (1957); Wilhelm Rössler, *Die Entstehung des modernen Erziehungswesens* (Stuttgart, 1961).

23. Quoted in Flitner, *Erziehung* (1957), p. 16. Werner K. Blessing, "Allgemeine Volksbildung und politische Indoktrination im bayerischen Vormärz. Das Leitbild des Volksschullehrers als mentales Herrschaftsinstrument," *ZfBL*, 37, no. 2 (1974): 479–568, is a fresh and stimulating attempt to gauge the state's impact on education in Bavaria during the first half of the century.

24. Harkort, *Schriften* (1969), pp. 34–35, 38. K. H. Scheidler, "Pädagogik," *StL* (1st ed.), 12:319–49. On the *StL*, see also Schumacher, "Ständebegriff" (1956), pp. 121 ff.

25. W. von Humboldt, *The Limits of State Action* (Cambridge, 1969), has a useful introduction by the editor, J. W. Burrow. See also Schnabel, *Geschichte* (1949–59), 1:291 ff., and S. Kaehler, *Humboldt und der Staat*, 2d ed. (Göttingen, 1963).

26. Harkort, *Schriften* (1969), p. 17. Droysen quoted in Birtsch, *Nation* (1964), p. 80. For another example, see Sybel, *Parteien* (1847), p. 18. On the issue of church and state, see: Schnabel, *Geschichte* (1949–59), 4:506 ff.; R. Lempp, *Die Frage der Trennung von Kirche und Staat im Frankfurter Parlament* (Tübingen, 1913), pp. 5 ff.; Schib, *Grundlagen* (1927), pp. 54–56, on Rotteck.

27. Quoted in Fritz Fischer, "Der deutsche Protestantismus und die Politik im 19. Jahrhundert," *HZ* 171, no. 3 (May 1951): 477. See also Friedrich Schleiermacher, "Über den Beruf des Staates zur Erziehung" (1814), *Pädagogische Schriften*, ed. E. Weniger (Düsseldorf and Munich, 1957), vol. 2.

28. The best treatment of this problem can be found in Reinhard Rürup, "Jewish Emancipation and Bourgeois Society," *Year Book of the Leo Baeck Institute* 14 (1969), pp. 67–91, and "Kontinuität und Diskontinuität der 'Judenfrage' im 19. Jahrhundert. Zur Enstehung des modernen Antisemitismus," in Wehler, ed., *Sozialgeschichte* (1974), pp. 338–415. See also: Jacob Katz, *Out of the Ghetto. The Social Background of Jewish Emancipation. 1770–1870* (Cambridge, Mass., 1973); Toury, *Orientierungen* (1966); Valentin, *Frankfurt* (1908), p. 15.

29. There is a good summary of List's views in Schnabel, *Geschichte* (1949–59), 3:297–336 ff.

Historians are divided on the question of whether state intervention made a positive contribution to German economic development. W. O. Henderson, *The State and the Industrial Revolution in Prussia, 1740–1870* (Liverpool, 1958), argues yes, R. Tilly, *Financial Institutions and Industrialization in the Rhineland, 1815–1870* (Madison, 1966) argues no. For a new look at this issue, see F. Tipton, "The National Consensus in German Economic History," *CEH* 7, no. 3 (September 1974): 195–224. Additional material on the role of the state in German economic life can be found in: W. Fischer, *Staat* (1962); U. Ritter, *Die Rolle des Staates in den Frühstudien der Industrialisierung* (Berlin, 1961); Kocka, "Staat" (1974); Landes, "Japan" (1965).

30. Hansen, *Briefe* (1967), p. 58 (of the introduction), and Hansen, *Mevissen* (1906) 1:171, 307 ff.

31. Köllmann, *Harkort* (1964), p. 125; Harkort, *Schriften* (1969), pp. 5–63; Schnabel, *Geschichte* (1949–59), 3:287 ff.

32. Hansemann (1840) quoted in Hansen, *Briefe* (1967), p. 218.

33. Paul Pfizer, "Gedanken über das Ziel und die Aufgabe des Deutschen

Liberalismus" (1832), reprinted in *Deutsche Literaturdenkmale*, no. 144 (Berlin, 1911), pp. 337–38. On Pfizer, see Cornelia Popitz, "Paul Pfizer und sein Briefwechsel Zweier Deutschen" (Unpubl. diss., Berlin, 1951); F. Meinecke, *Cosmopolitanism and the National State* (Princeton, 1970), pp. 241–42; Krieger, *Idea* (1957), pp. 317–22.

. 34. Anon, "Rückblick," *Gb* (1848), p. 1. See also Dahlmann (1832), as quoted in J. Celotti, "The Political Thought and Action of Friedrich Christoph Dahlmann" (Unpubl. diss., Stanford, 1970), p. 97.

35. Buhl, quoted in Mayer, "Anfänge" (1960), p. 64.

36. Paul Ludwig Weinacht, "'Staatsbürger': Zur Geschichte und Kritik eines politischen Begriffes," *Der Staat* 8, no. 1 (1969): 41–63. See also Koselleck, *Preussen* (1967), p. 60.

37. Krieger, *Idea* (1957), pp. 86 ff. (on Kant), 252 ff. (on Vormärz); Heffter, *Selbstverwaltung* (1950), pp. 174–75; Angermann, *Mohl* (1962), pp. 95 ff.

38. Dirk Blasius' recent study of the campaign for a jury trial shows that the impulse for some kind of popular participation was present even in efforts to reform the legal system itself: see his "Der Kampf um die Geschworenengerichte im Vormärz," in Wehler, ed., *Sozialgeschichte* (1974), pp. 148–61.

39. Anon., "Verfassungsfrage," *DV* (1846), pp. 309 ff.

40. Quoted in Christern, "Dahlmanns" (1921), p. 264. See also: Krieger, *Idea* (1957), pp. 305 ff.; Boldt, "Patrimonialismus" (1974), pp. 87 ff.; Dahlmann, *Politik* (1924), pp. 53 ff. For a similar contemporary viewpoint, see Droysen, *Schriften* (1933), pp. 114–15 (which reprints an essay written in 1847).

41. Prince Smith, "Über den politischen Fortschritt Preussens" (1844), *Schriften* (1877–80), 2:11.

42. An introduction to liberal attitudes about representative institutions can be found in Krieger, *Idea* (1957); Brandt, *Repräsentation* (1968); Fenske, *Wahlrecht* (1972), pp. 58 ff. Klaus von Beyme, "Repräsentatives und parlamentarisches Regierungssystem. Eine begriffsgeschichtliche Analyse," *PV* 6, no. 2 (1965): 143–59, puts the German experience in its European context.

43. Gall, *Constant* (1963), pp. 62–63, 135–36, 222–25. See also Gall, *Liberalismus* (1968), pp. 24 ff.

44. Quoted in Schib, *Grundlagen* (1927), p. 62. See also Rotteck's essay of 1818 reprinted in his *Schriften* (1814–43), vol. 2, and the discussions in Boldt, "Patrimonialismus" (1974), pp. 90 ff., and Bermbach, "Landstände" (1968), pp. 250 ff.

45. *StL* (1st ed.), 15:66–67.

46. On constitutional practice in Vormärz, see Huber, 2:376 ff., and Böckenförde's essays, "Verfassungstyp" (1972), especially pp. 148 ff., and "Einheit" (1972), pp. 30 ff. Georg Jellinek's "Regierung und Parlament in Deutschland," *Vorträge der Gehe-Stiftung* (Leipzig, 1909), 1:9 ff., provides an interesting analysis from the perspective of Wilhelmine Germany.

47. Theodor von Schön, quoted in Koser, "Charakteristik" (1908), p. 309. See also Sheehan, "Partei" (1974).

48. Like the concept of the *Rechtsstaat*, the notion of responsibility had its orgins within the bureaucracy itself. It was originally proposed in order to increase an official's accountability and as an antidote to the monarch's interference in administrative affairs. See Willard Fann, "The Rise of the Prussian Ministry, 1806–1827," in Wehler, ed., *Sozialgeschichte* (1974), pp. 119–29.

49. Otto Pflanze, "Judicial and Political Responsibility in Nineteenth Century

Germany," *The Responsibility of Power*, ed. F. Stern and L. Krieger (New York, 1967), pp. 162–82, and Franz Schnabel, "Geschichte der Ministerverantwortlichkeit in Baden," *ZGO* 75, no. 1–3 (1921): 87–110, 171–91, 303–31.

50. Angermann, *Mohl* (1962), pp. 388 ff.; Brandt, *Repräsentation* (1968), p. 242; Eulau, "Theories" (1963), pp. 45 ff.; Boldt, "Monarchie" (1973), pp. 613 ff.

51. Wilhelm, *Verfassung* (1928); Eulau, "Theories" (1963), pp. 44–45; Charles McClelland, *The German Historian and England* (Cambridge, 1971), p. 73.

52. Quoted in Brandt, *Repräsentation* (1968), p. 236. K. S. Zachariä's political ideas can be found in his *Vierzig Bücher vom Staate*, 7 vols. in 5 (Stuttgart and Tübingen, 1830–32), especially vol. 3. See also the discussion in Boldt, "Patrimonialismus" (1974), pp. 92 ff.

53. Quoted in Goessler, *Dualismus* (1932), pp. 49–50.

54. Welcker quoted in Gall, *Constant* (1963), p. 90; Murhard in Weidemann, "Murhard" (1926), p. 250. See also Karl Rosenkranz, *Über den Begriff der politischen Partei* (Königsberg, 1843), p. 20; Hansen, *Mevissen* (1906), 1:190; Birtsch, *Nation* (1964), pp. 93–95, on Droysen.

55. Weidemann, "Murhard" (1926), pp. 257, 267–68. On the tradition of obedience, see: Lewis Beck et al., "Symposium: Kant on Revolution," *JHI* 32, no. 3 (1971); Wieber, *Ideen* (1913), p. 37, on Jordan; Sybel, *Parteien* (1847), p. 63.

56. Liberal attitudes toward revolution are discussed at length in Neumüller, *Liberalismus* (1973).

Part II

1. Quoted in E. J. Hobsbawm, *The Age of Revolution, 1789–1848* (Cleveland and New York, 1962), p. 304. Two more examples: W. von Kügelgen, *Lebenserinnerungen des alten Mannes 1840–67* (Leipzig, 1923), p. 103, and Biedermann, *Leben* (1886), 1:215–22. Theodor Schieder has an excellent essay on the image of revolution in *Staat* (1958), pp. 11 ff.

The classic study of the revolution in Germany remains Veit Valentin's monumental *Geschichte* (1930–31). The best brief account is Stadelmann's *Geschichte* (1948). Thomas Nipperdey, "Kritik oder Objektivität? Zur Beurteilung der Revolution von 1848," *Archiv für Frankfurts Geschichte und Kunst*, no. 54 (1974), and Michael Stürmer, "1848 in der deutschen Geschichte," in Wehler, ed., *Sozialgeschichte* (1974), are stimulating essays which reflect recent historiographical concerns. Valentin's biography is the most complete list of older works, while newer trends in research can be followed in bibliographical articles by Hamerow, "History" (1954), and A. Dorpalen, "Die Revolution von 1848 in der Geschichtsschreibung der DDR," *HZ* 210, no. 2 (April 1970).

2. The problem of moving from the political world of Vormärz into the realities of the revolution is a central theme in many participants' memoirs. See, for example: Friedrich Theodor Vischer, "Mein Lebensgang," *Ausgewählte Schriften* (Stuttgart and Berlin, 1918), 3:64 ff.; Karl Rosenkranz, *Politische Briefe und Aufsätze, 1848–1856* (Leipzig, 1919), p. xiv; Haym, *Leben* (1902), p. 189; Pagenstecher, *Lebenserinnerungen* (1913), 2:56–57.

3. According to his son, Eduard von Simson, who served as president of the Nationalversammlung, "never stopped thinking of himself as a Prussian official"

(Simson, *Erinnerungen* [1900], p. 301). See also Ziebura, "Anfänge" (1963), pp. 188 ff.

Chapter 4

1. Jacoby, *Schriften* (1872), 2:21.
2. Anon, "Rückblick auf Preussen im Jahre 1847," *Gb* 7, no. 1 (1848), p. 4.
3. Helmut Asmus, "Die Verfassungsadresse der grossbürgerlichen-liberalen Opposition im preussischen Vereinigten Landtag von 1847," *ZfGW* 22, no. 12 (1974): 1326–40, has a good statement of liberal goals at the United Landtag. See also: Koselleck, *Preussen* (1967), pp. 367 ff., 387 ff.; Koser, "Charakteristik" (1908); Rosenberg, *Haym* (1933), pp. 105 ff. Two contemporary views: Engels, "Status Quo" (1964), p. 43, and Hansen, *Briefe* (1942), pp. 105 ff.
4. Hoffmann, "Die Öffentlichkeit der Gemeindeverhandlungen," *ZfGS* 4, no. 1 (1847): 89–120, is a representative contemporary view of political activity in cities. See also: P. Clauswitz, *Die Städteordnung von 1809 und die Stadt Berlin* (Berlin, 1908), pp. 203 ff., and Meyer, *Leben* (1912), pp. 67 ff., on Berlin; Falkson, *Bewegung* (1888), pp. 145 ff., on Königsberg; Stein, *Geschichte* (1884), p. 267, on Breslau.
5. Hamerow, *Restoration* (1958), and Tilly, "Disorders" (1970).
6. These developments are surveyed in Valentin, *Geschichte* (1930–31), vol. 1, chaps. 3, 4.
7. W., "Deutschland im Jahr 1847," *Gb* 7, no. 1 (1848): 24–32. On the contacts among liberals from various parts of Germany, see the material in Hansen, *Briefe* (1942).
8. The programs are reprinted in Huber, *Dokumente* (1961–66), 1:361–64. See also: Hebeisen, *Parteien* (1909), pp. 6 ff.; Hamerow, *Restoration* (1958), pp. 88–89; Angermann, "Mathy" (1955), pp. 504 ff.; Bergsträsser, "Lage" (1913). The best recent analysis is in Boldt, "Monarchie" (1973), pp. 561 ff.
9. See Walker, *Home Towns* (1971), p. 364.
10. Quoted in Noyes, *Organizations* (1966), p. 59. Krieger suggests a similar distinction, *Idea* (1957), pp. 330 ff. See also the formulation in Walker, *Home Towns* (1971), pp. 356 ff.
11. Stadelmann, *Geschichte* (1948), chaps. 1 and 2, and Noyes, *Organizations* (1966), chap. 1, provide introductions to the social movement in the spring of 1848. On the rural movement, see also: Günther Franz, "Die agrarische Bewegung im Jahre 1848," *Zeitschrift für Agrargeschichte und Agrarsoziologie* 6, no. 2 (October 1959): 176–93, and Hamerow, *Restoration* (1958), pp. 107 ff. On the cities, see: Repgen, *Märzbewegung* (1955), pp. 47 ff., and Walker, *Home Towns* (1971), pp. 364 ff.
12. On Berlin, see: Stadelmann, *Geschichte* (1948), p. 60, and the first-hand accounts in Paul Boerner, *Erinnerungen eines Revolutionärs: Skizzen aus dem Jahre 1848*, ed. E. Menke-Glückert, 2 vols. (Leipzig, 1920), and Born, *Erinnerungen* (1898). On Cologne see Gothein, *Wirtschaftsgeschichte* (1916), vol. 1, pt. 1, pp. 467 ff., and Noyes, *Organizations* (1966), pp. 62 ff.
13. Theodore Hamerow, for example, argues that liberalism "was never able again to win the allegiance of the masses whom it led to defeat in 1848" ("History" [1954], p. 28). Koselleck's formulation is closer to the mark: "the social crisis had

made it possible for the constitutional movement to get off the ground but also insured that it would not reach its destination'' (*Preussen* [1967], p. 620).

14. Camphausen (February 28, 1848) quoted in Repgen, *Märzbewegung* (1955), p. 16. See also: Mohl's remarks on March 9, quoted in Angermann, *Mohl* (1962), p. 59; Virchow's assessment of the situation in Berlin at the end of March, *Briefe* (1907), pp. 139–40. This fear of the *Volk* was one of the most important differences Fanny Lewald noted between the situation in Paris and Berlin: *Erinnerungen* (1850), pp. 74–75.

15. The quotation is from Julius Jolly (June 1848) in J. Heyderhoff, ed., ''Franz von Roggenbach und Julius Jolly. Politischer Briefwechsel 1848–1882,'' *ZGO*, 86, nos. 1–2 (1934): p. 90. See also Bennigsen's views in May 1848, cited in Oncken, *Bennigsen* (1910), 1:154–55. Valentin, *Geschichte* (1930–31), 1:565–66 has a number of contemporary statements, both optimistic and pessimistic, about Frankfurt.

16. There are useful summaries of political alignments in the opening stages of the revolution in Heffter, *Selbstverwaltung* (1950), pp. 292 ff., and Stadelmann, *Geschichte* (1948), pp. 83 ff.

The regional variety of developments can be seen in the following works: Edmund Silberner, ''Johann Jacoby in der Revolution von 1848/49,'' *AfS* 10 (1970): 153–260, on Königsberg; Kochhann, *Auszüge* (1906), 3:69 ff., and Born, *Erinnerungen* (1898), pp. 120 ff., on Berlin; Biedermann, *Leben* (1886), 1:244 ff., and Schmidt, *Blum* (1971), pp. 129 ff., on Leipzig; Weber, *Revolution* (1970), pp. 14 ff., on Saxony as a whole; Elben, *Lebenserinnerungen* (1931), pp. 115 ff., on Stuttgart; Hebeisen, *Partei* (1909), on Baden; Kastendiek, ''Bremen'' (1952), pp. 34 ff.; Repgen, *Märzbewegung* (1955), on the Rhineland; Carl Schurz, *Lebenserinnerungen*, 3 vols. (Berlin and Leipzig, 1912–30), 1:140 ff., on Bonn; Nickel, *Revolution* (1965), on Augsburg; Christa Graf, ''The Hanoverian Reformer, Johann Carl Bertram Stüve, 1798–1872'' (Unpubl. diss., Cornell, 1970), pp. 244 ff., on Osnabrück.

17. Langewiesche, *Liberalismus* (1974), pp. 108 ff. and 127 ff.

18. Quoted in Boldt, ''Monarchie'' (1973), p. 590. See also Huber, 2:593 ff., and the eyewitness account in Pagenstecher, *Lebenserinnerungen* (1913), 2:13 ff.

19. The suffrage law is reprinted in Huber, *Dokumente* (1961–66), 1:269–71. On the debate, see Hamerow, ''Elections'' (1961), and Schilfert, *Sieg* (1952), pp. 86 ff.

20. The best single treatment of the elections is Hamerow, ''Elections'' (1961). See also: Eyck, *Frankfurt* (1968), pp. 57–62; Vogel et al., *Wahlen* (1971), pp. 76–82; Schilfert, *Sieg* (1952), pp. 102 ff.

21. Eichmeier's dissertation, *Anfänge* (1968), has a good deal of useful information on organized political activity in the spring and early summer. See also: Weber, *Revolution* (1970), pp. 24 ff., 43 ff., on Saxony; Repgen, *Märzbewegung* (1955), on the Rhineland; Schulte, *Volk* (1954), pp. 197 ff.; Nickel, *Revolution* (1965), on Augsburg; Bellot, ''Leben'' (1951), on the Saar; Kaiser, *Strömungen* (1963), pp. 23 ff., on Bonn; Röttges, *Wahlen* (1964), pp. 58 ff., on Düsseldorf; Schierbaum, *Wahlen* (1960), pp. 21 ff., on Trier; Weinandy, ''Wahlen'' (1956), pp. 49 ff., on the area around Sieg and Gummersbach; Kastendiek, ''Liberalismus'' (1952), on Bremen; Pülke, *Geschichte* (1934), pp. 44–45, on Recklinghausen; Sonnemann, ''Oppermann'' (1922), pp. 132 ff., on Hanover.

22. Hamerow, ''Elections'' (1961), p. 32.

23. There is a good example of a radical program in Boldt, *Anfänge* (1971), pp. 103–5.

24. Haym, *Briefwechsel* (1967), p. 37. See also Boldt, *Anfänge* (1971), pp. 99–107, and the works just cited in n. 21.

25. Krabs, "Hamm" (1964), p. 15.

26. Matern, *Wahlen* (1959), p. 36, on Hildesheim; Virchow, letter of May 1, 1848, *Briefe* (1907), pp. 36 ff. For another example, see Schulte, *Volk* (1954), p. 200.

27. Quoted in Schulte, *Volk* (1954), p. 191. For some similar statements, see: Haym, *Briefwechsel* (1967), p. 38; Nickel, *Revolution* (1965), p. 72; L. Bamberger, *Erinnerungen* (1899), p. 21.

28. Only about 43 percent of those elected lived in or near their constituencies: Eyck, *Frankfurt* (1968), p. 93. See also Repgen, *Märzbewegung* (1955), p. 231. For the important role of cities as a source of candidates, see: Koselleck, *Preussen* (1967), pp. 583 ff.; Stein, *Geschichte* (1884), p. 340, on Breslau; Haym, *Leben* (1902), p. 183, on Halle; Nickel, *Revolution* (1965), p. 68, on Augsburg.

One sign of the scarcity of candidates is the large number of men who were elected because they seemed to be the only available alternative: Unruh, *Erinnerungen* (1895), pp. 88–89; Pagenstecher, *Lebenserinnerungen* (1913), 2:42 ff.; Thorwart, *Schulze-Delitzsch* (1913), p. 12.

29. O'Boyle, "Left" (1961), Koselleck, *Preussen* (1967), pp. 392–97, and Gillis, *Bureaucracy* (1971), chaps. 5 and 6, all discuss the role of educated men in the revolution. On the social composition of the parliaments, see: Sheehan, "Liberalism" (1973), pp. 584–86; Gertrud Beushausen, "Zur Strukturanalyse parlamentarischer Repräsentation in Deutschland vor der Gründung des Norddeutschen Bundes" (Unpubl. diss., Hamburg, 1926), pp. 97 ff.; Walker, *Home Towns* (1971), pp. 366 ff.

30. Schilfert, *Sieg* (1952), p. 314, and Gillis, *Bureaucracy* (1971), p. 242, have data on the Prussian parliament's social composition. For a contemporary comparison of Berlin and Frankfurt, see Unruh, *Erfahrungen* (1851), p. 122. The political character of the Berlin parliament is analyzed in Donald J. Mattheisen, "Voters and Parliaments in the German Revolution of 1848: An Analysis of the Prussian Constituent Assembly," *CEH* 5, no. 1 (March 1972): 3–22.

31. See, for example, the material on the *Wahlmänner* elected in Aachen and Düsseldorf in Repgen, *Märzbewegung* (1955), p. 227, and the analysis of organizations in Württemberg in Langewiesche, *Liberalismus* (1974), pp. 120 ff.

32. Gothein, *Wirtschaftsgeschichte* (1916), vol. 1, pt. 1, pp. 478–79, on the events in Cologne. For a sardonic and perhaps distorted view of the haphazard voting procedures, see Theodor Fontane's account of the elections in Berlin: *Zwanzig* (1967), pp. 354–59. The point is better made in Stephan Born's memoirs, which relate how he was invited to be a candidate by some moderate constitutionalists despite his own radical views: *Erinnerungen* (1898), pp. 131–32. For some other firsthand accounts of the voting, see: Peter Franz Reichensperger, *Erlebnisse eines alten Parlamentariers im Revolutionsjahre 1848* (Berlin, 1882), pp. 50 ff., on the Rhineland; Schorn, *Lebenserinnerungen* (1898), 1:31 ff., on Essen; Wilhelm Schrader, *Erfahrungen und Bekenntnisse* (Berlin, 1900), pp. 90 ff., on Brandenburg; J. D. H. Temme, *Erinnerungen* (Leipzig, 1883), pp. 268 ff., on Ragnit.

33. According to Eyck (*Frankfurt* [1968], p. 198), the political composition of the Nationalversammlung in June 1848 was approximately as follows: right, 43 (7.5 percent; right-center, 156 (27 percent); left-center, 121 (21 percent); left, 55 (9.5 percent); extreme left, 46 (8 percent); no affiliation 155 (27 percent).

Chapter 5

1. Bauer, *Untergang* (1849), p. 272.

2. Eyck, *Frankfurt* (1968), p. 155; Heiber, "Rhetorik" (1953), pp. 6 ff.; Mohl, *Lebenserinnerungen* (1902), 2:34 ff.

3. On the evolution of parliamentary procedures at Frankfurt, see: Ziebura, "Anfänge" (1963), pp. 194 ff.; Kramer, *Fraktionsbindungen* (1968), pp. 185 ff.; Boldt, *Anfänge* (1971), pp. 25 ff.; Heiber, "Rhetorik" (1953), pp. 80 ff. The debate can be found in Wigard, 1:163–65.

4. This sense of being among strangers is described in the following memoirs: Beseler, *Erlebtes* (1884), pp. 58–59; Wichmann, *Denkwürdigkeiten* (1890), p. 26; Mohl, *Lebenserinnerungen* (1902), 2:65.

5. Biedermann, *Erinnerungen* (1849), pp. 14 ff.

6. The following works describe the formation of factions at Frankfurt: Eyck, *Frankfurt* (1968); Stadelmann, *Geschichte* (1948), pp. 118 ff.; Valentin, *Geschichte* (1930–31), 2:20 ff.; Boldt, *Anfänge* (1971), pp. 68 ff., 163 ff.; Ziebura, "Anfänge" (1963), pp. 203 ff.; Kramer, *Fraktionsbindungen* (1968), pp. 74 ff., 271 ff.

The memoir literature on the revolution is very extensive. Among the works I consulted, the following seemed to be the most informative about the evolution of political alignments: Schorn, *Lebenserinnerungen* (1898), 2:1 ff.; Wichmann, *Denkwürdigkeiten* (1890), pp. 120 ff.; Lewald, *Erinnerungen* (1969), pp. 108 ff.; Mohl, *Lebenserinnerungen* (1902), 2:68 ff.; Biedermann, *Erinnerungen* (1849), pp. 168 ff., and *Leben* (1886), pp. 358–93; Pagenstecher, *Lebenserinnerungen* (1913), 2:68–70.

7. Quoted in Kramer, *Fraktionsbindungen* (1968), p. 175. See also Ziebura, "Anfänge" (1963), pp. 201–3.

8. Kramer, *Fraktionsbindungen* (1968), pp. 218 ff. Two contemporary assessments: Haym, *Nationalversammlung* (1848–50), 1:39, and Beseler, *Erlebtes* (1884), pp. 74 ff.

9. Eyck, *Frankfurt* (1968), pp. 140 ff. Schrader, "Fraktionen" (1923), p. 125, makes this point about the Prussian parliament.

10. See especially Boldt, *Anfänge* (1971), pp. 68 ff.

11. Remarks from August 1848, quoted in Kramer, *Fraktionsbindungen* (1968), p. 115. For another example of this reluctance to organize on the local level, see Langewiesche, *Liberalismus* (1974), pp. 113 ff.

12. By March 1849, the Märzvereine had 950 local organizations with about a half-million members: see Botzenhart, "Parlamentarismusmodelle" (1974), pp. 129 ff., and Fricke, 1:217–35.

13. Boldt, *Anfänge* (1971), pp. 31–32 and 70–71; Ziebura, "Anfänge" (1963), pp. 227 ff.; and Gebhart, *Revolution* (1974) provide a great deal of information on the efforts of the "constitutionalists" to form national organizations. Also worth reading on this subject are L. Bergsträsser's two articles, "Parteien" (1919) and "Entstehung" (1933), as well as the letters and other documents published in his *Parlament* (1929).

14. Kramer, *Fraktionsbindungen* (1968), pp. 233 ff.; Schrader, "Fraktionen" (1923); Valentin, *Geschichte* (1930–31), 2:44 ff. For a comparison of the social composition of the two parliaments, see Schilfert, *Sieg* (1952), p. 314.

15. There is a survey of state elections, Botzenhart, "Parlamentarismusmodelle" (1974), pp. 135–36, n. 45. Vogel et al., *Wahlen* (1971), pp. 79–81, has a table summarizing the different suffrage regulations. On various regional developments,

see: Weber, *Revolution* (1970), pp. 222 ff., on Saxony; Valentin, *Geschichte* (1930–31), 2:405, on Kurhessen; Heger, *Partei* (1927), pp. 20 ff., on Württemberg; Valentin, *Geschichte* (1930–31), 2:440, and Nickel, *Revolution* (1965), pp. 144 ff., on Bavaria.

16. Quotation from a group in Barmen, as given in Köllmann, *Sozialgeschichte* (1960), p. 225. See also Zunkel, *Unternehmer* (1962), pp. 170 ff. and Pagenstecher, *Lebenserinnerungen* (1913), 2:80–81.

17. On the left, see: Valentin, *Geschichte* (1930–31), vol. 2; Huber, 2:705 ff.; Noyes, *Organizations* (1966), pp. 260 ff.; Krause, *Partei* (1923), pp. 117 ff.; Lüders, *Bewegung* (1909).

18. Quotation from Boldt, *Anfänge* (1971), p. 82. His analysis of the development of political organizations is a good introduction to the problem.

19. Weinandy, "Wahlen" (1956), p. 71.

20. Valentin, *Geschichte* (1930–31), 2:447.

21. Noyes, *Organizations* (1966), pp. 221–22. My account owes a great deal to this monograph, especially chap. 9. See also: Volkmann, *Arbeiterfrage* (1968), p. 33, and Schneider, *Sozialpolitik* (1923), p. 16, on the petitions to Berlin. Repgen, *Märzbewegung* (1955), p. 308, analyzed the contents of 2,000 petitions sent to Frankfurt from 1,100 Rhenish cities; he found that a majority were about religious and social issues.

Fieker, "Liberals" (1972), pp. 84–217, summarizes liberal ideas about social problems during the revolution.

22. Huber, *Dokumente* (1961–66), 1:273. See also Noyes, *Organizations* (1966), pp. 93 ff.

The Committee of Fifty, which was elected at the Vorparlament to prepare for the Nationalversammlung, tried to provide some concrete proposals on the "social question." However, the report of its subcommittee on labor was pushed aside when the Frankfurt deliberations began. This report, which was drafted by Robert Blum, is reprinted in Arnold Duckwitz, *Denkwürdigkeiten aus meinem öffentlichen Leben von 1841–1866* (Bremen, 1877), pp. 248 ff.

23. Wigard, 1:195. The debate over establishing this committee is given on pp. 69 ff.

24. On the political and social composition of the committee, see Eyck, *Frankfurt* (1968), pp. 206 ff., and Noyes, *Organizations* (1966), pp. 228 ff. The deliberations of the committee are described in: Ludwig Ölsner, "Die wirtschafts-und sozialpolitischen Verhandlungen des Frankfurter Parlaments," *PJbb* 87, no. 1 (1897): 81–100; Hugo C. M. Wendel, *The Evolution of Industrial Freedom in Prussia, 1845–1849* (Allentown, Pa., 1918); Schneider, *Sozialpolitik* (1923); Ziebura, "Anfänge" (1963), pp. 220–27.

25. W. von Rimscha, *Die Grundrechte im süddeutschen Konstitutionalismus* (Cologne, 1973).

26. Wigard, 1:700–701; Eyck, *Frankfurt* (1968), pp. 210 ff.

27. These reports are printed in Wigard, 1:681–700; Huber, *Dokumente* (1961–66), 1:318 ff., has the final version passed by the parliament. See: Eyck, *Frankfurt* (1968), for a guide to the debate; H. Scholler, "Die sozialen Grundrechte in der Paulskirche," *Der Staat* 13, no. 1 (1974): 51–72; T. Mommsen, *Die Grundrechte des deutschen Volkes* (1849; reprinted Frankfurt, 1969).

28. My account owes a great deal to the analysis in Walker, *Home Towns* (1971), pp. 369 ff. On the debate, see Eyck, *Frankfurt* (1968), pp. 214 ff., and the speeches in

Wigard, 1:756 ff., and 2:847 ff. Heffter, *Selbstverwaltung* (1950), pp. 291–321, discusses the issue in the various states.

29. See, for example, the report of the Economics Committee on Article 1: Wigard, 1:690–91.

30. On the situation in various parts of Germany, see the literature cited above, chap. 2, n. 60.

31. Noyes, *Organizations* (1966), pp. 233 ff., and Schneider, *Sozialpolitik* (1923), pp. 33 ff. For a contemporary view, see Born, *Erinnerungen* (1898), pp. 135–37. Hamerow, *Restoration* (1958), chap. 8, has a great deal of interesting material on these issues. In my opinion, Hamerow overestimates the cohesion both of the artisans and of the delegates at Frankfurt. A summary of his views can be found in *Restoration*, pp. 154–55.

32. Noyes, *Organizations* (1966), pp. 238 ff.

33. Wigard, 7:5422–23, and Noyes, *Organizations* (1966), pp. 328 ff.

34. Wigard, 7:5100–20 and 5127–46.

35. See, for example, F. Vigener, *Ketteler* (Munich and Berlin, 1924), pp. 66 ff.

36. Eyck, *Frankfurt* (1968), pp. 228 ff., 245, and 321, provides a guide to the debate. On the issue of church and state, see also Richard Lempp, *Die Frage der Trennung von Kirche und Staat im Frankfurter Parlament* (Tübingen, 1913). Herbert Hömig, *Rheinische Katholiken und Liberale in den Auseinandersetzungen um die preussische Verfassung unter besonderer Berücksichtigung der Kölner Presse* (Cologne, 1971), describes relations between Catholics and liberals in the Rhineland.

37. See: Walker, *Home Towns* (1971), p. 385, on the defenders of local autonomy; Noyes, *Organizations* (1966), and Max Quarck, *Die erste deutsche Arbeiterbewegung: Geschichte der Arbeiterverbrüderung 1848/49* (1924; reprinted Glashutten, 1970), on workers and artisans; Konrad Repgen, "Klerus und Politik 1848," *Aus Geschichte und Landeskunde. Festschrift für Franz Steinbach* (Bonn, 1960), pp. 133–65, and Nickel, *Revolution* (1965), pp. 140 ff., for the Catholics. Krieger, *Idea* (1957), pp. 333 ff., has a concise formulation of this entire problem.

38. Volkmann, *Arbeiterfrage* (1968), pp. 14 ff., and Krause, *Partei* (1923), pp. 109 ff. For more on the democrats and the "social question" see: Noyes, *Organizations* (1966), especially 266 ff.; Lüders, *Bewegung* (1909); and the excellent account of the Württemberg situation in Langewiesche, *Liberalismus* (1974), pp. 208 ff. For a different view, see Conze and Groh, *Arbeiterbewegung* (1966), especially pp. 32 ff.

39. This formulation owes a good deal to Walker's analysis in *Home Towns* (1971). See especially p. 372.

40. Wigard, 1:700.

41. Huber, *Dokumente* (1961–66), 1:284 ff., and Joseph Celotti, "The Political Thought and Action of Friedrich Christoph Dahlmann" (Unpubl. diss., Stanford, 1970), pp. 189 ff. See also Droysen, *Aktenstücke* (1967), pp. 46 ff., and the remarks in Rudolf Stadelmann, "Deutschland und die westeuropäischen Revolutionen," *Deutschland und Westeuropa* (Laupheim, 1948), p. 30.

42. Boldt, "Monarchie" (1973), pp. 554 and 594, and Botzenhart, "Parlamentarismusmodelle" (1974).

43. Valentin, *Geschichte* (1930–31), 2:17, and Eyck, *Frankfurt* (1968), pp. 113 ff.

44. Valentin, *Geschichte* (1930–31), 2:29 ff., and Eyck, *Frankfurt* (1968), pp. 116 ff. and 194–95. The debate is in Wigard, 1:356 ff.

45. There is a full account of this in Valentin, *Geschichte* (1930–31), 3:3. For a

vivid firsthand description of the riots, see Moritz Hartmann, *Bruchstücke revo-
lutionärer Erinnerungen* (1861), vol. 10 in his *Gesammelte Werke* (Stuttgart, 1874),
pp. 23–29. Pagenstecher, *Lebenserinnerungen* (1913), 2:97 ff., and Ambrosch, in
Bergsträsser, *Parlament* (1929), pp. 23 ff., illustrate the impact of these events on the
delegates.

46. The remark was made by Bavaria's representative in Berlin and is quoted in
Valentin, *Geschichte* (1930–31), 2:291. On the Prussian constitution see Huber, 2:721
ff., and *Dokumente* (1961–66), 1:385 ff.

47. The classic analysis of these issues remains bk. 2 of F. Meinecke's *Cosmopolitanism and the National State* (Princeton, 1970). See also Valentin, *Geschichte*
(1930–31), 2:298 ff., and Heffter, *Selbstverwaltung* (1950), p. 291.

48. The leading members of this group are analyzed in Hock, *Denken* (1957).
Birtsch, *Nation* (1964), provides an excellent account of Droysen's ideas and corrects
Hock on a number of details. Robert H. Handy, "Johann Gustav Droysen: The
Historian and German Politics in the Nineteenth Century," (Unpubl. diss.,
Georgetown, 1966) is a clearly written but not especially original summary of
Droysen's thought.

49. The most convenient guide to these debates is in Eyck, *Frankfurt* (1968), pp.
363 ff.

50. Quoted in Droz, "Anschauungen" (1972), p. 203. In addition to Droz's essay,
see: Schilfert, *Sieg* (1952), especially pp. 48–49 and 76 ff.; Boberach, *Wahlrechtsfrage* (1959), pp. 115 ff.; Philippson, *Ursprung* (1913). For a contemporary
view, see Mevissen in March 1848, quoted in Hansen, *Mevissen* (1906), 2:351.

51. For the suffrage system discussed in the Constitutional Committee, see
Droysen, *Aktenstücke* (1967), pp. 370 ff.; the parliamentary debate is in Wigard,
7:5220 ff.; especially interesting is Hildebrandt's effort to define "independence" on
pp. 5285–87; the law is reprinted in Huber, *Dokumente* (1961–66), 1:324–26. G.
Rümelin's article of February 21, 1849, is a good example of the liberals' hostility to
universal suffrage: reprinted in Gustav Rümelin, *Aus der Paulskirche. Berichte an den
Schwäbischen Merkur aus den Jahren 1848 und 1849* (Stuttgart, 1892), pp. 173–77.

Carol Rose, "The Issue of Parliamentary Suffrage at the Frankfurt National Assembly," *CEH* 5, no. 2 (June 1972): 127–49, is an excellent analysis of the suffrage
question and emphasizes the dilemmas liberals faced when they tried to define "independent." See also: Schilfert, *Sieg* (1952), pp. 169 ff., and Vogel et al., *Wahlen*
(1971), pp. 82 ff.

52. A record of the discussion of these issues in the Constitutional Committee can
be found in Droysen, *Aktenstücke* (1967), pp. 111 ff.; Eyck, *Frankfurt* (1968), pp. 221
ff., 373, 377 ff., provides a good guide to the debates; the constitution is reprinted in
Huber, *Dokumente* (1961–66), 1:304 ff.

I found the following interpretations helpful for understanding the constitutional
debate and its outcome: Ziebura, "Anfänge" (1963), pp. 232 ff.; Boldt,
"Monarchie" (1973); Botzenhart, "Parlamentarismusmodelle" (1974); Donald J.
Mattheisen, "1848: Theory and Practice of the German juste milieu," *RP* 35, no. 2
(April 1973): 180–92.

53. There is a moving description of the parliamentarians' journey to Berlin and its
unhappy ending in E. von Simson, *Erinnerungen* (Berlin, 1900), pp. 174–74. For two
examples of the impact of Frederick William's refusal of the crown, see Gothein,
Wirtschaftsgeschichte (1916), 1, pt. 1:489, and Rümelin in Bergsträsser, *Parlament*
(1929), p. 131. There is a great deal of information about Prussia in the final stage of

the revolution in F. Fischer, *Preussen am Abschlusse der ersten Hälfte des 19. Jahrhunderts* (Berlin, 1876), especially pp. 17 ff. On the extent and character of the support for the constitution, see Christoph Klessmann, "Zur Sozialgeschichte der Reichsverfassungskampagne von 1849," *HZ* 218, no. 2 (April 1974): 283–337, and Bernhard Mann, "Das Ende der deutschen Nationalversammlung im Jahre 1849," *HZ* 214, no. 2 (April 1972): 265–309.

54. Valentin, *Geschichte* (1930–31), 2:8; Huber, 2:861 ff.; Noyes, *Organizations* (1966), pp. 341 ff.; Eyck, *Frankfurt* (1968), pp. 384 ff. Weber, *Revolution* (1970), pp. 327 ff., has a good account of the May uprising in Saxony; Balser, *Demokratie* (1962), p. 62, gives the social composition of those arrested in Leipzig in 1849.

55. Pagenstecher, *Lebenserinnerungen* (1913), 3:102. Some other examples: Duncker, *Briefwechsel* (1923), p. 51; Reinhard Eigenbrodt, *Meine Erinnerungen aus den Jahren 1848, 1849, und 1850*, ed. L. Bergsträsser (Darmstadt, 1914), p. 48 (of the introduction); Hansen, *Mevissen* (1906), 1:617–18; Beseler, *Erlebtes* (1884), p. 95; Anna Caspary, *Ludolf Camphausens Leben* (Stuttgart and Berlin, 1902), p. 390; Gustav Freytag, *Karl Mathy, Gesammelte Werke* (Leipzig, 1898), 22:360 ff.; Bein, *Hammacher* (1932), pp. 28 ff.

Part III

1. Engels, *Revolutions* (1967), p. 239. Cf. Hamerow, "History" (1954), p. 28: "Liberalism was dealt a blow from which it never recovered."

2. On the Prussian election of 1855, see Parisius, *Deutschlands* (1878), p. 16. Some other examples: Pülke, *Geschichte* (1934), p. 34; Matern, "Wahlen" (1959), pp. 65 ff.; Haas, "Wahlen" (1954), pp. 71 ff. Huber, 3:35–128 and 182 ff., has a useful summary of political developments in the fifties; see also G. Grünthal, "Konstitutionalismus und konservative Politik," in Ritter, *Gesellschaft* (1974), on Prussia after 1850.

3. The quotations are from: Lewald, *Erinnerungen* (1969), p. 147; Thorwart, *Schulze-Delitzsch* (1913), p. 50; Haym, *Briefwechsel* (1967), p. 127; Duncker, *Briefwechsel* (1923), p. 47.

4. Pagenstecher, "Lebenserinnerungen" (1919).

5. The most important change in the constitution was the substitution of the "three-class" suffrage system for the democratic voting procedures set down in the original version. On the origins and operation of the system, see Droz, "Anschauungen" (1972), pp. 195 ff.

6. For an example of the Crimean War's impact on Germany, see Droysen, "Zur Characteristik der Europäischen Krisis," *Schriften* (1933), pp. 307–42.

Chapter 6

1. Rochau, *Grundsätze* (1853; reprinted 1972), p. 141.

2. Quoted in K. Abraham, *Der Strukturwandel im Handwerk in der ersten Hälfte des 19. Jahrhunderts und seine Bedeutung für die Berufserziehung* (Cologne, 1955), p. 96.

3. On the development of the economy after 1850, see: Landes, *Prometheus* (1969), especially the data on p. 194; K. Borchardt, "The Industrial Revolution in

Germany," in C. Cipolla, ed., *The Fontana Economic History of Europe* (London and Glasgow, 1972), 4:63 ff.; Böhme, *Deutschlands* (1966), pp. 57 ff. R. Spree and J. Bergmann, "Die konjunkturelle Entwicklung der deutschen Wirtschaft, 1840–1864," in Wehler, ed. *Sozialgeschichte* (1974), pp. 289–325, argue convincingly that the critical period for mid-century economic development began in the mid-forties.

4. Hoffmann, "Take-Off" (1963), p. 118.

5. Köllmann, "Bevölkerung" (1968), p. 211; Walker, *Home Towns* (1971), pp. 397–98; P. Quante, *Die Abwanderung aus der Landwirtschaft* (Kiel, 1958), p. 5.

6. Köllmann, "Bevölkerung" (1968), p. 230. Schmoller's *Geschichte* (1870) has stood the test of time remarkably well; see especially pp. 281 and 307 for some useful data. Among the more recent works, Wolfram Fischer's essays are the best place to begin; they are collected in *Wirtschaft* (1972). See also the contributions by Henning and Schmidt in Abel et al., *Handwerkergeschichte in neuer Sicht* (Göttingen, 1970); G. Hermes, "Statistische Studien zur wirtschaftlichen und gesellschaftlichen Struktur des zollvereinten Deutschlands," *ASW* 63, no. 1 (1929), especially pp. 146 ff.; Birker, *Arbeiterbildungsvereine* (1973), pp. 11–12.

7. Zunkel, *Unternehmer* (1962), pp. 61–62, 99 ff.; Schramm, *Hamburg* (1943), chap. 8; Henning, *Bürgertum* (1972), pp. 40, 490–91; Böhme, *Deutschlands* (1966), p. 165. Bramstedt, *Aristocracy* (1964), discusses changing social values as they were reflected in literature; Rosenburg, *Weltwirtschaftskrise* (1934), pp. 76–77, has some data on the distribution of wealth; R. Engelsing, "Lebenshaltungen und Lebenshaltungskosten im 18. und 19. Jahrhundert in den Hansestädten Bremen und Hamburg," *IRSH* 11, no. 1 (1966): 87, describes changing patterns of consumption; Ayçoberry, "Strukturwandel" (1975), finds the beginning of a shift within the middle strata in the 1840s. For two contemporary statements, see Kiesselbach, "Generationen" (1860), and J. F. Faber, "Vom Dritten Stande," *DV* 27 (1865): 1–54.

8. Birker, *Arbeiterbildungsvereine* (1973), p. 115; Conze, "Arbeiter," in Brunner et al., *Grundbegriffe* (1972), 1:216 ff.; Balser, *Demokratie* (1962), pp. 143–44.

9. Kaelble, *Unternehmer* (1972), pp. 126 ff., and T. E. Carter, "Freytag's *Soll und Haben*: A National Liberal Manifesto as a Best Seller," *German Life and Letters*, 21, no. 4 (1968): 320–29.

10. Bebel, *Leben* (1961), p. 63.

11. Bein, *Hammacher* (1932), and Dorn, "Anfänge" (1922), pp. 10 ff., on Buhl.

12. Kaelble, *Unternehmer* (1972), p. 230.

13. See for example, the data on a thousand Hanoverians listed by the government as holding liberal views and on the signers of the Bavarian Fortschrittspartei electoral statement in 1863; Kurmeier, *Entstehung* (1923), p. 32 ff., and Dorn, "Anfänge" (1922), p. 69.

14. For an example, see Hofmann, *Stadtverordneten* (1964), pp. 82, 171.

15. Hentschel, *Freihändler* (1975), and Böhme, *Deutschlands* (1966), p. 88.

16. There are data on the social composition of the *Nationalverein* in L. O'Boyle, "Nationalverein" (1957), p. 334.

17. Quoted from a letter to Engels in D. McLellan, *Karl Marx. His Life and Thought* (New York, 1973), p. 319. The best analysis of the Prussian Landtage of the 1860s is in Hess, *Parlament* (1964). See also Eisfeld, *Entstehung* (1969), pp. 108 ff. Gillis, *Bureaucracy* (1971), pt. 3, discusses the Prussian civil service after 1850.

18. H. Jordan, *Die öffentliche Meinung in Sachsen, 1864–66* (Kamenz, 1918), p. 46; anon., *Die Fortschritt in der Bayerischen Abgeordneten Kammer* (Nördlingen, 1863); Gall, *Liberalismus* (1968), p. 62, and Becker, *Staat* (1973), p. 104, on Baden.

19. Hess, *Parlament* (1964), pp. 60 and 155, n. 61. See also Unruh, *Erinnerungen* (1895), p. 196.

20. V. Böhmert, *Rückblicke und Ausblicke* (Dresden, 1900), pp. 22 ff.; Philippson, *Forckenbeck* (1898); Eisfeld, "Anfänge" (1969), p. 84, on Becker; Dorn, "Anfänge" (1922), pp. 7 ff., on the importance of lawyers in Bavaria. For the literature on Schulze and Lasker, see below, n. 60 and chap. 11, n. 12.

21. See above, pp. 24–26.

22. On the Prussian elections, see E. Anderson, *Statistics* (1954), which reprints the returns for 1862 and 1863; F. W. C. Dieterici, "Über die Zahl der Urwähler im preussischen Staate und deren Verteilung nach Geschäften und Erwerbszweigen," *Mitteilungen des Statistischen Bureaus in Berlin*, 2, no. 2 (1849): 17–32, has some data on the composition of the voting classes; official returns were published in the *ZPSB* 2 (1862): 77–120, for the election of 1861 and in vol. 5 (1865): 41–86, for the elections of 1862 and 1863.

23. Eisfeld, *Entstehung* (1969), p. 109, has data on local leadership. See also: Köllmann, *Sozialgeschichte* (1960), pp. 236 ff., on Barmen; Hofmann, *Stadtverordneten* (1964), pp. 42 ff., on Bielefeld; Kaiser, *Strömungen* (1963), especially pp. 211 and 403, on Bonn.

24. Quoted in Zunkel, *Unternehmer* (1962), p. 181. See also Hansen, *Mevissen* (1906), 1:603 ff. Tipton, "Consensus" (1974), pp. 203 ff., raises some important questions about the conventional view that economic growth was encouraged by the diversion of energy from politics to economics.

25. Bamberger, *Erinnerungen* (1899), pp. 214 ff. Cf. Zucker, *Bamberger* (1975).

26. Quoted in Krieger, *Idea* (1957), p. 346.

27. Böhmert, "Entstehung" (1884), p. 211.

28. Quoted in Gall, *Liberalismus* (1968), pp. 175–76. Cf. the program of the Prussian liberals, reprinted in Parisius, *Deutschlands* (1878), pp. 33–34, and the Fortschrittspartei declaration of June 1861 in *EGK 1861*, p. 42.

29. Bluntschli, *Staatswörterbuch* (1857–70); *StL* (1st ed.), 6:667–70 and (3d ed.), 6:449–66. For another example, see J. Held's addition to Rotteck's article on "Naturrecht," *StL* (3d ed.), 10:447–54.

A similar set of changes can be observed in the *Zeitschrift für die gesamte Staatswissenschaft*, which, despite its title, became increasingly absorbed with economic matters: see volumes 7–22 (1850–66). W. H. Riehl, *Die Naturgeschichte des Volkes*, 3 vols. 4th ed. (Stuttgart and Augsburg, 1857–58), has some astute comments on the growing significance of social forces in German thought and action (see, for example, 2:4).

30. Quoted in Wolff, "Prince Smith" (1880), p. 323. See also Maenner, "Deutschlands" (1927), pp. 351 ff.

31. Tischlermeister Schwarze, in Centralverein für das Wohl der arbeitenden Klassen, "Vorbericht," *Der Arbeiterfreund*, 2:4 (1864). There are some additional examples in Hamerow, *Foundations* (1969–72), 1:84 ff. See also Schmoller, *Geschichte* (1870), p. 666.

32. *StL* (3d ed.), 10:740. See also G. Cohen, "Handelspolitik," *StL* (3d ed.), 7:381–405, and Böhmert as quoted by Hamerow, *Foundations* (1969–72), 1:95. Walker, *Home Towns* (1971), pp. 390 ff., has an interesting discussion of this process. Karl Rathgen, in "Die Ansichten über Freihandel und Schutzzoll in der deutschen Staatspraxis des 19. Jahrhunderts," *Die Entwicklung der deutschen Volks-*

wirtschaftslehre im neunzehnten Jahrhundert (Leipzig, 1908), covers some of the most important expressions of liberal economic thought.

33. There is a firsthand account of the Kongress in Böhmert, "Entstehung" (1884). Krieger, *Idea* (1957), pp. 407 ff., and Eisfeld, *Entstehung* (1969), pp. 15 ff., are both good, brief analyses. See also Hentschel, *Freihändler* (1975); Grambow, *Freihandelspartei* (1903); Hamerow, *Foundations* (1969–72), 1:340 ff.

34. J. Wiggers, *Aus meinem Leben* (Leipzig, 1901), pp. 220–21.

35. The quotations are from anon., "Übergang," *Gb* (1861), pp. 121 ff., 131; Schulze, *Schriften* (1909–13), 1:21–22; Hansen, *Mevissen* (1906), 1:619.

36. Rochau, *Grundsätze* (1853; reprinted 1972), pp. 27, 33. There is an excellent analysis of Rochau's ideas in Lees, *Revolution* (1974), 107 ff.

37. Huber, 3:143–44, summarizes the basic issues, which are further analyzed in Böhme, *Deutschlands* (1966), pp. 91 ff. Rosenberg, *Publizistik* (1935), pp. 559 ff., surveys the contemporary literature. The Handelstag debate over the Commercial Treaty is described in *EGK 1862*, pp. 97–98.

38. Hamerow, *Foundations* (1969–72), 1:369–71.

39. Mohl, "Staatswissenschaften" (1855), pp. 70, 101. On the article, see Klaus von Beyme's introduction ,to Mohl's *Schriften* (1966), pp. xiv–xxv, and Pankoke, *Bewegung* (1970), pp. 119–23, 158 ff.

40. Hegel's concept of "Corporation" is developed in his *Philosophy* (1952), pp. 152 ff.

41. Pankoke, *Bewegung* (1970), pp. 161 ff.; M. Riedel, "Der Staatsbegriff der deutschen Geschichtssschreibung des 19. Jahrhunderts in seinem Verhältnis zur klassisch—politischen Philosophie," *Der Staat* 2, no. 1 (1963): 50 ff.; Dorpalen, *Treitschke* (1957), pp. 47 ff.

42. Quoted in Heffter, *Selbstverwaltung* (1950), p. 395.

43. Bluntschli, in Bluntschli, ed., *Staatswörterbuch* (1857–70), vol. 6 (1861), pp. 16–17; Huber's article is in Bluntschli, vol. 9 (1865), the quotation is from p. 482.

44. Droysen, *Schriften* (1933), p. 324. See also Birtsch, *Nation* (1964), pp. 187 ff.

45. Kiesselbach, "Generationen" (1860).

46. Quotations from: Kiesselbach, "Generationen" (1860), p. 36; Hamerow, *Foundations* (1969–72), 1:136; Kapp, *Frühsozialisten* (1969), pp. 77–78.

47. Welcker, *StL* (3d ed.), 1:xxiii; *Gb* 20, no. 2 (1861): p. 519.

48. 'G,' "Parteien," *StL* (3d ed.), 11:326.

49. These views are discussed in Henning, *Bürgertum* (1972), pp. 22–27.

50. Rochau, *Grundsätze* (1853; reprinted 1972), pp. 141–43. For a somewhat different interpretation of Rochau's views, see Winkler, *Mittelstand* (1972), pp. 21 ff.

51. Lees, *Revolution* (1974), pp. 138 ff., and Fieker, "Liberals" (1972), pp. 220 ff., provide useful introductions to this problem.

52. J. Prince Smith, "Die sogenannte Arbeiterfrage," *VVK* 5, no. 4 (1864): 192–207.

53. Quoted in Gagel, *Wahlrechtsfrage* (1958), p. 33.

54. Weber, *Demokraten* (1962), p. 169; Schmierer, *Arbeiterbildung* (1970), pp. 95 ff.; Simon, *Demokraten* (1969), p. 11.

55. H. Oncken, *Lassalle*, 3d ed. (Stuttgart, 1920), is the classic biography; S. Na'aman, *Lassalle* (Hanover, 1970), is the most recent. For liberals' views of Lassalle, see Oncken, *Bennigsen* (1910), 1:670, and Thorwart, *Schulze* (1913), pp. 188 ff.

56. Bebel, *Leben* (1961), pp. 73 ff.

57. On liberals and workers, see the following: H. Lademacher, "Zu den Anfängen der deutschen Sozialdemokratie, 1863–1878," *IRSH* 4, nos. 2 and 3 (1959): 239–60, 367–93; Birker, *Arbeiterbildungsvereine* (1973); Reichard, *Birth* (1969), pp. 128–35, 182 ff.; E. Eyck, *Der Vereinstag deutscher Arbeitervereine, 1863–1868* (Berlin, 1904); Engelberg, *Widerstreit* (1970), pp. 203 ff. As usual, it is necessary to qualify and refine generalizations about national trends with local studies; on this issue, see: E. Bernstein, *Die Geschichte der Berliner Arbeiterbewegung* (Berlin, 1907–10), 1:108 ff.; Böttcher, *Anfänge* (1953), pp. 75 ff., on Bremen; Möllers, "Strömungen" (1955), pp. 42–43, on Essen; Eckert, *Sozialdemokratie* (1968), on Nuremberg.

58. Quoted in H. Schwab, "Von Düppel bis Königgrätz," *ZfG*, 14, no. 4 (1966): 591.

59. Vorländer, "Princip," *ZfGS* (1857): 3.

60. "After the contemporary political movement's defeat," wrote Schulze in 1850, "it has returned to its real point of departure—the social realm." *Schriften* (1909–13), 1:1. On Schulze, see the biography by Thorwart (1913); Conze, *Möglichkeiten* (1965); B. Schulze, "Zur linksliberalen Ideologie und Politik. Ein Beitrag zur politischen Biographie Schulze-Delitzschs," in Bartel and Engelberg, eds., *Reichsgründung* (1971), 271–307.

61. Thorwart, *Schulze* (1913), p. 132. On the evolution of cooperatives, see also H. Faust, *Geschichte der Genossenschaftsbewegung*, 2d ed. (Frankfurt, 1965).

62. Huber, "Assoziation," in Bluntschli, *Staatswörterbuch* (1857–70), 1:456–500; H. Oncken, *Lassalle*, 3d ed. (Stuttgart, 1920); F. Vigener, *Ketteler* (Munich and Berlin, 1924); Gerteis, *Sonnemann* (1970), pp. 35 ff.; Biedermann, "Socialismus," *StL* (3d ed), 13:423–33; Volkmann, *Arbeiterfrage* (1968), pp. 75 ff., on Harkort; Mommsen, *Miquel* (1928), pp. 159 ff.; Schmoller, "Die Arbeiterfrage," *PJbb* 14, nos. 3–4, and 15, no. 1 (1864–65); and Böhmert, *Briefe Zweier Handwerker* (Dresden, 1854), especially pp. 90 ff.

63. Quoted in Volkmann, *Arbeiterfrage* (1968), p. 75. Cf. Faucher's remark that "certainly the best way to improve the financial condition of the laboring stratum is to turn workers into capitalists" Centralverein für das Wohl der arbeitenden Klassen, "Vorbericht," *Der Arbeiterfreund*, 2:4 [1864], p. 428.

64. For example, Schmoller wrote that "only a moral solution of the worker question can save us from a social revolution" ("Die Arbeiterfrage," *PJbb*, 14, no. 4 [1864]: 423).

65. Like so many other liberals, Schulze continued to emphasize the importance of education: see, for example, *Schriften* (1909–13), 4:383 ff., and *StL* (3d ed.), 12:189–90.

66. On the strike movement in the sixties, see *EGK 1865*, p. 59 (Leipzig printers) and p. 83 (Hamburg).

67. Schulze, *Schriften* (1909–13), 2:25.

68. Quoted in Eisfeld, *Entstehung* (1969), p. 44. See also Birker, *Arbeiterbildungsvereine* (1973), pp. 53–54.

Chapter 7

1. Rochau, *Grundsätze* (1853; reprinted 1972), p. 57.

2. Quoted in Weinandy, "Wahlen" (1956), p. 149. For a guide to the contemporary literature, see Rosenberg, *Publizistik* (1935), pp. 1–19.

3. Gall, *Liberalismus* (1968), p. 61, n. 8.

4. On politics in the various states, see: Hess, *Reichstagswahlen* (1958), pp. 44 ff., on Hesse; *EGK 1862*, p. 93, on Hesse-Darmstadt; *EGK 1865*, p. 88, on Nassau; Bolland, *Bürgerschaft* (1959), pp. 37 ff., and *EGK 1865*, pp. 130 and 141, on Hamburg; Ehrenfeuchter, "Willensbildung" (1951), p. 56, on Hanover; Adam, *Jahrhundert* (1919), pp. 95–136, on Württemberg; Jordan, *Meinung* (1919), pp. 45–46, on Saxony; *EGK 1863*, p. 35 and *DAZ*, May 3, 1863, on Bavaria.

5. The liberals' activity in city government is chronicled in *EGK, 1862–66*: see, for example, *EGK 1863*, pp. 136–37, on the conflict between the Berlin city council and the government over the press ordinance. R. Lembcke, *Johannes Miquel und die Stadt Osnabrück* (Osnabrück, 1962), p. 8, provides another example.

6. See above, pp. 84–86.

7. Brief accounts of the Nationalverein can be found in Huber, 3:384 ff., and Fricke, 1:489 ff. See also Krieger, *Idea* (1957), 413 ff.; R. LeMang, *Der deutsche Nationalverein* (Berlin, 1909); W. Grube, *Die neue Ära und der Nationalverein* (Diss., Marburg, 1933); O'Boyle, "Nationalverein" (1957); Oncken, *Bennigsen* (1910), 1:313 ff.

8. There is a great deal of interesting information on these institutions in Hamerow, *Foundations* (1969–72), 1: chap. 8. See also: Eisfeld, *Entstehung* (1969), p. 125, on the *Abgeordnetentag*; D. Schäfer, "Der Deutsche Handelstag auf dem Weg zum wirtschaftlichen Verband," in Varain, *Interessenverbände* (1973), 120–38, and Fischer, *Unternehmerschaft* (1964), pp. 63 ff., on the *Handelstag*; Fricke, 1:520 ff., on the *Protestantverein*; and Weber, *Demokraten* (1962), and Fricke, 1:541 ff., 605 ff., on recreational societies. The annual meetings and programs of these organizations are reported in the *EGK, 1862–66*.

9. Quoted in Hamerow, *Foundations* (1969–72), 1:339.

10. On the growth of communications, see: W. Zorn, "Die wirtschaftliche Integration Kleindeutschlands in den 1860er Jahren und die Reichsgründung," *HZ* 216, no. 2 (April 1973): 304–34; Hoffmann, *Wachstum* (1965); Anderson, *Conflict* (1954), p. 15. *StL* (3d ed.), 5:46–48 has some excellent data on the railroads. J. Riesser, *The Great German Banks and Their Concentration in Connection with the Economic Development of Germany* (Washington, 1911), traces the evolution of commercial institutions. On newspapers, see Hamerow, *Foundations* (1969–72), 1:288–92. Rosenberg, *Publizistik* (1935), pp. 977–82, has a survey of leading periodicals.

11. These data are from: Grambow, *Freihandelspartei* (1903), p. 16, on the Kongress; Fricke, 1:489, 541, 605, on the Nationalverein and the gymnastic and singing societies.

12. Adam, "Liberalismus" (1933); Parisius, *Deutschlands* (1878), pp. 24 ff.; *Gb* 17, no. 3 (1858): 436–37.

13. Parisius, *Deutschlands* (1878), pp. 33–34, reprints the original statement of January 1861; the party program of June 1861 is given in *EGK 1861*, pp. 41–42. On the *Altliberalen*, see E. Fülling, *Die preussischen Altliberalen im Heeresreform -und Verfassungskampf* (Marburg diss., Bad Essen, 1933).

14. Quoted in Eisfeld, "Anfänge" (1969), p. 82. A similar remark is quoted in Pülke, "Geschichte" (1934), p. 95.

15. Quoted in Kaiser, *Strömungen* (1963), p. 136. The left wing's efforts to get a more precise and radical program are discussed in Parisius, *Deutschlands* (1878), pp. 44–45, and Uelsmann, "Beiträge" (1926), p. 113.

16. The following local studies give a good picture of the variety of political

alignments among liberals in Prussia: Bellot, "Leben" (1951), pp. 188 ff., on the Saar; Denk, "Wahlen" (1955), pp. 136 ff., on Cologne; Kaiser, *Strömungen* (1963), pp. 140 ff., on Bonn; Köllmann, *Sozialgeschichte* (1960), pp. 233 ff., on Barmen; Möllers, "Strömungen" (1955), p. 37, on Essen; Uelsmann, "Beiträge" (1926), p. 113, on the Niederrhein region.

17. Gall's excellent book, *Liberalismus* (1968), is the best account of the movement in Baden. For a summary of Gall's achievement and some thoughtful criticisms, see Thomas Nipperdey's review, *HZ* 210 (1970): 436–39. On the situation in Baden, see also H. Striebich, "Konfession und Partei. Ein Beitrag zur Entwicklung der politischen Willensbildung im alten Lande Baden" (Unpubl. diss., Heidelberg, 1955).

18. Gall, *Liberalismus* (1968), pp. 205 ff., 337 ff.; Becker, *Staat* (1973), pp. 167 ff.

19. Dorn, "Anfänge" (1922), and Schieder, *Partei* (1936).

20. Kurmeier, *Entstehung* (1923). The best account of Bennigsen's career is Oncken's massive biography (1910).

21. Hess, *Reichstagswahlen* (1958), pp. 44 ff., and White, *Party* (1976), pp. 23 ff.

22. Menzinger, *Verfassungsrevision* (1969), pp. 38 ff., surveys the situation in Württemberg. On the *Volkspartei*, see Heger, *Partei* (1927), and Runge, *Volkspartei* (1970).

23. Fricke, 1:285 ff.

24. E. Schmidt-Weissenfels, *Preussische Landtagsmänner* (Breslau, 1862). On Haym, see above, chap. 1, n. 54.

25. Welcker, preface to Rotteck, "Bewegungspartei," *StL* (3d ed.), 2:716–24, and 'G,' "Parteien," 11:311–27.

26. H. Pierer, *Universallexicon*, 4th ed. (Altenburg, 1857–62), vol. 10 (1860), p. 337.

27. *Landtagsmänner*, pp. 74–76.

28. Baumgarten (March 1862), HW, 1:84–85; the other quote is from Sybel, HW, 1:73. On the liberals' self-image, see Nipperdey, *Organisation* (1961), pp. 9 ff.

29. Quoted in Dorn, "Anfänge" (1922), p. 44.

30. Eisfeld, *Entstehung* (1969), pp. 25, 85. Another example of the hope for a unified movement can be found in Freytag, *Erinnerungen* (n.d.), p. 631.

31. J. Held, "Die politischen und socialen Wirkungen der verschiedenen politischen Wahlsystems," in August Freiherr von Haxthausen, ed., *Das constitutionelle Princip* (Leipzig, 1864), 2:1–86.

32. The atmosphere at the meetings of the Nationalverein is described with not so gentle irony in Wilhelm Raabe's novel *Gutmanns Reise* (1891; reprinted as vol. 18 in his *Sämtliche Werke*, Göttingen, 1963). A more reliable treatment can be found in Seyffardt, *Erinnerungen* (1900), p. 32.

33. Eisfeld, *Entstehung* (1969), pp. 48, 104, and idem, "Anfänge" (1969).

34. The best analysis of party organization remains Thomas Nipperdey's pioneering monograph, *Organisation* (1962) (on the Fortschrittspartei, see pp. 16 ff.). Eisfeld, *Entstehung* (1969), and Anderson, *Conflict* (1954), are also worth reading on this issue.

35. A contributor to the *Grenzboten* called indirect voting "a gentle kind of tutelage for the crowd by an aristocracy of electors." Quoted in Gagel, *Wahlrechtsfrage* (1958), p. 45. For an example of the system in operation, see Schierbaum, *Wahlen* (1960), pp. 178–80, on Trier.

36. *StL* (3d ed.), 10:742. For some other examples, see: Lees, *Revolution* (1974),

pp. 44 ff., on Sybel; R. Virchow, *Einheitsbestrebungen in der wissenschaftlichen Medizin* (Berlin, 1849); A. Wucher, *Theodor Mommsen: Geschichtsschreibung und Politik* (Göttingen, 1956), pp. 24–25. Hans Rosenberg has some astute comments on this issue in "Honoratiorenpolitik" (1970), p. 186.

37. Rochau, *Grundsätze* (1853; reprinted 1972), p. 45.

'38. Anderson, *Conflict* (1954), p. 279.

39. HW, 1:128, and J. Heyderhoff, "Ein Brief Max Dunckers an Hermann Baumgarten über Junkertum und Demokratie in Preussen (6. Juni 1858)," *HZ* 113, no. 2 (1914): 325, on Twesten; Bein, *Hammacher* (1932), p. 55; Bunsen, *Bunsen* (1900), p. 185.

40. Letter of December 1861, reprinted in E. von Simson, *Erinnerungen aus seinem Leben* (Berlin, 1900), p. 344.

41. Parisius, *Hoverbeck* (1897–1900), 1:150. For more on political style, see the following local studies: Schierbaum, *Wahlen* (1960), pp. 179–80, on Trier; Kochhann, *Auszüge* (1906), pp. 71 ff., on Berlin; Weinandy, "Wahlen" (1956), p. 194, on the Sieg-Gummersbach region; Mommsen, *Miquel* (1928), pp. 85 ff., on Göttingen; Hofmann, *Stadtverordneten* (1964), pp. 41 ff., 83 ff., on Bielefeld.

42. The best single work on the suffrage issue after 1848 is Gagel, *Wahlrechtsfrage* (1958).

43. Schulze, *Schriften* (1909–13), 4:414 ff., and Welcker, *StL* (3d ed.), 3:415–27.

44. Quoted in Gagel, *Wahlrechtsfrage* (1958), p. 33.

45. Bluntschli, *Staatswörterbuch* (1857–70), 8:595. His plan of 1851 is given in *Denkwürdiges aus meinem Leben* (Nördlingen, 1884), 2:117–20.

46. Quoted in Seier, *Staatsidee* (1961), p. 57. See also Hamerow, *Foundations* (1969–72), 1:164–65.

47. These problems can be clearly seen in the Prussian Landtag debate over suffrage regulations for city government, which is analyzed in Gagel, *Wahlrechtsfrage* (1958), pp. 22 ff., 63–72. Eisfeld, *Entstehung* (1969), p. 128, discusses the situation in Bavaria; Gall, *Liberalismus* (1968), p. 204, on Baden. See also the following contemporary treatments: *Gb* 18, no. 3 (1858): 488–89; G. Waitz, "Über die Bildung einer Volksvertretung," in A. Freiherr von Haxthausen, *Das constitutionelle Princip* (Leipzig, 1864), 2:181–218; Rochau, *Grundsätze* (1853; reprinted 1972), pp. 87 ff.

48. Quoted in Bauer, *Meinung* (1914), p. 49 (see also the remarks by Treitschke and Josef Held quoted on p. 50).

49. *Gb* 19, no. 4 (1860): 114, and Biedermann, *StL* (3d ed.), 14:369–70.

50. In 1858, for example, the *Kölnische Zeitung* referred to "all factions of the liberal party, that is, with few exceptions, the entire nation." Quoted in Denk, "Wahlen" (1955), p. 121.

51. Pagenstecher, *Lebenserinnerungen* (1913), 3:102.

52. Quoted in Balser, *Anfänge* (1959), p. 103.

Chapter 8

1. Rochau, *Grundsätze* (1853; reprinted 1972), p. 131.

2. Quoted in Celotti, "Thought" (1970), p. 285. For more on the liberal view of the revolution, see Neumüller, *Liberalismus* (1973), pp. 119 ff.

3. Unruh, *Erfahrungen* (1851), pp. 5 ff. For another example, see the two recent articles on Georg Gervinus: Charles McClelland, "History in the Service of Politics: A

Reassessment of G. G. Gervinus," *CEH* 4, no. 4 (December 1971): 371–89, and J. Wagner, "Georg Gottfried Gervinus: The Tribulations of a Liberal Federalist," ibid., pp. 354–70.

4. 'G,' "Parteien," *StL* (3d ed.), 11:325, and J. Held, "Organisation," ibid., p. 42.

5. Oncken, *Bennigsen* (1910), 1:361, and Rochau, *StL* (3d ed.), 1:85.

6. The Prussian constitutional conflict is one of the best-studied episodes in modern German history. Among the newer works, the following are especially valuable: Hess, *Parlament* (1964); Anderson, *Conflict* (1954); Winkler, *Liberalismus* (1964) and "Emanzipation" (1968); R. Wahl, "Der preussische Verfassungskonflikt und das konstitutionelle System des Kaiserreichs," in Böckenförde, ed., *Verfassungsge-schichte* (1972), pp. 171–94. F. Löwenthal, *Der preussische Verfassungsstreit 1862–1866* (Altenburg, 1914), gives a detailed narrative of events. Michael Gugel's *Indus-trieller Aufstieg und bürgerliche Herrschaft* (Cologne, 1975), appeared too late to be of use for the present chapter; he has some astute comments on the liberals' political goals, but does not, in my opinion, succeed in analyzing Prussian liberalism as part of a European process of "industrial growth and *bürgerliche Herrschaft*." A guide to contemporary publications can be found in Rosenberg, *Publizistik* (1935), pp. 159–202, 475 ff., 858 ff.

7. G. Craig, *The Politics of the Prussian Army* (New York and Oxford, 1956), chap. 4.

8. For a complete guide to the older literature on Bismarck, see K. E. Born, ed., *Bismarck Bibliographie* (Cologne and Berlin, 1966). His role in the conflict is well treated in Pflanze, *Bismarck* (1963), chaps. 7–14.

9. Some examples of the antiaristocratic ingredient in the constitutional conflict can be found in Anderson, *Conflict* (1954), pp. 20 ff. In my opinion, Winkler, "Emanzipa-tion" (1968), rather overestimates the Prussian *Bürgertum*'s opposition to the Junkers and the importance of this opposition for the *Bürgertum*'s political behavior.

10. The phrase is from a letter by Sybel in 1862, HW, 1:107. The classic formula-tion of the differences between civil servants and politicians is to be found in Max Weber, *Schriften* (1958), p. 95.

11. Quoted in Gall, *Liberalismus* (1968), pp. 122–23. Gall gives the best account of the political situation in Baden. Becker, *Staat* (1973), is also worth reading on the religious issue. G. Schmoller, "Rümelin" (1913), pp. 151–64, has some information on church-state relations in Württemberg.

12. Quoted in Ficker, *Der Kulturkampf in Münster* (Münster, 1928), p. 42. On the situation in the Rhineland, see Uelsmann, "Beiträge" (1926), pp. 123 ff.

13. H. Anders, *Der Kampf der Arbeiterklasse um die Koalitionsfreiheit in den 60er Jahren des 19. Jahrhunderts in Preussen* (Diss., Leipzig, 1961), p. 12.

14. Quoted in Rosenberg, *Weltwirtschaftskrise* (1934), p. 188. Böhme, *Deutsch-lands* (1966), pp. 78 ff., also has a good account of the depression.

15. See the data cited in Tilly, "Economy" (1966), p. 492 (see also p. 494 on tax policies). More on the state and the economy after 1850 in: Rosenberg, *Weltwirtschaftskrise* (1934); Zunkel, "Beamtenschaft" (1964), pp. 182 ff., and *Un-ternehmer* (1962); Kaelble, *Unternehmer* (1972), pp. 236 ff.; Hansen, *Mevissen* (1906), 1:701 ff.

16. Kaelble, *Unternehmer* (1972), pp. 247–49.

17. Maenner, "Deutschlands" (1927); Schunke, *Freihändler* (1916); Zunkel, *Un-*

ternehmer (1962), pp. 205 ff.; Böhme, *Deutschlands* (1966), pp. 100 ff.

18. Rochau, *Grundsätze* (1853; reprinted 1972), p. 68. On the national question after the revolution, see Lees, *Revolution* (1974), pp. 125 ff. For a list of contemporary publications, see Rosenberg, *Publizistik* (1935).

19. Haym, *Briefwechsel* (1967), p. 152; Krieger, *Idea* (1957), pp. 361 ff. has a good treatment of Haym's ideas. For some other examples, see: Oncken, *Bennigsen* (1910), 1:482–83; Gall, *Liberalismus* (1968), p. 123, on Roggenbach; K. W. Wippermann, "National-politische Bewegung," *StL* (3d ed.), 10:354–94.

20. E. Portner, *Die Einigung Italiens im Urteil liberaler deutscher Zeitgenossen* (Bonn, 1959), traces liberal views of Italian affairs; these can also be seen in the careful attention paid to Italy in the *EGK*. Heffter, *Selbstverwaltung* (1950), p. 365, notes a renewal of interest in the era of reforms and the wars of liberation during the 1850s.

21. For some examples of those who did view the *Volk* as the primary source and instrument of foreign policy, see Weber, *Demokraten* (1962), pp. 32, 42–43, and Gerteis, *Sonnemann* (1970), p. 33.

22. For example, Widenmann (1861), in HW, 1:55. This point is developed in Schweitzer, "Kritik" (1950).

23. Rochau, *Grundsätze* (1853; reprinted 1972), p. 191. See also Treitschke, quoted in Krieger, *Idea* (1957), pp. 366–67, and Droysen, whose ideas are analyzed in F. Gilbert, *Johann Gustav Droysen und die preussisch-deutsche Frage* (Munich and Berlin, 1931), pp. 121 ff.

24. Twesten and the *Nationalzeitung* quoted in Winkler, *Liberalismus* (1964), pp. 44, 78; Böhmert in Oncken, *Bennigsen* (1910), 1:647. For some other examples, see: Seier, *Staatsidee* (1961), p. 152, on Sybel; Haym, *Briefwechsel* (1967), p. 247, letter of May 1866; Bluntschli, *Denkwürdiges aus meinem Leben* (Nördlingen, 1884), 3:136; Wehrenpfennig, HW, 1:265, letter of November 1865.

25. Mommsen, *Miquel* (1928), p. 201; Treitschke quoted in Westphal, *Staatsauffassung* (1919), p. 302; Sybel in E. Schmidt-Weissenfels, *Preussische Landtagsmänner* (Breslau, 1862), pp. 153 ff.; Bluntschli in HW, 1:149, n. 1. Two other examples: Baumgarten, HW, 1:148–49, and Seyffardt, *Erinnerungen* (1900), pp. 20–21.

26. Mommsen, *Miquel* (1928), p. 237; Westphal, *Staatsauffassung* (1919), and Schroth, *Welt-und Staatsideen des deutschen Liberalismus in der Zeit der Einheits-und Freiheitskämpfe, 1859–1866* (Berlin, 1931), have useful discussions of the *Preussische Jahrbücher*; on Sybel, see Seier, *Staatsidee* (1961), pp. 14–15; on Bluntschli, see above, chap. 7, n. 18.

27. *EGK 1861*, p. 45. Another example: Kapp, *Frühsozialisten* (1969), pp. 76–77.

28. Three examples: Kaiser, *Strömungen* (1963), p. 147, quoting the *Kölner Blätter*; Baumgarten in HW, 1:112; Parisius, *Hoverbeck* (1897–1900), 2:pt. 2, pp. 53–54 (Hoverbeck in 1865). See also Krieger, *Idea* (1957), pp. 389 ff., and Hamerow, *Foundations* (1969–72), 1:269 ff., and 2:168.

29. Quoted in Weber, *Demokraten* (1962), p. 66. L. Dehio, "Die Taktik der Opposition während des Konflikts," *HZ* 140, no. 2 (1929): 279–347, argued that liberals hoped defeat would open the way to reform, but his evidence shows only that they believed reform was necessary for victory.

30. Hoverbeck, quoted in Winkler, *Liberalismus* (1964), p. 25.

31. Sybel (May 1863) in HW, 1:153 (cf. Sybel's comments in 1864 [p. 211] and Schulze-Delitzsch's in 1863 [pp. 160–61]. For more on this, see Eisfeld, *Entstehung*

(1969), pp. 118–19, and Winkler, *Liberalismus* (1964), pp. 23–24.

32. Oncken, *Bennigsen* (1910), 1:483 ff. Two other examples: Baumgarten (March 1861) and Sybel (1862), in HW, 1:61, 97.

33. Rochau, for example, had some critical remarks about those who overestimated the power of constitutionalism, but he did not question the need for representative institutions: Rochau, *Grundsätze* (1853; reprinted 1972), pp. 38–39. See also Lees' analysis of Biedermann in *Revolution* (1974), p. 105.

34. *StL* (3d ed.), 13:646. See also: Karl Biedermann, *Die Repräsentative-Verfassung mit Volkswahlen*, in A. Freiherr von Haxthausen, ed., *Das constitutionelle Princip* (Leipzig, 1864); Bluntschli, "Verantwortlichkeit," *Staatswörterbuch* (1857–70), 10:746 ff.; Max Rümelin, *Gustav Rümelin. Erinnerungen an meinen Vater* (Tübingen, 1927), p. 66.

35. As in the first half of the century, the liberals' rather distorted image of English institutions was a symptom of their own uncertainties: see Lamer, *Parlamentarismus* (1963).

36. The claim that liberals wanted a parliamentary regime was first made during the conflict itself: see the minister of the interior's communication of March 1862, quoted in *EGK 1862*, pp. 137 ff. It has been repeated frequently since then, usually by liberalism's conservative opponents: see, for example, A. Wahl, *Beiträge zur Geschichte der Konfliktszeit* (Tübingen, 1914), and Huber, 3:298, 333 ff. For a critique of this position, see L. Bergsträsser, "Kritische Studien zur Konfliktszeit," *HV* 19, no. 3 (1919): 343–76; and, most recently, the discussion in Ritter, *Gesellschaft* (1974), p. 17.

37. Sybel (July 1862), in HW, 1:105. Cf. *Gb* 17, no. 3 (1858): 481–90; Veronika Renner, "Karl Twesten" (Unpubl. diss., Freiburg, 1954), p. 30, n. 34; Lette, in Duncker, *Briefwechsel* (1923), p. 162. The official position of the liberal parties can be found in the following programs and electoral statements: Parisius, *Deutschlands* (1878), pp. 33–34, Declaration of January 13, 1861; *EGK 1861*, pp. 41–42, Program of June 9, 1861; *EGK 1861*, pp. 45–46, Electoral Statement of September 28, 1861; *EGK 1862*, pp. 131–32, Statement of March 14, 1862; *EGK 1863*, p. 122, Statement of March 1863.

38. Schulze, *Schriften* (1909–13), 4:250. Lasker's articles from 1862–63 are reprinted in his *Zur Verfassungsgeschichte Preussens* (Leipzig, 1874), pp. 297–382. On Lasker's background and career, see G. Mork, "The Making of a German Nationalist: Eduard Lasker's Early Years, 1829–1847," *Societas* 1, no. 1 (Winter 1971): 23–32, and A. Laufs, "Eduard Lasker und der Rechtsstaat," *Der Staat* 13, no. 3 (1974): 365–82.

39. Quoted in Seier, *Staatsidee* (1961), p. 25.

40. Quotations are from Mohl, "Repräsentativsystem" (1860), pp. 368, 394 ff., 439. His ideas on suffrage regulations can be found on pp. 381 ff. and 405 ff. See also: Angermann, *Mohl* (1962), pp. 415 ff., and Boldt, *Monarchie* (1973), pp. 613 ff.

41. Quoted in A. Wucher, *Theodor Mommsen* (Göttingen, 1956), p. 114. See also Heuss, *Mommsen* (1956), and G. Mosse, "Caesarism, Circuses and Monuments," *JCH* 6, no. 2 (1971): 167–82.

42. Bollmann is quoted in H. Gollwitzer, "Der Cäsarismus Napoleons III im Widerhall der öffentlichen Meinung Deutschlands," *HZ* 173, no. 1 (1952), p. 64; Unruh in Oncken, *Bennigsen* (1910), 1:525–56.

43. Quoted in L. Dehio, "Der preussische Demokratie und der Krieg von 1866. Aus dem Briefwechsel von Karl Rodbertus und Franz Ziegler," *FBPG* 39 (1927): 247,

251, and H. Neumann, "Franz Ziegler und die Politik der liberalen Oppositionsparteien von 1848–1866," *FBPG* 37 (1925): 271.

44. Quoted in Weber, *Demokraten* (1962), p. 270.

45. Haym (May 1866) in HW, 1:285. See J. Schuchardt, "Die Wirtschaftskrise von 1866," *JbW* (1962), pt. 2, pp. 91–141, and Schweitzer, "Kritik" (1950), pp. 49 ff.

46. Oncken, *Bennigsen* (1910), 1:686 ff.

47. Ibid., p. 693.

48. See, for example, Gall's account of the situation in Baden, *Liberalismus* (1968), pp. 337 ff.

49. A good sense of the situation in June and July can be acquired from the reports in *EGK 1866*. See also Spahn, "Entstehung" (1908), pp. 346 ff., 380 ff.; Winkler, *Liberalismus* (1964), pp. 83 ff.; Hamerow, *Foundations* (1969–72), 2:238 ff.

Chapter 9

1. Quoted in A. Wucher, *Theodor Mommsen* (Göttingen, 1956), p. 151.

2. See below, chap. 10, n. 20.

3. Huber, 3:351 ff.; Eisfeld, *Entstehung* (1969), pp. 178 ff.; Spahn, "Entstehung" (1908), pp. 440 ff.; F. Löwenthal, *Der preussische Verfassungsstreit* (Altenburg, 1914), pp. 303–8.

4. J. C. Bluntschli, quoted in Faber, "Realpolitik" (1966), p. 4. This article provides a good introduction to the impact of 1866 on German political thought. For a guide to the contemporary literature, see K. G. Faber, *Die nationalpolitische Publizistik Deutschlands von 1866 bis 1871*, 2 vols. (Düsseldorf, 1963).

5. Rochau, *Grundsätze* (1869; reprinted 1972), pp. 206, 220, 255. Some other examples: Baumgarten in HW, 1:374, 386; Seier, *Staatsidee* (1961), pp. 187–88, on Sybel; Haym, *Briefwechsel* (1967), pp. 258–59 and 271–72.

6. Quoted in Spahn, "Entstehung" (1908), p. 450.

7. Quoted in Winkler, *Liberalismus* (1964), p. 121. See also: Kapp, *Frühsozialisten* (1969), pp. 83 ff.; Herzfeld, *Miquel* (1938), 1:44 ff.; W. Mosse, "The Conflict of Liberalism and Nationalism and Its Effect on German Jewry," Leo Baeck Institute, *Year Book XV* (1970), pp. 125–39, and G. Mork, "Bismarck and the 'Capitulation' of German Liberalism," *JMH* 43, no. 1 (March 1971), especially pp. 62–63.

8. For example, see Schulze-Delitzsch's attitudes about the Prussian victory, *Schriften* (1909–13), 3:298.

9. Some examples: Parisius, *Hoverbeck* (1897–1900), vol. 2, pt. 2, p. 131, quoting a letter of December 1866; Eisfeld, *Entstehung* (1969), p. 197, quoting Rudolf Virchow; Oppenheim in *Gb* (1868), pp. 162 ff.

10. On the formation of the National Liberal faction, see: Spahn, "Entstehung" (1908), which contains a good deal of useful information on the Prussian situation; E. W. Mayer, "Aus der Geschichte der nationalliberalen Partei in den Jahren 1868 bis 1871," in Wentzcke, *Staat* (1922), 135–53, on the south; Schunke, *Freihändler* (1916), on the economic interests involved; Krieger, *Idea* (1957), pp. 438 ff.; Eisfeld, *Entstehung* (1969), pp. 173 ff.

11. Stoltenberg, *Reichstag* (1955), pp. 18 and 23, and T. Schieder, *Das Kaiserreich von 1871 als Nationalstaat* (Cologne and Opladen, 1961), p. 12.

12. See Eugen Richter's formulation of this point, quoted in Matthes, "Spaltung"

(1953), p. 13, and the three unsigned articles surveying liberalism in various parts of Germany published by *NZ*, November 9, 1870.

13. As early as 1869, Stephani spoke in terms of a possible split in National Liberalism: D. Sandberger, *Die Ministerkandidatur Bennigsens* (Berlin, 1929), p. 19. See also Mohl, *Lebenserinnerungen* (1902), 2:166–67, and A. Pfaff, *Zur Erinnerungen an Friedrich Oetker* (Gotha, 1883), p. 176.

14. Gall, *Liberalismus* (1968), and Becker, *Staat* (1973), have excellent accounts of Badenese liberalism from 1866 to 1870. Eisfeld, *Entstehung* (1969), p. 143, discusses party organization. There are various contemporary views and some important documents in *EGK 1868*, pp. 177–78 and 191–92, and *EGK 1869*, pp. 178–79. On Baden after 1870, see W. Fuchs, ed., *Grossherzog Friedrich I von Baden und die Reichspolitik* (Stuttgart, 1968), and Becker, *Staat* (1973), pp. 293 ff.

15. Eisfeld, *Entstehung* (1969), pp. 129 ff.; W. Zorn, "Parlament, Gesellschaft und Regierung in Bayern, 1870–1918," in Ritter, ed., *Gesellschaft* (1974), 299–315; F. Freiherr von Rummel, *Das Ministerium Lutz und seine Gegner, 1871–1882* (Munich, 1935); Schieder, *Partei* (1936). Some contemporary views and documents: *NZ*, October 28, 1870; a series of articles in *INR* (1871), vol. 1, pt. 2; *HW*, 2:15, 186.

16. Quoted in *EGK 1874*, pp. 193–94. On the Deutsche Partei, see: Eisfeld, *Entstehung* (1969), pp. 139 ff.; Langewiesche, *Liberalismus* (1974), pp. 385 ff.; and Lang, *Partei* (1891), which also reprints party programs and other documents. Elben's *Lebenserinnerungen* (1931) is a good firsthand account. For contemporary views and documents on the Volkspartei, see *EGK 1868*, pp. 169–73, and *EGK 1869*, p. 150. The most recent historical analysis is in Runge, *Volkspartei* (1970), and Langewiesche, *Liberalismus* (1974), pp. 410 ff.

17. Eisfeld, *Entstehung* (1969), pp. 153 ff.; Huber, 4:402 ff.; Otto Richter, *Geschichte der Stadt Dresden in den Jahren 1871–1902* (Dresden, 1903), pp. 9 ff.; Biedermann's *Leben* (1886), 2:295 ff., is a good source for Saxon political life. For other contemporary views and documents, see: *DAZ*, December 16, 1871, and October 5, 1873; *EGK 1871*, pp. 197–98, 249, and *EGK 1874*, p. 117; and the reports in *Gb* 31, no. 2 (1872): 148–54; 32, no. 2 (1873): 78–80; 32, no. 3 (1873): 427–38.

18. Eisfeld, *Entstehung* (1969), pp. 174 ff.; Hess, *Reichstagswahlen* (1958), pp. 54 ff.; White, *Party* (1976), chap. 1.

19. For a contemporary view of the liberals' regional diversity, see "Die Organisation der liberalen Nationalpartei," *Gb* 28, no. 3 (1869): 468 ff. There is a good summary of the situation in Maenner, "Liberalismus" (1927), p. 461. Naumann's essay, "Parteien" in *Werke* (1964), 4:169–70 is also worth reading.

20. Quoted in Robolsky, *Reichstag* (1893), p. 332.

21. The best analysis of these issues is Nipperdey, *Organisation* (1961). There is some additional information in Steinbrecher, *Parteiorganisation* (1960). There are examples of regional variety and the persistence of institutional fluidity in the following: "Eine Episode aus Karl Twestens Leben," *DR*, 25, no. 1 (1900): 78 ff., on Danzig; Bunsen, *Bunsen* (1900), pp. 226–27, on Solingen; J. Wiggers, *Aus meinem Leben* (Leipzig, 1901), p. 244, on Mecklenburg; Böttcher, *Stephani* (1887), p. 86, on Leipzig; Vitzthum, *Politik* (1971), pp. 39 ff., on Schleswig-Holstein; Kastendiek, "Liberalismus" (1952), pp. 71 ff., on Bremen; Denk, "Wahlen" (1955), pp. 170 ff., on Cologne; Hofmann, *Stadtverordneten* (1964), p. 57, on Bielefeld; Möllers, "Strömungen" (1955), pp. 119–20, on Essen.

22. The legal situation is summarized in Huber, 4:7 ff.

23. Mommsen, *Parteiprogramme* (1964), pp. 147, 151. See also the National

Liberals' electoral statement printed in *NZ*, October 7, 1873.

24. H. B. Oppenheim (July 1872), HW, 2:56. Siemens quoted in Nipperdey, *Organisation* (1961), p. 25. For another example, see E. Lasker (March 1871), HW, 2:9.

25. Forckenbeck and Stauffenberg in HW, 2:29–30, 107.

26. Hölder's position is discussed in a letter by H. Reuchlin of January 1873, HW, 2:72.

27. For example, see Theodor Lucas, November 1877, HW, 2:189 ff.

28. J. H. Loesch is now working on a roll-call analysis of the Reichstag which should significantly increase our knowledge about party alignments in that institution: "The Application of Roll-Call Analysis to the Study of German Parliamentary History," Unpublished paper (December 1973).

29. The constitution is described in Huber, 3: chaps. 12–17, and reprinted in Huber, *Dokumente* (1961–66), 2:227 ff. Pflanze, *Bismarck* (1963), pp. 337 ff., and K. E. Pollmann, "Vom Verfassungskonflikt zum Verfassungskompromiss: Funktion und Selbstverständnis des verfassungsberatenden Reichstags des Norddeutschen Bundes," in Ritter, ed., *Gesellschaft* (1974), 189–203, have good accounts of the debates. Additional material and a complete bibliography can be found in Böckenförde, ed., *Verfassungsgeschichte* (1972). See also Stürmer, *Regierung* (1974), pp. 36 ff., and passim.

30. Boldt, "Konstitutionalismus" (1970), pp. 126 ff., and E-W. Böckenförde, "Der Verfassungstyp der deutschen konstitutionellen Monarchie im 19. Jahrhundert," in Böckenförde, ed., *Verfassungsgeschichte* (1972).

31. For example, see Schulze-Delitzsch's speech of March 12, 1867, *Schriften* (1909–13), 4:543 ff.

32. Besides in the works cited in n. 29, the deliberations over the Reich executive are discussed in Otto Becker, *Bismarcks Ringen um Deutschlands Gestaltung* (Heidelberg, 1958), pp. 371 ff.; Morsey, *Reichsverwaltung* (1957), pp. 23 ff.; R. Wahl, "Der preussische Verfassungskonflikt und das konstitutionelle System des Kaiserreichs," in Böckenförde, ed., *Verfassungsgeschichte* (1972), p. 177.

33. The Fortschrittspartei's official explanation of its vote is given in Parisius, *Deutschlands* (1878), pp. 94–97.

34. W. Gerloff, *Die Finanz-und Zollpolitik des Deutschen Reiches* (Jena, 1913), is the classic account of German financial policies and is still an invaluable source: see especially pp. 12 ff. for 1860s and 1870s. Witt's *Finanzpolitik* (1969) emphasizes the early twentieth century but provides a useful analysis of the whole budget problem during the imperial era.

35. Stoltenberg, *Reichstag* (1955), pp. 82 ff.; Huber 4:545 ff.; Stürmer, *Regierung* (1974), pp. 65 ff., and "Militärkonflikt" (1974), especially pp. 225 ff. For a firsthand account of the military issue, see Eugen Richter, *Reichstag* (1894–96), 1:36.

36. Stürmer, "Militärkonflikt" (1974), pp. 235 ff., and *Regierung* (1974), pp. 118 ff. For the reaction of various liberal leaders, see: the letters in HW, 2:100 ff.; James Harris, "Eduard Lasker and Compromise Liberalism," *JMH* 43, no. 3 (September 1970): 352 ff.; Herzfeld, *Miquel* (1938), 2:272 ff.; Oncken, *Bennigsen* (1910), 2:257; Böttcher, *Stephani* (1887), p. 141; Richter, *Reichstag* (1894–96), 1:78 ff.

37. Huber, 3:373 ff., summarizes the most important debates on these issues. See also Morsey, *Reichsverwaltung* (1957), pp. 289–93.

38. Heffter, *Selbstverwaltung* (1950), on Treitschke; Angermann, *Mohl* (1962), pp. 92 ff.

39. McClelland, *Historian* (1971), p. 150, on Sybel; Gall, *Liberalismus* (1968), p.

446, on Jolly. For the German view of English institutions in this period, see Lamer, *Parlamentarismus* (1963). For more about liberal political thought in the seventies, see Fenske, *Wahlrecht* (1972), pp. 58 ff., and G. Seeber, "Die Bourgeoisie und das Reich. Zur politischen Konzeption der Bourgeoisie in den 70er Jahren," in Bartel and Engelberg, eds., *Reichsgründung* (1971), 2:127–69.

40. Quoted in *EGK 1872*, pp. 589–90.

41. For example, see the National Liberal statement of April 1870, reprinted in Robolsky, *Reichstag* (1893), p. 144.

42. The Fortschrittspartei program is in *EGK 1873*, p. 98. See also Vitzthum, *Politik* (1971), pp. 77–78; Matthes, "Spaltung" (1953), pp. 13–14, maintains that the liberal left wanted parliamentary government.

43. See, for example, Kapp, *Frühsozialisten* (1969), pp. 105 ff., which contains his letters from 1874. Max Weber's analysis of Bismarck and the liberals remains one of the best formulations of the problem: Weber, *Schriften* (1958), pp. 301–2.

44. Bamberger, *Schriften* (1894–98), 5:55.

45. Quoted in Rachfahl, "Richter" (1912), p. 291.

46. D. Albers, *Reichstag und Aussenpolitik von 1871–1879* (Berlin, 1927), has a useful summary of parliamentary views on foreign policy during the seventies. On the Fortschrittspartei, see: Seeber, *Bebel* (1965); Carl Schneider, "The Political Liberalism of the Progressive Parties in Germany, 1871–1914" (Unpubl. diss., Wisconsin, 1943); Schweitzer, "Kritik" (1950).

47. Huber, 4:140 ff., has a summary of this legislation. For an analysis see: Böhme, *Deutschlands* (1966), pp. 263 ff.; Volkmann, *Arbeiterfrage* (1968), pp. 184 ff.; Köllmann, "Anfänge" (1966), p. 50; H. Schwab, "Von Königgrätz bis Versailles. Zur Entwicklung der nationalliberalen Partei bis zur Reichsgründung und zum Charakter ihrer Politik," in Bartel and Engelberg, eds., *Reichsgründung* (1971), 1:315 ff. Tipton, "Consensus" (1974), pp. 206 ff., questions the conventional view that this legislation was important for economic development in the late sixties and early seventies.

48. There is an excellent discussion of Delbrück in Morsey, *Reichsverwaltung* (1957), pp. 40 ff. Delbrück's *Lebenserinnerungen*, 2 vols. (Leipzig, 1905) gives additional information on his background and ideas.

49. For example, Welcker, *StL* (3d ed.), 3:227.

50. The best treatment of this issue is Heffter's masterful *Selbstverwaltung* (1950). See also Huber, 4:352 ff., and Herzfeld, *Miquel* (1938), 1:310 ff.

51. The literature on the Kulturkampf is discussed in R. Morsey, "Probleme der Kulturkampf-Forschung," *HJb* 83, no. 2 (1963): 217–45. Stürmer, *Regierung* (1974), places the religious issue in the context of the participants' other political conflicts and objectives. Also valuable in this regard is Adolf Birke, "Zur Entwicklung und politischen Funktion des bürgerlichen Kulturkampfverständnisses in Preussen-Deutschland," in Kurze, ed., *Theorie* (1972), pp. 257–79. On the European dimensions of the conflict, see G. Franz, *Kulturkampf, Staat und Katholische Kirche in Mitteleuropa von der Säkularisation bis zum Abschluss des preussischen Kulturkampfes* (Munich, 1954). Felix Rachfahl, "Windthorst und der Kulturkampf," *PJbb* 134, no. 2 (1909): 213–53; 135, no. 3 (1909): 460–90; 136, no. 1 (1909): 56–73, is a good biography of the leading Catholic participant. The *EGK* followed the Kulturkampf very closely and provides a good sense of the liberals' perspective.

In order to understand the Kulturkampf, it is essential to remember that religious issues also continued to be important in the various *Mittelstaaten*. A survey of these events can be found in Huber, 4:746 ff. On Baden, see Gall, "Problematik" (1965), and Becker, *Staat* (1973), especially pp. 317 ff.; on Bavaria, Möckl, *Prinzregentenzeit* (1972), pp. 36 ff.

52. HW, 2:17. See also Faber, "Realpolitik" (1966), p. 35, and Birke, "Entwicklung" (1972), pp. 263–64. Bornkamm's "Staatsidee" (1950), pp. 48 ff., has other examples of liberal attitudes.

53. For a guide to Bismarck's goals, see R. Morsey, "Bismarck und der Kulturkampf," *AfK* 39, no. 2 (1957): 232–70. A good example of his position can be found in his *Herrenhaus* speech of April 1873, quoted in E. Foerster, *Adalbert Falk* (Gotha, 1927), p. 141.

54. This typology is based on Bornkamm, "Staatsidee" (1950), pp. 44–45. Huber, 4:693 ff., is a useful guide to the most important legislation.

55. Stoltenberg, *Reichstag* (1955), pp. 94 ff., on 1871; Heffter, *Selbstverwaltung* (1950), p. 567, on 1872; Stürmer, "Konservatismus" (1970), pp. 150–51, and *Regierung* (1974), on 1874. Cf. the situation in Baden as described in Becker, *Staat* (1973), pp. 236 ff. Schmidt, "Nationalliberalen" (1973), offers a different interpretation of these events.

56. For a concrete illustration of how the Kulturkampf encouraged bureaucratic growth, see H. Schiffers, *Kulturkampf in Stadt und Regierungsbezirk Aachen* (Aachen, 1929), p. 203.

57. Eyck, *Bismarck* (1941–44), 3:112 ff., 185 ff.; Stürmer, "Konservatismus" (1970), pp. 152–53.

58. A. Wahl, *Vom Bismarck der 70er Jahren* (Tübingen, 1920), p. 25, and R. Freiherr von Friesen, *Erinnerungen aus meinem Leben* (Dresden, 1910), 3:284–85.

59. Booms, *Partei* (1954). For some contemporary views, see *EGK 1876*, pp. 118, 171.

60. The reaction to Delbrück's dismissal is surveyed in *EGK 1876*, p. 114. See also Eyck, *Bismarck* (1941–44), 3:190 ff., and Lambi, *Trade* (1963), pp. 150 ff.

61. Rachfahl, "Richter" (1912), is a good introduction. See also: L. Ullstein, *Eugen Richter als Publizist und Herausgeber* (Leipzig, 1930); Nipperdey, *Organisation* (1961), pp. 31–32; Seeber, *Bebel* (1965); Matthes, "Spaltung" (1953), pp. 166 ff., including an excellent bibliography of Richter's works on pp. 346–47. The best summary of Richter's own views can be found in his memoirs, *Reichstag* (1894–96).

62. *EGK 1876*, pp. 48, 114 ff., 119 (on the railroads), 219–21 (on the *Justizgesetz*). See also Eyck, *Bismarck* (1941–44), 3:53 ff., 193–94, and Richter, *Reichstag* (1894–96), 1:149 ff., 160–63.

63. *EGK 1876*, p. 229.

64. For example, *INR* 5, no. 2 (1875): 1028–31, and *Gb* 36 (1877): 1 ff.

65. On Bavaria, see: *AZ*, July 13, 1875 (Liberal electoral program), and *EGK 1875*, pp. 109–10; on Lippe, *EGK 1876*, p. 96; on Saxony, *EGK 1875*, pp. 166, 176–77, and *DAZ*, September 14, 1875.

66. On the relationship between the liberal parties during the Landtag election campaign, see the reports in *NZ*, especially August 13 and 17 and October 11, 1876. The debate on the *Justizgesetz* is summarized in *EGK 1876*, pp. 222–28, and Oncken, *Bennigsen* (1910), 2:292 ff.

67. The parties' electoral statements are in *EGK 1876*, pp. 228–31. For two examples of local relationships, see: Böttcher, *Stephani* (1887), pp. 167 ff., on Leipzig, and Haym, *Briefwechsel* (1967), p. 298, on Halle.

68. *EGK 1877*, p. 55.

69. Kapp to E. Cohen, January 1875, in *Frühsozialisten* (1969), p. 107. See also Listemann (January 1875) and Oppenheim (November 1875) in HW, 2:115–16, 137.

70. Lasker's letters to Baerwald (November and December 1875), Memorandum of December 24, 1876, and letter to Marquardsen (January 1877), HW, 2:140, 163–64, 169.

71. Quoted in Steinbrecher, *Parteiorganisation* (1960), p. 32.

Chapter 10

1. Dieter Brosius, "Bodo von Hodenberg: Ein hannoverscher Konservativer nach 1866," *Niedersächisches Jahrbuch für Landesgeschichte* 38 (1966): 177.

2. The best overall treatment of political organization is Nipperdey's *Organisation* (1961). A guide to the literature can be found in G. A. Ritter, ed., *Parteien* (1973). A good brief introduction to the major issues is H. J. Puhle, "Parteien" (1970). On the theoretical literature, see J. La Palombara and M. Weiner, eds., *Political Parties and Political Development* (Princeton, 1966).

3. The course of the "participation revolution" can be charted by examining the changing proportion of eligible voters who actually went to the polls. In the elections for the constitutent Reichstag in 1867, about 63.7 percent of the eligible electorate voted; a few months later this dropped to 39.4 percent. (No official returns for 1867 are available; the best discussion is in Hamerow, *Foundations* [1969–72], 2:323–25, 334.) In 1871, 52 percent voted; in 1874, 61 percent; 1877, 61.6 percent; 1878, 63.4 percent; 1881, 56.3 percent; 1884, 60.5 percent; 1887, 77.5 percent. The most convenient source on elections after 1871 is Vogel et al., *Wahlen* (1971). The suffrage system and its effects are treated at length in Fenske, *Wahlrecht* (1972), see especially pp. 106 ff.

4. The remark about permanent electioneering is quoted in Pülke, "Geschichte" (1934), p. 123. Another contemporary view can be found in the description of the Reichstag elections of 1871 quoted in Robolsky, *Reichstag* (1893), p. 193. The following local studies are particularly useful for an understanding of political Catholicism: Paul Mazura, *Die Entwicklung des politischen Katholizismus in Schlesien von seinen Anfängen bis zum Jahre 1880* (Diss., Breslau, 1925); H. Neubach, "Parteien und Politiker in Oberschlesien zur Bismarckzeit," *Jb der Schlesischen Friedrich-Wilhelms Universität zur Breslau* 12 (1968): 193–231; Schiffers, *Kulturkampf* (1929), on Aachen; Ficker, *Kulturkampf* (1928), on Münster; Steil, *Wahlen* (1961), on Trier; Möllers, "Strömungen" (1955), on Essen.

5. See: Oswald Hauser, "Polen und Dänen im Deutschen Reich," in Schieder and Deuerlein, eds., *Reichsgründung* (1971), pp. 291–315; H-U. Wehler, "Die Polen im Ruhrgebiet bis 1918," in Wehler, ed., *Sozialgeschichte* (1966), pp. 437–55; Dan Silverman, "Political Catholicism and Social Democracy in Alsace-Lorraine 1871–1914," *Catholic Historical Review* 52, no. 1 (April 1966): 39–65; Evan Bukey, "The Guelph Party in Imperial Germany, 1866–1918," *The Historian*, 35, no. 1 (November 1972): 43–60.

6. In 1867, the Prussian Conservatives, like the north German liberals, split. The Free Conservatives, or Reichspartei, supported Bismarck's solution to the German question. On their origins and development, see Frederick Aandahl, "The Rise of German Free Conservatism" (Unpubl. diss., Princeton, 1955).On the Prussian (after 1876, German) Conservatives, see: Booms, *Partei* (1954); Nipperdey, *Organisation*

(1961), pp. 241 ff.; Robert Berdahl, "Conservative Politics and Aristocratic Landholders in Bismarckian Germany." *JMH* 44, no. 1 (March 1972): 1–20. When referring to both parties, I will use the term *conservative*, reserving the capital-C *Conservative* for the latter group.

7. Horst Lademacher, "Zu den Aufängen der deutschen Sozialdemokratie, 1863–1878. Probleme ihrer Geschichtsschreibung," *IRSH* 4, nos. 2 and 3 (1959): 239–60, 367–93, is a good place to begin reading about the origins of Social Democracy. Wachenheim, *Arbeiterbewegung* (1967) is a good narrative account. Nipperdey, *Organisation* (1961) describes early institutional developments. On the break between liberals and the labor movement, see: E. Eyck, *Der Vereinstag deutscher Arbeitervereine, 1863–1868* (Berlin, 1904), especially pp. 83 ff.; Mayer, "Trennung" (1969); Conze and Groh, *Arbeiterbewegung* (1966); Reichard, *Birth* (1969). Bebel's *Leben* (1961) and Julius Bruhns, "*Es klingt im Sturm ein altes Lied!" Aus der Jugendzeit der Sozialdemokratie* (Stuttgart and Berlin, 1921), are two useful firsthand accounts, both for the Socialist side. The best way to understand the variety and complexity of the relationships between liberals and workers is by reading some of the excellent studies which trace the emergence of the labor movement on the local level: Köllmann, *Sozialgeschichte* (1960), pp. 241 ff., on Barmen; Eckert, *Sozialdemokratie* (1968), on Nuremberg; Schneider, "Anfänge" (1956), on the Palatinate; Schadt, *Partei* (1971), on Baden; Schmitz, *Anfänge* (1968), on Düsseldorf. On the early electoral history of the party, see Wacker, *Entwicklung* (1903).

8. This is the theme of Mayer's classic study, "Trennung" (1912; reprinted 1969).

9. For a preliminary statement on this process, see Köllmann, "Entwicklung" (1964), and L. Uhen, *Gruppenbewusstsein und informelle Gruppenbildungen bei deutschen Arbeitern im Jahrhundert der Industrialisierung* (Berlin, 1964).

10. Conze and Groh, *Arbeiterbewegung* (1966), pp. 47, 69 ff., 125, and Schaarschmidt *Geschichte* (1934), on Crimmitschau.

11. For an example, see the remarks by one participant in the Dresden Handwerkertag, quoted in *EGK 1872*, p. 194.

12. H. Gollwitzer, "Die politische Landschaft in der deutschen Geschichte des 19/20. Jahrhunderts," in *Land und Volk. Karl A. von Müller zum 80. Geburtstag* (Munich, 1964).

13. *Gewerbefreiheit* was introduced in Hanover after its annexation by Prussia: *EGK 1867*, p. 98. On the situation in Bavaria, see Max Schwarz, "Die Fortschrittspartei und die sogenannte Sozialgesetzgebung Bayerns im Jahre 1868–1869" (Unpubl. diss., Munich, 1922), pp. 48 ff., and J. Kaizl, *Der Kampf um Gewerbereform und Gewerbefreiheit in Bayern von 1799–1868* (Leipzig, 1879), pp. 134 ff.

14. In the words of one contemporary: "the social question is liberalism's most vulnerable point, here is where the Center's sword will penetrate." Quoted in Möllers, "Strömungen" (1955), p. 217. See also Steil, "Wahlen" (1961); Edith Müller, "Die katholische Wirtschafts-und Gesellschaftsidee in der Politik des Zentrums im Reichstag von 1871–1879" (Unpubl. diss., Frankfurt, 1954), and [K. Bader], "Die badischen Wahlen zum Zollparlament," *Historisch-Politische Blätter*, 61, no. 1 (1868), 760–92.

Lothar Gall's discussion of the social dimensions of religious conflict in Baden is extremely suggestive: *Liberalismus* (1968), pp. 292 ff., and "Problematik" (1965), pp. 169 ff. See also Becker, *Staat* (1973), p. 64.

15. Böhme, *Deutschlands* (1966), pp. 214 ff., and Rosenberg, *Depression* (1967). For an example of the connection made by contemporaries between liberal policies

and the depression, see Pülke, "Geschichte" (1934), pp. 130–31.

16. On Bismarck's views see: R. Augst, *Bismarcks Stellung zum parlamentarischen Wahlrecht* (Leipzig, 1917); Karl Heinz Hagen, "Bismarcks Auffassung von der Stellung des Parlaments im Staat" (Unpubl. diss., Marburg, 1950), pp. 35 ff.; E. Zechlin, "Bismarcks Stellung zum Parlamentarismus bei der Gründung des Norddeutschen Bundes" (Unpubl. diss., Heidelberg, 1922). Two contemporary accounts: Unruh, *Erinnerungen* (1895), p. 272, n., and Gustav von Diest, *Aus dem Leben eines Glücklichen. Erinnerungen eines alten Beamten* (Berlin, 1904), pp. 368–70.

17. Quoted in Gagel, *Wahlrechtsfrage* (1958), p. 54. For some other hostile opinions, see: Duncker, *Briefwechsel* (1923), p. 437, and two articles in the *Grenzboten* 26, no. 1 (1867): 155, and 26, no 2 (1867): 445–55.

18. The debate is discussed in Gagel, *Wahlrechtsfrage* (1958), pp. 38 ff., 51 ff.; W, Scheffler, "Entwicklung und Lösung des Diätenproblems in England und Deutschland" (Unpubl. diss., Berlin, 1956); Clauss, *Staatsbeamte* (1906), pp. 159–66; T. Hamerow, "The Origins of Mass Politics in Germany, 1866–1867," in Geiss and Wendt, eds., *Deutschland* (1973), 105–20.

19. HW, 1:368.

20. *NZ*, June–July, 1866; Parisius, *Hoverbeck* (1897–1900), 2: pt. 2, pp. 93–95; Pflanze, *Bismarck* (1963), pp. 322–23.

21. On the Zollparlament elections, see: Pflanze, *Bismarck* (1963), pp. 395 ff.; G. Windell, *The Catholics and German Unity, 1866–1871* (Minneapolis, 1954), chap. 5; W. Schübelin, *Das Zollparlament und die Politik von Baden, Bayern und Württemberg, 1866–1870* (Berlin, 1935).

22. The difficulties liberals faced during the elections of 1870 are illuminated by the contemporary reports in *NZ*; see especially the summary of the campaign published on November 19, 1870. For some contemporary views of liberalism's growth thereafter, see Parisius, *Deutschlands* (1878), pp. 118, 139, 163, and *EGK 1876*, p. 187.

23. *NZ*, October 29, 1876.

24. For a guide to the various suffrage systems see Vogel et al., *Wahlen* (1971).

25. *EGK 1869*, p. 138, and Ehrenfeuchter, "Willensbildung" (1951), pp. 267–68, on Hanover; Ficker, *Kulturkampf* (1928), p. 117, on Münster; Schiffers, *Kulturkampf* (1929), pp. 156 ff., on Aachen.

26. Some examples of liberalism's strength in city government: Erich Höner, *Geschichte der christlich-konservativen Partei in Minden-Ravensberg von 1866–1896* (Diss., Münster, 1923), pp. 14–15; Köllmann, *Sozialgeschichte* (1960), p. 250, on Barmen; Zenz, *Selbstverwaltung* (1959), pp. 58 ff., on Trier; Lenk, "Katholizismus" (1960), pp. 384 ff., on Munich.

27. HW, 1:415. See also Kapp to Sybel, November 3, 1866, in Kapp, *Frühsozialisten* (1969), p. 88, and the comments in Gall, *Liberalismus* (1968), p. 448.

28. Quoted in Steil, "Wahlen" (1961), p. 141. Eckert, *Sozialdemokratie* (1968), p. 226, has a similar comment from a liberal newspaper in 1876.

29. HW, 2:172–73.

30. Kapp, *Frühsozialisten* (1969), p. 100, on a by-election of 1872; See also Nipperdey, *Organisation* (1961), pp. 42 ff., and H. Schwab, "Zur Wandlung von Funktion und Organisationsstruktur der deutschen bürgerlichen Parteien im Übergang zur imperialistischen Epoche," *Wissenschaftliche Zeitschrift der Universität Jena* 14, no. 2 (1965): 201–9.

31. Kaiser, *Strömungen* (1963), pp. 295 ff.; Schiffers, *Kulturkampf* (1929), pp.

126 ff.; Seyffardt, *Erinnerungen* (1900), p. 149; Möllers, "Strömungen" (1955), pp. 244 ff.

32. Nipperdey, *Organisation* (1961), p. 198. See also Wehrenpfennig to H. H. Meier, June 19, 1877, HW, 2:181.

33. In 1871, for example, Robert von Mohl agreed to run for the Reichstag on the condition that he not be expected to appear in his district; he was elected. Mohl, *Lebenserinnerungen* (1902), 2:160.

34. Quoted in Gall, *Liberalismus* (1968), p. 451. See also Langewiesche, *Liberalismus* (1974), pp. 363 ff.

35. Quoted in Dill, *Lasker* (1958), pp. 14–15. For a similar view, see Seyffardt, *Erinnerungen* (1900), pp. 51 ff.

36. Roggenbach in HW, 1:406.

37. Bluntschli, *Charakter* (1869), especially pp. 9–10. This point is made even more forcefully in Treitschke's article "Parteien und Fractionen" (1871). See also Hans Blum, *Lebenserinnerungen* (Berlin, 1907–8), 2:3. Lamer, *Parlamentarismus* (1963), pp. 63 ff., has more on the growing hostility to parties.

38. Miquel, "Briefe" 10, no. 1 (1912–13): 811; Freytag, *Erinnerungen* (n.d.), p. 646.

39. Schmoller, *Geschichte* (1870), pp. ix–x, xii. See also Sheehan, *Career* (1966), chap. 4.

40. One indication of this was the nostalgia many liberals soon felt for the North German Reichstag of 1867, which they often contrasted with the parliaments elected thereafter: R. von Delbrück, *Lebenserinnerungen* (Leipzig, 1905), 2:391; Elben, *Lebenserinnerungen* (1931), p. 199; E. Richter, *Jugenderinnerungen* (Berlin, 1892), p. 160. On the changing tone in the Reichstag, see Dill, *Lasker* (1958), pp. 155 ff.

41. For a forceful statement of the argument that the liberals lost their chance to build a popular base, see Schraepler, "Haltung" (1954).

42. Quoted in Rosenberg, *Depression* (1967), p. 124.

43. Kulemann, *Erinnerungen* (1911), pp. 14 ff., 27–28, on the situation in Braunschweig. Hombach, *Landtagswahlen* (1963), p. 124, has a similar example from the 1870 Landtag elections in Siegburg.

44. This point is developed in Sheehan, "Liberalism and the City" (1971). See also Steinbrecher, *Parteiorganisation* (1960), p. 90.

45. Quoted in Böttcher, *Anfänge* (1953), p. 96. See also Birker, *Arbeiterbildungsvereine* (1973), pp. 85–87.

46. See, for example, the discussion of the "red" and "black" internationals in *EGK 1871*, p. 527. Nipperdey, "Grundzüge" (1965), has a good analysis of this issue.

47. Gall, *Liberalismus* (1968), pp. 297, 427 ff., and "Problematik" (1965), pp. 171–72.

48. See above, pp. 135–37.

49. *EGK 1868*, pp. 89–90, 97. See also the summary of working-class parties in *EGK 1870*, pp. 76–78.

50. Quoted in Matern, "Wahlen" (1959), p. 155.

51. Braun (1870), quoted in Volkmann, *Arbeiterfrage* (1968), p. 197.

52. For example, see Eynern's letter to Sybel, February 1872, HW, 2:43. On the impact of the Commune, see G. Grützner, *Die Pariser Kommune. Macht und Karriere einer politischen Legende* (Cologne, 1963), pp. 26 ff., 89 ff., 99 ff., and Conze and

Groh, *Arbeiterbewegung* (1966), pp. 105 ff. There is more material on the evolution of the social question after 1871 in Sheehan, *Career* (1966), pp. 47 ff.

53. Wachenheim, *Arbeiterbewegung* (1967), pp. 100 ff., and Sheehan, *Career* (1966), pp. 22–45.

54. Schmoller, *Geschichte* (1870), p. 683.

55. Sheehan, *Career* (1966), pp. 50 ff., 84 ff. See also *Verhandlungen der Eisenacher Versammlung* (1873) and the reports of the meetings of the Verein in VfSP, *Schriften*.

56. Wachenheim, *Arbeiterbewegung* (1967), pp. 124, and 194; Seeber, *Bebel* (1965), pp. 14–15; Nipperdey, *Organisation* (1961), p. 64; Steinbrecher, *Parteiorganisation* (1960), pp. 168 ff. On the strike movement of the late sixties and early seventies, see the data in W. Steglich, "Eine Streiktabelle für Deutschland, 1864 bis 1880," *JbW* 2 (1960): 235–83. Parisius' *Deutschlands* (1878), p. xxxviii, is a good example of the Progressives' continued reluctance to recognize the problems posed by Social Democracy.

57. Schraepler, "Haltung" (1954), severely criticizes the liberals for failing to attract working-class support.

58. This controversy is analyzed in Sheehan, *Career* (1966), pp. 59 ff.

59. Oppenheim to Lasker, August 29, 1872, and Bamberger to Lasker, September 26, 1872: HW, 2:59–60. See also Zucker, *Bamberger* (1975), pp. 105 ff.

60. Reprinted as *Sozialismus und seine Gönner* (Berlin, 1875). See Dorpalen, *Treitschke* (1957), pp. 198 ff. For another example, see *Gb* 34, no. 2 (1875): 41 ff., 506 ff.

61. Rochau, *Grundsätze* (1869; reprinted 1972), p. 338; Bauer, *Meinung* (1914), pp. 134–35, on Gneist; Franz von Holtzendorff, *Wesen und Werth der öffentlichen Meinung* (Munich, 1879). Unruh's *Erinnerungen* (1895) records his reassessment of public opinion in the face of the new challenges of the seventies: see pp. 91–92 and 154–55.

62. Dorpalen, *Treitschke* (1957), p. 137; Bluntschli, *Charakter* (1869), pp. 105–6; Gagel, *Wahlrechtsfrage* (1958), pp. 59 ff. See also Gall, *Liberalismus* (1968), pp. 436 ff., on Baden and Menzinger, *Verfassungsrevision* (1969), pp. 51 ff., on Württemberg.

63. Mohl, "Phasen" (1871), pp. 51 ff., 67; Gagern's views are in a letter of May 1872, quoted in P. Wentzcke, "Ludwig von Edelsheim und Franz von Roggenbach. Aufzeichnungen und Briefe aus dem Nachlass Heinrich von Gagerns," *ZGO* 94, no. 4 (1951): 598; Prince Smith, "Der Staat und der Volkshaushalt" (1873), in *Schriften* (1877–80), 1:189–92.

64. H. von Treitschke, *Sozialismus und seine Gönner* (Berlin, 1875), p. 45; Haym, *Briefwechsel* (1967), pp. 301–2. See also Unruh, *Erinnerungen* (1895), pp. 147 ff., and the additional examples in Gagel, *Wahlrechtsfrage* (1958), pp. 87 ff.

65. Quoted in Stoltenberg, *Reichstag* (1955), p. 163.

66. Quoted in Krieger, *Idea* (1957), pp. 459–60.

67. G. Schmoller, "Die soziale Frage und der preussiche Staat" (1874), reprinted in *Zur Sozial-und Gewerbepolitik der Gegenwart* (Leipzig, 1890), pp. 37–63.

68. Sybel to Lasker, January 2, 1875, HW, 2:114. For the debate on the press law of 1873, see Stürmer, *Regierung* (1974), pp. 61 ff.

69. Kapp, *Frühsozialisten* (1969), p. 102.

70. Gagel, *Wahlrechtsfrage* (1958), pp. 75 ff., 97; Heffter, *Selbstverwaltung* (1950), p. 615; Seeber, *Bebel* (1965), p. 13. For some examples of liberal doubts

about democratic suffrage in local government, see: Philippson, *Forckenbeck* (1898), p. 276; Schulze-Delitzsch (1869), in *Schriften* (1909–13), 4:489 ff.; Seyffardt, *Erinnerungen* (1900), p. 204.

71. Stürmer, *Regierung* (1974), has a good analysis of the election on pp. 183 ff. For the rise of Social Democracy, see Henry Sloan, "The German Social Democrats in the Reichstag Elections, 1871–1912" (Unpubl. diss., New York University, 1962), pp. 52 ff., 64 ff., 79 ff.

72. Richter, *Reichstag* (1894–96), 2:1 ff., and Seeber, *Bebel* (1965), pp. 24 ff., 41–2. The Fortschrittspartei lost four seats to the Conservatives and four to the SPD.

73. Karl Friedrich to August Lamey, March 13, 1877, HW, 2:176.

74. Elben to Treitschke, February 22, 1877, HW, 2:173–74.

Chapter 11

1. Letter to Lasker, June 22, 1876, HW, 2:150.

2. Josef Edmund Jörg, *Geschichte der sozialpolitischen Parteien in Deutschland* (Freiburg, 1867), especially pp. 20 ff. See also Karl Heinz Grenner, *Wirtschaftsliberalismus und katholisches Denken. Ihre Begegnung und Auseinandersetzung in Deutschland des 19. Jahrhunderts* (Cologne, 1967).

3. W. Bauer, "Das Schlagwort als sozialpsychische und geistesgeschichtliche Erscheinung," *HZ* 132, no. 2 (1920): 189–240, discusses the changing meaning of liberalism. The best general introduction to the rise of antiliberal feeling in the seventies is Rosenberg, *Depression* (1967). See also the essays in Fritz Stern, *The Failure of Illiberalism. Essays on the Political Culture of Modern Germany* (New York, 1972).

4. Rosenberg, *Depression* (1967), pp. 88 ff. See also: Walter Boehlich, ed., *Der Berliner Antisemitismus Streit* (Frankfurt, 1965); Paul Massing, *Rehearsal for Destruction: A Study of Political Anti-Semitism in Imperial Germany* (New York, 1949); P. G. J. Pulzer, *The Rise of Political Anti-Semitism in Germany and Austria* (New York, 1964); Klemens Felden, *Die Übernahme des antisemitischen Stereotyps als soziale Norm durch die bürgerliche Gesellschaft Deutschlands (1875–1900)* (Diss., Heidelberg, 1963).

5. Glagau, quoted in Gerlach, "Agitation" (1956), p. 13. Angel-Volkov, "Function" (1974), pp. 416 ff., has some interesting comments on Glagau and on the connection between anti-Semitism and antiliberalism. For some other examples, see: Constantin Frantz, *Der Nationalliberalismus und die Judenherrschaft* (Munich, 1874); Rudolf Meyer, *Politische Gründer und die Corruption in Deutschland* (Leipzig, 1877); Georg Quirin, *Oberursel und seine Wähler* (Oberursel, 1964); C. Wilmanns, *Die Goldene Internationale* (Berlin, 1876).

6. Broszat, "Bewegung" (1953), p. 26, has some material on Catholic anti-Semitism. The *Kreuzzeitung* articles are reprinted in Robolsky, *Reichstag* (1893). On Treitschke, see Dorpalen, *Treitschke* (1957), pp. 241 ff.

7. There is a discussion of the methodological problems and the literature on parliamentary elites in Sheehan, "Quantification" (1972). For some general comments on trends within the Reichstag, see Sheehan, "Leadership" (1968).

8. The role of landed interests is discussed in O'Boyle, "Leadership" (1956). For an interesting comparative analysis, see Gustav Schmidt, "Politischer Liberalismus, 'Landed Interests,' und organisierte Arbeiterschaft, 1850–1880: Ein deutsch-englischer Vergleich," in Wehler, ed., *Sozialgeschichte* (1974), pp. 266–88.

9. There is an example of some of the problems businessmen still had to confront in Helfferich, *Siemens* (1921–23), 3:153 ff.

10. Böhme, *Deutschlands* (1966), p. 260. See also Carl Fürstenberg, *Die Lebensgeschichte eines deutschen Bankiers, 1870–1914* (Berlin, 1931), pp. 28–29.

11. The literature on Richter is given above, chap. 9, n. 61. On Hänel, see Vitzthum, *Politik* (1971), pp. 9 ff., 57 ff., and Kiehl, "Hänel" (1966), pp. 120 ff.

12. Dill, *Lasker* (1958), and the essays in Heinrich Rickert et al., *Eduard Lasker* (Stuttgart, 1884), testify to his extraordinary commitment to political life.

13. HW, 2:145 (letter of February 18, 1876). See also Bein, *Hammacher* (1932), pp. 64 ff.

14. Biedermann, *Leben* (1866), 2:342, and *DAZ*, September 23, 1873. In 1869, liberal candidates for the Saxon Landtag included: one judicial official, six local officials (11 percent), three teachers (5 percent), two physicians (3 percent), eighteen lawyers (34 percent), twelve businessmen (22 percent), ten landowners (19 percent). *DAZ*, May 30, 1869.

15. From 1868 to 1871, the liberal faction of the Hessian Landtag contained two judicial officers, three lawyers, one academic, three businessmen, three farmers, and one unknown. Hess, *Reichstagswahlen* (1958), p. 99.

16. Seyffardt, *Erinnerungen* (1900). See also: Croon, "Städtevertretung" (1958), on Krefeld and Bochum; Hofmann, *Stadtverordneten* (1964), on Bielefeld; Möllers, "Strömungen" (1955), pp. 267 ff., on Essen; Vitzthum, *Politik* (1971), p. 47, on Kiel.

17. Karl Hackenberg, *Der rote Becker* (Leipzig, 1899), pp. 272 ff., and Philippson, *Forckenbeck* (1898), pp. 234 ff.

18. Kulemann, *Erinnerungen* (1911), pp. 25 ff.

19. See, for example, the data on the Cologne city council in G. Neuhaus, *Die Entwicklung der Stadt Cöln von der Errichtung des Deutschen Reiches bis zum Weltkriege* (Cologne, 1916), pp. 529 ff., and on liberal electors in Trier (1873) in Steil, "Wahlen" (1961), p. 273.

20. Hofmann, *Stadtverordneten* (1964), p. 58, n. 23. Cf. the material on the Volkspartei in Württemberg: Heger, *Partei* (1927), p. 53; Runge, *Volkspartei* (1970), pp. 78 ff., 99, 125, 150 ff.; Langewiesche, *Liberalismus* (1974), pp. 370 ff.

21. Seeber, *Bebel* (1965), p. 101. Kiehl, "Hänel" (1966), has some data on the liberal committees in Kiel.

22. Two examples: Matern, "Wahlen" (1969), pp. 148 ff., on the election committee in Hildesheim (1866), and Stoffregen, *Geschichte* (1965), on the signers of a National Liberal electoral statement in Gandersheim (1878).

23. On these issues, see the general remarks in S. M. Lipset and S. Rokkan, eds., *Party Systems and Voter Alignments: Cross-National Perspectives* (New York, 1967); Milatz, "Reichstagswahlen" (1974), pp. 207 ff.; Thränhardt, *Wahlen* (1973), pp. 20 ff.

24. For more on research problems and a fuller bibliography, see Sheehan, "Quantification" (1972), and O. Büsch, "Parteien und Wahlen in Deutschland bis zum Ersten Weltkrieg," *Abhandlungen aus der Pädagogischen Hochschule Berlin* (Berlin, 1974), 1:178–264. There is a guide to the statistical material in N. Diederich, "Germany, " in S. Rokkan and J. Meyriant, eds., *International Guide to Electoral Statistics*, vol. 1, *National Elections in Western Europe* (The Hague, 1969), pp. 128–62. Unless otherwise noted, my analysis of the Reichstag elections is based on the published returns: *Statistik des Deutschen Reiches*, 1st ser., vol. 14, pt. 5 (for 1871 and

1874), vol. 37, pt. 6 (for 1877.and 1878), vol. 53, pt. 3 (for 1881); *Monatshefte zur Statistik des Deutschen Reiches*, (1885) no. 1 (for 1884), (1887) no. 4 (for 1887), (1890) no. 4 (for 1890); *Vierteljahrshefte zur Statistik des Deutschen Reiches*, (1893) no. 4 (for 1893), *Ergänzungshefte 1898* (for 1898), and *1907* (for 1907); *Statistik des Deutschen Reiches*, vol. 250 (for 1912).

• 25. Walter Schübelin, *Das Zollparlament und die Politik von Baden, Bayern und Württemberg 1866–1870* (Berlin, 1935), p. 101.

26. Kurt, *Wahlen* (1966), see especially the map on p. 42. Thränhardt, *Wahlen* (1973), pp. 48 ff., treats the relationship between religion and political alignments in Bavaria.

27. Quoted in Möllers, "Strömungen" (1955), pp. 170–71. See also Forckenbeck's comments on the situation in Breslau (April 1873), HW, 2:78–79, and Ehrenfeuchter, "Willensbildung" (1951), pp. 50, 96 ff., on Hanover.

Despite the obvious importance of religion for German social, political, and cultural history, there has been remarkably little research on the subject. For a survey of what is available, see Annemarie Burger, *Religionszugehörigkeit und soziales Verhalten. Untersuchungen und Statistiken der neueren Zeit in Deutschland* (Göttingen, 1964).

28. Ehrenfeuchter, "Willensbildung" (1951), pp. 54 ff., 66 ff., 77 ff., 88 ff.

29. Hess, *Reichstagswahlen* (1958), pp. 33 ff., on Hesse, and Thränhardt, *Wahlen* (1973), pp. 49 ff., on Bavaria.

30. The following districts in the small states elected a liberal candidate continually between 1867 and 1877: Mecklenburg (WKe 1, 2, 5, 6), Sachsen-Weimar (Wke 1, 2, 3), Mecklenburg-Strelitz, Oldenburg (Wke 1, 2), Braunschweig (Wke 1, 2, 3), Sachsen-Meiningen (Wke 1, 2), Sachsen-Altenburg, Sachsen-Koburg (Wke 1, 2), Anhalt (Wke 1, 2), Schwarzburg-Rudolstadt, Waldeck, Reuss jüngere Linie, Schaumberg-Lippe, and Lippe. For an example of political life in a *Kleinstaat*, see T. Klein, "Reichstagswahlen" (1968), on Anhalt.

31. The distribution of the parties can be seen in the following figures, which record the number of districts in which a party earned more than 25 percent of the vote in the elections of 1874. Figures on 1871 are given in parentheses: National Liberals 201 (199), Fortschrittspartei 63 (66), Conservatives 74 (101), Free Conservatives 47 (56), Center 141 (105), Poles 22 (24), Danes 3 (2), Guelphs 13 (16), Alsatians 15 (15), Social Democrats 43 (18). From Germany, *StJb*, 7 (1886): 161–62.

32. On the regional distribution of the Fortschrittspartei, see the report of February 1877 quoted in Steinbrecher, *Parteiorganisation* (1960), pp. 223–25.

33. Kapp, *Frühsozialisten* (1969), p. 114. Some examples: Seyffardt, *Erinnerungen* (1900), p. 155, on Krefeld in 1874 and 1877; O. Rückert, *Zur Geschichte der Arbeiterbewegung in Reichstag Wahlkreis Potsdam-Spandau-Osthavelland*, 3 parts (Potsdam, 1965), pp. 136.; Thränhardt, *Wahlen* (1973), pp. 68 ff., on Bavaria.

34. Wilhelm Blum to Lasker, July 1872, HW, 2:68–69.

35. Lavies, *Nichtwählen* (1973), pp. 131 ff., has some data on electoral participation and urbanization. See also: Hamerow, *Foundations* (1969–72), 2:327, on the elections of 1867; *EGK 1869*, p. 97, on the Saxon Landtag; Möllers, "Strömungen" (1955), p. 53, on Essen; Kaiser, *Strömungen* (1963), p. 332, on Bonn; Eckert, *Sozialdemokratie* (1968), p. 230, on Nuremburg; Vogel and Haungs, *Wahlkampf* (1965), p. 77, on Baden.

In 1871, participation in urban WKe was 36.4 percent, well below the national average of 52 percent. By 1877, 55.4 percent of the urban electorate voted, just a few points below the national average of 60.6 percent. Germany, *StJb*, 12 (1881): 134.

36. Möllers, "Strömungen" (1955), p. 174, on Essen in 1870; Seyffardt, *Erinnerungen* (1900), on Krefeld; Ficker, *Kulturkampf* (1928), pp. 286 ff., on Münster; Poll, *Selbstverwaltung* (1960), pp. 277–78, on Aachen; Kaiser, *Strömungen* (1963), on Bonn.

37. For some data on changes in the tax structure, see J. Riesser, *The Great German Banks* (1905; translated Washington, D.C., 1911), p. 98, and J. Müller and S, Geisenberger, *Die Einkommensstruktur in verschiedenen deutschen Ländern, 1874 bis 1913* (Berlin, 1972).

38. Hoffman, *Wachstum* (1965), p. 212. On the changing structure of enterprise, see: Böhme, *Deutschlands* (1966), pp. 331–33, and "Emil Kirdorf," *Tradition* 13, no. 6 (1968): 282–300, and 14, no. 1 (1969): 21–48; Zorn, "Typen" (1957), pp. 72 ff.; Köllmann, *Sozialgeschichte* (1960), pp. 116 ff.; David Landes, "The Structure of Enterprise in the Nineteenth Century: The Cases of Britain and Germany," in *Extrait des Rapports du XI. Congrès International des Sciences Historique* (Stockholm, 1960), pp. 107–28; G. Adelmann, "Führende Unternehmer im Rheinland und in Westfalen, 1850–1914," *RV* 35 (1971): 335–52; L. Schofer, "Modernization, Bureaucratization, and the Study of Labor History: Lessons from Upper Silesia, 1865–1914," in Wehler, ed., *Sozialgeschichte* (1974), 467–78.

39. H. Kaelble's article, "Sozialer Aufstieg in Deutschland, 1850–1914," *VSWG* 60, no. 1 (1973): 41–71, is the best place to begin an examination of the problem of social mobility in the second half of the nineteenth century. Zorn, "Typen" (1957), and Sachtler, *Wandlungen* (1937), pp. 24 and 41, have some preliminary conclusions on the background of entrepreneurs. W. Zorn, "Hochschule und höhere Schule in der deutschen Sozialgeschichte der Neuzeit," in *Spiegel der Geschichte (Festschrift für Max Braubach)* (Münster, 1964), p. 332, suggests a growing narrowness in the social backgrounds of Gymnasium students as this critically important institution became more exclusive. Finally, a number of local studies indicate that economic elites after 1871 were consolidating their positions: for example, see Crew, "Industry" (1975), chap. 3, on Bochum, and Zunkel, *Unternehmer* (1962), pp. 128 ff., on the Rhineland.

40. R. Michels, *Probleme der Sozialphilosophie* (Leipzig, 1914), p. 151. J. Sheehan, "Conflict" (1972), has a further discussion of this process and cites some additional literature. Morsey, *Reichsverwaltung* (1957), pp. 246–47, 273 ff., discusses government policy towards ennoblement. The classic analysis of the Junker's relationship to other social groups is Hans Rosenberg's "Die Pseudodemokratisierung der Rittergutsbesitzerklasse," in Wehler, ed., *Sozialgeschichte* (1966), pp. 287–308. For three examples of upward mobility and movement into the aristocracy, see: Kocka, *Unternehmensverwaltung* (1969), pp. 283 ff., 386 ff., on Wilhelm von Siemens; E. Foerster, *Adalbert Falk* (Gotha, 1927), p. 64; Mohl, *Lebenserinnerungen* (1902), 2:63–64.

41. Mack Walker, *Germany and the Emigration, 1816–1885* (Cambridge, Mass., 1964), chap. 7, and Angel-Volkov, "'Decline'" (1974).

42. Motteck, "Gründerkrise" (1966), and Böhme, *Deutschlands* (1966), especially pp. 320 ff.

43. The most influential interpretation is Rosenberg, *Depression* (1967). His views are supported and extended in Wehler, *Bismarck* (1969). For a critique, see A. Gerschenkron, "The Great Depression in Germany," in *Continuity in History and Other Essays* (Cambridge, Mass., 1968). Angel-Volkov "'Decline'" (1974), pp. 170–71, has a convenient summary of the most important economic data; her article

also provides an excellent analysis of the depression's impact on various social groups, especially among artisans.

44. Quoted in Rosenberg, *Depression* (1967), p. 56.

45. Quoted in Motteck, "Gründerkrise" (1966), p. 72.

46. Rupert Breitling, "Die zentralen Begriffen der Verbandsforschung: Pressure Group, Interessengruppen, Verbände," *PV* 1, no. 1 (1960): 47–73, discusses some important terms. There is an excellent bibliography in Varain, ed., *Interessenverbände* (1973).

Among recent works on the rise of interest politics, the following essays are especially noteworthy: H. Böhme, "Big Business Pressure Groups and Bismarck's Turn to Protectionism, 1873–1879," *HJ* 10, no. 2 (1967): 218–36; Nipperdey, "Interessenverbände" (1961); Fischer, "Staatsverwaltung" (1972); Kaelble, "Interessenverbände" (1971); G. Schulz, "Über Entstehung und Formen von Interessengruppen in Deutschland seit Beginn der Industrialisierung," *PV* 2, no. 2 (1961): 124–54.

47. H. A. Bueck's *Der Centralverband deutscher Industrieller 1876–1901*, 3 vols. (Berlin, 1902–5), is a highly biased but still indispensable source.

48. The continued importance of educated elites, especially in the Berlin parliaments, meant that many of liberalism's national spokesmen did not suffer from the depression because they lived on fixed incomes; in fact its deflationary impact probably caused an increase in their real earnings. On this point, see Rosenberg, *Depression* (1967), p. 125. Along these lines, it is quite remarkable to see how little attention a periodical such as *Im Neuen Reich* paid to economic affairs, even during the depths of the depression.

49. *NZ*, October 30, 1873.

50. Quoted in Vitzthum, *Politik* (1971), p. 47, n. 58.

51. Treitschke quoted in Parisius, *Deutschlands* (1878), p. xx, Hänel in Steinbrecher, *Parteiorganisation* (1960), p. 37. Both remarks were made in 1877.

52. Herzfeld, *Miquel* (1938), 1:363 ff.; Helfferich, *Siemens* (1921–23), 3:158, on Bamberger.

53. The potential disruptiveness of commercial and fiscal issues was foreshadowed in the debates of 1873 and 1875 on financial policy: see Stürmer, *Regierung* (1974), pp. 147–79.

54. *EGK 1876*, pp. 70–71.

55. Hardach, *Bedeutung* (1967), is the best introduction to these issues. Matthes, "Spaltung" (1953), pp. 57 ff., has a good brief account of their impact on the liberal parties. For some local examples, see: Möllers, "Strömungen" (1955), pp. 285–86; Ehrenfeuchter, "Willensbildung" (1951), pp. 71 ff.; J. Wiggers, *Aus meinem Leben* (Leipzig, 1901), p. 325.

It is important to keep in mind that the sharp impact of the tariff on public opinion was in part because changes in tariff policy usually had a direct and easily observable influence on prices: Nipperdey, "Interessenverbände" (1961), p. 265, n. 2.

56. The most subtle analysis of the relationship between interest and ideology in liberalism is Nipperdey, "Grundprobleme" (1973).

57. Parisius, *Deutschlands* (1878), pp. 223 ff. (The program is also given in *EGK 1876*, pp. 228–31). Cf. the program of March 1877, Parisius, pp. 226 ff.

58. There is an excellent summary of the National Liberals' position in Hardach, *Bedeutung* (1967), pp. 172–76. Significantly, the party's electoral declaration of December 1876 has no mention of economic issues except for a statement against new

taxes: Parisius, *Deutschlands* (1878), pp. 221–23.

59. Quoted in Meinecke, "Dove," *Werke* (1957–68), 7:404.

60. These ideas are carefully analyzed in Wehler, *Bismarck* (1969), especially pp. 112 ff., 135 ff.

61. S. Angel-Volkov's articles provide some excellent material on the relationship of craftsmen to liberalism. See "'Decline'" (1974) and "Funktion" (1974).

62. *Gb* 33, no. 1 (1874): 78–80.

63. Böttcher, *Stephani* (1887), p. 169.

64. Baumgarten, "Liberalismus" (1966). See also: Krieger, *Idea* (1957), pp. 440–41; G. Iggers, *The German Conception of History. The National Tradition of Historical Thought from Herder to the Present* (Middletown, Conn., 1968), pp. 122 ff.; Faber, "Realpolitik" (1966). For a somewhat similar statement, see Siemens' letters of July 1866, quoted in Helfferich, *Siemens* (1921–23), 1:63, 66.

65. Even those on the far right of the movement were uneasy about Baumgarten's praise for the nobility: Dorpalen, *Treitschke* (1957), pp. 113–14, and Freytag in *Gb* 27, no. 1 (1868): 1–8.

66. Erich Marcks, as quoted in Faber, "Realpolitik" (1966), p. 14 n.

67. *EGK 1876*, p. 177.

Part V

1. F. B. M. Hollyday, *Bismarck's Rival. A Political Biography of General and Admiral Albrecht von Stosch* (Durham, North Carolina, 1960), pp. 164 ff. See also J. Heyerdoff, ed., *Im Ring der Gegner Bismarcks. Denkschriften und politischer Briefwechsel Franz von Roggenbachs mit Kaiserin Augusta und Albrecht von Stosch, 1865–1896* (Leipzig, 1943).

2. Haym to W. Schrader, April, 20, 1877, HW, 2:178–80.

3. The importance of these events for the future development of the Reich has become one of the key assumptions in recent historical scholarship. For an early and belatedly influential statement of this issue, see the essays reprinted in Kehr, *Primat* (1965). Kehr's ideas have been extended and refined in Heffter, *Selbstverwaltung* (1950), pp. 654 ff.; Rosenberg, *Depression* (1967); Böhme, *Deutschlands* (1966); Wehler, *Bismarck* (1969); Stürmer, *Regierung* (1974). There is an interesting critique of these interpretations in Schmidt, "Nationalliberalen" (1973).

Chapter 12

1. HW, 2:230.

2. On Bismarck's position, see Ziekursch, *Geschichte* (1925–28), 2:309 ff.; Hardach, *Bedeutung* (1967), pp. 52–53, 185 ff., which is especially good for the connection between commercial and fiscal policy; Matthes, "Spaltung" (1953), pp. 48, 61; Maenner, "Deutschlands" (1927), especially pp. 364 ff.

3. Matthes, "Spaltung" (1953), p. 65, n. 1a, has a guide to the primary source material on the Bennigsen candidacy. D. Sandberger's monograph, *Ministerkandidatur* (1929), is informative but rather out of date. See also Oncken, *Bennigsen* (1910), 2:297 ff., and Herzfeld, *Miquel* (1938), 1:422 ff.

4. Morsey, *Reichsverwaltung* (1957), pp. 287 ff.; Eyck, *Bismarck* (1941–44),

3:216–17; Sandberger, *Ministerkandidatur* (1929), pp. 16 ff.; *EGK 1878*, pp. 64 ff.

5. Quoted in Stürmer, "Staatsstreichgedanken" (1969), p. 591. See also Matthes, "Spaltung" (1953), pp. 78 ff. A week later, Bismarck spoke of the need to turn public opinion toward economic matters so that in the next election "the vote can be directed to economic, not political, issues." Quoted in Maenner, "Deutschlands" (1927), p. 373. For a view of this tactic from the liberal camp, see C. Braun, *Randglossen zu den politischen Wandlungen der letzten Jahre* (Bromberg, 1878), pp. 253–54.

6. Quoted in Eyck, *Bismarck* (1941–44), 3:228. Huber, 4:1153, summarizes the parliamentary deliberations over the anti-socialist laws. The fullest account is in Pack, *Ringen* (1961). Gall, "Sozialistengesetz" (1963), and Stürmer, *Regierung* (1974), pp. 241 ff., are also valuable, as is Oncken's account of Bennigsen's role in *Bennigsen* (1910), 2:360 ff.

7. Quoted from a memorandum on the elections prepared for, and corrected by, Bismarck, published in H. Kohl, ed., *Bismarck-Jahrbuch* 1 (Berlin, 1894): 97–121. See also *EGK 1878*, pp. 100, 110, 124 ff., and the description of the campaign in one Prussian district given in Kapp, *Frühsozialisten* (1969), pp. 113–15.

8. The Fortschrittspartei statement is reprinted in Richter, *Reichstag* (1894–96), 2:68, the National Liberals' statement in HW, 2:201–3. For an example of right-wing pressure for action against the SPD, see Aegidi's letter to Treitschke of June 19, 1878, HW, 2:206–7, and Treitschke's article in the July 1878 issue of the *PJbb*.

9. Some examples: Bunsen, *Bunsen* (1900), pp. 284–85; Rickert, HW, 2:210; and the material in Oncken, *Bennigsen* (1910), 2:374 ff.

10. Bamberger to Stauffenberg, August 13, 1878, HW, 2:216. Cf. Bennigsen to Stauffenberg, August 12, 1878, HW 2:215.

11. The situation in Württemberg is discussed in a letter by J. Hölder of June 1878, HW 2:207–8. On Baden, see Gall, "Sozialistengesetz" (1963).

12. For example, Danzig WK 2, Marienwerder WK 4, Breslau WK 6, and Hanover WKe 5 and 11.

13. For some material on the voting in various districts, see: Kaiser, *Strömungen* (1963), pp. 379 ff., on Bonn; Möllers, "Strömungen" (1955), pp. 320 ff., on Essen; Steil, "Wahlen" (1961), pp. 174 ff., on Trier; Ehrenfeuchter, "Willensbildung" (1951), pp. 71 ff., 82 ff., 120 ff., 129 ff., on Hanover; Köllmann, *Sozialgeschichte* (1960), p. 252, on Barmen; Kiehl, "Hänel" (1966), pp. 314 ff., on Kiel.

14. "Nach dem Wahlen," *INR* 8, no. 2 (1878): 241–44.

15. For a guide to the debate in October, see *EGK 1878*, pp. 137 ff. Vernon Lidtke, *The Outlawed Party. Social Democracy in Germany, 1878–1890* (Princeton, 1966), is the best account of the law's impact on the labor movement.

16. Rachfahl, "Richter" (1912), pp. 297–99. See also Stürmer, *Regierung* (1974), pp. 265 ff. Hardach, *Bedeutung* (1967), has the best overall treatment of the tariff issue; M. Nitzsche's *Die handelspolitische Reaktion in Deutschland* (Stuttgart and Berlin, 1905), has been superseded in detail but remains worth reading.

17. *EGK 1878*, pp. 167–68; Hardach, *Bedeutung* (1967), pp. 154–56; Bein, *Hammacher* (1932), pp. 76 ff.

18. *EGK 1878*, pp. 173 ff.

19. The program is reprinted in H. Ritter von Poschinger, *Fürst Bismarck als Volkswirth* (Berlin, 1889–91), 1:170–1. See also Böhme, *Deutschlands* (1966), pp. 524 ff.

20. Bismarck, *Werke* (1923–33), 12:71.

21. On the debate, see: Maenner, "Deutschlands" (1927), pp. 465 ff.; Hardach,

Bedeutung (1967), pp. 172 ff.; *EGK 1879*, pp. 124 ff., 156–57; VfSP, *Schriften*, vol. 16, on the Verein meeting of April 1879.

22. *EGK 1879*, pp. 164 ff.; Lambi, *Trade* (1963), pp. 202 ff.; Matthes, "Spaltung" (1953), p. 114; Philippson, *Forckenbeck* (1898), pp. 316 ff.; Seyffardt, *Erinnerungen* (1900), pp. 313–17.

23. *EGK 1879*, pp. 132 ff.; Lambi, *Trade* (1963), pp. 212 ff.; Böhme, *Deutschlands* (1966), pp. 550 ff.; and the letters in HW, especially Lasker to Stauffenberg and Miquel, 2:252–53, 254 ff.

24. Oncken, *Bennigsen* (1910), 2:403 ff., and Matthes, "Spaltung" (1953), pp. 105 ff.

25. *EGK 1879*, p. 209. The amendment established a revenue-sharing plan between the Reich and the states. See: Lambi, *Trade* (1963), pp. 221 ff., and Block, *Krisis* (1930), pp. 48 ff.

26. Matthes, "Spaltung" (1953), pp. 115 ff.; Block, *Krisis* (1930), pp. 52–53; for a statement of the right-wing position, see *INR* 9, no. 1 (1879): 898–902.

27. Forckenbeck to Lasker and Lasker to Miquel, HW, 2:243, 248–49.

28. For a contemporary analysis, see the article entitled "Der Wendepunkt in der Entwicklung des Reiches," *NZ*, July 6, 1879. Rosenberg, *Depression* (1967), has a good account of the interventionist state which emerged after 1879. The major legislative developments are given in Huber, vol 4.

29. The classic account of this is Kehr's essay on Puttkamer in *Primat* (1965), pp. 64 ff. See also: Hintze, *Abhandlungen* (1962–67), 1:615 ff.; Morsey, *Reichsverwaltung* (1957), pp. 262 ff.; and Rosenberg, *Depression* (1967). H-J. Rejewski, *Die Pflicht zur politischen Treue im preussischen Beamtenrecht 1850–1918* (Berlin, 1973), pp. 83 ff., has a legalistic analysis of the officials' political position.

30. K. Oldenburg, *Aus Bismarcks Bundesrat* (Berlin, 1929), p. 76. For a similar view, see H. Rothfels, *Theodor Lohmann und die Kampfjahre der staatlichen Sozialpolitik* (Berlin, 1927), p. 62.

31. Bunsen, *Bunsen* (1900), p. 285.

Chapter 13

1. Miquel, *Reden* (1911–14), 3:134.

2. A. Gröning to H. Meier, July 5, 1879, HW, 2:250. Some other examples: HW, 2:256 ff.; Kapp, *Frühsozialisten* (1969), p. 122; Bein, *Hammacher* (1932), pp. 80–81, A. Dove, *Ausgewählte Aufsätze* (Munich, 1925), 2:72.

3. "Die Kandidaturen zur Abgeordnetenwahl," *NZ*, August 15, 1879.

4. Müller, *Strömungen* (1963), pp. 108–13, 118, 123.

5. Oncken, *Bennigsen* (1910), 2:418 ff.; Lasker to Stauffenberg, August 2, 1879, HW, 2:262; Herzfeld, *Miquel* (1938), 1:448–49. The party's electoral statement was published in *NZ* on September 6. The problems of the campaign were discussed at length in *NZ*, see especially July 13, 28, August 10, September 6, 13, and 26.

6. *EGK 1879*, p. 229; *NZ*, September 9 and 12, 1879.

7. Letter to Lasker, August 16, 1879, HW, 2:273.

8. The Fortschrittspartei lost thirteen seats in Ostpreussen, five in Westpreussen, and six in both Silesia and Prussian Saxony: Richter, *Reichstag* (1894–96), 2:141 ff. There is a very perceptive analysis of the voting in a series of anonymous articles in

INR 9, no. 2 (1879): 327–30, 542–44, 571–73. See also, *EGK 1879*, pp. 239–40; *VZ*, October 1, 1879; *NZ*, October 1, 2, 7, 8, 1879.

9. *NZ*, October 2, 1879; Müller, *Strömungen* (1963), pp. 124 ff.

10. Quoted in Block, *Krisis* (1930), p. 59. Cf. *VZ*, October 9, 1879.

11. Matthes, "Spaltung" (1953), p. 125.

12. Miquel made this point in a letter of October 15, 1879, HW, 2:278. See also Block, *Krisis* (1930), pp. 59 ff.

13. Oncken, *Bennigsen* (1910), 2:424 ff.; Matthes, "Spaltung" (1953), pp. 127 ff.; Block, *Krisis* (1930), pp. 62 ff.; Herzfeld, *Miquel* (1938), 1:450 ff.

14. This material is reprinted in HW, 2:307 ff. See also *EGK 1880*, p. 88, and Dill, *Lasker* (1958), p. 181. Forckenbeck expressed a similar view in February, HW, 2:292–93. Cf. Kapp, *Frühsozialisten* (1969), pp. 127–28.

15. Block, *Krisis* (1930), pp. 87 ff., and Matthes, "Spaltung" (1953), pp. 130–31. For an example of the kind of pressure Bismarck was putting on the liberals, see his Reichstag speech of May 8, 1880, reprinted in *Werke* (1923–33), 12:133 ff. By July, even Miquel was beginning to wonder if some measure of independence from the chancellor might not be necessary: HW, 2:325.

16. *EGK 1880*, pp. 210–11.

17. See the letters in HW, 2:333 ff. The Secessionists' formal declaration is reprinted on pp. 355–57. See also *EGK 1880*, pp. 214–15, and Mommsen, *Parteiprogramme* (1964), pp. 156–57. A right-wing critique can be found in *INR* 10, no. 2 (1880): 336–40, 405–9, 440–49.

18. In my opinion, Seeber overestimates the significance of *Grosskapital* in his otherwise very useful sketch of the Secessionist leaders: *Bebel* (1965), pp. 114 ff. See also Block, *Krisis* (1930), p. 22.

19. *EGK 1880*, pp. 81, 101–2, 110–11; Block, *Krisis* (1930), pp. 80–81.

20. Rickert to Stauffenberg, January 4, 1880, and Stauffenberg to Lasker, January 28, 1880, HW, 2:286, 290. On Stauffenberg's role in this period, see H. Steinsdorfer, *Franz Freiherr Schenk von Stauffenberg* (Diss., Munich, 1959).

21. "Die Sezession," in Bamberger, *Schriften* (1894–98), see especially 5:56, 75–76, 132–33. On the background for this essay, see HW, 2:372–73, and Zucker, *Bamberger* (1975), pp. 130 ff.

22. "Die natürliche Gruppierung deutscher Parteien," *Gb* 38, no. 3 (1879): 200–204, and "Das neue Abgeordnetenhaus," 38, no. 4:126–30.

23. J. Jolly, *Der Reichstag und die Parteien* (Berlin, 1880), quotations from pp. 70 and 156 ff. On Jolly's career, see H. Baumgarten and L. Jolly, *Staatsminister Jolly* (Tübingen, 1897).

24. For example, *INR* 11, no. 1 (1881): 36–40, and 11, no. 2:95–104, 201–11, 943–54. On the *PJbb*, see Hans Schleier, "Treitschke, Delbrück und die 'PJ' in den 80er Jahren des 19. Jahrhunderts," *JbG* 1 (1967), especially p. 147.

25. R. Fleischer, "Ein Blick auf das Parteileben in Deutschland," *DR* 3, no. 3 (1879): 232–40.

26. Haym, *Leben* (1902), p. 303. Some other examples: Baumgarten (1881), quoted in Bornkamm, "Staatsidee" (1950), p. 55. Wehrenpfennig, quoted in C. von Tiedemann, *Sechs Jahre Chef der Reichskanzlei unter dem Fürsten Bismarck* (Leipzig, 1909), p. 269; *Gb* 41, no. 1 (1882): 57–66. As usual, the best analysis is in Gagel, *Wahlrechtsfrage* (1958), pp. 90–92, 100 ff.

27. For some examples of Rümelin's earlier views, see his essays "Stadt und

Land" (1870) and "Über das Verhältnis der Politik zur Moral" (1874), in his *Reden* (n.d.), vol. 1, especially pp. 170–71 and 351–52. On his career, see Schmoller, "Rümelin" (1913).

28. Rümelin to Haym, December 30, 1879, in Haym, *Briefwechsel* (1967), p. 317.

29. Reprinted in Rümelin, *Reden* (n.d.), vol. 2, see especially pp. 588, 617 ff. In the 1878 version, Rümelin still hoped that Germany would be able to master these problems; by 1881 he was much less optimistic: see p. 624. For some similar views, see: Max Haushofer, "Die grossstädische Krankheit," *DR* 4, no. 2 (1879): 238–47; Adolf Lasson, "Der Streit der Interessen und die Gesellschaft," *DR* 6, no. 2 (1881): 180–93; *Gb* 42, no. 4 (1883): 386 ff.

30. Rümelin, "Über den Wahlmodus für den Reichstag" (1880), *Reden* (n.d.), vol. 2, and "Begriff der Gesellschaft" (1888), vol. 3.

31. Zunkel, *Unternehmer* (1962), pp. 225–26. The most complete analysis of entrepreneurs in German parliamentary life is Jaeger, *Unternehmer* (1967), which concentrates on the period after 1890.

32. For two contemporary expressions of these regional differences, see Marquardsen to Bennigsen, August 24, 1883, *HW*, 2:399, and Stephani to Bennigsen, September 4, 1882, in Oncken, *Bennigsen* (1910), 2:493. White, *Party* (1976), pp. 84 ff., has a good account of the divisions between north and south.

33. *EGK 1879*, p. 258, and *EGK 1881*, pp. 251, 259.

34. See Möckl, *Prinzregentenzeit* (1972), pp. 48 ff., on Bavaria. The results of the Saxon elections are in *EGK 1881*, pp. 219–20.

35. The best analysis of this is White, *Party* (1976). See also Kriegbaum, *Tätigkeit* (1962), pp. 52 ff.

36. Elben to Lasker, March 17, 1881, *HW*, 2:376. On the situation in Württemberg, see Lang, *Partei* (1891), pp. 72 ff.

37. The program is reprinted in Oncken, *Bennigsen* (1910), 2:467–69. See also: *EGK 1881*, pp. 305, 308; *EGK 1882*, pp. 108–9; Matthes, "Spaltung" (1953), pp. 142 ff.

38. Oncken, *Bennigsen* (1910), 2:497 ff.

39. The best treatment of Miquel remains Herzfeld's biography (1938), see especially 1:411 ff., and 2:11 ff.

40. The Heidelberg Declaration, together with Miquel's keynote speech, can be found in Miquel, *Reden* (1911–13), 3:114 ff. See also *EGK 1884*, pp. 37–38, and Miquel, "Briefe" (1912–13), pp. 813 ff. The best analysis of these developments is White, *Party*, especially pp. 93 ff.

41. *EGK 1884*, pp. 49–50. For some reactions, see the letters by Elben and Fries in *HW*, 2:409–11, 413–14.

42. Letter of April 23, 1884, *HW*, 2:404–5.

43. *NZ*, March 6, 7, 8, 1884.

44. *NZ*, March 18, 1884.

45. G. Köhler to Miquel, May 2, 1884, *HW*, 2:408–9.

46. *EGK 1884*, p. 59; *NZ*, May 19, 1884; Miquel, *Reden* (1911–14), 3:128 ff. See also Nipperdey, *Organisation* (1961), pp. 125–26, and White, *Party* (1976).

47. Ehrenfeuchter, "Willensbildung" (1951), pp. 52–53, and Müller, *Strömungen* (1963), pp. 189 ff.

48. This happened, for instance, to Ernst Bassermann in Baden: K. Bassermann, ed., *Ernst Bassermann* (Mannheim, n.d.), p. 67.

49. The standard work is Wehler, *Bismarck* (1969). For some examples of the

political uses of colonialism, see *EGK 1884*, pp. 4–5, 93, 415–70.

50. Two examples: Bein, *Hammacher* (1932), p. 88, and Herzfeld, *Miquel* (1938), 1:24–25, 37 ff. Wehler, *Bismarck* (1969), treats this process in great detail.

51. Hesse provides the best example of this situation: in 1881, one of the two conservative parties contested five of the state's nine WKe, whereas in 1884 they did not run any candidates. As a result, almost all of these conservative voters apparently shifted to the National Liberals. In Guben-Lübben (Prussia, Frankfurt WK 7), on the other hand, liberals moved to the right and supported the Free Conservatives but still had to face opposition from the Conservative party: see L. Maenner, *Prinz Heinrich zu Schoenaich-Carolath* (Stuttgart and Berlin, 1931), p. 46.

52. In 1881, the National Liberals competed with one of the conservative parties in seventy-two districts, in 1884 in only forty-two. At the same time, the number of contests between a National Liberal and a left liberal increased from sixty to ninety-nine. (I have omitted from these figures districts where any of the parties got less than five percent of the vote).

53. *EGK 1887*, pp. 7–57, 60; Oncken, *Bennigsen* (1910), 2:529 ff.; Herzfeld, *Miquel* (1938), 2:64 ff., 93 ff.; Stürmer, "Militärkonflikt" (1974), pp. 204 ff.

54. Miquel, "Briefe" (1912–13), p. 94.

55. Quoted in Müller, *Strömungen* (1963), p. 228. The party's electoral statement is in *EGK 1887*, pp. 60–61. For some local studies of the campaign, see: Steil, "Wahlen" (1961), pp. 236 ff., on Trier; Schneider, "Anfänge" (1956), pp. 100 ff., on the Palatinate; Nettmann, "Witten" (1972), pp. 130–31; Graf, *Entwicklung* (1958), pp. 21 ff., on Dortmund; Kurt, *Wahlen* (1966), pp. 35 ff., on Offenbach.

56. In Berlin (WK 3), the conflict between the two liberal parties was so intense that the National Liberals abstained rather than support the Fortschrittspartei against the SPD.

57. Stürmer, "Staatsstreichgedanken" (1969); John Röhl, "The Disintegration of the *Kartell* and the Politics of Bismarck's Fall from Power, 1887–1890," *HJ* 9, no. 1 (March 1966): 60–89; Herzfeld, *Miquel* (1938), 2:104 ff. See also Pack, *Ringen* (1961), for changing views of the anti-Socialist laws.

58. On the liberals in the Prussian Landtag elections, see *NZ*, October 2, 1885, and October 10, 17, 25, 26, 28, 1888. It is worth noting that by 1888 even the left-leaning *NZ* tried to downplay the importance of electoral agreements between National Liberals and Progressives.

59. *EGK 1885*, pp. 11–12; *NZ*, January 21, 1885, on Baden; and *AZ*, June 5–25, 1887, on Bavaria.

Chapter 14

1. Quoted in Wegner, *Barth* (1968), p. 4.

2. See Richter's statement of March 1877, printed in *Reichstag* (1894–96), 2:29. The party program of 1877 is given in *EGK 1877*, pp. 82–83.

3. The minutes of this convention were printed as Fortschrittspartei, *Parteitag* (1879). See also: *EGK 1878*, p. 187; Richter, *Reichstag* (1894–96), 2:85 ff.; Seeber, *Bebel* (1965), pp. 50 ff.; Gagel, *Wahlrechtsfrage* (1958), pp. 95 ff., and 104 ff.; Steinbrecher, *Parteiorganisation* (1960), pp. 28 ff.

4. Fortschrittspartei, *Parteitag* (1879), p. 53.

5. Vitzthum, *Politik* (1971), pp. 72 ff.

6. Fortschrittspartei, *Parteitag* (1879), pp. 20 ff., Virchow quoted on p. 22. On the vote in 1884, see Seeber, *Bebel* (1965), pp. 136 ff., and Pack, *Ringen* (1961), pp. 136 ff.

7. Fortschrittspartei, *Parteitag* (1879), pp. 30 ff.

8. Cf. Seeber, *Bebel* (1965), pp. 101 ff. for some data on local electoral organizations.

9. Fortschrittspartei, *Parteitag* (1879), pp. 46 ff. See also Seeber, *Bebel* (1965), pp. 53 ff.; Steinbrecher, *Parteiorganisation* (1960), pp. 45 ff.; Nipperdey, *Organisation* (1961), pp. 176 ff.

10. Steinbrecher, *Parteiorganisation* (1960), p. 19.

11. Richter to Lasker, September 7, 1880, HW, 2:360; Richter, *Reichstag* (1894–96), 2:174–75; Rachfahl, "Richter" (1912), pp. 311–12; Seeber, *Bebel* (1965), pp. 71 ff.

12. Bamberger called Richter's followers "the lowest form of electoral cattle [*Stimmvieh*]." Quoted in Matthes, "Spaltung" (1953), p. 148.

13. Nipperdey, *Organisation* (1961), pp. 32 ff. For some examples, see: White, *Party* (1976), on Hesse; Oncken, *Bennigsen* (1910), 2:435 ff.; Kastendiek, "Liberalismus" (1952), pp. 96 ff., on Bremen; and the letters in HW, 2:358 ff.

14. See their program reprinted in *EGK 1880*, pp. 256–57, and Stauffenberg in February 1881, HW, 2:375.

15. Rachfahl, "Richter" (1912), p. 317. See also Lasker's letters to Stauffenberg and Bennigsen, HW, 2:379–80, 470–73. Support for left-liberal unity from within the Fortschrittspartei was provided by Albert Hänel, in part because he wanted their help against right-wing liberalism in Schleswig-Holstein: see Kiehl, "Hänel" (1966), pp. 382 ff.

16. See above, pp. 191–95.

17. *EGK 1880*, pp. 185–86.

18. See, for example, "Zur Altenburger Wahl," *Gb* 40, no. 1 (1881): 49–50.

19. Seeber, *Bebel* (1965), pp. 58 ff.; Rachfahl, "Richter" (1912), pp. 312 ff.; Richter, *Reichstag* (1894–96), 2:167 ff., 228 ff. For an example of Richter's criticism of Bismarck, see his speeches in the debate on taxation policies during February 1881, as summarized in *EGK 1881*, pp. 77–88.

20. *EGK 1880*, pp. 72–73, 123.

21. See: Kaehler, "Stoeckers" (1922), and *EGK 1880*, pp. 239 ff., on Stoecker; Wawrzinek, *Entstehung* (1927), and Levy, *Downfall* (1975), chap. 1, on the other parties; the violence in 1881 is described in *EGK 1881*, pp. 222–23, 230.

22. See above, p. 198.

23. Richter quoted in *EGK 1881*, p. 279; Lasker in HW, 2:386–87.

24. For a criticism of Richter based on this assumption, see Seeber, *Bebel* (1965), p. 32. An argument similar to my own can be found in Matthes, "Spaltung" (1953), pp. 147 ff.

25. See: Phillips, ed., *Reichtags-Wahlen* (1883); Frank, *Brandenburger* (1934), pp. 83–84, 105, 132; and Rückert, *Geschichte* (1965), chap. 3, n. 144, on Potsdam-Spandau.

26. On voting behavior in 1881, see the following local studies: Ehrenfeuchter, "Willensbildung" (1951), especially p. 135, on Hanover; Kurt, *Wahlen* (1966), p. 34, on Offenbach; Müller, *Strömungen* (1963), pp. 140 ff., on Sieg, Mülheim, and Gummersbach; Steil, "Wahlen" (1961), on Trier; Nettmann, "Witten" (1972), pp. 88 ff.; Kastendiek, "Liberalismus" (1952), p. 96, Böttcher, *Anfänge* (1953), pp. 125–26, on

Bremen; Eckert, *Sozialdemokratie* (1968), pp. 236–37, on Nuremberg; and Graf, *Entwicklung* (1958), pp. 21 ff., on Dortmund.

27. On the relations among the liberal parties during the campaign, see *EGK 1882*, pp. 148–49, 151, 178–79. Disputes within the Fortschrittspartei are discussed on pp. 176–77.

28. Lasker, *Laskers* (1902), pp. 2 ff., discusses the causes and impact of the liberals' defeat in 1882. See also Steinbrecher, *Parteiorganisation* (1960), p. 83.

29. Seeber, *Bebel* (1965), pp. 128 ff.; Matthes, "Spaltung" (1953), pp. 151 ff.; Rachfahl, "Richter" (1912), pp. 321 ff. For some contemporary material see HW, 2:399 ff., and Bamberger, *Bismarcks* (1932), pp. 274–75, 288 ff.

30. *EGK 1884*, pp. 27 ff., 34. The program is reprinted in Mommsen, *Parteiprogramme* (1964), pp. 157–58, and analysed in Rubinstein, *Partei* (1935), pp. 17–21.

31. Nipperdey, *Organisation* (1961), pp. 206–17; Steinbrecher, *Parteiorganisation* (1960), pp. 61 ff.; Rachfahl, "Richter" (1912), pp. 334 ff.; Wegner, *Barth* (1968), especially p. 1, n. 3. For an example of the distrust with which Richter continued to be viewed, see Hellpach, *Wirken* (1948–49), 1:46. The liberal left was further divided by the Freisinnige Partei's failure to attract the South German Volkspartei: see *EGK 1885*, pp. 102–3.

32. The continuing debate over military policy is discussed in D. Dietz, *Die Heeresvorlage von 1880 und die liberalen Parteien* (Diss., Berlin, 1929). For differences within the left liberals' ranks, see Matthes, "Spaltung" (1953), pp. 214 ff., and the following examples: *EGK 1887*, pp. 61–62; *EGK 1889*, pp. 119, 148–49; *EGK 1890*, pp. 87, 101.

33. Rachfahl, "Richter" (1912), p. 335; Matthes, "Spaltung" (1953), pp. 185 ff. Seeber, *Bebel* (1965), pp. 143 ff., blames the Secessionists for this defeat, but it is more likely that the integration of the two parties was harmful to both of them.

34. These returns from Gumbinnen WKe 1 and 2 illustrate the shift away from the left.

	1881	1884	
	Gumbinnen Wk 1		
Forschrittspartei	50%	29%	(of votes cast)
Conservatives	49%	70%	(of votes cast)
Participation	61%	62%	(of eligible voters)
	Gumbinnen Wk2		
Fortschrittspartei	59%	21%	(of votes cast)
Conservatives	40%	78%	(of votes cast)
Participation	69%	58%	(of eligible voters)

For another example, see I. Dunger, *Wilhelmshaven 1870–1914* (Wilhelmshaven, 1962), pp. 130 ff.

35. Conze and Groh, *Arbeiterbewegung* (1966), p. 125, and Steinbrecher, *Parteiorganisation* (1960), p. 80.

36. The left liberals lost sixteen WKe to the conservative parties and twenty-five to the National Liberals.

37. Letter to Stauffenberg, February 25, 1887, HW, 2:429.

38. A. Dorpalen, "Emperor Frederick III and the German Liberal Movement," *AHR* 54, no. 1 (October 1948): 1–31, is a good discussion of the emperor's relation-

ship with the liberals. For some examples of the liberals' attitudes see: Schrader to
Stauffenberg, April 9, 1887, HW, 2:433–34; T. Barth, *Politische Porträts* (Berlin,
1904), pp. 84–93; E. Feder, *Politik und Humanität*. *Paul Nathan, Ein Lebensbild*
(Berlin, 1929), pp. 28, 48.
    39. Fraenkel, *Deutschland* (1968), p. 30.
    40. Stürmer, "Staatsstreichgedanken" (1969).
    41. Some examples: Elben, *Lebenserinnerungen* (1931), pp. 201 ff.; Schulze-
Delitzsch, *Schriften* (1909–13), 2:508 ff.; Heuss, *Mommsen* (1956), p. 205; Bunsen,
Bunsen (1900), pp. 291 ff.
    42. Letter of August 1884, in Kapp, *Frühsozialisten* (1969), pp. 137–38.
    43. Schrader to Stauffenberg, August 1884, HW, 2:418; Bennigsen quoted in *EGK
1888*, pp. 20–21.
    44. Dan White, "Hessen and the Reformulation of National Liberalism" (Unpubl.
diss., Harvard, 1966), p. 340.
    45. Helfferich, *Siemens* (1921–23), 3:223; Bamberger, *Bismarcks* (1932), p. 339,
entry of June 1887; Baumgarten quoted in Marcks, "Einleitung" (1894), p. cxviii.

Part VI

    1. On Bismarck's dismissal, see J. A. Nichols, *Germany after Bismarck. The
Caprivi Era. 1890–1894* (Cambridge, Mass., 1958), pp. 12–26, and John Röhl, *Germany without Bismarck. The Crisis of Government in the Second Reich, 1890–1900*
(London, 1967), chap. 2.
    2. A summary of social and economic developments can be found in K. E. Born,
"Der soziale und wirtschaftliche Strukturwandel Deutschlands am Ende des 19. Jahrhunderts," in Böckenförde, *Verfassungsgeschichte* (1972), pp. 451–70. On demographic trends, see Köllmann, "Grundzüge" (1959), and "Industrialisierung"
(1959). Hoffmann, *Wachstum* (1965), has some useful data, especially on economic
growth.

Chapter 15

    1. Quoted in Michels, "Sozialdemokratie" (1906), p. 474.
    2. In 1871, 4 million Germans (52 percent of those eligible) voted; by 1912, over
12 million (84.2 percent) went to the polls. The impact of this on parliamentary
alignments was somewhat weakened by the government's refusal to redraw the boundaries for the WKe. This led to an increasing underrepresentation of the most heavily
populated areas. In 1903, for example, the ten largest WKe had an average of 118,000
voters, while the ten smallest averaged 13,000. See Fenske, *Wahlrecht* (1972), especially pp. 115 ff., 134 ff., and Milatz, "Reichstagswahlen" (1974), pp. 208 ff.
    3. The best treatment of the labor movement's growth after 1890 remains G. A.
Ritter, *Die Arbeiterbewegung im Wilhelminischen Reich* (Berlin-Dahlem, 1963), especially pp. 67 ff. T. Wacker, *Entwicklung der Sozialdemokratie in den zehn ersten
Reichstagswahlen* (Freiburg, 1903), has some useful data on elections in the nineties..
    4. Even during the election of 1907, when all of the non-Socialist parties combined
against the Center, its position remained fairly stable: G. Crothers, *The German
Elections of 1907* (New York, 1941), pp. 180 ff. Otto Eitner, "Die Stärke der Protes-

tanten und Katholiken in den einzelnen Reichstagswahlkreisen und die Sozialdemo-kratie,'' *Historisch-Politische Blätter* 144 (1912): 687–93, has some interesting material on the Center's electoral base. For the party's overall development after 1890, see: Rudolf Morsey, *Die deutsche Zentrumspartei, 1917–1925* (Düsseldorf, 1966), and Ronald Ross, *Beleaguered Tower: The Dilemma of Political Catholicism in Wilhelmine Germany* (Notre Dame, Ind., 1976).

5. Matthes, ''Spaltung'' (1953), pp. 241 ff., 333–34.

6. WKe contested by both liberal parties: 1890: 113; 1893: 89; 1898: 68; 1903: 47; 1907: 29; 1912: 47. By 1912, contested districts were clustered in a few regions—Schleswig-Holstein (7 of 10 WKe), Hesse (6 of 9) and the smaller states and cities (11 of 50). In Prussia's eastern provinces, on the other hand, there were contests in only 5 of the 140 WKe. (In order to be included in these figures, the parties had to poll more than 5 percent of the votes cast.)

7. There is a guide to the various suffrage laws in Vogel et al., *Wahlen* (1971).

8. Kalkoff, *Fraktion* (1913), has a great deal of material on the parties, with particular emphasis on the National Liberals. Official election returns are available for the elections of 1903, 1908, and 1913: Evert, ''Landtagswahlen'' (1905); Evert, ''Landtagswahlen'' (1909); and Höpker, ''Landtagswahlen'' (1916).

9. Warren, *Kingdom* (1964), has material on Saxon political life. On the suffrage question, see *EGK 1896*, p. 21, and *EGK 1909*, p. 332.

10. Schadt, *Partei* (1971), discusses politics in Baden, with particular emphasis on the rise of Social Democracy. On the persisting importance of religious issues, see Manfred Stadelhofer, *Der Abbau der Kulturkampfgesetzgebung im Grossherzogtum Baden 1878–1918* (Mainz, 1969), and H. Köhler, *Lebenserinnerungen des Politikers und Staatsmannes, 1878–1949* (Stuttgart, 1964). On the elections of 1905, see the material in *EGK 1905*, pp. 124–25.

11. On Bavaria, see: Albrecht, *Landtag* (1968); Möckl, *Prinzregentenzeit* (1972); Thränhardt, *Wahlen* (1973). Material on the elections of 1899 and 1905 can be found in *EGK 1899*, pp. 118–19, and *EGK 1905*, p. 106.

12. See: Adam, *Jahrhundert* (1919); Menzinger, *Verfassungsrevision* (1969); G. Egelhaaf, *Lebenserinnerungen* (Stuttgart, 1960); and Simon, *Demokraten* (1969). The elections of 1895 are reported in *EGK 1895*, p. 34; the struggle for suffrage reform in *EGK 1905*, pp. 97 ff., and *EGK 1906*, pp. 18, 127, 143.

I did not see a copy of James Hunt's excellent book, *The People's Party in Württemberg and Southern Germany, 1890–1914* (Stuttgart, 1975), until after my manuscript was finished.

13. White, *Party* (1976), is the best single source on Hesse; Kurt, *Wahlen* (1966), discusses the situation in Offenbach. On Hessian anti-Semitism, see Broszat, ''Bewegung'' (1953), and R. Mack, ''Otto Böckel und die antisemitische Bauernbewegung in Hesse (1887–1894),'' *Wetterauer Geschichtsblätter* 16 (1967): 113–47.

14. Schramm, *Hamburg* (1943); Carl Schröder, *Aus Hamburgs Blütezeit, Lebenserinnerungen*, 2d ed. (Hamburg, 1921). R. A. Comfort, *Revolutionary Hamburg* (Stanford, 1966), and J. Schult, *Geschichte der Hamburger Arbeiter 1890–1919* (Hanover, 1967), discuss the labor movement. Bolland, *Bürgerschaft* (1959), has an account of parliamentary affairs; he reprints the most important local party programs on pp. 207–17. On the suffrage issue, see: *EGK 1906*, pp. 10, 18, and *KP* (1905), 5:253 ff., and (1913), 13:477–78.

According to the *EGK 1913* (p. 88), the political composition of the *Bürgerschaft* was: right 40; left, 39; left-center, 30; "United Liberals," 30; SPD, 20; Conservative, 1.

15. The thirty different laws regulating municipal affairs are listed in Otto Most, ed., *Die deutsche Stadt und ihre Verwaltung* (Berlin, 1912), 1:20–21. The best guide to the different suffrage systems is P. Hirsch and H. Lindemann, *Das kommunale Wahlrecht* (Berlin, 1905). *Kommunale Praxis* regularly featured articles on the techniques used to limit the power of the labor movement in local affairs.

16. Dressel, *Wahlen* (1961), pp. 245–47. There are a great many other examples in *KPB*.

17. There is a series of articles on cities and towns with a Socialist majority in *KP* (1913), 13:1185 ff. The following autobiographies provide valuable insights into the function of local government for the labor movement: P. Löbe, *Erinnerungen eines Reichstagspräsidenten* (Berlin, 1949), pp. 38 ff., on Breslau; G. Noske, *Erlebtes aus Aufstieg und Niedergang einer Demokratie* (Offenbach, 1947), pp. 17 ff., on Königsberg; Severing, *Lebensweg* (1950), 1:132 ff., on Bielefeld; Karl Ulrich, *Erinnerungen des ersten hessischen Staatspräsidenten* (Offenbach, 1953), pp. 60 ff., on Offenbach.

18. This issue is discussed in greater detail in Sheehan, "Liberalism and the City" (1971).

The following monographs treat urban political life during the imperial era: Croon, "Städtevertretung" (1958), on Krefeld and Bochum, and *Auswirkungen* (1960), on the Rhineland and Westphalia; Henning, *Geschichte* (1965), on Essen; Hofmann, *Stadtverordneten* (1964), on Bielefeld; Köllmann, *Sozialgeschichte* (1960), on Barmen; Kaufmann, "Strukturen" (1957), on Heidelberg; Schuckmann, *Willensbildung* (1966), on Cologne; VfSP, *Schriften* (1900–07), vols. 117–20, on a number of important cities.

19. On elections and the cost of campaigns, see Bertram, *Wahlen* (1964), pp. 173 ff., 190 ff. A good survey of the press can be found in Wernecke, *Wille* (1970); see also Koszyk, *Geschichte* (1966), and I. Rieger, *Die Wilhelminische Presse* (Munich, 1957).

20. *KPB* (1911), 2:1. For another example, see Eduard Spranger's remarks quoted in Knoll, *Führungsauslese* (1957), p. 179.

21. *Werke* (1964–), 4:90. See also Naumann's essays "Liberalismus und Organisation" (1905), and "Die Erneuerung des Liberalismus" (1906), in *Werke*, 4:258 ff., 270 ff. For some similar views, see: Link, "Nationalverein" (1964), and Blaustein, "Uneinigkeit" (1911), especially pp. 21–22.

22. Nipperdey, *Organisation* (1961), pp. 86 ff.; O'Donnell, "Liberalism" (1973), pp. 170 ff.; Reiss, *Bassermann* (1967), pp. 11 ff.

23. The split between the two wings of the Freisinnige Partei is discussed above, pp. 265–66.

24. Nipperdey, *Organisation* (1961), pp. 176 ff.; Robson, "Liberalism" (1966), pp. 92 ff.; Elm, *Fortschritt* (1968), pp. 212–13; Reimann, *Müller-Meiningen* (1968), p. 80.

25. Nipperdey, *Organisation* (1961), p. 86.

26. Quoted in O'Donnell, "Liberalism" (1973), p. 187.

27. See Reiss, *Bassermann* (1967), on policy-making in the *Fraktion*. There is an example of the local importance of established elites in Bertram, *Wahlen* (1964), pp. 142–43. The ratio of members to voters is from Huber, 4:22–23.

28. Huber, 4:22–23. For some local examples of the left's organizational problems, see: Brooks, "Clubs" (1900), p. 377, and Helfferich, *Siemens* (1921–23), 3:195. Michael Georg Conrad's *Wahlfahrten* (Munich, 1894), which describes an election campaign by a member of the Volkspartei in the nineties, illustrates the limited understanding of democratic organization which persisted even on the far left of the movement.

29. Simon, *Demokraten* (1969), pp. 17 ff., 21–22, 37.

30. An example of this is the hostility aroused by Gustav Stresemann among many of his National Liberal colleagues: A. Thimme, *Gustav Stresemann* (Hanover and Frankfurt, 1957), pp. 18–19, and Warren, *Kingdom* (1964), pp. 29–30.

31. Complaints about the alienation of the *Bürgertum* from politics are to be found in many contemporary accounts: Hugo Graf Lerchenfeld, *Erinnerungen und Denkwürdigkeiten 1843 bis 1925*, 2d ed. (Berlin, 1935), p. 264; Georg Reicke, *Ein Bürger zwischen Welt und Stadt* (Berlin, 1923), p. 48; August Stein [Irenäus], *Es war alles ganz anders. Aus der Werkstätte eines politischen Journalisten* (Frankfurt, 1922), pp. 141–43; W. Sombart, *Volkswirtschaft* (1909), p. 128.

32. F. Paulsen, *The German Universities and University Study* (New York, 1906), p. 355. Some other examples: Walther Goetz, *Historiker in meiner Zeit* (Cologne and Graz, 1957), p. 37, and Hellpach, *Wirken* (1948–49), 1:207–8. The classic statements of the problematic relationship between scholarship and politics are probably Max Weber's essays, "Politics as a Vocation" and "Science as a Vocation" (1918), reprinted in *From Max Weber*, ed. H. Gerth and C. W. Mills (New York, 1958). See also F. Ringer, *Decline* (1969), especially pp. 134 ff.

33. Georg Friedrich Knapp, as quoted in John Williamson, *Karl Helfferich, 1872–1924* (Princeton, 1971), p. 15. Knapp's daughter recalled that "politics" was never discussed in her parents' home: E. Heuss-Knapp, *Ausblick vom Münsterturm* (Berlin, 1934), p. 16.

34. Ulrich Scheuner, "Das Wesen des Staates und der Begriff des Politischen in der neueren Staatslehre," in K. Hesse et al., eds., *Staatsverfassung und Kirchenordnung. Festgabe für Rudolf Smend* (Tübingen, 1962), pp. 225–62; Theodor Schieder, "Wandlungen des Staates in der Neuzeit," *HZ* 216, no. 2 (April 1973): 274–75; Kurt Sontheimer, *Antidemokratisches Denken in der Weimarer Republik: Die politischen Ideen des deutschen Nationalismus zwischen 1918 und 1933* (Munich, 1962), pp. 82 ff.

35. Dieter Lindenlaub, *Richtungskämpfe im Verein für Sozialpolitik. Wissenschaft und Sozialpolitik im Kaiserreich* (Wiesbaden, 1967), 1:14, 22 ff.

36. See, for example, Hans-Heinz Krill, *Die Rankerenaissance. Max Lenz und Erich Marcks. Ein Beitrag zum historisch-politischen Denken in Deutschland 1880–1935* (Berlin, 1962).

37. Nipperdey, "Jugend" (1974), p. 92.

38. Quoted in R. H. Samuel and R. H. Thomas, *Education and Society in Modern Germany* (London, 1949), p. 120.

39. Henning, *Bürgertum* (1972), pp. 308 ff., 352 ff. Two examples: Brecht, *Nähe* (1966), pp. 43, 91 ff., and Georg Michaelis, *Für Staat und Volk. Eine Lebensgeschichte* (Berlin, 1922), p. 263.

40. *Franz Adickes. Sein Leben und sein Werk* (Frankfurt, 1929). Some other examples: Heinrich Tramm, *Heinrich Tramm. Stadtdirektor von Hannover 1854–1932: Ein Lebensbild* (Hanover, 1932), p. 16, and Friedrich Horstmann, "Dr. Wilhelm Schmiedling, Oberbürgermeister der Stadt Dortmund 1836–1910," *Beiträge zur Ge-*

schichte Dortmunds und der Grafschaft Mark, 58 (1962): 318.

41. Hans Luther, *Politiker ohne Partei: Erinnerungen* (Stuttgart, 1960). See also W. Hofmann, *Zwischen Rathaus und Reichskanzler. Die Oberbürgermeister in der Kommunal- und Staatspolitik des Deutschen Reiches von 1890 bis 1933* (Stuttgart, 1974).

42. Horst Schallenberger, *Untersuchungen zum Geschichtsbild der Wilhelminischen Ära und der Weimarer Zeit: Eine vergleichende Schulbuchanalyse deutscher Schulgeschichtsbücher aus der Zeit von 1888 bis 1933* (Ratingen-near-Düsseldorf, 1964), p. 57.

43. A good example of this is the *Deutsche Revue*, which I surveyed for the years 1890 to 1914. See also Bramstedt, *Aristocracy* (1964), on the *Gartenlaube*, and J. Haacke, *Julius Rodenberg und die Deutsche Rundschau* (Heidelberg, 1950), pp. 163 ff.

44. M. Stürmer, "Bismarck in Perspective," *CEH* 4, no. 4 (December, 1971): 291–331, has a brief discussion of the Bismarck cult.

45. Brecht, *Nähe* (1966), p. 17. Another example: Seyffardt, *Erinnerungen* (1900), p. 356.

46. Fontane, *Zwanzig* (1967), p. 270 n. Cf. Ulrich von Wilamowitz-Moellendorf, *My Recollections, 1848–1914* (London, 1930), p. 230.

47. Quoted in Dressel, *Wahlen* (1961), p. 225. Another example is quoted in Henning, *Geschichte* (1965), p. 37.

48. Otto Baumgarten, *Meine Lebensgeschichte* (Tübingen, 1928), pp. 216–17.

49. Otto Heinemann, *Kronenorden Vierter Klasse. Das Leben des Prokuristen Heinemann, 1864–1944* (Düsseldorf, 1969), pp. 93–94. Two other examples: *AZ*, July 4, 1905, quoting a National Liberal meeting in the Palatinate, and Möckl, *Prinzregentenzeit* (1972), pp. 292–93 n., on a meeting in Munich in 1889.

50. This intensity of affiliational loyalties among sectors of the middle strata leads me to have some reservations about Dahrendorf's dichotomy between public and private behavior in Germany (see *Society* [1969] pp. 258 ff.).

51. I have discussed the role of the VfSP as a substitute form of political action in *Career* (1966), especially in chap. 4.

52. K. A. von Müller, *Aus Gärten der Vergangenheit. Erinnerungen, 1882–1914* (Stuttgart, 1958), p. 396. Some similar comments can be found in: Hellpach, *Wirken* (1948–49), 1:396–98; E. Heuss-Knapp, *Ausblick vom Münsterturm. Erlebtes aus dem Elsass und dem Reich* (Berlin, 1934), p. 68; Ludwig Curtius, *Deutsche und antike Welt. Lebenserinnerungen* (Stuttgart, 1951), pp. 160 ff.; Meinecke, *Strassburg* (1949) in *Werke* (1957–68), 8:214.

53. Nipperdey, "Jugend" (1974), p. 94. For two examples of organizations seeking "cultural renewal," see: Daniel Gasman, *The Scientific Origins of National Socialism: Social Darwinism in Ernst Haeckel and the German Monist League* (London and New York, 1971), pp. 20 ff., and Gerhard Kratzsch, *Kunstwart und Dürerbund. Ein Beitrag zur Sozialgeschichte der deutschen Gebildeten in der Epoche des Imperialismus* (Göttingen, 1969), especially pp. 138 ff. Also of interest on these issues is Stern, "Consequences" (1960).

54. When a National Liberal newspaper declared in 1908 that business had to be "liberal or nothing," an interest-group executive pointed out that "industry as a whole does not need a political standpoint." Quoted in Bertram, *Wahlen* (1964), p. 30. The contemporary literature is filled with laments about the political "apathy" of German businessmen: J. Riesser, quoted in *EGK 1909*, pp. 198 ff.; Cecil, *Ballin* (1967), pp.

129 ff.; J. Williamson, *Karl Helfferich* (Princeton, 1971), p. 28; Kaelble, *Interessenpolitik* (1967), pp. 77 ff.

55. M. Lamberti, "The Attempt to Form a Jewish Bloc: Jewish Notables and Politics in Wilhelmian Germany," *CEH* 3, nos. 1–2 (March–June 1970): 73–93. See also I. Schorsch, *Jewish Reactions to German Anti-Semitism, 1870–1914* (New York, 1972).

56. Quoted in Knoll, *Führungsauslese* (1957), p. 95, n. 106. See also Sheehan, "Liberalism and the City" (1971).

57. G. von Diest, *Aus dem Leben eines Glücklichen* (Berlin, 1904), pp. 464–65, on Merseberg, and Emil Kraatz, *Aus dem Leben eines Bürgermeisters* (Leipzig, 1914), pp. 606 ff., on Naumburg. For some other examples, see: Schmitt, *Vereinsleben* (1963), and Meyer, *Vereinswesen* (1970). Hopwood, "Paladins" (1974), has some very useful comments on local organizations. See also L. Beutin, "Die 'Massengesellschaft' im 19. Jahrhundert," in *Gesammelte Schriften zur Wirtschafts- und Sozialgeschichte* (Cologne and Graz, 1963), pp. 337–38, and H. Staudinger, *Individuum und Gemeinschaft in der Kulturorganisation des Vereins* (Jena, 1913), especially pp. 79 ff.

58. For some contemporary views on *Vereinsmeierei*, see Schmitt, *Vereinsleben* (1963), p. 63, and especially Tucholsky's poem, "Das Mitglied," quoted on pp. 94–95.

59. The concept of "social milieu" is from M. R. Lepsius, "Parteisystem" (1966), and *Nationalismus* (1966).

Chapter 16

1. Quoted in Schwarz, "Attitudes" (1961), pp. 241–42.

2. On the National Liberals' Reichstag *Fraktion*, see: Kalkoff, *Parlamentarier* (1917), p. 53; Jaeger, *Unternehmer* (1967), pp. 47, 50–56; Bertram, *Wahlen* (1964), pp. 160–61; O'Donnell, "Liberalism" (1973), pp. 51 ff., 61 ff.

Molt, *Reichstag* (1963), is flawed in detail but is still of considerable interest.

3. Thieme, *Liberalismus* (1963), pp. 20 ff.; Kalkoff, *Fraktion* (1913), pp. 101–56, and *Parlamentarier* (1917), pp. 141–258; Jaeger, *Unternehmer* (1967), pp. 67 ff.; Kaelble, *Interessenpolitik* (1967), p. 116.

4. Kalkoff, *Parlamentarier* (1917), pp. 273, 305; Jaeger, *Unternehmer* (1967), p. 73 ff., and E. Heintz, *Der Beamtenabgeordnete im Bayerischen Landtag* (Berlin, 1966), pp. 83–84. On the other state parliaments, see Kalkoff, pp. 339 ff., 370 ff., 406 ff., and Jaeger, pp. 77–79.

5. Kriegbaum, *Tätigkeit* (1962), surveys Heyl's career. See Henning, *Bürgertum* (1972), p. 277, on Hanover, and pp. 352 ff., on the Rhineland; Schelm, *Volkspartei* (1964), p. 39 and n. 104, on Braunschweig. O'Donnell, "Liberalism" (1973), especially pp. 396 ff., has a good account of officials' political role in the western provinces of Prussia. Jaeger, *Unternehmer* (1967), p. 115, deals with businessmen on the local level.

6. Nipperdey, *Organisation* (1961), pp. 103 ff. See, for example, Henning, *Geschichte* (1965), appendix, table 3, on Essen.

7. Quoted in Reiss, *Bassermann* (1967), p. 17.

8. Quoted in Reimann, *Müller-Meiningen* (1968), p. 10.

9. Jaeger, *Unternehmer* (1967), pp. 121 ff., and Elm, *Fortschritt* (1968), pp. 18 ff.

10. Bertram, *Wahlen* (1964), pp. 161 ff. The social composition of the Progressive *Fraktion* in the Prussian Landtag can be found in the official returns for the elections of 1903, 1908, and 1913: Georg Evert, "Landtagswahlen" (1905) and (1909) and Höpker, "Landtagswahlen" (1916).

11. VfSP, *Schriften*, 117:125–29, on Berlin; Hellpach, *Wirken* (1948–49), 1:31 ff. Some other examples: O. Meyer, *Von Bismarck zu Hitler, Erinnerungen und Betrachtungen*, 2d ed. (Offenbach, 1948), pp. 71 ff.; Reimann, *Müller* (1968), p. 14; C. Funck, *Lebenserinnerungen* (Frankfurt, 1921).

12. Simon, *Demokraten* (1969), p. 28. Cf. data on Fortschrittliche Volkspartei in Robson, "Liberalism" (1966), p. 97.

13. See: *VZ*, November 2, 1911, on candidates for the Berlin city council; *KP* 4, no. 5 (1905): 107, on the Stuttgart city council; and VfSP, *Schriften*, 117: 114, on the Frankfurt city council.

14. As noted above, my calculations are based on the official returns unless another source is given. For a citation to these data, see above, chap. 11, n. 24.

15. Kurt, *Wahlen* (1966), pp. 42–43; Simon, *Demokraten* (1969), pp. 30 ff.; Ehrenfeuchter, "Willensbildung" (1951). Thränhardt, *Wahlen* (1973), has some useful material on Bavaria. He also calls attention to the dairy farmers in the Allgäu who, although staunchly Catholic, continued to vote liberal until the First World War: see *Wahlen*, pp. 71 ff.

16. The following regional clusters were apparent in 1912: the National Liberals, with a national total of 45 WKe, won 8 in Hanover, 8 in the Rhineland and Westphalia, 3 in Hesse, 4 in Baden, and 6 in the smaller states; the Progressives, with a total of 42 seats, won 5 in Liegnitz (eastern Prussia), 7 in Schleswig-Holstein, 6 in Württemberg, and 9 in the smaller states.

17. Schneider, "Anfänge" (1965), pp. 85 ff.

18. Here is the distribution of WKe won by the liberals in 1912 according to population:

WKe under 100,000 (61) : NL 4 (6.5%), FVP 10 (16.4%)
        100–150,000 (181) : NL 24 (13.2%), FVP 19 (10.5%)
        150–200,000 (85) : NL 12 (14.1%), FVP 11 (12.9%)
        over 200,000 (70) : NL 5 (7.1%), FVP 2 (2.8%)
Total   (397) : NL 45 (11.3%), FVP 42 (10.5%)

19. In Hanover in 1912, the National Liberals won 25 percent of the vote overall, 28.3 percent in rural areas and 17.3 percent in towns with more than 10,000 inhabitants. In the east Prussian district of Marienwerder, the situation was reversed: 20.7 percent overall, 17.2 percent in rural areas, and 39.2 percent in large towns and cities. The left liberals, on the other hand, usually did better in more urban regions: in Stralsund, for instance, they won 31.2 percent of the vote overall, 21 percent in rural areas, and 48.4 percent in the towns. For the situation elsewhere, see: Klein, "Reichstagswahlen" (1968); Ehrenfeuchter, "Willensbildung" (1951); Schelm, *Volkspartei* (1964), especially p. 39; Thränhardt, *Wahlen* (1973), especially pp. 68 ff.

20. In the Baden Landtag elections of 1905 and 1909, liberals won 35.8 percent and 32.1 percent of the total vote, but 43.5 percent and 38.2 percent in urban districts. Computed from Baden, *StJb* (1913).

21. O'Donnell, "Liberalism" (1973), p. 484.

22. Heberle, *Democracy* (1945), chap. 2; Rubinstein, *Partei* (1935), pp. 22 ff., on Liegnitz; Ehrenfeuchter, "Willensbildung" (1951), pp. 160 ff., 198, on Hanover;

Simon, *Demokraten* (1969), pp. 3–6, on Württemberg. For some general comments on politics in rural areas, see James Hunt, "Peasants, Grain Tariffs and Meat Quotas: Imperial German Protectionism Reexamined," *CEH* 7, no. 4 (December 1974): 311–31.

23. Ehrenfeuchter, "Willensbildung" (1951), pp. 165 ff.

24. Simon, *Demokraten* (1969), pp. 25–36. A somewhat similar pattern existed in Frankfurt, as can be seen in the data on voting in the local elections of 1904, given in VfSP, *Schriften*, 118:112–13. See also *KP* (1904), 4:403–6.

25. Elm, *Fortschritt* (1968), pp. 9 ff.; Zunkel, *Unternehmer* (1962), pp. 227–28; Wegner, *Barth* (1968), pp. 99–101.

26. One expression of this was the rather unfavorable ratio for both the liberal parties between total votes and delegates elected.

Reich average	30,750	voters / delegate
National Liberals	37,000	" / "
Fortschriftliche VP	35,000	" / "

Given in Bertram, *Wahlen* (1964), p. 215.

27. Hans Block, "Das Wahlergebnis in Sachsen," *Die neue Zeit* 25 (February 1907): 668ff. Cf. Ehrenfeuchter, "Willensbildung" (1951), p. 309, for a similar situation in Hanover.

28. Two examples of permanent shifts away from the liberals: Schneider, "Anfänge" (1956), p. 176, on the Palatinate, and Vogel and Haungs, *Wahlkampf* (1965), pp. 89 ff., on Heidelberg. On the general issue of Social Democracy and the "middle strata," see Michels, "Sozialdemokratie" (1906), pp. 502 ff., and R. Blank, "Die soziale Zusammensetzung der sozialdemokratischen Wählerschaft Deutschlands," *ASW* 20 (1905): 507–53, with the critical comments in G. A. Ritter, *Die Arbeiterbewegung im Wilhelminischen Reich* (Berlin-Dahlem, 1963), pp. 77–78 n.

29. In "Identification" (1972), p. 1221, n. 46, Phillips Shively describes the preliminary conclusions of his research on German elections from 1871 to 1912 in the following way: "Two major gulfs in party distance appear to have determined voting during the Empire—that between the Center Party and all other parties, and that between the Social Democrats and all other parties." He also finds some traces of urban-rural splits over constitutional issues but regards the distance between the non-Catholic, nonworking-class parties to be rather small. This meant that conservatives and liberals continually competed for the same sort of voters.

30. See, for example, the persistent restlessness reflected in the returns for Königsberg WKe 2 and 4, Gumbinnen WK 1, and Merseberg Wk 7.

31. On the Bund der Landwirte, see Puhle, *Interessenpolitik* (1966), especially pp. 193 ff. on the Bund and the National Liberals. For the situation in the southwest see Hunt, "Egalitarianism" (1975).

Richard Levy, *The Downfall of the Anti-Semitic Parties in Imperial Germany* (New Haven, 1975), discusses anti-Semitism's electoral support; see especially chaps. 2–4.

The best-studied case of the movement of liberal voters to the radical right is that of Hesse: in addition to White, *Party* (1976), see W. Schlau, *Politik und Bewusstsein. Voraussetzungen und Strukturen politischer Bildung in ländlichen Gemeinden* (Cologne, 1971), pp. 385 ff., and W. Menges and W. Toonen, "Deutsche Parteientwicklung und Wahlentscheidungen seit 1871, unter besonderer Berücksichtigung der Entstehung des politischen Bildes von Hessen," *Sociaal Kompas* 4, no. 2 (1956): 68–99.

32. E. Würzburger, "Die Partei der Nichtwähler," *JbbNS*, 3d ser., 33 (1907): 381–89. For more on this, plus a guide to the recent literature, see Lavies, *Nichtwählen* (1973).

33. Data on income, production, and the distribution of the labor force can be found in: G. Bry, *Wages in Germany, 1871–1945* (Princeton, 1960), and Hoffmann, *Wachstum* (1965). Frank B. Tipton, "Farm Labor and Power Politics: Germany, 1850–1914," *JEH* 34, no. 4 (December 1974): 951–79, is a good recent treatment of agricultural trends. Borchardt, "Wachstumsdifferenzierung" (1968), analyzes regional diversity.

On the uneven growth rate of different enterprises and branches, see Nussbaum, *Unternehmer* (1966), pp. 19 ff., and the figures in Germany, *StJb* (1914), pp. 59–60.

34. For example, Wilhelm Roscher wrote in 1892: "Unfortunately it appears that at the highest stages of civilization a division between a few very rich people and a huge proletariat is unavoidable." Quoted in Winkler, *Mittelstand* (1972), p. 26. Additional quotes can be found in Angel-Volkov, "'Decline'" (1974), pp. 166–67.

35. Wernicke, *Kapitalismus* (1907), pp. 186 ff., has data on retail trade. Hengel, "Warenhaus" (1952), p. 18, estimates that by 1908 only about 2 percent of retail trade was done by department stores; their share of the trade was growing, however, and was concentrated in a few large cities. On other small enterprises, see the essays by Fischer, *Wirtschaft* (1972), and the careful reconsideration of the problem in Angel-Volkov, "'Decline'" (1974). Also of use are: Winkler, *Mittelstand* (1972); A. Noll, "Wirtschaftliche und soziale Entwicklung des Handwerks in der zweiten Phase der Industrialisierung," in Rüegg and Neuloh, eds., *Theorie* (1971), 193–212; O. Thissen, *Beiträge zur Geschichte des Handwerks in Preussen* (Tübingen, 1901).

36. There are data on the distribution of arable land, as well as a good discussion of the problems involved in using them, in Karl Grünberg, "Agrarverfassung: Begriffliches und Zuständliches," *Grundriss der Sozialökonomik* (Tübingen, 1922), 7:137. For divisions within agriculture, see Hunt, "Peasants" (1974).

37. The best analysis of white-collar employees is Jürgen Kocka's masterful study of the Siemens firm, *Unternehmensverwaltung* (1969). See also: Fritz Croner, *Soziologie der Angestellten* (Cologne and Berlin, 1962); Heinz Potthoff, "Die deutsche Privatbeamtenschaft nach der Berufs-und Betriebszählung 1907," *ASGS* 32 (1911): 124–35; Emil Lederer, *Die Privatangestellten in der modernen Wirtschaftsentwicklung* (Tübingen, 1912). On the growth of the bureaucracy, see: John Röhl, "Higher Civil Servants in Germany, 1890–1900," *JCH* 2, no. 3 (1967): 101–22; Otto Hintze, "Der Beamtenstand," *Abhandlungen* (1962–67), 2:66–125; John P. Cullity, "The Growth of Governmental Employment in Germany, 1882–1950," *ZfGS* 123, no. 2 (April 1967): 201–17.

38. This process involved the acceleration of trends apparent since midcentury: see above, chaps. 6 and 11.

There are data on income inequalities in: David Crew, "Definitions of Modernity: Social Mobility in a German Town, 1880–1901," *JSH* 7, no. 1 (Fall 1973): 51–74; Helmuth Croon, "Die Einwirkungen der Industrialisierung auf die gesellschaftliche Schichtung der Bevölkerung im rheinisch-westfälischen Industriegebiet," *RV* 20, no. 3 (1955): 301–16; Rolf Engelsing, "Die wirtschaftliche und soziale Differenzierung der deutschen kaufmännischen Angestellten im In- und Ausland, 1690–1900," in Engelsing, *Sozialgeschichte* (1973), pp. 51–111; W. Gutsche, "Die Veränderungen in der Wirtschaftsstruktur und der Differenzierungsprozess innerhalb des Bürgertums der

Stadt Erfurt in den ersten Jahren der Herrschaft des Imperialismus (Ende des 19. Jahrhunderts bis 1914)," *JbG* 20 (1974): 343–71.

Social mobility and education are discussed in H. Kaelble, "Chancenungleichheit und akademische Ausbildung in Deutschland, 1910–1960," *GuG* 1, no. 1 (1975): 121–49. Ringer, *Decline* (1969), treats the differences within educated elites.

In a careful study of officials in Düsseldorf, Otto Most shows how difficult it was for state employees to maintain a "respectable" style of life in the face of rising costs: "Zur Wirtschafts- und Sozialstatistik der höheren Beamten in Preussen," *SJb* 39, no. 1 (1915): 181–218.

39. A list of interest groups representing employers, employees, and wage earners, together with data on their membership and income, can be found in Germany, *Reichsarbeitsblatt*, special no. 2 (1915). These data are summarized in Germany, *StJb* (1914), pp. 430 ff.

40. Quoted in Gerhard Kessler, *Die deutschen Arbeitgeberverbände* (VfSP, *Schriften*, vol. 124 [Leipzig, 1907]), p. 7.

41. Kaelble, *Interessenpolitik* (1967), and "Interessenverbände" (1971); H. König, *Entstehung und Wirkungsweise von Fachverbänden der Nahrungs- und Genussmittelindustrie* (Berlin, 1965); H. Schmitt, *Enstehung und Wandlungen der Zielsetzungen, der Struktur und der Wirkungen der Berufsverbände* (Berlin, 1966); Wein, *Verbandsbildung* (1968).

The Arbeitgeberverbände were formed to assist employers in dealing with organized labor, especially with strikes. Kessler's monograph (see n. 40 above) is out of date, but still informative. See also Stegmann, *Erben* (1970), pp. 34–37, and, for a specific case, Karl Werner, "Gründung des Deutschen Arbeitgeberbundes für das Baugewerbe 1899 und seine Entwicklung bis 1910," in Varain, ed., *Interessenverbände* (1973), 197–203.

42. Nussbaum, *Unternehmer* (1966), pp. 38 ff.

43. See H. J. Varain, *Freie Gewerkschaften, Sozialdemokratie und Staat* (Düsseldorf, 1956), on the unions; Puhle, *Interessenpolitik* (1967), on the Bund der Landwirte; Winkler, "Mittelstand" (1971) and *Mittelstand* (1972), on the craftsmen and shopkeepers.

44. Emil Lederer, "Die ökonomische Element und die politischen Ideen im modernen Parteiwesens," *ZfP* 5, no. 4 (1912): 557. For some similar statements, see: A. Thimme, *Hans Delbrück als Kritiker der Wilhelminischen Epoche* (Düsseldorf, 1955), p. 23, n. 6, quoting Delbrück in 1896; Otto Richter, *Geschichte der Stadt Dresden in den Jahren 1871–1902* (Dresden, 1903), p. 127; Hermann Krueger, "Historische und kritische Untersuchungen über die freien Interessenvertretungen von Industrie, Handel und Gewerbe in Deutschland," *SJb* 32, no. 4 (1908): 325–58; 33, no. 2 (1909): 189–240.

45. This problem is discussed in Sheehan, "Leadership" (1968), Nipperdey, "Grundzüge" (1965), and the essays by Fraenkel, *Deutschland* (1968). Gustav Schmidt has recently argued that just before 1914 the parties were beginning to reassert themselves vis-à-vis the *Verbände*: "Blockbildungen" (1972), pp. 17 ff.

46. On the relationship between business interests and the National Liberals, see Thieme, *Liberalismus* (1963), pp. 34 ff. Albert Ballin is a good example of the restlessness many entrepreneurs felt with the liberal parties: see Cecil, *Ballin* (1967).

47. Quoted in Winkler, *Mittelstand* (1972), p. 219, n. 83. Winkler's monograph and his article on "Mittelstand" (1971) are good analyses of this process.

48. O'Donnell, "Liberalism" (1973), p. 77.

49. In 1912, 26 National Liberal delegates and 27 Progressives lived outside of the districts in which they were elected; 10 National Liberals and 9 Progressives lived in Berlin: Blaustein, "Abteilung" (1912), pp. 370 ff.

50. Electoral statement of January 1890, *EGK 1890*, p. 11. See the similar views expressed at the party convention of 1891, *EGK 1891*, p. 93, and in the declaration of 1896 reprinted in Mommsen, *Parteiprogramme* (1964), pp. 164 ff.

51. Quoted in Seyffardt, *Erinnerungen* (1900), pp. 595–96.

52. Quoted in Eschenburg, *Kaiserreich* (1929), p. 122. See also the articles on parties and interests in *NZ*, April–May 1908, especially May 14.

53. Reprinted in Mommsen, *Parteiprogramme* (1964), pp. 168 ff.

54. Quoted in Elm, *Fortschritt* (1968), p. 16. See also Richter's last speech in the Prussian Landtag (June 1904), quoted in Rachfahl, "Richter" (1910), p. 370.

55. Elm, *Fortschritt* (1968), pp. 18 ff.; Wegner, *Barth* (1968), pp. 99–101; Rachfahl, "Richter" (1912), pp. 347–48. On the situation in the south, see Simon, *Demokraten* (1969), pp. 42–43.

56. Quoted in Struve, *Elites* (1973), p. 99. The literature on Naumann is cited below, chap. 17, n. 46.

57. Quoted in Robson, "Liberalism" (1966), p. 101.

58. Mommsen, *Parteiprogramme* (1964), pp. 173, 178.

59. Gustav Schmoller, *Was verstehen wir unter dem Mittelstande?* (Göttingen, 1897). See Winkler, *Mittelstand* (1972), p. 24.

60. Leo Müffelmann, *Die moderne Mittelstandsbewegung* (Leipzig and Berlin, 1913); Wernicke, *Kapitalismus* (1907), pp. 327–28.

61. Quoted in Winkler, "Mittelstand" (1971), p. 173. See also the material in Kocka, *Unternehmensverwaltung* (1969), p. 520, and A. Noll, "Wirtschaftliche und soziale Entwicklung des Handwerks in der zweiten Phase der Industrialisierung," in Rüegg and Neuloh, eds., *Theorie* (1971), pp. 206 ff.

62. Some examples: anon., "Bürgertum," *DR* 20 (1895): pp. 81 ff.; F. von Schulte, "Nationalsünden," *DR* 21 (1896): 89–97, 291–99, and "Bürgertum," *DR* 31 (1906): 65 ff. Sombart, *Volkswirtschaft* (1909), pp. 508–9; Hugo Preuss, *Entwicklungsgeschichte der deutschen Städteverfassung* (Leipzig, 1906), p. 374.

63. "Der Nationalstaat und die Volkswirtschaftspolitik" (1895), in *Schriften* (1958), p. 20. On this famous speech, see A. Bergstraesser, "Max Webers Antrittsvorlesung in zeitgeschichtlicher Perspektive," *VfZ* 5, no. 3 (July 1957): 209–19. My own view of Weber has been most influenced by the work of W. J. Mommsen; see especially: *Weber* (1959) and *The Age of Bureaucracy. Perspectives on the Political Sociology of Max Weber* (Oxford, 1974).

64. Fritz Friedrich in *PJbb* (1907), quoted in W. Hock, *Liberales Denken* (1957), p. 69. Cf. Weber's remarks in 1893, quoted in R. Bendix, *Max Weber: An Intellectual Portrait* (New York, 1959), p. 30.

65. Meinecke, "Alfred Dove und der klassische Liberalismus im Neuen Reich" (1925), in *Werke* (1957–69), 7:411. See also Meinecke's obituary for Dove (1916), in *Werke*, 7, especially pp. 382–83, and his "Erlebtes," in *Werke*, 8:101.

66. A. Mitzman, *Sociology and Estrangement. Three Sociologists of Imperial Germany* (New York, 1973), and G. Lukács, *Die Zerstörung der Vernunft* (Neuwied, 1962), pp. 512 ff.

67. Some examples: Robert Gaupp, "Die wachsende Nervösität unserer Zeit," *DR* 39 (1909): 154–66; Dietrich Schäfer, "Die Grossstadt," *Jb der Gehe- Stiftung*, 9

(1903); D. Gasman, *The Scientific Origins of National Socialism: Social Darwinism in Ernst Haeckel and the German Monist League* (London and New York, 1971), pp. 22–23. See also: A. Lees, "Debates" (1975); Schwarz, "Attitudes" (1961), pp. 206 ff.; Klaus Bergmann, *Agraromantik und Grossstadtfeindschaft* (Meisenheim-am-Glan, 1970); Dietrich Rüschemeyer, "Modernisierung und die Gebildeten im kaiserlichen Deutschland," in Ludz, ed., *Soziologie* (1972), 515–29.

68. Ringer, *Decline* (1969).

69. Rudolf Gneist, *Die nationale Rechtsidee von den Ständen und das Dreiklassenwahlsystem* (Berlin, 1894), especially chap. 16, and Karl Helfferich, *Deutschlands Volkswohlstand 1888–1913* (Berlin, 1913).

70. A good example of these mixed feelings can be found in the book prepared to celebrate the twenty-fifth anniversary of William II's coronation: S. Korte et al., eds., *Deutschland unter Wilhelm II*, 4 vols. (Berlin, 1916). See also: a speech from 1911 reprinted in Theodor Spitta, *Aus meinem Leben. Bürger und Bürgermeister in Bremen* (Munich, 1969), pp. 60 ff., and Meinecke, "Strassburg," in *Werke* (1957–69), 8:212, 220.

Additional material can be found in Schwarz, "Attitudes" (1961); Lees, "Debates" (1975); Michael Salewski, "'Neujahr 1900.' Die Säkularwende in zeitgenossischer Sicht," *AfK* 52, no. 2 (1971): 335–81; Bruno Seidel, "Zeitgeist und Wirtschaftsgesinnung in Deutschland der Jahrhundertwende." *SJb* 83, no. 2 (1963): 129–52; Karl Heinrich Höfele, "Selbstverständnis und Zeitkritik des deutschen Bürgertums vor dem ersten Weltkrieg," *Zeitschrift für Religions- und Geistesgeschichte* 8, no. 1 (1956): 40–56.

71. Wehler, "Sozialdarwinismus" (1973), and Struve, *Elites* (1973), pp. 46 ff. For an example, see Kocka's description of Wilhelm von Siemens in *Unternehmensverwaltung* (1969), pp. 385–86.

72. Sheehan, *Career* (1966), pp. 161 ff.

73. This is based on F. Blaich, "Die Anfänge der deutschen Antikartellpolitik zwischen 1897 und 1914," *JbS*, 21, no. 2 (1970): 127–50, and idem, *Kartell- und Monopolpolitik im kaiserlichen Deutschland* (Düsseldorf, 1973).

74. Sheehan, *Career* (1966), p. 159.

Chapter 17

1. Kulemann, *Erinnerungen* (1911), p. 241.

2. Some examples: Paul Busching, "Der Liberalismus in Bayern," *Süddeutsche Monatshefte* 6, no. 2 (November 1909): 590–600; Blaustein, *Uneinigkeit* (1911); Otto Harnack, "Die Zukunft des deutschen Liberalismus," *März*, 4, no. 7 (1910): 1–4.

3. Richter's remark is quoted in Pachnicke, *Männer* (1930), p. 32; Bassermann in Eschenburg, *Kaiserreich* (1929), p. 21.

4. There is a good account of this process in White, *Party* (1976). See also O'Donnell, "Liberalism" (1973), pp. 204 ff.

5. The best treatment of Miquel during this period remains Herzfeld's biography (1938); see also Miquel, "Briefe" (1912–13), especially 10, no. 1:171.

The classic analysis of the Sammlung is in E. Kehr, *Schlachtflottenbau und Parteipolitik, 1894–1901* (Berlin, 1930). See also John Röhl, *Germany without Bismarck: The Crisis of Government in the Second Reich, 1890–1900* (London, 1967), pp. 246 ff.; Stegmann, *Erben* (1970), pp. 63 ff. There is a useful critique of this literature in

Barkin, *Controversy* (1970), pp. 274–75, n. 1, and W. J. Mommsen, "Domestic Factors in German Foreign Policy before 1914," *CEH* 6, no. 1 (March 1973): 3–43.

6. Herzfeld, *Miquel* (1938), 2:526.

7. Quoted in Stegmann, *Erben* (1970), p. 66.

8. Miquel was ennobled in 1897; his daughter married an aristocratic landowner, one son became a cavalry officer, another a bureaucrat, a third joined the diplomatic corps.

Lamar Cecil, "The Creation of Nobles in Prussia, 1871–1918," *AHR* 75, no. 3 (February 1970): 757–95, has shown that direct ennoblement was rather infrequent, but the chance of obtaining honors, medals, and orders was much greater. For some examples, see: Paul Hermann Mertes, "Zum Sozialprofil der Oberschicht im Ruhrgebiet. Dargestellt an den Dortmunder Kommerzienräten," *Beiträge zur Geschichte Dortmunds und der Grafschaft Mark*, 67 (1971): 165–226, and Joachim Remak, *The Gentle Critic: Theodor Fontane and German Politics 1848–1898* (Syracuse, 1964), p. 67. For more on this issue, see Sheehan, "Conflict" (1972).

9. On the foreign political aspects of the Sammlung, see my Conclusion and the literature cited in n. 4.

10. The number of WKe which moved back and forth between National Liberals and one of the conservative parties increased from two in 1890 to nine in 1912. For some examples of regional diversity, see Ehrenfeuchter, "Willensbildung" (1951), pp. 166 ff. (Hanover WK 19), and 202–3 (Hanover WK 4).

11. Heckart, *Bassermann* (1974), greatly overestimates the chances for a *Grossblock* on the national level, but she does provide a great deal of interesting information on its origins and development; see especially pp. 91 ff. Schlemmer, "Rolle" (1953), pp. 73 ff., discusses Social Democracy in Baden. Jürgen Thiel, *Die Grossblockpolitik der Nationalliberalen Partei Badens 1905 bis 1914* (Stuttgart, 1976) appeared too late for me to use it. On Bavaria, see: Möckl, *Prinzregentenzeit* (1972); Otto Gessler's memoir of prewar liberalism in *Reichswehrpolitik in der Weimarer Zeit* (Stuttgart, 1958), pp. 543–45; Link, "Nationalverein" (1964).

12. When educational or religious issues became important in national politics, the same kind of pressure for an alliance to the left could operate in the Reichstag. See, for example, the controversy in 1900 over the "Lex Heinze" as described in *EGK 1900*, pp. 23 ff., 40, 51, 73 ff.

13. White, *Party* (1976), especially p. 151.

14. On the tariff controversy, see: Barkin, *Controversy* (1970); G. Schöne, *Die Verflechtung wirtschaftlicher und politischer Motive in der Haltung der Parteien zum Bülowschen Zolltarif* (1901–2) (Diss., Halle, 1934); Jaeger, *Unternehmer* (1967), pp. 116 ff.; Stegmann, *Erben* (1970), pp. 80 ff. The canal controversy at the turn of the century generated a similar but not identical set of conflicts: see Hannelore Horn, *Der Kampf um den Bau des Mittellandkanals: Eine Politologische Untersuchung über die Rolle eines wirtschaftlichen Interessenverbandes im Preussen Wilhelms II* (Cologne and Opladen, 1964), especially pp. 291 ff.

15. On Sozialpolitik after 1890, see: K. E. Born, *Staat und Sozialpolitik seit Bismarcks Sturz* (Wiesbaden, 1957), and Born and P. Rassow, *Akten zur staatlichen Sozialpolitik in Deutschland* (Wiesbaden, 1959). The National Liberals' response to the so-called *Umsturzvorlage* of 1894 is a good example of their divisions on this subject: J. A. Nichols, *Germany after Bismarck* (Cambridge, Mass., 1958), pp. 331 ff.; Born, *Staat* (1954), pp. 112 ff.; *EGK 1895*, p. 5 (Bennigsen's speech on the law), and pp. 134 ff. (final vote).

Some other examples of National Liberal views on social policy: Herzfeld, *Miquel* (1938), 2:289 ff.; Bein, *Hammacher* (1932), pp. 124 ff.; Kulemann, *Erinnerungen* (1911), pp. 152 ff.

16. Kaelble, *Interessenpolitik* (1967) and "Interessenverbände" (1971), have a great deal of useful information on conflicts within the industrial establishment. See also Nussbaum, *Unternehmer* (1966), and F. Blaich, *Kartell* (1973).

17. The handicrafts law is analyzed in Linke, "Rolle" (1955), pp. 110 ff. and 138 ff., and Winkler, *Mittelstand* (1972), pp. 44 ff. For other efforts by the National Liberals to attract the proprietary *Mittelstand*, see: Linke, "Rolle" (1955), pp. 172 ff.; Wein, *Verbandsbildung* (1968), pp. 82 ff.; Hengel, "Warenhaus" (1952), pp. 78 ff.

18. Warren, *Kingdom* (1964), has a good account of Stresemann's career in Saxony. Stresemann himself has a brief description of Saxon politics in Kalkoff, *Parlamentarier* (1917); his views on other political and social issues can be seen in the collection of his speeches and articles published as *Wirtschaftspolitische Zeitfragen* (Dresden, 1911). See also H. A. Turner, *Stresemann and the Politics of the Weimar Republic* (Princeton, 1963), chap. 1.

19. Eschenburg, *Kaiserreich* (1929), pp. 11 ff.; Nipperdey, *Organisation* (1961), pp. 96 ff.; *EGK 1903*, p. 128 (on their convention of 1903), and *EGK 1906*, p. 161 (on their membership). Kulemann's *Erinnerungen* (1911), pp. 194 ff., is a sympathetic contemporary view. The Young Liberal program is reprinted in Salomon, *Parteiprogramme* (1931–32), 2:54–55.

20. The best account of Bassermann's career is in Eschenburg, *Kaiserreich* (1929), especially pp. 13 ff. See also Karola Bassermann, ed., *Ernst Bassermann* (Mannheim, n.d.), and Elisabeth von Roon, *Ernst Bassermann* (Berlin, 1925). Nussbaum, *Unternehmer* (1966), p. 192, n. 461, lists his corporate affiliations. Wernecke, *Wille* (1970), p. 33, has a revealing quotation giving his views on foreign policy.

21. Quoted in Eschenburg, *Kaiserreich* (1929), p. 21. Meinecke recalled Bassermann as being like a "helmsman who was uncertain whether to turn left or right" ("Strassburg" [1949] in *Werke* [1957–68], 8:217).

22. I think both Eschenburg, *Kaiserreich* (1929), and Walter Koch, *Volk und Staatsführung vor dem ersten Weltkrieg* (Stuttgart, 1935), overestimate the bloc's potential for resolving Germany's political problems. On the elections of 1907, see Crothers, *Elections* (1941), and D. Fricke, "Der deutsche Imperialismus und die Reichstagswahlen von 1907," *ZfG* 9, no. 3 (1961): 538–76. Karl Jakob, "Landtagswahlen und Reichstagswahlen in Württemberg," *Süddeutsche Monatshefte* 4, no. 4 (1907): 517–24, is an interesting contemporary view of the bloc's impact on local politics.

23. On the divisions within the bloc, see: Stegmann, *Erben* (1970), pp. 146–66; Nipperdey, "Interessenverbände" (1961); Nussbaum, "Hintergrund" (1965). The financial issue is treated with great care in Witt, *Finanzpolitik* (1969). Eschenburg, *Kaiserreich* (1929), pp. 239 ff. describes the bloc's final dissolution.

24. "Let us remember," the program of the Bauernbund declared, "that it was the large landowners who once took away the peasantry's freedom. . . . We want to protest the way in which they now present themselves as the peasantry's leaders." Quoted in U. Lindig, "Der Einfluss des Bundes der Landwirte auf Politik des wilhelminischen Zeitalters, 1893–1914" (Unpubl. diss., Hamburg, 1954), pp. 73–74. See also Bertram, *Wahlen* (1964), pp. 100 ff.

25. "Hansabund Aufgaben," reprinted in Stresemann, *Wirtschaftspolitische Zeitfragen* (Dresden, 1911), pp. 193 ff. The Hansabund program is in *EGK 1909*, pp. 198

ff., and Riesser, *Der Hansabund* (Jena, 1912), especially pp. 43–44.

26. On the Hansabund, see: Bertram, *Wahlen* (1964), pp. 102 ff. and 155, for the elections of 1912; Kaelble, *Interessenpolitik* (1967), pp. 181 ff.; Winkler, *Mittelstand* (1972), pp. 55 ff.; Wein, *Verbandsbildung* (1968), pp. 121 ff.; Eschenburg, *Kaiserreich* (1929), pp. 242 ff.; *EGK 1910*, p. 325, and *EGK 1911*, p. 121 ff. My account was written without the benefit of S. Mielke's *Der Hansa-Bund für Gewerbe, Handel und Industrie, 1909–1914* (Göttingen, 1975), which is now the definitive treatment of this organization.

27. *EGK 1911*, p. 125, and Stegmann, *Erben* (1970), pp. 208 ff., 239–41.

28. Kaelble, *Interessenpolitik* (1967), p. 145; Thieme, *Liberalismus* (1963), pp. 34–37; Bertram, *Wahlen* (1964), p. 154.

29. The strike movement before the war is described in H. Kaelble and H. Volkmann, "Konjunktur und Streik während des Übergangs zum organisierten Kapitalismus in Deutschland," *Zeitschrift für Wirtschafts- und Sozialwissenschaften* 92, no. 5 (1972). On the Kartell, see Stegmann, *Erben* (1970), pp. 269 ff., 305 ff., 352 ff., and F. Fischer, *Krieg der Illusionen* (Düsseldorf, 1969), pp. 384–412.

30. See: Thieme, *Liberalismus* (1963), on Prussia; Heckart, *Bassermann* (1974), pp. 257 ff., on Baden; Möckl, *Prinzregentzeit* (1972), pp. 17, 543, Albrecht, *Landtag* (1968), pp. 35 ff., and Reimann, *Müller-Meiningen* (1968), pp. 142 ff., on Bavaria.

31. Bertram, *Wahlen* (1964), pp. 28 ff.; Reiss, *Bassermann* (1967), pp. 150 ff.; Stegmann, *Erben* (1970), pp. 206 ff., 312, 318 ff.

32. Bassermann made this position clear in his speech to the Kassel Parteitag in October 1910: *EGK 1910*, pp. 353–54. See also: Reiss, *Bassermann* (1967), pp. 23–24; Stegmann, *Erben* (1970). pp. 223 ff.

33. Reiss, *Bassermann* (1967), pp. 90 ff., is a good summary of the party's condition on the eve of the war. For a contemporary view, see Meinecke, "Partei" (1912), in *Werke* (1957–68), 2:55 ff.

34. Quoted in Stegmann, *Erben* (1970), p. 443.

35. Rudolf von Campe, quoted in Heckart, *Bassermann* (1974), p. 229.

36. Gagel, *Wahlrechtsfrage* (1958), pp. 126 ff., surveys liberal attitudes on the suffrage issue. The official position can be found in the National Liberals' electoral declaration of 1911, reprinted in Mommsen, *Parteiprogramme* (1964), p. 177. Some examples of right-wing liberal views: R. Gneist, *Die nationale Rechtsidee von den Ständen und das preussische Dreiklassenwahlsystem* (Berlin, 1894); Wippermann in *Kommunale Rundschau* (1908), 1:341–44; G. Meyer, *Das parlamentarische Wahlrecht* (1901); Eugen Schiffer's memorandum of 1909, published in B. von Hutten-Czapski, *Sechzig Jahre Politik und Gesellschaft* (Berlin, 1936), 2:8–12. The continued failure of suffrage reform after 1914 is described in R. Patemann, *Der Kampf um die preussische Wahlrechtsreform im Ersten Weltkrieg* (Düsseldorf, 1964), especially pp. 143 ff.

37. Quoted in Reiss, *Bassermann* (1967), p. 109. Cf. Jellinek, *Regierung* (1909), p. 36.

There is a useful summary of National Liberal attitudes toward constitutional reform in Grosser, *Konstitutionalismus* (1970), pp. 69 ff. Heckart, *Bassermann* (1974), p. 257, points out the ambivalence toward the state in the party at the time of the Zabern crisis. For the persistence of these attitudes after 1914, see: Grosser, pp. 168 ff.; U. Bermbach, "Aspekte der Parlamentarismus-Diskussion im kaiserlichen Reichstag. Die Erörterung im Interfraktionellen Ausschuss, 1917–1918," *PV* 8, no. 1 (March

1967): 51–70, and K. Epstein, "Der Interfraktionelle Ausschuss und das Problem der Parlamentarisierung," *HZ* 191, no. 2 (1960): 562–84.

38. The party programs are in Salomon, *Parteiprogramme* (1931–1932), 1:68–72. On the origins and development of the division, see: Rachfahl, "Richter" (1912), pp. 344–61; Elm, *Fortschritt* (1968), pp. 4 ff.; Matthes, "Spaltung" (1953), pp. 250 ff.; and Nipperdey, *Organisation* (1961), pp. 213 ff.

39. J. A. Nichols, *Germany after Bismarck: The Caprivi Era, 1890–1894* (Cambridge, Mass., 1958) is a good account of the Caprivi regime.

40. Rachfahl, "Richter" (1912), and Nipperdey, *Organisation* (1961), pp. 180, 217–24.

41. Quoted from *Die Nation*, July 22, 1893, in Sheehan, *Career* (1966), p. 137. See also Wegner, *Barth* (1968), and Nipperdey, *Organisation* (1961), pp. 224–30.

42. There is a detailed defense of this position in Wernicke, *Kapitalismus* (1907). On left-liberal attitudes to specific items of legislation, see: Linke, "Rolle" (1955), pp. 41 ff., 110 ff., 172; Wein, *Verbandsbildung* (1968), pp. 79 ff.; Hengel, "Warenhaus" (1952), pp. 89 ff.

43. Barkin, *Controversy* (1970), pp. 186 ff.; Sheehan, *Career* (1966), pp. 132–33, 136, 141 ff. For an example of this point of view, see the early essays by Hugo Preuss reprinted in his *Staat, Recht und Freiheit* (Tübingen, 1926).

44. Quoted in Helfferich, *Siemens* (1921–23), 3:219. On the Handelvertragsverein, see Anderson, *Background* (1939), pp. 155 ff., and Nussbaum, *Unternehmer* (1966), pp. 151 ff.

45. Heuss, *Mommsen* (1956), pp. 212 ff., and *EGK 1902*, pp. 182–83. Sheehan, *Career* (1966), pp. 137 ff., discusses Barth's relationship to Brentano. For a more critical view, see Elm, *Fortschritt* (1968), pp. 29 ff., 103 ff.

46. Naumann has attracted a great deal of scholarly attention; indeed he may soon acquire more monographs than he did supporters. The standard biography remains Theodor Heuss's sympathetic treatment, *Friedrich Naumann: der Mann, das Werk, die Zeit*, 2d ed. (Stuttgart and Tübingen, 1949). A bibliography of works by and about him has been compiled by A. Milatz, *Friedrich Naumann Bibliographie* (Düsseldorf, 1957). There is a good edition of Naumann's writings, *Werke* (1964–). Two worthwhile brief treatments of his career are Richard Nürnberger, "Imperialismus, Sozialismus und Christentum bei Friedrich Naumann," *HZ* 180, no. 3 (October 1950): 525–48, and Werner Conze, "Friedrich Naumann. Grundlagen und Ansatz seiner Politik in der national-sozialen Zeit (1895–1903)," in Hubatsch, ed., *Schicksalswege* (1950), 355–86.

47. The most recent work on the National Socials is Dieter Düding, *Der National-soziale Verein* (Munich, 1972). Sheehan, *Career* (1966), pp. 137 ff., discusses Naumann's relationship with Barth.

48. Rachfahl, "Richter" (1912), pp. 363 ff. See also: *EGK 1894*, pp. 137–39, 151, for the program and Parteitag of 1894; *EGK 1903*, pp. 103, 164, for a polemic against the SPD and the Parteitag of 1903.

49. Simon, *Demokraten* (1969), pp. 40–41. See also the party's convention of 1903 as reported in *EGK 1903*, p. 164.

50. Elm, *Fortschritt* (1968), pp. 103 ff., 129 ff., and Nipperdey, *Organisation* (1961), p. 226. For an example of these divisions, see the conflict between Naumann and Pachnicke as reported in *Die Hilfe* (1905), no. 41.

51. In 1893, the Freisinnige Vereinigung won 3 seats on the first ballot, 7 in runoffs

against the SPD, 5 in runoffs against the right. In 1898, these figures were 1, 5, and 8; in 1903, 0, 7, and 6. See Wegner, *Barth* (1968), pp. 144–45.

52. On Prussia, see the official returns cited above, chap. 15, n. 8. Examples from the south can be found in: Simon, *Demokraten* (1969), pp. 72 ff., on Württemberg; Reimann, *Müller-Meiningen* (1968), pp. 36 ff., 83 ff., on Bavaria.

53. Reimann, *Müller-Meiningen* (1968), pp. 42 ff.; Elm, *Fortschritt* (1968), pp. 170 ff.; Simon, *Demokraten* (1969), pp. 81 ff.; Robson, "Liberalism" (1966), pp. 48 ff.

54. The elections of 1907 provide another illustration of the right-left pull created within liberalism by the incongruence of local and national institutions: in 1907, the Volkspartei joined with other parties against the Social Democrats during the Reichstag elections but joined with the SPD against the right in the Württemberg state elections. Heckart, *Bassermann* (1974), p. 69.

55. Sheehan, *Career* (1966), pp. 168 ff., discusses this and cites the relevant literature. See also Fricke, 1:280–84, on the organization Barth created.

56. The new party program is reprinted in Mommsen, *Parteiprogramme* (1964), pp. 173 ff. For a discussion of the fusion, see: Nipperdey, *Organisation* (1961), pp. 187 ff.; Robson, "Liberalism" (1966), chap. 3; Simon, *Demokraten* (1969), pp. 90 ff.; Reimann, *Müller-Meiningen* (1968), pp. 61 ff.; Elm, *Fortschritt* (1968), pp. 208 ff.

57. Gagel, *Wahlrechtsfrage* (1958). Some examples of local conflicts between left liberals and Socialists on the voting laws: P. Hirsch and H. Lindemann, *Das kommunale Wahlrecht* (Berlin, 1905), pp. 8–9; *KP* (1904), 4:403–6, and (1909), 9:1223–24.

58. The best place to follow the complex local relationships between liberals and the SPD is in the pages of *KP*. Also of interest are the following autobiographies of labor leaders: Karl Ulrich, *Erinnerungen des ersten hessischen Staatspräsidenten* (Offenbach/Main, 1953), pp. 60 ff.; G. Noske, *Erlebtes aus Aufstieg und Niedergang einer Demokratie* (Offenbach, 1947), pp. 17 ff.; P. Löbe, *Erinnerungen eines Reichstagspräsidenten* (Berlin, 1949), pp. 38 ff.; Carl Severing, *Lebensweg* (1950), 1:132 ff. Sheehan, "Liberalism and the City" (1971), treats this problem somewhat more extensively.

59. For a good example of the workers' social and political isolation, see Hellpach, *Wirken* (1948–49), 1:38 ff.

60. Bertram's analysis of the runoff in *Wahlen* (1964), pp. 221–41, suggests some important revisions to Schorske, *Social Democracy* (1955), pp. 226 ff., but I think the main lines of Schorske's argument remain intact. For another view, see Robson, "Liberalism" (1966), pp. 89 ff. Severing, *Lebensweg* (1950), 1:183 ff., has a good account of the liberals' failure to control their constituency in one district.

61. Mommsen, *Parteiprogramme* (1964), p. 174.

62. Grosser, *Konstitutionalismus* (1970), pp. 60 ff., 163 ff., and H. Wasser, *Parlamentarismuskritik vom Kaiserreich zur Bundesrepublik* (Stuttgart, 1974), pp. 31–34, provide good introductions to left-liberal attitudes about constitutional reform.

63. On left liberals' response to the *Daily Telegraph* affair, see: Eschenburg, *Kaiserreich* (1929), pp. 166 ff.; Pachnicke, *Männer* (1930), p. 88; Reimann, *Müller-Meiningen* (1968), p. 58. On Zabern, see A. Dorpalen, "Wilhelminian Germany—A House Divided Against Itself," *JCEA* 15, no. 3 (October 1955): 244.

64. F. Payer, *Von Bethmann Hollweg bis Ebert* (Frankfurt, 1923), p. 15. Cf. the quotation in Fenske, *Wahlrecht* (1972), p. 15.

65. Friedrich Naumann, *Demokratie und Kaisertum*, 3d ed. (Berlin-Schöneberg, 1904). See also Naumann's article "Pessimistischer Liberalismus-Kaiserpolitik" in *Die Hilfe* (1900), no. 16, pp. 1–2.

66. Quoted in Struve, *Elites* (1973), p. 124. On left-liberal political thought after 1890, see: P. Gilg, *Die Erneuerung des demokratischen Denkens im Wilhelminischen Deutschland* (Wiesbaden, 1965), pp. 102 ff., 107 ff., 220 ff.; Vitzthum, *Politik* (1971), pp. 84 ff., on Hänel; Wegner, *Barth* (1968), pp. 65 ff.; G. Schwarz, *Theodor Wolff und das "Berliner Tageblatt"* (Tübingen, 1968), pp. 52 ff.

67. There is a survey of the liberals' influence on the Weimar constitution in Fenske, *Wahlrecht* (1972), pp. 339 ff., and Portner, *Verfassungspolitik* (1973). Gustav Schmidt, *Deutscher Historismus und der Übergang zur parlamentarischen Demokratie. Untersuchungen zu den politischen Gedanken von Meinecke, Troeltsch, Max Weber* (Lübeck and Hamburg, 1964), examines the "retarding elements inherent in democratic theory" at the end of the imperial era. See also Mommsen, "Wandlungen" (1975), pp. 141–42.

68. Some stimulating ideas about the state of German politics in 1914 can be found in three recent articles by Gustav Schmidt, "Deutschland am Vorabend des ersten Weltkriegs," in Stürmer, ed., *Deutschland* (1970), pp. 397–434, "Blockbildungen" (1972), and "Parlamentarisierung oder 'Praventive Konterrevolution'?" in Ritter, *Gesellschaft* (1974), pp. 249–78. See also Ritter's introduction to this volume, especially pp. 41 ff.

Conclusion

1. T. Schieder, *Das deutsche Kaiserreich von 1871 als Nationalstaat* (Cologne and Opladen, 1961), especially pp. 72 ff.; Mosse, *Nationalization* (1975); K. H. Höfele, "Selbstverständnis und Zeitkritik des deutschen Bürgertums vor dem ersten Weltkrieg," *Zeitschrift für Religions- und Geistesgeschichte* 8, no. 1 (1956): 40–56; Schwarz, "Attitudes" (1961), especially chap. 2. There are some interesting remarks on the problem of nationalism in Robert Berdahl, "New Thoughts on German Nationalism," *AHR* 77, no. 1 (February 1972): 65–80.

2. For good brief statements of Treitschke's position, see Krieger, *Idea* (1957), pp. 363 ff., and Dorpalen, *Treitschke* (1957). His views were anticipated in Rochau, *Grundsätze* (1853; reprinted 1972), p. 35.

3. Faber, "Realpolitik" (1966).

4. On the liberals and imperialism before 1890, see above, chap. 13. On the Wilhelmine era, see Mommsen, "Wandlungen" (1975), and the other essays in Holl and List, *Liberalismus* (1975), especially the critique of Mommsen by Lothar Gall. Also worth reading is M. Messerschmidt, "Reich und Nation im Bewusstsein der wilhelminischen Gesellschaft," in *Marine und Marinepolitik im kaiserlichen Deutschland, 1871–1914*, ed. H. Schottelius and W. Diest (Düsseldorf, 1972).

5. A good introduction to the patriotic societies can be found in K. Schilling, *Beiträge zu einer Geschichte des radikalen Nationalismus in der Wilhelminischen Ära 1890–1909* (Diss., Cologne, 1968), and H. Pogge von Strandmann, "Nationale Verbände zwischen Weltpolitik und Kontinentalpolitik," in *Marine und Marinepolitik im kaiserlichen Deutschland, 1871–1914*, ed. H. Schottelius and W. Diest (Düsseldorf, 1972). There are articles on the individual organizations in Fricke. For the *Kriegervereine*, see: H. Henning, "Kriegervereine in den preussischen Westprovinzen. Ein

Beitrag zur preussischen Innenpolitik zwischen 1860 und 1914," *RV* 32, nos. 1–4
(1968): 430–75, and K. Saul, "Der 'Deutsche Kriegerbund': Zur innenpolitischen
Funktion eines 'nationalen' Verbandes im kaiserlichen Deutschland," *Militärge-
schichtliche Mitteilungen* (1971), pp. 97–143.

6. Mosse, *Nationalization* (1975), p. 2.

7. Quoted in H-U. Wehler, *Das deutsche Kaiserreich* (Göttingen, 1973), p. 195.

8. Quoted in O'Donnell, "Liberalism" (1973), p. 309.

9. O'Donnell, "Liberalism" (1973), p. 199.

10. Reimann, *Müller-Meiningen* (1968), pp. 26 ff., and 74 ff.; Elm, *Fortschritt*
(1968); Simon, *Demokraten* (1969), pp. 98 ff., 118–19; Anderson, *Background*
(1939), pp. 98 ff.; Wernecke, *Wille* (1970), pp. 34, 294, discusses the left-liberal
press.

11. Ludwig Frank, quoted in Stegmann, *Erben* (1970), p. 113.

12. Mommsen, *Weber* (1959). See also Meinecke, "Sammlungspolitik" (1910), in
Werke (1957–68), 2:40–41.

13. Otto Hintze, for example, began from the same premise as Naumann and
Weber, but used it to defend the status quo. See his essay "Das monarchische Prinzip
und die konstitutionelle Verfassung" (1911), reprinted in *Abhandlungen* (1962–67),
1:359–89.

14. B. Malinowski, *Magic, Science and Religion* (Garden City, N.Y., 1954), p.
129. On the distinction between ideology and myth, see W. Mullins, "On the Concept
of Ideology in Political Science," *APSR* 66, no. 2 (1972), esp. p. 505.

15. Fraenkel, *Deutschland* (1968), p. 28, and H. Arendt, *The Origins of To-
talitarianism* (New York, 1951), pp. 254–55, both call attention to this relationship
between domestic disunity and the assertion of national cohesion. See also Mommsen,
"Wandlungen" (1975).

16. Emil Lederer quoted in G. Feldman, *Army. Industry and Labor in Germany,
1914–1918* (Princeton, 1966), p. 27.

17. Quoted in Stern, "Consequence" (1960), p. 129. For Meinecke's memories of
the August Days, see "Strassburg" in *Werke* (1957–69), 8:222 ff.

18. V. Turner, *Dramas, Fields and Metaphors* (Ithaca, N.Y., 1974), pp. 166 ff.

19. J. Kocka's *Klassengesellschaft im Krieg. Deutsche Sozialgeschichte 1914–
1918* (Göttingen, 1973), is the best general introduction to the social impact of the war.
On the "middle strata" after 1918, see: Charles Maier, *Recasting Bourgeois Europe:
Stabilization in France, Germany, and Italy in the Decade after World War I* (Prince-
ton, 1975), especially pp. 256 ff., on the inflation; Winkler, *Mittelstand* (1972); W. T.
Angress, "The Political Role of the Peasantry in the Weimar Republic," *RP* 31, no. 3
(July 1959): 530–49; W. Kaltefleiter, *Wirtschaft und Politik im Deutschland. Kon-
junktur als Bestimmungsfaktor des Parteiensystems* (Cologne, 1966), pp. 22 ff., and
H. Lebovics, *Social Conservatism and the Middle Classes in Germany 1914–1933*
(Princeton, 1969). Theodor Geiger's *Die soziale Schichtung des deutschen Volkes*
(Stuttgart, 1932) is a classic contemporary account.

20. On the elections of 1919 and 1920, see: Gerhard A. Ritter, "Kontinuität und
Umformung des deutschen Parteisystems, 1918–1920," in Ritter, ed., *Entstehung*
(1970), pp. 267 ff.; Albertin, *Liberalismus* (1972), pp. 138 ff., 153 ff.; and Hartenstein, *Anfänge* (1962), pp. 59 ff., 224 ff.

A general introduction to the electoral history of Weimar can be found in A. Milatz,
Wähler und Wahlen in der Weimarer Republik (Bonn, 1965), and Fenske, *Wahlrecht*
(1972), chaps. 7–9.

21. Quoted in Schumacher, *Mittelstandsfront* (1972), p. 115. See also Winkler, *Mittelstand* (1972), pp. 121 ff.

On the development of liberalism after 1918, see: S. Neumann, *Die deutschen Parteien* (Berlin, 1932), pp. 46 ff.; G. Fischenberg, "Der deutsche Liberalismus und die Entstehung der Weimarer Republik" (Unpubl. diss., Münster, 1958); Portner, *Verfassungspolitik* (1973); Albertin, *Liberalismus* (1972). For the Deutsche Demokratische Partei, see especially: Robson, "Liberalism" (1966); E. Portner, "Der Ausatz zur demokratischen Massenpartei im deutschen Liberalismus," *VfZ* 13, no. 2 (April 1965): 150–61; W. Stephan, *Aufsteig und Verfall des Linksliberalismus 1918–1933* (Göttingen and Zürich, 1973); B. Frye, "The German Democratic Party, 1918–1930," *The Western Political Quarterly* 16, no. 1 (March 1963): 167–79. For the Deutsche Volkspartei, see: Booms, "Die Deutsche Volkspartei," in Matthias and Morsey, *Ende* (1960), pp. 523–39; Hartenstein, *Anfänge* (1962); L. Döhn, *Politik und Interesse. Die Interessenstruktur der Deutschen Volkspartei* (Meisenheim-am-Glan, 1970).

22. The best regional study remains Heberle's work on Schleswig-Holstein, *Democracy* (1945), and the longer, German version *Landbevölkerung* (1963). Schumacher, *Mittelstandsfront* (1972), deals with the Wirtschaftspartei; G. Opitz, *Der Christlich-soziale Volksdienst. Versuch einer protestantischen Partei in der Weimarer Republik* (Düsseldorf, 1969), pp. 223 ff., discusses the Protestant parties. Hopwood, "Paladins" (1974), pp. 223 ff., has some fascinating information about the decline of the traditional parties on the local level.

23. The concept of "social milieu" is defined in Lepsius, *Nationalismus* (1966), especially pp. 24, 27.

24. The last elections of the Weimar era have been studied with some intensity. The best place to begin examining this literature is probably Milatz's essay in Matthias and Morsey, *Ende* (1960). S. M. Lipset's essay in *Political Man* (1963), is a very influential attempt to see the relationship between fascism and the political "Middle." Shively, "Identification" (1972), and Burnham, "Immunization" (1972), also use national election returns to explain shifts in voting preference. While all of these articles contain useful insights, they must be supplemented with detailed regional studies. For some examples of this, see: Heberle's works just cited (in n. 22) and the interesting reconsideration of his research in T. Tilton, *Nazism, Neo-Nazism, and the Peasantry* (Bloomington, Ind., 1975); G. Pridham, *Hitler's Rise to Power: The Nazi Movement in Bavaria, 1923–1933* (New York, 1973); Allen, *Seizure* (1965); Faris, "Takeoff" (1975); J. Noakes, *The Nazi Party in Lower Saxony, 1921–1933* (New York, 1972).

25. This process can be seen in the data on state elections given in Milatz, "Ende" (1960), pp. 759, 766.

26. The most effective criticism of Lipset from this point of view is Winkler's thoughtful article "Extremismus der Mitte? Sozialgeschichtliche Aspekte der national-sozialistischen Machtergreifung," *VfZ* 20, no. 2 (April 1972): 175–91.

27. Quoted from Berelson et al., *Voting*, by Thränhardt, *Wahlen* (1973), p. 20, n. 11. Heberle's work is cited above, n. 22.

28. Burnham, for example, argues that "when crisis comes, the crucial differentiation lies not in the length of exposure before the crisis, but in the relative intensity of political commitment to traditional parties" ("Immunization" [1972], p. 15).

29. Schumacher correctly points out this connection when he calls the Nazis the heirs of the splinter parties: *Mittelstandsfront* (1972), p. 112.

30. K. D. Bracher et al., *Die Auflösung der Weimarer Republik*, 3d ed. (Villingen, 1960), p. 355, and the article "Staatspartei" in Matthias and Morsey, *Ende* (1960), pp. 31 ff.

31. There is a particularly good portrayal of this in Allen, *Seizure* (1965). See also Faris, "Take-Off" (1975), pp. 160–61, on the Nazis' use of the Young Plan campaign. On the general problem of nationalism and its political uses, see Lepsius, *Nationalismus* (1966).

32. For some other efforts to understand the relationship between liberalism and the rise of fascism in Germany, see: Dahrendorf, *Society* (1969); Lepsius, "Demokratie" (1969); Winkler, *Mittelstand* (1972), especially pp. 157–59; O'Donnell, "Liberalism" (1973), especially pp. 1 ff., 461 ff.

Bibliography

Adam, Albert. *Ein Jahrhundert württembergischer Verfassung*. Stuttgart, 1919.

Adam, Reinhard. "Johann Jacobys politischer Werdegang, 1805–1840." *HZ* 143, no. 1 (1930): 48–76.

———. "Der Liberalismus in der Provinz Preussen zur Zeit der neuen Ära und sein Anteil an der Entstehung der Deutschen Fortschrittspartei." In *Altpreussische Beiträge. Festschrift zur Hauptversammlung des Gesamtvereins der deutschen Geschichts- und Altertums-Vereine zu Königsberg*. Königsberg, 1933, pp. 145–81.

Albertin, Lothar. *Liberalismus und Demokratie am Anfang der Weimarer Republik. Eine vergleichende Analyse der Deutschen Demokratischen Partei und der Deutschen Volkspartei*. Düsseldorf, 1972.

Albrecht, Willy. *Landtag und Regierung in Bayern am Vorabend der Revolution von 1918. Studien zur gesellschaftlichen und staatlichen Entwicklung Deutschlands von 1912–18*. Berlin, 1968.

Allen, William S. *The Nazi Seizure of Power. The Experience of a Single German Town, 1930–1935*. Chicago, 1965.

Allgemeine Zeitung (Munich). 1866–1912.

Anderson, Eugene N. *The Social and Political Conflict in Prussia, 1858–1864*. Lincoln, Nebraska, 1954.

———. *The Prussian Election Statistics, 1862 and 1863*. Lincoln, Nebraska, 1954.

Anderson, Pauline. *The Background of Anti-English Feelings in Germany, 1890–1902*. Washington, D.C., 1939.

Angel-Volkov, Shulamit. "The Decline of the German Handicrafts: Another Reappraisal." *VSWG* 61, no. 2 (1974): 165–84.

———. "The Social and Political Function of Late 19th Century Anti-Semitism: The Case of the Small Handicraft Masters." In Wehler, ed. *Sozialgeschichte*. 1974, pp. 416–31.

Angermann, Erich. "Karl Mathy als Sozial- und Wirtschaftspolitiker (1842–1848)." *ZGO*, new series, 64, no. 2 (1955): 492–622.

———. *Robert Mohl. 1799–1875. Leben und Werk eines altliberalen Staatsgelehrten*. Neuwied, 1962.

Aris, Reinhold. *History of Political Thought in Germany, 1789–1815*. London, 1936.

Ayçoberry, Pierre. "Probleme der Sozialschichtung in Köln im Zeitalter der Frühindustrialisierung." In W. Fischer, ed. *Wirtschaftsgeschichte*. 1968, pp. 512–28.

———. "Der Strukturwandel im Kölner Mittelstand, 1820–1850." *GuG* 1, no. 1 (1975): 78–98.

Baden. *Verhandlungen der Stände Versammlung*. Karlsruhe, 1868 and 1874.

Baden. *Statistisches Jahrbuch für Grossherzogtum Baden, 1913*. Karlsruhe, 1913.

Balser, Frolinde. *Die Anfänge der Erwachsenenbildung in Deutschland in der ersten Hälfte des 19. Jahrhunderts*. Stuttgart, 1959.

———. *Sozial Demokratie 1848/49–1863: die erste deutsche Arbeiterorganisation*. 2 vols. Stuttgart, 1962.

Bamberger, Ludwig. *Gesammelte Schriften*. 5 vols. Berlin, 1894–98.

———. *Erinnerungen*. Berlin, 1899.

———. *Bismarcks grosses Spiel. Die geheimen Tagebücher Ludwig Bambergers*. Ed. Ernst Feder. Frankfurt, 1932.

Barkin, Kenneth. *The Controversy over German Industrialization, 1890–1902*. Chicago, 1970.

Bartel, Horst, and Engelberg, E., eds. *Die grosspreussisch-militarische Reichsgründung 1871: Voraussetzung und Folgen*. 2 vols. Berlin, 1971.

Bauer, Wilhelm. *Die öffentliche Meinung und ihre geschichtlichen Grundlagen*. Tübingen, 1914.

Baumgarten, Hermann. "Der deutsche Liberalismus. Eine Selbstkritik." *PJbb* 18, nos. 5 and 6 (1866): 455–517, 575–628.

Beau, Horst. *Das Leistungswissen des frühindustriellen Unternehmertums in Rheinland-Westfalen*. Cologne, 1959.

Bebel, August. *Aus meinem Leben*. 3d ed. Berlin, 1961.

Becker, Josef. *Liberaler Staat und Kirche in der Ära von Reichsgründung und Kulturkampf. Geschichte und Strukturen ihres Verhältnisses in Baden, 1860–1876*. Mainz, 1973.

Bellot, Josef. "Das politische Leben in den Saarkreisen zwischen der Revolution von 1848/49 und dem deutsch-französischen Krieg von 1870/71." Unpubl. diss., Bonn, 1951.

———. *Hundert Jahre politisches Leben an der Saar unter preussischer Herrschaft (1815–1918)*. Bonn, 1954.

Bein, Alex, and Hans Goldschmidt. *Friedrich Hammacher. Lebensbild eines Parlamentariers und Wirtschaftsführer, 1824–1904*. Berlin, 1932.

Bergsträsser, Ludwig. "Die Parteipolitische Lage beim Zusammentritt des Vorparlaments." *ZfP* 6 (1913): 594–620.

———. "Kritische Studien zur Konfliktszeit." *HV* 19, no. 3 (1919): 343–76.

———. "Parteien von 1848." *PJbb* 177, no. 2 (1919): 180–211.

————, ed. *Das Frankfurter Parlament in Briefen und Tagebüchern: Ambrosch, Rümelin, Hallbauer, Blum.* Frankfurt, 1929.

————. "Entstehung und Entwicklung der Parteikorrespondenzen in Deutschland im Jahre 1848/49." *Zeitungswissenschaft* 8, no. 1 (1933): 12–25.

Bermbach, Udo. "Über Landstände, Zur Theorie der Repräsentation im deutschen Vormärz." In *Sprache und Politik: Festgabe für D. Sternberger.* Ed. C. J. Friedrich and B. Reifenberg. Heidelberg, 1968, pp. 241–62.

Bertram, Jürgen. *Die Wahlen zum Deutschen Reichstag vom Jahre 1912: Parteien und Verbände in der Innenpolitik des Wilhelminischen Reiches.* Düsseldorf, 1964.

Beseler, Georg. *Erlebtes und Erstrebtes, 1809–1859.* Berlin, 1884.

Biedermann, Karl. *Erinnerungen aus der Paulskirche.* Leipzig, 1849.

————. *Mein Leben und ein Stück Zeitgeschichte.* 2 vols. Breslau, 1886.

Bigler, Robert. *The Politics of German Protestantism. The Rise of the Protestant Church Elite in Prussia, 1815–1848.* Berkeley, Los Angeles, and London, 1972.

Birker, Karl. *Die deutschen Arbeiterbildungsvereine, 1840–1870.* Berlin, 1973.

Birtsch, Günter. *Die Nation als sittliche Idee. Der Nationalstaatsbegriff in Geschichtsschreibung und politischer Gedankenwelt Johann Gustav Droysens.* Cologne and Graz, 1964.

Bismarck, Otto von. *Die gesammelten Werke.* 15 vols. Berlin, 1923–33.

Blättner, Fritz. *Das Gymnasium. Aufgaben der höheren Schule in Geschichte und Gegenwart.* Heidelberg, 1960.

Blaich, Fritz. "Die Anfänge der deutschen Antikartellpolitik zwischen 1897 und 1914." *JbS* 21, no. 2 (1970): 127–50.

————. *Kartell- und Monopolpolitik im kaiserlichen Deutschland. Das Problem der Marktmacht im deutschen Reichstag zwischen 1879 und 1914.* Düsseldorf, 1973.

Blaustein, Arthur. *Von der Uneinigkeit der Liberalen bei den Reichstagswahlen, 1867–1910.* Munich, 1911.

————. "Soziologisch/Statistische Abteilung." *ZfP*, Supplement 1 (1912): 351–80.

Block, Hermann. *Die parlamentarische Krisis der nationalliberalen Partei, 1879–80.* Hamburg, 1930.

Blum, Hans. *Auf dem Wege zur deutschen Einheit. Erinnerungen und Aufzeichnungen eines Mitkämpfers aus den Jahren 1867 bis 1870.* 2 vols. Jena, 1893.

Bluntschli, Johann Casper, ed. *Deutsches Staatswörterbuch.* 11 vols. Stuttgart and Leipzig, 1857–70.

————. *Charakter und Geist der politischen Parteien.* Nördlingen, 1869.

————. *Denkwürdiges aus meinem Leben.* 3 vols. Nördlingen, 1884.

Boberach, Heinz. *Wahlrechtsfrage im Vormärz; Die Wahlrechtsanschauung im Rheinland, 1815–1849, und die Entstehung des Dreiklassenwahlrechts.* Düsseldorf, 1959.

Böckenförde, Ernst-Wolfgang, ed. *Moderne Deutsche Verfassungsgeschichte (1815–1918).* Cologne, 1972.

————. "Die Einheit von nationaler und konstitutioneller politischer Bewegung im deutschen Frühliberalismus." In Böckenförde, ed., *Verfassungsgeschichte.* 1972, pp. 27–39.

————. "Der Verfassungstyp der deutschen konstitutionellen Monarchie im 19. Jahrhundert." In Böckenförde, ed., *Verfassungsgeschichte.* 1972, pp. 146–70.

Böhme, Helmut. *Deutschlands Weg zur Grossmacht: Studien zum Verhältnis von Wirtschaft und Staat während der Reichsgründungszeit, 1848–1881.* Cologne and Berlin, 1966.

————. *Probleme der Reichsgründungszeit, 1848–1879.* Cologne and Berlin, 1968.

Böhmert, Carl Victor. "Die Entstehung des volkswirtschaftlichen Kongresses vor 25 Jahren. Zur Erinnerung an Schulze–Delitzsch und Huber, Lette und Prince Smith." *Vierteljahrsschrift für Volkswirtschaft, Politik und Kulturgeschichte* 21, no. 1 (1884): 193–225.

Böttcher, Friedrich. *Eduard Stephani. Ein Beitrag zur Zeitgeschichte.* Leipzig, 1887.

Böttcher, Ulrich. *Anfänge und Entwicklung der Arbeiterbewegung in Bremen von der Revolution 1848 bis zur Aufhebung des Sozialistengesetzes, 1890.* Bremen, 1953.

Boldt, Hans. "Deutscher Konstitutionalismus und Bismarckreich." In Stürmer, ed., *Deutschland.* 1970, pp. 119–42.

————. "Zwischen Patrimonialismus und Parlamentarismus. Zur Entwicklung vorparlamentarischer Theorien in der deutschen Staatslehre des Vormärz." In Ritter, ed., *Gesellschaft.* 1974, pp. 77–100.

Boldt, Werner. *Die Anfänge des deutschen Parteiwesens. Fraktionen, politische Vereine und Parteien in der Revolution 1848.* Paderborn, 1971.

————. "Konstitutionelle Monarchie oder parlamentarische Demokratie. Die Auseinandersetzung um die deutsche Nationalversammlung in der Revolution von 1848." *HZ* 216, no. 3 (June 1973): 553–622.

Bolland, Jürgen. *Die hamburgische Bürgerschaft in alter und neuer Zeit.* Hamburg, 1959.

Booms, Hans. *Die deutschkonservative Partei. Preussischer Charakter, Reichsauffassung, Nationalbegriff.* Düsseldorf, 1954.

Borchardt, Knut. "Zur Frage des Kapitalmangels in der ersten Hälfte des 19. Jahrhunderts." *JbbNS* 173 (September 1961): 401–21.

————. "Regionale Wachstumsdifferenzierung in Deutschland im 19. Jahrhundert unter besonderer Berücksichtigung des West- Ost-Gefälles." In

F. Lütge, ed., *Wirtschaftliche und soziale Probleme der gewerblichen Entwicklung im 15.–16. und 19. Jahrhundert.* Stuttgart, 1968, pp. 115–30.

Born, Karl Erich, ed. *Probleme deutscher Wirtschaftsgeschichte.* Cologne and Berlin, 1966.

Born, Stephan. *Erinnerungen eines achtundvierzigers.* 2d ed. Leipzig, 1898.

Bornkamm, Heinrich. "Die Staatsidee im Kulturkampf." *HZ* 170, nos. 1 and 2 (1950): 41–72 and 273–306.

Botzenhart, Manfred. "Die Parlamentarismusmodelle der deutschen Parteien 1848–49." In Ritter, ed., *Gesellschaft.* 1974, pp. 121–43.

Bramstedt, E. K. *Aristocracy and the Middle Classes in Germany: Social Types in German Literature, 1830–1900.* Rev. ed. Chicago and London, 1964.

Brandt, Hartwig. *Landständische Repräsentation im deutschen Vormärz. Politisches Denken im Einflussfeld des monarchischen Prinzips.* Neuwied, 1968.

———. "Gesellschaft, Parlament, Regierung in Württemberg, 1830–1840." In Ritter, ed., *Gesellschaft.* 1974, pp. 101–18.

Brecht, A. *Aus nächster Nähe. Lebenserinnerungen, 1884–1927.* Stuttgart, 1966.

Briefs, Goetz. *The Proletariat.* New York, 1937.

Brooks, Robert. "Political Clubs in Prussian Cities." *Municipal Affairs* 4, no. 2 (June 1900): 375–84.

Broszat, Martin. "Die antisemitische Bewegung im wilhelminischen Deutschland." Unpubl. diss., Cologne, 1953.

Brunner, Otto, et al. *Geschichtliche Grundbegriffe. Historisches Lexikon zur politisch–sozialen Sprache in Deutschland.* 2 vols. Stuttgart, 1972 ff.

Bullik, Manfred. *Staat und Gesellschaft im hessischen Vormärz: Wahlrecht, Wahlen, und öffentliche Meinung in Kurhessen, 1830–1848.* Cologne and Vienna, 1972.

Büttner, S. *Die Anfänge des Parlamentarismus in Hessen–Darmstadt und das duThilsche System.* Darmstadt, 1969.

Bunsen, Marie von. *Georg von Bunsen: Ein Charakterbild aus dem Lager der Besiegten.* Berlin, 1900.

Burger, Annemarie. *Religionszugehörigkeit und soziales Verhalten. Untersuchungen und Statistiken der neueren Zeit in Deutschland.* Göttingen, 1964.

Burnham, Walter D. "Political Immunization and Political Confessionalism: The United States and Weimar Germany." *Journal of Interdisciplinary History* 3, no. 1 (Summer 1972): 1–30.

Bussmann, Walter. "Zur Geschichte des deutschen Liberalismus im 19. Jahrhundert." *HZ* 186, no. 3 (December 1958): 527–57.

Cecil, Lamar. *Albert Ballin. Business and Politics in Imperial Germany, 1888–1918.* Princeton, 1967.

Celotti, Joseph. "The Political Thought and Action of Friedrich Christoph Dahlmann." Unpubl. diss., Stanford, 1970.

Christern, Hermann. "Friedrich Christoph Dahlmanns politische Entwicklung bis 1848. Ein Beitrag zur Geschichte des deutschen Liberalismus." *Zeitschrift der Gesellschaft für Schleswig-holsteinische Geschichte*. 50 (special issue) (1921), pp. 146–392.

Clauss, Wilhelm. *Der Staatsbeamte als Abgeordneter in der Verfassungsentwicklung der deutschen Staaten*. Karlsruhe, 1906.

Conze, Werner, ed. *Staat und Gesellschaft im deutschen Vormärz, 1815–1848*. Stuttgart, 1962.

———. "Das Spannungsfeld von Staat und Gesellschaft im Vormärz." In Conze, ed. *Staat*. 1962, pp. 207–69.

——— et al. "Nation und Gesellschaft. Zwei Grundbegriffe der revolutionären Epoche." *HZ* 198, no. 1 (1964): 1–43.

———. *Möglichkeiten und Grenzen der liberalen Arbeiterbewegung in Deutschland. Das Beispiel Schulze-Delitzschs*. Heidelberg, 1965.

———. "Vom 'Pöbel' zum 'Proletariat.' Sozialgeschichtliche Voraussetzungen für den Sozialismus in Deutschland." In Wehler, ed. *Sozialgeschichte*. 1966, pp. 111–36.

———, and Groh, Dieter. *Die Arbeiterbewegung in der nationalen Bewegung. Die deutsche Sozialdemokratie vor, während und nach der Reichsgründung*. Stuttgart, 1966.

Crew, David. "Industry and Community: The Social History of a German Town, 1860–1914." Unpubl. diss., Cornell, 1975.

Croon, Helmuth. "Die Einwirkungen der Industrialisierung auf die gesellschaftliche Schichtung der Bevölkerung im rheinisch-westfälischen Industriegebiet." *RV* 20, no. 3 (1955): 301–16.

———. "Die Städtevertretung von Krefeld und Bochum im 19. Jahrhundert." In *Forschungen zu Staat und Verfassung. Festgabe für Fritz Hartung*. Berlin, 1958, pp. 289–306.

———. *Die gesellschaftlichen Auswirkungen des Gemeindewahlrechts in den Gemeinden und Kreisen des Rheinlandes und Westfalens im 19. Jahrhundert*. Cologne and Opladen, 1960.

———. "Bürgertum und Verwaltung in den Städten des Ruhrgebiets im 19. Jahrhundert." *Tradition* 9, no. 1 (1964): 23–41.

Crothers, George C. *The German Elections of 1907*. New York, 1941.

Dahlmann, F. C. *Die Politik auf den Grund und das Mass der gegebenen Zustände zurückgeführt*. 2d ed., 1847; reprinted Berlin, 1924.

Dahrendorf, Ralf. *Society and Democracy in Germany*. New York, 1969.

Denk, Heinz. "Die Wahlen zum preussischen Abgeordnetenhaus und zum Konstituierenden Reichstag des Norddeutschen Bundes in der Stadt Köln in den Jahren 1849–1867." Unpubl. diss., Bonn, 1955.

Deutsche Allgemeine Zeitung (Leipzig). 1863–77.

Deutsche Revue (Berlin). 1877–1922.

Deutsche Vierteljahrs-Schrift. 1838–1850.

Dill, Richard Walker. *Der Parlamentarier Eduard Lasker und die parlamentarische Stilentwicklung der Jahre 1867–1884. Ein Beitrag zur Geistesge-*

schichte des politischen Stils in Deutschland. Diss. Erlangen, 1958.

Dorn, Karl. "Die Anfänge der deutschen Fortschrittspartei in Bayern." Unpubl. diss., Munich, 1922.

Dorpalen, Andreas. *Heinrich von Treitschke.* New Haven, 1957.

Dressel, Hilmar. *Die politischen Wahlen in der Stadt Trier und in den Eifel- und Moselkreisen des Regierungsbezirks Trier 1888–1913.* Diss. Bonn, 1961.

Droysen, Johann Gustav. *Aktenstücke und Aufzeichnungen zur Geschichte der Frankfurter Nationalversammlung.* Ed. by R. Hübner. Osnabrück, 1967. (Reprint of 1924 ed.)

————. *Politische Schriften.* Ed. by F. Gilbert. Munich and Berlin, 1933.

Droz, Jacques. "Liberale Anschauungen zur Wahlrechtsfrage und das preussische Dreiklassenwahlrecht." In Böckenförde, ed. *Verfassungsgeschichte.* 1972, pp. 195–214.

Duncker, Max. *Zur Geschichte der Deutschen Reichsversammlung in Frankfurt.* Berlin, 1849.

————. *Politischer Briefwechsel aus seinem Nachlass.* Ed. by J. Schultze. Stuttgart and Berlin, 1923.

Eckert, Hugo. *Liberal- oder Sozialdemokratie. Frühgeschichte der Nürnberger Arbeiterbewegung.* Stuttgart, 1968.

Ehrenfeuchter, Bernhard. "Politische Willensbildung in Niedersachsen zur Zeit des Kaiserreiches. Ein Versuch auf Grund der Reichstagswahlen von 1867–1912, insbesonders seit 1890." Unpubl. diss., Göttingen, 1951.

Eichmeier, Jens Peter. *Anfänge liberaler Parteibildung (1847 bis 1854).* Diss., Göttingen, 1968.

Eisfeld, Gerhard. *Die Entstehung der liberalen Parteien in Deutschland 1858–70. Studie zu den Organisationen und Programmen der Liberalen und Demokraten.* Hanover, 1969.

————. "Die Anfänge liberaler Parteien in Dortmund 1858–1870." *Beiträge zur Geschichte Dortmunds und der Grafschaft Mark* 65 (1969): 81–86.

Eitner, Otto. "Die Stärke der Protestanten und Katholiken in den einzelnen Reichstagswahlkreisen und die Sozialdemokratie." *Historisch-Politische Blätter* 149 (1912): 687–93.

Elben, Otto. *Lebenserinnerungen, 1823–1899.* Stuttgart, 1931.

Elm, Ludwig. *Zwischen Fortschritt und Reaktion. Geschichte der Parteien der Liberalen Bourgeoisie in Deutschland, 1893–1918.* Berlin, 1968.

Engelberg, Ernst, ed. *Im Widerstreit um die Reichsgründung. Eine Quellensammlung zur Klassenauseinandersetzung in der deutschen Geschichte von 1849 bis 1871.* Berlin, 1970.

Engels, Friedrich. "Der Status Quo in Deutschland" (1847). *Karl Marx–Friedrich Engels Werke.* Berlin, 1964. Vol. 4, pp. 40–57.

————. *The German Revolutions: The Peasant War in Germany and Germany: Revolution and Counter-Revolutions.* Chicago and London, 1967.

Engelsing, Rolf. *Massenpublikum und Journalistentum im 19. Jahrhundert in Nordwestdeutschland.* Berlin, 1966.

————. "Zur politischen Bildung der deutschen Unterschichten, 1789–1803." *HZ* 206 (April 1968): 337–69.

————. "Probleme der Lebenshaltung in Deutschland im 18. und 19. Jahrhundert." *ZGS* 126, no. 2 (1970): 290–308.

————. *Zur Sozialgeschichte deutscher Mittel- und Unterschichten.* Göttingen, 1973.

Epstein, Klaus. *The Genesis of German Conservatism.* Princeton, 1966.

Eschenburg, Theodor. *Das Kaiserreich am Scheideweg: Bassermann, Bülow, und der Block.* Berlin, 1929.

Eulau, Heinz. "Early Theories of Parliamentarism." *Journeys in Politics.* Indianapolis and New York, 1963.

Evert, Georg. "Die preussischen Landtagswahlen des Jahres 1903 und frühere Jahre." *ZPSB*, Supplement 23 (1905).

————. "Die preussischen Landtagswahlen von 1908 and aus früheren Jahren." *ZPSB*, Supplement 30 (1909).

Eyck, Erich. *Bismarck.* 3 vols. Erlenbach-Zürich, 1941–44.

Eyck, Frank. *The Frankfurt Parliament, 1848–1849.* London, 1968.

Faber, Karl Georg. "Realpolitik als Ideologie: Die Bedeutung des Jahres 1866 für das politische Denken in Deutschland." *HZ* 203, no. 1 (1966): 1–45.

————. *Die Rheinlande zwischen Restauration und Revolution: Probleme der rheinischen Geschichte von 1814 bis 1848 im Spiegel der zeitgenössischen Publizistik.* Wiesbaden, 1966.

————. "Strukturprobleme des deutschen Liberalismus im 19. Jahrhundert." *Der Staat* 14, no. 2 (1975): 201–28.

Falkson, Ferdinand. *Die liberale Bewegung in Königsberg 1840–1848.* Breslau, 1888.

Faris, Ellsworth. "Takeoff Point for the National Socialist Party. The Landtag Election in Baden, 1929." *CEH* 8, no. 2 (June 1975): 140–71.

Fenske, Hans. *Wahlrecht und Parteisystem. Ein Beitrag zur deutschen Parteiengeschichte.* Frankfurt, 1972.

Ficker, Ludwig. *Der Kulturkampf in Münster.* Ed. by Otto Hellinghaus. Münster, 1928.

Fieker, Charles. "German Liberals and the Labor Question, 1844–1858." Unpubl. diss., Minnesota, 1972.

Fischer, Wolfram. *Handwerksrecht und Handwerkswirtschaft um 1800. Studien zur Sozial- und Wirtschaftsverfassung vor der industriellen Revolution.* Berlin, 1955.

————. "Der Volksschullehrer: Zur Sozialgeschichte eines Berufsstandes." *Soziale Welt* 12, no. 1 (1961): 37–47.

————. *Der Staat und die Anfänge der Industrialisierung in Baden, 1800–1850.* Vol. 1, *Die Staatliche Gewerbepolitik.* Berlin, 1962.

————. "Staat und Gesellschaft Badens im Vormärz." In Conze, ed., *Staat* (1962), pp. 143–71.

————. *Unternehmerschaft, Selbstverwaltung und Staat. Die Handelskam-*

mern in der deutschen Wirtschafts- und Staatsverfassung des 19. Jahrhunderts. Berlin, 1964.

―――. "Konjunkturen und Krisen im Ruhrgebiet seit 1840 und die wirtschaftspolitische Willensbildung der Unternehmer." *Westfälische Forschungen* 21 (1968): 42–53.

―――. *Wirtschaft und Gesellschaft im Zeitalter der Industrialisierung: Aufsätze, Studien, Vorträge*. Göttingen, 1972.

―――. "Das Verhältnis von Staat und Wirtschaft in Deutschland am Beginn der Industrialisierung." In *Wirtschaft*. 1972, pp. 60–74.

―――. "Staatsverwaltung und Interessenverbände im Deutschen Reich, 1871–1914." In *Wirtschaft*. 1972, pp. 194–213.

―――. "Innerbetrieblicher und sozialer Status der frühen Fabrikarbeiterschaft." In *Wirtschaft*. 1972, pp. 258–84.

―――. "Das deutsche Handwerk in der Frühphase der Industrialisierung." In *Wirtschaft*. 1972, 315–37.

―――. "Die Rolle des Kleingewerbes im wirtschaftlichen Wachstumsprozess in Deutschland 1850 bis 1914." In *Wirtschaft*. 1972, pp. 338–48.

―――. "Ansätze zur Industrialisierung in Baden 1770–1870." In *Wirtschaft*. 1972, pp. 358–91.

―――. "Karl Mez (1808–1877) ein badischer Unternehmer im 19. Jahrhundert." In *Wirtschaft*. 1972, pp. 443–63.

―――, and Bajor, G. *Die Soziale Frage. Neuere Studien zur Lage der Fabrikarbeiter in den Frühphasen der Industrialisierung*. Stuttgart, 1967.

Flathmann, J. *Die Reichstagswahlen in der Provinz Hannover, 1867–1896*. Hanover, 1897.

Flitner, Andreas. *Die politische Erziehung in Deutschland: Geschichte und Probleme, 1750–1880*. Tübingen, 1957.

Fontane, Theodor. *Von Zwanzig bis Dreissig*. Vol. 15, *Werke*. Munich, 1967.

Fortschrittspartei. *Der erste Parteitag der deutschen Fortschrittspartei. Verhandlungen, Programm, und Organisation*. Berlin, 1879.

Fraenkel, Ernst. *Deutschland und die westlichen Demokratien*. 3d ed. Stuttgart, 1968.

Frank, Robert. *Der Brandenburger als Reichstagswähler*. Diss., Berlin, 1934.

Freytag, Gustav. *Erinnerungen aus meinem Leben*. 2d series, vol. 8, *Gesammelte Werke*. Leipzig, n.d.

―――. *Karl Mathy*. Vol. 22, *Gesammelte Werke*. Leipzig, 1898.

Fricke, Dieter, et al., eds. *Die bürgerlichen Parteien in Deutschland. Handbuch der Geschichte der bürgerlichen Parteien und andere bürgerlicher Interessenorganisationen vom Vormärz bis zum Jahre 1945*. 2 vols. Leipzig, 1968; Berlin, 1970.

Gagel, Walter. *Die Wahlrechtsfrage in der Geschichte der deutschen liberalen Parteien 1848–1918*. Düsseldorf, 1958.

Gagern, Heinrich von. *Deutscher Liberalismus im Vormärz: Heinrich von Gagern. Briefe und Reden, 1815–1848.* Berlin, Frankfurt, and Göttingen, 1959.

Gall, Lothar. "Sozialistengesetz und innenpolitischer Umschwung. Baden und die Krise des Jahres 1878." *ZGO* 111, no. 2 (1963): 473–577.

———. *Benjamin Constant. Seine politische Ideenwelt und der deutsche Vormärz.* Wiesbaden, 1963.

———. "Die partei- und sozialgeschichtliche Problematik des badischen Kulturkampfes." *ZGO* 113, no. 1 (1965): 151–96.

———. "Das Problem der parlamentarischen Opposition im deutschen Frühliberalismus." In Kluxen and Mommsen, eds., *Ideologien.* 1968, 153–70.

———. *Der Liberalismus als regierende Partei. Das Grossherzogtum Baden zwischen Restauration und Reichsgründung.* Wiesbaden, 1968.

———. "Liberalismus und 'Bürgerliche Gesellschaft': Zu Charakter und Entwicklung der Liberalen Bewegung in Deutschland." *HZ* 220, no. 2 (1975): 324–56.

———, ed. *Liberalismus.* Cologne, 1976.

Gause, Fritz. *Die Geschichte der Stadt Königsberg in Preussen.* 2 vols. Cologne, 1965–68.

Gebhardt, Hartwig. *Revolution und liberale Bewegung. Die nationale Organisation der konstitutionellen Partei in Deutschland 1848/49.* Bremen, 1974.

Geiss, Imanuel, and Bernd Wendt, eds. *Deutschland in der Weltpolitik des 19. und 20. Jahrhunderts. Fritz Fischer zum 65. Geburtstag.* Düsseldorf, 1973.

Gerlach, Hans Christian. "Agitation und parlamentarische Wirksamkeit der deutschen Antisemitenparteien, 1873–1895." Unpubl. diss., Kiel, 1956.

Germany. *Statistik des Deutschen Reichs.* 1873–1914.

Germany. *Vierteljahrshefte zur Statistik des Deutschen Reichs, 1873–1876.* 1892–1914.

Germany. *Monatshefte zur Statistik des Deutschen Reichs.* 1877–1891.

Germany. *Statistisches Jahrbuch.* 1880–1914.

Gerteis, Klaus. *Leopold Sonnemann. Ein Beitrag zur Geschichte des demokratischen Nationalstaatsgedankens in Deutschland.* Frankfurt, 1970.

———. "Bildung und Revolution: Die deutschen Lesegesellschaften am Ende des 18. Jahrhunderts." *AfK*, 53, no. 1 (1971): 127–39.

Gerth, Hans. *Die sozialgeschichtliche Lage der Bürgerlichen Intelligenz um die Wende des 18. Jahrhunderts. Ein Beitrag zur Soziologie des deutschen Frühliberalismus.* Diss., Frankfurt, 1935.

Gervinus, G. Gottfried. *Leben, von ihm selbst* (1860). Leipzig, 1893.

Gillis, John R. *The Prussian Bureaucracy in Crisis, 1840–1860. Origins of an Administrative Ethos.* Stanford, 1971.

Goessler, Peter. *Der Dualismus zwischen Volk und Regierung im Denken der vormärzlichen Liberalen in Baden und Württemberg.* (Diss., Tübingen.) Schramberg, 1932.

Gothein, E. *Verfassungs- und Wirtschaftsgeschichte der Stadt Cöln vom Untergange der Reichsfreiheit bis zur Errichtung des Deutschen Reiches.* Vol. 1, pt. 1 of *Die Stadt Cöln im ersten Jahrhundert unter preussischer Herrschaft. 1815–1915.* Cologne, 1916.

Graf, Hans. *Die Entwicklung der Wahlen und politischen Parteien in Gross-Dortmund.* (Diss., Marburg, 1955.) Marburg, 1958.

Grambow, Ludolf. *Die deutsche Freihandelspartei zur Zeit ihrer Blüte.* Jena, 1903.

Grenzboten. 1842–1922.

Griewank, Karl. *Deutsche Studenten und Universitäten in der Revolution von 1848.* Weimar, 1949.

Grösser, L. *Der gemässigte Liberalismus im bayerischen Landtag von 1819–1848.* Diss., Augsburg, 1929.

Grosser, Dieter. *Vom monarchischen Konstitutionalismus zur parlamentarischen Demokratie: Die Verfassungspolitik der deutschen Parteien im letzten Jahrzehnt des Kaiserreiches.* The Hague, 1970.

Haas, Armin. "Die Wahlen zum preussischen Abgeordnetenhaus im Regierungsbezirk Aachen von der deutschen Revolution 1848/49 bis zum deutsch-französischen Krieg von 1870/71." Unpubl. diss., Bonn, 1954.

Habermas, Jürgen. *Strukturwandel der Öffentlichkeit. Untersuchungen zu einer Kategorie der bürgerlichen Gesellschaft.* Neuwied, 1962.

Haferland, Hans. *Mensch und Gesellschaft in Staatslexikon von Rotteck-Welcker. Ein Beitrag zur Gesellschaftstheorie des Frühliberalismus.* Diss., Berlin, 1957.

Hamerow, Theodore S. "History and the German Revolution of 1848." *AHR* 60, no. 1 (October 1954): 27–44.

———. *Restoration, Revolution, Reaction. Economics and Politics in Germany, 1815–1871.* Princeton, 1958.

———. "The Elections to the Frankfurt Parliament." *JMH* 33, no. 1 (March 1961): 15–32.

———. *The Social Foundations of German Unification, 1858–1871.* 2 vols. Princeton, 1969–72.

Hansen, Joseph. *Gustav von Mevissen. Ein rheinisches Lebensbild 1815–1899.* 2 vols. Berlin, 1906.

———. *Rheinische Briefe und Akten zur Geschichte der politischen Bewegung, 1830–1850.* Vol. 1, *1830–1845* (1919). Osnabrück, 1967.

———. *Rheinische Briefe und Akten zur Geschichte der politischen Bewegung 1830–1850.* Vol. 2, *1846–1850. (Part 1: 1846–April 1848.)* Bonn, 1942.

Hardach, Karl. *Die Bedeutung wirtschaftlicher Faktoren bei der Wiedereinführung der Eisen- und Getreidezölle in Deutschland 1879.* Berlin, 1967.

Harkort, Friedrich. *Schriften und Reden zu Volksschule und Volksbildung.* Paderborn, 1969.

Hartenstein, Wolfgang. *Die Anfänge der deutschen Volkspartei, 1918–1920.* Düsseldorf, 1962.

Haseloff, W. "Die politischen Parteien und die Wahlen in Waldeck 1867–1953." Unpubl. diss., Marburg, 1955.

Haym, Rudolf. *Aus meinem Leben. Erinnerungen. (Aus dem Nachlass.)* Berlin, 1902.

———. *Ausgewählter Briefwechsel Rudolf Hayms.* Ed. by H. Rosenberg. 1930; reprinted Osnabrück, 1967.

Hebeisen, Gustav. *Die radikale und die konstitutionelle Partei in Baden am Vorabend des Frühjahresaufstandes von 1848.* Diss., Freiburg, 1909.

Heberle, Rudolf. *From Democracy to Nazism. A Regional Case Study on Political Parties in Germany.* Baton Rouge, 1945.

———. *Landbevölkerung und Nationalsozialismus. Eine soziologische Untersuchung der politischen Willensbildung in Schleswig-Holstein. 1918 bis 1932.* Stuttgart, 1963.

Heckart, Beverly. *From Bassermann to Bebel. The Grand Bloc's Quest for Reform in the Kaiserreich, 1900–1914.* New Haven and London, 1974.

Heffter, Heinrich. *Die deutsche Selbstverwaltung im 19. Jahrhundert: Geschichte der Ideen und Institutionen.* Stuttgart, 1950.

Hegel, G. W. F. *Philosophy of Right.* Translated with notes by T. M. Knox. London, 1952.

Heger, Klaus. *Die deutsche Demokratische Partei in Württemberg und ihre Organisation.* Leipzig, 1927.

Heiber, Helmut. "Die Rhetorik der Paulskirche." Unpubl. diss., Berlin, 1953.

Heintz, Eckard. *Der Beamtenabgeordnete im Bayerischen Landtag. Eine politische Studie über die Stellung des Beamtentums in der parlamentarischen Entwicklung Deutschlands.* Diss., Berlin, 1966.

Helfferich, Karl. *Georg von Siemens. Ein Lebensbild aus Deutschlands grosser Zeit.* 3 vols. Berlin, 1921–23.

Hellpach, Willy. *Wirken in Wirren. Lebenserinnerungen.* 2 vols. Hamburg, 1948–49.

Henderson, W. O. *The Zollverein.* Cambridge, 1939.

Hengel, Peter. "Das Warenhaus als parteipolitisches Problem." Unpubl. diss., Tübingen, 1952.

Henning, Hansjoachim. "Preussische Sozialpolitik im Vormärz?" *VSWG* 52, no. 4 (December 1965): 485–539.

———. *Das westdeutsche Bürgertum in der Epoche der Hochindustrialisierung 1860–1914. Soziales Verhalten und soziale Strukturen.* Pt. 1, *Das Bildungsbürgertum in den preussischen Westprovinzen.* Wiesbaden, 1972.

Henning, Wilhelm. *Geschichte der Stadtverordnetenversammlung von Essen (1890–1914).* Essen, 1965.

Hentschel, Volker. *Die deutschen Freihändler und der volkswirtschaftliche Kongress 1858 bis 1885*. Stuttgart, 1975.

Herzfeld, Hans. *Johannes von Miquel*. 2 vols. Detmold, 1938.

Hess, Adalbert. *Die Landtags- und Reichstagswahlen im Grossherzogtum Hessen, 1865–1871*. Oberursel, 1958.

————. *Das Parlament das Bismarck widerstrebte: Zur Politik und sozialen Zusammensetzung des preussischen Abgeordnetenhauses der Konfliktszeit (1862–1866)*. Cologne and Opladen, 1964.

Heuss, Alfred. *Theodor Mommsen und das 19. Jahrhundert*. Kiel, 1956.

Heyderhoff, Julius, and Wentzcke, Paul. *Deutscher Liberalismus im Zeitalter Bismarcks: Eine politische Briefsammlung*. 2 vols. Bonn and Leipzig, 1925–26.

Hintze, Otto. *Gesammelte Abhandlungen*. 2d ed. 3 vols. Göttingen, 1962–67.

Hock, Wolfgang. *Liberales Denken im Zeitalter der Paulskirche. Droysen und die Frankfurter Mitte*. Münster, 1957.

Höpker, Heinrich. "Die preussischen Landtagswahlen von 1913." *ZPSB*, Supplement 43. Berlin, 1916.

Hoffmann, W. G. "The Take-Off in Germany." In W. W. Rostow, ed, *The Economics of Take-Off into Sustained Growth*. New York, 1963, pp. 95–118.

————. *Das Wachstum der deutschen Wirtschaft seit der Mitte des 19. Jahrhunderts*. Berlin, Heidelberg, and New York, 1965.

Hofmann, Wolfgang. *Die Bielefelder Stadtverordneten. Ein Beitrag zu bürgerlicher Selbstverwaltung und sozialem Wandel 1850–1914*. Lübeck and Hamburg, 1964.

Holl, Karl, and List, Günther, eds. *Liberalismus und imperialistischer Staat: Der Imperialismus als Problem liberaler Parteien in Deutschland 1890–1914*, Göttingen, 1975.

Hombach, Heinz-Jürgen. "Reichs- und Landtagswahlen im Siegkreis sowie in den Kreisen Mülheim-am-Rhein, Wipperfürth, Gummersbach und Waldbröl, 1870–1878." Unpubl. diss., Bonn, 1963.

Hopwood, Robert. "Paladins of the Buergertum: Cultural Clubs and Politics in Small German Towns, 1918–1925." Canadian Historical Association, *Historical Papers* (1974), pp. 213–35.

Hubatsch, Walther, ed. *Schicksalswege deutscher Vergangenheit*. Düsseldorf, 1950.

Huber, Ernst Rudolf. *Deutsche Verfassungsgeschichte*. 4 vols. Stuttgart, 1957–69.

————. *Dokumente zur Deutschen Verfassungsgeschichte*. 3 vols. Stuttgart, 1961–66.

Hunt, James C. "Peasants, Grain Tariffs, and Meat Quotas: Imperial German Protectionism Reexamined." *CEH* 7, no. 4 (December 1974): 311–31.

————. "The Egalitarianism of the Right. The Agrarian League in Southwest Germany, 1893–1914." *JCH* 10, no. 3 (1975): 513–30.

Im neuen Reich. 1871–81.

Jacoby, Johann. *Gesammelte Schriften und Reden*. 2 vols. Hamburg, 1872.

Jaeger, Hans. *Unternehmer in der deutschen Politik, 1890–1918*. Bonn, 1967.

Jantke, Carl. *Der vierte Stand: Die gestaltenden Kräfte der deutschen Arbeiterbewegung im XIX. Jahrhundert*. Freiburg, 1955.

———, and Hilger, Dietrich, eds. *Die Eigentumslosen. Armutsnot und Arbeiterschicksal in Deutschland in zeitgenössischen Schilderungen und kritische Beobachtungen bis zum Ausgang der Emanzipationskrise des 19. Jahrhunderts*. Munich, 1965.

Jolly, Julius. *Der Reichstag und die Parteien*. Berlin, 1880.

Jordan, Herbert. *Die öffentliche Meinung in Sachsen, 1864–66*. Kamenz, 1918.

Julku, Kyösti. *Die revolutionäre Bewegung im Rheinland am Ende des achtzehnten Jahrhunderts*. 2 vols. Helsinki, 1965–69.

Kaehler, Siegfried. "Stoeckers Versuch eine christlich-soziale Arbeiterpartei in Berlin zu begründen." In *Deutscher Staat und deutsche Parteien (Meinecke Festschrift)*. Ed. by P. Wentzcke. Berlin, 1922, pp. 227–65.

Kaelble, Hartmut. *Industrielle Interessenpolitik in der Wilhelminischen Gesellschaft: Centralverband Deutscher Industriellen 1895–1914*. Berlin, 1967.

———. "Industrielle Interessenverbände vor 1914." In W. Rüegg and O. Neuloh, eds., *Zur soziologischen Theorie und Analyse des 19. Jahrhunderts*. Göttingen, 1971, pp. 180–92.

———. "Kommunalverwaltung und Unternehmer in Berlin während der frühen Industrialisierung." In O. Büsch, ed., *Untersuchungen zur Geschichte der frühen Industrialisierung*. Berlin, 1971, pp. 371–415.

———. *Berliner Unternehmer während der frühen Industrialisierung. Herkunft, sozialer Status und politischer Einfluss*. Berlin, 1972.

Kaiser, Renate. *Die politischen Strömungen in den Kreisen Bonn und Rheinbach 1848–1878*. Bonn, 1963.

Kalkoff, Hermann. *Die nationalliberale Fraktion des Preussischen Abgeordnetenhauses, 1866–1913*. Berlin, 1913.

———, ed. *Nationalliberale Parlamentarier des Reichstages und der Einzellandtage, 1867–1917*. Berlin, 1917.

Kant, Immanuel. *Political Writings*. Cambridge, 1970.

Kapp, Friedrich. *Vom radikalen Frühsozialisten des Vormärz zum liberalen Parteipolitiker des Bismarckreichs. Briefe, 1843–1884*. Ed. by H. U. Wehler. Frankfurt, 1969.

Kastendiek, Hermann. "Der Liberalismus in Bremen." Unpubl. diss., Kiel, 1952.

Kaufmann, Karlheinz. "Soziale Strukturen im politischen Feld dargestellt am Beispiel Heidelbergs und der sozialdemokratischen Parteiorganisation in dieser Stadt." Unpubl. diss., Heidelberg, 1957.

Kehr, Eckart. *Der Primat der Innenpolitik: Gesammelte Aufsätze zur preussisch-deutschen Sozialgeschichte.* Ed. by H-U. Wehler. Berlin, 1965.

Kiehl, Hans-Georg. "Albert Hänel und der Linksliberalismus in Reichstagswahlkreis Kiel-Flendsburg-Plön, 1867–1884." Diss., Kiel, 1966.

Kiesselbach, Wilhelm. "Drei Generationen." *DV* 23, no. 3 (1860): 1–37.

Klein, Thomas. "Reichstagswahlen und Abgeordnete der Provinz Sachsen und Anhalt 1867–1918." In W. Schlesinger, ed., *Festschrift für Friedrich Zahn.* Vol. 1. Cologne-Graz, 1968, 65–141.

Klein-Hattingen, Oskar. *Die Geschichte des deutschen Liberalismus.* 2 vols. Berlin-Schöneberg, 1911–12.

Kluxen, Kurt, and Mommsen, Wolfgang J., eds. *Politische Ideologien und nationalstaatliche Ordnung. Festschrift für Theodor Schieder.* Munich and Vienna, 1968.

Knoll, J. H. *Führungsauslese in Liberalismus und Demokratie.* Stuttgart, 1957.

Kochhann, Heinrich Eduard. *Auszüge aus seinen Tagebüchern.* 4 vols. Berlin, 1906.

Kocka, Jürgen. *Unternehmensverwaltung und Angestelltenschaft am Beispiel Siemens 1847–1914. Zum Verhältnis von Kapitalismus und Bürokratie in der deutschen Industrialisierung.* Stuttgart, 1969.

———. "Preussischer Staat und Modernisierung im Vormärz: Marxistisch-leninistische Interpretationen und ihre Probleme." In Wehler, ed. *Sozialgeschichte.* 1974, pp. 211–28.

Köllmann, W. "Industrialisierung, Binnenwanderung und 'Soziale Frage.' Zur Entstehungsgeschichte der deutschen Industriegrossstadt im 19. Jahrhundert." *VSWG* 46, no. 1 (1959): 45–70.

———. "Grundzüge der Bevölkerungsgeschichte Deutschlands im 19. und 20. Jahrhundert." *Studium Generale* 12, no. 6 (1959): 381–92.

———. *Sozialgeschichte der Stadt Barmen im 19. Jahrhundert.* Tübingen, 1960.

———. "Politische und soziale Entwicklung der deutschen Arbeiterschaft 1850–1914." *VSWG* 50, no. 4 (1964): 480–504.

———. *Friedrich Harkort.* Vol. 1, *1793–1838.* Düsseldorf, 1964.

———. "Die Anfänge der staatlichen Sozialpolitik in Preussen bis 1869." *VSWG* 53, no. 1 (March 1966): 28–52.

———. "Bevölkerung und Arbeitskräftepotential in Deutschland, 1815–1865. Ein Beitrag zur Analyse der Problematik des Pauperismus." Landesamt für Forschung, Nordrhein-Westfalen, *Jahrbuch* (1968), pp. 209–54.

Kommunale Praxis. Vols. 1–14. 1900–14.

Kommunale Rundschau. Monatsschrift für städtische Bau- und Bodenpolitik, Kommunaltechnik und Verwaltungswesen. 1907–14.

Kommunalpolitische Blätter. 1910–14.

Koselleck, Reinhart. *Kritik und Krise. Ein Beitrag zur Pathogenese der bürgerlichen Welt.* Freiburg and Munich, 1959.
————. "Staat und Gesellschaft in Preussen 1815–1848." In Conze, ed., *Staat.* 1962, pp. 79–112.
————. *Preussen zwischen Reform und Revolution. Allgemeines Landrecht. Verwaltung und soziale Bewegung von 1791 bis 1848.* Stuttgart, 1967.
————. "Begriffsgeschichte und Sozialgeschichte." In Ludz, ed., *Soziologie.* 1972, 116–31.
Koser, Reinhold. "Zur Charakteristik des Vereinigten Landtags von 1847." In *Beiträge zur brandenburgischen und preussischen Geschichte. Festschrift für Gustav Schmoller.* Leipzig, 1908.
————. "Die Anfänge der politischen Parteibildung in Preussen bis 1849." In *Zur preussischen und deutschen Geschichte. Aufsätze und Vorträge.* Stuttgart and Berlin, 1921, pp. 376–400.
Köster, Johanna. *Der rheinische Frühliberalismus und die soziale Frage.* Berlin, 1938.
Koszyk, Kurt. "Carl d'Ester als Gemeinderat und Parlamentarier (1846–1849)." *AfS* 1 (1960): 43–60.
————. *Geschichte der deutschen Presse.* Vol. 2, *Deutsche Presse im 19. Jahrhundert.* Berlin, 1966.
Krabs, Otto. "Hamm. Beiträge zur Geschichte der Stadt im 19. Jahrhundert." Unpubl. diss., Göttingen, 1964.
Kramer, Helmut. *Fraktionsbindungen in den deutschen Volksvertretungen 1819–1849.* Berlin, 1968.
Krause, Hans. *Die demokratische Partei von 1848 und die soziale Frage. Ein Beitrag zur Geschichte der ersten deutschen Revolution.* Frankfurt, 1923.
Kremer, Willy. *Der soziale Aufbau der Parteien des Deutschen Reichstages von 1871–1918.* Emsdetten, 1934.
Kriegbaum, Günther. *Die parlamentarische Tätigkeit des Freiherrn C. W. Heyl zu Herrensheim.* Meisenheim (Glan), 1962.
Krieger, Leonard. *The German Idea of Freedom: History of a Political Tradition.* Boston, 1957.
Kulemann, Wilhelm. *Politische Erinnerungen: Ein Beitrag zur neueren Zeitgeschichte.* Berlin, 1911.
Kurmeier, Karl. *Die Entstehung der nationalliberalen Partei Hannovers.* Diss., Göttingen, 1923.
Kurt, Alfred. *Wahlen und Wähler im Wahlkreis Offenbach. Eine historisch-statistische Untersuchung zur politischen Struktur der Stadt und des Landkreises Offenbach.* Offenbach, 1966.
Kurze, Dietrich, ed. *Aus Theorie und Praxis der Geschichtswissenschaft. Festschrift für Hans Herzfeld zum 80. Geburtstag.* Berlin, 1972.
Lambers, Hanno. *Die Revolutionszeit in Hagen. Die politische Entwicklung von 1917 bis 1924 in Hagen und Haspe.* Hagen, 1963.
Lambi, Ivo. *Free Trade and Protection in Germany, 1868–1879.* Wiesbaden, 1963.

Lamer, Reinhard. *Der englische Parlamentarismus in der deutschen politischen Theorie im Zeitalter Bismarcks (1857–1890).* Lübeck and Hamburg, 1963.

Landes, David S. "Japan and Europe: Contrasts in Industrialization." In W. Lockwood, ed., *The State and Economic Enterprise in Japan.* Princeton, 1965, pp. 93–182.

———. *The Unbound Prometheus. Technical Change and Industrial Development in Western Europe from 1750 to the Present.* Cambridge, 1969.

Lang, Wilhelm. *Die deutsche Partei in Württemberg, 1866–1891.* Stuttgart, 1891.

Langewiesche, Dieter. *Liberalismus und Demokratie in Württemberg zwischen Revolution und Reichsgründung.* Düsseldorf, 1974.

Lasker, Eduard. "Aus Eduard Laskers Nachlass. Sein Briefwechsel aus den Jahren 1870/71." *DR* 17, nos. 2, 3 and 4, (1892): 46–64, 166–86, 296–317; 59–82, 157–77, 283–301; 60–76, 190–203, 352–66.

Lasker, Eduard. *Aus Eduard Laskers Nachlass.* Ed. by W. Cahn. Berlin, 1902.

Lavies, Ralf-Rainer. *Nichtwählen als Kategorie des Wahlverhaltens: Empirische Untersuchung zur Wahlenthaltung in historischer, politischer und statistischer Sicht.* Düsseldorf, 1973.

Lebovics, Herman. *Social Conservatism and the Middle Classes in Germany, 1914–1933.* Princeton, 1969.

Lees, Andrew. *Revolution and Reflection: Intellectual Change in Germany during the 1850's.* The Hague, 1974.

———. "Debates about the Big City in Germany, 1890–1914." *Societas* 5, no. 1 (Winter 1975): 31–47.

Lenk, Leonhard. "Katholizismus und Liberalismus. Zur Auseinandersetzung mit dem Zeitgeist in München, 1848–1918." In *Der Monch im Wappen.* Munich, 1960.

Lepsius, M. Rainer. "Parteisystem und Sozialstruktur: zum Problem der Demokratisierung der deutschen Gesellschaft." In W. Abel et al., eds., *Wirtschaft, Geschichte und Wirtschaftsgeschichte. Festschrift zum 65. Geburtstag von Friedrich Lütge.* Stuttgart, 1966, 371–93.

———. *Extremer Nationalismus. Strukturbedingungen von der nationalsozialistischen Machtergreifung.* Stuttgart, 1966.

Lewald, Fanny. *Erinnerungen aus dem Jahre 1848* (1850). Ed. by Dietrich Schaefer. Frankfurt, 1969.

Link, Werner. "Der Nationalverein für das liberale Deutschland. (1907–1918)." *PV* 5, no. 4 (December 1964): 422–44.

Linke, Wolf-Dieter. "Die Rolle des Reichstages bei der Einschränkung der Gewerbefreiheit: Ein Beitrag zum Problem 'Handwerk und Parlament.'" Unpubl. diss., Berlin, 1955.

Ludz, Peter Christian, ed. *Soziologie und Sozialgeschichte. (Kölner Zeitschrift für Soziologie und Sozialpsychologie*, Supplement 16). Opladen, 1972.

Lüders, Gustav. *Die demokratische Bewegung in Berlin in Oktober 1848.* Berlin and Leipzig, 1909.

Lütge, Friedrich, ed. *Die wirtschaftliche Situation in Deutschland und Österreich um die Wende vom 18. zum 19. Jahrhundert.* Stuttgart, 1964.

Maenner, Ludwig. "Deutschlands Wirtschaft und Liberalismus in der Krise von 1879." *Archiv für Politik und Geschichte* 9, nos. 11 and 12 (1927): 347–82, 456–88.

Manheim, Ernst. *Die Träger der öffentlichen Meinung. Studien zur Soziologie der Öffentlichkeit.* Brunn, 1933.

Marquardt, Frederick D. "A Working Class in Berlin in the 1840's?" In Wehler, ed., *Sozialgeschichte.* 1974, pp. 191–210.

———. "Sozialer Aufstieg, sozialer Abstieg und die Entstehung der Berliner Arbeiterklasse, 1806–1848." *GuG* 1, no. 1 (1975) pp. 43–77.

Matern, Norbert. "Politische Wahlen in Hildesheim, 1848 bis 1867." Unpubl. diss., Bonn, 1959.

Matthes, Heinz Edgar. "Die Spaltung der Nationalliberalen Partei und die Entwicklung des Linksliberalismus bis zur Auflösung der Deutsch-Freisinnigen Partei (1878–1893): Ein Beitrag zur Geschichte der Krise des deutschen politischen Liberalismus." Unpubl. diss., Kiel, 1953.

Matthias, Erich, and Morsey, Rudolf, eds. *Das Ende der Parteien 1933.* Düsseldorf, 1960.

Mayer, Gustav. *Radikalismus, Sozialismus und bürgerliche Demokratie.* Ed. by H-U. Wehler. Frankfurt, 1969.

———. "Die Trennung der proletarischen von der bürgerlichen Demokratie in Deutschland, 1863–1870" (1912). In *Radikalismus.* 1969, pp. 108–78.

———. "Die Anfänge des politischen Radikalismus im vormärzlichen Preussen." (1913). In *Radikalismus.* 1969, pp. 7–107.

McClelland, Charles E. *The German Historian and England: A Study in Nineteenth-Century Views.* Cambridge, 1971.

Meinecke, Friedrich. *Werke.* Ed. by H. Herzfeld et al. 8 vols. Munich, 1957–69.

———. "Alfred Dove und der klassische Liberalismus im Neuen Reich." (1925). *Werke,* 7:386–412.

———. "Erlebtes. 1862–1901." *Werke,* 8:3–136.

———. "Strassburg, Freiburg, Berlin. 1901–1919." *Werke,* 8:137–322.

Menzinger, Rosemarie. *Verfassungsrevision und Demokratisierungsprozess im Königreich Württemberg. Ein Beitrag zur Entstehungsgeschichte des parlamentarischen Regierungssystems in Deutschland.* Stuttgart, 1969.

Meyer, Dora. *Das öffentliche Leben in Berlin im Jahr vor der Märzrevolution.* Berlin, 1912.

Meyer, Wolfgang. *Das Vereinswesen der Stadt Nürnberg im 19. Jahrhundert.* Nuremberg, 1970.

Michels, Robert. "Die deutsche Sozialdemokratie, I: Parteimitgliedschaft und soziale Zusammensetzung." *ASW* 23 (1906): 471–556.

Milatz, Alfred. "Das Ende der Parteien im Spiegel der Wahlen 1930 bis 1933." In Matthias and Morsey, eds., *Ende*. 1960, pp. 741–793.

———. "Die linksliberalen Parteien und Gruppen in den Reichstagswahlen von 1871–1912." *AfS* 12, no. 2 (1972): 273–92.

———. "Reichstagswahlen und Mandatsverteilung 1871 bis 1918. Ein Beitrag zu Problemen des absoluten Mehrheitswahlrechts." In Ritter, ed., *Gesellschaft*. 1974, pp. 207–23.

Miquel, Johannes von. *Reden*. 4 vols. Halle, 1911–14.

———. "Die Briefe Miquels an Marquardsen." *Süddeutsche Monatshefte* 10, no. 1 (1912–13): 807–16, and 10, no. 2 (1912–13): 90–96, 163–71.

Möckl, Karl. *Die Prinzregentenzeit. Gesellschaft und Politik während der Ära des Prinzregenten Luitpold in Bayern*. Munich and Vienna, 1972.

Möllers, Paul. "Die politischen Strömungen im Reichstags-Wahlkreis Essen zur Zeit der Reichsgründung und des Kulturkampfes (1867–1878)." Unpubl. diss., Bonn, 1955.

Mohl, Robert von. "Die Staatswissenschaften und die Gesellschaftswissenschaften" (1851). *Die Geschichte und Literatur der Staatswissenschaften*. Erlangen, 1855, 1:69–110.

———. "Drei deutsche Staatswörterbücher." *PJbb* 2, no. 3 (1858): 243–67.

———. "Das Repräsentativsystem, seine Mängel und die Heilmittel." *Staatsrecht, Völkerrecht und Politik*. Tübingen, 1860, 1:367–458.

———. "Die geschichtlichen Phasen des Repräsentativsystems in Deutschland." *ZfGS* 27, no. 1 (1871): 1–69.

———. *Lebenserinnerungen. 1799–1875*. 2 vols. Stuttgart and Leipzig, 1902.

———. *Politische Schriften. Eine Auswahl*. Ed. by Klaus von Beyme. Cologne and Opladen, 1966.

Molt, Peter. *Der Reichstag vor der improvisierten Revolution*. Cologne and Opladen, 1963.

Mommsen, Wilhelm. *Johannes Miquel*. Vol. 1, *1828–1866*. Berlin and Leipzig, 1928.

———. *Stein, Ranke, Bismarck. Ein Beitrag zur politischen und sozialen Bewegung des 19. Jahrhunderts*. Munich, 1954.

———. *Deutsche Parteiprogramme*. 2d ed. Munich, 1964.

———. *Grösse und Versagen des deutschen Bürgertums*. 2d ed. Munich, 1964.

Mommsen, Wolfgang J. *Max Weber und die deutsche Politik, 1890–1920*. Tübingen, 1959.

———. "Wandlungen der liberalen Idee im Zeitalter des Imperialismus." In Holl and List, eds., *Liberalismus*. 1975, pp. 109–47.

———. "Liberalismus und liberale Idee in Geschichte und Gegenwart." In Kurt Sontheimer, ed., *Möglichkeiten und Grenzen liberaler Politik*. Düsseldorf, 1975, pp. 11–45.

Morsey, Rudolf. *Die oberste Reichsverwaltung unter Bismarck, 1867–1890.* Münster, 1957.

Mosse, George L. *The Nationalization of the Masses. Political Symbolism and Mass Movements in Germany from the Napoleonic Wars through the Third Reich.* New York, 1975.

Motteck, H., et al. *Studien zur Geschichte der industriellen Revolution in Deutschland.* Berlin, 1960.

————. "Die Gründerkrise: Produktionsbewegung, Wirkungen, theoretische Problematik." *JbW 1* (1966): 51–128.

Müller, Friedrich. *Korporation und Assoziation: Eine Problemgeschichte der Vereinigungsfreiheit im deutschen Vormärz.* Berlin, 1965.

Müller, Klaus. *Politische Strömungen in den rechtsrheinischen Kreisen der Regierungsbezirks Köln (Sieg, Mülheim, Wipperfürth, Gummersbach und Waldbröl) von 1879 bis 1906.* Diss., Bonn, 1963.

Na'aman, Shlomo. *Demokratische und soziale Impulse in der Frühgeschichte der deutschen Arbeiterbewegung der Jahre 1862/63.* Wiesbaden, 1969.

Nationalzeitung (Berlin). 1862–1914.

Naumann, Friedrich. *Werke.* 6 vols. Cologne and Opladen, 1964–.

Nettmann, Wilhelm. "Witten in den Reichstagswahlen des deutschen Reiches, 1871–1918." *Jahrbuch des Vereins für Orts- und Heimatkunde. Grafschaft Mark,* 70 (1972), pp. 77–165.

Neumüller, Michael. *Liberalismus und Revolution. Das Problem der Revolution in der deutschen liberalen Geschichtsschreibung des neunzehnten Jahrhunderts.* Düsseldorf, 1973.

Nickel, Dietmar. *Die Revolution 1848/49 in Augsburg und bayerisch-Schwaben.* Augsburg, 1965.

Nipperdey, Thomas. "Interessenverbände und Parteien in Deutschland vor dem ersten Weltkrieg." *PV* 2, no. 3 (1961): 262–80.

————. *Die Organisation der deutschen Parteien vor 1918.* Düsseldorf, 1961.

————. "Über einige Grundzüge der deutschen Parteigeschichte." In *Festschrift für Hans Carl Nipperdey.* Munich, 1965, 2:815–41.

————. "Volksschule und Revolution im Vormärz." In Kluxen, ed., *Ideologien.* 1968, pp. 117–42.

————. "Carl Bernhard Hundeshagen. Ein Beitrag zum Verhältnis von Geschichtsschreibung, Theologie und Politik im Vormärz." In *Festschrift für Hermann Heimpel zum 70. Geburtstag.* Göttingen, 1971, 1:368–409.

————. "Verein als soziale Struktur in Deutschland im späten 18. und frühen 19. Jahrhundert." In H. Boockmann et al., eds., *Geschichtswissenschaft und Vereinswesen im 19. Jahrhundert.* Göttingen, 1972, pp. 1–44.

————. "Grundprobleme der deutschen Parteigeschichte im 19. Jahrhundert." In G. A. Ritter, ed., *Parteien.* 1973, pp. 32–55.

————. "Jugend und Politik um 1900." In W. Rüegg, ed., *Kulturkritik und Jugendkult.* Frankfurt, 1974, pp. 87–114.

Noyes, P. H. *Organizations and Revolution: Working-Class Associations in the German Revolutions of 1848–49.* Princeton, 1966.

Nussbaum, Helga. *Unternehmer gegen Monopol. Über Struktur und Aktionen antimonopolistischer bürgerlicher Gruppen zu Beginn des 20. Jahrhunderts.* Berlin, 1966.

O'Boyle, Lenore. "Liberal Political Leadership in Germany 1867–1884." *JMH* 28, no. 4 (December 1956): 338–52.

———. "The German Nationalverein." *JCEA* 16, no. 4 (January 1957): 333–52.

———. "The Democratic Left in Germany, 1848." *JMH* 33, no. 4 (1961): 374–83.

———. "The Middle Class in Western Europe, 1815–48." *AHR* 71, no. 3 (1966): 826–45.

———. "The Image of the Journalist in France, Germany, and England, 1815–1848." *CSSH* 10, no. 2 (1968): 290–317.

———. "The Problem of an Excess of Educated Men in Western Europe, 1800–1850." *JMH* 42, no. 4 (1970): 471–95.

O'Donnell, Anthony. "National Liberalism and the Mass Politics of the German Right, 1890–1907." Unpubl. diss., Princeton, 1973.

Oncken, Hermann. *Rudolf von Bennigsen. Ein deutscher liberaler Politiker.* 2 vols. Stuttgart and Leipzig, 1910.

Pachnicke, Hermann. *Führende Männer im alten und im neuen Reich.* Berlin, 1930.

Pack, Wolfgang. *Das parlamentarische Ringen um das Sozialistengesetz Bismarcks, 1878–1890.* Düsseldorf, 1961.

Pagenstecher, C. H. Alexander. *Lebenserinnerungen.* 3 vols. Leipzig, 1913.

———. "Aus den Lebenserinnerungen des Dr. med. C. H. Alexander Pagenstecher (1860–1866)." *ZGO* 73, no. 2 (1919): 227–56.

Pankoke, Eckart. *Sociale Bewegung, Sociale Frage, Sociale Politik. Grundfragen der deutschen Socialwissenschaft im 19. Jahrhundert.* Stuttgart, 1970.

Parisius, Ludolf. *Leopold Freiherr von Hoverbeck: Ein Beitrag zur vaterländischen Geschichte.* 2 vols. Berlin, 1897–1900.

———. *Deutschlands politische Parteien und das Ministerium Bismarck.* Berlin, 1878.

Petermeier, Karl. "Balthasar Daller. Politiker und Parteiführer, 1835–1911. Studien zur Geschichte der bayerischen Zentrumspartei." Unpubl. diss., Munich, 1956.

Pflanze, Otto. *Bismarck and the Development of Germany: The Period of Unification, 1815–1871.* Princeton, 1963.

———. "Judicial and Political Responsibility in Nineteenth Century Germany." In F. Stern and L. Krieger, eds., *The Responsibility of Power.* New York, 1967, pp. 162–82.

Philippson, Johanna. *Über den Ursprung und die Einführung des allgemeinen gleichen Wahlrechtes in Deutschland mit besonderer Berücksichtigung der Wahlen zum Frankfurt Parlament im Grossherzogtum Baden.* Berlin and Leipzig, 1913.

Philippson, Martin. "Briefe Max von Forckenbecks." *DR* 23, no. 2 (1898): 1–16, 141–58; 29, nos. 1 and 2 (1899): 129–46, 164–74.

———. *Max von Forckenbeck: Ein Lebensbild.* Leipzig, n.d. (1898).

Phillips, Adolf, ed. *Die Reichstags-Wahlen von 1867 bis 1883: Statistik der Wahlen zum konstituierenden und norddeutschen Reichstage, zum Zollparlament, sowie zu den fünf ersten Legislatur-Perioden des deutschen Reichstages.* Berlin, 1883.

Piechocki, Werner. "Die kommunalpolitische Wirksamkeit Arnold Ruges in Halle während der Jahre 1831 bis 1841." *Wissenschaftliche Zeitschrift der Universität Halle.* Gesellschafts- und Sprachwissenschaftliche Reihe, 16, nos. 2/3 (1967): 173–96.

Poll, Bernhard. "Die neuere kommunale Selbstverwaltung Aachens. Ein Beitrag zur rheinischen Städteordnung 1856–1918." In *Im Schatten von St. Gereon. Erich Kiephal zum 1. Juli 1960.* Cologne, 1960, pp. 259–84.

Portner, Ernst. *Die Verfassungspolitik der Liberalen 1919.* Bonn, 1973.

Prince Smith, John. *Gesammelte Schriften.* 3 vols. Berlin, 1877–80.

Pülke, Engelbert. "Geschichte der politischen Parteien in Kreis Recklinghausen bis zum Ende des Kulturkampfes 1848–1889." *Vestische Zeitschrift* 41 (1934): 3–163.

Puhle, Hans-Jürgen. *Agrarische Interessenpolitik und preussischer Konservatismus im wilhelminischen Reich (1893–1914).* Hanover, 1967.

———. "Parlament, Parteien und Interessenverbände, 1890–1914." In Stürmer, ed. *Deutschland.* 1970, pp. 340–77.

Rachfahl, Felix. "Eugen Richter und der Linksliberalismus im neuen Reiche." *ZfP* 5, nos. 2/3 (1912): 261–374.

Rapp, Alfred. *Die badischen Landtagsabgeordneten, 1905–1929.* Karlsruhe, 1929.

Reichard, Richard W. *Crippled From Birth. German Social Democracy, 1844–1870.* Ames, Iowa, 1969.

Reimann, Joachim. *Ernst Müller-Meiningen senior und der Linksliberalismus in seiner Zeit. Zur Biographie eines bayerischen und deutschen Politikers (1866–1944).* Munich, 1968.

Reiss, Klaus-Peter, ed. *Von Bassermann zu Stresemann. Die Sitzungsberichte des nationalliberalen Zentralvorstandes, 1912–1917.* Düsseldorf, 1967.

Renner, Veronika. "Karl Twesten, Vorkämpfer der liberalen Rechtsstaatsidee. Studien zu seiner politischen Entwicklung." Unpubl. diss., Freiburg, 1954.

Repgen, Konrad. *Märzbewegung und Maiwahlen des Revolutionsjahres 1848 im Rheinland.* Bonn, 1955.

Richter, Eugen. *Im alten Reichstag: Erinnerungen.* 2 vols. Berlin, 1894–96.

Ringer, Fritz. *The Decline of the German Mandarins. The German Academic*

Community, 1890–1933. Cambridge, Mass. 1969.

Ritter, Gerhard A. "Kontinuität und Umformung des deutschen Parteisystems 1918–1920." In Ritter, ed., *Entstehung*. 1970, pp. 342–84.

———. "Entwicklungsprobleme des deutschen Parlamentarismus." In Ritter, ed., *Gesellschaft*. 1974, pp. 11–54.

———, ed. *Entstehung und Wandel der modernen Gesellschaft. Festschrift für Hans Rosenberg*. Berlin, 1970.

———. *Die deutschen Parteien vor 1918*. Cologne, 1973.

———. *Gesellschaft, Parlament und Regierung. Zur Geschichte des Parlamentarismus in Deutschland*. Düsseldorf, 1974.

Robolsky, Hermann. *Der deutsche Reichstag. Geschichte seines fünfundzwanzigjährigen Bestehens, 1867–1892*. Berlin, 1893.

Robson, S. T. "Left-wing Liberalism in Germany, 1900–1919." Unpubl. diss., Oxford, 1966.

Rochau, Ludwig August von. *Grundsätze der Realpolitik* (1853–69). Ed. by H. U. Wehler. Frankfurt, Berlin, and Vienna, 1972.

Röttges, Otto. *Die politische Wahlen in den linksrheinischen Kreisen des Regierungsbezirkes Düsseldorf, 1848–1867*. Kempen-Niederrhein, 1964.

Rohr, Donald. *The Origins of Social Liberalism in Germany*. Chicago and London, 1963.

Rosenberg, Hans. "Geistige und politische Strömungen an der Universität Halle in der ersten Hälfte des 19. Jahrhunderts." *Deutsche Vierteljahrsschrift für Literaturwissenschaft und Geistesgeschichte* 7, no. 3 (1929): 560–86.

———. "Theologischer Rationalismus und vormärzlicher Vulgärliberalismus." *HZ* 141, no. 3 (1930): 497–541.

———. *Rudolf Haym und die Anfänge des klassischen Liberalismus*. Munich and Berlin, 1933.

———. *Die Weltwirtschaftskrise von 1857–1859*. Stuttgart, 1934.

———. *Die nationalpolitische Publizistik Deutschlands. Vom Eintritt der Neuen Ära in Preussen bis zum Ausbruch des deutschen Krieges. Eine kritische Bibliographie*. 2 vols. Munich and Berlin, 1935.

———. *Bureaucracy, Aristocracy, and Autocracy. The Prussian Experience, 1660–1815*. Cambridge, Mass., 1958.

———. *Grosse Depression und Bismarckzeit. Wirtschaftsablauf, Gesellschaft, und Politik in Mitteleuropa*. Berlin, 1967.

———. "Honoratiorenpolitik und 'Grossdeutsche' Sammlungsbestrebungen im Reichsgründungsjahrzehnt." *JbGMO* 19 (1970): 155–233.

———. *Politische Denkströmungen im deutschen Vormärz*. Göttingen, 1972.

Rosenkranz, Karl. *Über den Begriff der politischen Partei*. Königsberg, 1843.

———. *Aus einem Tagebuch. Königsberg Herbst 1833 bis Frühjahr 1846*. Leipzig, 1854.

———. *Politische Briefe und Aufsätze, 1848–1856*. Ed. by Paul Herre. Leipzig, 1919.

Rosskopf, Josef. "Johann Adam von Itzstein. Ein Beitrag zur Geschichte des badischen Liberalismus." Unpubl. diss., Mainz, 1954.

Rotteck, Carl von. *Gesammelte und nachgelassene Schriften mit Biographie und Briefwechsel.* Ed by H. von Rotteck. 5 vols. Pforzheim, 1841–43.

Rubinstein, Adolf. *Die Deutsch-Freisinnige Partei bis zu ihrem Auseinanderbruch (1884–1893).* Diss., Basel, 1935.

Rückert, Otto. *Zur Geschichte der Arbeiterbewegung im Reichstag Wahlkreis Potsdam-Spandau-Osthavelland.* 3 pts. Potsdam, 1965.

Rüegg, Walter, and Neuloh, O., eds. *Zur soziologischen Theorie und Analyse des 19. Jahrhunderts.* Göttingen, 1971.

Rümelin, Gustav. *Aus der Paulskirche. Berichte an den Schwäbischen Merkur aus den Jahren 1848 und 1849.* Stuttgart, 1892.

————. *Reden und Aufsätze.* 3 vols. Freiburg and Leipzig, n.d.

Runge, Gertrude. *Die Volkspartei in Württemberg von 1864 bis 1871. Die Erben der 48er Revolution im Kampf gegen die preussisch-kleindeutsche Lösung der nationalen Frage.* Stuttgart, 1970.

Sachtler, Heinz. *Wandlungen des industriellen Unternehmers in Deutschland seit Beginn des 19. Jahrhunderts.* (Diss., Halle.) Berlin, 1937.

Salomon, Felix. *Deutsche Parteiprogramme.* 2d ed. 3 vols. Leipzig and Berlin, 1931–32.

Sandberger, Dietrich. *Die Ministerkandidatur Bennigsens.* Berlin, 1929.

Saxony. *Statistisches Jb.* Vols. 40–41. Dresden, 1912–13.

Schaarschmidt, Erich. *Geschichte der Crimmitschauer Arbeiterbewegung.* Diss., Dresden, 1934.

Schadt, Jörg. *Die sozialdemokratische Partei in Baden. Von den Anfängen bis zur Jahrhundertwende (1868–1900).* Hanover, 1971.

Schelm-Spangenberg, Ursula. *Die deutsche Volkspartei im Lande Braunschweig. Gründung, Entwicklung, soziologische Struktur, politische Arbeit.* Braunschweig, 1964.

Schib, Karl. *Die staatsrechtlichen Grundlagen der Politik Karl von Rottecks. Ein Beitrag zur Geschichte des Liberalismus.* (Diss., Basel.) Mulhouse, 1927.

Schieder, Theodor. *Die kleindeutsche Partei in Bayern in den Kämpfen um die nationale Einheit, 1863–1871.* Munich, 1936.

————. *Staat und Gesellschaft im Wandel unserer Zeit.* Munich, 1958.

————. "Partikularismus und nationales Bewusstsein im Denken des Vormärz." In Conze, ed., *Staat.* 1962, pp. 9–38.

Schieder, Theodor, and Deuerlein, Ernst, eds. *Reichsgründung, 1870/71.* Stuttgart, 1970.

Schieder, Wolfgang. *Anfänge der deutschen Arbeiterbewegung.* Stuttgart, 1963.

Schierbaum, Hansjürgen. *Die politischen Wahlen in den Eifel- und Moselkreisen des Regierungsbezirks Trier, 1849–1867.* Düsseldorf, 1960.

Schiffers, Heinrich. *Kulturkampf in Stadt und Regierungsbezirk Aachen.* Aachen, 1929.

Schilfert, Gerhard. *Sieg und Niederlage des demokratischen Wahlrechts in der deutschen Revolution, 1848/49*. Berlin, 1952.

Schlemmer, Hannelore. "Die Rolle der Sozialdemokratie in den Landtagen Badens und Württembergs und ihr Einfluss auf die Entwicklung der Gesamtpartei zwischen 1890 und 1914." Unpubl. diss., Freiburg, 1953.

Schlumbohm, Jürgen. *Freiheit–Die Anfänge der bürgerlichen Emanzipationsbewegung in Deutschland im Spiegel ihres Leitworte*. Düsseldorf, 1975.

Schmidt, Gerhard. *Die Staatsreform in Sachsen in der ersten Hälfte des 19. Jahrhunderts*. Weimar, 1966.

Schmidt, Gustav. "Deutschland am Vorabend des Ersten Weltkrieges." In Stürmer, ed., *Deutschland*. 1970, pp. 397–434.

———. "Innenpolitische Blockbildungen am Vorabend des Ersten Weltkrieges." *Das Parlament*. Supplement 20 (May 13, 1972): 1–32.

———. "Die Nationalliberalen-eine regierungsfähige Partei? Zur Problematik der inneren Reichsgründung 1870–1878." In Ritter, G. A., ed., *Parteien*. 1973, pp. 208–23.

Schmidt, Siegfried. *Robert Blum: Vom Leipziger Liberalen zum Märtyrer der deutschen Demokratie*. Weimar, 1971.

Schmierer, Wolfgang. *Von der Arbeiterbildung zur Arbeiterpolitik. Die Anfänge der Arbeiterbewegung in Württemberg, 1862/63–1878*. Hanover, 1970.

Schmitt, Heinz. *Das Vereinsleben der Stadt Weinheim an der Bergstrasse. Volkskundliche Untersuchung zum kulturellen Leben einer Mittelstadt*. Weinheim, 1963.

Schmitz, Heinrich Karl. *Anfänge und Entwicklung der Arbeiterbewegung im Raum Düsseldorf. Die Arbeiterbewegung in Düsseldorf 1859–1878*. Hanover, 1968.

Schmoller, Gustav. "Die Arbeiterfrage." *PJbb* 14, nos. 4 and 5 (1864): 393–422, 513–47; 15, no. 1 (1865): 32–62.

———. *Zur Geschichte des deutschen Kleingewerbes im 19. Jahrhundert*. Halle, 1870.

———. *Was verstehen wir unter dem Mittelstande? Hat er im 19. Jahrhundert zu-oder abgenommen?* Göttingen, 1897.

———. *Umrisse und Untersuchungen zur Verfassungs–, Verwaltungs–und Wirtschaftsgeschichte*. Leipzig, 1898.

———. "Gustav Rümelin. Ein Lebensabriss des schwäbischen Staatsmannes, Statistikers und Sozialphilosophen." In *Charakterbilder*. Munich and Leipzig, 1913, 141–88.

Schnabel, Franz. *Deutsche Geschichte im neunzehnten Jahrhundert*. 3d ed. 4 vols. Freiburg, 1949–59.

Schneider, Erich. "Die Anfänge der sozialistischen Arbeiterbewegung in der Rheinpfalz, 1864–1899. Ein Beitrag zur süddeutschen Parteiengeschichte." Unpubl. diss., Mainz, 1956.

Schneider, Franz. *Pressefreiheit und politische Öffentlichkeit. Studien zur politischen Geschichte Deutschlands bis 1848*. Neuwied and Berlin, 1966.

Schneider, Walter. *Wirtschafts–und Sozialpolitik im Frankfurter Parlament*. Frankfurt, 1923.

Schorn, Karl. *Lebenserinnerungen: Ein Beitrag zur Geschichte des Rheinlands im 19. Jahrhundert*. 2 vols. Bonn, 1898.

Schorske, Carl E. *German Social Democracy, 1905–1917. The Development of the Great Schism*. Cambridge, Mass., 1955.

Schottelius, Herbert, and Diest, W., eds. *Marine und Marinepolitik im kaiserlichen Deutschland 1871–1914*. Düsseldorf, 1972.

Schrader, Richard. "Die Fraktionen der preussischen Nationalversammlung von 1848." Unpubl. diss., Leipzig, 1923.

Schrader, Wilhelm. *Erfahrungen und Bekenntnisse*. Berlin, 1900.

Schraepler, Ernst. "Die politische Haltung des liberalen Bürgertums im Bismarckreich." *GWU* 5, no. 9 (September 1954): 529–44.

———. "Linksliberalismus und Arbeiterschaft in der preussischen Konfliktszeit." In *Forschungen zu Staat und Verfassung. Festgabe für Fritz Hartung*. Berlin, 1958, pp. 385–401.

Schramm, Percy Ernst. *Hamburg, Deutschland und die Welt*. Munich, 1943.

Schuckmann, G. von. *Die politische Willensbildung in der Grossstadt Köln seit der Reichsgründung im Jahr 1871*. Cologne, 1966.

Schulte, Wilhelm. *Volk und Staat. Westfalen im Vormärz und in der Revolution, 1848/49*. Regensberg and Münster, 1954.

Schulthess, Heinrich, ed. *Europäischer Geschichtskalender*. Nördlingen, 1861–1914.

Schultze, Johanna. *Die Auseinandersetzung zwischen Adel und Bürgertum in den deutschen Zeitschriften der letzten drei Jahrzehnte des 18. Jahrhunderts (1773–1806)*. Berlin, 1925.

Schulze-Delitzsch, Hermann. *Schriften und Reden*. Ed. by F. Thorwart. 5 vols. Berlin, 1909–13.

Schumacher, Martin. "Gesellschafts-und Ständebegriff um 1846. Ein Beitrag zum sozialen Bild des süddeutschen Liberalismus nach dem Rotteck-Welckerschen Staatslexikon." Unpubl. diss., Göttingen, 1956.

———. *Mittelstandsfront und Republik. Die Wirtschaftspartei, Reichspartei des deutschen Mittelstandes, 1919-1933*. Düsseldorf, 1972.

Schunke, Werner. *Die preussischen Freihändler und die Entstehung der nationalliberalen Partei*. Leipzig, 1916.

Schwarz, Georg. "Political Attitudes in the German Universities during the Reign of Wilhelm II." Unpubl. diss., Oxford, 1961.

Schweitzer, Carl Christoph. "Die Kritik der westlich-liberalen Oppositionsgruppen an der Aussenpolitik Bismarcks von 1863 bis 1890." Unpubl. diss., Freiburg, 1950.

Schwemer, Richard. *Geschichte der Freien Stadt Frankfurt am Main (1814–1866)*. 3 vols. (in 4). Frankfurt, 1910–18.

Seeber, Gustav. *Zwischen Bebel und Bismarck. Zur Geschichte des Linksliberalismus in Deutschland 1871–1893*. Berlin, 1965.

Seidel, Friedrich. *Das Armutsproblem im deutschen Vormärz bei F. List.* Cologne, 1970.

Seier, Hellmut. *Die Staatsidee Heinrich von Sybels in den Wandlungen der Reichsgründungszeit, 1862/71.* Lübeck and Hamburg, 1961.

Sell, Friedrich. *Die Tragödie des deutschen Liberalismus.* Stuttgart, 1953.

Sengle, Friedrich. *Biedermeierzeit. Deutsche Literatur im Spannungsfeld zwischen Restauration und Revolution 1815–1848.* 2 vols. Stuttgart, 1971–72.

Severing, Carl. *Mein Lebensweg.* 2 vols. Cologne, 1950.

Seyffardt, Ludwig Friedrich. *Erinnerungen.* Leipzig, 1900.

Sheehan, James J. *The Career of Lujo Brentano: A Study of Liberalism and Social Reform in Imperial Germany.* Chicago and London, 1966.

————. "Political Leadership in the German Reichstag, 1871–1918." *AHR* 74, no. 2 (December 1968): 511–28.

————. "Liberalism and the City in Nineteenth-Century Germany." *PP,* no. 51 (1971): 116–37.

————. "Quantification in the Study of German Social and Political History." In Lorwin, V., and Price, J., eds., *Dimensions of the Past.* New Haven, 1972, pp. 301–32.

————. "Conflict and Cohesion among German Elites in the Nineteenth Century." In Bezucha, Robert, ed., *Modern European Social History.* Lexington, Mass., 1972, pp. 3–27.

————. "Liberalism and Society in Germany, 1815–1848." *JMH* 45, no. 4 (December 1973): 583–604.

————. "*Partei, Volk,* and *Staat*: Some Reflections on the Relationship between Liberal Thought and Action in Vormärz." In Wehler, ed., *Sozialgeschichte.* 1974, pp. 162–74.

Shively, W. Phillips. "Party Identification, Party Choice, and Voting Stability: The Weimar Case." *APSR* 66, no. 4 (December 1972): 1203–25.

Simon, Klaus. *Die württembergischen Demokraten. Ihre Stellung und Arbeit im Parteien-und Verfassungssystem in Württemberg und im Deutschen Reich 1890–1920.* Stuttgart, 1969.

Snell, John L. *The Democratic Movement in Germany, 1789–1914.* Edited and completed by Hans Schmitt. Chapel Hill, North Carolina, 1976.

Sombart, W. *Die deutsche Volkswirtschaft im neunzehnten Jahrhundert.* 2d ed. Berlin, 1909.

Sonnemann, Theodor. "Heinrich Albert Oppermann und der hannoversche Liberalismus." Unpubl. diss., Rostock, 1922.

Spahn, Martin. "Zur Entstehung der nationalliberalen Partei." *ZfP* 1, no. 3 (1908): 346–470.

Staatslexikon. Ed. by Karl von Rotteck and Karl Theodor Welcker. 1st ed. 15 vols., Altona, 1834–43. Supplement, 4 vols., Altona, 1846–48. 2d ed. 12 vols., Altona, 1845–48. 3d ed. 14 vols., Leipzig, 1856–66.

Stadelmann, Rudolf. *Soziale und politische Geschichte der Revolution von 1848.* Munich, 1948.

Stadelmann, Rudolf, and Fischer, W. *Die Bildungswelt des deutschen Handwerks um 1800*. Berlin, 1955.

Der Stadtverordnete. 1911–14.

Stegmann, Dirk. *Die Erben Bismarcks. Parteien und Verbände in der Spätphase des wilhelminischen Deutschlands*. Cologne and Berlin, 1970.

Steil, Hans-Willi. "Die politischen Wahlen in der Stadt Trier und in den Eifel–und Moselkreisen des Regierungsbezirkes Trier 1867–1887." Diss., Bonn, 1961.

Stein, Hans. "Pauperismus und Assoziation. Soziale Tatsachen und Ideen auf dem westeuropäischen Kontinent vom Ende des 18. bis zur Mitte des 19. Jahrhunderts, unter besonderer Berücksichtigung des Rheingebiets." *IRSH* 1, no. 1 (1936): 1–120.

Stein, Julius. *Geschichte der Stadt Breslau im neunzehnten Jahrhundert*. Breslau, 1884.

Steinbrecher, Ursula. *Liberale Parteiorganisation unter besonderer Berücksichtigung des Linksliberalismus 1871–1893. Ein Beitrag zur deutschen Parteigeschichte*. Diss., Cologne, 1960.

Stern, Fritz. "The Political Consequences of the Unpolitical German." *History* 3 (1960): 104–34.

Stillich, Oskar. *Die politischen Parteien in Deutschland*. 2 vols. Leipzig, 1908–11.

Stoffregen, Albert. *Die Geschichte der politischen Parteien und Wahlen im Gebiet des Kreises Gandersheim und der Stadt Salzgitter von 1867 bis 1963*. Diss., Marburg, 1965.

Stoltenberg, Gerhard. *Der deutsche Reichstag, 1871–1873*. Düsseldorf, 1955.

Stresemann, Gustav. *Wirtschaftspolitische Zeitfragen*. Dresden, 1911.

Striebich, Heinz. "Konfession und Partei. Ein Beitrag zur Entwicklung der politischen Willensbildung im alten Lande Baden." Unpubl. diss., Heidelberg, 1955.

Struve, Walter. *Elites Against Democracy. Leadership Ideals in Bourgeois Political Thought in Germany, 1890–1933*. Princeton, 1973.

Stürmer, Michael. "Machtgefüge und Verbandsentwicklung in Deutschland." *Neue Politische Literatur* 14, no. 4 (1969): 490–507.

———. "Staatsstreichgedanken im Bismarckreich." *HZ* 209, no. 3 (December 1969): 566–615.

———. "Konservatismus und Revolution in Bismarcks Politik." In Stürmer, ed., *Deutschland*. 1970, pp. 143–67.

———. "Bismarck in Perspective." *CEH* 4, no. 4 (December 1971): 291–331.

———. "Bismarckstaat und Cäsarismus." *Der Staat* 12, no. 4 (1973): 467–98.

———. "Militärkonflikt und Bismarckstaat. Zur Bedeutung der Reichsmilitärgesetze 1874–1890." In Ritter, ed., *Gesellschaft*. 1974: 225–48.

————. *Regierung und Reichstag im Bismarckstaat, 1871–1880. Cäsarismus oder Parlamentarismus.* Düsseldorf, 1974.

————. ed. *Das kaiserliche Deutschland, Politik und Gesellschaft, 1870–1918.* Düsseldorf, 1970.

Sybel, Heinrich von. *Die politischen Parteien der Rheinprovinz.* Düsseldorf, 1847.

Thieme, Hartwig. *Nationaler Liberalismus in der Krise. Die nationalliberale Fraktion der preussischen Abgeordnetenhauses, 1914–1918.* Boppard, 1963.

Thomas, R. Hinton. *Liberalism, Nationalism, and the German Intellectuals (1822–1847): An Analysis of the Academic and Scientific Conferences of the Period.* Cambridge, 1951.

Thorwart, Friedrich. *Hermann Schulze-Delitzsch.* (vol. 5 of Schulze, *Schriften und Reden*). Berlin, 1913.

Thränhardt, Dietrich. *Wahlen und politische Strukturen in Bayern, 1848–1953.* Düsseldorf, 1973.

Tilly, Richard. "The Political Economy of Public Finance and the Industrialization of Prussia, 1815–1866." *JEH* 26, no. 4 (1966): 484–97.

————. "Germany 1815–1870." In Cameron, Rondo, ed., *Banking in the Early Stages of Industrialization.* New York, 1967, pp. 151–82.

————. "Soll und Haben: Recent German Economic History and the Problem of Economic Development." JEH 29, no. 2 (June 1969): 298–319.

————. "Popular Disorders in Nineteenth-Century Germany: A Preliminary Survey." *JSH* 4, no. 1 (1970): 1–40.

Tipton, Frank B. "The National Consensus in German Economic History." *CEH* 7, no. 3 (September 1974): 195–224.

Toury, Jacob. *Die politischen Orientierungen der Juden in Deutschland von Jena bis Weimar.* Tübingen, 1966.

Treitschke, Heinrich von. "Parteien und Fraktionen." *PJbb*, 27, nos. 2 and 3 (1871): 175–208, 347–67.

————. *Sozialismus und seine Gönner.* Berlin, 1875.

————. *History of Germany in the Nineteenth Century.* 7 vols. London, 1915–19.

Uelsmann, Erich. "Beiträge zur niederrheinischen Parteigeschichte, insbesondere zur Neuen Ära und zum Verfassungskonflikt (1858–1863)." *Annalen des Historischen Vereins für den Niederrhein* 109 (1926): 93–144.

Unruh, Hans Viktor von. *Erfahrungen aus den letzen drei Jahren. Ein Beitrag zur Kritik der politischen Mittelparteien.* Magdeburg, 1851.

————. *Erinnerungen.* Ed. by H. von Poschinger. Stuttgart, 1895.

Valentin, Veit. *Frankfurt am Main und die Revolution von 1848/49.* Stuttgart and Berlin, 1908.

————. *Geschichte der deutschen Revolution, 1848–1849.* 2 vols. Berlin, 1930–31.

Valjavec, Fritz. *Die Entstehung der politischen Strömungen in Deutschland, 1770–1815.* Munich, 1951.

Varain, Heinz Josef. *Freie Gewerkschaften, Sozialdemokratie und Staat.* Düsseldorf, 1956.

————., ed. *Interessenverbände in Deutschland.* Cologne, 1973.

Verein für Sozialpolitik. *Schriften.* Leipzig, 1873–1914.

Verhandlungen der Eisenacher Versammlung zur Besprechung der sozialen Frage am 6. und 7. Oktober 1872. Leipzig, 1873.

Vierhaus, Rudolf. "Politisches Bewusstsein in Deutschland vor 1789." *Der Staat* 6, no. 2 (1967): 175–96.

Virchow, Rudolf. *Briefe an seine Eltern 1839 bis 1864.* Ed. by M. Rahl. 2d. ed. Leipzig, 1907.

Vitzthum, Stephan Graf. *Linksliberale Politik und materiale Staatsrechtslehre. Albert Hänel, 1833–1918.* Freiburg and Munich, 1971.

Vogel, Bernhard, and Haungs, P. *Wahlkampf und Wählertradition. Eine Studie zur Bundestagswahl von 1961.* Cologne and Opladen, 1965.

Vogel, Bernhard; Nohlen, Dieter; and Schultze, Rainer-Olaf. *Wahlen in Deutschland. Theorie, Geschichte, Dokumente, 1848–1970.* Berlin, 1971.

Volkmann, Heinrich. *Die Arbeiterfrage im preussischen Abgeordnetenhaus, 1848–1869.* Berlin, 1968.

Volkszeitung (Berlin). 1879, 1910–14.

Vopelius, Marie Elisabeth. *Die altliberalen Ökonomen und die Reformzeit.* Stuttgart, 1968.

Wachenheim, Hedwig. *Die deutsche Arbeiterbewegung 1844 bis 1914.* Cologne and Opladen, 1967.

Wacker, Theodor. *Entwicklung der Sozialdemokratie in den zehn ersten Reichstagswahlen.* Freiburg, 1903.

Walker, Mack. *German Home Towns: Community, State, General Estate, 1648–1871.* Ithaca, New York, 1971.

Warren, Donald. *The Red Kingdom of Saxony. Lobbying Grounds for Gustav Stresemann.* The Hague, 1964.

Wasser, Hartmut. *Parlamentarismuskritik vom Kaiserreich zur Bundesrepublik.* Stuttgart, 1974.

Weber, Max. *Gesammelte politische Schriften.* 2d ed. Tübingen, 1958.

Weber, Rolf. *Kleinbürgerliche Demokraten in der deutschen Einheitsbewegung, 1863–1866.* Berlin, 1962.

————. *Die Revolution in Sachsen 1848/49. Entwicklung und Analyse ihrer Triebkräfte.* Berlin, 1970.

Wegner, Konstanze. *Theodor Barth und die Freisinnige Vereinigung.* Tübingen, 1968.

Wehler, Hans-Ulrich. "Die Polen im Ruhrgebiet bis 1918." In Wehler, ed., *Sozialgeschichte.* 1966, pp. 437–55.

————. *Bismarck und der Imperialismus.* Cologne and Berlin, 1969.

————. "Theorieprobleme der modernen deutschen Wirtschaftsgeschichte, 1800–1945." In Ritter, G. A., ed., *Entstehung.* 1970, pp. 66–107.

————. *Krisenherde des Kaiserreichs. Studie zur deutschen Sozial-und Verfassungsgeschichte.* Göttingen, 1970.

――――. *Das Deutsche Kaiserreich, 1871–1918*. Göttingen, 1973.

――――. "Sozialdarwinismus im expandierenden Industriestaat." In Geiss, I., and Wendt, J., eds., *Deutschland in der Weltpolitik des 19. und 20. Jahrhunderts. Fritz Fischer zum 65. Geburtstag*. Hamburg, 1973, pp. 133–42.

――――, ed. *Moderne deutsche Sozialgeschichte*. Cologne and Berlin, 1966.

――――, ed. *Sozialgeschichte Heute. Festschrift für Hans Rosenberg zum 70. Geburtstag*. Göttingen, 1974.

Weidemann, Wilhelm. "Friedrich Murhard (1778–1853) und der Altliberalismus." *Zeitschrift des Vereins für Hessische Geschichte* 55 (1926): 229–76.

Wein, Josef. *Die Verbandsbildung im Einzelhandel*. Berlin, 1968.

Weinacht, Paul Ludwig. *Staat. Studien zur Bedeutungsgeschichte des Wortes von den Anfängen bis ins 19. Jahrhundert*. Berlin, 1968.

Weinandy, Klaus. "Die politischen Wahlen in den rechtsrheinischen Kreisen Sieg, Mülheim, Wipperfürth, Grummersbach und Waldbröl des Regierungsbezirkes Köln in der Zeit von 1849 bis 1870." Unpubl. diss., Bonn, 1956.

Wentzcke, Paul, ed. *Deutscher Staat und deutsche Parteien: Beiträge zur deutschen Partei–und Ideengeschichte (Meinecke Festschrift)*. Munich and Berlin, 1922.

Wernecke, Klaus. *Der Wille zur Weltgeltung. Aussenpolitik und Öffentlichkeit im Kaiserreich am Vorabend des ersten Weltkrieges*. Düsseldorf, 1970.

Werner, Karl Gustav. "Gründung des Deutschen Arbeitgeberbundes für das Baugewerbe 1899 und seine Entwicklung bis 1910." In Varain, ed., *Interessenverbände* 1973, pp. 197–203.

Werner, Lothar. *Der Alldeutsche Verband, 1890–1918*. Berlin, 1955.

Wernicke, J. *Kapitalismus und Mittelstandspolitik*. Jena, 1907.

Westphal, Otto. *Welt–und Staatsauffassung des deutschen Liberalismus. Eine Untersuchung über die Preussischen Jahrbücher und den konstitutionellen Liberalismus in Deutschland von 1858 bis 1863*. Munich and Berlin, 1919.

White, Dan. *The Splintered Party. National Liberalism in Hessen and the Reich, 1867–1918*. Cambridge, Mass., 1976.

Wichmann, W. *Denkwürdigkeiten aus dem ersten deutschen Parlament*. Hanover, 1890.

Wieber, Walter. *Die politischen Ideen von Sylvester Jordan*. Tübingen, 1913.

Wigard, Franz. *Stenographischer Bericht über die Verhandlungen der Deutschen constituierenden Nationalversammlung zu Frankfurt*. 9 vols. Leipzig, 1848–49, and Frankfurt, 1849–50.

Wiggers, Julius. *Aus meinem Leben*. Leipzig, 1901.

Wilhelm, Theodor. *Die englische Verfassung und der vormärzliche deutsche Liberalismus*. Stuttgart, 1928.

――――. *Die Idee des Berufsbeamtentums. Ein Beitrag zur Staatslehre des deutschen Frühkonstitutionalismus*. Tübingen, 1933.

Winkler, Heinrich August. *Preussischer Liberalismus und deutscher Nationalstaat*. Tübingen, 1964.

————. "Bürgerliche Emanzipation und nationale Einigung. Zur Entstehung des Nationalliberalismus in Preussen." In Böhme, ed., *Probleme*. 1968, pp. 226–42.

————. "Der rückversicherte Mittelstand. Die Interessenverbände von Handwerk und Kleinhandel im deutschen Kaiserreich." In Rüegg and Neuloh, eds., *Theorie*. 1971, pp. 163–79.

————. *Mittelstand, Demokratie und Nationalsozialismus: Die politische Entwicklung von Handwerk und Kleinhandel in der Weimarer Republik*. Cologne, 1972.

————. *Pluralismus oder Protektionismus. Verfassungspolitische Probleme des Verbandswesen im deutschen Kaiserreich*. Wiesbaden, 1972.

————. "Extremismus der Mitte? Sozialgeschichtliche Aspekte der national-sozialistischen Machtergreifung." *VfZ* 20, no. 2 (April 1972): 175–91.

Witt, Peter Christian. *Die Finanzpolitik des Deutschen Reiches, 1903–1913*. Lübeck and Hamburg, 1969.

Zeitschrift des Königlich Preussischen statistischen Bureaus. 1861–1914.

Zeitschrift des Königlich Sächsischen statistischen Bureaus. 1903–09.

Zeitschrift für die gesamte Staatswissenschaft. 1844–1871.

Zeitschrift für Politik. Supplement 1, *Die Parteien* (1912).

Zenz, Emil. *Die kommunale Selbstverwaltung der Stadt Trier seit Beginn der preussischen Zeit 1814–1949*. Trier, 1959.

Ziebura, Gilbert. "Anfänge des deutschen Parlamentarismus (Geschäftsverfahren und Entscheidungsprozess in der ersten deutschen Nationalversammlung 1848/49)". In Ritter, G. A., and Ziebura, G., eds., *Faktoren der politischen Entscheidung (Festgabe für Ernst Fraenkel)*. Berlin, 1963, pp. 185–236.

Ziekursch, Johannes. *Politische Geschichte des neuen deutschen Kaiserreiches*. 3 vols. Frankfurt, 1925–28.

Zorn, Wolfgang. "Typen und Entwicklungskräfte des deutschen Unternehmertums im 19. Jahrhundert." *VSWG* 44, no. 1 (March 1957): 57–77.

————. "Gesellschaft und Staat im Bayern des Vormärz." In Conze, ed., *Staat*. 1962, pp. 113–42.

————. "Wirtschafts-und sozialgeschichtliche Zusammenhänge der deutschen Reichsgründungszeit (1850–1879)." *HZ* 197, no. 2 (October 1963): 318–42.

————. "Parlament, Gesellschaft und Regierung in Bayern, 1870–1918." In Ritter, ed., *Gesellschaft*. 1974, pp. 299–315.

Zucker, Stanley. *Ludwig Bamberger: German Liberal Politician and Social Critic, 1823–1899*. Pittsburgh, 1975.

Zunkel, Friedrich. *Der Rheinisch-Westfälische Unternehmer 1834–1879: Ein Beitrag zur Geschichte des deutschen Bürgertums im 19. Jahrhundert*. Cologne and Opladen, 1962.

————. "Beamtenschaft und Unternehmertum beim Aufbau der Ruhrindustrie." *Tradition* 9, no. 6 (1964): 261–77.

Index